LINES DRAWN ACROSS THE GLOBE

MCGILL-QUEEN'S STUDIES IN THE HISTORY OF IDEAS
Series Editor: Philip J. Cercone

72 The Culturalist Challenge
    to Liberal Republicanism
    Michael Lusztig

73 God and Government: Martin
    Luther's Political Thought
    Jarrett A. Carty

74 The Age of Secularization
    Augusto Del Noce
    Edited and Translated
    by Carlo Lancellotti

75 Emancipatory Thinking:
    Simone de Beauvoir
    and Contemporary
    Political Thought
    Elaine Stavro

76 Life Embodied:
    The Promise of Vital Force
    in Spanish Modernity
    Nicolás Fernández-Medina

77 The Aesthetics of Fear
    in German Romanticism
    Paola Mayer

78 Objectively Engaged Journalism:
    An Ethic
    Stephen J.A. Ward

79 Progress, Pluralism, and Politics:
    Liberalism and Colonialism,
    Past and Present
    David Williams

80 Beyond Tragedy
    and Eternal Peace:
    Politics and International
    Relations in the Thought
    of Friedrich Nietzsche
    Jean-François Drolet

81 Inequality in Canada: The
    History and Politics of an Idea
    Eric W. Sager

82 Attending: An Ethical Art
    Warren Heiti

83 Imperial Paradoxes:
    Training the Senses and Tasting
    the Eighteenth Century
    Robert James Merrett

84 The Problem of Atheism
    Augusto Del Noce
    Edited and Translated
    by Carlo Lancellotti

85 The Etruscans in the
    Modern Imagination
    Sam Solecki

86 The Communion of the Book:
    Milton and the Humanist
    Revolution in Reading
    David Williams

87 Dying for France:
    Experiencing and Representing
    the Soldier's Death, 1500–2000
    Ian Germani

88 Religion and the Post-
    revolutionary Mind: Idéologues,
    Catholic Traditionalists,
    and Liberals in France
    Arthur McCalla

89 The Domination of Nature,
    New Edition
    William Leiss

90 Lines Drawn across the Globe:
    Reading Richard Hakluyt's
    Principal Navigations
    Mary C. Fuller

Lines Drawn across the Globe

Reading Richard Hakluyt's *Principal Navigations*

Mary C. Fuller

McGill-Queen's University Press
Montreal & Kingston • London • Chicago

© McGill-Queen's University Press 2023

ISBN 978-0-2280-1676-2 (cloth)
ISBN 978-0-2280-1841-4 (ePDF)

Legal deposit third quarter 2023
Bibliothèque nationale du Québec

Printed in Canada on acid-free paper that is 100% ancient forest free (100% post-consumer recycled), processed chlorine free

---

Library and Archives Canada Cataloguing in Publication

Title: Lines drawn across the globe: reading Richard Hakluyt's Principal navigations / Mary Fuller.

Names: Fuller, Mary C., author.

Series: McGill-Queen's studies in the history of ideas ; 90.

Description: Series statement: McGill-Queen's studies in the history of ideas ; 90 | Includes bibliographical references and index.

Identifiers: Canadiana (print) 20230137512 | Canadiana (ebook) 20230137520 | ISBN 9780228016762 (cloth) | ISBN 9780228018414 (ePDF)

Subjects: LCSH: Hakluyt, Richard, 1552?-1616. | LCSH: Principall navigations, voiages, and discoveries of the English nation. | LCSH: Voyages and travels—Early works to 1800. | LCSH: Discoveries in geography—English.

Classification: LCC G240 .F85 2023 | DDC 910.941—dc23

This book was typeset by Marquis Interscript in 10/13 New Baskerville.

For my brother, Edward Grayson Fuller

Contents

Acknowledgments ix

Abbreviations xiii

1 Opening the Work 3

PART ONE NORTH AND NORTHEAST

2 Remembering the North: Hakluyt's Medieval Materials 25
3 Imagining the Arctic 76
4 Encounters with the North 109

PART TWO SOUTH AND SOUTHEAST

5 The Levant and Beyond: Duration, Interruption, Repetition 155
6 West Africa and Beyond: Into the Tropics 207
7 Belligerent Materials: Sea Fights in the Atlantic 267

PART THREE AMERICAS AND THE PACIFIC

8 The Relations of Strangers: Covering the Americas 317
9 Voyages in Search of a Northwest Passage: Identities at High Latitudes 372
10 Famous Voyages: The Caribbean and the Pacific 412

Afterword 462

Appendices

1 Contents of Volume 2(ii), in Order of Appearance   471

2 West African Materials in Volume 3 (By Subheading)   475

3 Eden's Narrative of John Lok's Voyage to Guinea (1554), in *Decades* and in *Principal Navigations*   477

4 The Anglo-Spanish Sea War in Volumes 1 and 2   479

5 Authorship and Editing in Hakluyt's Materials on the Anglo-Spanish Sea War   483

6 Spanish Manuscripts in *Principal Navigations*, Volume 3 (Item Numbers from "c&s")   486

7 Materials on Eastern Canada in Volume 3   488

8 *Principal Navigations* Materials Related to Drake's Activities at Sea   491

9 *Principal Navigations* Materials Related to Drake, by Voyage   494

10 Preachers and Voyages   497

Tables, Figures, and Plates   499

Bibliography   505

Index   549

Acknowledgments

This book has taken more than twenty years to complete, and would never have existed without the communities on which it depends. My debts to past scholars sometimes feel like living friendships, but I'm grateful that some of this book's deepest intellectual debts are personal as well as scholarly. Fellow travailers in the field of Hakluyt and early modern geography, interlocutors, and companions who made the work both better and happier: Dan Carey, Surekha Davies, Matthew Day, Claire Jowitt, Peter Mancall, Anthony Payne, Joan-Pau Rubiés, Bill Sherman, Nicolás Wey Gómez. Especially kind supporters of the book and its author: Mary Campbell, Peter Hulme, Frank Lestringant, Joyce Lorimer, Stephen Orgel, Bruce Smith, Laurier Turgeon, Sarah Tyacke. Successive presidents of the Hakluyt Society, whose publications have been the invaluable bedrock of the project, and hospitable convenors of scholarly exchange: Mike Barritt, Jim Bennett, Gloria Clifton – and Will Ryan, a helpful voice at editorial workshops.

Sharers of networks, references, invaluable expertise, and sometimes convivial tables: Patricia Akhimie, Reginald Auger, Julia Boffey, Joyce Chaplin, Nandini Das, Jeannine DeLombard, Anthony Edwards, Margaret Garber, Stephen Johnston, Ian MacLaren, Alex Marr, Nabil Matar, Bruce Moran, Joyce Millen, Marcy Norton, Tara Nummedal, David Sacks, Jyotsna Singh, Sebastian Sobecki, Scott Stevens, Henry Turner. Sylvia Sumira and Lesley Whitelaw helped me gain access to the Middle Temple's fascinating copy of the Molyneux globe. Anonymous readers for the press read the manuscript with great care; Kenda Mutongi and Anthony Payne kindly cast their expert eyes over particular chapters. They are not responsible for the finished product, but it is better for their recommendations.

Germaine Warkentin's invitation to a conference on early modern Canada many years ago began to create the interdisciplinary networks that made a project like this possible. Talks related to the book benefited from audiences at the University of Michigan, Princeton, MLA, RSA, the Université de Laval, Trinity College Oxford, the USC-Huntington Early Modern Studies Institute, the University of Hong Kong, the National Maritime Museum, the Clark Library, the University of New Hampshire, the University of Basel, UCLA, the Hakluyt Society, Oxford University, the Oxford Forum in the History of Mathematics, the Mahindra Humanities Center at Harvard, the School of Earth and Space Exploration (ASU), the University of Grenoble, McGill University, Seikei University, Boston University, and the Shakespeare Association of America. I'm grateful for invitations from Lindy Elkins-Tanton, Fuhito Endo, Alan Greer, Keith Hannabuss, Peter Mancall, Alex Marr, Paul Smethurst, Nigel Smith, Mark Somos and Ioannis Evrigenis, Scott Stevens, Carl Thompson, and Tim Youngs. The participants in my 2011 NEH Summer Seminar were wonderful interlocutors, and I have drawn on their subsequent scholarship. I would like to express my appreciation to Christine Goettler for her invitation to a stimulating set of conversations at the 2016 summer school, "Border Regimes," sponsored by the University of Luzerne, Utrecht University, and the University of Bern, as well as to the participants and to Sandro Mezzadra for his thought-provoking comments. Jim Bennett's invitation to give the Hakluyt Society's Annual Lecture earlier that year provided the occasion when I began to think there was a light at the end of this tunnel, and an audience that would one day read this book.

My work with Hakluyt's book began at the John Carter Brown Library, which under the direction of Norman Fiering and Neil Safier has been a place of many human connections as well as a storehouse of books, knowledge, and time. Susan Danforth, Bertie Mandelblatt, Dan Slive, and Rick Ring were all generous with their expertise. The hospitality of Roy Ritchie at the Huntington helped make it a great place to work. The Master and fellows of Balliol College kindly welcomed me on two occasions for an extended stay. I'm also grateful for the assistance and expertise of staff at the Bodleian Libraries, the Boston Public Library, the British Library, the Hayden Library at MIT, the Houghton Library, the Huntington Library, and the Newberry Library. While residential fellowships and visits to a number of rare book collections afforded me rich networks, access to specialized expertise, and evidence from material texts, visionary efforts by libraries and publication societies to digitize collections and provide online access made it possible to complete much of this book during a period when no library was physically accessible. The publications of the Navy Records Society, in particular, came as a happy surprise.

Janet Sonenberg was a generous and inspiring listener, who helped me find the words I needed. Life has been made better by Sam Allen and Annie Fowler, Barbara Britton and David Halprin, Isidro Castineyra, Mary Crane, David Farrell, Lissa Gifford, Barbara Goldoftas, Vu Ha and Catherine Lefebvre, Heather Hendershot and Mauricio Cordero, Diana Henderson, Marina Leslie, Jana Murray, David Smilow, Charles Shadle, Jayne Tan, Chris Wong, and Jeffrey Light. Harriet Ritvo gave me a push at the right time. My colleagues in the Literature Section were the kind first auditors for a book they have been living next to for many years, and which bears the impress of its community. In particular, I learned unexpected things from the work of Arthur Bahr, Genie Brinkema, and Stephanie Frampton. Sometimes the writing travelled, and I want to thank the friends who helped it find a home away from home: Amrita Daniere, Cath Davies and Clodagh Brook, Jenny Davis, Lindy Elkins-Tanton and James Tanton, Stephen Tapscott, Seohyung Kim and Alex Donnelly, Shankar Raman and Lianne Habinek, Emma Teng.

Although none of this book's chapters have been previously published, during the twenty odd years of its composition, invitations to contribute to edited collections and special issues provided valued opportunities to do other things with the same evidence, asking different questions or pursuing a particular topic more widely or deeply than the book would accommodate. In many cases, these publications were the trace of lively exchanges or became an introduction to vital new scholarship, and I list their venues with gratitude here: Peter C. Mancall, ed., *Bringing the World to Early Modern Europe: Travel Accounts and Their Audiences* (Leiden; Boston: Brill, 2007); Julia Kuehn and Paul Smethurst, ed., *Travel Writing, Form, and Empire: The Poetics and Politics of Mobility* (New York: Routledge, 2009); Kent Cartwright, ed., *A Companion to Tudor Literature* (Chichester, UK; Malden, MA: Wiley-Blackwell, 2010); Nandini Das, ed., *Yearbook of English Studies* 41 (2011), special issue on prose romance; Daniel Carey and Claire Jowitt, eds., *Richard Hakluyt and Travel Writing in Early Modern Europe* (New York: Routledge, 2012); Frédéric Regard, ed., *The Quest for the Northwest Passage: Knowledge, Nation and Empire 1576–1806* (London: Pickering and Chatto, 2013); Bruce R. Smith, ed., *The Cambridge Guide to the Worlds of Shakespeare* (New York: Cambridge University Press, 2016); "Experiments in Reading Richard Hakluyt's *Principal Navigations*," Hakluyt Society Annual Lecture (London: Hakluyt Society, 2017); Patricia Akhimie and Bernadette Andrea, ed., *Travel and Travail: Early Modern Women, English Drama, and the Wider World* (Lincoln, NE: University of Nebraska Press, 2019); Jyotsna G. Singh, ed., *A Companion to the Global Renaissance*, 2nd ed. (Chichester, UK; Malden, MA: Wiley-Blackwell, 2021); Mark Somos and Anne Peters, ed.,

The State of Nature: Histories of an Idea (Leiden; Boston: Brill, 2022); and Allan Greer, ed., *Before Canada: Northern North America in a Connected World* (Montreal; Kingston: McGill-Queen's University Press, forthcoming).

Generous support for the project was provided by the MIT Literature section, under the leadership of Peter Donaldson, James Buzard, and Shankar Raman, as well as by the SHASS Dean's Office, under Philip Khoury, Deborah Fitzgerald, and Melissa Nobles. I also acknowledge with gratitude the support of James A. Levitan and Ruth Levitan, the Margaret MacVicar family, and the MIT-Balliol Exchange. Alicia Mackin, Marc Jones, Erminia Piccinonno, Daria Johnson, Albert Wang, and Chad Galts provided indispensable support for the varied kinds of work one does within an institution. My research was also supported – more than once, and when very much needed – by funding from the National Endowment for the Humanities, as well as by fellowships offered by the Huntington Library, the Newberry Library, the Folger Library, and the John Carter Brown Library.

Kate Johnson, Sarah Carr, Rebecca Herrmann, and Kim Foster helped to keep my own equipment working. The team at Loyal Nine provided a place to eat, drink, and think during a global pandemic. Kyla Madden showed me what an editor can be. Finally, I want to acknowledge the love and support of my family: Mark, Kim, Jane, and Sarah Lackley; Julia and George Crawford; Dorothy and Amy Heggie; Martha Helbein; Jennifer and Peter Allen; my mother, Nancy Grayson, who generously supported acquiring rights to some of my illustrations; and finally my brother, Edward Grayson Fuller, a secret scholar and artist who has kept the home fires burning.

Abbreviations

BL Catalogue	British Library, Explore Archives and Manuscripts Catalogue, https://searcharchives.bl.uk
"C&S"	David B. Quinn and Alison M. Quinn, "Contents and Sources of the Three Major Works"
"Chronology"	David B. Quinn and Alison M. Quinn, "A Hakluyt Chronology"
DV	Richard Hakluyt, *Divers Voyages*
ESTC	English Short Title Catalogue
Guide	Anthony Payne, *Richard Hakluyt: A Guide to His Books*
NAW	David B. Quinn, ed. *New American World*
ODNB	Brian Harrison and H.C.G. Matthew, *Oxford Dictionary of National Biography* (online edition)
OED	*Oxford English Dictionary* (online)
OW	E.G.R. Taylor, ed. *Original Writings and Correspondence of the Two Richard Hakluyts*
PD	Richard Hakluyt, *A Particuler Discourse*, ed. David B. Quinn
Pilgrimes	Samuel Purchas, *Hakluytus Posthumus, or Purchas His Pilgrimes*
PN (1589)	Richard Hakluyt, *Principall Navigations, Voyages and Discoveries of the English Nation*
PN (1903–5)	Richard Hakluyt, *Principal Navigations, Voyages, Traffiques & Discoveries of the English Nation*, 12 vols. (Glasgow: J. MacLehose and sons, 1903–5)
PN	(1598–1600) or PN [volume number: page number] Richard Hakluyt, *Principal Navigations, Voyages, Traffiques, and Discoveries of the English Nation* [...], 3 vols.
TNA	The National Archives, Kew

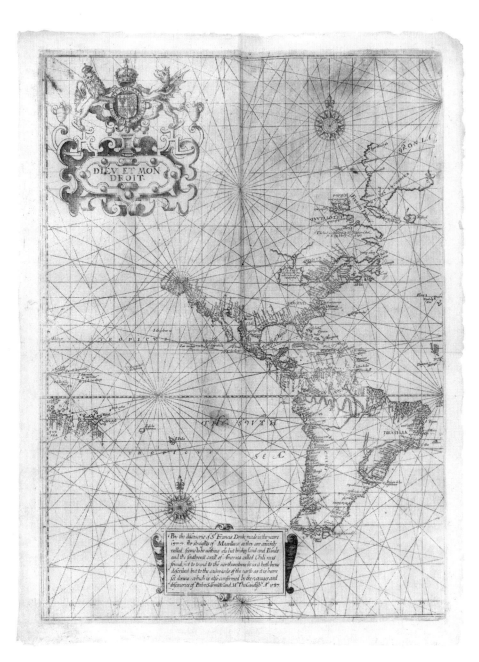

Figures 0.1 and 0.2 Edward Wright's fold-out world map (1598) appears in some copies of *Principal Navigations*.

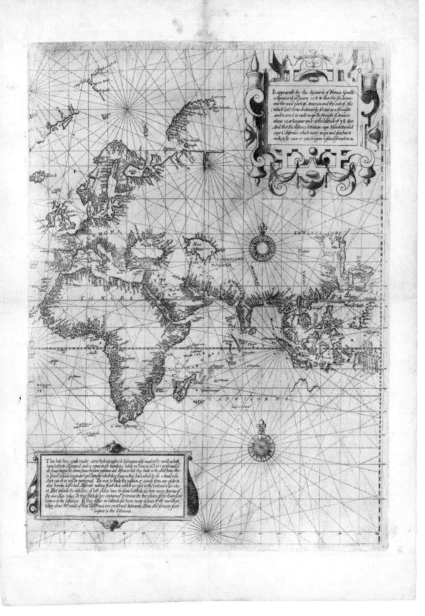

LINES DRAWN ACROSS THE GLOBE

1

Opening the Work

These magnificent volumes [Hakluyt's *Voyages*] are not often, perhaps, read through. Part of their charm consists in the fact that Hakluyt is not so much a book as a great bundle of commodities loosely tied together, an emporium, a lumber room strewn with ancient sacks, obsolete nautical instruments, huge bales of wool, and little bags of rubies and emeralds ... these odds and ends of priceless value and complete worthlessness, were the fruit of innumerable voyages, traffics, and discoveries to unknown lands in the reign of Queen Elizabeth.

Virginia Woolf[1]

THIS IS A BOOK ABOUT A BOOK: Richard Hakluyt's compilation of geographic and mercantile documents, *The Principal Navigations, Voyages, Traffiques and Discoveries of the English Nation*, printed over the years 1598 to 1600.[2] In its own way, this book is a world. Or at least, it tells us something about *how* the world appeared to England in 1600, through the observations and experiences of English merchants, mariners, and travellers, as well as through the ancient and foreign sources available to them. Within the book's covers are documents in or from a multitude of languages, drawn from printed books, government and corporate archives, private libraries, personal collections, and oral testimony. It is a massive material object, spanning three volumes and roughly 2,000 pages. Expanding on a shorter version published in 1589, the final version of *Principal Navigations* fell between the defeat of

---

1 Woolf, "Elizabethan Lumber Room," 61.
2 Subsequently cited as *Principal Navigations*, PN (1598–1600), or PN (volume number: page number). I am grateful to Sarah Tyacke for prodding me to think about the implications of terms like "anthology," which imply a selection of "best" or "representative" texts. I have found it useful to think about the work as a compilation: to paraphrase a medievalist's definition, a compilation is "the assemblage of multiple discrete works into a larger structure"; that structure itself adds to the content of its components a variety of effects produced by the "formal interplay of textual and material parts" (Bahr, *Fragments and Assemblages*, 10).

the Armada and the first voyages of the East India Company, after Roanoke and before Jamestown.[3]

Over the centuries, the perceived importance of *Principal Navigations* has fluctuated. For a time eclipsed by later travel collections, by the end of the nineteenth century (if not earlier), Hakluyt's compilation began to be characterized as a founding document of English national identity.[4] It also remains a massive and crucial piece of evidence on the origins of empire, on settler and Indigenous societies, and on cultures and environments that the voyages of the fifteenth and sixteenth centuries first put into sustained contact. Yet it so far awaits completion of a modern critical edition, and the most extensive single-authored study of the compilation and its author is almost a century old.[5] Modern indexes, produced in 1905 for the three-volume second edition, and in 1965 for the earlier 1589 edition of the work, give an imperfect idea of its contents, foregrounding some lines of inquiry while affording little encouragement for others.[6] Constantly alluded to, it is frequently subject to generalization, while its voluminous size challenges detailed engagement. Woolf's characterization of *Principal Navigations* provides a charming image that is equally true to the experience of reading the work: frequently anthologized and reprinted jewels sit amid a great diversity of contents, some of which

---

[3] *Principall Navigations* (1589), subsequently cited as PN (1598), is generally distinguished from the second edition by the alternate spelling of "Principall." A useful guide to the single-volume first edition, its preparation, and its contents is provided by the editors of the Hakluyt Society facsimile edition (see D. Quinn and Skelton, "Introduction").

[4] On Hakluyt's reputation and on his successors, see D. Quinn, "Hakluyt's Reputation"; Steele, "From Hakluyt to Purchas"; Dew, "Reading Travels in the Culture of Curiosity"; Holtz, "Hakluyt in France"; Day, "'Honour to Our Nation.'"

[5] Parks, *Hakluyt and the English Voyages*. Important studies and reference sources include Taylor, *Original Writings and Correspondence of the Two Richard Hakluyts*; D. Quinn, *Hakluyt Handbook*; Carey and Jowitt, *Richard Hakluyt and Travel Writing*; Mancall, *Hakluyt's Promise*; Payne, *Guide*. (Claire Jowitt and Daniel Carey are the general editors of a projected critical edition now in progress at Oxford University Press.) A still valuable overview of Hakluyt criticism through 1974 is provided in Pennington, "Secondary Works on Hakluyt." Another tradition views Hakluyt's works through the lens of political and legal history, frequently with a focus on manuscript sources; see, for instance, Armitage, *Ideological Origins*; Fitzmaurice, *Sovereignty*; Grotius, *Free Sea*; MacMillan, *Sovereignty*; Tomlins, *Freedom Bound*; Tuck, *Rights of War and Peace*.

[6] Hakluyt, PN *1903–05*, vol. 12; A. Quinn, "Modern Index to the 'Principall Navigations.'" Alison Quinn's prize-winning index provides a granular level of detail, but covers only the much shorter 1589 edition.

are dull indeed, but contribute mass and volume to the whole.[7] We can discern logics of connection between what Woolf implies were chance assemblies – the wool that was Elizabethan England's great export, the jewels it hoped to find in the East Indies, the navigational instruments that enabled journeys of exchange – yet the lumber room with its layers of casual deposition belies the actual agency of Richard Hakluyt as the author of "Hakluyt," that term for the bundle or emporium that barely rises to the quality of a book.

Hakluyt was an Oxford-educated geographer and cleric; deeply connected with the practice and policy of English voyages in his day as well as with continental geographers, he was able to print for the first time sources on voyages as unusual as the circumnavigation of Sir Francis Drake and as mundane as England's medieval trade in fish at Bergen.[8] His compilation was organized on the model provided by the earlier compilation of Giovanni Battista Ramusio, dividing its materials into three broad geographical categories: voyages to the North and Northeast, to the South and Southeast, and to the West and around the world.[9] In the first edition of 1589, Hakluyt had gathered materials into a single folio volume. As he expanded and altered the text to produce the larger second edition of *Principal Navigations* with which this book is concerned, each of these geographical categories was expanded to make an entire volume of its own.

The contents of *Principal Navigations* are famously heterogeneous, including price lists and vocabularies, charters and royal letters, logs and journals, and excerpts from medieval manuscripts; even many previously printed books were hungrily digested within its covers. This diversity was in part generated by the activities, plans, and investments that the work records. Across regions and cultures contacted, the English perceived different possibilities of action and engagement, ranging from careful diplomacy and settled trade, to violence, to solitary exploration. These activities were accompanied with different writing practices as well as different conditions of retention and dissemination for the writing that was produced. Some voyages had to be reconstructed

---

7 For assessments of *Principal Navigations* as dull, and a response, see Lewis, *English Literature in the Sixteenth Century*, 438; Parks, "Tudor Travel Literature"; Fuller, "Dullness in Hakluyt's Collections."

8 On Hakluyt's life, see Mancall, *Hakluyt's Promise*; Quinn and Quinn, "Chronology"; Taylor, ow.

9 On Ramusio's *Navigationi et Viaggi* (1550–59), see Parks, *Contents and Sources of Ramusio's Navigationi*; Rubiés, "Rise of a Modern Genre"; Small, "World Seen through Another's Eyes"; Horodowich, *Venetian Discovery of America*, chap. 3.

from oral testimony, or represented by brief mentions in secondary sources. Others generated rich surrounds of theory, celebration, and legal authorization, as well as multiple narratives, both in manuscript and in print. Many additional non-narrative documents were drawn by the editor from state and company archives.

These contents, on their own, only tell part of the story; we also need what is missing from Woolf's metaphor, the story of how these materials came to be assembled into a single-authored book. That is, the story of Hakluyt's work as author: what he chose to include or not include; where he located particular documents in the compilation, and with what accompanying materials; the context and emphasis he provided (or didn't provide); where he sought materials with particular energy; where he was or was not given access; where his selections reflected the agendas of associates or patrons; where he was incurious or mistaken. These elements, as much as the habits of authors and the actions they wrote about, are part of the book's topography.

This study *is* the story of a book more than of an age, even if – given its monumental status – a detailed study of Hakluyt's book *as* a book can contribute to broader historical thinking.[10] Hakluyt's book, and even more the activities and tendencies that it records, have had lasting and consequential effects on the world outside its pages, and these effects are in large part why it demands attention. Yet I believe that we have to understand what the book tells us, as book, before it can effectively serve as witness to what is outside it, or be placed into a history of what comes after it. Textual evidence is by no means all the evidence that matters (and Hakluyt's compilation provides a far from complete picture of the histories it begins to document) – but it is the most fundamental evidence that the nature of the object affords.

Studying this book as a book presents obvious challenges, however. At just under two thousand pages in folio, the book's scale in and of itself is difficult to manage, not only in the linear sense of how long it might take to read all of *Principal Navigations*, but – since it is an edited compendium of many individual documents – because the number of parts reflecting on each other,

---

10 While readers will come away with some awareness of "what's there" in each of the work's geographically focused volumes, they will not find a narrative history of the activities we read about in Hakluyt's book: the trade and diplomacy of the Levant and Muscovy companies, forms of trade along the African coast, the search for the Northwest Passage, or the activities of Elizabethan privateers and colonists. Sources for these histories are provided in the notes.

and thus potentially affecting interpretation at multiple scales, creates daunting complexity. We open its pages to encounter many authors other than Hakluyt – largely, ones who composed their texts in ignorance that they would ever form part of such a book. These documents must be considered on their own terms (as referred to the individual authors, in Hakluyt's words), as part of the collection as a whole, and as part of groupings formed by Hakluyt within the larger architecture of *Principal Navigations*.[11] Each document, in a sense, demands multiple layers of attention, which may extend to their original print or manuscript contexts, histories of preservation and reception, or an archive of competing narratives. And while the book itself has remained constant, our sense of the information it provides has expanded. In studying both *Principal Navigations* and other early modern books, we have learned to "read" not only the contents of the text, but also printed marginalia, running heads, layout, and other features of the physical book. A text like *Principal Navigations* presses us to look for formal regularities and organizing systems, both explicit and implicit, as a way to manage this scale and complexity.

Thinking about the work as an assemblage of discrete texts within a larger structure captures the multiple scales on which *Principal Navigations* demands to be read. Close reading of individual texts forms a ready point of entry, and remains one of the fundamental methods for approaching the work. Yet some of the best-known and most frequently studied works within *Principal Navigations* – Woolf's "little bags of rubies and emeralds" – may be outliers rather than representative samples of its content. While it would be equally misleading to avoid the most celebrated parts of Hakluyt's book, we would certainly come away with an incomplete understanding of it should we fail to attend to some of its plainer and more obscure pages.[12] The texts for close study in this book are often ones that can function as examples for forms of writing represented across the compilation: shipboard logs and journals, for

---

11 In the first edition of his compilation, Hakluyt promised that he had "referred every voyage to his Author, which both in person hath performed and in writing hath left the same"; authors bore both the credit and the responsibility for the contents of their writing (Hakluyt, "Preface to the Reader (1589)," sig. *3v).

12 Examples would include Walter Ralegh's "Last Fight of the *Revenge*" and "Discoverie of Guiana"; Thomas Harriot's "Briefe and True Report"; the "Famous Voyage" account of Drake's circumnavigation; and George Best's "True Discourse" on the three voyages of Martin Frobisher. All except for "Famous Voyage" were previously printed; all but "Last Fight of the *Revenge*" appear in Hakluyt's third volume, an index of how uneven attention to the collection has been.

instance (chapters 4 and 9), captivity narratives (chapters 5 and 6), accounts of battles at sea (chapter 7), and instructions for how to write (chapters 4 and 10).

Attending to phenomena on a larger scale than that of the sentence, the page, or even the individual document directs us beyond the documents to the organizing principles that operate *in* the collection. *Principal Navigations* assembles a heterogeneous mass of documents relating to travel and to the description of foreign places. Let's imagine that the documents sit in front of us in a heap. How do we sort them? Several significant possibilities would offer themselves, beyond the simply alphabetic: for instance, according to nationality. English activities and authors might be differentiated from those of the French, or the Spanish. Despite some discussion in Hakluyt's prefaces, however, language and nationality are largely invisible as a sorting principle – documents written by, or about the voyages of, other nations are simply interspersed with others under the uniform heading, Principal Navigations ... of the *English* Nation.

It would also be possible to organize the contents of *Principal Navigations* by kind: letters, lists, logs, patents, narrative documents. Such generic groupings were meaningful for Hakluyt: the tables of contents for each volume make visible a rudimentary distinction along generic lines, dividing each major section of the collection into a "catalogue of ... Voyages" and "a Catalogue of the ambassages, treatises, privileges, letters, &c." But these categories are fairly slippery: a number of voyage narratives fall under the second heading. Further, these genre categories are visible as such only in the table of contents of the volumes: the distinction between voyages and diplomacy, treatises, privileges, and so on does not organize the placement of documents within the collection, or clarify the order in which *readers* will encounter them. Hakluyt's idea of genre is both hard to pin down, and not the highest priority in organizing the text.

Chronology organizes the materials more visibly, and at a variety of scales. In the first part of volume 2, for instance, temporal categories are emphasized in the table of contents as well as in the editor's preface, where Hakluyt distinguishes early forms of travel (pilgrimage and crusade) from later ones (travel for trade and diplomacy). Within documents, Hakluyt's marginalia often draw attention to chronological boundaries and landmarks, and time sequence is an especially important and visible structuring feature of many texts produced by the kinds of travel recorded in the collection. The requirements of navigation, for instance, shaped a writing practice that mandated regular recording, without requiring the authors of such records to tell a

¶ A Catalogue of the English Voyages made by and within the Streight of *Gibraltar*, to the South and Southeast quarters of the world, conteined in the first part of this second volume.

Voyages before the Conquest.

1. The voyage of *Helena* the Empresse, daughter of *Coelus* king of *Britain*, and mother of *Constantine* the Great, to *Ierusalem*. An. 337. pag. 1.2
2. The voyage of *Constantine* the Great, Emperour and king of *Britaine*, to *Greece*, *Ægypt*, *Persia*, and *Asia*, Anno 339. pag. 2.3
3. The voyage of *Pelagius Cambrensis*, vnder *Maximus* king of the *Britaines*, into *Ægypt* and *Syria*, Anno 390. pag. 4
4. The voyage of certaine Englishmen sent by the French king to *Constantinople*, vnto *Instinian* the Emperour, about the yeere of our Lord 500. pag. 4
5. The memorable voyage of *Sighelmus* bishop of *Shirburne*, sent by king *Alphred* vnto S. *Thomas* of *India*, An. 883. confirmed by two testimonies. pag. 5
6. The voyage of *Iohn Erigen*, vnder king *Alphred*, to *Athens*, in the yeere of our Lorde 885. pag. 5.6
7. The voyage of *Andrew Whiteman*, aliàs *Leucander*, vnder *Canutus* the Dane, to *Palastina*, Anno 1020. pag. 6
8. The voyage of *Swanus* one of the sonnes of Earle *Godwin*, vnto *Ierusalem*, Anno 1052. pag. 6
9. A voyage of three Ambassadours sent in the time of king *Edward* the Confessor, vnto *Constantinople*, and from thence vnto *Ephesus*, Anno 1056. pag. 7
10. The voyage of *Alured* bishop of *Worcester* vnto *Ierusalem*, Anno 1058. pag. 8
11. The voyage of *Ingulphus*, afterward Abbat of *Croiland*, vnto *Ierusalem*. An. 1064. pag. 8.9

Voyages since the Conquest.

12. A Voyage made by diuerse of the honourable family of the *Beauchamps*, with *Robert Curtois* the sonne of *William* the Conquerour, to *Ierusalem*, Anno 1096. pag. 10
13. The voyage of *Gutuere* an English Lady married vnto *Baldwine* brother of *Godfrey* duke of *Bouillon*, toward *Ierusalem*, An. 1097. 10.11
14. The voyage of *Edgar* the soone of *Edward*, which was the sonne of *Edmund* surnamed *Ironside*, brother vnto king *Edward* the Confessor (being accompanied with valiant *Robert* the sonne of *Godwine*) to *Ierusalem*, Anno 1102. 11
15. The voyage of *Godericus* a valiant Englishman, who trauailed with his ships in an expedition vnto the holy land, Anno 3. *Hen.1*. 12
16. The voyage of *Hardine* an Englishman, and one of the principall commaunders of 200 sayles of Christians ships, which arriued at *Ioppa*, Anno 1102 12.13
17. A voyage by sea of Englishmen, Danes, and Flemings, who arriued at *Ioppa* in the holy land, the seuenth yeere of *Baldwine* the second, king of *Ierusalem*, and in the 8. yeere of *Henry* the first, king of *England*, pag. 13,14,15
18. The voyage of *Athelard* of *Bathe* to *Ægypt* and *Arabia*, in the yeere of our Lord 1130 pag. 15,16
19. The voyage of *William* Archbishop of *Tyre* to *Ierusalem* and to the citie of *Tyre* in *Phœnicia*, Anno 1130. 16
20. The voyage of *Robert Ketenensis*, vnder king *Stephen*, to *Dalmatia*, *Greece*, and *Asia*, Anno 1143. 16
21. A voyage of certaine Englishmen vnder the conduct of *Lewis* the French king, vnto the holy land, Anno 1147. 17
22. The voyage of *Iohn Lacy* to *Ierusalem*, Anno 1173. 17

23 The

Figure 1.1 In volume 2, part 1 of *Principal Navigations* (1598–1600), Hakluyt distinguished voyages "before" and "after" the Norman Conquest (*PN* 2[i], *5r).

M.Wil.Towrson. Traffiques and Discoueries. 335

The colde and moyst aire doth somewhat offend them. Yet doubtlesse men that are borne in hot Regions may better abide colde, then men that are borne in colde Regions may abide heate, forasmuch as vehement heate resolueth the radicall moysture of mens bodies, as colde constraineth and preserueth the same. · Colde may be better abiden then heate.

This is also to be considered as a secret worke of nature, that throughout all Africke, vnder the Æquinoctial line, and neere about the same on both sides, the regions are extreeme hote, and the people very blacke. Whereas contrarily such regions of the West Indies as are vnder the same line are very temperate, and the people neither blacke, nor with curlde and short wooll on their heads, as they of Africke haue, but of the colour of an Oliue, with long and blacke heare on their heads: the cause of which varietie is declared in diuers places in the Decades.

It is also worthy to be noted that some of them that were at this voyage told me: That is, that they ouertooke the course of the Sunne, so that they had it North from them at noone, the 14. day of March. And to haue said thus much of these voyages, it may suffice.

The first voyage made by Master VVilliam Towrson Marchant of London, to the coast of Guinea, with two Ships, in the yeere 1555.

Pon Sunday the thirtieth day of September wee departed from the Isle of Wight, out of the hauen of Neuport with two good shippes, the one called the Hart, the other the Hinde, both of London, and the Masters of them were Iohn Ralph, and William Carter, for a voyage to bee made vnto the Riuer de Sestos in Guinea, and to other hauens thereabout. · September.

It fell out by the varietie of windes, that it was the foureteenth day of October before wee could fetch Dartmouth: and being there arriued wee continued in that roade sixe dayes, and the 20. of October we warpt out of the hauen, and set saile, directing our course towards the Southwest, and the next morning we were runne by estimation thirty leagues. · October.

The first of Nouember we found our selues to be in 31. degrees of latitude by the reckoning of our Master. This day we ranne about 40. leagues also. · Nouember.

The second day we ranne 36. leagues.

The third day we had sight of Porto Santo, which is a small Island lying in the sea, about three leagues long, and a league & a halfe broad, & is possessed by Portugals. It riseth as we came from the Northnorthwest like two small hilles neere together. The East end of the same Island is a high land like a saddle with a valley, which makes it to beare that forme. The West end of it is lower with certaine small round hillocks. This Island lyeth in thirty and three degrees. The same day at 11. of the clocke we rayled the Isle of Madera, which lieth 12. leagues from Porto Santo, towards the Southwest: that Island is a faire Island and fruitfull, and is inhabited by Portugals, it riseth afarre off like a great whole land and high. By three of the clocke this day at after noone we were thwart of Porto Santo, and we set our course Southwest, to leaue the Isle of Madera to the Eastward, as we did Porto Santo. These two Islands were the first land that we saw since wee left the coast of England. About three of the clocke after midnight wee were thwart of Madera, within three leagues of the West ende of it, and by meanes of the high hilles there, we were becalmed: We suppose we ranne this day and night 30. leagues. · Porto Santo. · Madera.

The fourth day wee lay becalmed vnder the Isle of Madera, vntill one of the clocke at afternoone, and then, the winde comming into the East, we went our course, and ranne that day fifteene leagues.

The 5. day we ranne 15. leagues more.

The 6. day in the morning we rayled the Isle of Tenerif, otherwise called the Pike, because it is a very high Island, with a pike vpon the top like a loafe of suger. The same night we raised the Isle of Palma, which is a high land also, and to the Westward of the Isle of Tenerif. · Tenerif. · Palma.

The 7. day we perceiued the Isle of Gomera, which is an Island standing betwixt Tenerif and Palma, about 12. leagues Eastward from Palma, and 8. leagues Westward from Tenerif: and for feare of being becalmed with the Isle of Tenerif, we left both it, and Gomera to the Eastward of vs, and went betwixt Palma and Gomera. We ranne this day and night 30. leagues. · Gomera.

Note that these Islands be 60. leagues from Madera, and that there are 3. Islands more to the Westward of Tenerif, named the Grand Canaria, Forte-ventura, & Lancerot, of which Islands we came not in sight: they be inhabited by Spaniards.

This day also we had sight of the Isle of Ferro, which is to the Southwards 13. leagues from the other Islands, and is possessed by Spaniards. All this day and night by reason of the winde we · Ferro.

Figure 1.2 Hakluyt frequently marked temporal divisions with headings and marginalia, as in this 1555 voyage to West Africa by William Towerson.

connected story. Time-based recording is native to many of Hakluyt's documents, and sometimes (though not always) supervenes over the causal connections and selections characteristic of narrative.

Time thus functions as an organizing principle at multiple scales, from the style of individual documents to large groupings within the collection. We can easily imagine a version of *Principal Navigations* that would be organized historically, and indeed reorganizing Hakluyt's materials by year can allow us to perceive features that are not otherwise easy to see.[13] In the end, however, spatial thinking – not only by region but by route – is the collection's highest-order organizing category. It supervenes on all the other categories (of genre and time), and corresponds with the work's most prominent boundary marker, its division into "three several volumes, according to the positions of the Regions, whereunto they were directed." A division into three physical volumes was not absolutely necessitated by the size of the collection, and may not have been Hakluyt's original plan, but it provided the editor with an opportunity to align the physical boundaries of his volumes with spatial categories.[14] Pagination, title pages, and discrete sets of introductory materials all reinforce the spatial division of materials announced in Hakluyt's titles.

Many materials within each of the regional groupings marked in the paratext are engaged with common externalities of geography and culture, may record voyages organized by the same network of people, have related aims, and reflect similar resources and difficulties. This spatial organization invites us to consider Hakluyt's regional categories as bounded sets, to think of their contents as having something more than accidentally in common, and to look for shared properties and axes of comparison within these groups. There is also much to be understood by following threads of person, place, or source that cut across paratextual groupings. Drake's voyages, for instance, are distributed into several regional sections of volume 3, but the use of "first" and "last" in their headings alerts us to a sequence that overgoes regional categories; similarly, headings often name investors whose many and varied projects can be traced across the collection. Lacking an index, the second edition offers less assistance in following such connections than does the first edition of 1589, but Hakluyt's prefaces and marginal comments provide some indication of his own web of global thinking; the decline of confessional war in the near East, for instance, occasions a long digression promoting the settlement of

---

13 See, for instance, chapter 3, tables 3.1 to 3.2.
14 I am grateful to Anthony Payne for speaking with me about the production process of volume 2, with caveats about Hakluyt's intentions.

North America in the preface to volume 2, otherwise focused on voyages to the South and Southeast. Hakluyt's interest in both itineraries and individual actors means that while accepting the broad coherence of spatial categories, we also have to hold together what they separate. There are compelling historical and intellectual reasons to do so; as Joan-Pau Rubiés comments in a larger study of early modern travel collections, "separating America from parallel developments in Asia and Africa distorts a perspective from which the growth of geographical literature and its effects in Europe can best be understood."[15]

In organizing this book, I wanted to follow the contours of Hakluyt's own organizing systems, precisely because those systems are themselves a form of evidence and a topic of inquiry. Organization is information, whether it works to highlight the links between similar objects or to obscure them. More, the editor's active organization and selection of materials contributed to shaping the world as Hakluyt's readers would experience it through the mediation of his book. Across regions and across scales, some recurring questions will come to the surface: questions about the nature of authorship and the writing process; questions about the conceptual mapping of other regions and peoples, and the frameworks of climate, civility, and value that it evokes; questions about collective identity and how it is shaped, from the scale of a ship's crew to the scale of the nation. We will encounter these questions again and again from different angles.

Each of the three sections of this book focuses on one volume of *Principal Navigations*, joining together a regional geography, a set of projects, actors, and trajectories, and a category of the paratext. In addition to the particularities of activities, documents, and access associated with each volume, each of Hakluyt's volumes also exhibits particularities of method, and presents distinctive problems and opportunities. Before opening the book, some orientation to Hakluyt's volumes may be useful; readers who prefer to begin at chapter 2 may want to bookmark the overview and return to it as needed.

PART 1/VOLUME 1: VOYAGES TO THE NORTH AND NORTHEAST

Each of *Principal Navigations*'s three volumes opens with a selection of medieval texts. These older documents were among Hakluyt's major additions to the collection published in 1589. They represent an explicit new mandate for

---

15 Rubiés, "New Worlds and Renaissance Ethnology," 157.

the editor, who was now concerned not only with England's recent achievements but with *both* "our ancient and late navigations ... voyages ... and traffiques": "Which worke of mine I have not included within the compasse of things onely done in these latter dayes, as though litle or nothing woorthie of memorie had bene performed in former ages; but mounting aloft by the space of many hundred yeeres, have brought to light many rare and worthy monuments, which long have lien miserably scattered in mustie corners, & retchlessly hidden in mistie darknesse."[16] This change in editorial principles had the sharpest impact in volume 1, where a third of the volume's total page count (200 of 606 in total) concerns events before 1500.[17] George B. Parks calculates that as Hakluyt expanded the single volume *Principall Navigations* of 1589 into three volumes, volume 1 grew by roughly 275,000 words, of which the lion's share (more than 170,000 words) came from newly added medieval documents.[18]

The second distinctive feature of volume 1 was geographical. In 1589, the editor had committed to focusing on travels and trade beyond the boundaries of Europe, not relying "upon any action perfourmed neere home, nor in any part of Europe commonly frequented by our shipping." This commitment forced him to omit actions that any author of English maritime history would be hard-pressed to overlook, like "that victorious exploit not long since atchieved in our narow Seas agaynst that monstrous Spanish army under the valiant and provident conduct of the right honourable the Lord Charles Howard high Admirall of England" as well as English raids on Lisbon and Cádiz, and the taking of the *Madre de Deus* carrack. These "singular and happy voyages of our renowned countrymen" had to be excluded, "as things distinct and without the compass of my prescribed limits.[19] In preparing the second edition of *Principal Navigations*, Hakluyt reversed course, including all of the actions listed in the 1589 preface and many more. While most of the naval actions were added to volume 2, the largest number of European

16 Hakluyt, "Epistle Dedicatorie (1598)," 1: sig. *2r.
17 The "total pages" figure does not include "The honourable voyage to Cadiz," which appears in some copies at the end of volume 1. See chapter 7 for a discussion of this text; the bibliographical situation is examined in Payne, *Guide*.
18 Parks, *Hakluyt and the English Voyages*, 175n4. By contrast, volume 2 gained 185,000 words compared to the 1589 edition, of which 5,000 were from medieval documents; and volume 3 gained 540,000 words, of which 6,000 were from medieval documents. The *total* size of volume 1's medieval materials, 175,000 words, also dwarfs that of volumes 2 (65,500) and 3 (7,350). (Figures are those provided by Parks, ibid.)
19 Hakluyt, "Preface to the Reader (1589)," sig. *3v.

materials can be found in volume 1, which begins with medieval accounts of English voyages to and trade with continental Europe and concludes with accounts of the Armada battle and the raid on Cádiz.

Chapter 2 surveys medieval and earlier materials on the British Isles, along with medieval missionary accounts of Central Asia; Hakluyt's versions of domestic history and his accounts of medieval Europe's furthest peripheries suggest various understandings of near and far, self and other, where the boundaries of inside and outside are placed. Chapter 3 looks at Robert Thorne's proposals for northern exploration in the early decades of the sixteenth century as part of Hakluyt's effort to construct a genealogy for the northern voyages of the 1550s, and to represent them as a national project that was both prestigious and world-historical; his biography suggests some of what this effort made *less* visible. Chapter 4 examines writing associated with the Northeast Passage search of 1553 and its sequels: instructions for writing, forms of writing actually produced, and the collision of ideas about the Arctic with actual encounters.

PART 2/VOLUME 2: VOYAGES TO THE SOUTH AND SOUTHEAST, WITHIN AND WITHOUT THE STRAIT OF GIBRALTAR

As we have seen, Hakluyt joined a new set of materials on England's ancient history and medieval trades with Europe to his materials on northern voyages, and the resulting volume became the first in the compilation as a whole, giving literal precedence to a national history absent from *PN* (1589). Volume 2 of the second edition begins with the travels to the Holy Land that had opened the first edition of 1589, but the dedication announces another important change to the compilation's organizational scheme.[20] While the first edition had intermingled voyages to the Mediterranean, the Near East, West Africa, and South Asia in chronological sequence, under the common heading of voyages to the South and Southeast, the second edition would divide these materials into two distinct parts: voyages "through and within" and "without" the Strait of Gibraltar, categories that correspond roughly (though not exactly) with the Islamic Mediterranean and Near East, in part 1,

---

20 Hakluyt, "Epistle Dedicatorie (1599)," sig. *3v.

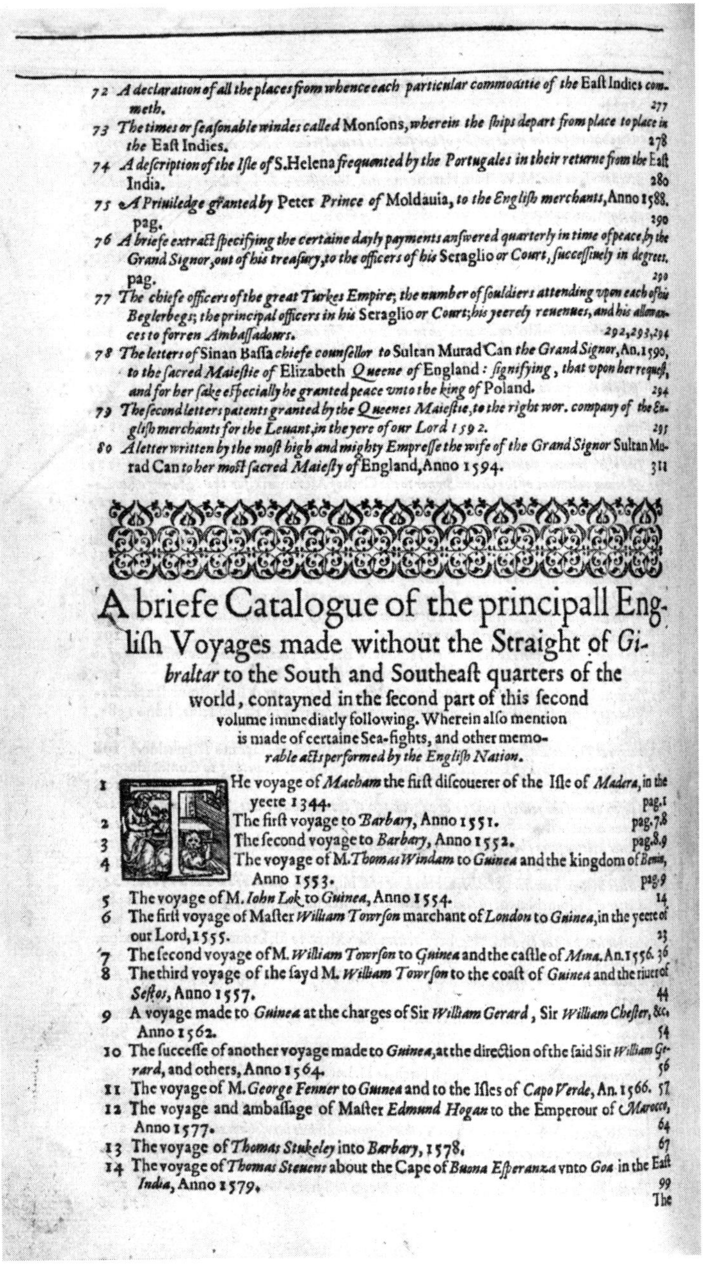

72 *A declaration of all the places from whence each particular commoditie of the East Indies commeth.* 277
73 *The times or seasonable windes called* Monsons, *wherein the ships depart from place to place in the East Indies.* 278
74 *A description of the Isle of S.* Helena *frequented by the Portugales in their returne from the East India.* 280
75 *A Priuiledge granted by* Peter *Prince of Moldauia, to the English merchants,* Anno 1588. pag. 290
76 *A briefe extract specifying the certaine dayly payments answered quarterly in time of peace, by the Grand Signor, out of his treasury, to the officers of his* Seraglio *or Court, successiuely in degrees.* pag. 290
77 *The chiefe officers of the great Turkes Empire; the number of souldiers attending vpon each of his Beglerbegs; the principal officers in his Seraglio or Court; his yeerely reuenues, and his allowances to forren Ambassadours.* 292,293,294
78 *The letters of* Sinan Bassa *chiefe counsellor to* Sultan Murad Can *the Grand Signor,* An.1590, *to the sacred Maiestie of* Elizabeth *Queene of England: signifying, that vpon her request, and for her sake especially he granted peace vnto the king of Poland.* 294
79 *The second letters patents granted by the Queenes Maiestie, to the right wor. company of the English merchants for the Leuant, in the yere of our Lord* 1592. 295
80 *A letter written by the most high and mighty Empresse the wife of the Grand Signor* Sultan Murad Can *to her most sacred Maiesty of* England, Anno 1594. 311

A briefe Catalogue of the principall English Voyages made without the Straight of *Gibraltar* to the South and Southeast quarters of the world, contayned in the second part of this second volume immediatly following. Wherein also mention is made of certaine Sea-fights, and other memorable acts performed by the English Nation.

1 The voyage of *Macham* the first discouerer of the Isle of *Madera*, in the yeere 1344. pag.1
2 The first voyage to *Barbary*, Anno 1551. pag.7,8
3 The second voyage to *Barbary*, Anno 1552. pag.8,9
4 The voyage of M. *Thomas Windam* to *Guinea* and the kingdom of *Benin*, Anno 1553. pag.9
5 The voyage of M. *Iohn Lok* to *Guinea*, Anno 1554. 14
6 The first voyage of Master *William Towrson* marchant of *London* to *Guinea*, in the yeere of our Lord, 1555. 23
7 The second voyage of M. *William Towrson* to *Guinea* and the castle of *Mina*. An.1556. 36
8 The third voyage of the sayd M. *William Towrson* to the coast of *Guinea* and the riuer of *Sestos*, Anno 1557. 44
9 A voyage made to *Guinea* at the charges of Sir *William Gerard*, Sir *William Chester*, &c. Anno 1562. 54
10 The successe of another voyage made to *Guinea*, at the direction of the said Sir *William Gerard*, and others, Anno 1564. 56
11 The voyage of M. *George Fenner* to *Guinea* and to the Isles of *Capo Verde*, An. 1566. 57
12 The voyage and ambassage of Master *Edmund Hogan* to the Emperour of *Marocco*, Anno 1577. 64
13 The voyage of *Thomas Stukeley* into *Barbary*, 1578. 67
14 The voyage of *Thomas Steuens* about the Cape of *Buona Esperanza* vnto *Goa* in the East India, Anno 1579. 99

The

Figure 1.3 The table of contents for volume 2, like the title page, emphasizes its division into two parts.

and West Africa below the Sahara, in part 2 – with travel to the Indian Ocean and South Asia distributed according to the route travelled.[21]

Hakluyt underlined this new geographical division in several aspects of the organization and presentation of volume 2. The first and second parts of the volume share a dedicatory epistle, but are assigned distinct lists of contents that appear in sequence at the beginning of the volume, with headings identifying the materials that follow as belonging to "the first part" or "the second part" of the volume.[22] The first part of the volume, on "voyages ... by and within the Streight of Gibraltar to the South and Southeast," concludes on page 312. On the following page, the second part of the volume begins with a general heading that echoes the grander presentation of travels "through and within the Streight of Gibraltar" on the volume's title page. This break is also marked by separate pagination: following page 312, the following page is numbered page 1.

There could be a number of motivations for Hakluyt's decision to organize the volume in this bifurcated way, not all of which would be conceptually important: for instance, the editor may have felt the need to impose order on an increasingly large volume of materials, or there may have been delays in the editor's access to or in the preparation of materials from different sources or at the hands of different assistants. The *fact* of the volume's division, however, has the effect of drawing distinct borders around groups of materials that each have a regional focus. This feature of the paratext invites readers to think regionally – and invites critical readers to reflect on the meanings and effects of thinking that has been organized by such borders around regions, borders which are never "given" or simply natural but are products of human actions and choices, whatever the nature of the physical terrain.[23]

---

21 These regional categories index the bulk of each part's contents without comprehensively describing them. The first half of volume 2 – hereafter, 2(i) – includes travels as far as India and Ceylon, when these were initiated through the Mediterranean; the second half, volume 2(ii), includes materials on China and Japan, as well as one long voyage around Africa and into the Indian Ocean. Other materials on Persia can be found in volume 1; these resulted from travels that passed through Muscovy, and thus were grouped by Hakluyt with "voyages to the North and Northeast."

22 The two "catalogues" of the volume's contents appear in sequence on sig.*5r to *7v and sig.*7v to *8v.

23 On "sub-Saharan Africa" as a category, and a view of the Sahara as space of communication rather than dividing line, see Lydon, "Saharan Oceans."

Chapters 5 and 6 follow Hakluyt in treating materials from the volume's two parts as distinct sets, centring on the circum-Mediterranean world and on sub-Saharan Africa respectively. The third and last chapter, chapter 7, turns to a set of narratives on maritime conflict with Spain in the Atlantic; these materials, present occasionally in volume 1 and the first half of volume 2, cluster most densely among the African materials in the second part of volume 2. Many common threads can be traced across these different landscapes and seascapes: narrating encounter, seeking trade, recruiting foreign expertise, narrating violence. The volume's categories and juxtapositions invite us to observe their variation across regions.

PART 3/VOLUME 3: VOYAGES TO THE WEST

The first two sections of this book largely follow (or scrutinize) Hakluyt's organizing principles, focusing on groups of materials defined by paratextual interventions that, in turn, reflect spatial and temporal logics. (For instance, as we have seen, volume 2 distinguishes between Africa below and above the Sahara, associating the latter with the Mediterranean and further differentiating it into two chronological categories characterized by different modes of interaction.) For the two earlier volumes, looking at the materials as Hakluyt chose to associate them presented an opportunity to think about how spatial and textual geographies took on meaning both for the editor and for his travellers and authors. The *copia* of volume 3 – both in numbers of documents and numbers of headings – resists this approach.

The third volume of *PN* (1598–1600) – focused on the Americas and westward voyages into the Pacific – had properties that distinguished it from volumes 1 and 2, calling for a different approach from the editor as well as in this book. The chief difference highlighted by Hakluyt was the abundance of materials available to him on the Americas and the Pacific: he was "much more plentifully furnished with matter."[24] Using George B. Parks's count of 819,350 words, volume 3 is more than twice as long as the two parts of volume 2 combined, and longer than volume 1 by 329,000 words. Of this considerable total, only 7,350 words were devoted to medieval materials; the weight of the contemporary is thus far greater than in either of the two previous volumes. In fact, the sum of contemporary materials in volumes 1 and 2 together would still fall significantly short of those contained in volume 3.

---

24 Hakluyt, "Epistle Dedicatorie (1600)," sig. A2v.

That copious supply required or permitted a much finer-grained organizational strategy. Rather than creating the broad, spatio-temporal categories we saw in the first two volumes of the collection, Hakluyt grouped his materials into fourteen regional "branches," beginning with the Arctic and moving clockwise around the Americas to conclude with voyages of circumnavigation. Each regional category has its own heading in the volume's "General Catalogue," and each is divided by the "Catalogue" into two sub-categories of voyages and associated documents: these are variously characterized as letters, rutters, patents, instructions, intercepted letters, observations, advertisements, and intelligences.

Volume 3 also has a second distinctive feature. While there is a clear spatial logic to the volume's organization, the kinds of materials that populate its categories are wildly disparate in nature, because English contacts with different regions of the Americas were not uniform in nature or intensity. In consequence, because Hakluyt's copious supply of materials by English hands was not evenly distributed across the hemispheric region he set out to cover, this volume of the "English voyages" contains an especially high proportion of texts in translation that describe the discoveries of (especially) the Spanish and the French in the Americas, as well as Portuguese materials on East Asia (a small number of other such materials are found in the second half of volume 2). These materials, as typical for the collection, are varied in nature; many are excerpts (and thus present some of the problems characterizing medieval sources, in that a surrounding context has to be understood), some have also generated extensive bibliographies, and all have, of course, been translated through a variety of means.

The substantial presence of these materials in translation, and on the travels and discoveries of other nations, highlights a critical point: Hakluyt's *Principal Navigations*, innovative in its national focus, is nonetheless *not* exclusively either an account of English travels or a collection of English sources. The editor's use of non-English sources (of both kinds) has not always been adequately appreciated; indeed, both the title "Principal Navigations ... of the *English Nation*" and Hakluyt's own prefatory comments encourage readers to focus their attention elsewhere. Yet Hakluyt's engagement with travel knowledge and travel writing in other languages was both an important feature of the collection and a major theme in his career. The first chapter of this section, chapter 8, examines the practice and politics of translation in *PN* (1598–1600) and in the editor's career more generally, examining Hakluyt's work with foreign sources and informants of various nationalities, and his own sole effort to publicize English voyages in languages other than English, de Bry's *America*, part 1.

While the English had little or no direct experience of some regions of the Americas, others were intensive targets of English activities or claims; thus, along with a wealth of materials in translation, volume 3 is *also* especially rich in substantial narrative accounts of English travel, many now very well known, some with their own histories of publication before and after Hakluyt's collection. Some of these narrative texts (and the haloes of manuscript, visual, and material evidence that surround them) have generated an extensive, nuanced, and multidisciplinary literature: examples include Walter Ralegh's account of his explorations in Guiana, Thomas Harriot's tract on the attractions of the English settlement at Roanoke, the "Famous Voyage" account of Francis Drake's circumnavigation, and the various accounts of Martin Frobisher's three Northwest Passage searches by George Best, Dionyse Settle, and Thomas Ellis.[25] Thus, while the earlier sections of this book aimed at giving readers a general sense of the kinds of contents they might find in different parts of a volume, both the expansive contents and extensive secondary literature associated with volume 3 make such an approach seem less plausible and useful: a matter of ploughing over a large number of fields ably covered by a growing body of focused scholarship.

Rather than following Hakluyt's divisions of the Americas by region, the second and third chapters on volume 3 take a different approach. Chapter 9 turns to a set of acts and documents that were both far flung and largely self-contained. The records of the well-documented but less well-studied voyages of John Davis, into the high latitudes of the Arctic and the Straits of Magellan, recount important encounters with the Inuit in Western Greenland; they also offer a look at the behaviours of shipboard communities under stress, when the supporting context of home was very far away. The plural voice of maritime writing invites us to think about the implications of both dynamics for how collective identities were articulated, challenged, and remade in the crucible of distant voyages. Chapter 10, on the Caribbean and the Pacific, examines the other side of the coin: voyages that joined new navigations with triumphant aggression against the far-flung empire of Spain. For readers familiar with Hakluyt's work in the form of anthologies, these narratives may present its most familiar face: raids on the Spanish Indies and incursions into the Pacific

---

25 Ralegh, "Voyage of Sir Walter Ralegh"; Harriot, "Briefe and True Report" (*PN*); "Famous Voyage"; Best, "True Discourse"; Settle, "Second Voyage of Frobisher, 1577"; Ellis, "Third Voyage unto Meta Incognita, 1578." All but "Famous Voyage" were previously published as individual works, and in some cases subsequently in other collections that included illustrations. (For a discussion of the 1590 Harriot, see chapter 7).

through the Straits of Magellan, both exemplified in the career of Sir Francis Drake. Drake's voyages return us to questions about authorship, national and confessional identity, and the nature of what made its way into the print record.

My interest in Hakluyt's work has long been animated by the need to look beyond well-trodden readerly and critical paths that leave much of its contents untouched. Some familiar questions and topics thread through the book: how a common identity is shaped; how nationally defined selves and communities address what is foreign to them; how the stories of conflict, exchange, and accommodation that negotiate across that boundary are told. These are questions on which Hakluyt's career, and the evidence of *Principal Navigations*, have often been brought into evidence, and I hope to contribute to those discussions. Yet however the conclusions of this book fare in the marketplace of ideas, I hope that – practically speaking – it will also provide an orienting overview and guide to readers that will complement the detail we can anticipate from a critical edition.

My larger aspiration is to provide an account of the work that can displace the ideas about it inherited from an earlier era. While I began with a passage from Virginia Woolf, the nineteenth-century historian James Froude's description of *Principal Navigations* as the "prose epic of the English nation" has long framed discussions of Hakluyt's book. The tenacious hold of such ideas is considerable, and continued citation of Froude by scholars working in a very different historical moment testifies to our shared need for a summary perspective on this sprawling work and its legacy.[26] Yet if this is a work to which national communities can turn for powerful narratives of identity and origin, more than a century of historical change divides the needs of Froude's time from those of our own. Hakluyt's book is not simply a thoroughly controlled and rationalized expression of nationalism imbued with Protestant zeal, but nor is it a casual accretion of all the geographical materials available to a diligent English researcher of the late Elizabethan age. Such descriptions can be supported only by a highly selective reading of a work whose gargantuan length and heterogeneous contents both demand and challenge summary. With more than a century of scholarship to build on, it is time to develop and make use of a new perspective on Hakluyt's work.

---

26 Froude, "England's Forgotten Worthies," 361. See also Raleigh, "English Seamen." For a more extended discussion of Froude and Raleigh, see Fuller, *Voyages in Print*, chap. 4.

NOTE ON REFERENCES

Since questions of authorship, provenance, and editorial handling all affect our understanding of a given content, the component documents of *Principal Navigations* are treated as discrete items for reference purposes, with citation by author (if known), item title, volume, and page number in the original text of PN (1598–1600). The frequent use of twentieth-century editions with distinct pagination and volume divisions in earlier scholarship sometimes left readers without access to the particular edition cited unable to identify, locate, or consult the material being discussed. The modern advent of digital text has made possible a standard of reference that was always needed. Providing item titles and other search terms should also enable readers without access to the original (digital or otherwise) to locate materials in existing editions. As other scholars have shown, moreover, Hakluyt's document titles can themselves be an interesting form of evidence. In elevating the specificity of the compilation's component texts, I hope also to provide greater clarity about Hakluyt's own specific interventions as editor and compiler.[27] Hakluyt's older cousin of the same name, Richard Hakluyt the lawyer, has been cited as "Hakluyt, Esq." to distinguish him from the editor.

Most early modern sources, for similar reasons, are cited in the original. While *Principal Navigations* is paginated in modern style, sources that are not paginated are referenced either by signature (the discrete gatherings of pages assembled to make a book), page number, and side (sig. A2r, for instance, the recto side of the second leaf in signature A) or, where appropriate for a particular book, by leaf number and side (fo. 160v, the verso side of leaf 160). While signatures are usually ordered alphabetically, signatures containing the front matter to a volume were often designated using non-alphabetic characters (*, **, or ¶, most frequently). Original spelling has been maintained except for the silent interchange of u/v and i/j.

---

27 On Hakluyt's paratext, valuable contributions include Day, "Richard Hakluyt's 'Principal Navigations' (1598–1600) and the Textuality of Tudor English Nationalism"; Day, "Hakluyt, Harvey, Nashe"; Schleck, "Forming the Captivity of Thomas Saunders"; MacCrossan, "Framing 'the English Nation.'"

PART ONE

North and Northeast

THE
PRINCIPAL NAVI-
GATIONS, VOIAGES,
TRAFFIQVES AND DISCO-
ueries of the English Nation, made by Sea
or ouer-land, to the remote and farthest distant quarters of the Earth, at any time within
the compasse of these 1500. yeeres: Deuided
into three seuerall Volumes, according to the
positions of the Regions, whereunto
they were directed.

This first Volume containing the woorthy Discoueries,
&c. of the English toward the North and Northeast by sea,
as of *Lapland, Scriksinia, Corelia,* the Baie of *S. Nicolas,* the Isles of *Col-
goieue, Vaigatz,* and *Noua Zembla,* toward the great riuer *Ob,*
with the mighty Empire of *Russia,* the *Caspian* sea, *Geor-
gia, Armenia, Media, Persia, Boghar* in *Bactria,*
and diuers kingdoms of *Tartaria:*

Together with many notable monuments and testimonies of the ancient forren trades, and of the warrelike and
other shipping of this realme of *England* in former ages.

VVhereunto is annexed also a briefe Commentarie of the true
state of *Island,* and of the Northren Seas and
lands situate that way.

And lastly, the memorable defeate of the Spanish huge
Armada, Anno 1 5 8 8. and the famous victorie
atchieued at the citie of *Cadiz, 1 5 9 6.*
are described.

By RICHARD HAKLVYT Master of
Artes, and sometime Student of Christ-
Church in Oxford.

¶ Imprinted at London by GEORGE
BISHOP, RALPH NEWBERIE
and ROBERT BARKER.
1598.

2

Remembering the North: Hakluyt's Medieval Materials

THE FIRST VOLUME OF RICHARD HAKLUYT'S *Principal Navigations, Voyages, Traffiques and Discoveries of the English Nation* (1598–1600) is bracketed with rousing stories of national achievement: concluding with the defeat of the Spanish Armada (and in some copies, the 1596 raid on Cádiz), the volume opens with King Arthur's conquest of Ireland and Iceland, and the voluntary submission to him of kingdoms in "all the other islands" of the North Atlantic, as far as Lapland in the East and the Pole in the North.[1] The appeal to myth has an undeniable rhetorical impact: we all "know" King Arthur, even if the legend of his northern conquests may not be the most familiar part of Arthur's story.[2] The legibility of this opening moment invites extrapolation towards a sense of knowing Hakluyt (or at least his book). Yet as other excerpts from medieval texts follow, a modern reader's sense of familiarity and coherence may fade, confronting materials that are often obscure, are certainly fragmentary, and obey a logic of selection that is often less readily apparent. The first volume of *Principal Navigations*, from its opening pages, thus begins to introduce us to some of the compilation's distinctive challenges and questions. If

---

1 Geoffrey of Monmouth, "Voyage of Arthur K. of Britaine"; Lambarde, "A Testimonie of M. Lambard." David and Alison Quinn identify Hakluyt's source for Geoffrey's text as Jerome Commelin, *Rerum Brittanicum* [...] *scriptores* (Heidelberg, 1587) ("c&s"). Hakluyt's accounts of the Armada and the voyage to Cádiz are discussed in chapter 7, with other materials on the Anglo-Spanish sea war.
2 Hakluyt was far from alone in continuing to treat Geoffrey as a useful source, and the story of Arthur was not easily abandoned despite a long history of skepticism. I discuss his use of Arthurian and other fabulous material in Fuller, "Arthur and Amazons." On the sixteenth-century debate on the historicity of King Arthur, see, for example, Kendrick, *British Antiquity*; Carley, "Polydore Vergil and John Leland on King Arthur"; McKisack, *Medieval History in the Tudor Age*; Levy, *Tudor Historical Thought*.

some highly visible or recognizable documents suggest a clear agenda for the compilation as a whole, more detailed attention to its contents will destabilize the clarity that, for example, the opening and closing moments of volume 1 might appear to offer.[3] Myth and ideology are interwoven with a discourse of fact; if Hakluyt has been famous for his commitment to the latter, we can't be confident that his editorial standards were uniformly applied. Claims about Arthur's conquest of Ireland, Iceland, Orkney, and other North Atlantic territories in the sixth century CE also point us to two features that distinguish volume 1 within *Principal Navigations* as a whole: sustained attention to the longer past before 1500, and inclusion of what was geographically near at hand as well as what was distant. The substantial group of medieval materials in volume 1, including domestic and European trade as well as distant travels, will be the focus of this chapter.

By opening his compilation of distant voyages with older materials on England's maritime and commercial history, Hakluyt sought to provide the achievements of his contemporaries with a past, "that no man should imagine that our forren trades ... have not bene of any long continuance."[4] The motives for this broader work of historical recovery were both legal – providing plausible grounds for rights to settle, explore, or trade – and rhetorical, seeking to maintain that the English were not latecomers compared to Portugal and Spain, but had long been at sea making voyages and discoveries of their own, and engaging in the kinds of adventurous trade that Hakluyt would document.[5] A volume beginning with the conquests of King Arthur and ending with the defeat of the Armada seems well aligned with these aims. Yet the older materials that follow the Arthur excerpt, both local and distant ones, raise more inwardly focused questions: What were the limits and extent of the national community that was to be celebrated? What was the nature of its boundaries,

---

3 The volume's concluding documents are discussed in chapter 7. For an alternate account, see Boruchoff, "Piety, Patriotism, and Empire," 829–50.

4 Hakluyt, "Preface to the Reader (1598)," sig. *5v.

5 Hakluyt's interest in claiming rights of discovery in North America shaped his selection of materials in clear and important ways, and is expressed most explicitly in his 1584 manuscript treatise, "A Particuler Discourse" (also known as "Discourse of Western Planting"); see *PD*. On English thinking about rights of discovery, trade, travel, and settlement, see also Benton, *A Search for Sovereignty*; Tomlins, *Freedom Bound*; Fitzmaurice, *Sovereignty*; MacMillan, *Sovereignty*. Lauren Benton indeed suggests a legal dimension to Hakluyt's decision "to assemble first-person voyage accounts as if they constituted an array of evidence instead of composing a comprehensive narrative of English overseas travel" (Benton, *A Search for Sovereignty*, 28).

and what were the contours of the "us" to be distinguished from an either distant or proximate "them"?

The medieval materials of volume 1 also invite us to engage with questions of editorial treatment and aims. *Principal Navigations* typically presents its constituent documents with little of the explicit framing and connecting text provided in compilations of travels by near contemporaries, like the *Navigationi et viaggi* (Venice, 1550–59) of Giovanni Battista Ramusio (on which Hakluyt relied for a number of items) or Samuel Purchas's *Hakluytus Posthumus or Purchas his Pilgrimes* (London, 1626), which, as the name indicates, drew on Hakluyt's continued collecting efforts. Hakluyt's treatment of medieval materials adds an additional challenge to this absence of editorial comment. Rather than reproducing whole documents (as he does elsewhere in the compilation), Hakluyt populated the medieval sections of *Principal Navigations* in large part with paragraph-length excerpts from longer works, providing both Latin and English versions but leaving readers to guess at context. The discontinuity and fragmentary nature of these medieval materials present issues that are native to the book as a whole in especially acute form.[6]

On the other hand, Hakluyt's medieval materials present us with distinctive opportunities and forms of information. Each of *Principal Navigations*'s medieval documents had a rich history of transmission and reception, extended across the centuries in which manuscripts were read, copied, disseminated, collected, forgotten, and rediscovered. Reading older documents critically invites us to retrace their origins and trajectories, as physical and cultural objects created at an earlier moment, and eventually – by a variety of means – reaching Hakluyt's hands. For each such item, there are in effect three stories to take into account: first, *what* happened, and why it mattered; second, *when* a record of "what happened" was produced, where, and for what reason; third, *where* a document was located in the late sixteenth century – both in intellectual history, and as a unique object held in a particular repository – and how it came to Hakluyt's attention, and into his hands. Questions of provenance and selection loom larger because the editor had centuries' (rather than decades') worth of events and documents to choose from; following the trail of materials as Hakluyt accessed them can tell us more about how (and perhaps why) he chose them. The rich medieval materials in volume 1, with their histories of

---

6 The question of PN's coherence – or lack thereof – has become a classic question in studies of Hakluyt's work. See, inter alia, Das, "Hakluyt's Two Indias"; Sacks, "Rebuilding Solomon's Temple"; Sacks, "Richard Hakluyt's Navigations in Time"; Mancall, *Hakluyt's Promise*.

ownership, circulation, and use, thus promise insights about how the work as a whole was assembled.

Had Hakluyt's own books and papers survived, we might have ampler resources for thinking about such questions. Early modern readers often left a trail of evidence, using their books in ways far more vigorous and interactive than a silent, solitary scanning of the printed page.[7] Much of what we understand about reading in Elizabethan England comes from studying readers who left a trail of explicit, written evidence about their reading: writing in the margins, noting their reading in diaries or commonplace books, leaving lists of books and manuscripts they owned (or hoped to own). Hakluyt's predecessor Richard Eden, whose *Decades of the Newe World* (1555) included the first original narratives of new English voyages, left a densely annotated copy of the work by Pietro Martire d'Anghiera that formed the core of his compilation. Other readers cut up and disassembled books and manuscripts in order to reassemble their parts into new forms and new combinations, a practice closely akin to Hakluyt's own editorial work: the collection's internal fragmentation and discontinuity may well have reflected and harmonized with the ways early modern readers read.[8] Yet Hakluyt himself left almost no trail of physical texts. He obviously read widely: he complained in a dedication to the 1598 volume about the "great charges and infinite cares" of seeking out his materials and the "mustie corners" in which he found them.[9] Samuel Purchas would later complain about the difficulty and expense of acquiring Hakluyt's collection after the earlier editor's death, and his own compilation carefully noted many items originally acquired (but not previously printed) by Hakluyt. But beyond its afterlife in Purchas's printed collection, Hakluyt's

---

    7 The vast and growing literature on early modern annotation practices resists summary here; key points of orientation for me have been Sherman, *Used Books*; Orgel, *Reader in the Book*. Both a useful overview of the literature and a fascinating database *of* early modern annotations can be found at https://archaeologyofreading.org.

    8 Eden's copy of *De orbe novo* (1533) is held at Johns Hopkins Special Collections (Garrett Library Ei41.A51 1533 QUARTO); for a brief description, see Havens, "Americana Vetustissima." On cutting as a reading practice, see, for instance, Fleming, *Graffiti and the Writing Arts of Early Modern England*; Fleming, "Afterword." On readers' marks in surviving copies of *PN*, see Day, "Richard Hakluyt's 'Principal Navigations' (1598–1600) and the Textuality of Tudor English Nationalism."

    9 Hakluyt, "Epistle Dedicatorie (1598)," sig. *2v.

personal library has disappeared almost entirely.[10] Hakluyt's reading manifests almost entirely through his authorship.[11] In place of the working collection that once existed, we have the results in *Principal Navigations*, a compilation not only adapted to the practice of early modern readers, but itself the evidence of what one man read.

Both as the editor of *Principal Navigations* and in his professional life more broadly, Hakluyt can usefully be regarded as a manager of information: a collector, selector, and sorter, annotating, organizing, and sometimes translating texts that others had written. With contemporary materials, he could sometimes solicit oral or written accounts directly from travellers; for older materials, his work necessarily relied on prior acts of collection and selection by editors, compilers, and owners of libraries.[12] Some choices were in effect made not at the scale of the individual document, but by incorporating sources already accorded importance by Hakluyt's acquaintances and patrons. The editor's replication of materials sometimes amplified selections and priorities that to some extent existed before and outside the boundaries of his own work.

Hakluyt had published a shorter first edition of the compilation, *Principall Navigations* (1589); in the earlier work the bulk of Hakluyt's pre-modern materials had related to voyages of pilgrimage and crusade ("voyages to the

10 See Purchas, *Pilgrimes*, 1: sig. 4v. The contents list of *Pilgrimes* identifies with an "H" 121 items collected but not printed by Hakluyt, and more have been traced by scholars (Steele, "From Hakluyt to Purchas," 74). One of the few surviving items traceable to Hakluyt is a Mexican book, the *Codex Mendoza*, which passed with the rest of his papers to Purchas, from Purchas' son to John Selden, and thence to the Bodleian Library, where it is today. What remains of Hakluyt's library and the work of collecting and reading associated with it, must largely be reconstructed through his bibliography. A list of publications by or associated with Hakluyt is provided in Payne, *Guide*. (Anthony Payne's *Bibliography of Richard Hakluyt* is forthcoming from the Hakluyt Society.)

11 For instance, William Sherman considers Hakluyt's "Particuler Discourse" (1584) as "evidence of ... reading practices" such as "summarizing, epitomizing, abridging, and collecting" (*John Dee*, 65). Intriguing connections between Hakluyt and Gabriel Harvey, one of the most well-studied of early modern readers, are explored in Day, "Hakluyt, Harvey, Nashe." Although *Principal Navigations* contains numerous and often significant printed marginalia, not all are the editor's. Some texts came to Hakluyt already annotated, and these annotations are simply reproduced; the "Libelle of Englyshe Polycye" is one example of such a document. The printed text of *Principal Navigations* does not clearly distinguish Hakluyt's marginalia from that present in the original documents.

12 Examples of Hakluyt's wide-ranging and energetic search for early sixteenth-century materials include his efforts to seek out and interview aged survivors of a 1533 voyage into the eastern Mediterranean, or a 1536 voyage to Newfoundland ("Voyage to the Iles of Candia and Chio, 1534 [and] 1535"; "Voyage of M. Hore").

south and south-east," in his organizing scheme), and many were drawn from a single source: the mid-century compilation of John Bale, *Scriptorum illustrium maioris Brytanniae ... catalogus* (Basle, 1557–59).[13] The second edition reflected a broader and more wide-ranging program of research that was especially active for materials relating to the history of Britain itself; its fruits are thus especially visible in volume 1. Excerpts (often of a page or less) taken from medieval chroniclers like Geoffrey of Monmouth, John of Worcester (misidentified as Florence), and the venerable Bede tell us that Edwin, King of Northumberland, had dominion over both Britain and the surrounding islands (624 CE); that King Edgar made an annual practice of circumnavigating the British Isles with his navy (973 CE); or that the daughter of Harold Godwinson, after his defeat at the Battle of Hastings, married the Duke of Russia (1067 CE). Extended accounts of two missions to the Mongol Khan in the mid-1200s, one by an Italian and one by a Fleming, are given in Latin as well as English, and prefaced by a brief account of an Englishman who had served the Mongols as a translator; materials on the Mongols occupy almost one hundred folio pages in volume 1, close to half of the space devoted to medieval travels.[14] Following these longer materials, English shipping and English travellers of the fourteenth century are registered through (again) a number of brief excerpts. A new subheading (not in the table of contents) introduces materials on "the original, proceedings and successe of the Northren domestical and forren trades and traffiques of this Isle of Britain from the time of Nero the Emperor ... untill this present time." (In fact, the section covers through 1462.)[15] From monks drinking mare's milk on the way to Karakoram, readers are plunged into charters, leagues, safe conducts, trade negotiations with the Baltic, and letters about the fish and textiles that English merchants carried there. The early materials in volume 1 were widely varied in topic, type, length, and geographical reference. Nonetheless, they will allow for some general observations about Hakluyt's methods and the provenance of his materials, which – while various – exhibit some marked patterns.

---

13 Quinn and Quinn, "C&S." On Bale's bio-bibliography of English authors, dedicated to Elizabeth shortly after her accession, see, inter alia, Warner, "Savior of Books." The medieval materials in *PN* (1589) on the North included the same excerpts from Commelin, John Dee, and William Lambard that would appear in volume 1 of the second edition. On the differences between the two compilations of 1589 and 1598–1600, see D. Quinn and Skelton, "Introduction."

14 These documents are discussed in the last section of this chapter.

15 On the timespan covered, see Ramsay, "Northern Europe."

Most of Hakluyt's medieval documents narrated *events* from earlier centuries and also were *composed* in earlier centuries by chroniclers like Bede (672–735), Geoffrey of Monmouth (ca. 1100–1155), William of Malmesbury (ca. 1090–1142), or John of Worcester (f. 1095–1140). Yet apart from documents found in the Patent Rolls and similar bureaucratic repositories, Hakluyt typically read his medieval history in forms that were quite up to date, including recent editions by Matthew Parker (Matthew Paris, 1571; Thomas Walsingham, 1574), Lord William Howard (John of Worcester, *Chronicon*, 1592), Henry Savile (William of Malmesbury, 1591), and Jerome Commelin (Geoffrey of Monmouth, 1587), as well as works by William Lambarde (1568, 1596) and William Camden (1594) that drew extensively on earlier materials.[16] Hakluyt's selection of medieval materials was in dialogue with a particular context of intellectual work and exchange *about* the past during the Tudor period, from which these editions emerged.

The sixteenth century saw important changes in both what English people knew (or thought they knew) about their history, and how they came to know it. Broadly speaking, the dissolution of the monasteries by Henry VIII (1536–41) put into circulation centuries-old collections of manuscripts, the largest libraries then existing in England. The outflow of monastic manuscripts, and their obvious vulnerability to loss and destruction, stimulated some important efforts of collection and scholarship (those of Bale and Lambarde among them). New libraries were formed, in the houses of men like William Cecil, Matthew Parker, and (later) Robert Cotton; under their incitement and patronage, others sought out valuable manuscripts, learned how to read them, and began to assimilate, sift, and compile their information. Historical sources, in turn, were combined with attention to other kinds of evidence: place names, inscriptions, coins, artifacts. William Camden's historical geography, the *Brittania* (in various editions from 1594), was one important outcome of such projects. In this context of active scholarship, mythic histories like those of Britain's foundation by the Trojan Brutus or the conquests of King Arthur received skeptical scrutiny in some quarters even as other scholars searched diligently and hopefully for corroborating evidence. Myth was not the only target of Tudor historians. With Henry VIII's break from Rome to found the Church of England in 1533, new arguments about the past became necessary, in order to make the case that the English church represented not schismatic

---

16 For editions consulted by Hakluyt, see Quinn and Quinn, "c&s." (This source is likely to be superseded in many details by the forthcoming Oxford edition of *Principal Navigations* when it appears.)

innovation but continuity, the return to a primitive English church from which Catholic practices had degenerated. A new history was necessary, in other words, to legitimate Protestant practice and belief, and the scholarship behind it was enabled by access to sources that the break with Rome had dispersed from their monastic repositories, even as some proportion of those sources was ignored or destroyed.[17]

Hakluyt evidently had some direct contact with the agents of this antiquarian scholarship – indeed, Camden wrote one of the dedicatory poems to *Principal Navigations*.[18] Yet even though the second edition on *Principal Navigations* paid increased attention to travels before 1500, the energy and resourcefulness apparent in the editor's acquisition of sixteenth-century materials are rather less evident in his approach to the earlier period. Hakluyt's original research focused largely on government archives.[19] For other materials – with a few exceptions discussed later in this chapter – Hakluyt largely followed in the footsteps of other, more active readers of history, relying on the editions and collections of his contemporaries.

A significant group of Hakluyt's medieval sources can be connected with one such active reader: the mathematician and magus John Dee.[20] Dee collected one of the largest private libraries of the period, and drew on his collection to advise the crown on the legal, geographical, historical, and policy dimensions of England's rights of discovery and potential claims to sovereignty beyond its shores; he also consulted on several voyages of northern

---

17 For a broader account of monastic libraries and their contents in the sixteenth century, see Summit, *Memory's Library*. On the revival of Anglo-Saxon in the sixteenth century, see Frantzen, *Desire for Origins*.

18 On Camden, see Herendeen, *William Camden*. Camden's commendatory verse appears at *PN* 1: sig. **3v.

19 Hakluyt included numerous documents from the Patent Rolls in volume 1 especially; the forthcoming Oxford edition may shed more light on his use of government archives. Hakluyt printed a small number of important medieval texts from manuscript; see below for more detailed discussion of manuscript sources in volume 1.

20 Dee's wide-ranging career can be traced in Parry, *Arch-Conjuror of England*. William Sherman's study of Dee focuses more closely on his writing and reading practices, where Dee's views on the importance of historical precedents for English exploration and trade were clearly articulated. As Sherman characterizes his views, "the British discovery and recovery enterprise entailed, further a *temporal* or *historical reconnaissance*. In order to persuade the Queen and her counsel to pursue an Imperial policy, as well as to persuade other countries to tolerate it, Dee needed to build his vision on historical foundations. In accordance with Tudor historiographical convention, he amassed a collection of precedents for territorial (re)possession and for Empire itself" (Sherman, *John Dee*, 151).

exploration, and secured letters patent for a voyage ultimately undertaken by others.[21] Unlike the case of Hakluyt, Dee's textual remains provide rich evidence both of his views and of the reading and collecting that helped shape them. We know nothing directly of Dee's relationship with Hakluyt the editor; Dee is not among those named in Hakluyt's prefaces as having furthered his research. Yet the mathematician was certainly connected with the editor's cousin and guardian of the same name, Richard Hakluyt the lawyer: Dee noted in a diary entry for June 1578 that the elder Hakluyt heard him explain that "King Arthur, and King Malgo both of them, did conquer Gelandium, lately called Friseland." In *General and Rare Memorials* (1577), he praised the lawyer's public-spirited interest in fisheries.[22] Hakluyt the lawyer might have introduced the two men as the younger Hakluyt was entering on his geographical career, or they may have been drawn by shared interests into common circles of friendship and advising: all three men were advisors to the Muscovy Company on a voyage of northern exploration set forth in 1580.[23] Dee and Hakluyt the editor were actually employed in different places on the continent during the years leading up to publication of *Principal Navigations*'s

21 On Dee's efforts to organize a voyage of exploration with Adrian Gilbert and John Davis, see chapter 9.

22 Fenton, *Diaries of John Dee*, 3. Dee's "diaries" were a series of memoranda written in the margins of two almanacs, covering the period "from the mid-1570s ... through to the end of his life" (Sherman, *John Dee*, 4). "Friseland" was one of several apocryphal islands believed to lie north and west of England, originally conquered by King Arthur, and in consequence, Dee would argue, to be recovered as part of England's North Atlantic empire; he had "declared to the Q[ueen] her title to Greenland &c., Estotiland, Friseland" (Fenton, *Diaries of John Dee*, 2). Place names cited in the diary entry were derived from the largely apocryphal narrative of a voyage by Venetian brothers (see chapter 8). Of the elder Hakluyt, Dee wrote that "all such matter [concerning domestic fisheries], is declared unto some of the higher powers of this kingdom, and made manifest [note: R. H.], by an other honest Gentleman of the Middle Temple. Who, very discretely and faithfully hath dealt there in, and still travaileth, (and by divers other wayes also) to farder the Weale-Publik of England, so much as in him lyeth" (Dee, *General and Rare Memorials*, 7). Although the elder Hakluyt evidently sought information on the Newfoundland fishery, his consulting on domestic fisheries is otherwise unrecorded (on Newfoundland, see Parkhurst, "Letter Written to M. Richard Hakluyt of the Midle Temple, 1578"). Both Dee and the elder Hakluyt contributed guidance to the Northeast Passage search undertaken by Charles Jackman and Arthur Pet in 1580 (see chapter 4).

23 Sherman, *John Dee*, 173. Hakluyt later wrote that he gave lectures on geography at Oxford, probably after receiving his MA in spring of 1577; he dates his interest in geography to the late 1560s, and positive evidence of that interest can be traced from 1577 onwards ("Chronology").

1589 first edition: Hakluyt in Paris, Dee in Poland and what is now the Czech Republic. It is nonetheless evident that in preparing that first edition, Hakluyt had access to at least some manuscript materials derived from Dee, and he would add more in the second edition.

Hakluyt's selection of medieval materials, in particular, often followed Dee's own priorities and choices of emphasis, and that is especially true for materials on the North. His collections disseminated more broadly sources and combinations of sources also found in Dee's writing, either in manuscript or in print treatises of very limited circulation.[24] The brief set of materials I will discuss next, which include testimony by Dee, were clearly animated by his views and interests; they were among those marshalled by Dee in briefings supplied to the Queen and her advisors. Hakluyt's fragments thus emerged from a matrix in which they were decidedly part of an argument. They were also the subject of correspondence between Dee, the atlas-maker Gerhard Mercator, and Hakluyt himself. Slight in themselves, these texts are rich with information about the Elizabethan circulation of medieval texts and the use of these texts in assembling geographical and historical knowledge.

---

24 Materials almost certainly derived from Dee include, for instance, two letters from 1586 relating to Dee's prospective employment by the tsar in the 1580s (*PN* 1: 508). Edward Dyer, whom Hakluyt thanked for his assistance in making connections to "those, who ... have much steeded me," was Dee's "most consistent patron," and the godfather of his son Arthur; he visited Dee and his associate Edward Kelley during Dee's time in Prague in the later 1580s (Hakluyt, "Preface to the Reader [1589]," sig. *4v; Sherman, *John Dee*, 130; Parry, *Arch-Conjuror of England*, 201–4). Two naval miscellanies originating with Dee, BL MSS Harley 167 and Cotton Otho E 8, contain a number of items also represented in *PN* (1598–1600). Dee also vigorously annotated Bale's compilation, which figured so importantly in the first volume of *PN* (1589) (Sherman, *John Dee*, 92). Dee's annotated copy of Bale's *Scriptorum illustrium maioris Brytanniae* is held at Christ Church Library (Wb.4.8). Ken MacMillan suggests that Dee's manuscript "Of Famous and Rich Discoveries" (1577) was in Hakluyt's possession at some point before parts were published by Samuel Purchas (MacMillan, *Limits*, 3). In short, although we have no specific information connecting Dee with Hakluyt the editor, Hakluyt's access to Dee's materials and amplification of Dee's agenda in many details strongly suggests a connection or collaboration, even while there is no evidence that Hakluyt shared either Dee's mystical interests or his mathematical expertise.

POLAR ROMANCE: ARTHUR'S CONQUEST AND MERCATOR'S MAP

1 The voyage of Nicholaus de Linna, a Franciscan Friar, and an excellent Mathematician of Oxford to all the regions situate under the North pole, Anno 1360 (121–2)
2 A testimony of master John Dee touching the voyage of Nicholas de Linna to the North pole (122)[25]
3 The letter of Gerard Mercator to Richard Hakluyt of Oxford [1580] (443–5)

Among the Dee materials to which Hakluyt gave far wider circulation were several relating to the Arthurian conquest of the Arctic, the topic Dee had discussed with Hakluyt's cousin. William Sherman identifies Geoffrey of Monmouth's chronicle as Dee's "most influential source" on Arthur, and Arthur's supposed conquests in the North helped animate Dee's contention that the Queen's title extended from North America, to "the most northen ilandes great and small," eastward to the boundaries of "the Duke of Moscovia his domynions," and over the northern seas and islands that English mariners were exploring with increasing intensity from the 1550s onward.[26] If Arthur had at one time extended British rule over territories in the North Atlantic, Dee advised the Queen, other documents could provide confirming evidence both that such conquests had happened, and that they had resulted in the kind of *persisting* presence that would strengthen claims of sovereignty in the North. Among such sources were obscure indications of a journey towards the pole by an Oxford friar named Nicholas of Lynn, said to have taken place in 1360; the friar's voyage also offered testimony about descendants of Arthurian colonists still settled in the North. In the larger context of Dee's writings, the documents we will examine here supported a political and legal argument concerning the extent of English sovereignty in the late sixteenth century; within *Principal Navigations*, they provide a kind of after-history for the

---

25 Quinn does not give a provenance for Dee's testimony, which is not listed in Hakluyt's table of contents; on Dee's correspondence with Mercator, however, see Taylor, "A Letter Dated 1577," 68. Dee transcribed the letter both in "Famous and Rich Discoveries" and in "Brytanici Imperii Limites" (transcribed and edited by Ken Macmillan in *Limits*). Macmillan's introduction to the volume provides valuable context.
26 Sherman, *John Dee*, 92; MacMillan, *Limits*, 43.

opening celebration of Arthur's conquests in volume 1.[27] The first source in this group is a legend taken from the polar inset to Mercator's 1569 world map (given in both Latin and English), the second a brief, related "testimony" by Dee, and the third a letter from Mercator to Hakluyt, in response to a query about the evidence underlying the map legend.

Mercator's text credits the Oxford friar as the ultimate source for the cartographic representation of the polar regions that it accompanies: "touching the description of the North parts ... a certaine English Frier, a Franciscan, and a Mathematician of Oxford ... described all those places that he sawe, and tooke the height of them with his Astrolabe, according to the forme that I (Gerard Mercator) have set downe in my mappe."[28] Mercator's map represents the pole itself as a massive rock (*rupes nigra et altissima*) surrounded by four islands between which powerful currents drew ships "into an inward gulfe or whirlepoole." Dee's testimony confirmed that the friar, "being a good Astronomer ... described all the Northerne Islands, with the indrawing seas" from 54 degrees north to the pole. The first layer of interest in the text was thus its geographical information on the physical features of the polar regions. Mercator, for instance, compared the friar's description of a polar whirlpool with a description by Gerald of Wales of a whirlpool that swallowed up ships "as it were, into a bottomlesse pit." Hakluyt's marginal annotation added comparison to "a notable whirlepoole on the coast of Norway, called Malestrande [Maelstrom], about the latitude of 68." Mercator's legend incidentally provides a representative example of the way maps are used in *Principal Navigations*: that is, as sources of text. Extracting text from the map allowed Hakluyt, here and elsewhere, to attribute cartographic information to observations made at a particular time and by a particular person. As Sarah Tyacke

---

27 "Brytanici Imperii Limites" (BL Add MS 59681), in which Dee transcribed the letter, reproduces documents and advice prepared for the queen in 1577 and 1578 regarding her title to the North Atlantic; MacMillan describes "Limites" as a manuscript compilation prepared under the author's supervision in 1593 (MacMillan, *Limits*, 5). See also the discussion by Sherman, *John Dee*, 182–92.

28 Mercator, "Voyage of Nicholaus de Linna," 1: 122. Margaret Small traces the influence of Nicholas of Lynn's lost book on cartographic representations of the Polar regions, from Johannes Ruysch's 1508 world map through Oronce Fine's 1531 map (Small, "Jellied Seas," 332).

has noted, Hakluyt's energy in collecting, organizing, and preserving written records did not extend to graphical records of any kind.[29]

Not only geographical information was at issue, though. Roughly half the text cited from Mercator's map actually describes the *source* of what he knew. This provenance proves to have been more complicated than simply naming the traveller credited with making observations, because Mercator's knowledge relied on a sequence of information transfers. His description of the Arctic was taken "out of the voyage of James Cnoyen of Hartzevan Buske, which alleageth certaine conquests of Arthur king of Britaine: and the most part, and chiefest things among the rest, he learned of a certaine priest in the King of Norwayes court, in the yeere 1364. This priest was descended from them which King Arthur had sent to inhabit these Islands." Mercator's source was a book by the fourteenth-century Dutch writer Jacobus Cnoyen of 's-Hertogenbosch; Cnoyen's book drew in turn on an anonymous book about King Arthur's conquests, *and* recorded information transmitted to him orally by "a certain priest" (descended from Arthurian colonists) at the Norwegian court in 1364. That priest testified to Cnoyen both that he was a descendant of Arthurian colonists in the Arctic, and that he had personally met an English friar making a voyage towards the pole. On that voyage, the friar had himself visited islands still inhabited by descendant communities. Dee's accompanying testimony refers to a second presumptive source derived from the friar's voyage, containing the description of "all those places that he saw": "the record thereof at his return [the friar] delivered to the King of England. The name of which book is Inventio Fortunata ... qui liber incipit a gradu 54. usque ad polum."[30] The appearance of independent witness is illusory, however. A 1577 letter from Mercator to Dee, transcribed by Dee, indicates that Mercator had himself told Dee about "*Inventio fortunata*" in response to Dee's inquiry about the map legend. (Dee and Mercator's warm friendship dated to Dee's studies on the continent in 1547 to 1550.)[31] The web of sources concerning the friar's voyage to the Arctic was in fact quite problematic.

29 Tyacke, *Before Empire*, 3. Hakluyt also referenced "Gerardus Mercator ... his generall mappe" in the marginalia to de Rubriquis, "Journall of Frier William," 1: 107. On Hakluyt's use of maps more broadly, see Mancall, "Visual World of Early Modern Travel Narratives"; Skelton, "Hakluyt's Maps"; Wallis, "Edward Wright and the 1599 World Map."

30 Dee, "Testimony Touching the Voyage of Nicholas de Linna." On Dee and Mercator's relationship, see Crane, *Mercator*, 145–59, 242–4; Parry, *Arch-Conjuror of England*, 12, 16–18.

31 See Taylor, "A Letter Dated 1577"; MacMillan, *Limits*, 21–2, 83–7; Sherman, *John Dee*, 5–6.

Mercator's information involved several famous lost books. First of these was the book by Cnoyen. Mercator's later letter to Hakluyt related that "The historie of the voyage of Jacobus Cnoyen Buschoducensis throughout al Asia, Affrica, and the North, was lent me in time past by a friend of mine at Antwerpe. After I had used it, I restored it againe: after many yeeres I required it again of my friend, but hee had forgotten of whom hee had borrowed it."[32] Second was *Inventio fortunata*, the book written by the friar to describe his voyage and said to have been given by him to Edward III; its title was cited in numerous late-fifteenth and early-sixteenth-century sources, but it is otherwise unknown to posterity. Cnoyen himself relied both on the oral testimony of the priest he met in Bergen and – as Mercator told Dee – on a third lost or unknown book, *Gestae Arthuri*, that contained additional information relating to the purported Arthurian colony in the Arctic.[33] Kirsten Seaver has offered a conjectural reconstruction of the events that might have been refracted through this complicated chain of transmission as follows: circa 1360, a Minorite (Franciscan) friar visited the Norse settlements in Western Greenland on a voyage further up the coast, and this voyage was reported independently in a book (*Inventio fortunata*) and by a priest (Seaver tentatively identifies him as Ivar Bárdarson) who returned to Bergen from Greenland in 1364.[34] These accounts were later conflated with each other and with additional Arthurian material by Cnoyen. Once Cnoyen's materials reached English hands, they underwent a few additional transformations: Dee associated the friar with Bishop's Lynn, and Hakluyt publicized Dee's identification of the previously unnamed Minorite friar with Nicholas of Lynn, an Oxford cosmographer who was actually a Carmelite.[35] The friar's story thus came to offer additional opportunities to its English readers, over and above its apparent observations of Arctic hydrography: it attributed Mercator's information to the voyage of an Englishman (for Hakluyt, a fellow Oxonian), and associated Geoffrey

---

32 "Letter of Gerard Mercator," 1: 445.

33 Seaver, *Frozen Echo*, 134–5. "The anonymous *Arthuri Gestis* is a lost work that depicts King Arthur as an explorer and colonist of the Arctic regions" (MacMillan, *Limits*, 138 n. 81). On the trope of lost books in Tudor responses to Geoffrey of Monmouth's Arthur story, see Escobedo, "Tudor Search for Arthur."

34 Seaver, *Frozen Echo*, 132–8. (Seaver's book discusses Ivar's travels extensively.)

35 Ibid., 134. Dee adds that the Norfolk town of Lynn long had a "very common and usual trade" with Iceland and that the nearby town of Blakeney had a similar involvement with the Iceland fishery, evident from a privilege granted by Edward III. Hakluyt's marginalia link these comments to An. 2, 4, and 31 of Edward III's reign, but no related documents appear in *PN* (1598–1600).

of Monmouth's claims about Arthur's dominion over northern lands and seas with independent testimony of a continued British presence. Through this chain of transmission, what might be thought of (however tentatively) as historical voyages and contacts were reframed as part of a corpus of materials about the deeds of King Arthur – parts of which were, in turn, grafted onto the explorations of the Elizabethan era as an enabling precedent. Nominally, the editor's methods were careful: information was attributed to sources, as best they could be identified, signed for by two important authorities, Mercator and Dee, and further reliant on Mercator's authoritative atlas.[36] But the impression of impartial scholarship does not survive examination.

This particular instance of antiquarian exchange in the late 1570s had a second, practical context. The late 1570s saw several major initiatives in Arctic exploration by the English, and older texts might promise to inform on the regions in question. Even as he assembled sources on the Queen's title, and corresponded with Mercator about their provenance, Dee also wrote to Abraham Ortelius, inquiring specifically "about the northern coast of the Atlantic." This more geographical inquiry may have arisen in connection with Martin Frobisher's second voyage in search of a Northwest Passage later that year; Ortelius's visit to England a few months later, according to Hakluyt, was "to no other ende but to prye and looke into the secretes of Frobishers voyadge."[37] (Dee provided advice to Frobisher's investors as well as some late tuition in navigation to the mariners.) For Dee, the Elizabethan voyages held out a promise of confirming the ancient settlement of the Arctic by English colonists. Taking seriously the apocryphal Arctic voyages of the Zeno brothers, who claimed to have contacted urbanized and literate societies in the Arctic, Dee expressed the hope in that libraries in "Friseland ... Icaria, Iseland, Groenland, or in Estotiland" might yet yield textual evidence of "the Brytish

---

36 A point also made by Mercator's biographer (Crane, *Mercator*, 244).

37 MacMillan, *Limits*, 9; Hakluyt, *PD*, 76; Taylor, *OW*, 1: 12. Frobisher made three voyages in search of a Northwest Passage to Asia, in 1576 to 1578; these are thoroughly documented in volume 3 of *Principal Navigations*. On Dee's engagement with the Frobisher voyages, see Sherman, "John Dee's Role." Dee appears to have served as a consultant for the voyages, and after the fact "possessed his own manuscript copies of several central documents" produced by the voyagers (Sherman, "John Dee's Role," 287–9, 293). Ortelius was another point of connection between Dee and the two Hakluyts. Hakluyt the lawyer had been in correspondence with Ortelius since as early as 1567, and Ortelius's visit to England in 1577 allowed him to see Camden and (at least) Hakluyt the younger in London before travelling to Dee's house in Mortlake (Taylor, *OW*, 1: 76–83; Baldwin, "John Dee's Interest," 99).

antiquities and your highnes royalties." Frobisher's reports appear to have dashed these hopes.[38] (The Zeno materials nonetheless appeared in all three of Hakluyt's compilations.) Hakluyt was also attentive to the ways these older documents might inform on contemporary voyages in the Arctic, if in more practical terms. His correspondence with Mercator about the Cnoyen text in 1580 coincides with the Northeast Passage search of Arthur Pet and Charles Jackman in that year, and Mercator's reply indicates that Hakluyt's inquiry was indeed connected with this voyage.[39] As we will see, Hakluyt also viewed other medieval narratives as trustworthy sources of information relevant to contemporary projects of exploration and trade.

The sources concerning "Nicholas de Linna" were first printed by Hakluyt in 1589, several years after Frobisher's ships had returned from the Arctic devoid of anything resembling the settlements alluded to in Mercator's map legend. Glyn Parry suggests that the supposed Arthurian conquests vanished from arguments about the Queen's title, by Dee and others, after the last of these voyages, in 1578.[40] By the time the second edition of *Principal Navigations* began to appear in 1598, English interest in northern exploration had ebbed to the degree that Hakluyt conceded primacy in northern discoveries to the Dutch, albeit "with the proviso, that our English nation ... brake the yce before them."[41] With the evacuation of their authority or relevance for legal arguments about title, as well as their value as actionable information, the documents persist largely as evidence of early initiative, and as traces of the arguments and correspondence in which they had once been embedded. They serve as one example of how Hakluyt read history: in this case, as refracted through the hands of others who found and transmitted it.

One final aspect of the exchanges around these sources calls for attention, however: namely, that both Dee and Hakluyt *could* appeal to Mercator (or Ortelius) for information, even concerning a British hero and evidence of British sovereignty. Hakluyt's and Dee's work, animated by national interest, was nonetheless cosmopolitan in its engagements. Such international

---

38 MacMillan, *Limits*, 52; Parry, *Arch-Conjuror of England*, 144. On the voyages of the Zeno brothers and their circulation, see chapter 8.

39 Hakluyt's letter to Mercator does not survive, but the reply printed in PN (1598–1600) appears to continue a conversation about the 1580 voyage; it begins with an expression of regret that Pet had not "bene informed before his departure of some speciall points" ("Letter of Gerard Mercator," 1: 444).

40 Parry, *Arch-Conjuror of England*, 144–5.

41 Hakluyt, "Preface to the Reader (1598)," sig. *5v.

connections were woven into other nationalist projects of the Elizabethan period. Engravers for the county maps in Christopher Saxton's *Atlas of the Counties of England and Wales* (London, 1579) were "mainly emigrés from Flanders or northwest Germany"; the landmark globe commissioned by William Sanderson, produced by Emery Molyneux and presented to Elizabeth in 1591 – described by Helen Wallis as the cartographic counterpart to *Principal Navigations* – was engraved by Jodocus Hondius, who would take the plates to Amsterdam, dedicating later editions to Maurice of Nassau.[42] Camden's *Britannia* (illustrated, in later editions, with some of Saxton's maps) had its origin in a suggestion by Ortelius, and Ortelius, in turn, made prominent use of materials provided him by the Welsh antiquary Humphrey Llwyd, an important figure in the transmission of the legend concerning a medieval Welsh discovery of the Americas.[43] As we'll see in later chapters, Mercator and Ortelius were only two of Hakluyt's own collaborators and interlocutors across the channel and in London's émigré communities.[44]

The transnational provenance of Nicholas of Lynn's voyage, as we'll see, was far from an anomaly within the compilation. Indeed, Hakluyt's methods and interests ensured that foreign expertise and texts would be prominent in his book. Whether we consider the sources of *Principal Navigations*, the scholarship behind it, or the travels it records, Hakluyt's compilation had a more expansive scope than its titular focus on the navigations of the English nation would suggest. The geographer Robert Mayhew's comment about Camden's ties with scholars on the continent surely applies to Hakluyt as well: "Whilst *Brittania* has clear patriotic intent ... its author was able to balance his sense of national identity with full participation in the Europe-wide Republic of letters ... As for most Renaissance characters to whom we look today for the flowering of modern nationalism, Camden was able to hold on to several

---

42 Barber, "Mapmaking in England," 1629; Wallis, "First English Globe," 275. On Saxton's atlas as providing English readers with "visual and conceptual possesson of the physical kingdom in which they lived," see Helgerson, *Forms of Nationhood*, chap. 3. On Hondius's globes, see Krogt, *Globes of Hondius*.

43 See Camden, *Britain*, sig. [+]4r., cited in Mayhew, "William Camden and Brittania." In the 1595 edition of his atlas, Ortelius credited Llwyd for the map of England used in the 1570 edition of *Theatrum Orbis Terrarum*. Hakluyt's version of the Madoc legend appears in volume 3.

44 See chapter 8 for more on Hakluyt's circle.

forms of identity at several geographical scales."[45] The exchanges surrounding the friar's voyage to the Arctic index the compilation's multiple identities as national celebration and work of cosmopolitan intellectual exchange.

BRITAIN'S BOUNDARIES

1 "The voyage of King Edgar with 4000, shippes round about his large Monarchie, Anno 973" (6–8)
2 "Libellus de politia conservativa Maris. Or, the pollicy of keeping the Sea" (187–208)[46]
3 "Chronicle of the Kings of Man" (10–16)
4 "The voyage of Octher to the north parts beyond Norway" (4–5)

The first volume of *Principal Navigations* includes not only documents that trace the extension of British presence elsewhere, but also documents relating to the history of the realm itself; it is the only one of the compilation's three volumes that explicitly engages with what is close at hand as well as what is far away. Uniquely, volume 1 thus puts into play questions about the nature and place of Britain's boundaries: how far did the realm itself extend, and how firm or permeable were its borders? The Arthurian materials direct our attention outward, to a notional empire far beyond Britain's shores. Other documents within the volume's medieval section will bring our attention closer in, exactly to the boundaries of Britain and who was at home within them. The four documents considered here all emerge from the late Tudor circulation and reading of medieval manuscripts, and the new encounter with sources for British history in Hakluyt's time. Yet the itineraries, uses, and implications of the documents point in quite different directions, shedding light on Hakluyt's methods but also raising questions about national identity and the relationships between inside and outside that appear to be taken for granted in materials relating to an Arthurian empire in the North Atlantic.

---

45 Mayhew, "William Camden and Brittania," xiv. An older habit of referring to the compilation as the "English voyages" may have helped to foster mistaken characterizations of it as including *only* English materials.

46 Hakluyt's source had not been identified by the date of Quinn and Quinn, "c&s." "Sixteen manuscripts of different versions of *The Libelle of English Policy* have hitherto been recorded, some of them fragmentary" (Edwards, "New Manuscript of The Libelle," 444–5). The manuscripts are discussed further below.

The first text, drawn from Dee's *General and Rare Memorials* (1577) and titled "The voyage of King Edgar" by Hakluyt, offers a panegyric in praise of King Edgar (r. 959–74) as embodying "the selfe same Idaea" of naval power recommended to the Queen by Dee "for the godly prosperitiee of this British Empire."[47] This text, of course, provides another example of the editor's reliance on Dee's thinking about the past and its uses. *Memorials*, Hakluyt's source text, offered "pragmatic counsel for the development of British naval power."[48] It had a strictly limited press run, and had been "stayed" by the Queen after publication; indeed, Sherman has suggested that Dee's close control of the text's production and circulation argue for regarding *Memorials* as closer to a manuscript than a printed book.[49]

Drawing on a variety of medieval sources, Dee described a monarch whose "prosperous pastimes" were annual circumnavigations of the island of Britain with some part of his navy of "4000. saile at the least," a spectacular enactment of dominion that "made evident to the whole world, that as he wisely knew the ancient bounds and limits of this British Empire, so that he could and would royally, justly, and triumphantly enjoy the same, spite of the devil, and maugre the force of any forreine potentate."[50] For Dee, Edgar was (like Arthur) "one of the perfect Imperial Monarchs of this British Empire," exercising rights and powers that he urged the Queen and her advisors "discreetly and valiantly [to] recover and enjoy."[51] To recover: that is, to return to the conditions of an earlier period in which England enjoyed a form of power lost to the present,

47 Dee, "Voyage of King Edgar," 1: 7. The in-text title of the item describes it as "taken out of Florentius Wigorniensis, Hoveden, and M. Dee his discourse of the Brittish Monarchie, pag. 54, 55, &c."

48 Sherman, *John Dee*, 153. Ken McMillan suggests more specifically that *General and Rare Memorials* "was written in 1576 to promote [Martin] Frobisher's voyage and the trading goals of the Muscovy Company" (MacMillan, *Limits*, 2). Andrew Escobedo argues that Dee's treatment of Arthur and Edgar in *Memorials* registers the complexity of England's British and Saxon pasts; Dee commented in a marginal note to his treatment of Edgar that "King ARTHUR ... was a Thorne in the Saxons eyes" (Escobedo, "Tudor Search for Arthur," 148).

49 Sherman, *John Dee*, 156. Figures of 50 and 100 printed copies are given, respectively, by Glyn Parry and Ken McMillan; MacMillan notes that Dee's 1583 library catalogue found 60 copies still in his possession (Parry, *Arch-Conjuror of England*, 105–6; MacMillan, *Limits*, 2). Hakluyt's familiarity with a text that cannot have circulated widely adds another piece of evidence about, at least, the shared interests, relationships, and intellectual alignment of the two men.

50 Dee, "Voyage of King Edgar," 1: 7–8.

51 Ibid., 1: 7, 6.

and to ennoble the present by affiliating it to this past. As Dee glosses Edgar's style ("Ego Aedgarus Anglorum Basileus, omniumque Regum, Insularum, Oceaniquae Brittaniam circumiacentis, cunctarumque nationum, quae infra eam includuntur, Imperator, Et Dominus"): "Note the Queen's Majesties royalty over the British Ocean sea, round about the British Empire."[52]

Current scholarship on Edgar's reign credits him with administrative reforms that included requirements for the supply of ships and manpower by his subjects; these came during a brief respite from the Scandinavian raids and invasions that had devastated England during previous reigns and would again do so under his successors, when they encountered an English fleet that (*pace* later accounts of Edgar's enormous navy) was not in fact large enough to provide effective defence.[53] In the *Anglo-Saxon Chronicle*, Edgar was principally remembered for his energetic interest in ecclesiastical administration. Later historians, however, began to remember Edgar as a king who exercised a broad and distinctively maritime dominion, and Hakluyt's headnote on the sourcing of Dee's history makes clear both men's reliance on twelfth century, rather than pre-conquest, sources: "taken out of Florentius Wigorniensis, Hoveden, and M. Dee his discourse of the British Monarchy, pag. 54, 55, & c."[54] How did this version of Edgar's reign emerge from the sources?

Celebration of Edgar as naval hero had its foundations in a ceremony associated with Edgar's (late) consecration as king in 972 or 973. The *Anglo-Saxon Chronicle* (D, E, and F versions) relates that "the king led his whole raiding ship-army to Chester, and there 6 kings came to meet him, and all pledged that they would be allies on sea and on land."[55] Anglo-Norman historians elaborated what some sources characterized as homage, but others as treaty making, into a ceremony of power. As one maritime historian describes this

---

52 Ibid., 1: 9. The gloss is Dee's rather than Hakluyt's.
53 Rodger, *Safeguard of the Seas*, 19; Williams, "Edgar, King of England."
54 "Voyage of King Edgar," 1: 6.
55 Swanton, *Anglo-Saxon Chronicle*, 119. Rodger cites Pauline Stafford on the view that this was "a conference to discuss common measures against the Viking threat; a sort of 10th century NATO" (Rodger, *Safeguard of the Seas*, 514 n. 15; Stafford, *Unification and Conquest*, 12). Whitelock translates slightly differently: the kings "all gave him pledges that they would be his allies on sea and on land" (Whitelock, *Anglo-Saxon Chronicle*, 77). Ann Williams specifies that "the Anglo-Saxon Chronicle suggests no more than that the kings made a treaty with Edgar (*trywsodon*), [but the] language implies that they did homage (*gebugon*) to him." John of Worcester (fl. 1095–1140) was "the source of most subsequent accounts" of Edgar actually being rowed by the other kings (Williams, "Edgar, King of England").

development of the story, Edgar "cruised with his fleet from the Severn round to the Dee, where he was rowed in state by the rulers of North and South Wales, Man, the Hebrides, Strathclyde and Galloway, while he took the helm ... The symbolism is unmistakable: princes from around the shores of the Irish Sea submitted to the sea power of the English king."[56] But the details of this account – the identity of the kings, the detail that they rowed the ship, indeed that they submitted to Edgar at all – were elaborations introduced into the twelfth-century *Chronicon ex chronicis* attributed to John of Worcester.[57] Similarly, the style cited and glossed by Dee derived from a charter dated to 964 but "most likely forged at Worcester in the early 1140s." The ceremony of maritime dominion as well as Edgar's annual circumnavigation were later traditions resting "on a series of intricately connected documents, many ... either forged in the twelfth century or ... believed to be of dubious authenticity." Indeed, Sebastian Sobecki characterizes the legend of Edgar's maritime dominion as "the by-product of deliberate rewriting and forgery."[58]

Dee's historical interests are well attested, and he owned at least one important Anglo-Saxon manuscript, the Old English Orosius (discussed below).[59] Yet his inclination appears to have been to rely on Anglo-Norman sources, and (at least in this instance) to use them selectively. For instance, he consulted William of Malmesbury (?1090–?1142) for a charter expressing "Edgar's claim to the entire archipelago's overlordship."[60] (William also elaborated the ceremony of submission, not present in Hakluyt's excerpt.) Other material in William's text, however, would have challenged Dee's narrative: for instance,

---

56   Rodger, *Safeguard of the Seas*, 20.

57   Sobecki, "Edgar's Archipelago," 18–19. See also David Thornton, "Edgar and the Eight Kings, AD 973: textus et dramatis personae," *Early Medieval Europe*, 10 (2001): 49–79 (cited in Sobecki, "Edgar's Archipelago"). The chronicle's traditional attribution to Florence of Worcester has been questioned by modern scholars.

58   Sobecki, "Edgar's Archipelago," 9–10, 7. Other scholarship on the charter is cited in Sobecki's notes.

59   On Dee's use of historical sources, see Sherman, *John Dee*, 90–5. The sources covered by "& c." in Hakluyt's headnote to "Voyage of Edgar" include passages from the state papers of Henry II ("Charta regia, Henrici secundi," r. 1133–1189), Matthew of Westminster's *Flores historiarum* (a chronicle composed from 1188 through 1235), Ranulph of Higden ("Ranulphus Cestrensis," main author of the *Polychronicon*, d. 1364), and the charters of Worcester and Ely Cathedrals. Dee's ownership of BL Add MS 47967 is tentatively attributed "according to George Hickes (b. 1642, d. 1715), librarian of the Duke of Lauderdale's library and clergyman" (BL catalogue).

60   The authenticity of this charter is also viewed as doubtful (Sobecki, "Edgar's Archipelago," 23).

he repeats a comment from the *Anglo-Saxon Chronicle* that Edgar loved foreign things: he "attracted ... foreigners and ... harmful people to this country" and brought in "evil foreign customs." William complained that Edgar's xenophilia corrupted the "native simplicity" of the English with the vices of other nations – a characterization at odds with Dee's image of Edgar as effectively monitoring and controlling access to England's shores.[61]

The image of Edgar as the paradigmatic figure of British maritime power, and defender of national integrity, was, as Sobecki comments, already "a result of an accrual of myths, forgeries, and the rewriting of archives." *Principal Navigations* amplified this version of the past; if the research and motivated presentation were largely Dee's responsibility, the story's wider dissemination and perpetuation were certainly Hakluyt's, and it would be taken up with alacrity by later writers as "the foundation myth of maritime Englishness."[62] If not fact, what was Hakluyt transmitting with this story about King Edgar? The exemplary story of a monarch who sought "invincibly to fortify the chiefe and uttermost walles of his Islandish Monarchie, against all forreine encombrance possible" had two important components, each with implications for Elizabeth's policy: first, the delineation of expansive territorial limits for the British monarchy, limits that included the contiguous territories of England, Scotland, and Wales, as well as the smaller islands around them and the waters off their shores; and second, the attentive policing of these limits by naval

---

61 Whitelock, *Anglo-Saxon Chronicle*, 75. William of Malmesbury: "[Edgar's] fame being noised abroad, foreigners ... frequently sailed hither, and were on terms of intimacy with Edgar, though their arrival was highly prejudicial to the natives: for from the Saxons they learned an untameable ferocity of mind; from the Flemings an unmanly delicacy of body; and from the Danes drunkenness; though they were before free from such propensities, and disposed to observe their own customs with native simplicity rather than admire those of others. For this history justly and deservedly blames him" (*Chronicle of the Kings of England*, 148). Ann Williams suggests that, like Alfred, Edgar employed Viking mercenaries, and that the *Chronicle* author had this practice particularly in mind (Williams, "Edgar, King of England"). Hakluyt cites William for testimony that Edgar was "not onely soveraigne lord of all the British seas, and of the whole Isle of Britaine it selfe, but also that he brought under his yoke of subjection, most of the Isles and some of the maine lands adjacent" ("Preface to the Reader [1598]," sig.**1v).

62 Sobecki, "Edgar's Archipelago," 25, 5. Equally, a story about the origins of English naval power, or of British "imperial" rule, might have been grounded in the reigns of other monarchs. The non-appearance of Alfred in *Principal Navigations* is a little surprising, as Alfred would come to be identified as "the founder of the British navy" (Rodger, *Safeguard of the Seas*, 12). On the arc of Alfred's reputation, see Parker, "Ruling the Waves." For another early naval monarch, see Foot, "Æthelstan [Athelstan] (893/4–939)."

power.[63] Dee's panegyric was framed to support policy recommendations made in *General and Rare Memorials* that the Queen create a naval patrol to secure England's shores. Sherman sums up the concerns to which these recommendations responded: "Dee's international perspective rested on two fears about the boundaries of Britain: they seemed alarmingly permeable by foreigners while at the same time the natives and their rulers were all but bound in."[64] Both fears were explicitly articulated in the next document to be considered, which falls towards the end of the volume's medieval materials; this one, however, can be associated more specifically with Hakluyt's personal priorities and research.

In the preface to volume 1, Hakluyt called attention to an additional source concerning the "victorious Saxon prince king Edgar" and his "huge fleet": "the libel of English policie, pag. 202 and 203. of this present volume."[65] The "Libelle of Englyshe Polycye" is an early-fifteenth-century verse treatise advocating for a commercial and naval policy both aggressive and impressively xenophobic, an echo of the concerns we can discern in Dee. Although "Libelle" was printed for the first time in Hakluyt's compilation, the survival of many inexpensively produced manuscript copies suggests that its appeal "was broadly based," and continued demand for such copies was reflected by ongoing production of manuscripts into the sixteenth century.[66]

"Libelle" is anonymous in surviving manuscripts.[67] Written around the time of the siege of Calais, still but uneasily an English possession during the

63 Dee, "Voyage of King Edgar," 1: 8.
64 Sherman, *John Dee*, 157.
65 Hakluyt, "Preface to the Reader (1598)," sig. **1v.
66 Meale, "Libelle of Englyshe Polycye," 223, 225. (I am grateful to Sebastian Sobecki for kindly providing a copy of Meale's article.) One manuscript (BL MS Add. 40673) was owned and annotated by William Cecil (Taylor, "Some Manuscripts of the 'Libelle of Englyshe Polycye,'" 377–8). Another manuscript in the College of Arms associates the work with heralds like William Camden (Edwards, "New Manuscript of The Libelle"). A few decades beyond 1598, the poem was cited by John Selden in *Mare Clausum* (1635), his response to Hugo Grotius's *Mare Liberum* – a text Hakluyt translated (Taylor, *Tudor Geography*, 379). The poem is written mostly in rhymed couplets, with a prologue in rhyme royal and "an elaborate system of marginal glosses in Latin and English" reproduced by Hakluyt (Meale, "Libelle of Englyshe Polycye," 208–9). For editions, see Warner, *Libelle of English Polycye*; Bale and Sobecki, *Medieval English Travel*.
67 Carol Meale locates its origins in the London mercantile community, noting that the poem is especially "well-informed on ... contemporary trade," bespeaking "a set of values and priorities different to those which would normally be expected to concern a martial elite" (Meale, "Libelle of Englyshe Polycye," 214). More recently, Sebastian Sobecki

prolonged minority of Henry VI, the poem recalled Edgar and his navy approvingly in the context of an argument that England must maintain control over both sides of the Channel. Keeping Calais would allow England to control the movement of goods to and from Flanders, "the staple of Christendom."[68] Equally, "Libelle" argued England could at need restrict supply of its own export goods, commodities such as cloth, wool, and tin. While England's exports satisfied universal needs, the author of "Libelle" argued, the goods England imported from other European nations were merely luxuries that might well be abjured. In succeeding "chapters," the poem enumerates the goods imported from each of the nations and regions with which England traded: Spain and Flanders, Portugal, Brittany, Scotland, Prussia and the Baltic, Genoa, Venice and Florence, Brabant, Zealand and Hainault, Ireland, and finally Iceland.[69] Goods from beyond the boundaries of Europe were brought in only by Genoese, Venetian, and Florentine merchants, and these – far from being the locus of desire or motive for exploration that they would become for Hakluyt's contemporaries – allowed Italian merchants to "fetely blere our eye," blinding English consumers to their own interests. Costly luxuries were imported by a carrying trade from the Mediterranean: silk, cloth of gold, "Apes, and Japes, and marmosets tailed, nifles and trifles." Spices were the only cargo of significance, and these served principally as medicine, purgative aids for "voiding humors"; for this unglamorous purpose, the author comments, "things ... that growen here" might well be employed.[70]

has emphasized the poem's legal and bureaucratic dimensions, concluding that it should be attributed to the clerk of the Privy Council, Richard Caudray (Sobecki, *Last Words*, chap. 3).

68 "Libelle" regards Flanders as England's main economic competitor, and backs up economic self-interest with xenophobic disgust:

Yee have heard that two Flemings togider
Will undertake ere they goe any whither
Or they rise once to drinke a Ferkin full,
Of good Beerekin: so sore they hall and pull.
Under the board they pissen as they sit
("Libelle," 1: 192)

69 With the exception of Iceland, these were all places too near at hand for discussion anywhere in the post-medieval sections of *Principal Navigations*, but their discussion here sits comfortably among the statutes and charters Hakluyt collected to document England's long history of foreign trade.

70 Sugar is the one exception to the author's general condemnation of luxury foodstuffs: "if they should except be anything / *It were but sugar*, trust to my saying" – a harbinger of the massive colonial expansion to come (emphasis mine; "Libelle," 1: 193).

When such exotic wares were purchased from foreign merchants, the poem claims, what was truly purged was England's gold: "they bere the gold out of this land, / And sucke the thrift away out of our hand."[71] The poem's admiration for Edgar, a monarch who ruled the waves but sailed no further than his own coasts, accompanied a fear that foreign imports could only lead to loss and corruption. (The other use for luxury goods mentioned by the poem is bribery.)[72] And foreigners themselves were not to be trusted: Hakluyt highlights the poem's "subtile discovery of outlandish merchants fraud, and ... the sophistication of their wares."[73]

The policy recommendations made in "Libelle" sought to restrict rather than expand trade, imagining the sea around England not as a space of passage but as a wall.

Kepe than the sea about in speciall,
which of England is the towne wall.
As though England were likened to a citie,
and the wall environ were the see.
Kepe then the sea that is the wall of England:
And than is England kept by Goddes hande;
That as for anything that is without,
England were at ease withouten doubt.[74]

This England – oddly in a poem about foreign trade – seems firmly self-enclosed. Such pessimism about the consequences of maritime exchange between England and its neighbours stands in sharp contrast to the famous, formative geography lesson described in the preface to *Principall Navigations* (1589), occasioned by the schoolboy Hakluyt's curiosity about a universal map that he found lying open in his cousin's chambers at the Middle Temple. "He seeing me somewhat curious in the view thereof, began to instruct my ignorance ... he pointed with his wand to all the known Seas, Gulfs, Bays,

---

71 "Libelle," 1: 194.
72 On Edgar, see "Libelle," 1: 202–4. On bribery:
   Beware ye men that bear the great in hand
   That they destroy the policy of this land,
   by gift and good, and the fine golden clothes,
   And silk, and other ...
   whereby stopped should be good governance ("Libelle," 1: 168)
73 Hakluyt, "Preface to the Reader (1598)," sig. *6v.
74 "Libelle," 1: 206–7.

Straights, Capes, Rivers, Empires, Kingdoms, Dukedoms, and Territories of each part, with declaration also of their special commodities, & particular wants, which by the benefit of traffic, & intercourse of merchants, are plentifully supplied."[75] In this pedagogic moment, commerce is shown to have been designed by providence to ensure that human beings would need each other, a view of trade that is hard to reconcile with Hakluyt's praise of "Libell."[76]

Yet Hakluyt's esteem for the poem's "true and sound policy" occasioned one of the editor's rare metaphors. He wrote in the volume's preface that he "could not more fitly compare" the treatise to anything other than "the Emperour of Russia his palace called the golden Castle." Hakluyt alludes to wondering descriptions of Muscovy's Golden Palace by early English travellers, who discovered that, beyond a "homely" outward appearance, the palace was "beautified and adorned with the Emperour his majesticall presence, with the honourable and great assembly of his rich-attired Peers and Senatours, with an invaluable and huge masse of gold and silver plate, & with other princely magnificence."[77] Like the Golden Palace, whose unprepossessing exterior belied the magnificence and triumphant celebration of power within, the language and style of "Libelle" – its "outward appearance" – were "homely" and "harsh." Indeed, Hakluyt continued, its style "may seem to have been whistled of Pan's oaten pipe," and its "olde dialect ... to have proceeded from the mother of Evander." Such attention to aesthetics may be unique not only in *Principal Navigations*, but in the whole body of Hakluyt's work. Nowhere else does the *language* of an otherwise valuable narrative generate this level of explicit comment. Hakluyt's metaphor thus signals not only admiration for the poem's "true and sound prescriptions" about foreign trade, but a striking uneasiness with the particular linguistic form those prescriptions take: namely, a slightly older English.

With the pastoral figures of Pan and Evander, Hakluyt evoked a genre that some Elizabethan theorists cast as the most primordial of all poetic forms.[78] Attributing the poem's dialect to Evander's *mother* emphasizes its antiquity and rusticity even further: this was not the urbane language, Hakluyt suggests, of modern (male) humanists, but a sub-vernacular or mother tongue whose rhetorical and aesthetic inadequacy were to be disavowed. His use of the trope

---

75 Hakluyt, "Epistle Dedicatorie (1589)," sig. *2r.
76 For this idea in the context of intellectual history, see Sacks, "Blessings of Exchange."
77 Hakluyt, "Preface to the Reader (1598)," sig. *6v.
78 George Puttenham's chapter on pastoral debunks the genre's supposed rusticity, however (*Arte of English Poesie*, chap. 18).

can be compared with the position of Edmund Spenser, who defends a "good and natural" older vocabulary in the preface to *Shepheardes Calendar*: "Other some not so wel seene in the English tonge as perhaps in other languages, if them happen to here an olde word albeit very naturall and significant, crye out streight way, that we speak no English, but gibbrish, or rather such, as in old time Evanders mother spake."[79] Hakluyt was evidently of the party Spenser criticized for their fastidiousness and preference for other languages; despite the editor's interest in presenting the maritime activities of his contemporaries as rooted in a legitimating past, this poet's "olde dialect" did not add to the poem's value as witness, but required explanation and apology.

It's not hard to see why materials such as Dee's account of Edgar, or the vision of Britain ruling the (commercial) waves provided in "Libelle," would lead to something like James Froude's characterization of *Principal Navigations* as "the prose epic of the English nation," a foundational text for the empire proleptically imagined by Dee.[80] Both valued a coherent, insular Britain, able to project power outwards by virtue of its strength by sea, naval as well as mercantile, without fear of influence or invasion from without. Indeed, the nineteenth-century revival of interest in Hakluyt and his own project of documenting England's maritime past rested on related presuppositions about the legitimating value of rootedness in the past. At the same time, Hakluyt's apology for the language and style of an earlier vernacular work – even granted the rapidity of linguistic change in the period – suggests some discomfort with the very past he sought to memorialize. (So, perhaps, does Dee's disinclination to make use of Anglo-Saxon sources for his history.) At the least, these moments suggest a perceptual ambiguity about what *was* natively English, and the kinds of origins with which these learned men wished to claim affiliation.

That uncertainty is another story that the compilation might be understood to tell: that is, the story not of a coherent and bounded national identity securely grounded in a known past, but one that was far more fluid, less clearly demarcated, and requiring ongoing negotiation by acts of assertion, selection, and persuasion on every scale, from the management of ship's crews to the visible and invisible work of historians and of Hakluyt as editor. This story, too, can be found in Hakluyt's medieval and domestic materials, which offer other versions of the English past less aligned with Dee's triumphal vision. Two other

---

79 Spenser, *Shepheardes Calender*, sig. ¶2v. The Norton editors of the work trace the allusion to an anecdote in Aulus Gellius, *Noctes Atticae* 1.10.2 (Spenser, *Edmund Spenser's Poetry*, 503n5).

80 Froude, "England's Forgotten Worthies."

documents recall moments when Britain's boundaries were thoroughly porous: an excerpt from the *Chronicle of Man* (ca. 1261) and another from the Anglo-Saxon version of Paulus Orosius's *Historiae* (860–930).

The Isle of Man was one of the liminal territories whose rulers were said to have been subject to Edgar, thus among the "lesser Isles next adjacent" included in Edgar's annual circumnavigation of his realm.[81] The island appears several times in volume 1: an excerpt from Bede, for instance, noted that Man and other islands in the Irish Sea had been subjected by Edwin of Northumberland in 624.[82] The *Chronicle of Man* is by far the most extensive source, however. Hakluyt's immediate source was Camden's *Brittania* (1594), which treated the Isle of Man, along with the Orkneys, the Shetlands, and other *insulae minores in Oceano Britannico* as part of an archipelagic British geography and history. This textual incorporation of England's peripheries echoed and supported the campaigns of territorial expansion undertaken by both military and political means under the Tudors. Camden's original introduction to the *Chronicle* made evident how contested this incorporation was. Man was "possessed by the Britains" originally, but subject to repeated invasions by "northern nations" (Scots and Norwegians) both before and again after Edwin subjected the island. "About which Isle, and namely to whether of the two countries it ought of right to appertaine, there arose no small doubt among those in ancient times ... Howbeit, the inhabitants both in language and manners come nighest to the Irish, yet so as they therwith savour somewhat of the qualities of Norvegians."[83] Camden suggested that a history of contested possession at the level of rights was accompanied by difficulty in assigning Manx culture and language unambiguously to a single source: who *were* the Manx? Geographically, politically, culturally, and linguistically, Man appears to have been *on* rather than *inside* Britain's border.

Hakluyt translated and reprinted an excerpt from the *Chronicle* directly focused on Manx history. In the year 1066, as his text begins, Harald Godwinson had succeeded Edward as king of England, and defeated Harald Hardråde, king of Norway, at Stamford Bridge, "where the English ... put all the

---

81 Dee, "Voyage of King Edgar," 1: 9; Rodger, *Safeguard of the Seas*, 20.

82 Bede, "Conquest of the Isles of Anglesey and Man," 1: 3. Hakluyt used Jerome Commelin's edition of Bede's "Ecclesiastical History," *Rerum britannicarum* [...] *scriptores* (Heidelberg, 1587).

83 Camden, *Britain*, 2: 204. The original for Camden's text, "Cronica regum Mannie et insularum" (1361), is found in BL MS Cotton Julius A.VII, ff. 30–51.

Norwegians to flight."[84] The Anglo-Saxon king was related to both the Danish and Norwegian royal families; he would soon lose his throne to Viking-descended William of Normandy, who was in turn related to Harald's Anglo-Saxon royal house. From this battle a man named Godred Crovan, said by the *Chronicle* to be the son of an Icelander, fled to take refuge with the ruler of Man, Godred Sigtrygsson – whose name speaks to his Norse parentage. On the death of Godred Sigtrygsson, Godred Crovan was able to seize Man, followed by Dublin (itself ruled by Norse Gaels until the late twelfth century). After his death, and his sons falling out, the *Chronicle* records that the throne was held successively by a son of the king of Dublin and by a designate of the king of Norway. The *Chronicle of Man* thus recalls a time when some regions of the British Isles were as much Norse as Saxon or British, and even domestic wars were between factions of the Norse and more or less naturalized Norse descendants: outsiders and insiders could hardly be disentangled.[85]

Camden's text also receives notice in Hakluyt's preface, where it is recommended to readers both for the the light it sheds on a "dolefull" history, and the information it offers of "the most ordinarie and accustomed navigations, through those very seas, and amidst ... the Hebrides."[86] This second aspect of its content served as an example of successful seafaring to the editor's contemporaries, necessary because "most of our Navigators at this time bee (for want of trade and practice that way) either utterly ignorant, or but meanely skilfull, in the true state of the Seas, Shoulds, and Islands, lying between the North part of Ireland and of Scotland."[87] Hakluyt's provision of the *Chronicle* was thus directed at contemporary mariners who had not mastered, even navigationally, the waters of the Irish Sea and the Hebrides. Following the expansive assertions of ancient British sea power associated with Arthur and Edgar, these native mariners who were said to be still "at sea" immediately off England's shores add another layer to a story which, itself, troubled the notions not only that borders had been fortified against foreigners, but that Britons were entirely at home within them.

---

84 Camden, "Chronicle of the Kings of Man," 1: 10.

85 In Hakluyt's time, the islands north of Scotland would still have been in large part culturally Norse: Orkney and Scotland were Norse possessions until 1468, when they were pledged to Scotland as part of a dowry, and the local Norse dialect persisted into the nineteenth century. Dionyse Settle's account of touching at the Orkneys en route to Baffin Island with Martin Frobisher testifies to how foreign Englishmen found them.

86 Hakluyt, "Preface to the Reader (1598)," sig. *1v.

87 Ibid., sig. *1v.

Hakluyt's only document of Anglo-Saxon origins, the "Voyage of Octher," dates from the reign of King Alfred (848/49–99), another moment when Norse and Saxons both lived and fought each other on English soil. Ohthere was a Norseman who provided Alfred with an account of his voyage around the North Cape of Norway and into the White Sea. He described the voyage as motivated largely by curiosity, in order to see how far north the land continued, and whether, since he was "the furthest north of any Norseman," anyone else lived to the north of him.[88] He sailed north into lands where there was no settlement, then south again, stopping only because he saw signs of habitation; the implication is that settled land would belong to someone else already. In the lands between were nomadic "Finnas" (Sámi) who, by implication, did not possess the land in the same way as Ohthere did because they were not settled upon it in permanent dwellings. Just as the Finnas were foreign to Ohthere, being migratory herders rather than settled cultivators, the nature of Ohthere's own possessions marked him as foreign to his Anglo-Saxon auditors: he owned not cattle but wild deer. Ohthere's relation was, as Sealy Gilles has commented, "in effect, a tale told to King Alfred *by* a stranger *about* strangers."[89] Taking Alfred's court as a normative centre, it maps gradations of difference northwards on a declining scale of civility measured in ways of dwelling on and using the land. It is followed by a second piece of Ohthere's testimony, separately titled by Hakluyt as "The second voyage of Ohthere into the Sound of Denmark." This time, Ohthere sailed south and then east from his home in Halgoland, and at the furthest point of his journey, he or the narrator notes, "In that countrey dwelt English men, before they came into this land."[90] Extending history backwards revealed that Alfred and his courtiers had once been strangers to the land themselves.

Ohthere's account, punctuated by the "he said" of its origins in oral testimony, was incorporated by Alfred's scribes into the Anglo-Saxon translation of Orosius's *Historia adversos Paganos*. The interpolation of his narrative accompanied significant revisions aimed at expanding and reconceiving the geographical information provided by the fifth-century original, and to provide the resulting text in the Anglo-Saxon vernacular.[91] Both the narrative itself and its manuscript context testify to a larger Alfredian project of appropriating

---

88 "Voyage of Octher," 1: 4; Niels, "Ohthere." See also the essays in Bately and Englert, *Ohthere's Voyages*.
89 Gilles, "Territorial Interpolations," 88.
90 "Second Voyage of Ohthere," 1: 6.
91 Gilles, "Territorial Interpolations," 83–5.

foreign knowledge within and for an emergent national culture.[92] Like "Libelle" and the Mongol relations we will examine in the last part of this chapter, the "Voyage of Octher" was first printed in the pages of *Principal Navigations*, but the path by which it arrived there was quite different.[93]

Both of the surviving Orosius manuscripts had known early modern owners (Dee is said to have owned what is now BL MS Add. 47967, while BL MS Cotton Tiberius B 1 belonged to William Bowyer and his son Robert). The manuscripts themselves were only one mode of access to Ohthere's relation for English readers, however. In the 1560s, the antiquarian and cartographer Lawrence Nowell (then part of William Cecil's household) borrowed a copy of the Orosius manuscript, making transcriptions and translations of some parts of it.[94] Humphrey Gilbert credited Nowell's translation for the summary of Ohthere's narrative given in his *Discourse of a discoverie*; he cited it as evidence supporting his belief in the existence of navigable passages north of Asia and the Americas. "I have for the better assurance of those proofes, set downe some part of a discourse, written in the Saxon tongue, and translated into English by M. Nowel servant to Sir William Cecil, lord Burleigh, and lord high treasurer of England. Wherein there is described a Navigation, which one Octher made, in the time of King Alfred, King of Westsaxe Anno.871."[95] After describing Ohthere's voyage around the North Cape, Gilbert connected it to the northeast passage searches of his contemporaries: "he went the very same way, that we now do yearly trade by St. Nicholas into Muscovy, which way no man in our age knew, for certainty to be sea, until it was since discovered by our Englishmen, in the

---

92 On this broader Alfredian context, see Gilles, "Territorial Interpolations," 82.
93 See Bately, "Introduction."
94 For circulation of the Old English Orosius in the sixteenth century, see Brewer, "Sixteenth, Seventeenth, and Eighteenth Century References to the Voyage of Ohthere." (I am grateful to Tony Edwards for this reference.) On Lawrence Nowell's activities, see Flower, "Laurence Nowell." Flower proposes that the manuscript used by Nowell was that in Bowyer's collection, now Tiberius B.1 (Flower, "Laurence Nowell," 69). Nowell's transcriptions from MSS C, D, and E of the *Anglo-Saxon Chronicle*, along with part of the Old English Orosius, are found in BL Add MS 43704; contra Flower, the BL catalogue entry notes that "the text [of Orosius] does not agree with those found in Cotton MS Tiberius B 1 ... or Add. MS 47967 (the Helmingham Hall Orosius)" (otherwise known as the Tollemache Orosius).
95 Gilbert, "Discourse," 3: 13. The text is lightly revised from the earlier print version, adding Cecil's titles.

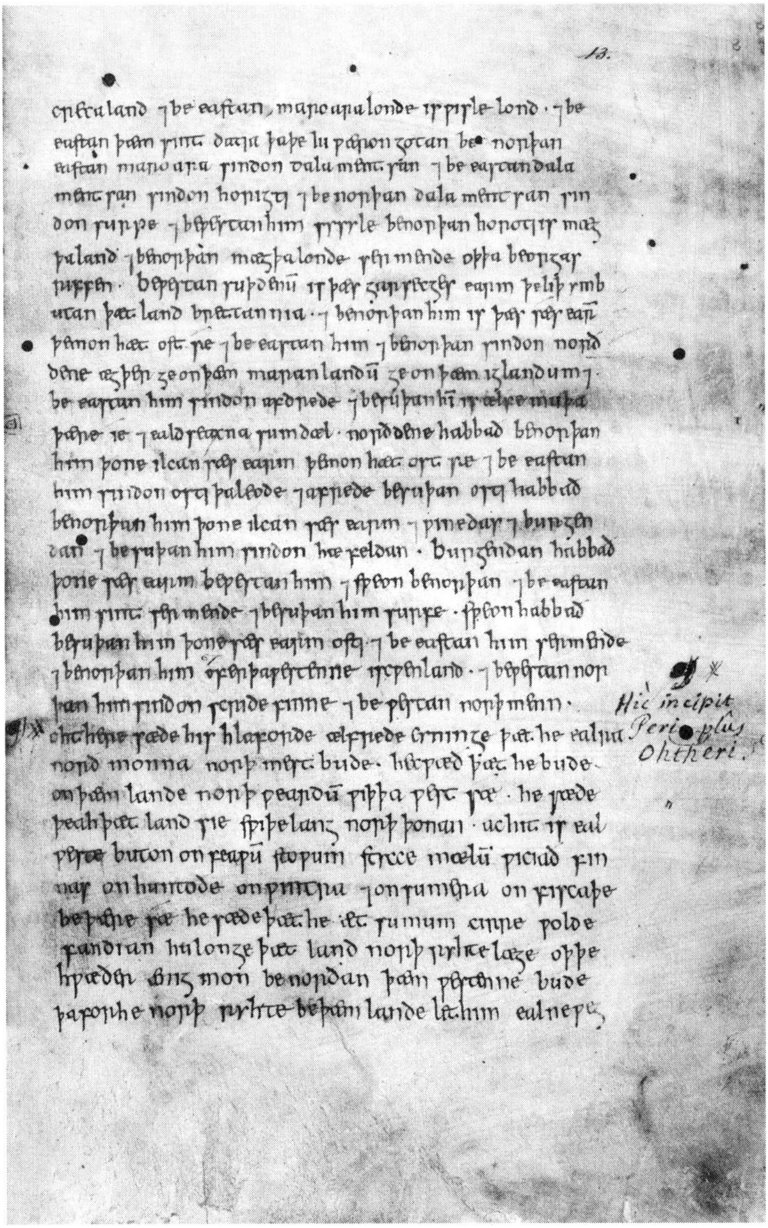

Figure 2.1 The voyage narrative added to Orosius's work in the eighth century begins at "Hic incipit periplus Ohthere." This manuscript belonged to John Dee.

time of King Edward the sixth."[96] (Hakluyt's marginal note identifies the excerpt provided by Gilbert as "a perfect description of our Muscovy voyage.")

Gilbert's references to Ohthere's voyage point back even further. The voyage narrative had been known to at least some part of the reading public since the 1550s, when the seemingly disparate disciplines of Anglo-Saxon studies and applied mathematics met in the "trading zone" where voyages into new regions were planned, financed, equipped, executed, documented, and conceptualized.[97] The antiquarian and mathematician Robert Recorde, an early consultant to the Muscovy Company, owned an important library rich in manuscripts that he plumbed for historical and geographical information.[98] His references to Ohthere appeared in two mathematical treatises: *The Castle of Knowledge* (1556) and *The Whetstone of Witte* (1557). (*Castle* went into numerous editions in the sixteenth century, and was one of the books included in Frobisher's ship's library.)[99] The dialogue that comprises *Castle of Knowledge* refers to Ohthere as "the first discoverer of the North voyage towards Muscovy." In his dedication of *Whetstone* to the Muscovy Company, sponsor of northeastern exploration, Recorde again made explicit the connection between Ohthere's voyage and the ventures of his own day, promising to produce "a booke of Navigation" in which he "will not forgett specially to touche, bothe the olde attempte for the Northlie Navigations, and the later good adventure, with the fortunate successe in discoveryng that voiage, sith the tyme of kyng Alurede his reigne. I meane by the space of 700.yere. Nother ever any before that tyme, had passed that voiage, excepte onely Ohthere,

---

96 Ibid., 3: 13. Originally drafted ca. 1566, Gilbert's *Discourse* was published in 1576, soon before he received a patent for discovery; Hakluyt reprinted the text in both editions of *Principal Navigations*.

97 I borrow the term from Pamela O. Long, who provides a history of the term. "The trading zones that developed in Europe in the sixteenth century and beyond constituted arenas in which substantive communication occurred between artisanally trained and university-trained men, with the latter almost always from more socially elevated backgrounds than the former ... In a trading zone, each party has a particular knowledge or skill that the other side values as something they would like to possess or use in their own work or thinking" ("Trading Zones," 844). Dee's house at Mortlake was doubtless one physical space where different kinds of skills and knowledge converged around the new voyages, the newly constructed hall of the Middle Temple another. But I use the term here to indicate the confluence of learned and practical knowledges organized around the sixteenth-century enterprises Hakluyt documents.

98 Williams, "Lives and Works of Robert Recorde," 18–21.

99 Michael Lok's accounts for the first voyage (TNA, E 164/35, fols. 9–26), transcribed in D. Quinn, *NAW*, 4: 197.

that dwelte in Halgolande: whoe reported that jorney to the noble kyng Alurede: As it doeth yet remaine in auntiente recorde of the olde Saxon tongue."[100] This particular story, in short, had been circulating among Englishmen interested in a northern route to China since the 1550s, and circulating in *English* since at least 1566.

The voyage narratives taken from the Old English Orosius appear to be the only Anglo-Saxon materials Hakluyt did not access through Elizabethan editions of Norman histories. Yet the document does *not* tell us that Hakluyt was either conversant with or interested in the Anglo-Saxon past. Hakluyt appears to have consulted a manuscript of the relation in Anglo-Saxon – perhaps the one in Dee's library – instead of or in addition to Nowell's translation into modern English.[101] If so, however, he did so almost certainly because this fragment of the Old English Orosius had already become a commonplace within the network of people interested in northern geographies and English projects related to them, repeatedly referenced and circulating in transcripts and translations. Moreover, Hakluyt did not provide the original, as he routinely did for medieval texts in Latin.[102] For the Mongol relations we'll discuss later in this chapter, he stressed the importance of providing the originals, both to preserve rare and valuable sources and in case "the translation should chance to swerve in ought."[103] That he provided no original for Ohthere's relation suggests that it had value for its informational contents, and the claims these enabled – but somewhat less as an ancient English text that was linguistically even more alien than the "homely" late Middle English of "Libelle."

We don't have to turn to scholars like Lambarde or Nowell to find a very different treatment of the Anglo-Saxon inheritance than Hakluyt's: John Foxe,

---

100 Recorde, *Castle of Knowledge*, 213; Recorde, *Whetstone of Witte*, sig. A3r–v.

101 Sebastian Sobiecki, personal communication. Brewer notes that Hakluyt and Gilbert both insert a "C" into Ohthere's name, rendering it as Octher, Ochther (Brewer, "Sixteenth, Seventeenth, and Eighteenth Century References to the Voyage of Ohthere," 208–11).

102 Hakluyt was sufficiently fluent to translate modern texts from French, Spanish, Latin, and Portuguese, but only occasionally provided originals. (For instance, both Spanish and English texts were provided for a source that Hakluyt had published in the original language, "Voyage of Antonio de Espeio.") Without performing an exhaustive inventory, it can be noted that intercepted letters in Spanish and Portuguese, materials from Ramusio, and French texts on Canada and Florida are generally provided only in English translation. Hakluyt's use of sources in other European vernaculars is discussed in chapter 8.

103 Hakluyt, "Preface to the Reader (1598)," sig. **1r.

although he confessed not to understand the language, included an Easter sermon by Ælfric in its original language, "in order to support the belief that the vernacular documents of native English Christianity" were superior to the Latin of the Church of Rome.[104] Unlike Foxe, although he was a patriot and a nationalist, Hakluyt appears to have been more at ease with the cosmopolitan context of learned culture and exchange than with England's indigenous past, a past he accessed principally in translation and at several removes. The case of Ohthere calls our attention to how complicated Hakluyt's genealogical project became as he tracked "English" enterprises into a past preceding the Norman conquest. Hakluyt sought to root an account of his compatriots' achievements in a long and dense history – but how unsettling that history proved to be! The resort of strangers to England's shores figured as lively trade in multiple classical and medieval examples: authors from Tacitus to William of Malmesbury are cited as testimony to London's prominence as a market town. Yet this presence also appears in the form of invasion or commercial predation, and the deeper the documents draw readers into the past, the harder it becomes to draw the distinction between ancestors and strangers.

Hakluyt did not simply suppress traces of this unruly past: for instance, his materials on trade privileges include an agreement secured by Cnut in 1027 for the benefit of his English and Danish subjects travelling to Rome. Such traces of Norse invasion and settlement coexist in the collection with myth-making, to which scholars who did engage more closely with Anglo-Saxon sources were no less prone than Hakluyt himself. Lambarde's account of Arthur's conquests, for instance, seems designed precisely to rework the problematic era of Norse invasion and settlement with which the *Chronicle of Man* and Ohthere's relation were connected. According to Lambarde, Arthur had not only subdued all of Norway and its associated territories but also converted them to Christianity. Having converted, the Norse nobles married British women, and thus "the Norses say, that they are descended from the race and blood of this kingdome." Therefore "the Norses say, that they ought to dwell with us in this kingdome ... for which cause ... many cruell battles have been ... fought between the Englishmen and the people of Norway, and ... the Norse have possessed many lands and Islands of this Empire, which unto this day they do possess, neither could they ever afterwards be fully expelled."[105] The Norse occupation of British territories, on this account,

---

104 King, *Foxe's Book of Martyrs*, 121.
105 Lambarde, "A Testimonie of M. Lambard," 1: 2–3.

resulted from their conquest by King Arthur, and testified to their cultural assimilation and desire to return "home."

Both Dee's account of Edgar and the policy prescriptions of "Libelle" suggest that Britain did or, with appropriate policies, *could* enjoy boundaries that were both expansive and firmly controlled. The *Chronicle of Man* raises the question not only of where those boundaries lay but how to identify who belonged inside them. Finally, Ohthere's relation of his travels at the court of Alfred forgets a reign actually famous for heroic defence against Scandinavian invasion in order to present such a "knowledge transaction" as unremarkable. The politics of the larger source text, which sought to frame geographical knowledge for English audiences in the English vernacular, was resonant with Hakluyt's project – yet the Old English Orosius was couched in a language the editor declined to recognize as ancestrally akin to his own.[106]

The sixteenth-century context may have one more thing to tell us about the meanings of Ohthere's relation. Early modern readers might well have connected its framing structure with a famous and consequential knowledge transaction of their own era: Columbus's "offer" of his discovery to Ferdinand and Isabella. A voyage (and voyage narrative) by an Italian became the intellectual and practical property of Spain, both the foundation of a Spanish Empire and the exemplary instance of prowess in geographical discovery. Ohthere's offer of geographical testimony to Alfred also provided Hakluyt with the solution to a particular problem – namely, that the English were not the first to know of the White Sea route to Muscovy "discovered" in the 1550s, a discovery celebrated in the more contemporary materials in volume 1. This route had been described in Sigismund von Herberstein's *Rerum Muscovitarum commentarii* (1549); Herberstein's book was excerpted in Ramusio's *Navigationi et viaggi*. Neither text was unfamiliar to interested English readers; indeed, Hakluyt printed excerpts from Herberstein's book, and one author in *Principal Navigations* concludes a letter about Muscovy by telling his reader, "if thou list, to know the Russians well, to Sigismund's book repair, who all the truth can tell."[107] This ninth-century voyage related to Alfred, however, provided Hakluyt and others with a claim for anterior discovery of the White Sea route, albeit

---

106 I borrow the term from Jardine and Sherman, "Pragmatic Readers."

107 See Turberville, "Certaine Letters in Verse," 1: 389. Alison Quinn's index for *PN* (1589) identifies the text Turberville refers to as an unidentified book on Russia by Sigismund II, king of Poland; I believe that in this case she was mistaken. Herberstein's *Rerum Moscoviticarum* went into "seventeen editions, 1551–89," and relied on visits to Muscovy in 1517 and 1526 (Simmons, "Russia," 1: 162). Hakluyt's brief excerpt from

one that was mediated through several linguistic relays. Rights to the White Sea route were neither actively contested nor defended, and thus the rhetorical payoff of Ohthere's discovery comes to the fore, making the implicit case that the English had always been patrons of voyages and collectors of geographical information. In the latter part of volume 1, Hakluyt would draw on sixteenth-century materials to advance that case in the present, supporting through a mass of documents his contention in the preface that England's explorations of northern seas, and particularly their search for a northeastern passage to China, were achievements comparable to the maritime discoveries of Spain and Portugal in the South.

BARBARIAN ETHNOGRAPHERS

1 "The voyage of a certaine Englishman into Tartaria, and from thence into Poland and Hungary, Anno 1243" (20–1)[108]
2 "Libellus historicus Johannis de Plano Carpini" (21–37)[109]
3 "The long and wonderfull voyage of Friar John de Plano Carpini ... 1246" (37–53 [Latin], 53–71 [English])[110]
4 "The journall of Frier William de Rubricis, Anno 1253" (71–92 [Latin], 93–117 [English])[111]

Herberstein, on northern peoples, appears later in the volume (Herberstein, "Voyage to the Northeast").

108 From Matthew Paris, *Angli historia maior*, ed. Matthew Parker (1571).

109 Chapters i to viii of Giovanni del Pian di Carpini, "Liber Ta[r]tarorum," BL MS Royal 13 A XIV, fo. 198–213. The text is printed in Latin only, not Latin and English as indicated in "C&S"; the manuscript used by Hakluyt includes the first eight chapters of John's text (BL catalogue). I have adopted the English version of the friar's name, John of Plano Carpini.

110 Hakluyt's source for item 3, an excerpt from Vincent de Beauvais, is mistakenly given as BL MS Royal 13 A XIV in Quinn and Quinn, "C&S." Hakluyt's contents list ("Catalogue") can also be confusing for the sources relating to John's travels. "Libellus historicus," the first text on John de Plano Carpini's travels, appears in the category of "Ambassages, Treatises, Priviledges, Letters, and other observations," and the second, "The long and wonderfull voyage," appears in the category of "Voyages." However, the entry for "The long and wonderfull voyage" provides three discrete page references ("21, 37, 53"), the first for "Libellus Historicus" and the second and third for the Latin and English versions of "The long and wonderfull voyage."

111 "'Itinerarium fratris Willelmi de Rubrukis de ordine fratrum minorum anno gratie m°cc°liii ad partes orientales," BL MS Royal 14 C XIII, fo. 225–36.

We have been looking at fragments. A large proportion of Hakluyt's medieval sources, however, coheres around the geographical topic of Central Asia and its peoples, and here Hakluyt provided several texts as he found them. Four thirteenth-century texts about the Mongols occupy roughly ninety-five pages: a significant part of volume 1 as a whole. Little in the rest of the compilation resembles them. Unlike the surrounding documents in volume 1, the bulk of this lengthy section on the Mongols is neither about England, nor about an Englishman, nor by an Englishman; the brief excerpt from Matthew Paris presents a different kind of problem, in that its titular English protagonist was a Mongol collaborator. The ongoing search for new routes to East and Southeast Asia, the central focus of the more contemporary materials in volume 1, made the geography of the Mongol territories sharply relevant to Hakluyt and his contemporaries. Despite their antiquity, these documents thus promised to make a substantial contribution to geographical knowledge of northern Asia in particular.

Three of Hakluyt's Mongol documents narrate missions to the Mongols, including geographic information about the regions traversed: one undertaken in 1245–47 by John de Plano Carpini on behalf of Pope Innocent, the second by William de Rubriquis in 1253–55 on behalf of Louis IX. John's first-person narrative ("Libellus historicus"), given by Hakluyt in Latin only, provides an account of the author's travels from Lyons through Kyiv to Karakoram and then back to Kyiv. A second account, "The long and wonderful voyage of Friar John de Plano Carpini," was compiled by Vincent of Beauvais from the first narrative along with other sources, and printed by Hakluyt in both Latin and English.[112] A third document contains part of William's report to Louis of France.[113] William's narrative begins with his travel from Constantinople across the Black Sea as far as the "new world" of the Mongol empire (chapter 1). The travel narrative is paused for an account of Mongol culture (chapters 2

---

112 Hakluyt's excerpt from Vincent's *Speculum Historiale* includes a chapter of introduction followed by an account of the Mongols' land and culture (chapters 3 to 7), an account of their history (chapters 8 to 18), and finally the narrative of John's travel to and from the court of Güyük Khan (chapters 19 to 33). For Vincent's handling of John de Plano Carpini's *Ystoria Mongalorum* and Simon of Saint Quentin's now lost *Historia Tartarorum*, see Guzman, "Vincent of Beauvais and His Mongol Extracts."

113 On William's mission and his relationship with Louis, see Jackson and Morgan, *Mission of Friar William*, 44.

to 10), and resumes with William's travel towards Karakoram, breaking off somewhere in the Uighur territories of present-day Mongolia.[114]

Both friars' travels were known in some form to Hakluyt's contemporaries. Information derived from John had been disseminated through the maps and globes of Martin Behaim and Martin Waldseemüller, and would continue to figure in the atlases of Hakluyt's contemporaries.[115] Yet the accounts of both missionaries were principally known through the widely read compilations and summaries of Vincent of Beauvais (for John de Plano Carpini) and Roger Bacon (for William de Rubriquis).[116] In other words, these texts were both famous and unread, in anything like their original form, by early modern geographers. Mercator wrote to Hakluyt that "the writings of ... Joannes de Plano Carpini I never saw: onely I found certaine pieces of them in other written hand bookes."[117] The two original narratives appeared in print for the first time in the pages of *Principal Navigations*. Hakluyt describes his presentation of the documents as something of a scholarly coup, since both Mercator and Ortelius "were many years very inquisitive, and could not for all that attain unto [these relations]; and ... they have been of so great account with those two famous cosmographers, that according to some fragments of them they have described in their maps a great part of those northeastern regions."[118] Despite this note of rivalry, Seaver suggests that Hakluyt's publication of the documents was done as "a service to his two cartographer friends," a favour exchanged within a cosmopolitan network of scholars.[119] If these narratives did not testify to the prowess of Englishmen as travellers, they certainly spoke to the sophistication and wealth of English libraries. For William's text, four of the five important manuscripts were in England.[120]

---

114 Hakluyt's text of William de Rubriquis was incomplete, a fault that would be remedied by Samuel Purchas (Purchas, *Pilgrimes*, 3: 1–52; Parker, "Contents and Sources of 'Pilgrimes,'" 2: 422).

115 Van Duzer, "A Northern Refuge of the Monstrous Races"; Goldenberg, "Russian Cartography to ca. 1700," 1878.

116 Bacon made "wide use" of William's information in the "geographical sections" of his *Opus Maius*, in particular for Scythia and Tartary (Campbell, *Witness and the Other World*, 1988, 9; Jackson and Morgan, *Mission of Friar William*, 51).

117 Mercator, "Letter of Gerard Mercator," 1: 445.

118 Hakluyt, "Preface to the Reader (1598)," sig. **1r. Hakluyt may, again, be echoing John Dee quite closely; Dee made a similar assertion in chapter 12 of "Famous and Rich Discoveries" (Sherman, *John Dee*, 178).

119 Seaver, *Maps, Myths, and Men*, 266.

120 Jackson and Morgan, *Mission of Friar William*, 51–3. The manuscripts of both William de Rubriquis and John de Plano Carpini are also discussed in Beazley, *Texts and*

The inclusion of these documents also speaks to other relationships. Hakluyt found the originals of both the friars' narratives (as well as Parker's 1571 edition of Matthew Paris) in the library of John, Lord Lumley.[121] Hakluyt made particular note both of the place where he read and copied these "jewels" and of the patronage to which their presence in his collection testified: "for these two rare jewels, as likewise for many other extraordinary courtesies, I must here acknowledge myself most deeply bounden unto the right reverend, grave, and learned Prelate, my very good lord the Bishop of Chichester, and L. high Almner unto her Majestie; by his friendship and meanes I had free accesse unto the right honor. my L. Lumley his stately library, and was permitted to copy out of ancient manuscripts, these two journals and some others also."[122] We can compare the acknowledgment prefacing a medieval text in Camden's *Brittania*. Camden's book was already in press when Lord William Howard, "for the love that he bears unto the studies of antiquity, willingly imparted unto me the manuscript annals of Ireland" from 1152 through 1370. Next to Gerald of Wales, Camden knew nothing extant "better in this kind," but the annals also had value "because, so noble and worthy a person whose they were by right in private before, permitted so much. Unto whom, the very same thanks in manner are duly to be yielded for bringing them to light, that were to be given unto the author himself, who first recorded them in writing."[123] Camden compliments Howard both as a generous patron and as a fellow antiquary engaged in the labour, commensurate with his own, of "bringing ...

Versions. Later, the colonist John Smith would silently incorporate passages from William de Rubriquis's narrative into his autobiography, *True Travels*; so it might be said that at least one of these texts *became* the account of an English traveller in due course (Smith, *Complete Works of Captain John Smith*, 3: 191 n. 2).

121 Hakluyt, "Preface to the Reader (1598)," sig. **1v. The Lumley library is not known to have contained a copy of Vincent's *Speculum Historiale* (for the 1609 catalogue of the collection, see Sears and Johnson, *Lumley Library*). Lumley's library was also the source for Hakluyt's account of Odoricus's travels in volume 2(i), now part of BL Royal 14 C XIII, and for a sixteenth-century account by Richard Chancellor, "Booke of the Emperor of Russia."

122 Hakluyt, "Preface to the Reader (1598)," sig. **1v. The bishop referred to is Anthony Watson, appointed through Lumley's patronage in 1596 (Richardson, "Watson, Anthony").

123 Cited from Camden, *Britain*, 2: 149. (Note: although the work is in one volume, the section on Scotland is paginated separately.) Howard's transmission of the manuscript was only one facet of his activities as an antiquarian and in support of Camden's enterprise. Howard had been tutored by Hakluyt's brother Edmond (Ovenden and Handley, "Howard, Lord William"; Taylor, *ow*, 2: 414).

to light" lost records of the past in order that their records may be preserved.[124] For Camden and Hakluyt alike, these manuscripts had value *both* as records of a past threatened with loss, *and* as tokens stemming from and (in their print form) acknowledging a patronage relationship in the present.

Hakluyt clearly intended his Mongol materials to be put to use. Marginal annotations to the texts in *Principal Navigations* provide some indication of how they were expected to be read. Many highlight common categories of information by copying them in the margin next to the text:[125] place names (the North Ocean, 54; "the citie of Matriga," 93); topical headings ("The military discipline of the Tartars," 62); dates ("the 7. day of November," 113); persons ("Boleslaus duke of Silesia," 63); events ("He entreth into the territories of Mangu-Can," 113); identification of scriptural passages ("*Deut.* 32.*v.*21," 112); and distances ("Iaic twelve days journey from the Volga," 111). Names of rivers are sometimes indexed to alternative names in the margins, using the mark "‡" (65). Distinctive or unfamiliar customs and physiologies are also indexed by marginalia ("De monstrosis mulieribus & canibus monstrosa narratio," 28; "their custom of drinking at the sound of music," 65); for the Latin version of Vincent of Beauvais's text, these are occasionally in Greek ("polygamy," "taking of bribes," and "atheism," but also "treasure-bearing" and "obedience to command"; 26 and 39, 24 and 40, 24).[126]

Some annotations belonged to the text Hakluyt transcribed; others can probably be attributed to him, such as comparisons with the work of later authors: "This history of Presbyter John in the Northeast, is alleged at large by Gerardus Mercator in his general map" (107).[127] Others are directly or indirectly linked to Hakluyt's interests as a practical geographer interested in the routes taken by the travellers, and the territories along that route. The frequent marginal notes highlighting distances travelled would have been relevant to Hakluyt, if they were not indeed his own. Some marginal comments correct the author's geography: when William writes that a river "is the limit

---

124 Camden, *Britain*, 2: 149. This concern with the preservation of ephemeral records can be heard again in Camden's introduction to the *Chronicle*: a "brief history I will here put down word for word out of an old manuscript, least it should be utterly lost, which is entitled *The Chronicle of Man*" (Camden, *Britain*, 2: 205).

125 Page numbers refer to volume 1.

126 Polygamia, 26, 39; doorodokia, 39; athestes, 24, 40; ethelothreiskeia, 24, 39; peitharchia, 39.

127 These cross-references are generally distinguished by the marks "*"or "¶." Other authors cited include Marco Polo (1: 41), Sigismund von Herberstein (1: 39, 44), and Peter Martyr (1: 42).

of the East part of Russia, and it springs out of the fens of Maeotis, which fens stretch unto the North Ocean," a marginal comment reads, "He is much deceived" (104; see also 65). Other annotations highlight concerns and practices of sixteenth-century explorers: "The benefit of a painter in strange countries" (95) glosses William's regretful comment to Louis that "I would write willingly have painted all things for you, have my skill been all in the art."[128] Evidence about the Mongols as potential consumers of English textiles is repeatedly highlighted: "Cloth is the chief merchandise in Tartary" (102; see also 99). Finally, a small but pointed set of marginal comments connect customs observed by the missionaries to others recorded by sixteenth-century accounts of the New World: the women of Meta Incognita (modern Baffin Island) dress themselves like Mongol women (27), the Mongols wear clothes "like unto Frobisher's men" (54; see also 30), the same manner of burial is used in Florida (96; see also 74). The first two comments in particular invite speculation on geography: if Mongol and Inuit women were seen to wear similar dress, might that indicate that these regions were at no great distance from each other?[129]

Both Hakluyt's marginalia and the surrounding print context of the compilation invite us to compare the medieval encounter with the Mongols with early modern encounters, especially in the Americas. Both William and John attentively recorded ethnographic observations (manners, laws and customs, material culture, "superstitions"), and the accounts of their travels add additional details of Mongol culture, implied and explicit. Most striking, however, is the degree to which the friars themselves are embodied observers, who

---

128 John White would have been the most noteworthy example for Hakluyt; the editor provided White's drawings to Theodor de Bry, who used them for the engravings that illustrate his edition of Thomas Harriot's *Briefe and True Report* (1590). See also instructions for Thomas Bavin on a planned voyage to North America, ca. 1582; Bavin was charged with keeping instruments for navigation, plotting maps and charts, and drawing "each kinde of thing that is strange to us in England" (D. Quinn, NAW, 3: 242-4).

129 The friars are sometimes considered as being in some sense ethnographers *avant la lettre*. Mary Campbell describes the dominant tone of William's narrative as one of "disinterested naturalism" (*Witness and the Other World*, 1988, 114). Jás Elsner and Joan-Pau Rubiés point out that for John and William, as for their successors in the Americas, "a historical analysis of human cultural diversity [was] increasingly seen as a precondition for effective methods of evangelization." Failing in their diplomatic and evangelical aims, the missionaries nonetheless created "a new standard of ethnographic analysis" (*Voyages and Visions*, 32). All three note that the narratives of William and John mark an important stage in the development of emergent reporting practices based on observation.

frequently referenced their own suffering and incapacity.[130] Mary Campbell argues that William's vows of poverty helped give meaning to his "many months of cold, hunger, humiliation, and disillusionment," rendering his experiences "an important spiritual initiation."[131] William framed incapacity as allied to spiritual discipline when he explained to Sartach Khan that he was unable to present the expected gifts due to his vows of poverty.[132] And yet plain descriptions of cold, or extreme hunger, impoverishment, or disgust, characterize at least the surface of these narratives far more than explicit claims to the meaningfulness of those experiences as spiritual offering or ascetic practice. Much of what was unbearable to the narrators (for instance, Mongol hygienic practices) seems less a matter of heroic suffering than of chronic annoyance, bearing with what was enormously "irksome and tedious."[133] This feature of the narratives contrasts with the general confidence exhibited by later English travellers to the Americas: Thomas Harriot at Roanoke, Francis Drake on the Pacific coast of North America, Walter Ralegh in Guiana.

Unlike those later travellers, both men also emphasized the difficulty of communicating across language differences. William repeatedly complained of the barriers provided by the "silly" and often tired or recalcitrant interpreter Homo Dei.[134] Both men also experienced (and described) the inadequacy of the best linguistic instruments produced by Latin Christianity, as the letters they brought with them (those from the pope in Latin, those from the Byzantine emperor in Greek, those from Louis of France translated into "Arabic and Syriake") still required, in order to be read, a further translation.[135] Güyük Khan's scribes provided John and his companions with letters in Latin

---

[130] "We were so feeble in bodie, that we were scarce able to ride" ("Voyage of Friar John," 1: 66). On the friars' inability to drink mares' milk, or to "endure" the quantities of ale that "they compelled us to drink," see also 1: 67.

[131] Campbell, *Witness and the Other World*, 1988, 117–18.

[132] de Rubriquis, "Journall of Frier William," 1: 105.

[133] Ibid., 1: 103.

[134] Ibid., 1: 103, 106, 110, 112, 115. John commented on being received by the first in a succession of progressively more powerful Mongol leaders that "our interpreter whome we had hired and brought with us from Kiow was not sufficiently able" to translate the pope's letters, nor was anyone else competent to do so; at the court of Batu, however, the friars requested and received interpreters who "translated our sayd letters into the Russian, Tartarian, and Saracen languages" ("Voyage of Friar John," 1: 64–6). The acknowledged challenge of communicating across language barriers in Asia contrasts sharply with later narratives in the Americas.

[135] "Voyage of Friar John," 1: 64; "Journall of Frier William," 1: 101, 106. On written documents and translation, see also "Voyage of Friar John," 1: 65.

and "Saracen," but asked whether any of the pope's retinue understood Russian, Saracen, or the Tartar language, John and his companions had to confess, "we had none of those letters or languages."[136] For the two friars, it was not a question of confronting the actual or supposed linguistic incapacity of others, speakers who could be conceived as not *knowing* how to speak.[137] The incapacity was theirs, as they encountered an empire that, extending from eastern Europe to western China, had the speakers of many languages at its disposal. In the end, the missionaries relied on this cosmopolitanism, on court scribes, interpreters, and visitors to the court, in order both to communicate and to understand.

One of the implicit stories told by these encounters contrasts the poverty and incapacity of the narrators with the Mongols' extraordinary wealth, both linguistic and material. This wealth is unmistakable in the friars' narratives. John observed Güyük Khan receiving from ambassadors "such abundance of gifts ... that they seemed to be infinite ... And we were demanded whether we would bestow any gifts upon him or no? But we were not of ability so to do, having in a manner spent all our profession."[138] Such disparities of sophistication and material wealth did not hamper the cultural confidence of the two friars, based on a shared conviction that they professed the only true faith. John concluded, after a description of Mongol beliefs, that "they know nothing concerning eternal life, and everlasting damnation"; for William, Islam was a "damnable religion," the Mongols "a people which is no people," raised up by God to provoke lawbreakers.[139] Hakluyt's version of the text concludes with what William describes as a triumphant routing of several Buddhist priests in a debate on the nature of God (triumphant, at least, until his interpreter tired, and "I was constrained to keep silence").[140]

Despite the doctrinal confidence that enabled the friars to manage the various constraints and incapacities of their position, they bore witness that Christianity in Asia was a decaying faith. William met Christians who were "ignorant of all things appertaining to Christian religion, except only the name

---

136 "Voyage of Friar John," 1: 70.

137 Stephen Greenblatt traces a "denial of Indian language or of the language barrier" through early European accounts of the encounter with the Americas (Greenblatt, *Learning to Curse*, 28).

138 "Voyage of Friar John," 1: 69.

139 Ibid., 1: 56; "Journall of Frier William," 1: 109, 112.

140 "Journall of Frier William," 1: 115. On communication and confidence in the friars' narratives, see also Montalbano, "Misunderstanding the Mongols."

of Christ."[141] Others "had sometime bene after a sort Cleargie men"; one "could as yet sing many songs without booke," while another had enough Latin grammar to understand the friars' speech but not to answer them. William was himself so impoverished in material terms that, unable to provide those he met with the books they requested, he had to borrow pen and ink to copy the hours of the Blessed Virgin and the office for the dead from his breviary.[142] The friars were not so much the spearhead of a triumphantly expansionist faith as impoverished travellers across a landscape of depleted Christianities, the reflux and ebb of earlier, exhausted waves of evangelization.

John's narrative makes the Mongols not only the objects of ethnographic description, but observers themselves: another divergence from later sources on the Americas. In chapters 11 to 16 of his text, the monstrous races associated by Pliny with extreme climates and distant geographies appear within a history of the Mongols' rise to power, as their antagonists and eventual subjects. As the Mongol armies travelled through the "desert places" of Central Asia, they are said to have come upon and, often, defeated in battle, a race whose men are "like unto dogges"; "very deformed" people who ate their own deceased fathers; the "Parositae," whose small stomachs require them to be nourished solely by the steam from boiling meat; "certaine monsters, who in all things resembled the shape of men, saving that their feete were like the feete of an oxe, and they had indeed mens heads but dogges faces"; and finally "monsters in the shape of men, which had each of them but one arme & one hand growing out of the midst of their breast, and but one foote."[143] Although John described the Mongols as "in outward shape ... unlike to all other people," particularizing the differences in the shape of their noses and eyelids, the length of their hair and their feet, such "unlikeness" seems trivial in comparison with the more flamboyantly unusual physiognomies and practices of those they conquered.[144] Of normative human configuration themselves, the Mongols – broad cheekbones and all – were fit to exercise dominion over the deformed races of Asia's margins. By implication, they were for Asia the natural rulers that Aristotle and Pliny held the Greeks and Romans to be

---

141 "Journall of Frier William," 1: 101, 102.
142 Ibid., 1: 111. See also ibid., 1: 114: "I conjectured that they were indeede Christians, but for lacke of instruction they omitted [a] ceremonie."
143 "Voyage of Friar John," 1: 58, 61. See also ibid., 1: 57, "wilde men ... which cannot speake at all, and are destitute of joynts in their legges."
144 Ibid., 1: 54.

within the order of Europe, able to "bear sovereign rule, and sway Empires and Monarchies, which those uttermost nations never had."[145]

In the context of Hakluyt's collection, John's and William's descriptions of the Mongol empire might be considered not only alongside other ethnographies, but also among ambivalent reckonings with other, more powerful empires and centres of power that England at once derogated, negotiated with, and hoped to imitate: Spain, for instance, Muscovy, the Ottoman Empire, China. But if in one sense the Mongols mastered and contained the frightening otherness that classical geographers and their heirs imagined to exist beyond the Caspian, in another they were its most extreme and dangerous avatars. Numerous late medieval texts and maps conflated the Mongols' invasion of Europe in the mid-thirteenth century with a tradition concerning the apocalyptic destroyers, Gog and Magog. This tradition elaborated on two Biblical texts: Ezekiel's prophecy that, in "latter days," Gog from the land of Magog would "come from thy place in the north parts ... against my people of Israel" (Ezekiel 38:15–16), and a passage from the Book of Revelation, associating these names with the supernatural forces gathered in end times: "Satan shall be loosed out of his prison, And shall go out to deceive the nations which are in the four quarters of the earth, Gog, and Magog, to gather them together to battle" (Revelation 20:7–8). In late antiquity, legend credited Alexander the Great with locking up "unclean races" found in the east behind a mountain barrier. These races came to be identified with Gog and Magog, and located in the northeastern regions of Asia; the thirteenth-century Ebstorf map, for instance, locates them there, as cannibals who "nourish themselves with the flesh of humans and drink blood."[146] Marco Polo suggested that the names "Gog" and "Magog" were versions of "Ung" and "Mongul," and this

---

145 Pliny, *Historie of the World*, 37. For an extended discussion of this geopolitics, see Wey Gómez, *Tropics of Empire*, 69–86. John's account of Central Asia's various monstrous races attributes his information to Russian clerics at the Mongol court but was derived ultimately from Pliny and other classical sources (chapters 15 to 16). Although Hakluyt's comments in the volume preface register some reservations about "some particulars which hardly will be credited," at least some of the races described by John continued to appear on sixteenth-century maps; the maps and atlases of Martin Waldseemüller, Gerhard Mercator, and Abraham Ortelius all gave credence (and, thus, renewed authority) to aspects of his marvellous ethnography (Hakluyt, "Preface to the Reader (1598)," sig. **1r).

146 "[G]og et magog quos comites habebit antichristus. hii humanis carnibus vescuntur et sanguinem bibunt" (Gow, "Gog and Magog," 62–3). This discussion of Gog and Magog draws on Gow's essay throughout.

conflation of the Mongols with Gog and Magog persisted on maps through the sixteenth century and beyond. On Juan de la Cosa's world map (1500), for instance, Gog and Magog appeared in the northeast corner of Asia in the guise of cannibals and dog-headed men. Legends on Mercator's 1569 world map located Gog and Magog similarly, adding the identification with the Mongols made by Marco Polo: "Mongol which we call Magog," "Ung which we call Gog" ("Mongul que a no Magog dicitur"; "Ung quae a nostris Gog dicitur").[147] These figures could be found in successive editions of Mercator's atlas as late as 1636.[148]

The identification of the Mongols with the scriptural races of Gog and Magog hovers between the lines of William's narrative. As he crossed into the Mongols' realm, "taking our journey directly toward the North," he "thought that we had passed through one of hell gates."[149] As he passed the river Don ("Tanais" in the text), William noted that Derbent was a site of a wall built by Alexander the Great "which, together with the rocks of Caucasus, served to restrain those barbarous and bloodthirsty people from invading the regions of the South."[150] His description of them as "devils" resonates richly with a long and many-stranded tradition that would make such a description almost literal.

The cluster of geographical, Biblical, cosmographic, and ethnographic associations that placed the cannibalistic "Magog als Mongol" at the far margins of the Asian continent suggests the persistence of a science that associated climates outside the temperate zone of the Mediterranean with aberrations in nature.[151] In the north, as Andrew Gow comments, "'septentrionalism' complements and potentiates 'orientalism.'"[152] The Mongols' location in Central Asia – to Europeans, a region of extreme climate and mysterious geography – comported well with the idea that they were precisely *not* the temperate, normative, natural rulers of John's early chapters, but themselves unnatural and, indeed, possibly inhuman.

---

147 Ibid., 86. Gow references a discussion of the map in Shirley, *Mapping of the World*, 140–1.
148 Ibid., 74, 86. Purchas acquired a copy of Marco Polo translated by Hakluyt, but preferred Ramusio's version of the text for use in *Pilgrimes* (Parker, "Contents and Sources of 'Pilgrimes,'" 2: 423).
149 de Rubriquis, "Journall of Frier William," 1: 102.
150 Ibid., 1: 105.
151 See Ortelius, *Theatrum Orbis Terrarum*.
152 Gow, "Gog and Magog," 65. For a survey of traditions concerning the North Atlantic and their influence on early modern cosmography and cartography, see Small, "Jellied Seas."

Figure 2.2 The text "Mongul als Ma-gog" and "Ung als Gog" can be seen in northeastern Siberia, on either side of the Arctic Circle. Gerhard Mercator and Rumold Mercator, "Asia," in *Atlas sive Cosmographicae meditationes de fabrica mvndi et fabricati figvra* (Dvisbvrgi Clivorvm, 1595).

In Matthew Paris's text, the Mongols were clearly relegated to this status at or beyond the extreme limits of the human: they were the *most* barbarous and savage, an apocalyptic punishment visited upon Christian Europe. And yet it is here that the unique English presence in this set of narratives appears, in the person of a failed crusader who became an interpreter for the Mongols during their invasion of Hungary. The Englishman's story appears as a confession, transcribed by a renegade French priest in a letter subsequently included by Paris in his chronicle; he is never named. Banished from England for unspecified crimes, he lost his money at dice one winter in Acre.[153] Compelled by hunger, wearing a shirt, shoes, and hair cap,

> shaven like a foole, and uttering an uncoth noise as if he had bene dumbe, he tooke his journey, and so traveiling many countreyes, and finding in divers places friendly enterteinment, he prolonged his life in this maner for a season ... At length, by reason of extreame travaile, and continuall change of aire and of meats in Caldea, he fell into a grievous sicknesse, insomuch as he was wearie of his life. Not being able therefore to go forward or backeward, and staying there awhile to refresh himselfe, he began (being somewhat learned) to commend to writing those wordes which hee heard spoken, and within a short space, so aptly to pronounce, and to utter them himselfe, that he was reputed for a native member of that countrey: and by the same dexteritie he attained to manie languages. This man the Tartars having intelligence of by their spies, drew him perforce into their societie: and being admonished by an oracle or vision, to challenge dominion ouer the whole earth, they allured him by many rewards to their faithfull seruice, by reason that they wanted Interpreters.[154]

The Englishman also served as the Khan's envoy to the Hungarians, but was taken prisoner by the Austrians when the Mongol general Batu retreated to Central Asia after Ögödei Khan's death, where John and William would later meet him.

The unnamed Englishman arrived at the "bad eminence" of his position through forms of disgrace, impoverishment, illness, and accident – and served the Mongol project of universal conquest, accompanied as it was by what were reported as atrocities of unprecedented horror. Their advance into eastern Europe was accompanied by "the hideous lamentations of ... Christian subjects ... with whose carcasses, the Tartarian chieftains, and their brutish and savage followers, glutting themselves as with delicious cates ... old, and deformed women they gave, as it were, for daily sustenance, unto their

---

[153] Gabriel Ronay suggests that this might have been around the time of the fifth crusade, and that his "crimes" might have been participation in the barons' rebellion against King John (*Tartar Khan's Englishman*).

[154] "The Voyage of a Certaine Englishman," 1: 20–1.

cannibals: the beautiful devoured they not, but smothered them lamenting and screeching, with forced and unnatural ravishments. Like barbarous miscreants, they quelled virgins unto death, and cutting off their tender paps to present for dainties unto their magistrates, they engorged themselves with their bodies."[155] (Raymond Beazley notes that "in the MSS a representation of the Tartars eating human victims is inserted here, at the foot of the page.")[156] The Englishman's cosmopolitanism, distant travel, and success in foreign contexts – some of the qualities for which Hakluyt hoped to create a genealogy – were *contingent* on his complicity with the Mongols precisely at the point of their condemnation as the ultimate barbarians. If not precisely the "war criminal" or "traitor" that Gabriel Ronay calls him, neither is the Englishman easy to assimilate to a record of national achievement.

If Hakluyt had the broadly celebratory patriotic intentions he claims and which we attribute to him, what work could this astonishing story about the Mongols' English interpreter be doing in the compilation? This document may be the clearest example of a larger fact: many of the component parts of *Principal Navigations* stand in an uneasy relation to a celebration of the achievements of England as a "nation blessed of JEHOVAH."[157] We can't simply ignore such texts – whatever picture of Hakluyt's great volumes we are to form, in the end, it must include (as much as possible) what they contain and not only what is contained in our ideas of them. This story of the Mongol's Englishman certainly invites us to ask: Where are the limits of the editor's commitment to celebrate *English* travel, and what are the limits of his commitment to *celebrate* it?[158]

If this shorter text poses questions that will re-emerge periodically as we work our way through the compilation's parts, the two longer relations had a clear role in preparing the ground for later materials; their interest was more than simply antiquarian. Hakluyt marshalled the manuscript accounts of John de Plano Carpini's and William de Rubriquis's travels into printed form in order to shed light on regions that were newly an object of attention in the

---

155 Ibid., 1: 20.

156 Beazley, *Texts and Versions*, 248 n. 7.

157 Hakluyt, "Preface to the Reader (1598)," sig. **2r. Hakluyt refers specifically to the 1588 defeat of the Spanish Armada, which appears near the end of volume 1. See chapter 7.

158 For a more contemporary example of an English traveller known to but *not* celebrated by Hakluyt, whose treatment implied "a refusal to include him in the 'us' of the British nation," see Steggle, "Charles Chester and Richard Hakluyt," 75.

second half of the sixteenth century, as the English began to explore new routes to the East. These accounts could be mined for observational information about distances, weather, culture, and ecology, and Hakluyt's annotations indicate this kind of use. The missionaries' accounts also offer more general ideas about the *kind* of place the north was: a place that gave rise to barbarous and monstrous races. Seemingly, such ideas were out of date, and certainly Hakluyt warns the reader that the friars related "some particulars which hardly will be credited."[159] Yet as the English began to make their own contacts both with the Eurasian Arctic and the African tropics from the 1550s onwards, theories of place that made such claims credible would play an unpredictable but persisting role in English theory, planning, and perhaps even understandings of experience. Finally, the imposing presence of these Mongol relations speaks to the scarcity and uncertain quality of information on the North available to Hakluyt and his contemporaries: on maps of Northern Asia in the Mercator and Ortelius atlases, Pliny and Marco Polo still figured as key sources. Rare in their original form, these texts had value as an object of exchange in Hakluyt's correspondence with continental geographers and planners.[160] Such exchanges with interlocutors outside England's borders will be another persisting thread through Hakluyt's book.

---

159 Hakluyt, "Preface to the Reader (1598)," sig. **1r.
160 Hakluyt corresponded about John de Plano Carpini's text with Emmanuel van Meteren, to aid the latter in planning the Northeast Passage search by Willem Barentsz; see chapter 8 (Taylor, *OW*, 2: 419–20).

3
Imagining the Arctic

Will it not in all posteritie be as great a renown unto our English nation, to have been the first discoverers of a Sea beyond the North cape (never certainly known before) and of a convenient passage into the huge empire of Russia ... as for the Portugals to have found a Sea beyond the Cape of Buona Esperanza [Cape of Good Hope] and so consequently a passage by Sea into the East Indies; or for the Italians and Spaniards to have discovered unknown lands so many hundred leagues Westward and southwestward of the Straits of Gibraltar, & of the pillars of Hercules?

Hakluyt, "Preface to the Reader," *PN* (1: sig. 4*r)

AROUND THE MIDDLE OF THE SIXTEENTH CENTURY, the landscape (or seascape) of England's overseas ambitions and capabilities shifted dramatically; this shift would ultimately make a work such as *Principal Navigations* conceivable and possible, both because of the increased tempo of activity and because this activity began to be systematically recorded. At the time of the publication of volume 1 in 1598, none of the projects inaugurated in the 1550s appeared to be at the centre of English activities and interests. In the prefatory material to volume 1, however, Hakluyt framed one of these projects – the search for a Northeast Passage to China, and the contacts that ensued from it – as world historical in its achievement and significance. If the voyages to be documented in volume 1 were no longer at the cutting edge of England's overseas commerce and discovery, the editor insists that they were nonetheless worthy to be celebrated and remembered.

The opening lines of the preface to the reader in volume 1 compare the English navigator Richard Chancellor to the Portuguese explorer Vasco da Gama, and his colleagues Sir Hugh Willoughby, Stephen Borough, Arthur Pet, and Charles Jackman to Christopher Columbus. All were associated with a series of voyages in the years 1553 to 1580 that aimed at finding a route into the Pacific by sailing to the north of Scandinavia and Asia. Hakluyt presents the voyages actually accomplished as contributions to that (unachieved) larger project. Were these achievements not comparable to the discoveries of da Gama, Verrazano, and Columbus, he asks? The answer to the editor's rhetorical question has to be no – neither the renown of these English voyages into and beyond the White Sea, nor their consequences, were comparable to those other discoveries of routes that linked Europe by sea to the Indian Ocean and to the Americas. Yet if not of the world-historical stature the editor claimed for them, the voyages *were* pivotal in more local terms, building the range of organizational, financial, and practical expertise that would be necessary for other new ventures as well as generating the kind of textual record that never seems to have existed for exploration and trade under the two King Henrys. In both respects, these northeastern voyages of the 1550s and following inaugurated much of what made Hakluyt's own project possible.

Hakluyt's celebratory presentation sought not only to equate these northeastern voyages with the landmark discoveries of Columbus and da Gama, but also to suggest they were part of a long-continued English project of exploring the North. Invoking a legendary past of Arthurian empire in the Arctic made Elizabethan initiatives into a project of recovering what England had already known and possessed in the past; in the same way, Ohthere's "Relation" was understood as documenting both a precedent for Elizabethan voyages to Muscovy and a "discovery" proffered to an English king by a foreign navigator, like the later discoveries made on behalf of the Spanish and Portuguese crowns. (A marginal comment to Willoughby's log of the 1553 voyage confirms the connection from the other direction: "In this land dwellt Octher as it seemeth.")[1] Connecting the voyages of the 1550s and beyond to the past, and making them the latest part of a longer sequence, meant that England no longer had to be viewed as a latecomer to the arena of discovery, obliged (in the language of Hakluyt's precursor Richard Eden) to "stoop" in deference to the achievements of Spain.[2]

This was a challenging case to make. Arthur and Ohthere were precedents from a distant, at least partly legendary past, and the recent past – the half century or so between John Cabot's voyage of 1497, and the Chancellor-Willoughby voyage of 1553 – was largely characterized by sporadic activity and an impoverished documentary record. Both posed challenges for an editor concerned with telling his story through the provision of primary sources; indeed, since Cabot's western voyage appeared in volume 3, the category of *voyages* in the contents list of volume 1 is simply empty for the span from 1391

1 Willoughby, "True Copie," 1: 235.
2 Eden, *Decades*, sig. biv.

to 1553. (Hakluyt filled the interval with materials on English commerce with Northern Europe, including the long poem on foreign trade that we examined in the previous chapter.) Not only in volume 1, but over the span of the compilation as a whole, the early Tudor period is quite poorly represented, and only vestigial traces are legible of many enterprises that would seem to fall squarely within the collection's mandate of gathering together and incorporating "into one body the torn and scattered limmes of our ancient and late Navigations by See, our voyages by land, and traffiques of merchandise by both."[3]

Yet this earlier history would frame the voyages of 1553 and following as both epochal *and* the natural successor to a long history of distant voyages and trades: "That no man should imagine that our forren trades of merchandise have bene comprised within some few yeeres, or at least wise have not bene of any long continuance; let us now withdraw our selves from our affaires in Russia, and ... take a sleight survey of our traffiques and negotiations in former ages."[4] Gaps in the record thus had to be negotiated. After the celebrated yet poorly documented voyage for which Henry VII granted a patent to John Cabot, *Principal Navigations* yields a smattering of information about voyages under the two Henrys, and Hakluyt took evident pains to scour his sources for what he could find. (Notably, these findings did not include any significant information about any of the Cabot voyages, even though in 1582, Hakluyt could still name the owner of Sebastian Cabot's papers, and expected them to be published shortly.)[5] Two early voyages into the eastern Mediterranean (1534–35) appear in volume 2, transcribed by the editor from the account of an aged survivor. The remainder can be found in volume 3: voyages to the northwest in 1527, and to Newfoundland in 1536 (the second again transcribed by Hakluyt from oral testimony); brief mentions of Sebastian Cabot's 1516 voyage to Brazil and the Caribbean, extracted from the writings of Richard Eden and Robert Thorne; a handful of trading voyages to Brazil in the 1530s and early 1540s by William Hawkins; and "A voyage of two Englishmen to the river of Plate in the company of Sebastian Cabota, 1527." The title of the last

---

[3] Hakluyt, "Preface to the Reader (1598)," 1: sig. *4r.
[4] Ibid., 1: sig.*5v.
[5] "Shortly, God willing, shall come out in print all his owne mappes & discourses drawne and written by himselfe, which are in the custodie of the worshipfull Willia[m] Worthington one of her Majesties Pensioners, who (because so worthie monumentes shoulde not be buried in perpetuall oblivion) is very willing to suffer them to be overseene and published in as good order as may bee" (Hakluyt, *DV*, sig. A4r).

item suggests something more substantial, but it was in reality a short passage excerpted from a longer document that appears in its entirety in volume 1: a response by the Anglo-Spanish merchant Robert Thorne (1492–1532) to questions about the Indies posed by Edward Lee (or Ley), the English ambassador to Spain. Both in *Principal Navigations* and in the manuscript record, Thorne's text is joined with a second by his hand, a discourse addressed to Henry VIII.[6] In this documents, Thorne laid out a strategy for England to pursue discoveries in the North – seeking a sea route to China either to the north of Asia or over the pole – as an explicit response to the Spanish and Portuguese discoveries of routes to the southwest and southeast. His proposals, in other words, advised Henry VIII to pursue precisely what Hakluyt would argue had been undertaken by his successors.

In the 1598 volume, Thorne's proposals for the exploration of the North, dated to the late 1520s, appear as the first set of properly post-medieval texts, and Thorne's "Persuasion" and "Discourse" are among the few documents found in all three of Hakluyt's collections: *Divers Voyages* (1582), *Principall Navigations* (1589), and *Principal Navigations*, volume 1 (1598). In *Divers Voyages*, Thorne appears on the list of "certaine late writers of Geographie," in the illustrious company of Peter Martyr and Gerhard Mercator; Hakluyt also included one of his rare maps, drawn from Thorne's "Carde" (see figure 3.2).[7] In 1589, he added a copy of Thorne's epitaph, and by 1598, he was able to draw additional information on the activities of the Thorne family from the ledger book of Robert Thorne's late brother, Nicholas. As with the excerpt on Cabot's voyage, the ledger materials appear in multiple places. Thorne's proposals themselves, printed in full in volume 1, are referenced or excerpted in the sections in volume 3 on the Northwest Passage, Newfoundland, the Antilles, and Brazil. The marks of Thorne's importance to Hakluyt are thus both early and persisting. In particular, I would argue, Hakluyt used Thorne's documents to fill the gap between 1497 and 1553 with geographical theory and strategy. These documents themselves merit attention, and so too does Hakluyt's use of them, with his implicit claim for their influence on the undertakings that followed. Despite his reticent habits as an editor, Hakluyt did more than simply transmit the writings of others. Even given the paucity of documents for the period during which Thorne was active, the highlighting

---

6 The texts are found together in BL MS Cotton Vitellius C VII fo. 329r–45r and Lansdowne MS 100/7 (Dalton, *Merchants*, 133).

7 On the map printed by Hakluyt (which does not survive in the manuscript record), see D. Quinn, *Richard Hakluyt, Editor*, 17–19.

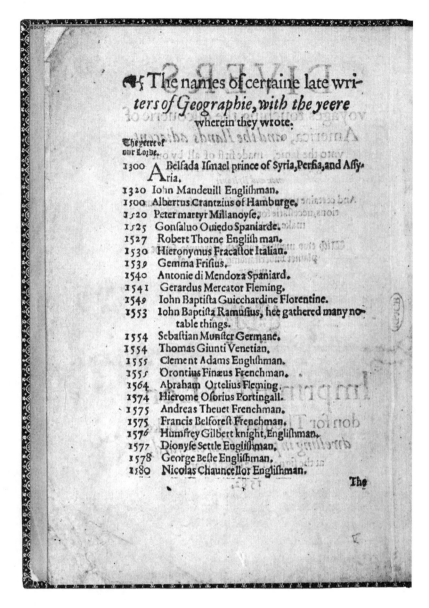

Figure 3.1 Robert Thorne's name appeared with those of other prominent authorities in Hakluyt's early compilation, *Divers Voyages* (1582).

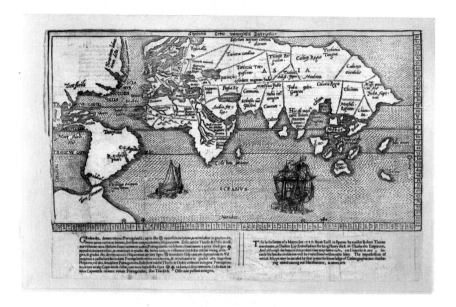

Figure 3.2 Robert Thorne's "Carde," which appeared in *Divers Voyages* (1582), was one of the few maps published in Hakluyt's works.

of Thorne's proposals both covers some surprising absences in the record and leaves other areas in relative shadow. Overall, Hakluyt's presentation of materials from 1500 to 1560 will provide several reminders (if any were needed) that his collections cannot be treated as a neutral repository of information.

This chapter will examine the inception of the northern project, the content of Thorne's proposals, and, finally, some of the context around those proposals that Hakluyt does not provide. That context is both biographical, placing Thorne in the context of early sixteenth-century Seville and its Atlantic connections, and bibliographical, looking at the ways Hakluyt's work shapes our understanding of English activities in the period. The 1550s, after all, inaugurated *two* sets of voyages. The first were the voyages of northeastern exploration that resulted in a direct trade with Muscovy and, for a time, Persia. The second were voyages of trade with West Africa, undertaken at the same time and by a group of investors, planners, and mariners whose membership included many names familiar from the northern voyages. (Thorne's biography will remind us how close these two projects actually were in their origins.) Both enterprises produced a documentary record that appeared in printed forms both in and prior to the appearance of Hakluyt's collection. This record allows us to compare Hakluyt's framing of contemporaneous projects in two distinct regions. In the end, Hakluyt's representation of the North as a privileged sphere of English activity *under*represents the ways this activity depended on what we might broadly call the resources of the South.

In the early 1550s, a group of London merchants and gentry came together to plan, fund, and organize a voyage intended to search for a Northeast Passage to China. The resulting voyage of 1553 was led by Sir Hugh Willoughby and the pilot Richard Chancellor – a protégé of Sir Henry Sidney who had been trained by John Dee and Roger Bodenham. Unlike the scattering of earlier voyages by the Cabots, Hawkins, or other, even more obscure figures, the enterprise of 1553 mobilized a diverse group of investors, including both merchants and gentry, with the participation of the crown: two hundred and forty individual people contributed 25 pounds each towards the expenses of the voyage, while Edward VI provided diplomatic letters addressed to "the Kings, Princes, and other Potentates of the Northeast."[8] Willoughby and Chancellor sailed in May of 1553. In late July, Chancellor's *Edward Bonaventure* became separated from the other two ships on the northern coast of Norway; Willoughby's two ships, lacking anyone with the navigational skills that had led to Chancellor's appointment as chief pilot, sailed on, uncertain where they were in relation to their charts and missing a rendezvous at Vardø, Norway. They are believed to have sailed as far as Novaya Zemlya before turning back, eventually to land on an uninhabited part of the Kola Peninsula. There they died over the ensuing winter.[9] Meanwhile, Chancellor continued from Vardø into the White Sea, to land near the mouth of the Dvina River; he then travelled overland and by river to the court of the Muscovite Tsar. He returned to England in 1554 with a letter from Tsar Ivan IV to Edward, "welcoming the prospect of trade."[10] By this time, Edward had died, to be succeeded by his sister; Mary and Philip granted a charter to "the Merchant Adventurers ... for the discovery of lands and territories unknown," generally known as the Muscovy Company, early in 1555. Despite the loss of Willoughby's ship and crew, the initial voyage to Muscovy was quickly repeated; later that year,

8 "Letters of King Edward the Sixt," 1: 230–2.
9 Barbara Gordon has suggested, from the evidence of a contemporary document, that the men died not of cold, but from carbon monoxide poisoning subsequent to using sea-coal for heat in a closed environment (Gordon, "Fate of Sir Hugh Willoughby and His Companions").
10 Loades, *England's Maritime Empire*, 167. "The Letters of the Emperour of Russia."

Chancellor returned to Muscovy with merchants who would remain as factors to manage trade over the ensuing years. In 1558, Anthony Jenkinson extended the reach of the Company's interests, travelling south from Muscovy to Bukhara; there, he opened trade and diplomatic relations with the Shah that bypassed the series of Mediterranean commercial powers through whose mediation English goods had previously reached Persia. The Muscovy Company would also continue to plan and dispatch voyages of exploration in search of a Northeast Passage; in the last of these recorded in *PN* (1598–1600), Arthur Pet and Charles Jackman reached Vaigatz (on the Arctic coast of Russia) before turning back.

The events of the voyage, and the organizational structures enabling it, were momentous in several ways. David Loades describes the Privy Council's involvement with Willoughby and Chancellor's voyage of 1553 as itself "a turning-point in the maritime history of England, the importance of which can hardly be over emphasized."[11] Nor was the innovation only on the side of government: with this voyage and those that followed it, "the City for the first time witnessed and took part in a long-distance, heavily capitalized trade, run by a joint stock company."[12] Sophus Reinert views the nascent Muscovy Company as a case study in the emergence of economic expertise. Experience gained in these voyages – including their failures – taught Tudor planners that successful long-distance trade required "certain clusters of knowledge ... not only in terms of navigation and Arctic survival but in the judicious selection of middlemen, envoys, and more generally the logistics and management of economic agents and resources on an imperial scale."[13] The novel organizational structures supporting the voyage of 1553 would enable enterprises of trade, diplomacy, and exploration in the decades that followed. The documents produced by these enterprises, recording the experiences of English merchants and diplomats in Muscovy and, eventually, Persia, as well as continued exploration east along Russia's Arctic coast, made up (in Hakluyt's words) "the chief contents of this present volume."[14]

What lay behind these developments? In the words of Clement Adams, the voyage's first chronicler, "[O]ur merchants perceived the commodities and wares of England to be in small request with the countries and people about us, and neere unto us, and that those merchandises which strangers in the

[11] Loades, *John Dudley*, 246–7.
[12] Andrews, *Trade, Plunder, and Settlement*, 69.
[13] Reinert, "Authority and Expertise at the Origins of Macro-Economics," 117.
[14] Hakluyt, "Epistle Dedicatorie (1598)," *2v.

time and memory of our ancestors did earnestly seek and desire, are now neglected, and the price thereof abated, although by us carried to their own ports, and all foreign merchandises in great account, and their prices wonderfully raised."[15] England faced growing problems with the market for its main export good of woollen cloth in Antwerp (problems that would be amplified with the rise of conflict in the Low Countries over ensuing decades), and intersecting problems arising from the debasement of the coinage, a strategy employed by Henry VIII to pay for his numerous wars and one that affected the price of English goods abroad. London merchants also sought "better access to the ultimate sources of supply" for distant goods imported through intermediate markets at Antwerp and on the Iberian Peninsula.[16] For both these problems – the need for new export markets, and the need for precious metals – the globalizing empires of Spain and Portugal offered appealing models for solution. Perhaps exploration would enable English merchants to emulate their Luso-Iberian counterparts. Accordingly, Adams continues, "certain grave citizens of London, and men of great wisdom, and careful for the good of their country, began to think with themselves, how this mischief might be remedied. Neither was a remedie (as it then appeared) wanting ... for seeing that the wealth of the Spaniards and Portingales, by the discovery and search of new trades and countries was marvelously increased, supposing the same to be a course and mean for them also to obtain the like, they thereupon resolved upon a new and strange navigation." In short, a crisis in English foreign trade and monetary policy pushed merchants to innovate, ultimately stimulating the willingness to risk such a "new and strange navigation."[17]

These voyages were highly speculative, not only financially risky but venturing into a part of the world whose contours were almost entirely unknown to the investors (and navigators). Hakluyt's headnote describes the Chancellor-Willoughby voyage as "intended" for Cathay, itself a region which the English conceived of only indistinctly.[18] For the coasts of northern and eastern Asia, by which they hoped to travel, maps of the period remained especially

---

15 Adams, "Newe Navigation, 1553," 1: 243.

16 Brenner, *Merchants and Revolution*, 5. For an account of the voyages and their inception in economic and political context, see (for instance) Loades, *England's Maritime Empire*, 52–74; Reinert, "Authority and Expertise at the Origins of Macro-Economics"; Brenner, *Merchants and Revolution*, 6–21.

17 Adams, "Newe Navigation, 1553," 1: 243.

18 For a stimulating account of how to read fragmentary references to another region in East Asia, see Das, "Encounter as Process." A helpful overview of sixteenth-century European sources on China is provided in Padrón, *Indies of the Setting Sun*.

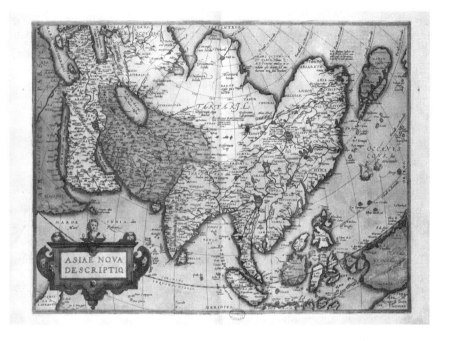

Figure 3.3 Ortelius's map of Asia compressed the distance between Beijing ("Cambalu") and the easternmost part of Siberia; such ideas informed plans for a 1580 voyage aimed at reaching Beijing by sailing around the northern and eastern coasts of Asia.

misleading. The atlases of Gerhard Mercator (1595) and Abraham Ortelius (1570), for instance, relied for their information about Siberia on "partly legendary materials by Pliny, Strabo, Giovanni de Plano Carpini, Marco Polo, and the Bible."[19] Neither Western Europeans nor the Russian travellers and cartographers whose materials they may have used understood the contours of Asia's northern and eastern coastlines accurately. Ortelius's map of 1570 (see figure 3.3), for instance, overestimated the northern extent of the Siberian coastline, but smoothed out the long peninsulas of Kamchatka and Korea in the east, compressing the distance between Beijing ("Cambalu") and the easternmost extent of Siberia. (Granted the capacity to navigate far northern waters, such a map made the Northeast Passage appear more plausible than

19 Goldenberg, "Russian Cartography to ca. 1700," 1877–8.

it would prove in reality.) Those charged with planning the voyage to Cathay were thus operating on scant, antiquated, and inadequate information, a situation that they were unable to remedy short of simply sending ships to discover how the coasts lay. We have already seen Hakluyt's attempts to extract usable information from the Mongol narratives. An anecdote from Adams brings the dearth of information on Central Asia into immediate view:

the companie growing to some silence, it seemed good to them that were of greatest gravity amongst them, to inquire, search and seeke what might be learned & knowen, concerning the Easterly part or tract of the world. For which cause two Tartarians, which were then of the kings Stable, were sent for, & an interpreter was gotten to be present, by whom they were demaunded touching their Countrey and the maners of their nation. But they were able to answere nothing to the purpose: being in deede more acquainted (as one there merily and openly said) to tosse pottes, then to learne the states and dispositions of people.[20]

Positive knowledge of northern geography and hydrography was in short supply, and Adams's grave merchants consulted the drunken grooms to no avail.

They were more successful in recruiting general expertise. Sebastian Cabot had made several voyages under a patent of exploration granted to his father by Henry VII before emigrating to Spain after 1512, where he became pilot major, charged with overseeing navigational training at the Casa de la Contratación in Seville. Shortly after the death of Henry VIII, the Privy Council allocated money to bring Cabot and his family back to England from Spain.[21] Cabot returned to England sometime in 1548, and was active in planning and promoting voyages for the remaining nine years of his life – in particular, voyages for the discovery of a northeast passage. His personal experience included voyages to Newfoundland (probably) in 1497, and to Brazil in 1526; another voyage to subarctic Canada in 1508 is possible but uncertain. Although Cabot could add little, if anything, to the general dearth of geographic information concerning the Eurasian Arctic, he did bring considerable experience in navigation, in training navigators, and in the logistics of managing long voyages in little-known waters. The "moon-shot" project of finding a third passage to the Indies seems to have engaged his enthusiasm. Stephen Borough's

20 Adams, "Newe Navigation, 1553," 1: 244.
21 For a detailed account of Cabot's career, see Ash and Sandman, "Trading Expertise."

journal of a 1556 voyage of northern exploration records that Cabot feasted them on the eve of their departure, and danced "for very joy that he had to see the towardnes of our intended discovery."[22]

Critically, northern voyages trained a cohort of English mariners in the kinds of expertise that Cabot had brought with him from Spain. Hakluyt's marginal comment highlights the name of William Borough, among the 1553 list of mariners on Chancellor's *Edward Bonaventure*, as "nowe comptroller of her Maiesties navie." Among the roster of mariners, officers, and merchants who sailed with Chancellor are many other names that would recur prominently in connection with later voyages and trade missions, as captains, agents, and often also as authors of documents: these include the mariners Borough (master of Chancellor's ship) and Pet, as well as the merchants Arthur Edwards, John Hasse, and Richard Johnson. Borough and Pet would lead subsequent Arctic voyages of exploration in 1556–57 and 1580, respectively, and others would go on to serve the Muscovy Company in other ways.[23] (All produced documents printed by Hakluyt.) The impacts of the 1553 voyage, and its successors, were thus considerable.

We know the details of the Chancellor-Willoughby voyage and its circumstances largely courtesy of Adams's lengthy narrative, *Anglorum navigatio ad Muscovitas* (London, 1554), which survives only in Hakluyt's compilations and a later edition.[24] Adams was a mapmaker as well as tutor to Edward VI's companions; his narrative was published within a year of Chancellor's return from

---

22 Borough, "Voyage of Stephen Burrough, 1556," 1: 274–5.

23 Willoughby, "True Copie," 1: 233. For Borough's and Pet's voyages, see Borough, "Voyage of Stephen Burrough toward the River of Ob ... 1556," "Voyage of the Aforesaide Stephen Burrough, 1557"; Smith, "Discoverie of the Northeast Parts, 1580."

24 In PN (1598–1600), Hakluyt provided only an English translation of Adams's Latin original; both appear in PN (1589). The Latin text later appeared in C. Marnius and J. Aubrius, eds., *Rerum Moscoviticarum auctiores varii* (Frankfurt am Main, 1600) (Simmons, "Russia," 162n2). No originals of Adams's work are known to have survived, but Richard Eden's comments suggest that his text would be readily available to readers: "I shall not neede here to describe that viage, forasmuche as the same is largely and faythfully written in the Laten tongue by that lerned young man Clement Adams" (Eden, *Decades*, fo. 256r). However, James McDermott writes that "the Russia Company jealously guarded Adams's handwritten notes until 1589, when Hakluyt reproduced them in the first edition of his *Principall Navigations*" (McDermott, "Chancellor, Richard"). Chancellor's first-person account, "The booke of the great and mighty Emperor of Russia," appears only in the second edition, PN (1598–1600), and is not differentiated from Adam's third-person narrative either in Hakluyt's "Catalogue" or in David and Alison Quinn's "Contents and Sources."

the first voyage.[25] Richard Helgerson has commented on Adams's innovative use of "humanist eloquence" to celebrate what he sees as an essentially mercantile endeavour, calling attention to a critical point: Adams narrates a kind of action that had not previously been the subject of narrative in England.[26] Significant aspects of English overseas travel and trade before 1553 were unavailable half a century later in part because they were not documented in the same ways or in the same places as later voyages. Thus it is noteworthy both that the Adams narrative exists at all, and that the voyage was *documented* in a lasting and public way – not only by this narrative, printed again in both editions of *Principal Navigations*, but also, eventually, by two additional participant accounts discovered and published by Hakluyt.[27] (We will examine these different narratives and forms of narrative in chapter 4.)

The redundant (and in part public) documentation of the 1553 voyage marks a departure from practices on earlier long-distance voyages. John Cabot's 1497 voyage of westward discovery had resulted in a land claim that put England, literally, "on the map" of the Americas only five years after Columbus's voyage of 1492; records show that he received letters patent and later a reward and pension from Henry VII "for discovery of the new found isle" in 1497, and made another westward voyage in 1498.[28] But the elder Cabot's undertakings – unlike those of Columbus, or (later) Hernán Cortés – did not produce narrative accounts that were circulated in print, and much about them is still unknown. Neither memorialized nor succeeded by a concerted push to settle or explore, by the later sixteenth century Cabot's voyages in the 1490s had been so thoroughly obscured by time and the dearth of documentation that Hakluyt attributed them to Sebastian, his son.[29] Facts about English voyages

---

25 Adams is said to have engraved a revised version of Sebastian Cabot's 1546 cosmographic world map; his son Robert collaborated with Augustine Ryther to produce detailed maps of the Armada battle (see chapter 7).

26 Helgerson, *Forms of Nationhood*, 179–81.

27 Willoughby, "True Copie"; Chancellor, "Booke of the Emperor of Russia."

28 D. Quinn, NAW, 1: 93–102.

29 In the second edition of his collection, Hakluyt printed letters patent and a bill licensing John Cabot to make the discovery, followed by excerpts from Ramusio, Peter Martyr, and López de Gómara attributing the discovery to Sebastian (Hakluyt, PN [1598–1600], 3: 5–10). Peter Pope suggests that Hakluyt and other writers had difficulty distinguishing multiple voyages by the father and son, conflating (for instance) John's voyage to Newfoundland in 1497 with Sebastian's sub-Arctic voyage of 1508; he also suggests that the long-lived Sebastian may have sought to take credit for his father's endeavours after John's death (Pope, *Many Landfalls*, 43–68).

towards the west in the late fifteenth and early sixteenth centuries are still being pieced together by archival research in the twenty-first century, a far cry from the multilingual print publicity given to the voyages of Columbus in the 1490s, or Thomas Harriot's narrative of the short-lived English colony at Roanoke in the 1580s.[30] The northeastern voyage of 1553 marked a watershed in English history simply by being durably recorded and remembered rather than forgotten. Looking back from 1553, Thorne's proposals stand out against a background of missing or fragmentary sources – complete, written in the first person, pointed and apparently prescient as harbingers of what was to come.

THE POLAR PROPOSALS OF ROBERT THORNE

1 "A persuasion of Robert Thorne merchant of Bristol [...] to king Henry the eight [...] to set out and further Discoveries toward the North" (212–14)
2 "The discourse of [...] Robert Thorne, written, to Doctor Leigh the Kings Ambassador in Spaine" (214–20)

Hakluyt's headnote identifies Robert Thorne as a Bristol merchant "who dwelt long in the citie of Sivil in Spaine." In 1527, Thorne wrote to Edward Lee, the English ambassador to Spain, to inform him more fully on the parts of the world newly discovered by Spain and Portugal. Portugal's exclusive rights over the East Indian spice trade had been challenged by Spain's discovery of a westward route to Asia in 1522, following the return of Magellan's *Victoria*. A letter to Thomas Wolsey reported that Charles V's claim to the East Indies was potentially for sale, possibly to England, and the debate over territorial limits would be settled by the lease of Spain's "rights" in the East Indies to Portugal in the Treaty of Zaragoza in 1529.[31] Thorne was well positioned to brief Lee on these matters, by his familiarity with Spanish navigators and his own involvement with Atlantic commerce; as he told Lee, he had also invested in a 1526 voyage by Sebastian Cabot that would attempt to follow Magellan's route. Thorne

---

30 On the Cabots, see Pope, *Many Landfalls*; Jones and Condon, *Cabot and Bristol's Age of Discovery*. (The book by Condon and Jones stems from an ongoing research project that has made significant archival discoveries.) Non-narrative documents on voyages under the two Henries can be found in D. Quinn, NAW.
31 Taylor, *Brief Summe*, xxv–xxvi. On the context for Thorne's letter, see also Dalton, *Merchants*, 72.

told Lee that the Spanish Indies and "our New Found lands" were "all one maine land."[32] But America was not the principal region in question; Thorne's exposition centres on "the new trade of Spicery of the Emperour," which Thorne understood to span the Pacific.[33] While the "principall spicerie" of Portugal was "a headland called Malaca," from there to the east were "many islands, which be Islandes of the Spiceries of the Emperour. Upon which the Portingals and he be at variance."[34] Thorne appears to speculate on the relations between these Indies and the northern Americas: east of the Moluccas, the Asian coast turned to the north, "which coast not yet plainely knowen, I may joint to the Newfound lande found by us, that I spake of before." Thorne's geographical exposition, originally accompanied by a map resembling that found in *Divers Voyages*, is followed by a history of discoveries and of subsequent negotations over how to specify the "division of the world" agreed in the Treaty of Tordesillas. He concludes his exposition with the opinion that "to the Indias [that is, the West Indies] it should seeme that we have some title," or at least "might trade thither as other doe" – but that the Americas are "nothing neere the Spicerie."

Here, however, the document takes a turn: should the seas to the north of "the sayd New found lands" be navigable, England too had a potential route to the other side of the world, "a much shorter way" than ones diverted around the southern tips of Africa and South America. Thorne claimed a personal knowledge of English discovery in the North, telling Lee that his father and another merchant of Bristol had discovered "the New found lands" west of England, and (more importantly) would have continued south to claim other, richer regions of the Americas had their mariners not refused to proceed: "my father ... with another marchant of Bristow named Hugh Eliot, were the discoverers of the New found lands, of the which there is no doubt, (as nowe plainely appeareth) if the mariners would then have bene ruled, and followed their Pilots minde, the lands of the West Indies (from whence all the gold commeth) had bene ours. For all is one coast, as by the Carde appeareth, and

---

32 Thorne, "Discourse to Doctour Leigh," 1: 216.

33 For a detailed account of how this geography was imagined by Spanish authors and cartographers – that is, the East Indies as an extension of Spanish empire in the west – see Padrón, *Indies of the Setting Sun*.

34 Thorne, "Discourse to Doctour Leigh," 1: 216.

is aforesayd."[35] Thorne's regretful comment about the unruly mariners conveys the sense that only a series of unlucky accidents had prevented England from gaining the empire that Spain in fact had.

The "inclination or desire" for northern exploration that Thorne claimed to have inherited from his father motivated a project he then outlined in a proposal to Henry VIII, the first in order of the two texts by Thorne but chronologically the second to be written. Addressing the king, Thorne described the world as divided into four parts, of which "three parts are discovered by other Princes." The Spanish had discovered to the west and south, "the Indies and Seas Occidentall"; the Portuguese to the south and east, "the Indies and Seas Orientall." What remained to be discovered were "the said North parts, the which it seemeth to me, is only your charge and duty. Because the situation of this your realm is thereunto nearest and aptest of all other: and also for that you have already taken it in hand."[36] England had a particular opportunity to explore these regions of the world, with the incentive of opening a new route to the rich regions already accessed by the Spanish and Portuguese, and perhaps others not yet discovered. Thorne imagined a route crossing the pole and then descending in three possible directions: to the east, passing by the northern coasts "of all the Tartarians" before reaching China, Malaca, and the East Indies, returning through the Indian Ocean and the Cape of Good Hope; to the west, sailing along the Pacific coast of the Americas, "the back side of the new found land ... until they come to the back side ... of the Indies Occidental," returning through the Straits of Magellan; and finally, directly over the North Pole and then south, right "toward the Pole Antarctic, and then ... toward the lands and islands situated between the Tropikes, and under the Equinoctiall, without doubt they shall finde ... the richest lands and Islands of the world of golde, precious stones, balmes, spices, and other thinges that we here esteeme most."[37] All of these possibilities would be explored in the reigns of Edward VI and Elizabeth: John Davis's voyages in search of a Northwest Passage included attempts to sail directly north.[38]

35 Ibid., 1: 219. Thorne's "Carde" was printed by Hakluyt in *DV*, opposite sig. B4v. On the western voyages of Elyot and Thorne the elder, see the documents in D. Quinn, *NAW*, chap. 11. Some context is provided in Seaver, *Frozen Echo*, 294–302.

36 Thorne, "Persuasion to King Henry the Eight," 1: 213. Hakluyt's marginal note identifies the previous voyage here alluded to as Sebastian Cabot's sub-Arctic voyage of 1508.

37 Ibid., 1: 213.

38 Davis believed a polar route was possible and even practical, but found his way barred by ice as he sailed north between Greenland and Canada's Arctic archipelago; in *Worldes Hydrographical Discription* (1595), he continued to advocate for a polar route.

Thorne's proposal that England seek a passage in the North rested on what was then – in the 1520s – still a relatively new understanding that the Arctic might be, in fact, tractable and navigable rather than an insuperable barrier to passage. This understanding arose from the challenges to an existing model of the world posed by the empirical evidence of voyages to another region altogether. The zones of high and low latitude (regions between the Arctic and Antarctic circles and the poles, and or between the Tropics of Cancer and Capricorn around the equator) had been thought to be sufficiently extreme in climate that they could be neither inhabited nor traversed by ordinary human beings. Yet Columbus's discoveries in the Caribbean had found a temperate nature and human beings of ordinary configuration in the torrid zone south of the Tropic of Cancer; these discoveries overturned established ideas of cosmography and geography, and challenged the linkage between the two.

This idea that zones defined by the sun's movement could inform on the nature of what was to be found in any terrestrial region rested on the supposition that both organic and inorganic bodies were generated and nurtured by (especially) the heat of the sun, receiving their nature from its period and intensity. A scientific tradition originating in ancient Greece predicted that climates hotter or colder than the temperate Mediterranean were uninhabitable, or would at best give rise to aberrant bodies and degraded political systems.[39] We have seen traces of these ideas in John de Plano Carpini's description of the monstrous races located in the far reaches of northern Asia; such peoples were also routinely represented on medieval maps of Africa.

One aspect of the cosmography inherited by the sixteenth century was a mathematical discipline of increasing utility to navigators for finding position by the sun and stars rather than by known landmarks, and to cartographers

---

[39] "Climate," on this model, had a specific referent. Five climates or zones were delineated by the limits of the sun's apparent movement over the course of the year: the polar zones of the Arctic and Antarctic, defined by the line of latitude above which for one day or more each year, the sun does not set or rise; the temperate zones, extending from the polar circles to the tropics of Cancer and Capricorn, respectively the northern and southern limits of the sun's declination (where, for one day a year, the sun is directly overhead); and the torrid zone extending from the equator south and north to the tropics. An important vehicle for the transmission of these ideas in the period was Sacrobosco's *Tractatus de sphera*, which Lynn Thorndike desribes as the "most used textbook in astronomy and cosmography from the thirteenth to the seventeenth century" (Thorndike, *Sphere of Sacrobosco*, 1). On Sacrobosco and the theory of climates, see, for example, Portuondo, *Secret Science*, 26–8.

concerned with devising accurate projections of a three-dimensional object onto two-dimensional maps. (Robert Recorde's publications in the 1550s are an example of this mathematical cosmography.) In another aspect, cosmography aspired to systematic, universal description, including qualitative information on the earth's human and physical geography; linked to the "Ptolomaic grid" of latitude and longitude, such a project continued to rely both on new observations by mariners and on textual sources of heterogeneous age and quality, as well as the predictive models inherited, along with the mathematics, from antiquity. This inheritance contributed a long-standing set of associations between latitude and physiology, natural resources, and political forms, built on the understanding that these were systematically affected by the influence of the sun and other planets.[40]

Thorne and his contemporaries grappled with the uses and defects of these models as a way to describe and understand a rapidly expanding world. If experiences of the Portuguese and the Spanish in West Africa, the Caribbean, and the East Indies had begun to discredit the prediction of an uninhabitable zone surrounding the equator, Thorne argued that this newly acquired knowledge of regions under the "burning zone of the equator" to the *south* had implications for the still unexplored *north*. As Thorne writes, "it is a generall opinion of Cosmographers, that passing the seventh clime [i.e., the Arctic Circle], the sea is all ice, and the colde so much that none can suffer it. And hitherto they had all the like opinion, that under the line Equinoctiall [i.e., around the equator] for much heate the land was unhabitable. Yet since (by experience is proved) no land so much habitable nor more temperate. And to conclude, I thinke the same should be found under the North."[41] The prediction that the Arctic would be navigable worked by analogy with the earlier discovery that the tropics also were navigable, and moreover sufficiently temperate and fruitful to support human populations. This particular articulation of the challenge to cosmography's model of the world – false at the equator, therefore false at the pole – would be echoed by English writers through the end of the century, from scholars like Recorde and Eden in the 1550s, to theoretically inclined mariners like George Best and John Davis

---

40 See, inter alia, Portuondo, *Secret Science*, chap. 1; Cosgrove, "Images of Renaissance Cosmography"; Wey Gómez, *Tropics of Empire*. On the early modern rediscovery of Ptolomy's geography, see Dalché, "Reception of Ptolomy's Geography," 285–364.

41 Thorne, "Discourse to Doctour Leigh," 1: 219.

in the 1570s and 1590s.[42] It also comported with a belief that God would not create the earth such that parts were unusable. To paraphrase Thorne's ringing phrase, no land was uninhabitable, no sea innavigable.[43]

Yet even while Thorne framed his proposal as a rejection of cosmography, not all of its predictions were cast aside. Particularly persistent (and not at all challenged by the new discoveries) were understandings that rich goods – not only fruits and spices, but also metals – would be most abundant between the tropics because they were generated and ripened by the sun. Thorne explained the wealth of the Indies in precisely these latitudinal terms. As Thorne writes, the islands of the East Indies abounded "with golde, Rubies, Diamondes ... and other stones & pearles, *as all other lands, that are under and neere the Equinoctiall* ... For as with *us and other, that are apparted from the said Equinoctiall*, our mettals be Lead, Tinne, and Iron, so theirs be Gold, Silver, and Copper. And as our fruits and graines bee Apples, Nuts and Corne, so theirs be Dates, Nutmegs, Pepper, Cloves and other Spices" (emphasis mine). Thorne clearly considered that latitude was as predictive for mineral resources as it was for agriculture.[44]

On the one hand, Thorne's repudiation of the climate model made the Arctic conceptually open for navigation; on the other, his lingering embrace of *some* parts of the climate-based theory predicted that it would be empty of

---

[42] See also item 32 of Sebastian Cabot's instructions for the 1553 voyage ("Ordinances, 1553," 1: 229).

[43] Thorne, "Discourse to Doctour Leigh," 1: 219. George Best gave voice to this theory in his "Treatise of the sphere," a theoretical preface to Frobisher's three voyages in search of a Northwest Passage: "I cannot thinke that the divine providence hath made any thing uncommunicable, but to have given such order to all things, that one way or other the same should be imployed, and that every thing and place should be tollerable to the next: but especially all things in this lower world be given to man to have dominion and use thereof" (Best, "True Discourse," 56). In his 1595 treatise on navigation, John Davis still found it necessary both to describe and refute the theory of climates, both from his own experience of the equatorial and Arctic regions and on the principle that God would not have created large regions of the earth to be "to no purpose" for man's use (*Seamans Secrets*, sig. J5v). For a broader context, see Small, "From Thought to Action."

[44] Thorne, "Discourse to Doctour Leigh," 1: 214. Several decades later, when false assays taken from Martin Frobisher's Arctic voyages of the 1570s briefly suggested the existence of gold in the North, some of the resulting excitement had to do with the theoretical implications of this find: "where it was supposed, that the golden mettall had his beginning and place in the East and West India, neare unto the hote Zone, ... it is now approved ... that the same golden mettall dothe also lie in corporate in the bowelles of the Norweast parties" (preface to López de Gómara, *Pleasant Historie*, A2v).

valuable resources. If the North was reserved for the English, it had value chiefly as a privileged point of access to points south. As Thorne argued, a northern route should be particularly attractive to the English king not only because "the situation of this your Realme is therunto neerest and aptest of all other" but also because "considering well the courses, the ... way is shorter to us, then to Spaine and Portugall."[45] On each of the known routes around the Cape of Good Hope or through the Straits of Magellan – those claimed by Portugal and Spain respectively – ships were constrained by a very large landmass to sail far to the south and then north again towards destinations that lay closer to the equator. Yet Thorne's map, as Hakluyt reproduced it in *Divers Voyages*, represented the Asian continent with a flat northern coastline trending south from the White Sea, and extending only 110 degrees east from England. (On the globe as we know it, the northern coast of Russia is punctuated by promontories reaching roughly 6 degrees further north than the North Cape of Norway, and Siberia extends more than 180 degrees to the east of Greenwich.) Had Thorne been correct, a northern route from England to China and Indonesia would indeed be shorter and more direct than the first two, especially if additionally – as Thorne suggests – this route were to pass over the pole rather than hugging the northern coast of Asia. Thorne's argument for a polar route implies that he was thinking in terms of the globe, calculating distances on the surface of a sphere rather than on the kind of planar map accompanying his text. The polar route he proposed traversed precisely the space that planar maps (including his own) do not allow to be visualized. By Hakluyt's day, and with heightened interest in the northern coasts of Asia and North America, mathematical cartographers like Mercator and Dee were drawing circumpolar maps to remedy this defect (see plates 1 to 2).[46]

Thorne's hypothetical polar route also had the advantage of being largely free from the frictions of experience, crossing a geography that had still to be imagined. This was not true for the other routes it promised to displace; in 1526, the intransigent difficulties of the Pacific route would have been vivid to well-informed contemporaries. (The alternate route by the Cape of Good Hope would not be practiced by English mariners until late in Elizabeth's reign, and the initial attempt by James Lancaster in 1591 would illustrate its challenges.)[47] Absent comparable experience of waters north of Newfoundland,

---

45 Thorne, "Persuasion to King Henry the Eight," 1: 213.
46 Baldwin, "John Dee's Interest," 100–1.
47 Hakluyt and Barker, "Memorable Voyage of M. James Lancaster, 1591."

Thorne could simply *assert* that a route through the Arctic would present little difficulty: "it is very cleere and certaine, that the Seas that commonly men say, without great danger, difficulty and perill, yea rather it is impossible to passe, that those same Seas be navigable and without anie such danger." To the extent there might be difficulty, it would be only for "this little way which they named so dangerous (which may be two or three leagues before they come to the Pole, and as much more after they pass the Pole)."[48]

One might say that such assertions about the Arctic were simply that. But Thorne did actually have a good predictive model for one aspect of Arctic navigation: the mathematical components of cosmography allowed him to predict that angle and period of the sun's light for any given place at a given date or season. (Indeed, making such calculations took up considerable space in manuals of cosmography and navigation published later in the century.) For Thorne (as for us), the Arctic was definitionally the region above the line of latitude where for one day or more each year, the sun does not set or rise. Even without observational information, he could thus be confident in expectations of a prolonged polar day that would last for several months in summer. Thorne predicted that such conditions of uninterrupted light would enable navigators to see their way with a clarity not possible in lower latitudes: "shippes may passe and have in them perpetuall clerenesse of the day without any darkenesse of the night: which thing is a great commoditie for the navigants, to see at all times round about them, as well the safegards as dangers ... Yea what a vantage shal your Graces subjects have also by this light to discover the strange lands, countries, and coastes: For if they that be discovered, to saile by them in darkenesse is with great danger, much more then the coastes not discovered be daungerous to travell by night or in darkenesse." Not only would polar conditions allow navigators to *see*, Thorne believed that once over the pole, it would be "at the will and pleasure of the mariners to choose whether they will sayle by the coastes, that be colde, temperate, or hote. For they being past the Pole, it is plaine, they may decline to what part they list."[49] Navigators at the pole, in other words, would enjoy a position granting both a privileged ability to see clearly at all times, and a privileged ability to access any and all directions, thus to pass into any regions of the world. The pole offered not commodities so much as the absence of impediment, along with more abstract abilities to see, to know, and to choose one's direction. The world lay all below it, where to choose.

48 Thorne, "Persuasion to King Henry the Eight," 1: 213.
49 Ibid., 1: 216.

Thorne's proposal that England focus its maritime exploration in the North resonated with Hakluyt's own agenda of celebrating those voyages of northern exploration that, by his time, had already taken place. We can also hear echoed by the editor and other writers Thorne's core idea that since more southerly routes to China by the east and by the west (that is, by the Cape of Good Hope and either Panama or the Straits of Magellan) had been monopolized by the Spanish and Portuguese, a northern route was what remained or was reserved for the English to discover.[50] By the time of writing, however, the experience provided by actual voyages had made some elements of Thorne's proposals implausible.

Thorne had predicted conditions of polar light that would favour both literal vision and navigational mastery of space. Yet, as Hakluyt writes, English navigators later in the century found Arctic seas to be "stern and uncouth," obscured with "darke mistes and fogs" along with "divers other fearefull inconveniences."[51] Like Thorne, Hakluyt translated empirically descriptive language about the conditions of visibility at northern latitudes into metaphors about knowledge – but when he characterized northern seas as "misty," southern ones as "lightsome," the poles (so to speak) were reversed. While the Spanish were afforded "much light" in their western discoveries by classical geographers, Hakluyt wrote, the English "were either altogether destitute of such clear lights and inducements, or if they had any inkling at all, it was as misty as they found the northern seas."[52] Northern regions were not only obscure, but also impoverished in the rich trades found by the Portuguese along the African coast as they sought a route to the Indies; this absence made these unrewarding ventures all the more deserving of praise. In Hakluyt's text, the North was difficult, and the hardships, poverty, and "darkness" of the Arctic route – both literal and figurative – defined the achievement he sought to celebrate. He echoed Thorne, however, in one final proposition: "it is high time for us to weigh our ancre, to hoise up our sails, to get cleare of these boistrous, frosty, and misty seas," and to reach towards the riches of the South.[53] Voyages into and across the North were useful to point to as examples of

50 See, for instance, Davis, *Worldes Hydrographical Discription*.
51 Hakluyt, "Preface to the Reader (1598)," 1: sig. *4v.
52 Ibid., 1: sig. *4v. Hakluyt is being somewhat disingenuous: in addition to the relation of Octher, the White Sea route had been described by Sigismund von Herberstein in a book excerpted later in the volume.
53 Ibid., 1: sig. *4v–*5r. Further east, Pet and Jackman encountered Russian fishermen who traded regularly along Russia's Arctic coast.

initiative and accomplishment, providing Hakluyt an example of a place where the English *could* be argued to have been first. That being done, the North was not a destination but a space to pass through, once having (in some rhetorically plausible way) mastered it.

Thorne's early ideas about the Arctic may have been challenged by the experience of actual voyages in the second half of the century, but Hakluyt's editorial treatment nonetheless accorded considerable prominence to both these ideas and their author. Further, Hakluyt suggests that the proposals were more than simply ideas, assembling fragmentary references to a voyage to "the North partes" by a ship named the *Dominus Vobiscum* in 1527 to demonstrate "that [Thorne's] motion tooke present effect."[54] The voyage to which he refers, John Rut's exploration of the American coast from Newfoundland south to the Caribbean, probably took place before Thorne wrote his proposal to Henry VIII, rather than resulting from it.[55] Indeed, Thorne's proposal appears never to have been delivered to the king, and no resulting voyages are known to have taken place.

Hakluyt's foregrounding of Thorne's proposals might induce us to follow the editor's lead and to suppose that they were, in fact, strongly influential, evidence for a continuity of English thinking and activity dating back to the early decades of the sixteenth century, if not before. Yet the prominence of these materials appears to result more clearly from a much later circulation. In the 1570s or perhaps a little earlier, Cyprian Lucar – a mathematician whose father, Emanuel, had been Thorne's apprentice – began to disseminate copies of the two texts later printed by Hakluyt. (In *Divers Voyages*, Hakluyt appended a comment to Thorne's texts that these were "friendly imparted unto me by master Cyprian Lucar.") Three surviving copies were owned by Hakluyt's contemporaries, including one annotated by Dee.[56] Yet even if Thorne's reputation was to some extent a back-formation of later decades, recovering

---

54 Hakluyt, "Voyage of the Dominus Vobiscum."

55 Rut sailed in May 1527. E. G. R. Taylor argues that this is the voyage referred to in Thorne's "Persuasion," when he writes that Henry had "already taken ... in hand" the project of northern discovery (*Brief Summe*, xliii).

56 Extant manuscripts of Thorne's proposals are BL MS Cotton Vitellius C VII fo. 329r–45r (Dee's copy), BL MS Lansdowne 100/7 (Burghley papers), and Hatfield House, Cecil 245/5. On the evidence of watermarks, the Hatfield House manuscript appears to date from 1530, while the first two manuscripts are much later copies (Dalton, *Merchants*, 196; Taylor, *Brief Summe*, xxvi–vii). In a hint of earlier circulation, E.G.R. Taylor notes that Anthony Jenkinson's 1565 proposals for a Northeast Passage search exhibit a similarity of

the details surrounding the composition of the documents found in volume 1 tells a different and equally intriguing story about the unfolding of English geographical thinking from the early sixteenth century onward, one that will also shed additional light on Hakluyt's research.

These ideas about the North, in effect, were dependent on knowledge in the South. In these textual remnants associated with Thorne, Hakluyt brushed up against a history of English trade and knowledge exchange in the Iberian world, coincident and clearly engaged with the early stages of Spanish discovery, colonization, and trade with the Americas. Like the details of westward voyages before 1550, this history is poorly represented in the print record, and not readily perceptible to readers of *PN* (1598–1600). So far, we have examined Thorne's texts of the 1520s as a means by which Hakluyt assembled a genealogy for the more recent voyages celebrated in this volume, a bridge between the Arctic discoveries of King Arthur, Ohthere, and Nicholas of Lynn, and the Muscovy Company voyages of Willoughby, Chancellor, Borough, and others that began in the year of Hakluyt's birth. In the concluding section of this chapter, we will examine some of the historical context that Hakluyt did not provide for the Henrician period, and reflect on what it can add to our understanding of both the editor's methods and choices.

BETWEEN THE ARCTIC AND THE TROPICS: ENGLISH MERCHANTS AND COSMOGRAPHERS IN SEVILLE

Not long after Hakluyt had published Lucar's materials in *Divers Voyages*, he travelled to Thorne's former home in Bristol to generate interest in western voyages among merchants there; correspondence between Francis Walsingham and the mayor of Bristol records one such visit in March 1583.[57] He became a prebendary at Bristol Cathedral in 1586, and attended chapter meetings there through the mid-1590s; in 1603, although his parish was in Suffolk, he remained close enough to Bristol's merchant community to engage them with an expedition to New England in that year.[58] One tangible result of these

---

phrasing and argument that suggest "he had before him [the Thorne papers] which were in the possession of Emanuel Lucar"; William Bourne's *Regiment of the Sea* (London, 1577) also echoed the idea of a polar route (*Tudor Geography*, 98; Taylor, *Brief Summe*, xxix).

57 See *PN* 3: 181. Other materials possibly related to this visit are identified in "Chronology," 1: 277. Hakluyt's *DV* was entered into the Stationer's Register 21 May 1582.

58 "Chronology," 289–90, 319. See also Hakluyt's "Briefe Note of the Morse."

connections was access to the Thorne family papers. Notes by Hakluyt drawn from the ledger book of Robert's older brother, Nicholas Thorne, appear in volumes 2 and 3 of *PN* (1598–1600). As he writes in one of these:

it appeareth out of a certaine note ... written 1526 by master Nicholas Thorne the elder, a principall merchant of Bristol unto his friend and factour ... at S. Lucar in Andaluzia: that before the sayd yeere one Thomas Tison an Englishman had found his way to the West Indies, and was there resident ... This Thomas Tison (so farre as I can conjecture) may seeme to have bene some secret factour for M. Thorne and other English marchants in those remote parts; whereby it is probable that some of our marchants had a kinde of trade to the West Indies even in those ancient times and before also.[59]

Hakluyt's treatment of the ledger's contents suggests, again, a perception of its value; the information concerning Tison appears twice, once with materials on the Antilles and also appended to evidence of early English trade with the Canaries, equally drawn from Nicholas Thorne's ledger. According to Heather Dalton, Tison served as one of Robert Thorne's factors in Hispaniola from November 1526, and later returned to Bristol, where he traded in wine and cloth, serving as sheriff of Bristol in 1552.[60] These biographical details suggest a degree of prominence; yet Hakluyt's note retains only a trace of Tison's mobility and the Thorne family's commerce both in Spain and its new colonies. His language of conjecture and probability, of "seeming" and of qualification ("a kinde of trade"), signals that the "ancient times" of the 1520s were remote and difficult of access. As the editor complained in his notice of Rut's voyage, "thus much (by reason of the great negligence of the writers of those times...) is all that hitherto I can learn."[61]

The gaps and uncertainties of Hakluyt's apparent knowledge become quite striking when we consider that men like Tison – associates of Thorne – lived on into the 1550s as important figures in Bristol's merchant community, a community known to Hakluyt. Dalton, indeed, suggests that Hakluyt chose

---

59 Hakluyt, "Voyage of Thomas Tison." See also Hakluyt, "Briefe Note Concerning the Canarie Isles, 1526."

60 Dalton, *Merchants*, 50, 110, 152–3, 172–3.

61 Hakluyt, "Voyage of the Dominus Vobiscum." Later, a letter surfaced that had been sent to Henry VIII from Rut, then in Newfoundland; the letter is printed by Purchas in a small group of materials titled "Discoveries made by English-men to the Northwest" (Purchas, *Pilgrimes*, 3: 806–14).

deliberately to suppress information about Thorne and other English merchants in Seville.[62] His manipulation of the Thorne materials, on this view, suppressed a positive history of English trade in Spain in order to encourage "the idea ... that England's empire would be constructed in opposition to the Spanish," with the mistreatment of English merchants as a repeated *casus belli*. The second edition of *Principal Navigations* is indeed distinguished from the first by the addition of numerous materials documenting not only naval conflict between England and Spain, but also hostile encounters between English merchant vessels and Spanish galleys. (These narratives are the subject of chapter 7, below.) Yet even if we suppose Hakluyt's suppressions to have been deliberate, they came at a distinct cost: surrendering the opportunity to register precisely the kinds of achievements by English merchants, navigators, and cosmographers that the collection sought to celebrate. Detailing some of what did not appear in PN (1598–1600) – or Hakluyt's other works – will make apparent the scope of these gaps.

Thorne had told the ambassador Lee that he belonged to a group of investors who had set forth a 1526 voyage aimed at exploring the westward route identified by Magellan only a few years earlier. Sebastian Cabot served as captain general of this voyage, intended for the Moluccas, though, in fact, reaching no further than the coast of Brazil.[63] Thorne's investment allowed him to arrange that two Englishmen "somewhat learned in cosmographie" should "goe in the same shippes," to bring him "certaine relation of the situation of the countrey, and to be expert in the navigation of those seas."[64] Spanish sources have been more informative: the two men mentioned (but not named) in Thorne's letter have been identified as Roger Barlow and

---

62 Heather Dalton and Gustav Ungerer suggest, if for different reasons, that Hakluyt was thoroughly conversant with Thorne's activities in Seville but chose to suppress much of his information (Dalton, *Merchants*, 200–1; Ungerer, *Apprenticeship*, 69). I am enormously indebted to their archival research and rich accounts of the English merchant community in Seville, but disagree on the point that Hakluyt knew more than he indicated. The apparent lacunae in Hakluyt's account of English trade and exploration before 1550 are many, and generally tend to weaken his overall case for English activity and sophistication rather than otherwise. The materials Hakluyt did print on the slave trade in the 1560s do not comport with Ungerer's suggestion that he sought to "protect his compatriots against being lumped together with the ignominious record of the Spanish and Portuguese" (see chapter 6).

63 The voyage and its aftermaths are discussed in Dalton, *Merchants*, chaps. 5–7. See also Taylor, *Brief Summe*, xix–xliii.

64 Thorne, "Discourse to Doctour Leigh," 1: 215. Hakluyt reprinted this passage as well in his section on the Antilles, without any additional detail.

Henry Patmer or Latimer, while four other Englishmen were among the company in lesser roles. Thorne's phrasing might lead us to think of Barlow and Latimer as passengers sent at his charges to observe and learn, but their roles were in fact quite central to the voyage. Barlow served as supercargo on Cabot's flagship, "instrumental in provisioning the fleet and responsible for selling cargoes and acquiring goods throughout the voyage"; he also invested in the voyage himself. Latimer served as navigator on Cabot's next largest ship, a highly skilled role.[65] Dalton and E.G.R. Taylor concur that the proposal to Henry VIII attributed by Hakluyt to Thorne alone was likely written after Barlow's return from the voyage with Cabot in November 1528 and composed by Thorne and Barlow together.[66] By 1530, both men had left Seville to return to Bristol, and both spent the rest of their lives in England.

Thorne died in 1532. In the following years, it was Barlow who revived their proposals for a polar voyage, addressing Henry VIII in a text included with his translation of Martin de Enciso's *Suma de geographia* (Seville, 1519), a navigational manual and treatise on cosmography; the textual resemblances to the earlier proposal are striking.[67] This time, the proposal was delivered. Rumours of a voyage followed; none was made.[68] In 1547, as we have seen, Sebastian Cabot was brought back to England at the charges of the Privy Council; in 1550 and 1551 there were more rumours of northern voyages. Barlow died in December of 1553; among his executors was Edward Prynne, a founding member of what would become the Muscovy Company.[69] Neither Thorne nor Barlow are mentioned in the compilations of Eden, *Treatyse of the Newe India* (1553) and *Decades* (1555), although Eden was closely connected to Cabot and the Muscovy Company, and included Edward VI's letters for the 1553 voyage in *Decades*; Eden also failed to secure a narrative from Cabot, of course, who was personally known to him. If we are to understand that the proposals for northern exploration associated with Thorne's name "took present effect," in the sense of resulting in actual voyages, Barlow seems likely to have been the immediate agent, and well after Thorne's own death. Yet Barlow's text – although he had requested it be printed – remained in the Royal Library, "scarcely glanced at"; it was not located by Hakluyt, in particular,

---

65 Dalton, *Merchants*, 80–4. For Patmer, see ibid., 26–7, 84, 122–3.
66 Taylor, *Tudor Geography*, 50–2; Dalton, *Merchants*, 134.
67 The single known copy of Barlow's work is now BL MS Royal 18 B xxviii. On Barlow's manuscript materials, see the introduction to Taylor, *Brief Summe*.
68 Dalton, *Merchants*, 166; Taylor, *Brief Summe*, l–li.
69 Dalton, *Merchants*, 185.

and as a result not by others until it was edited for the Hakluyt Society by E.G.R. Taylor in 1933.[70] The texts from 1527 to 1528, provided to Dee and Hakluyt by Lucar, stood in its place. These details of transmission and attribution are of interest because they bear on Hakluyt's practice as a scholar and editor. Here, he overlooked a document arguably of more immediate significance than those he chose to print. He also missed the opportunity to celebrate Barlow and Latimer's expert skills and distant travel with Cabot in 1526; the Spanish archives are far more voluble on this voyage than *Principal Navigations*. Perhaps the issue was one of availability, as Lucar circulated the texts under Thorne's name while Barlow's work slept in the archive. Perhaps Thorne's proposals simply offered the attractive prospect of antedating English intentions in the Arctic by several decades.

The context that brought together the two authors of the proposal attributed to Thorne has more to tell us, however, both about their knowledge and about Hakluyt's editorial practice.[71] Thorne and Barlow were close associates in Seville's community of foreign merchants, both members of families that had traded in the Mediterranean for generations; they were thoroughly networked with Genoese merchants, joining in undertakings like the Cabot voyage to Brazil, and their connections included relatives and colleagues of Columbus, Magellan, and Cortés. English merchants in Seville participated in old and new trades, and dealt with both old and new markets. Thorne himself dealt in a variety of goods, among them soap, cloth, woad, and pearls; his family had "traded with the Genoese in Rhodes, Cyprus, and Seville for at least three generations."[72] Thorne and his brother Nicholas also had trading interests in the Atlantic, with the Canaries and Azores, and the port of San Domingo in the new Spanish colony of Hispaniola; Tison was only one of several factors employed there at different times.[73]

---

70 Taylor, *Brief Summe*, lvi. Heather Dalton proposes an alternate explanation for Barlow's invisibility in Hakluyt's collections: his grandson Charles Chester, a likely informant on Barlow's activities, was known to Hakluyt but actually "personally attacked" by him in PN (1598–1600), an episode related by Matthew Steggle (Dalton, *Merchants*, 210–12; "Charles Chester and Richard Hakluyt").

71 For the following discussion of Thorne and Barlow's social and professional context, I have relied on Dalton's research, in the previously cited book and two articles: "Negotiating Fortune: English Merchants in Early Sixteenth-Century Seville"; "'Into Speyne.'"

72 Dalton, "'Into Speyne,'" 117.

73 Canaries and Azores: Baldwin, "Robert Thorne." San Domingo: Dalton, *Merchants*, 50.

The Americas were one area of interest for these English merchants working in Spain; North and West Africa were another. Barlow's translation of Enciso is rich in detailed descriptions of the West African coasts, its trades, and its peoples; interpolations suggest he himself may have visited São Thomé, a centre of Portuguese sugar production and slave trading, and certainly present-day Agadir in Morocco, again observing the Portuguese sugar trade there; not long after Barlow died, other Anglo-Spanish merchants would open regular trade with Morocco.[74] Thorne co-owned a soap factory in Seville with the Genoese merchant Leonardo Cataño and other colleagues, and employed as one of the masters an enslaved Berber known as Juan Fernandez, whom he had purchased from another Englishman, Thomas Maillard, in 1522 and would manumit (along with another Berber master, Juan Torne) on his return to England.[75] The soap production itself, according to both Dalton and Gustav Ungerer, was undertaken by African slaves. In 1526 and 1528, Thorne's purchase of three persons is documented, at least two of whom were sub-Saharan Africans; at his departure for England, documents apparently relating to the sale of Thorne's share in the soap factory record the sale of thirteen enslaved Africans; finally, his will indicates that at his death, he retained ownership of both a house in Seville and several slaves there.[76] In Dalton's summary, Barlow, Thorne, and their colleagues both used slave labour and bought and sold African slaves. Among their associates were "Genoese merchants involved in the forced transatlantic transportation of large groups of people from the African coast between the river Gambia and Sierra Leone."[77] While Hakluyt and others have assiduously traced the filiation of northern voyages at mid-century to the proposals of Thorne and his associates, the idea of a bright and frictionless polar voyage – promoted by Barlow and Thorne, later put in motion by Cabot – floats against the weightier background of the ways these men

---

74 Taylor, *Brief Summe*, 104–8; Blake, *Europeans in West Africa*, 1: 62. For the inception of English trade with Morocco, see especially Alday, "First Voyage to Barbary, Anno 1551"; Thomas, "Second Voyage to Barbary, Anno 1552." The Anglo-Spanish merchant Roger Bodenham cites the "great losse and hindrance by that new trade … in the city of Fez" as motivation for a voyage to the West Indies in 1564 ("Voyage of M. Roger Bodenham, 1564," 455).

75 Ungerer, *Apprenticeship*, 24, 68–9.

76 Details and transcriptions of sale and manumission records can be found in Ungerer, *Apprenticeship*, 24–5, 113–20. For Thorne's will, see Dalton, *Merchants*, 136–7.

77 Dalton, "'Into Speyne,'" 92. On the involvement of the Cataño family with the slave trade, see Dalton, 117–18.

made their money, and the uses to which they put their knowledge.[78] As Dalton and Ungerer have pointed out, Thorne's and Barlow's engagement with the Luso-Iberian slave trade not only preceded by decades John Hawkins's slaving voyages in the 1560s but dates to the early decades of the Atlantic trade itself; this knowledge and its profits were among the resources they brought home.

Once Thorne's and Barlow's proposals are placed into the broader context of their social and professional lives, we begin to hear the reverberations of a question that emerges more powerfully in later volumes of Hakluyt's collection. In decades when English writers regularly decried Spanish treatment of captives as "cruel" and "inhumane," and deployed these accusations in an argument about their own national identity, what gave Englishmen the *conceptual* license to enslave, and gave it most freely in relation to sub-Saharan Africa?[79] The question will present itself more insistently as we read materials in later sections of the collection that relate to West Africa and the Caribbean, but it is not *absent* from volume 1 so much as obscured. When Hakluyt enjoined his readers that it was time to get clear of the North and "direct our course for the milde, lightsome, temperate, and warme Atlantick Ocean, over which the Spaniards and Portugales have made so many pleasant prosperous and golden voyages," among allurements of those warmer waters was the "getting of *slaves* ... sugar ... Elephants teeth, grains, silver, [and] gold" (emphasis mine).[80]

We can observe what is *not* present in *Principal Navigations*. Trying to reconstruct what information was and was not transmitted to Hakluyt (in papers or in conversation), what might have been available but was not found or not sought out by him, what he might have known but did not chose to include in the compilation, involves us in irreducible uncertainties. If Hakluyt failed to uncover all he might have about Thorne and Barlow, he also failed to discover very much about the voyages of the Cabots, to which he accorded great importance both for claims of England's history of voyages and for legal rights of discovery to North America.[81] What *is* present in *Principal Navigations*, and

---

78 As Spain's pilot major, Cabot was charged with licensing the export of slaves; on the 1526 voyage for Thorne and his associates, he purchased fifty or sixty slaves on behalf of his investors (Dalton, *Merchants*, 38, 115–16).

79 The classic study of anti-Spanish discourse in the period is William Maltby, *Black Legend in England*. (Some of the book's claims about Hakluyt will be revisited in chapter 10.) See also chapter 7.

80 Hakluyt, "Preface to the Reader (1598)," sig. *5r.

81 Hakluyt, *PD*, chap. 18.

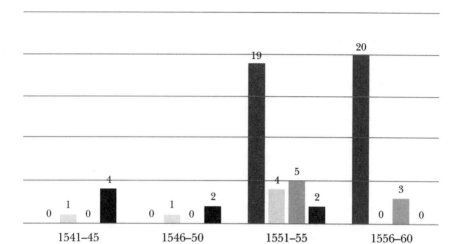

Figure 3.4 Documents by decade in *PN* (1598–1600), 1541–60.

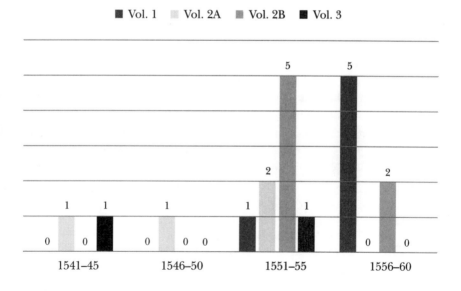

Figure 3.5 English voyages by decade in *PN* (1598–1600), 1541–60.

how, offers more objective evidence of Hakluyt's editorial choices.[82] Another measure of comparison is offered by Hakluyt's selection of documents on the Arctic and on the African tropics, the two most distant regions of English activity in the earliest years for which the editor found durable and relatively complete evidence. Figures 3.4 and 3.5 look at the distribution of Hakluyt's materials by five-year period for the years 1541 to 1560. Figures for documents and voyages are broken down by volume (and thus by geographical areas, as Hakluyt defined them), with the two parts of volume 2 (voyages to the southeast through the Mediterranean and through the Atlantic) represented separately. The figures visualize the footprint of the period's two new enterprises in *Principal Navigations* from two different angles: in figure 3.4, the total number of *documents* for each five-year period; in figure 3.5, the total number of English *voyages* represented by at least one document.

The results tell several stories. The first of these is clear: as we would expect, for both documents *and* voyages, the 1550s saw a very marked increase in numbers over the 1540s. More voyages of the kind that interested Hakluyt were undertaken, and more pages of the collection were devoted to the documents they produced. Most of this increase is seen in volume 1 and the second half of volume 2: that is, in materials relating to the northeast and to sub-Saharan Africa. Again, this only confirms what we know about the directions of English long-distance trade in the period. What may be more interesting, however, are the differences between the two tables.

For each five-year period, numbers of *documents* are greater than numbers of English voyages. There are several reasons for this discrepancy. First, Hakluyt's materials included some documents in translation, describing non-English voyages; for instance, five of six documents from the 1540s were connected with French or Spanish voyages to the Americas. Second, Hakluyt sometimes printed *many* documents relating to a single voyage: thus, the Chancellor-Willoughby voyage of 1553 was represented by no fewer than nineteen items, each with a separate entry in Hakluyt's table of contents. Third, this editorial habit varied sharply across region: during the 1550s, a

---

82 Hakluyt's choices of emphasis are consequential: Ungerer argues that this particular invisibility – that is, the non-appearance in PN (1598–1600) of Thorne's experience with slaveholding – was "instrumental" in creating the broader perception that Africans were not present as servants or slaves in English households in any significant numbers before 1600, either at home or abroad, a perception that has been called into question by recent scholarship. In addition to the works cited by Dalton and Ungerer, see especially Knutson, "A Caliban in St. Mildred Poultry"; Habib, *Black Lives in the English Archives*.

greater number of *voyages* were made into the *southeastern* region of sub-Saharan Africa, but the greater number of *documents* relate to the *northeastern* region of Muscovy, Persia, and the Northeast Passage. In short, voyages into the tropics are under-documented in PN (1598–1600) relative to the Muscovy voyages of the same decade, and the difference in documentation is a difference not only of numbers but kinds of documents. For both regions, Hakluyt printed primary sources on voyages made by English seafarers, merchants, and diplomats. For Muscovy and Persia, he provided a far greater number of ancillary documents: instructions, charters and privileges, diplomatic correspondence, letters from resident factors, accounts of weights and measures, and so on. Little that is comparable can be found in the second half of volume 2: some notes of meetings and instructions from the 1560s, a handful of patents from the 1580s, and some diplomatic correspondence with the emperor of Morocco that post-dated the inception of trade by several decades. The copious and attentive documentation of enterprises in the North suggests their continuity with the national myth of an Arthurian empire in the North. In the South, the documentary armature – procedural, theoretical, diplomatic – that scaffolds and adds meaning to the northern voyages is simply absent.

These gestures of framing, inclusion, and exclusion are taxing to read. Yet Hakluyt's editing silently shapes our vision of the world that *Principal Navigations* offers us: all the more reason to pay sharp attention to how it does so. This brief overview suggests that "cold" materials on voyages to the northeast and "hot" materials on voyages to equatorial Africa have quite different profiles in the compilation. The result was a celebration of the North as a space of possibility, where Englishmen could rival Spanish and Portuguese achievements in maritime discovery without acknowledging intellectual or practical dependence. No longer a cosmopolitan merchant leveraging connections from Seville outwards to Africa and the West Indies, Hakluyt's Thorne became the early theorist of mastery over the Arctic, looking towards the pole as the conduit to an English global empire. Yet the North seems everywhere to be imagined within an *implicit* framework anchored in the South, whether networks of knowledge and commerce in early modern Seville or a cosmography that tried to harmonize climate theory, the grid of mathematical cartography, and newly encountered regions and societies across the band of the tropics. We will return to African materials in more detail in chapter 6. In the next chapter, we will turn our attention more closely to the documents produced by the northeastern project in 1553 and following.

4

Encounters with the North

HOWEVER WE DESCRIBE ITS INTELLECTUAL PATERNITY, the northern voyage of 1553 gave rise to a multiplicity of ongoing undertakings: most centrally, trade and diplomacy with Muscovy, but also a commercial and diplomatic initiative with Persia that was functionally an extension of this. Alongside these, the Muscovy Company – chartered to capitalize on the route Richard Chancellor had found – intermittently continued the search for a northern sea route to China. Copious documents arising from these enterprises make up the bulk of the contemporary materials in volume 1. Many of the documents compiled by Hakluyt are reports of varying length by the Muscovy Company's agents; some appear to have been sent as letters from the field, while others are accounts of travel by sea (both kinds of travel, by land and by sea, are identified as "voyages" in Hakluyt's headnotes). Hakluyt amplified this quasi-narrative core of letters and reports with other kinds of documents, strikingly diverse in nature: a representative if not comprehensive sample would include charters, commissions and oaths, genealogies, letters patent, correspondence between monarchs, excerpts from Giovanni Battista Ramusio's *Navigationi et viaggi* and other texts by continental writers, a letter written to Mercator, ethnographic notes, word lists, depositions, advice, textual extracts from maps, lists of weights and measures, poetry, and lists of distances and directions. The impression is of completeness as well as abundance: for instance, headnotes present materials relating to the trade with Persia inaugurated in 1561 as a continuously numbered series of "voyages," up through the "6. voyage in the yeeres 1579. 1580. and 1581" by Christopher Borough, son of the navigator Stephen Borough, whose work for the Muscovy Company had begun with the initial voyage of 1553.¹ The exceptional "adequacy ... in number, content, and genre" of the documents has led scholars to surmise that the editor might have been given direct access to the Muscovy Company's archives, though since the archive does not survive, this conjecture cannot be verified.² Certainly Hakluyt had personal connections with central actors in this project, men like Anthony Jenkinson and William Borough who were important both to conceptualizing and executing travel under the aegis of the company; in the preface to *PN* (1589), he acknowledged both Jenkinson and Borough as having "much pleasured me" in preparing his northern materials.³

This chapter will examine the forms this documentation took, the practices that shaped it, and the evidence it provides about the mental maps that travellers brought to the North in particular.⁴ The initial voyage of 1553 was narrated in three very different ways: a shipboard journal kept aboard Sir Hugh Willoughby's ship; the humanist narrative by Clement Adams, which drew on Chancellor's information; and Chancellor's own account of the voyage, centred on economic geography, apparently written in response to inquiries by a relative or patron. Behind the first of these documents (and many others like it) lie instructions from the company that told voyagers when, how, and sometimes where to write. Hakluyt printed numerous such instructions, which have a broader interest in suggesting some of the principles and practices behind the profuse documentation that would eventually fill his compilations. The instructions reveal other expectations as well, both for how the voyagers would conduct themselves and about the peoples they would encounter. We will conclude by looking at accounts of northern environments, as these confronted the expectations of travellers from warmer latitudes.

---

1 C. Borough, "Voyage of Christopher Burrough, 1579," 1: 419.
2 Simmons, "Russia." See also D. Quinn and Skelton, "Introduction," xxxviii–xxxix. G.B. Parks, however, suggests that "[t]he fact that the voyages described a steady trade with Russia, which became an annual routine, may have ... induced Hakluyt to omit many of them ... an adequate idea of this travel needs to be fitted together from many more documents than these narratives" (Parks, "Tudor Travel Literature," 1: 106).
3 Hakluyt, "Preface to the Reader (1589)," sig. *4v.
4 Sources on the history of English commercial and diplomatic engagement with Muscovy include Willan, *Muscovy Merchants of 1555*; Willan, *Early History of the Russia Company*; Andrews, *Trade, Plunder, and Settlement*, chap. 3; Poe, *A People Born to Slavery*; Maclean, "East by North-East."

HOW TO WRITE ABOUT THE NORTH: DOCUMENTS AND GENRES FROM 1553

1 "The true copy of a note found written in one of the two ships ... which wintered in Lappia, where Sir Hugh Willoughby and all his company died ... Anno 1553" (232-7)[5]
2 Clement Adams, "The newe Navigation and discoverie of the kingdome of Moscovia, by the Northeast, in the yeere 1553" (243-55)
3 Richard Chancellor, "The booke of the great and mighty Emperor of Russia, and Duke of Moscovia, and of the dominions orders and commodities thereunto belonging" (237-42)[6]

What kinds of writing should travel produce? What kinds of information should travellers record, and in what form? These were among the new questions to be answered by those engaged with the Northeast Passage search of 1553. Each of the three accounts of the voyage printed by Hakluyt in the second edition of *Principal Navigations* responds in a different way.[7]

The three documents in question differ in what they are able to describe: Willoughby and Chancellor parted company off the coast of Norway, only a

---

5 BL MS Cotton Otho E VIII, fo. 11–16v is a transcript of the log annotated by John Dee (BL catalogue).

6 Hakluyt's "Catalogue" gives the two narratives by Adams and Chancellor a single heading with two page numbers: "The voyage of Richard Chancellor Pilote major [...] Anno 1553, 237, 243"; I have used Hakluyt's in-text headings in order to distinguish clearly between them. David and Alison Quinn's "Contents and Sources" gives a page number for Chancellor's "Booke" in PN (1598–1600) but does not clarify source. Hakluyt writes that he is "beholding unto the excellent Librarie of the right honorable my lord Lumley" for Chancellor's narrative "penned by himselfe" (Hakluyt, "Preface to the Reader [1598]," sig. *5r); Sears and Johnson's catalogue of the collection lists the manuscript as no longer extant (*Lumley Library*).

7 Hakluyt's representation of the voyage evolved modestly between the first and second edition. As we saw in chapter 3, the Willoughby/Chancellor voyage of 1553 had been quickly documented by Clement Adams, although scholars are not sure whether his account was printed. In 1589, Hakluyt printed both the original Latin and an English translation of Adams's narrative, prefaced by Richard Eden's comment that it was "faithfully written ... by that learned young man ... as he received it at the mouth of the said Richard Chancellor," along with a transcription of Willoughby's log and some accompanying documents. In PN (1598–1600), he printed only the English translation of Adams, adding Chancellor's own text addressed to "the right worshipful and my singular good uncle," Christopher Frothingham.

few months into the timeline of the voyage, and only Chancellor and his men survived. The three accounts were also composed with different aims: both the narrative prepared for print by Adams and the manuscript account addressed by Chancellor to a relative were based on Chancellor's testimony and have some overlap in topics and content, but they offer different information at different length. To a literary eye, the differences in *form* among the documents are also striking, particularly given that two are among the earliest extant examples of a whole class of writing. Willoughby's account, written during the voyage, is considered to be among the earliest extant logbooks (printed or otherwise).[8] Adams's *Anglorum navigatio ad Muscovitas*, composed by a humanist scholar to promote the new enterprise that resulted from the voyage, may have been the first account of English travel in print. (Chancellor's account, whose context is the least well understood, appears to be a kind of briefing document.) All three not only provide witness to a pivotal enterprise, but are inaugural exercises in composing the kinds of documents on which Hakluyt's collection largely relies.

These three accounts of the 1553 voyage pose interesting problems of method for critical readers. George Parks's survey of Tudor travel literature for the *Hakluyt Handbook* finds all three "highly unsatisfactory," casual in their observations, lacking "basic facts of the voyage," and overly focused (in the case of Adams) on panegyric or (in the case of Willoughby) on the weather, while Chancellor is criticized for writing "a report on Russia, not on his voyage."[9] While readers may disagree on the merits of the texts or, indeed, the criteria one might use to assess them, Parks's comments frame an issue of broader interest. Hakluyt's documents often neither tell us all we would wish to know, nor deliver what they do tell us as a well-shaped, engaging narrative. This is not to indict these documents as inadequate so much as to suggest they have goals and rationales of their own that we should seek to understand. The texts by Willoughby, Adams, and Chancellor each answer the question of how to document or write about travel in a different way, diverging in content and method, as well as from the expectations of at least

---

8 Schotte, "Expert Records," 311 n. 26. Purely as a navigational document, Willoughby's journal was largely a record of confusion; Chancellor's expertise was not duplicated on the other two ships. Although I am not aware of an extant manuscript version, Stephen Borough's 1556 log gives a better idea of the records kept by technically advanced English navigators in the 1550s ("Voyage of Stephen Burrough, 1556").

9 Parks, "Tudor Travel Literature," 1: 107.

one twentieth-century reader. What can we learn from paying attention to these documents both individually and as a set?

Chancellor's "Book of the [...] Emperor of Russia" opens with a comment about what is expected of travellers: "Forasmuch as it is meete and necessary for all those that minde to take in hande the travell into far or strange countreys, to endeavour themselves not onely to understande the orders, commodities, and fruitfulnesse thereof, but also to applie them to the setting foorth of the same, whereby it may incourage others to the like travaile: therefore have I nowe thought good to make a briefe rehearsall of the orders of this my travaile in Russia and Moscovia, and other countreys thereto adjoyning."[10] As also suggested by its headnote title – "The booke of the great and mighty Emperor of Russia" – the text that follows is not actually a narrative of travel, despite Hakluyt's omnibus title in the Catalogue, "The voyage of Richard Chanceller." Rather, Chancellor's text provides a brief account of Muscovy's economic, political, and cultural geography, with observation of the court occupying one full page (of six in total). Chancellor's text responds to the expectations he articulated, that it was the civic duty of travellers to gain knowledge, to share, and to encourage others to follow their example. By implication, this useful knowledge was to be gathered principally by travel on land, to "strange countreys," and not as such from travel across the unpopulated sea (or land, for that matter).

Chancellor's actual voyage appears only in a subordinate clause introducing a brief description of Russian cities and their trade: "because *it was my chance to fall with the North partes of Russia before I came towards Moscovie,* I will partly declare my knowledge therein" (emphasis mine).[11] His only sustained attention to "my travaile" occurs in a lengthy section on the Muscovite court that begins with Chancellor's summons to attend the tsar. "Now to declare my coming before his Majestie: After I had remained [in Moscow] twelve daies, the Secretary which hath the hearing of strangers did send for me, advertising me that the Dukes pleasure was to have me to come before his Ma. with the

---

10 Chancellor, "Booke of the Emperor of Russia," 1: 237. This comment gestures towards a genre of methods for travel writing (see Rubiés, "Instructions for Travellers"). Chancellor's account is not clearly related to Cabot's instructions for the voyage (discussed below); these in turn drew on Spanish instructions for travellers (for a discussion of Cabot and contemporaneous ethnographic questionnaires in the Spanish context, see Carey, "Hakluyt's Instructions," 171–4).
11 Chancellor, "Booke of the Emperor of Russia," 1: 237.

kings my masters letters."[12] In the scene that follows, Chancellor's movements and interactions, *as well as* his observations, are described in meticulous detail, as he is ushered from "the utter chamber" into the presence of the tsar, who "bade me to dinner," and then "unto the Secretaries chamber, where I remained two hours" before being summoned "unto another palace" and to a hall where the dinner was to take place. James McDermott suggested that the minutia of this description had a pragmatic rationale: "the data [Chancellor] supplied to his employers provided a manual of business etiquette for the English merchants who followed him."[13] Perhaps the glamour of the scene in which he found himself also had an appeal – as it did to later English observers, who repeatedly made similar observations. Beyond his movement through these courtly spaces, however, Chancellor's own actions and indeed presence register only faintly among those he observed and described. Of the specific moments and interactions that underlie general observations – such as his assertion that Muscovites are "naturally given to hard living" – only a single, passing comment remains, on the "miserable life" of the Russian poor: "*I have seene* them eate the pickle of Hearring and other stinking fish" (emphasis mine).[14]

The related narrative by Adams, as printed by Hakluyt, is a little more than twice as long as Chancellor's own account. Some of this length is devoted to the voyage: half a page brings the small fleet from Deptford to Harwich, another half page from Harwich to the coast of Norway (with the consultation among the officers setting Vardø as a rendezvous in case of accident), then to the region of Tromsø, where a storm separated Chancellor's *Edward Bonaventure* from his consorts. Another half page has Chancellor and his men first lingering at Vardø, and then resolving to press on. The voyage onwards from Vardø into the White Sea and into harbour at St Nicholas – precisely that part of the enterprise that was, truly, "new" – occupies only seven lines (in which Adams notes their experience of "no night at all but the continuall light and brightnesse of the Sunne," conditions predicted by cosmography and now observed and recorded for the first time by English mariners).[15] In short, travel is given its due along with observation – but Adams dwells

---

12 Ibid., 1: 238.
13 McDermott, "Chancellor, Richard." On court ceremonies as a form of information management, see Poe, *A People Born to Slavery*, 40–8. On the conduct of emissaries as performance, see Müller, "William Harborne's Embassies."
14 Chancellor, "Booke of the Emperor of Russia," 1: 241.
15 Adams, "Newe Navigation, 1553," 1: 246.

considerably longer on the fleet's movements past familiar points on the English coast than on their exploration of strange waters. A single phrase tersely sums up Chancellor's 1,500-mile journey from the White Sea coast down the Dvina to Moscow as "long and most troublesome."[16]

Both the accounts relying on Chancellor's memory share an attention to ethnography, and cover some of the same topics, which Adams organized under headings: "Of the discipline of warre among the Russes," "Of the Ambassadors of the Emperour of Moscovie," and "Of the forme of their private houses." Both texts offer a detailed description of Chancellor's reception by the tsar, followed immediately by a discussion of the Muscovite "discipline of war." Yet the order and emphasis of material frequently differ between the two texts: for instance, Adams's brief paragraph on penalties for theft corresponds to an extended discussion of Russian legal culture in Chancellor's shorter "Booke." Overall, the nature and extent of differences between the texts suggest that while both draw on Chancellor's memory and sense of what mattered, these are distinct and independent texts.

The most significant of their differences lies in Adams's attention to the voyage itself, and even earlier, to the events that occasioned and prepared for it. In all, two and a half pages of his text (of twelve in total) deal with preparations preceding the moment when the voyagers "committed themselves to the sea, giving their last adieu to their native Countrey."[17] (These included the conferences and deliberations among merchants described in chapter 3, above.) Adams also devotes attention to practical preparations, from acquiring "very strong and well seasoned planks" for the three ships being fitted out, to the "troublesome and necessary" matter of provisioning the ships for a voyage anticipated to last as long as eighteen months, as well as the choice of Willoughby and Chancellor as captain and chief navigator, respectively. (Adams includes an "oration" about Chancellor's qualifications by Sir Henry Sidney, one of his patrons.)[18] As these excerpts suggest, the framing material recognizes as part of the narrative the actions of merchants and shipwrights, as well as those of the voyagers themselves. When the narrator wonders "whether I may more admire the care of the merchants or the diligence of the shipwrights," *all* those who participated are lauded for their part in a shared enterprise, including those who stayed home.

16 Ibid., 1: 247.
17 Ibid., 1: 245.
18 Ibid., 1: 244.

Adams also tells a story of exemplarity, in which his compatriots did exactly as they ought, from paying for the ships, to building and bravely sailing them into unknown waters. (Perhaps we should infer some defensiveness: after all, two of the three ships failed to return.) This story encompasses not only actions, but also the *feelings* of the voyagers – what we might characterize as "interiority" – which his third-person narrative describes in considerable detail. We learn that Chancellor was "not a little grieved" over the state of provisions on his ship, troubled by "natural and fatherly affection" for his children and by "care for his company." After losing touch with Willoughby he was pensive and sorrowful, swallowed up with "good will and love" for his company and fearing to endanger them through any mistake. Similarly, as the company left the coast of England, "Many of them looked oftentimes backe, and could not refraine from teares." When Chancellor determined to go onwards from Vardø after losing sight of Willoughby, his company was "troubled" but nonetheless resolute.[19]

Adams's omniscient access to the affective experience of the mariners contrasts sharply with Chancellor's manuscript account, in which the first-person "I" (when it appears) is less a feeling subject, or even a doing subject, than a subject who judges and observes. He uses the first person almost exclusively to characterize opinions or in phrases that mark his role in shaping the narrative: "what shall I farther say … I will stand no longer in … I will in part declare."[20] The functional role of "Chancellor" is thus distinctly different in these two texts: in the manuscript account over his name, his "I" is a kind of punctuation mark to the observed and written material being presented; in Adams's richer narrative, the figure of Chancellor provides readers with a point of affective identification, inviting them to participate in the navigator's actions and feelings. In the preface to *Principall Navigations* (1589), Hakluyt characterized his method as drawing especially on the relations of those who were "paynefull and personall travellers," identified by name: "That every man might answere for himselfe, justifie his reports, and stand accountable for his own doings, I have referred every voyage to his Author, which both in person hath performed, and in writing hath left the same."[21] These early documents begin to suggest the range of roles to be played by the first person, who was the foundation of travel writing's authority.

---

19 Ibid., 1: 245.
20 Chancellor, "Booke of the Emperor of Russia," 1: 228–36.
21 Hakluyt, "Preface to the Reader (1589)," sig. *3v.

(In later chapters, we will examine some of the complexities of authorial attribution and identity in Hakluyt's sources.)

The accounts by Chancellor and Adams were both composed after the fact; the third account of the 1553 voyage, Willoughby's "bare log," was written in the course of the voyage itself. (Chancellor, the most expert pilot on the voyage, surely kept a similar log but it was manifestly not the basis for either of the two texts already discussed.) The log begins with the expedition's departure from Deptford, on 11 May 1553, saluting King Edward VI as they passed Greenwich, and ends with the ships at harbour near modern Murmansk, preparing to overwinter; there the members of the expedition would die. Headings and comments provided by Hakluyt indicate that this document was part of a pamphlet, which also included a list of the ships (with their weight, and names of officers and crew), the oath administered to the captain, and the oath administered to the master. Hakluyt concludes his presentation of the document by transcribing "two notes ... written upon the outside of this Pamphlet, or Book":

1 The proceedings of Sir Hugh Willoughbie after he was separated from the *Edward Bonaventure*
2 Oure shippe being at anker in the harbor called *Sterfier* in the Iland *Lofoote*[22]

Neither note is readily intelligible as a title either for the narrative or for other associated materials included under the larger heading, "The true copie of a note found in one of the two ships [...] which wintred in Lappia." Willoughby's narrative was thus framed by the formal, founding documents of the voyage, as well as traces of the material form in which it was found.[23] Hakluyt's editorial decisions (particularly the transcription of the two notes) suggest a desire to reproduce with unusual fidelity what he allows us, equally unusually, to glimpse as a material text: a pamphlet that, with the frozen bodies of its author and his companions, was found by Russian fishermen and recovered by a later English voyage.

22 According to Adams, Willoughby summoned the "chiefest men" of the fleet to a conference soon after they left the Lofoten Islands, off the coast of Norway; the ships were later separated somewhere north of modern Tromsø (Adams, "Newe Navigation, 1553," 1: 245).

23 The Quinns' "C&S" describes these items as "continuations" of Cabot's instructions for the voyage; however, in Hakluyt's text they appear under the common title, "The true copie of a note found in one of the two ships [...]."

The pathos suggested by this treatment has no counterpart in the log's entries, however. Closest of the three narratives to the events of the voyage and, indeed, to the suffering of the men who died, Willoughby's log is *formally* the most distant and impersonal even though a marginal note to the printed text comments that it "was written in [Willoughby's] own hand." The log is written exclusively in the collective voice of the first person *plural*: "we ran still along the coast ... we thought it best to return unto the harbor ... we sent out three men ... to search if they could find people."[24] Even command decisions are not attributed to (or claimed by) Willoughby as an individual. The log provides no "I," and nothing like the illusion of access to the thoughts and feelings of the travellers which the Adams narrative provides.[25] (A transcription of the original by John Dee has a marginal comment, next to the last entry: "The Haven of Death.")[26]

George B. Parks was correct: no one of these three narratives (or even the three together) tells a complete story of what happened on this 1553 voyage, a story that would have been complex in any event as Chancellor's and Willoughby's courses diverged, eventually with fatal consequence. But if the documents won't tell us all we want to know about what happened, perhaps they can tell us something else. These early accounts provide a revealing example of the systems and protocols by which voyage narratives were produced – by different kinds of hands, for different purposes, and for different audiences. The question of "how" rather than "what" becomes especially attractive in the context of volume 1, because this volume of *Principal Navigations* is especially rich in instructions for travellers. These are not the more general expectations of the kind that may lie in the background of Chancellor's narrative, a genre that directed young men of rank into making travel an educational rather than merely a recreational experience.[27] Rather, Hakluyt included instructions, produced under the aegis of the Muscovy Company, that were directed specifically to ships' officers and merchants in their

---

24 Willoughby, "True Copie," 1: 236–7.

25 Compare the gritty details we have of Henry Hudson's last days or the tragic writing-to-the-minute of the later Scott expedition to the South Pole. On Hudson, see documents 673–7, particularly "Examination of the survivors of the *Discovery* on the half of Trinity House," in D. Quinn, NAW, 4: 277–96. On Scott, see Apsley Cherry-Garrard, *Worst Journey in the World* (London, 1922). For further discussion of pronoun use in maritime writing, see chapters 7 and 9.

26 BL Cotton MS Otho E. VIII, fo. 16.

27 In addition to the essays by Carey and Rubiés, Justin Stagl provides a broad overview of instructions for travellers in *History of Curiosity*.

professional capacities, and in them, writing emerges as a point of particular emphasis. These instructions bear on the Muscovy and Persia documents, to be sure, but they open a revealing window onto how many of Hakluyt's documents came to be produced, as well as why they took the forms they did.

HOW TO TRAVEL IN THE NORTH: INSTRUCTIONS FOR VOYAGES AND VOYAGERS

1 The excellent orders and instructions of Sebastian Cabot [1553] (226–30)
2 The Commission given to the merchants Agents resiant in Russia (259–62)
3 Instructions given to the Pursers of the Moscovie voyage [1556] (272–4)
4 Instructions given to the Masters and mariners [...] Anno. 1557 (295–7)
5 Instructions given to the discoverers [1568] (383–4)[28]
6 Directions given by M. Richard Hakluyt Esquire to M. Morgan Hubblethorne, dier (432)
7 Rules and orders [...] to be observed in that Discovery [William Borough, for Arthur Pet and Charles Jackman, 1580] (435–7)
8 Brief advices given by M. John Dee [1580] (437)
9 Notes in writing, besides more privie by mouth, that were given by M. Richard Hakluyt [...] Esquire, Anno 1580, to M. Arthur Pet, and to M. Charles Jackman (437–42)[29]
10 Instructions given by the Moscovie Company [1582] (453–4)

Willoughby's log was the product of writing practices explicitly described in the instructions for the 1553 voyage, prepared by Sebastian Cabot. Item seven of Cabot's instructions mandated daily and weekly writing on shipboard:

---

28 These instructions, dated 1588 in the text, are corrected to 1568 in Quinn and Quinn, "c&s." Andrews attributes the instructions to William Borough, and notes that "the voyage did not take place as far as we know" (Andrews, *Trade, Plunder, and Settlement*, 71).

29 The elder Hakluyt's instructions to factors in Constantinople, found in volume 2(i), are discussed in chapter 5.

that the marchants, and other skilful persons in writing, shal daily write, describe, and put in memorie *the Navigation of every day and night, with the points [of the compass, i.e. headings sailed on], and observation of the lands, tides, elements, altitude of the sunne [latitude], course of the moon and starres,* and the same so noted by the order of the Master and pilot of every ship to be put in writing, the captaine generall assembling the Masters together once every weeke (if wind and weather shal serve) to conferre all the observations, and notes of the said ships, to the intent it may appeare wherein the notes do agree, and wherein they dissent, and upon good debatement, deliberation, and conclusion determined, to put the same into a common leger, to remain of record for the company: the like order to be kept in proportioning of the Cardes, Astrolabes, and other instruments prepared for the voyage, at the charge of the companie. (emphasis mine)[30]

The process must have worked something like this, at least in theory: the masters and pilots provided navigational information in rough form to the merchants or other designated scribes, who kept a daily record of the requested data; once a week, these daily records were conferred together, discrepancies reconciled, and from these three journals kept on board each ship, a single record was produced and transcribed in the "common ledger" aboard Willoughby's ship – perhaps the "pamphlet" that survived.[31]

Cabot's instructions were representative of the information English navigators of the time used to estimate their position. As ships' logs became more common, they would come to be (to some extent) regularized, and – as specified in 1553 – data gathered would typically include compass heading, distance travelled, and weather, as well as depth and ground.[32] Later instructions, like those prepared by William Borough in 1568 and 1580, would add expectations for frequent observations of latitude and compass variation; in the absence of known landmarks, navigators could check a position estimated by dead reckoning against a north-south position fixed by celestial observation.[33] The log

---

30 Cabot, "Ordinances, 1553," 1: 226.

31 The records and record-keeping methods of masters and pilots are a more technical subject, depending also on methods and instruments for navigation that were in rapid evolution over the course of the sixteenth century; see Waters, *Art of Navigation*; Schotte, "Expert Records."

32 John Law notes that observations of depth and the kind of ground under a ship's position were particularly important for navigation in the North Atlantic, where conditions (of depth, tides, visibility) differed from those prevailing in the Mediterranean (Law, "Methods of Long-Distance Control," 242–3).

33 W. Borough, "Necessarie Notes, 1568"; W. Borough, "Instructions and Notes, 1580."

for a Northeast Passage search by Borough's brother Stephen in 1556 included such observations of latitude and variation at regular intervals; and although Chancellor's own log for the 1553 voyage does not survive, he was considered an expert in the use and design of instruments for celestial observation as well as in the mathematics required for navigating by the sun and stars.[34]

Both Borough and Chancellor were at the leading edge of a significant evolution in English navigational practice, however, rather than representing the typical capacities of English ships' masters in the 1550s. Willoughby, a soldier, is highly unlikely to have had this facility, and the virtual absence of latitude observations after the ships under his command were separated from Chancellor suggests that his remaining masters were equally inexpert. The information provided by Willoughby's log does not allow us to reconstruct his course with certainty, even now.[35] On its own, this kind of written record was not a good or even adequate technology for knowing (or recording) position in unfamiliar waters. But it also served a second purpose: in addition to navigational data, instructions requested (and logs included) writing about "other things of note."[36] While records of navigational and hydrographic information had a practical function for the mariners as well as providing information for the company, who might wish to send others after them, the narrative of events did not have the same immediately practical function – rather, it served the company's interest in understanding what it could not directly see.

Additional kinds of written records were expected to be kept for a similar purpose: Cabot's instructions required a weekly account of provisions used, and regular inventories of munitions. These requirements for inventory would become even more varied and intense on subsequent voyages, as we can see in instructions to the pursers for a later voyage of trade in 1556, when written records tracked the movements of goods, persons, letters, and money on and off the ship and explicit processes were specified for crosschecking, copying, and submitting these records. It was the navigational logs, however, and *their* record of events, that would come to form the basis of the "travel narrative." Many of Hakluyt's documents – Willoughby's text among them – exhibit the stylistic marks of having originated in the kind of utilitarian practice these

---

34 See S. Borough, "Voyage of the Aforesaide Stephen Burrough, 1557." Dee, an expert mathematician, referred to Chancellor as an "incomparable" navigator (*General and Rare Memorials*, sig. ε.iii.r, cited in Ash, *Power, Knowledge, and Expertise*, 112).

35 Ash, *Power, Knowledge, and Expertise*, 112.

36 Several decades later, John Davis's tabular log included a column for general observations; see Davis, "Traverse-Book"; Davis, *Seamans Secrets*, sig. G5r.

Figure 4.1 Traverse boards allowed mariners to keep track of the courses steered during a watch before making a written log entry. Although use of the board was viewed as a conservative technique in the late sixteenth century, this later example (ca. 1800) suggests that it continued to be a useful tool.

instructions describe. Although the records printed by Hakluyt (as well as others in manuscript) presented their information in continuous prose, the frequent provision of dates in the margins, an aid to readers, also recalls the narratives' original context of production as a daily record kept on shipboard; surviving traverse boards used on shipboard suggest that logs may have translated into written form as a kind of reckoning whose material basis was neither verbal nor numeric. Later, the navigator John Davis would recommend that logs be kept in a tabular format, with column headings indicating and

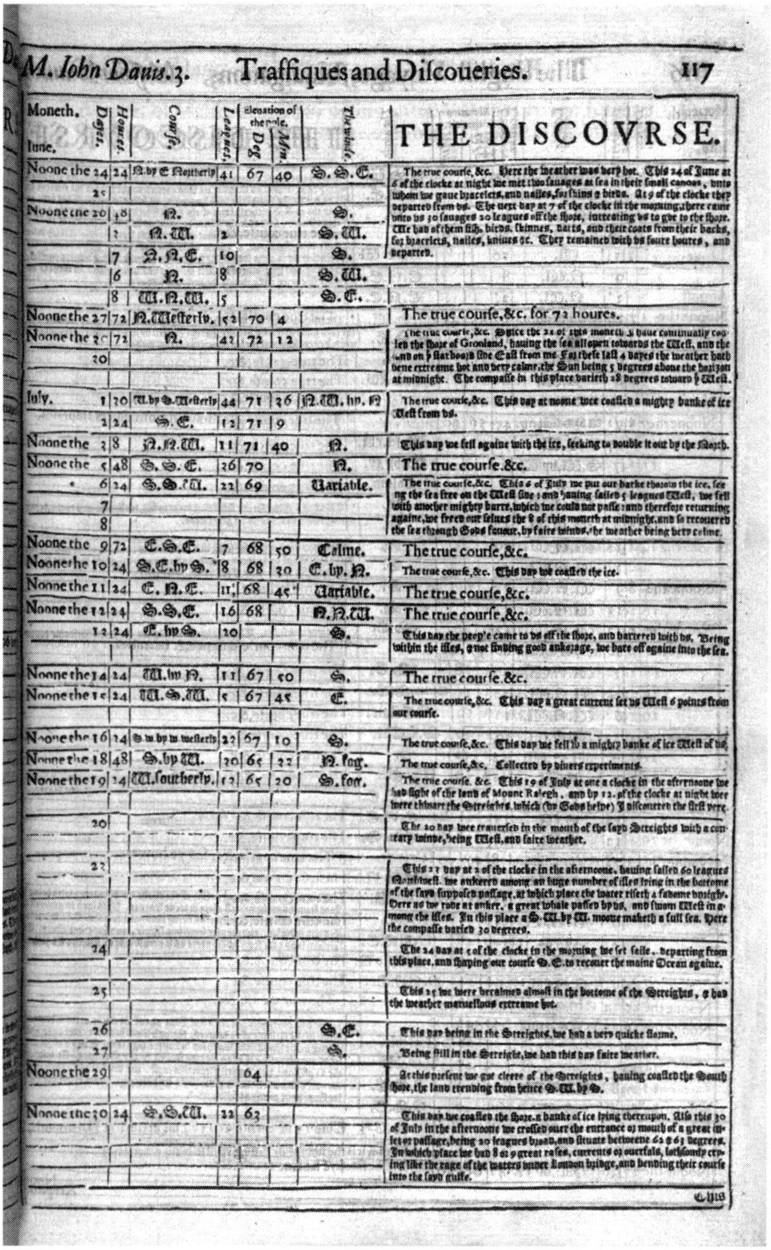

Moneth.	Dayes.	Houres.	Course.	Leagues.	Eleuation of the pole. Deg.	Min.	The winde.	THE DISCOVRSE.
Iune. Noone the	24	24	N. by E Northerly	41	67	40	S.S.E.	The true course, &c. Here the weather was very hot. This 24 of Iune at 6 of the clocke at night we met two sauages at sea in their small canoas, vnto whom we gaue bracelets, and nailes, for skins & birds. At 9 of the clocke they departed from vs. The next day at 7 of the clocke in the morning, there came vnto vs 30 sauages 20 leagues off the shore, intreating vs to goe to the shore. We had of them fish, birds, skinnes, darts, and their coats from their backs, for bracelets, nailes, kniues &c. They remained with vs foure houres, and departed.
	25							
Noone the	26	48	N.				S.	
		2	N.W.	2			S.W.	
		7	N.N.E.	10			S.	
		6	N.	8			S.W.	
		8	W.N.W.	5			S.E.	
Noone the	27	72	N. Westerly.	52	70	4		The true course, &c. for 72 houres.
Noone the	28	72	N.	42	72	12		The true course, &c. Since the 21 of this moneth I haue continually coasted the shore of Gronland, hauing the sea all open towards the West, and the land on the starboord side East from me. For these last 4 dayes the weather hath bene extreme hot and very calme, the Sunne being 5 degrees aboue the horizon at midnight. The compasse in this place varieth 28 degrees towards the West.
	30							
Iuly.	1	20	W. by S. Westerly	44	71	36	N.W. by N.	The true course, &c. This day at noone wee coasted a mighty banke of ice West from vs.
	2	24	S.E.	12	71	9		
Noone the	3	8	N.N.W.	11	71	40	N.	This day we fell againe with the ice, seeking to double it out by the North.
Noone the	5	48	S.S.E.	26	70		N.	The true course, &c.
	6	24	S.S.W.	22	69		Variable.	The true course, &c. This 6 of Iuly we put our barke thorow the ice, seeing the sea free on the West side: and hauing sailed 5 leagues West, we fell with another mighty barre, which we could not passe: and therefore returning againe, we freed our selues the 8 of this moneth at midnight, and so recouered the sea through Gods fauour, by faire windes, the weather being very calme.
	7							
	8							
Noone the	9	72	E.S.E.	7	68	50	Calme.	The true course, &c.
Noone the	10	24	S.E. by S.	8	68	20	E. by N.	The true course, &c. This day we coasted the ice.
Noone the	11	24	E.N.E.	11	68	45	Variable.	The true course, &c.
Noone the	12	24	S.S.E.	16	68		N.N.W.	The true course, &c.
	12	24	E. by S.	20			S.	This day the people came to vs off the shore, and bartered with vs. Being within the isles, & not finding good ankorage, we bare off againe into the sea.
Noone the	14	24	W. by N.	11	67	50	S.	The true course. &c.
Noone the	15	24	W.S.W.	5	67	45	E.	The true course, &c. This day a great current set vs West 6 points from our course.
Noone the	16	24	S by W westerly	22	67	10	S.	The true course, &c. This day we fell into a mighty banke of ice West of vs.
Noone the	18	48	S. by W.	20	65	22	N. fog.	The true course, &c. Collected by diuers experiments.
Noone the	19	24	W. southerly.	12	65	20	S. fog.	The true course, &c. This 19 of Iuly at one a clocke in the afternoone we had sight of the land of Mount Ralegh, and by 12 of the clocke at night wee were thwart the Streights, which (by Gods helpe) I discouered the first yere.
	20							The 20 day wee trauersed in the mouth of the sayd Streights with a contrary winde, being West, and faire weather.
	21							This 21 day at 1 of the clocke in the afternoone, hauing sailed 60 leagues Northwest, we ankered among an huge number of isles lying in the bottome of the sayd supposed passage, at which place the water riseth 4 fadome vpright. Here as we rode at anker, a great whale passed by vs, and swam West in among the isles. In this place a S.W. by W. moone maketh a full sea. Here the compasse varied 30 degrees.
	24							The 24 day at 5 of the clocke in the morning we set saile, departing from this place, and shaping our course S.E. to recouer the maine Ocean againe.
	25							This 25 we were becalmed almost in the bottome of the Streights, & had the weather maruellous extreame hot.
	26						S.E.	This day being in the Streights, we had a very quicke storme.
	27						S.	Being still in the Streights, we had this day faire weather.
Noone the	29				64			At this present we got cleere of the Streights, hauing coasted the South shore, the land trending from hence S.W. by S.
Noone the	30	24	S.S.W.	22	63			This day we coasted the shore, & banke of ice lying thereupon. Also this 30 of Iuly in the afternoone we crossed ouer the entrance or mouth of a great inlet or passage, being 20 leagues broad, and situate betweene 62 & 63 degrees. In which place we had 8 or 9 great races, currents or ouerfals, loathsomly crying like the rage of the waters vnder London bridge, and bending their course into the sayd gulfe.

This

Figure 4.2 John Davis advocated for systematic recording of navigational data, including observations that might form the basis of a narrative account.

distinguishing different kinds of data.[37] Logs collected a sequence of regular but discontinuous observations, which might then be smoothed to produce either a charted course, or a prose journal. Yet whatever continuities might be interpolated at a later stage of processing, the nature of logs privileged time over event as the stimulus for writing, and this had consequences both for logs themselves and for the other written forms that used them as source texts.

The group of instructions considered here addressed disparate kinds of actors and activities under the company's aegis, from navigators entering unknown Arctic waters to an individual clothworker charged with seeking commercial intelligence in Persia, and were composed by a variety of individuals with different forms of expertise, as well as in the corporate voice of the company itself. The articulation of a schedule for the production of writing emerges as one of the strongest regularities among *all* these varied instructions. Borough's instructions expected masters and pilots to "note" latitude "as often … as you may possible," but other navigational information was to be recorded "at the ende of every four glasses," or at the very least, "at the end of every watch, or eight glasses at the farthest" – in other words, every two to four *hours*.[38] Instructions for merchants were equally explicit in requiring written records to be produced on a daily or weekly basis; the elder Hakluyt's "directions" for a clothworker sent to Persia to gather commercial intelligence instruct him less formally to "Set down in writing whatsoever you shall learn from day to day lest you should forget."[39] These time-based writing practices were deeply consequential for Hakluyt's collection as a whole, and in collecting some of the documents produced by these practices, *Principal Navigations* provides us with a look at a mode of recording that accompanied every voyage, and virtually every maritime travel narrative, but had not been represented in published form.

---

37 On mariners' conservative preference for traverse boards, see Wright, *Certaine Errors in Navigation*, sig. ¶4r. On their use, see Bennett, *Navigation*, 68–9. Davis, a practitioner and advocate of newer methods, discusses the tabular log in *Seamans Secrets*, sig. G5r.

38 W. Borough, "Instructions and Notes, 1580," 1: 436. A glass generally measured thirty-minute intervals (*OED*).

39 Muscovy Company, "Articles, 1555," 1: 260; Hakluyt, Esq., "Directions to M. Morgan Hubblethorne," 1: 432.

At the macroscopic level of the collection, temporal sequence organizes documents within volumes and sections whose larger categories are those of space. At this scale, chronology allows (or even invites) readers to infer larger-scale continuities that link documents as parts of an implied historical narrative: for instance, "development," or other such arcs. At the more granular level of the documents, chronological order often has a different effect. The imperative to produce writing at frequent, regular intervals competed with (and usually dominated) narrative interests in causation, emphasis, and framing. With its commitment to chronological regularity over narrative significance or causation, the particular practice of writing on shipboard contributes to the affective "blankness" that we notice in these texts, albeit without exhaustively accounting for it.[40] By comparison, documents organized (like Chancellor's account) by topic are less frequent in the collection, and such organization by subject categories often occurs in combination with some form of chronological narrative. Narratives that, like the first half of Adams's account, include descriptions of thinking and feeling are less frequent still in the collection: one exceptional example is the unattributed account of Francis Drake's circumnavigation ("Famous Voyage").[41]

Instructions tell us about the *kind* of writing insisted on by the Muscovy Company's instructions, but they also provide valuable evidence about the material dimension of writing, its associated actions and artifacts. Eric Ash comments on William Borough's instructions for a later voyage, that "so concerned was Borough with data collection ... that he used some variant of the word *note* in every single paragraph of his brief instructions, six times in the first paragraph alone, and a total of twenty-three times throughout."[42] To note something might be simply to attend, to notice; almost everywhere, however, instructions specify a note to be made *in writing*, making reference not only to the act of inscription ("keepe a note thereof in your booke") but to the physical media of writing ("the plats that I have given you," "the paper books that we give you") and sometimes even to a designated scribal function

---

40 I borrow the term from Stephen Greenblatt's astute reading of a passage from John Sarracoll, "Voyage of M. Robert Withrington, and M. Christopher Lister, 1586" (Greenblatt, *Renaissance Self-Fashioning*, 194). This passage is discussed in chapter 6.

41 Examples of organization by topic include Harriot, "Briefe and True Report" (PN); Best, "True Discourse." Examples of affect include Ralegh, "Fight Betweene the Revenge and an Armada, 1591"; Ralegh, "Voyage of Sir Walter Ralegh." All but "Famous Voyage" were individually published before their inclusion in Hakluyt's collection.

42 Ash, *Power, Knowledge, and Expertise*, 238n77.

(decisions were "to be written by the secretary of the company in a book to be provided for that purpose").[43]

Designating particular physical media as the repository for the records requested seems to have fulfilled several functions. One such function might be technical.[44] In 1580, the captains Arthur Pet and Charles Jackman were each supplied by the Muscovy Company with a copy of William Borough's "description in plat of spiral lines" of the Russian coast as it ran east from Vaygach Island into a presumed northern passage, along with "one other sailing card, and a blank plat for either of them."[45] With the provision of these blank media – paper books and charts – the mariners were to create a record of their navigation that was both textual and graphic, as Borough's detailed instructions specify: the masters were to draw coastlines from several positions, using a sailing compass for orientation, estimating distance, marking important features with capital letters, and then repeating these observations after the ship had sailed "1. 2. 3. or 4. glasses (at the most)," with an estimate of distance and heading sailed. The various records produced – both drawings and notes – would be subject to calculation: "If you carefully with great heede and diligence, note the observations in your booke, as aforesaid, and afterwards make demonstration thereof in your plat, you shall thereby perceive howe farre the land you first sawe … was then from you, and consequently of all the rest: and also how farre the one part was from the other, and upon what course or point of the Compass the one lieth from the other."[46] The resulting product would be a coastal outline that could be copied onto "the plats, that I have given you."

Borough's specification of "the plats that I have given you" as the repository of Pet and Jackman's observations may suggest that these "blank plat[s]" were modelled on the charts provided to them. The characterization of Borough's chart as a "description in plat of spiral lines" (loxodromes), suggests that it

---

43 Muscovy Company, "Certaine Instructions 1556," 274; Borough, "Instructions and Notes, 1580," 1: 436; Muscovy Company, "Commission to Pet and Jackman, 1580," 1: 433; Muscovy Company, "Articles, 1555," 1: 260.

44 Compare Borough's instruction "to observe with the instrument which I deliver you here with … the true platformes, and distances" (Borough, "Necessarie Notes, 1568," 1: 384).

45 Muscovy Company, "Commission to Pet and Jackman, 1580," 1: 433; Waters, *Art of Navigation*, 209–11. Sarah Tyacke's census of English charts, 1560–1660, lists seven charts attributed or conjecturally attributed to Borough, of which three (one now incomplete) cover parts of the "Northeast Passage" voyages (Tyacke, "Chartmaking in England and Its Context, 1500–1660," 1748–9).

46 Borough, "Instructions and Notes, 1580," 1: 436.

Figure 4.3 Hugh Smith accompanied Arthur Pet and Charles Jackman on their Arctic voyage of 1580, and wrote an account printed in volume 1 of *Principal Navigations*; his map was among John Dee's papers.

was a circumpolar chart, like those drawn by Mercator and Dee (see plates 1 to 2); for a ship sailing far enough to the north, maps drawn on a regular grid of longitude and latitude were insufficient. As the north-south meridians grew closer together, a line of constant bearing drawn on a polar chart would appear to describe a spiral as it approached the pole (see plate 3).[47] Borough's insistence that Pet and Jackman's "whole travel" be transferred to the particular media supplied to them suggests that the plats provided had been prepared in a manner that Borough had mastered, but the two captains had not. The surviving chart provided to Dee by Hugh Smith, however, was a plain sketch.

The Muscovy Company's interest in the use of particular "paper bookes" for records produced by merchants had somewhat different purposes, organized by a concern with creating and preserving a uniform, stable written record of transactions and decisions. Navigational data were not the only information being funnelled into a single "common ledger": instructions for merchants resident in Russia instructed that accounts and household expenses were to be summarized weekly and "firmed by the said Agents hands," then reconciled, copied, and sent home once a month.[48] Records of decisions taken by groups were also to be centrally recorded. Instructions to the masters of a large fleet sailing to St Nicholas in 1582 directed that any decision "which you shall agree upon, or that which most of you shal consent unto, cause it to be set down in writing for record, which may serve for an acte amongst your selves to binde you all to observe the same."[49] The suggestion that the resulting document would "serve for an acte" with binding force on the contributors recalls the frequent requests that other records (such as weekly accounts) be signed or "firmed," and the indications that the originals of other Muscovy Company documents were sealed or notarized.[50] Attention to the material

---

[47] For a more professional explanation, see Bennett, *Navigation*, 54–5. My thanks to Sarah Tyacke for helping me find the example in plate 3, and answering naïve questions about plats.

[48] Muscovy Company, "Articles, 1555," 1: 260.

[49] Muscovy Company, "Instructions, 1582," 1: 454.

[50] The commission for Pet and Jackman, for instance, notes that Borough's instructions were annexed to it "under our seal," that Pet and Jackman each possessed a sealed copy, and that a third copy remained "with us the saide companie, sealed and subscribed by you the said Arthur Pet, and Charles Jackman" (Muscovy Company, "Commission to Pet and Jackman, 1580," 1: 235). A similar procedure was followed in 1555. Another account of the shipwreck suffered by a Russian ambassador to England in 1556 was represented by a memorial "written, and autentikely made, and by the sayde Ambassadour his servants, whose names be underwritten, and traine in presence of the Notarie, and

form of these documents was associated with their testamentary, instrumental, or contractual functions.

If the physical books serving as authoritative records of navigations, transactions, decisions, and agreements were distinct from the more varied written records that they summarized and reconciled, what happened to these other artifacts of writing, distinct from and, in a way, superseded by the common ledger and its harmonized record? A number of such variant reports can be found in *Principal Navigations* or in the manuscript record, and the Pet and Jackman voyage provides one example.[51] In PN (1589), Hakluyt printed two journals kept on board Pet's *George* during the exploratory voyage of 1580, one by Nicholas Chancellor, a merchant who was the voyage's designated writer, and the other by Hugh Smith, apparently master of the *George*.[52] Although the two accounts are broadly similar in content, and at times verbally identical, the journal by Chancellor – printed only in PN (1589) – provides more detail on some critical points. Over two days at the end of July, the officers of Jackman's *William* came on board the *George* to confer on how to proceed, given that the way forward appeared to be blocked by ice; the eventual decision was to turn back towards "Vaigats" (Vaygach Island, to the south of Novaya Zemlya), "and there to conferre further" on what to do.[53] As they passed Vaygach on 17 August, however, "the Masters came not together to confer," and a marginal note remarks "this was Arthur Pets fault"; the two ships

witnesses under named, recognized, and acknowledged" ("Honourable Receiving of the First Ambassador from Russia, 1556," 1: 289). This "instrument" was retained in the Muscovy Company archive, and represented by copies on ships sailing to Muscovy.

51 The voyages of Drake (1577–1580), Fenton (1582–1583), and Cavendish (1591–1593) provide rich examples of "other" records. See chapter 10, and Fuller, "Writing the Long-Distance Voyage."

52 Chancellor names Smith among the officers who conferred aboard the *George* on 28 July, and Smith's own journal records on 10 June that "I found the pole to be elevated 62. deg.," suggesting that he had some navigational skills (Chancellor, "Journal of Arthur Pet and Charles Jackman, 1580," 479; Smith, "Discoverie of the Northeast Parts, 1580," 1: 445). Nicholas Chancellor had served as purser on Frobisher's three voyages to the Arctic, as well as spending several years in Russia at the instance of the Muscovy Company; he was Richard Chancellor's son (McDermott, "Chancellor, Richard"). He would later serve as purser on Edward Fenton's attempted voyage to the Moluccas in 1582, and died in Sierra Leone (Taylor, *Troublesome Voyage*, xxxiv–v, 109, 159). On materials by Chancellor and Smith, see Sherman, *John Dee*, 173, 244 n. 84.

53 Chancellor, "Journal of Arthur Pet and Charles Jackman, 1580," 479. Smith records a conference between Pet and Jackman only, and only on the 28th, albeit with the same conclusion: namely, to turn back and confer again at Vaygach Island.

continued to sail west, and the *George* lost sight of her consort for good on 22 August.[54] In *PN* (1598–1600), only Hugh Smith's log was printed, and with some cuts: a curious decision given Hakluyt's interest in celebrating the voyages of discovery in the northeast. Perhaps the details of the voyage seemed either less interesting or actually inconvenient relative to the larger argument made about them in Hakluyt's preface; without further evidence, we can only speculate.

Both journals depict Pet and Jackman's voyage as a long, repetitive nightmare of warping from iceberg to iceberg in thick fog. Their principal drama stems from the outcome known to readers: the separation between the two ships on 2 July, their reunion on 25 July ("a great benefit of God for our mutuall comfort"), and their final failure to meet and subsequent separation on 22 August are all fraught with our knowledge of the *William*'s eventual loss. Yet this narrative of ships moving together, apart, together, and apart again speaks to a second set of preoccupations in the instructions, which join three distinct but related concerns: the abilities of the small fleets sent out to move together, to make decisions collectively, and to act – and feel – as a unified body. Pet and Jackman had been instructed on the importance of keeping company (an instruction they disregarded quite early in the voyage); so too were mariners in 1553, 1557, and 1582. Particular practices were recommended for ensuring that ships were able to "keep together, and not separate themselves asunder, as much as by winde & weather may be done or permitted"; in 1582, the mariners were required to give a bond of a hundred pounds "to keepe company together."[55] Keeping company enabled another important item in the instructions: meetings of officers held on a regular schedule aboard the principal ship, to confer on position and reach decisions about course, trade, or any disciplinary matters. Cabot's instructions mandated several occasions for such conferences:

6 Item ... that the Captaines, Pilots & masters shall speedily come aboord the Admiral, when and as often as he shall seeme to have just cause *to assemble them for counsaile or consultation* to be had concerning the affaires of the fleete and voyage. 7 Item, that the marchants ... shall daily write, describe, and put in memory the Navigation ... the captain general *assembling the masters together* once every weeke ... *to confer* all the observations, and notes ... 8 Item, that all

---

54 Ibid., 1: 481.
55 Cabot, "Ordinances, 1553," 1: 226; Muscovy Company, "Instructions, 1582," 454.

enterprises and exploits of discovering or landing ... to be searched, attempted, and enterprised by *good deliberation, and common assent.* (emphasis mine)[56]

The instructions of 1555, 1556, 1557, 1580, and 1582 all explicitly call for similar conferences, such that decision making – at least in theory – required actual proximity of the council's members and of the ships in which they sailed.

Presumably, such meetings and discussions lay behind the "we decided" of Willoughby's log. His invariant use of "we" thus looks like an accurate representation of the practice described, in which both decisions and written records were collectively produced by a group of "counsellors" in which the principal captain might have an extra vote. (Not all records produced by captains or masters or even others were so modest in abandoning altogether the singular "I.")[57] Merchants on land were also instructed to convene regularly to "conferre and consult together" and to reconcile their records.[58] But the instructions to captains and masters stress both the anticipated practical *challenges* of keeping ships together, and the *costs* of failing to doing so: a ship lost from sight might be a ship whose company would never be seen alive again.

Finally, both officers and ships' companies were instructed to consider each other as part of a united group, "willing and ready to help one the other."[59] Cabot told the voyagers of 1553 that "no conspiracies, parttakings, factions ... [were] to be suffered, but the same ... to be chastened charitably with brotherly love, and alwaies obedience to be used ... by al persons in their degrees ... considering and alwaies having present in your mindes that you be all one most royall kings subjects."[60] The masters of Muscovy Company ships travelling to Russia in 1557 were told that they should "conserve of *societie,* to be kept indissolubly and not to be severed" (emphasis mine); the practical instruction to "travaile together in one flote" resonated with the implied bonds of shared culture and identity.[61] Pet and Jackman were told to act as "deere friends and brothers," two barks and two companies but "wholy of one minde."[62] Such injunctions, with their affective language of national and

56 Cabot, "Ordinances, 1553," 1: 226.
57 See chapter 9. The most detailed account of processes for collective decision-making is given in documents related to Edward Fenton's voyage of 1582; see Taylor, *Troublesome Voyage.*
58 Muscovy Company, "Articles, 1555," 1: 260.
59 Muscovy Company, "Instructions, 1582," 1: 454.
60 Cabot, "Ordinances, 1553," 1: 229.
61 Muscovy Company, "Instructions to the Masters and Mariners, 1557," 1: 295.
62 Muscovy Company, "Commission to Pet and Jackman, 1580," 1: 433.

family ties, hint at a perception that mariners needed to be given instruction about identity, about the community of which they should consider themselves a part, and how they should feel about it.

Taken together, the instructions provided by the Muscovy Company reflect concerns with managing English ships and those who travelled inside them, both mariners and merchants. The company sought to gain knowledge of the physical environment, to set norms of behaviour for their personnel, and to track the movement of resources and goods into and out of the spaces they considered theirs (ships, warehouses, etc.) as these were expended, exchanged, or acquired. Their instructions were also aimed at producing unity in multiple registers: written record, common decisions, coordination of movement at the scale of ships and fleet, spatial practices of regularly gathering for common tasks, and finally conduct, identity, and feeling. By and large, they do *not* inform us about expectations regarding the people beyond Muscovy with whom the first and several subsequent voyages were intended to make contact and initiate diplomatic and commercial exchange.

Only two sets of instructions explicitly envision encounters with new peoples and cultures: those by Cabot prior to the voyage of 1553, and by Hakluyt the lawyer prior to the Pet and Jackman voyage of 1580. Both presume that a passage in high latitudes would be bordered by nations of "savages." Cabot appears to have been projecting onto the North what he had experienced and imagined decades earlier in Brazil, as well as even earlier memories of voyages to the northwest with his father.

28 Item if people shall appeare gathering of stones, gold, mettall, or other like, on the sand, your pinnesses may drawe nigh, marking what things they gather, using or playing upon the drumme, or such other instruments, as may allure them to harkening, to fantasie, or desire to see, and heare your instruments and voyces, but keepe you out of danger, and shewe to them no poynt or signe of rigour and hostilitie...

30 Item if you shall see them wear Lyons or Beares skinnes, having long bowes, and arrowes, be not afraid of that sight: for such be worne often times more to feare strangers, then for any other cause.[63]

He warned particularly against cannibals in the water: "people that can swimme ... naked ... coveting to draw nigh your ships, which if they shall finde

63 Cabot, "Ordinances, 1553," 1: 229.

not wel watched, or warded, they will assault, desirous of the bodies of men, which they covet for meate."[64] The exchanges Cabot imagined would take place without language, across a gap in sophistication that markedly favoured the English voyagers. His instructions focused on "islands" and coastlines rather than on populous cities and courts – they appear to have been aimed at guiding the voyagers' conduct on the way through the hypothesized northern passage, a region still imagined more than known.

The elder Hakluyt, although taking into consideration how "the Savage" who inhabited that passage might "bee made able to purchase our cloth," focused his instructions on what was to be observed and done once English ships arrived in Cathay. The companies were to bring a long list of goods including taffeta caps, perfumed gloves, shoes of Spanish leather, ivory combs, and silk handkerchiefs "for a shew of our commodities."[65] The exchange would be bilateral, bringing not only profit, but delight: just as the "seeds of [East Asian] fruits and herbs ... will delight the fansie of many for the strangenesse," so an English book of plants "may much delight the great Can, and the nobilitie, and also their merchants ... all things in these partes so much differing from the things of those regions."[66] Books featured repeatedly in the instructions given by the elder Hakluyt: "bring thence the mappe of the countrey ... [and] some old printed booke, to see whether they have had print there before it was devised in Europe."[67] In return, Pet and Jackman would offer maps of England and London, along with printed books like those of Joannes Boemus ("The booke of the attire of all Nations"), Abraham Ortelius ("Ortelius booke of Mappes"), and Rembert Dodoens ("the new Herball"), with their encyclopedic accounts of the peoples, regions, and plants known to Europe.[68] Yet another list in the instructions detailed the supplies to be brought "for bankketing on shipboord persons of credite": perfumes, figs, "olives to make them taste their wine," fine biscuits, French vinegar, and

64 Ibid., 1: 229.
65 Hakluyt, Esq., "Notes to Pet and Jackman, 1580," 1: 440.
66 Ibid., 1: 439.
67 Ibid., 1: 439.
68 Ibid., 1: 441. Hakluyt might have referred to one of several English versions of Johann Boemus, *Omnium gentium mores, leges, & ritus* (1520). The older *Fardel of facions* (1555) translated the original books 1 and 2, on Africa and Asia, but Hakluyt might also have referred to John Frampton's 1580 translation, via Spanish, of parts relating to northern Asia and China specifically (Boemus, *A Discouerie of the Countries of Tartaria, Scithia, & Cataya*). In his discussion of the lawyer's instructions, Peter Mancall suggests that the costume book was probably Hans Weigel, *Habitus Praecipuorum Popularum*

cinnamon water. "With these and such like, you may banket where you arrive the greater and best persons. Or with the gift of these Marmelades in small boxes, or small vials of sweet waters you may gratifie by way of gift, or you may make a merchandise of them."[69] The instructions speak eloquently to what its backers hoped and expected to find once *through* the Northeast Passage: a culture whose technology, power, and indeed civility might be in advance of Europe.

On the 1580 voyage for which the elder Hakluyt composed these instructions, Pet and Jackman encountered neither sea-borne cannibals, nor people they could gratify with gifts of marmalades in small boxes; in fact, east of Vardø they appear to have encountered no other people at all. (Traces of local knowledge in place names and routes can be plausibly attributed to the information of earlier voyages, in particular Stephen Borough's exploratory voyages of 1556.) While they penetrated further to the east than their predecessors, they came nowhere close to the court of the Chinese emperors who had succeeded to the Mongol Khans encountered by John de Plano Carpini and William de Rubriquis. That court would be represented in *Principal Navigations* only through the mediation of texts translated from the Portuguese.[70] Many records of the Muscovy Company voyages, and not only the early accounts by Chancellor and Adams, concerned themselves with describing the cultures that were encountered: the buildings, possessions, laws, resources, religion, and conduct of the Russians and Persians received detailed attention in print. But what of peoples actually encountered beyond the capital of Muscovy, along the northern periphery of the continent where the English sought to explore? This was, after all, the region privileged by both Richard Eden and Hakluyt as the part of the world left for the English to explore.

(Nuremberg, 1577) (Mancall, *Hakluyt's Promise*, 82–6). The other two books would have been Dodoens, *A Niewe Herball*; Ortelius, *Theatrum Orbis Terrarum*. On the elder Hakluyt's botanical interests, see chapter 5.

69 Hakluyt, Esq., "Notes to Pet and Jackman, 1580," 1: 441.

70 A number of translated sources on East and Southeast Asia came to Hakluyt through Richard Willes's revision and expansion of Eden's earlier collection, *History of Travayle*. Willes was a former Jesuit whose vocation had connected him with important geographers of the East within the order (Payne, "Willes, Richard"). See chapter 8 for further discussion of Hakluyt's use of translated materials on China and Japan.

SOCIETIES AND ENVIRONMENT IN THE NORTH: EXPERIENCES AND MODELS

1 Hugh Smith, "The discoverie made by M. Arthur Pet, and M. Charles Jackman, of the Northeast parts [...] 1580" (445–53)
2 Sigismund Herberstein, "The description of the regions, people, and rivers, lying North and East from Moscovia" (492–5)
3 Giovanni Battista Ramusio, "A speciall note [...] out of the Arabian Geographie of Abilfada Ismael" (495)
4 Stephen Borough, "The voyage of Stephen Burrough toward the River of Ob, intending the discovery of the Northeast passage, Anno 1556" (274–83)
5 Richard Johnson, "Certaine notes unperfectly written by Richard Johnson [...] which was in the discoverie of Vaigatz [...] 1556, and afterwards among the Samoedes" (283–5)
6 Arngrímur Jónsson, "A briefe commentarie of Island: wherin the errours of such as have written concerning this Island, are detected" (515–90)

Pet and Jackman failed to reach the merchants and courtiers for whom Hakluyt's cousin had prepared them. Neither did they encounter, along the Siberian coastline that was their voyage's furthest extent, the "marvelous races" of whom John de Plano Carpini had heard from Russian clerics at the court of the khan. That is not to say that such ideas of extreme geography as linked to human extremes were quarantined by the editor within John's account; indeed, Hakluyt printed two documents that lent credence to the belief that the far northeastern regions of Asia were home to beings of an unusual nature.

The first was an excerpt from Sigismund von Herberstein, an imperial emissary to Muscovy whose account of the sea route north of Scandinavia in *Rerum Muscovitaram commentarii* (1549) predated the English "discovery" of that route in 1553. (Herberstein's account of "The navigation by the frosen sea" had appeared in English among materials from "the bookes of Sigsmundus Liberus" in Eden's 1555 *Decades*.)[71] Hakluyt excerpted a different part of Herberstein's commentary, however, which dealt with the lands "North and

---

[71] Eden, *Decades*, fo. 289r, 303r–06r. George Turberville's verse letters from Muscovy also reference Herberstein in conclusion: "if thou list to know the Russes well, To Sigismundus booke repaire, who all the trueth can tell" ("Certaine Letters in Verse," 1: 389).

East of Muscovy" that a traveller towards China would presumably encounter. Hakluyt followed the excerpt from Herberstein with "A speciall note gathered by ... M. John Baptista Ramusius out of the Arabian Geographie of Abilfada Ismael, concerning the trending of the Ocean see from China Northward, along the coast of Tartary and other unknown lands, and then running Westwards upon the Northern coast of Russia, and so farther to the Northwest."[72] The geography sketched in this item described an open and passable sea north of the Asian continent. It also embeds a small story about the editor's use of sources that is worth pausing over briefly.

As the headnote indicates, Hakluyt printed a short passage from Ramusio, derived from the work of Abū al-Fidā, a Kurdish/Syrian geographer of the fourteenth century. Hakluyt appears to have been eager to locate the original text, as suggested in a letter addressed to him from Aleppo by John Newbery (1583): "Since my coming to Tripolis I have made very earnest inquirie both there and here, for the booke of Cosmographie of Abilfada Ismael, but by no meanes can heare of it. Some say that possibly it may be had in Persia, but notwithstanding I will not faile to make inquirie for it, both in Babylon, and in Balsara, and if I can finde it in any of these places, I will send it you from thence."[73] A few years later, in a private letter from Hakluyt to Emanuel van Meteren in 1594, Hakluyt offered to assist Jacob Valcke, the treasurer of Zeeland, in accessing copies in Arabic or Latin that he knew could be found in the libraries of several friends on the continent; another letter from Ortelius to William Camden in 1588 claimed that Hakluyt was on the verge of publishing an edition of the text.[74] Yet in both editions of the compilation, rather than using the superior materials to which he apparently had gained access, Hakluyt simply reproduced what he found in Ramusio's comments on the voyage of Marco Polo. This choice serves as a reminder that the editor's *stated*

---

72 The text is extracted from *Navigationi et viaggi* (Venice, 1559). Dee also cited Ramusio's excerpt from Abū al-Fidā in several texts for its information on the coastline of northern Asia (MacMillan, *Limits*, 40; Sherman, *John Dee*, 178).

73 Newbery, "A Letter of M. John Newbery Sent from Alepo to M. Richard Hakluyt of Oxford, Ann. 1583," 2(i): 246. Hakluyt's access to Arabic, Hebrew, Persian, and Turkish materials was generally negligible; see Allen, "Caspian," 1: 174–5. Another letter from Mercator indicates he had learned from Hakluyt that "the Epitomie of Abelfada is translated" (Mercator, "Letter of Gerard Mercator," 1: 445).

74 Van Meteren's letter to Jacob Valcke and his translation of Hakluyt's letter to Valcke (both translated or retranslated into English) are found in Taylor, *ow*, 2: 417–20. For documents subsequently transmitted by Hakluyt and now found in the Dutch archives, see "Chronology," 1: 307. I return to this exchange in chapter 8.

preference for using what we would think of as primary source material, in "the same termes wherein it is originally written," does not guarantee that, in practice, he always did so.[75]

Both these sources had particular things to say about the North and the peoples to be found there. Herberstein's account of Siberia drew on what he described as a "booke" or "journey which was delivered to me in the Moscovites tongue." In a geography whose focus moved progressively further from Muscovy, the nature and conformation of Asian peoples appeared progressively more unusual, beginning around the latitude of Novaya Zemlya with "Samoged (that is) such as eate themselves."[76] (Herberstein translated a derogatory Russian term for the Indigenous peoples of Siberia.) Among the "monstrous shapes of men" described in the text were "black men, lacking the use of common speech" who died each year in November and revived again near the end of April, "a marveilous thing and incredible"; "men of prodigious shape, of whom some are overgrown with hair like wild beasts, other have heads like dogs, and their faces in their breasts, without necks, and with long hands also and without feet"; and "a certain fish, with head, eyes, nose, mouth, hands, feet, and other members utterly of human shape, and yet without any voice, and pleasant to be eaten."[77] As Hakluyt did with the reports of John de Plano Carpini, Herberstein expressed reservations about the journal's fabulous elements – as well as frustration with his inability to confirm its claims through eyewitness testimony. Nevertheless, he wrote, the narrative merited publication "to give further occasion to other to search the truth of these things."[78]

The short passage that follows Herberstein in *Principal Navigations* derived ultimately (but not immediately) from Abū al-Fidā's *Taqwīm al-buldān* ("Locating the lands," 1321), and traces the coastline of the Asian continent north and east from China as it passes "the Gogi and Magogi, that is ... the confines of the uttermost Tartars" before reaching "the Northerne coasts of Russia." This short excerpt echoes traditions about the northeastern regions of Asia already outlined in chapter 2, in connection with the missions of William and John. The excerpt from Abū al-Fidā thus added to Herberstein's Siberia, populated by monstrous races, elements of the

75 Hakluyt, "Preface to the Reader (1589)," sig. *3v.
76 Herberstein, "Voyage to the Northeast," 1: 492, 494, 495.
77 Ibid., 1: 493, 494. For Hakluyt's reservations, see Hakluyt, "Preface to the Reader (1598)," sig. **1r.
78 Ibid., 1: 492, 494.

tradition that "evil comes from the North."[79] Both are surprising to find in a work apparently dedicated to reliable, first-hand accounts and in a volume that portrayed the northern regions of the world as among those providentially "reserved for the English to possesse," potentially sites of trade and habitation as well as passage.[80]

Hakluyt did offer first-hand witness of people along the northern fringes of Eurasia, however, in accounts by two men who had travelled with Chancellor in 1553 and numerous Muscovy Company ventures thereafter: the navigator Stephen Borough, who wrote journals of his voyages in 1556 and 1557, and the merchant Richard Johnson, who accompanied Borough in 1556 and made notes of his observations on the voyage and the winter following.[81]

In 1556, Borough's company sailed east roughly as far as Vaygach Island, to the south of Novaya Zemlya. His journal of the voyage, grounded in daily observations of sailing conditions, latitude, and variations, records friendly interactions with Russian fishermen, who provided information about the way forward as well as practical assistance (Borough's pinnace had a deeper draft than their light vessels, and was more reliant on wind).[82] Gabriel, a Russian fishing captain Borough described as "my friend," introduced him to one "Samoed, which was but a young man: his apparel was then strange unto us, and he presented me with three young wild geese, and one young barnacle." Borough represented his knowledge of Indigenous northerners as otherwise entirely mediated by his Russian counterparts; he later records that he sent men on shore at Vaygach "to see if they might speake with any of the Samoeds, but could not."[83] On 3 August, Borough went on shore with Loshak, another fisherman who had earlier given him some indications of the onward route

79 Gow, "Gog and Magog," 65. See chapter 2.

80 Hakluyt's marginal comment to Hayes, "Voyage by Sir Humfrey Gilbert," 144. The kinds of habitation imagined in the Asian North looked more like fortified outposts than colonies; for instance, see the cautionary tone in which the elder Hakluyt advised Pet and Jackman to seek out "some small Island in the Scithian sea, where we might plant, fortifie, and staple safely" (Hakluyt, Esq., "Notes to Pet and Jackman, 1580," 1: 437).

81 Stephen Borough was the elder brother of William Borough, whose instructions are discussed above. Both are understood to have studied mathematics with John Dee; Richard Eden praised Stephen Borough's expertise and dedication to advancing English knowledge of navigation in his preface to Cortés, *Arte of Navigation*. For the two brothers' importance in the development of English expertise in navigation, see Ash, *Power, Knowledge, and Expertise*, 113–34.

82 See, for instance, the incident described in S. Borough, "Voyage of Stephen Burrough, 1556," 1: 277.

83 Ibid., 1: 279, 281. The citations that follow are to the same passage.

to the Gulf of Ob, to the east of Vaygach Island. Loshak showed him "a heap of the Samoeds idols," before characterizing the material culture and behaviour of the Indigenous groups Borough would meet further along the coast ("these ... were not so hurtful as they of Ob are"). Some of the ethnographic material attributed to Loshak echoes Ohthere's relation in its account of northern culture as absence: "they have no houses," "they have no other beastes to serve them, but Deere only," "bread and corne they have none," "they know no letter."[84] But Borough's response to the objects he actually observed was more visceral, as indexed both by the amount of detail he provides (the idols receive a full paragraph in the text) and by the language in which he describes them: marked with blood that suggests sacrifice, they are also "the worst and the most unartificiall worke that ever I saw," "very grossly wrought," heaped up amidst other "broken" and "spoyled" objects of daily life. Borough understood what Loshak told him and showed him about the Arctic people he did not, himself, encounter in terms of what they failed to have, and what they failed to achieve: order, cleanliness, beauty. Negation and disorder emerge as the thematic principles of this description.

Johnson's notes began with an account of the same voyage, sharply different from Borough's text. Borough's log for the voyage out provided detailed and careful navigational information; Johnson's account of the route's human geography equally carefully distinguished different peoples along the western coast of Norway and into the White Sea, noting political affiliations, language, religion, and even alphabets with an attention that was uncommon in the archive of Muscovy Company documents appearing in *Principal Navigations*. (Once past the coast along which he had sailed with both Borough and Chancellor, Johnson painted regions to the south, east, and north of Muscovy in broader strokes, relying on information provided by others.) His notes on Arctic Siberia proceed from comments that the people of the Pechora Gulf were liable to eat strangers "as we are told by the Russes," to a description of Indigenous Siberian religious practice in the generalizing present tense: "they will make sacrifices in manner following."[85]

Yet what initially appears as something akin to the exoticizing and derogatory reports passed on by Herberstein quickly becomes something quite different. The text shifts from "they" to "I," and from the present into the narrative past tense, to give a detailed account of a shamanic ritual among the people that Johnson observed during the winter following the voyage of

84 On such lists of negatives and ideas of civility, see Fuller, "Missing Terms."
85 Johnson, "Certaine Notes," 1: 284.

exploration described by Borough. Not only an eyewitness, Johnson recorded that he personally measured and touched the sword which a priest had to all appearances thrust through his own body: "hee tooke a sworde of a cubite and a spanne long, (I did mete it my selfe) and put it into his bellie halfeway ... Then he ... thrust it through his bodie, as I thought, in at his navill and out at his fundament: the poynt being out of his shirt behinde, I layde my finger upon it." Even more strikingly, Johnson was able to speak with those around him, and seek better understanding of what he saw and heard: the account of the ritual is punctuated by "I asked" and "he/they answered." He reported that most of the Indigenous Siberians he met "can speake the Russe tongue to bee understood: and they tooke me to be a Russian."[86] Only three years after the English had first, accidentally, contacted Russia, Johnson's fluency was remarkable. (Perhaps his language also played a role in the other contribution under Johnson's name, a collection of "certain notes" taken from Russian travellers about the way east; although Johnson is credited in a headnote as having "gathered" the series of short texts that follow, these merge seamlessly into an excerpt from Ramusio such that it is not clear when his own gathering ends.)[87]

Johnson's detailed, curious, and dialogic account of the shamanic performance he witnessed contrasts sharply with the response of a near contemporary to a comparable scene in western Greenland. (Observing what he believed to be a ritual with magical intent, John Davis wrote that "I ... willed one of my company to tread out the fire, & to spurne it into the sea, which was done to shew them that we did contemne their sorcery.")[88] In Johnson's curiosity and sophistication, a life story beckons, one of the strange objects in the attic of *Principal Navigations*. Two years after he sailed with Borough, Johnson accompanied Anthony Jenkinson's initial expedition from Muscovy to Bukhara (in present day Uzbekistan) in 1558. This journey still seems extraordinary in its ambition, and resulted briefly in the opening of trade between England and the Shah of Persia.[89] In 1565, Johnson became the Muscovy Company's agent

---

86 Ibid., 1: 284, 285.
87 Johnson, "Notes of the Severall Wayes from Russia to Cathay," 1: 335.
88 Davis, "Second Voyage of John Davis, 1586," 3: 104.
89 To give one small example of the travellers' resourcefulness, when Jenkinson, Johnson, and another Englishman found cables, anchors, and sails missing from the boat they had left on the shores of the Caspian, they wove ropes from hemp, made a sail from cotton cloth, and improvised an anchor out of a cartwheel before buying one from another bark (Jenkinson, "Voyage of Anthony Jenkinson to Boghar, 1558," 1: 333).

in Bukhara, overseeing other company employees. Subsequently, a series of reports and letters from other English merchants complained of Johnson in both veiled and open terms, decrying his "vicious living" (by implication, drunkenness) and inability to "rule and governe himselfe" as damaging to the company's interests. Even these recognize his linguistic skills: "if he were honest he might do your worships good service because of his Russian tongue."[90] Johnson's biography is otherwise obscure, confining us to speculation about the combination of traits that left a fragmentary if intriguing trail of evidence across this section of the volume. Within that evidence, the disorder of "unartificiall" idols and other objects that Borough found so repellent echoes the disorder ascribed to Johnson's own conduct; even Hakluyt's headnote characterized his fuller account of Siberian religious culture as "unperfectly written."[91]

Overall, then, *Principal Navigations* treats the peoples of the Eurasian Arctic with some reserve, both in its sparse selection of documents and the particular content they offer. The Russians said that Indigenous Siberians were cannibals, while older sources suggested they might be monsters; if Johnson was more inquisitive than repulsed, his textured and closely informed observations about their culture (and the furs they offered in trade) may have been coloured for their original audience by the imputations of other company employees about his own character. While the elder Hakluyt could hypothesize from London about the eager market for woollens that would necessarily exist among the peoples bordering the Northeast Passage, none of the travellers sent out by the Muscovy Company appear to have considered these peoples with any attention, or – except for Johnson – interacted with them to any significant extent.[92] Lacking what southerners recognized as civility, or the dazzle of Muscovite gold and power, they were relegated to the edges of English travellers' mental maps – where the half-fabulous materials of Herberstein and Abū al-Fidā still passed current.

The new navigations of the 1550s to the 1580s allow us to linger longer on the experiences of actual travel which, if terse in their accounts of culture, provide ample descriptions of environment. *As* environment, the North was

---

90 Additional specific complaints include Johnson's carelessness with financial documents, and the charge that he kidnapped a Persian boy; other, less specific dissatisfactions are implied by Arthur Edwards (Cheney, "Voyage into Persia, 1563," 1: 354; Edwards, "Certaine Letters of Arthur Edwards," 1: 357).

91 Johnson, "Certaine Notes," 1: 283.

92 Hakluyt, Esq., "Notes to Pet and Jackman, 1580," 1: 439.

of course different in real ways – differing culturally in part because it differed ecologically or environmentally from regions further to the south. In his journal of Pet and Jackman's voyage, Hugh Smith described a landscape that was literally inhuman. Day after day, as the expedition's two ships struggled to pass into the Kara Sea, they were enclosed by ice, unable to move freely. Often the men could not distinguish land from ice or either from fog, discern distance from land (except by inference from constant sounding), or see in the "mistie darknesse" of an Arctic summer, past icebergs stretching above the ships' topmasts. This experience could not have been further from Robert Thorne's projection of an open polar sea lit by constant day, affording the opportunity "at the will and pleasure of the mariners, to choose" their course, since once "past the Pole, it is plaine, they may decline to what part they list."[93] The landscape Smith described resisted forward movement and frustrated choice of direction, leaving those ships that remain the iconic emblem of English sea power locked in ice and fog for days at a time. Pet and Jackman encountered neither cannibals, nor headless men, nor apocalyptic evil. Yet if the Siberian Arctic was not discernibly supernatural, the mariners' inability to assign what they saw around them to the organizing categories of sea/land, day/night, winter/summer, solids and air – much less to see or move freely – suggests that this environment was deeply uncanny for voyagers from lower latitudes.

As we near the end of volume 1, a final document informs us about ideas of northern environments and peoples from a very different perspective, one not directly connected with the Northeast Passage search which figures so prominently in Hakluyt's materials. Arngrímur Jónsson's *Brevis commentarius de Islandia* (Copenhagen, 1593), translated as "A briefe commentarie of Island," was an extended diatribe against the false and defamatory claims about Iceland promulgated by both learned and popular writers on the continent. The lengthy "Briefe commentarie," printed in both Latin and English, was not about the travels of Englishmen or indeed about a territory that England hoped to explore and claim, or even to traverse; indeed, Jónsson disclaimed knowledge of physical facts like "the true longitude & latitude of the said Iland."[94]

---

93 Thorne, "Persuasion to King Henry the Eight," 213. Smith's empirical descriptions echo classical sources that described the northern seas as "unexplorable, neither dense enough to walk on, nor liquid enough to navigate" (Small, "Jellied Seas," 321).

94 Jónsson, "Briefe commentarie of Island," 554. England is mentioned three times in "Briefe commentarie": English ships are said to fish at Iceland in the spring; an Englishman served as bishop in the fifteenth century; Hakluyt's marginal comment "The ancient traffique of England with Island" highlights a passing comment that "certain Cities of

His text is nonetheless richly informative both on European beliefs about Iceland, and the cultural and natural facts that falsified them.

Paratextual materials provide some modest suggestions of how and why the text came to Hakluyt's notice. The reverend Hugh Branham of Harwich, an ecclesiastical colleague of the editor's whose parish was some forty miles from Hakluyt's own seat of Wetheringsett, apparently obtained a copy of Jónsson's *Brevis commentarius* and wrote to the Icelandic bishop whose preface opens the work. Hakluyt printed a reply from the bishop, Guðbrandur Þorláksson; the letter indicates that Branham had found Þorláksson's name in Jónsson's text, and written to him enquiring about "the monuments of antiquitie which are ... thought to be extant" in Iceland, as well as about Iceland's "neighbour countries," including both Norway and Greenland. Þorláksson is also known as the source for a map of Iceland adapted by Ortelius in *Theatrum Orbis Terrarum* (1570); populating the waters around it with monsters, this well-circulated map "spread the image in Europe of Iceland as an exotic, extreme, and remote land inhabited by strange creatures and strange men," and Jónsson took a few swipes at Ortelius's version on his bishop's behalf (see plate 4).[95] Þorláksson's response is dated 1595; we can only speculate how Branham came to read a work on Iceland that had been published in Copenhagen only two years earlier. The letter provides no precise information about the "monuments" about which Branham had inquired; perhaps he shared Dee and Hakluyt's interest in the stories of an ancient English presence in the Arctic suggested by materials on King Arthur, Nicholas of Lynn, or the voyages of the Zeno brothers, and hoped that the "ancient records" mentioned by Jónsson might provide confirming evidence.[96] If so, no evidence was forthcoming. Branham's involvement may explain how the

---

England" had in the past benefited from Iceland's commodities (Jónsson, "Briefe commentarie of Island," 555, 575, 589). The texts of the "Briefe commentarie" and an associated letter occupy pp. 515–91, following the Muscovy Company materials, and preceding two narratives of the sea war with Spain that end the volume. For a longer discussion of the "Briefe commentarie" in the context of Hakluyt's other materials on English contact with Iceland, see Fuller, "Placing Iceland."

95 Thorláksson, "Letter by Gudbrandus Thorlacius," 591; Jónsson, "Briefe commentarie of Island," 1: 567. On the map, see Oslund, *Iceland Imagined*, 39.

96 Jónsson, "Briefe commentarie of Island," 1: 572. The apocryphal Arctic voyages of the Zeno brothers featured prominently in Dee's arguments for English title to regions in the North, and were printed by Hakluyt in volume 3, adjacent to the Arctic voyages of Martin Frobisher and John Davis (Zeno, "Voyage of M. Nicolas Zeno"). See chapter 8.

Brevis commentarius came to Hakluyt's notice, but not how and why it was of interest to the editor, or might have been to his audiences.

As we have seen, the far North depicted in volume 1 had so far not been associated with civility, let alone with learning. In the preface "To the reader" in volume 1, Hakluyt suggested that the "Briefe commentarie" would be valuable to readers in part because its provenance belied such expectations: "it commeth from that Northren climate which most men would suppose could not affourd any one so learned a Patrone for it selfe."[97] The main thrust of Jónsson's argument was indeed to challenge claims that Iceland's nature and culture were defective or aberrant, and to defend his native country in a manner David Koester has suggested had parallels with Hakluyt's own project.[98] Hakluyt's description of Jónsson as his country's learned *patron* indeed emphasizes that the author of "Briefe commentarie" was a disputant more than a geographer, entering the lists to "withstand the unjust violence of others" against Iceland.[99] The "Briefe commentarie" owed its inception to Þorláksson's desire for a refutation of the slanders contained in a frequently reprinted German poem: Gories Peerse's "Van Yslandt" (Hamburg, 1561). The text also sought to intervene in learned discourse about Iceland. Written in Latin by an Icelandic scholar educated in Denmark, it sought to correct errors commonly (and repetitiously) found in the publications of bold-face names like Sebastian Münster, Olaus Magnus, Albert Krantz, Gemma Frisius, and Abraham Ortelius.[100] Margaret Small notes that "the northern limits" of European geography were "the last to be challenged ... even educated Germans living relatively close to Scandinavia had ill-conceived ideas of the region."[101] Systematic misconceptions and distortions about a place located at the northern fringes of European space spanned the range of geographic writing, from sensational pamphlets to learned cosmography and cartography. In the 1520s, Thorne may have celebrated the opening of conceptual and actual possibilities to the north, in the wake of voyages that disproved predictions of an uninhabitable torrid zone. Yet the very need to respond, in 1593, to a series of authoritative publications over the intervening decades demonstrates how

---

97 Hakluyt, "Preface to the Reader (1598)," sig. **2v.

98 Koester, "Power of Insult," 10, 26.

99 Jónsson, "Briefe commentarie of Island," 1: 553. David Koester's valuable essay on the "Briefe commentarie" sharpened this point for me.

100 Ortelius is alluded to circuitously in connection with his edition of Þorláksson's map (which Jónsson criticizes as sloppy and irresponsible): for instance, as "a certaine Cosmographer in his Map of Island" (Jónsson, "Briefe commentarie of Island," 1: 567).

101 Small, "Jellied Seas," 315.

tenaciously predictions of an aberrant North nonetheless endured (including in *Principal Navigations*, as we have seen).[102]

Governed by Denmark in the period, Iceland would have been familiar to one subset of early modern Europeans as the site of a prolific cod fishery, visited regularly by English, German, and Danish ships.[103] Yet Jónsson had to begin by refuting a purely geographical claim that located Iceland at the extreme borders of the known world, belying its political, demographic, and economic connections to the continent: "The Isle of Island being severed from other countreys an infinite distance, standeth farre into the Ocean, and is scarse knowen unto Sailers."[104] Iceland's alleged location "upon the extreme northerly parts almost of the whole earth" organized a series of exaggerated claims about its physical geography: not only was its distance from Europe "infinite," but its mountains touched the sky, its pastures were so fertile as to threaten livestock with surfeit, its horses had extraordinary endurance, its whales passed for islands, and sea ice surrounded it for most of the year.[105] Even Iceland's size and population had been inflated by continental geographers. The paradox of snow-covered mountains whose "roots boil with everlasting fire" served as metonymy for a land of marvelous extremes, itself at the extreme northern edge of the known world.

Iceland was also imagined as a threshold space between the worlds of nature and the supernatural. According to the "Briefe commentarie," both Münster and Gemma Frisius claimed the souls of the dead were tormented both in the ice that ringed the island for most of the year and within the volcanic Mount Hekla, a gateway to hell through which the damned could be heard. Monstrous in its extremes, uncanny in its apertures to the supernatural world, Iceland in the work of cosmographers was a site of "miracles ... besides and against all nature."[106] Mocking these claims for their inconsistency with both religious doctrine and observed experience, Jónsson redescribed Iceland's geysers, icebergs, and volcanos as natural phenomena. Volcanoes, he reminded readers, could also be found in the temperate and tropical South; yet while cosmographers were perfectly able to understand volcanoes in Sicily or Mexico *as*

---

102 Perceptions of Iceland as a remote, liminal space whose nature and culture were fundamentally different from those of Europe endured in various forms well beyond the early modern period; see Oslund, *Iceland Imagined*.

103 Jónsson, "Briefe commentarie of Island," 1: 555.

104 Ibid., 1: 553. On the fishery, see Jones, "England's Icelandic Fishery in the Early Modern Period."

105 Jónsson, "Briefe commentarie of Island," 1: 555–7.

106 Ibid., 1: 569.

natural, Hekla was relegated to different systems of explanation: "In a fiery hill of West India they search for gold, but in mount Hecla of Island they seeke for hel."[107]

The second half of the text is devoted to a defence of Iceland's people and culture, and here Jónsson engaged a different kind of claim. Unlike the marvelous races of Arctic Asia, Icelanders were not said to be of unusual configuration or to enjoy extra-human abilities. Instead, continental writers emphasized the abnormal and deficient character of local customs and practices. Jónsson countered the more scandalous claims made in Peerse's poem by specifying that if the German saw the discreditable behaviours he described, it was because he had only frequented "the coast of Island, whither a confused rout of the meanest common people, in fishing time do yerely resort, who being naught as well through their owne leudnesse, as by the wicked behaviour of outlandish mariners, often times doe leade a badde and dishonest life."[108] Peerse described as *custom* practices that violated principles of order: use of chamber pots at the dinner table, toleration of adultery, employing urine for washing. Jónsson's reply attributed this disorder, if it existed, to elements that were socially marginal, probably foreign, and (literally) liminal.[109]

Peerse and others also found "matter for reproach" (or misrepresentation) in the absences or poverty that characterized Iceland's material culture. Diet was a key topic of rhetorical struggle, combining ideas about environment and resources, technologies of transformation, and the humoural constitution of bodies; Jónsson accords repeated and extensive attention to allegations about diet in sections 3, 4, and 9 of part 2 of "Briefe commentarie," devoted to culture, before announcing that he will deal in section 15 with "these reproches, which strangers do gather from the meats and drinks of the Islanders."[110] These were found both in the writings of cosmographers, and the popular work by Peerse.

---

107 Ibid., 1: 561.

108 Ibid., 1: 586.

109 Such treatment of the seasonal fishery was unique neither to Iceland nor to the "scurrilous rimer." Even as English writers praised the Atlantic fishery for its role as a nursery of seamen, they seem to have viewed it as a decivilizing force, and maritime cultures as virtually no culture at all; see Pope, *Fish into Wine*, 435–6.

110 Jónsson, "Briefe commentarie of Island," 1: 584. In the first mention of these allegations about diet, Jónsson indeed uses aberrant food practices as a metaphor for the defective textual practices of unexamined repetition and plagiarism with which he charged European cosmographers: "These be the things ... which Krantzius hath champed, and put into Munsters mouth ... [Munster] casteth up the verie same morsels

As Koester has pointed out, Jónsson did not dispute the "simple description of dietary facts": in an environment rich on marine resources and dairy products, an Icelandic diet was poor in salt and cereals, and thus relied little on the processes of preservation and fermentation that required them. (One allegation debunked by Jónsson was that Icelanders had until recently been ignorant of "the arte of brewing their water with corne"; another, that they "use stockefish instead of bread.")[111] Icelanders did drink water and eat fish dried and preserved without salt (stockfish); his text affirms these and other customs as testaments to God's providential care in endowing them with the ingenuity to manage a restricted set of resources.[112] Jónsson was nonetheless aware that these facts had meaning in a larger discourse of ethnographic categories and hierarchies, so that dietary fact became the stuff of insult.

Salt and bread were not just sustenance; they were marks of higher status that had been transferred into the realm of the discourse of national characteristics ... The descriptive categories of travel writing and cosmography – diet, housing, language, child-rearing practices, and so on – constituted an axis of selection comprised of status-marked possibilities ... Each category had European standards that ... expressed Christianity and/or civilization: houses were expected to be *built* and made of sturdy, durable materials; food included bread, salt, and meat ... For each category there were dishonorable variants that established the low status of the people described.[113]

More was at stake than mere insult; these allegations reflected systemic ideas that civility manifested in the ability to transform nature in particular ways, and in doing so, to create a "refined and complex way of life" testifying to the use of reason and understanding of natural law.[114] If Icelanders relied on foods preserved by drying rather than salt, had little use of fermented drinks, or built with whale bone, lived in caves, and shared their dwellings with

---

undigested and rawe against our nation, in his fourth booke of Cosmographie cap. 8" (Jónsson, "Briefe commentarie of Island," 1: 578).
 111 Ibid., 1: 580–4.
 112 Koester, "Power of Insult," 20; Jónsson, "Briefe commentarie of Island," 1: 588.
 113 Koester, "Power of Insult," 20–1. For an expansive discussion of these categories and hierarchies in European views of New World societies, see also Pagden, *Fall of Natural Man*, chap. 4.
 114 Francisco de Vitoria, *De temperantia* (1537), cited in Pagden, *Fall of Natural Man*, 88.

livestock, these customs could be seen not simply as adaptations to a particular environment, but as a failure to transform that environment, a failure to *be* cultivated. Borough's characterization of Indigenous Siberians in terms of negation and disorder echoes in allegations about the supposed absence of practices like fermentation and the use of money, or the gross and improper behaviours associated with the seasonal fishery. On a broader scale, the evaluative categories of this discourse, in turn, could be deployed – and were deployed elsewhere – to justify the dispossession or subjection of societies that failed to be or seem civil enough.

In the North Atlantic, however, as Karen Oslund notes, "It was not only the Europeans who had the privilege of observing the natives but the natives who looked back at Europe."[115] If location, environmental conditions, and an economy centred on marine resources left Iceland subject to insult and misrepresentation, it remained a country with a literate, Christian population of European descent, endowed with a printing press and the wherewithal to send scholars such as Jónsson to study – and publish – on the continent (where Jónsson's work was originally published). Citing Iceland's chronicles and ancient records, Jónsson could provide a list of Icelandic bishops dating back to 1056. Even better, a "sincere and simple" Icelandic Christianity had originally been implanted before the "poison of poperie" had infected the church, and the Reformation had since restored this original purity of doctrine.[116] The same language of "holy simplicitie" with which Jónsson celebrated Icelandic Christianity could also be deployed to manage the poverty of its material environment. A quotation from Saxo Grammaticus provided useful framing, claiming of Icelanders that "by reason of the native barrenness of their soile, wanting nourishments of riot, they do exercise the duties of continuall sobrietie, and use to bestow all the time of their life in the knowledge of other mens exploits, they supply their want by their wit."[117] The positive case set forth in "Briefe commentarie" rested on the virtuous austerity and ingenuity of Icelandic life, and was supported (as Hakluyt emphasized) by the very fact of its authorship.

Yet even as he placed Iceland on a knowable map rather than at an infinite distance, Jónsson adopted a conceptual schema that situated it on the European periphery, "in the extreme northerly parts almost of the whole earth." His privative list – "we have no corne, nor meale, nor yet salt" – echoes Borough,

---

115 Oslund, *Iceland Imagined*, 18.
116 Jónsson, "Briefe commentarie of Island," 1: 570–6.
117 Ibid., 1: 573

and indeed a long tradition associating such strings of negatives with societies in a pre-civil condition.[118] And indeed, in his prefatory supplication to Christian IV, Jónsson complained that "many ... things ... are wanting in our country," petitioning the monarch for remedy: presumably, these include some of the lacks described in his texts, practically and symbolically valuable goods such as grain for bread and wood for building.[119] Although affirming that "Our wits are not altogether so grosse and barren, as the philosophers seeme to assigne unto this our aier, and these nourishments," he complained (or conceded) that "envious poverty" prevented more Icelanders from proving in action that the air and diet of their country did not preclude cultivation.[120] The Iceland represented in Jónsson's corrected account may have served as reassurance that civility *could* flourish in the kind of northern lands which had been "reserved for the English nation to possesse."[121] As the qualification suggests, Jónsson's defence nonetheless largely accepted that North Atlantic environment and society could be characterized in terms of distance, scarcity, and absence.

Like Jónsson, Hakluyt made a defensive case for his northern, Protestant nation. The originating impulse for *Principal Navigations* itself was indeed to respond to "the obloquy of our nation," as Hakluyt explained in the 1589 dedication:

I both heard in speech, and read in books other nations miraculously extolled for their discoveries and notable enterprises by sea, but the English of all others for their sluggish security, and continual neglect of the like attempts especially in so long and happy a time of peace, either ignominiously reported, or exceedingly condemned ... Thus both hearing, and reading the obloquy of our nation, and finding few or none of our own men able to reply herein: and further, not seeing any man to have care to recommend to the world, the industrious labors, and painful travels of our country men: for stopping the mouths of the reproachers, myself ... determined notwithstanding all difficulties, to undertake the burden of that work.[122]

118 Ibid., 1: 551, 558.
119 Ibid., 1: 551. Jónsson refers to "letters supplicatory of the chiefe men of our nation" for particulars.
120 Ibid., 1: 588.
121 Marginal comment, Hayes, "Voyage by Sir Humfrey Gilbert," 3: 144.
122 Hakluyt, "Epistle Dedicatorie (1589)," sig. *2r–v.

One would not want to press the analogy too far: early modern England was no longer the remote, cold, and backward periphery it may have been for the ancient Mediterranean world, and Hakluyt's project was to make the positive case for his countrymen's "painful travels" as expansively as possible rather than to defend England itself as a temperate place of abundance and civility. But there is one aspect in which it may be productive to dwell on the analogy with Iceland a moment longer.

The distribution of Icelandic materials within *Principal Navigations* testifies to its uncertain place in early modern geography. Hakluyt put materials on Iceland in both the first and last volume of his compilation: definitively in the North, but straddling East and West, Eurasian and North American space. Jónsson's text itself invites readers to consider whether Iceland formed part of Europe, albeit a peripheral part, or belonged to some other natural and cultural order; to consider, in effect, where we draw the lines. Oslund has argued, across a longer time-span, that Iceland has occupied a liminal space in the "mental geographies" of Europeans, calling basic categories of thought into question: "in the North Atlantic, a region considered both 'close' and 'small' in the European imagination, the categories of 'self' and 'other,' 'home' and 'away' became less distinct."[123] Within volume 1, the "Briefe commentarie" bridges materials on the distant voyages sponsored by the Muscovy Company and two final documents that return the geographical focus of the volume to European waters. While volume 1 concludes with English maritime history in its most triumphalist form, this lengthy, ante-penultimate document on Iceland recalls some of the boundary issues we have already encountered between its opening and closing pages, and the changing definitions of near and far, us and them that can be traced in Hakluyt's selection of materials.

LOOKING FORWARD

If Pet and Jackman had reached Beijing in 1580, the first volume of Hakluyt's collection might have concluded very differently. Such contacts would have fulfilled the expectation Hakluyt voiced in a 1587 dedication to Sir Walter Ralegh, that English voyagers would "throw open the doors to China."[124] Considerations of place and time, if consistently applied, might have also resulted in a volume whose final pages looked quite different. But they were not applied, yielding to a different kind of consideration altogether. Jónsson's

---

123 Cronon, "Foreword," xi; Oslund, *Iceland Imagined*, 9.
124 Hakluyt, "Epistle Dedicatorie to Sir Walter Ralegh, 1587," 3: 301.

narrative is followed by an account of the 1588 Armada battle by Emanuel van Meteren and, in some copies, an account of the 1596 sack of Cádiz, drawn from a manuscript narrative by Roger Marbecke. Neither of these two narratives sits easily within the volume's spatio-temporal parameters for post-medieval voyages: van Meteren's narrative, taking place off the coast of England, contravenes a principle implicitly governing the rest of the volume (and collection), that domestic "voyages" and "traffiques" were to be included only for periods before 1500. On the basis of geography, Marbecke's account of the voyage to Cádiz would be more appropriately located in volume 2 of the collection among voyages to the south and southeast "without the strait of Gibraltar," where it would sit alongside Anthony Wingfield's account of the "Portugal voyage" of 1589 and other geographically and topically similar materials.

Both the Armada battle and the voyage to Cádiz pertained to the Lord Admiral Charles Howard, who was both the dedicatee of Hakluyt's volume and his brother's patron. Their appearance functions as a compliment to him, and appears to turn the volume back towards the nationally focused history exemplified in a pure form by the conquests of Arthur on page 1. Yet the apparent coherence of such a summary is also somewhat deceptive. The presence of the Cádiz narrative in only some copies of *Principal Navigations* registers an official sense that the circulation of narrative about a contentious and debated enterprise might not serve the national interest. Hakluyt's interest in telling the Cádiz story, alongside the state's interest in controlling its circulation, indicates how difficult it was to decide either what the story was, or whose interests it served. The defeat of the Armada could more safely be represented as a victory for national unity as well as over a national enemy. Yet Hakluyt's decision to use material translated from another language and from the history of another country (the *Historia Belgica*) adds a layer of complexity to its representation in the collection.[125] The unruliness of Hakluyt's organizing categories defies mapping to a neutral, coordinate-based system; the paratextual category of "the North" was both shaped by the actual vectors of English travel, and inflected by the conditions of the editor's patronage, affiliation, and access. Considering the end of volume 1, one can't help observing how unsatisfactory is *any* single account of what belongs in a volume on the North, and why.

---

125 By some measures out of place in volume 1, these texts will call for more detailed scrutiny later in this study, along with other documents from the Anglo–Spanish sea war (chapter 7).

PART TWO

South and Southeast

THE SECOND VOLVME OF THE PRINCIPAL NA-VIGATIONS, VOYAGES, TRAF-

fiques and Discoueries of the *English Nation*, made by Sea or ouer-land, to the South and South-east parts of the World, at any time within the compasse of these 1600. yeres: Diuided into two seuerall parts:

Whereof the first containeth the personall trauels, &c. of the *English*, through and within the Streight of *Gibraltar*, to *Alger*, *Tunis*, and *Tripolis* in *Barbary*, to *Alexandria* and *Cairo* in *AEgypt*, to the Isles of *Sicilia*, *Zante*, *Candia*, *Rhodus*, *Cyprus*, and *Chio*, to the Citie of *Constantinople*, to diuers parts of *Asia minor*, to *Syria* and *Armenia*, to *Ierusalem*, and other places in *Iudæa*; As also to *Arabia*, downe the Riuer of *Euphrates*, to *Babylon* and *Balsara*, and so through the *Persian* gulph to *Ormuz*, *Chaul*, *Goa*, and to many Ilands adioyning vpon the South parts of *Asia*; And likewise from *Goa* to *Cambaia*, and to all the dominions of *Zelabdim Echebar* the great *Mogor*, to the mighty Riuer of *Ganges*, to *Bengala*, *Aracan*, *Bacola*, and *Chonderi*, to *Pegu*, to *Iamahai* in the kingdome of *Siam*, and almost to the very frontiers of *China*.

The second comprehendeth the *Voyages*, *Trafficks*, &c. of the *English Nation*, made without the Streight of *Gibraltar*, to the Islands of the *Açores*, of *Porto Santo*, *Madera*, and the *Canaries*, to the kingdomes of *Barbary*, to the Isles of *Capo Verde*, to the Riuers of *Senega*, *Gambra*, *Madrabumba*, and *Sierra Leona*, to the coast of *Guinea* and *Benin*, to the Isles of *S. Thomé* and *Santa Helena*, to the parts about the Cape of *Buena Esperança*, to *Quitangone* neere *Mozambique*, to the Isles of *Comoro* and *Zanzibar*, to the citie of *Goa*, beyond *Cape Comori*, to the Isles of *Nicubar*, *Gomes Polo*, and *Pulo Pinaom*, to the maine land of *Malacca*, and to the kingdome of *Iunsalaon*.

¶ By RICHARD HACKLVYT Preacher, and sometime Student of Christ-Church in Oxford.

¶ Imprinted at London by *George Bishop*, *Ralph Newbery*, and *Robert Barker*.
ANNO 1599.

5

The Levant and Beyond: Duration, Interruption, Repetition

WITH VOLUME 2, WE LEAVE NORTHERN EUROPE BEHIND. Hakluyt divided the second volume of *Principal Navigations* into two parts, focused respectively on voyages to the southeast "within" and "without" the Strait of Gibraltar; this bifurcation used the routes taken by travellers as a way of organizing the vast geographical scope of his materials, which range from the Azores to Japan.[1] The hodological (or path-governed) division of materials in volume 2 had several consequences for the compilation's representations *of* geography: each part of the volume offers clusters of materials on a particular region (the Ottoman Empire in part 1, West Africa in part 2), along with a wider distribution of other sources. The strongest effect of elevating route over region comes with materials relating to Southeast Asia. Travel to Southeast Asia begun from the Mediterranean and proceeding over land falls in the first half of the volume 2, while travel to the same region by sea, around the tip of Africa, falls in the second half. Hakluyt's ordering also produced some other, second-order consequences in the temporal span of the volume's two parts. Materials in the second half of volume 2 largely date to after 1550, when London merchants inaugurated a series of risky and challenging voyages to West Africa. The first half of volume 2, by contrast, begins in the fourth century, defining a more expansive temporal reach and placing the commercial and diplomatic activities of Hakluyt's own day in dialogue with different and older modes of encounter. Covering the eastern Mediterranean and all the regions that English travellers contacted by travelling through the Mediterranean to the East, its materials include pilgrimages, crusades, trade and diplomacy with the Ottoman Empire,

---

[1] For additional detail, see the overview of each volume's structure in my introduction.

and more distant commercial exploration across the Ottoman Empire and Persia into India and Southeast Asia.[2]

This chapter examines the first half of the volume: travel and trade through the Mediterranean. This temporally expansive set of materials also foregrounds time as an organizing principle, both in the volume introduction and in the categories of the paratext. All of *Principal Navigations* is organized by chronology at some scale, but the explicit emphasis in volume 2(i) on time and temporality – temporal sequence, duration, discontinuity, or repetition – stands out as distinctive within the compilation. Temporal categories appear prominently in the volume's opening pages; the "Catalogue of voyages" for 2(i), for instance, distinguishes "Voyages before the Conquest" from "Voyages after the Conquest." These distinctively temporal categories responded in part to the long duration of English knowledge about the circum-Mediterranean world; contact with Muscovy or the Americas, by contrast, was too recent to be organized into distinct eras. Indeed, the Levant itself was perceived by English travellers as old, its landscapes layered with ruins and deposits that materialized an impressive temporal depth. John Lok wrote of Cyprus, for example, that "when they digge, plowe, or trench they finde sometimes olde antient coines, some of golde, some of silver, and some of copper, yea and many tombes and vautes with sepulchers in them." John Evesham described modern Alexandria as literally hollow, "an old thing decayed or ruinated, having bene a faire and great citie neere two miles in length, being all vauted underneath for provision of fresh water." Laurence Aldersey wrote that "the part that is destroyed of [the city], is sixe times more then that part which standeth."[3] English presence in the circum-Mediterranean world was also of considerable antiquity. Hakluyt wrote in the dedication to *PN* (1589) that "the *oldest* travels as well of the ancient Britains, as of the English, were ordinarie to Judea which is in Asia, termed by them the Holy land" (emphasis mine).[4] The earlier version of the compilation, *PN* (1589), opened to the story of Empress Helena's pilgrimage in the fourth century CE; early dates for the accounts of pilgrimage and crusade that would occupy the opening pages of *PN* (1598–1600), volume 2, had accorded them pride

---

2 The geographical extent of volume 2(i) also coincides fairly closely with regions mentioned in the letters patent granted to the Levant Company (Elizabeth I, "Second Letters Patents to English Merchants for the Levant, 1592," 297).

3 "Voyage of M. John Lok," 108; "Voyage of M. John Evesham 1586," 281; "Voyage of M. Laurence Aldersey, 1586," 284.

4 Hakluyt, "Preface to the Reader (1589)," sig. *3v.

of place in the first edition. The second edition as a whole demoted the importance of time, reversing the order of presentation for materials on the Southeast and on the North so that the compilation opens with the conquests of King Arthur rather than Helena's earlier pilgrimage; within volume 2(i), however, time retains its organizing importance.

The eras into which Hakluyt organizes his materials in 2(i) did more than simply organize an especially wide temporal distribution (as, in volume 3, a larger number of geographical headings organize a larger number of sources). Hakluyt's epistle dedicatory indicates that the boundary of the Norman Conquest, which divides materials in the "Catalogue," also marked off distinct modes of engagement. Narratives of pilgrimage and enriching travel were dated to the years before "the comming of the Normans, in the yeere 1096 [*sic.*]"; after 1066, travel to the east was focused on crusade – "the succour of Jerusalem," and the expulsion of "Saracens and Mahumetans" by military means. Hakluyt distinguished these two earlier forms of travel to the Levant, whether purely devotional or (also) military, from the commercial and diplomatic travel of his own time. The dedication dates this third phase by "our auncient trade and traffique with … the Ilands of Sicilie, Candie, and Sio, which … I find to have bene begun in the yeere 1511."[5] Drawing lines between time-bound modes of engagement with the Muslim world – first pilgrimage, then crusade, now diplomacy and trade – afforded Hakluyt a way to join materials that were in other ways uncomfortable neighbours. The pre-Reformation practice of pilgrimage challenged Protestant identity even as it extended English travel centuries back in time; religious conflict, which generated narratives of heroic action and endurance against perfidious enemies, provided forms of symbolic profit that Hakluyt was not willing to relinquish even while he celebrated the "new trade with Turkes and unbelievers" undertaken in the second half of the sixteenth century. Behind this sequence of differentiated modes of engagement were historical and geopolitical realities left silent by the editor: perhaps the largest of these was the Reformation, consequential for devotional practices like pilgrimage and religious war, as well as for the political and economic conditions that led England to look for new allies and markets in the East.

Hakluyt's temporal categories, with their chronology of pilgrimage, conflict, and commerce, invite both attention and objective scrutiny. The division of materials by chronological categories in Hakluyt's contents list ("Voyages

---

5 Hakluyt, "Epistle Dedicatorie (1599)," 2(i): sig. *3r.

before the Conquest ... Voyages since the Conquest"), and his description of English trade in the Mediterranean as "auncient," "new," or "interrupted," foregrounds the *dis*continuities of English contacts with the Levant as well as their long temporal duration.[6] Yet the clean conceptual lines of the divisions sketched by the editor – first pilgrimage, then military conflict, followed in modern times by commerce – are blurred by the materials they claim to organize. Accounts of pilgrimages by British bishops in 1231 and 1417 are interspersed among the later military narratives, and an excerpt from William Camden's *Brittania* (1594) with mentions of British participation in the ancient wars of Europe actually precedes John Bale's account of the empress Helena's pilgrimage, no longer the opening document on the region.[7] Siege and captivity narratives, contemporaneous with the reinvigoration of English commerce with the eastern Mediterranean, extend the story of religious conflict into Hakluyt's own day, while English travellers continued to travel the pilgrimage route to and within the Holy Land, even after the Reformation discredited pilgrimage as a devotional practice.[8]

England's diplomatic and commercial relations with the Ottoman Empire after 1577 generated an archive to which Hakluyt appears to have had excellent access; his editorial sensitivity to the interests of the Levant Company (or at least some members of it) amplifies our sense of his close connections with merchants trading in the region.[9] Yet while the correspondence, charters, and price lists that fill out volume 2(i) amply document these contemporary modes of engagement, very little takes *narrative* form. In contrast to the Muscovy Company materials in volume 1, Hakluyt did not draw on this the archive for accounts of travel by merchants or navigators acting for the company, and the compilation includes almost no accounts of Constantinople or the Ottoman court to compare with the detailed and sometimes

---

6 Hakluyt refers to England's "auncient trade" with Sicily, Candia, and Chios, the "renuing ... of our interrupted trade in all the Levant," and "our new trade with Turkes and misbeleevers" (ibid., sig. *3r–v).

7 Camden, "Testimony."

8 Morris writes that post-Reformation England "no longer had the same reverence for pilgrimage to the Holy Land, and ... its geographical interests were being shaped by voyages on the great oceans"; Hakluyt's collection nonetheless "presented English exploration as being rooted in the former world of pilgrimage" (Morris, "Pilgrimage to Jerusalem," 161–2).

9 On Hakluyt's preferential treatment of the Turkey and Levant companies, see Payne, "Hakluyt's London," 19–20.

opinionated descriptions provided by Richard Chancellor or George Turberville.[10] Nor does this archive yield comparable instructions for company employees. The only instance of mercantile travel described at length in PN (1598–1600) was thus an unusual expedition narrated by Ralph Fitch, an attempt to access Indian and East Indian trade by a largely overland route; I will spend some time on this expedition and its associated documents, which give a sense of Elizabethan efforts to manage the dramatic risks and rewards evident in medieval materials on "the East." Finally, while Hakluyt provides no sample of the Turkey Company's or Levant Company's instructions, his elder cousin's papers yielded two sets of instructions he had prepared for commercial travellers to Constantinople. These have their own interest, going beyond many examples of the genre in reflecting openly on the implications of trade for national culture and identity. But we will follow Hakluyt's own temporal schema, and begin by following the thread of pilgrimage from the Middle Ages into post-Reformation travels to Jerusalem by the editor's near contemporaries.

PILGRIMAGE

1 "The voyage of Alexander Whiteman, alias Leucander, under Canutus the Dane, to Palestine, Anno 1020" (6)
2 "The voyage of Swanus one of the sons of Earl Godwin, unto Jerusalem, Anno 1052" (6)
3 "The voyage of Ingulphus, afterward Abbot of Croiland, unto Jerusalem, An. 1064" (8–10)
4 "The voyage of M. Laurence Aldersey to the cities of Jerusalem, and Tripolis, in the year 1581" (150–4)
5 "The voyage of M. John Lok to Jerusalem, Anno 1553"[11] (101–12)

The medieval materials populating the early pages of volume 2 share some of the challenging features presented by the early pages of volume 1. The brevity of the documents makes some of them more mentions than narratives:

---

10 See, however, short accounts of William Harborne's and Edward Barton's arrival and reception in Constantinople ("Voyage of the Susan, 1582," 169–71; Wrag, "Voyage to Constantinople, 1593").
11 Sources for the first three items are given by David and Alison Quinn in "Contents and Sources" as Bale, *Scriptorum Illustrium Maioris Brytanniae Catalogus*; Savile, *Rerum Anglicarum scriptores*.

for instance, one item consists merely of a three-sentence epitaph.[12] Extracted from longer sources, the earlier "voyages" are decontextualized fragments. "Voyages before the Conquest" gains in length by repetition, however; as in volume 1, with scattered exceptions, Hakluyt provided the medieval materials of volume 2(i) twice, in Latin and English. These older materials on the near East have a markedly different character from those on the North in another regard, however. The varied provenance of the early materials in volume 1 had things to tell us about the editor's priorities, relationships, and access to archives. The provenance of early materials in volume 2(i) is far more uniform, drawing on a small number of print compendia assembled by Hakluyt's contemporaries and near-contemporaries.[13]

In the volume's dedication, Hakluyt credited himself with the labour of discovering and assembling these medieval materials: "The memorable enterprises in part concealed, in part scattered, and for the most part unlooked after, I have brought together in the best Method and brevitie that I could devise."[14] The work was largely that of extracting from and occasionally comparing bulky print sources. Of the first twenty items listed in the volume's list of contents, for instance, eight were taken from Bale's *Scriptorum majoris Brytannie* (1557/1587), six from Henry Savile's *Rerum Anglicarum Scriptores* (1596), four from the *Chronicon Hierosolymitanum* (1583), and one from Raphael Holinshed's *Chronicles* (1587); only a passage from Procopius cannot be traced to one of these sources.[15] Hakluyt's one important manuscript source for this part of the compilation, the Asian travels of Friar Odoric (1316–30), came from the same volume in the Lumley library that contained

---

12 "Voyage of Peter Read to Tunis, 1538." This memorial of an Englishman knighted by Charles V for his efforts in the battle of Tunis, 1535, provides one example of the ways in which the volume's actual contents blur Hakluyt's temporal sequence of pilgrimage, crusade, and commerce.

13 In *PN* (1589), Hakluyt had relied almost exclusively on the prior compendium of John Bale. Quinn writes in his introduction to the modern edition of *PN* (1589), "it cannot be said that, in this area [of medieval travel] ... he either went very far afield to look for materials or showed any exceptional degree of critical competence in handling them"; they are reprinted "uncritically." For instance, Hakluyt "did not attempt to go behind Bale to his sources" (D. Quinn and Skelton, "Introduction," xxv). Quinn's judgement is echoed in C.F. Beckingham's essay on Hakluyt's treatment of the Near East ("Near East, North and North-East Africa," 1: 178). While a broader range of sources can be found in the 1599 volume, Hakluyt seems to have done little archival research on the region.

14 Hakluyt, "Epistle Dedicatorie (1599)," sig. *2v. On this metaphor, see the thoughtful discussion in Das, "Hakluyt's Two Indias."

15 Quinn and Quinn, "c&s."

the travels of William de Rubriquis, included in volume 1.[16] While this section of *PN* (1598–1600) marks a modest advance on the comparable part of the 1589 first edition in that it moves beyond the earlier edition's virtually exclusive reliance on Bale, the paucity of manuscript sources suggests that Hakluyt did little original research on travel to this region for the period before 1520.

The very "auncient" character of these travels may have suggested to the editor that little new work was necessary. Unlike the majority of the voyages collected in *PN* (1598–1600), the travels of volume 2(i) were not a journey into the unknown, but entered a region thoroughly documented in scripture and classical geography, as well as through a tradition of other travels and texts. As C.F. Beckingham notes, many of the countries encompassed in the first half of volume 2 "had belonged to the Roman Empire and had therefore been familiar to the geographers of classical antiquity ... They were not unexplored and there was no need for Hakluyt to collect topographical descriptions."[17] What Hakluyt really had to show, in this case, was less the new geographies apparent in other parts of the compilation than the simple fact of English activities, both recently and long ago, in the circum-Mediterranean world. That being so, his omission of any sampling from the substantial tradition of pre-Reformation pilgrimage literatures makes for a noteworthy if silent choice.[18]

Colm MacCrossan has pointed out that a significant dimension of Hakluyt's editorial work with his sources, and particularly excerpts from longer works, was to frame them homogeneously in the paratext, insisting on their identity, significance, and common shape as "voyages of ...," whatever the bearing of their original context.[19] Fragmentary though they are, many of the earlier texts in 2(i) might be said to have a more particular, if schematic, narrative shape within their broader, attributed identification as "voyages." In Hakluyt's presentation at least, travels to the East (especially though not only to the Holy Land) catalyzed a transformation of the traveller. Some travellers returned from their voyages with spiritual wealth. In 1020, under "Canutus the Dane," one Andrew Whiteman or Leucander had "an incredible desire to see those places with his eyes, wherein Christ our Sauiour performed and wrought all

---

16 BL MS Royal 14.C XIII.
17 Beckingham, "Near East, North and North-East Africa," 1: 176.
18 Pilgrimage narratives are discussed in Morris, "Pilgrimage to Jerusalem," 143–50.
19 MacCrossan, "Framing 'the English Nation,'" 143.

the mysteries of our redemption ... Whereupon he began his journey, and went to Jerusalem a witnesse of the miracles, preaching, and passion of Christ, and being againe returned into his countrey, he was made the aforesayd Abbat [of the Abbey of Ramsey]."[20] Whiteman satisfied his devotion by witnessing places that the narrative equates with the historical actions performed in them; he became a witness to those actions, and his appointment as abbot, following his return, seems to confirm the value of that witnessing. Other travels were characterized by material loss and mortification. In the next document, one Swanus arrived at Jerusalem in 1052 as the terminal point in a devolving career of alienation and criminality. "Of a perverse disposition, and faithlesse to the king," he disagreed with his family and "afterwards proov[ed] a pirate." Finally, guilty of murdering one or possibly two kinsmen, "he travailed unto Jerusalem: and in his return home, being taken by the Saracens, was beaten, and wounded unto death."[21] In this fragment, crime was followed by a mixture of punitive misfortune and penitential travel.[22]

A few pages later, one of the longer and more engaging early accounts – noted by Hakluyt as "right worthy of memorie" – combines the two trajectories of devotion and mortification. Ingulf's narrative was written (unusually) in the first person; Hakluyt excerpted the pilgrimage from a longer history of the Benedictine house at Croyland, printed by Savile, and now recognized as a fifteenth-century forgery attributed to the eleventh-century abbot Ingulf that drew on a mix of spurious and authentic charters.[23] According to the pseudo-Ingulf's narrative, he had been born in London, educated at Westminster and Oxford, and "excelled divers of mine equals" in the study of Aristotle and Cicero. These exceptional abilities were followed by disdain for his familial, social, and geographical origins, and a thirst for worldly advancement and its trappings. "As I grewe in age, disdayning my parents meane estate, and forsaking mine owne natiue soyle, I affected the Courts of kings

---

20 "Voyage of Alexander Whiteman," 6. David and Alison Quinn identify Bale as Hakluyt's source ("c&s").

21 "Voyage of Swanus," 6. MacCrossan discusses the Swanus excerpt in "Framing 'the English Nation,'" 143–5.

22 On pilgrimage as penance, see Sumption, *Pilgrimage*, chap. 7. Hakluyt's selection from the *Chronicle of Man* notes the penitential pilgrimage of Godred Crovan's son Lagman, who "repenting him that he had put out the eyes of his brother, did of his owne accord relinquish his kingdome, and taking upon himself the crosse, he went on pilgrimage to Jerusalem, in which journey also he died" (Camden, "Chronicle of the Kings of Man," 1: 10).

23 See Hakluyt, "Epistle Dedicatorie (1599)," sig. *2r; King, "Ingulf."

and princes, and was desirous to be clad in silke, and to weare brave and costly attire."[24] Attaching ("intruding") himself into the company of William I, then Duke of Normandy, Ingulf left London with him to become his secretary, and governed William's court. But his restlessness and ambition were not yet satisfied: "being carried with a youthfull heat and lustie humour, I began to be wearie even of this place, wherein I was advanced so high above my parentage, and with an inconstant minde, and affection too too ambitious, most vehemently aspired at all occasions to climbe higher." When he heard that "divers Archbishops of the Empire, and secular princes" had determined to go to Jerusalem on pilgrimage, inconstancy and ambition moved Ingulf to join them. The company he joined, some seven thousand strong, passed through Constantinople only to meet with thieves in Lycia. By these, they were despoiled of "infinite summes of money" and lost many of their people, barely escaping with their lives. (Little wonder Jerusalem appeared to these travellers as the "most wished citie.") Ingulf describes the visit to Jerusalem in terms of tears and sighs, both expressing devotion, and mourning over its damaged monuments. The pilgrims' burning desire to be washed in the sacred River Jordan was frustrated by the presence of more "theevish Arabians." Ingulf describes a return home which was at once joyful ("taking our leaves with unspeakable thanks") and castigated: "at length, of thirty horsemen which went out of Normandie fat, lusty, and frolique, we returned thither skarse twenty poore pilgrims of us, being all footmen, and consumed with leannesse to the bare bones."[25] The narrative takes shape as a moral tale organized around the pivot of Ingulf's pilgrimage; successive alienations from family, class, country, and patron, caused by pride, led to a material and spiritual mortification which brought Ingulf's restless movement to a proper end.

These travels to Jerusalem, by Whiteman, Swanus, and Ingulf, are surrounded by accounts of travel further east and narratives of secular enrichment, material and intellectual. Sighelmus, a bishop of Sherborne said to have been sent by King Alfred to visit Saint Thomas of India in 883, returned with "many strange and precious unions and costly spyces." John Eriugena allegedly returned from studies in Athens and France replete with the knowledge of Greek, Chaldean, Arabic, and Latin, translating Aristotle and tutoring King Alfred and his sons; his learning antagonized less elevated students at the Abbey of Malmesbury, who "misliking and hating him, rose against him,

---

24 "Voyage of Ingulphus," 9–10.
25 "Voyage of Ingulphus," 10.

and slue him in the yeere of Christ, 884."[26] For all their concision (or perhaps as an effect of it), this set of short narratives offer a sense of travel to the East as a transformational experience: the traveller brought back with him satisfied devotion, unheard-of riches, and a wealth of learning – or returned (if at all) altered by morally corrective dispossession and mortification. Hakluyt's selection and framing of his excerpts reinforced as repeated features of these narratives the paired elements of potentially rich material or spiritual profit, and the ordeal of danger, loss, and privation that accompanied such very distant voyages.[27] The extraordinary risks, drain on resources, and promise of transforming gain sharply distinguish these materials from the representation in volume 1 of early trade with Northern Europe, largely documented with the kinds of diplomatic materials, charters, and agreements that would dominate Hakluyt's later materials on contemporary trade in the East.

The earliest sixteenth-century trading voyage to the eastern Mediterranean recorded by Hakluyt nonetheless shares the earlier documents' sense of ordeal, and of extraordinary payoff; it also demonstrates the energy he could sometimes bring to bear on locating relevant materials. The voyage of the *Holy Crosse* and *Matthew Gonson* to Candia (Crete) and Chios in 1534 was taken down by Hakluyt from the account of a ship's cooper still living in 1592.[28] The cooper told him that the voyage took a full year to perform. The cargo returned was rich: oils, spices, "Turkey carpets," and "very excellent" wines "the like whereof were seeldome seemed before in England." Yet the casks were so weakened that they could not be unloaded, but had their contents drawn on shipboard, while the *Holy Crosse* was so "shaken" that it was laid up in dock and never sailed again. The English might have been trading directly

---

26 "Voyage of Sighelmus," 5; "Voyage of John Erigen," 6. Hakluyt's version of the life of John Scottus Eriugena was "almost entirely the invention of ... William of Malmesbury" (Marenbon, "John Scottus"). The historical John Scottus, conjecturally an Irishman, was attached to the court of Charlemagne but not otherwise said to have visited England.

27 Actual pilgrimages to the Holy Land were indeed a challenging undertaking. "Every hazard which a mediaeval traveller could encounter is exemplified in the experiences of those who walked three thousand miles or endured six weeks in a tiny, unstable boat, in order to visit the Holy Places." Not only taxing and dangerous, it also imposed a daunting cost: "A pilgrim who intended to visit Jerusalem in the style that befitted his station, might expect to pay at least a year's income" (Sumption, *Pilgrimage*, 181, 204, 206). Simply, "[t]ravel to Jerusalem was hugely more expensive and more dangerous" than other pilgrimages (Morris, "Pilgrimage to Jerusalem," 141).

28 Hakluyt, "Voyage to the Iles of Candia and Chio, 1534 [and] 1535." The editor also scanned merchants' ledgers for further evidence of English trade in the eastern Mediterranean.

with Chios since the middle of the fifteenth century, but this first voyage recorded in *PN* (1598–1600) gives the impression that trade with the region was just the same kind of dangerous and transformative venture sketched out by medieval voyages and travels in the opening pages of the volume.[29] (The difficulties encountered on the voyage of 1532 may have been transient; the second ship, the *Matthew Gonson*, reappears later in the volume making subsequent trading voyages.)[30]

The ordeals and reward of this early voyage may have been in part an artifact of narration, and the aim of commerce would certainly be to render such voyages *less* novel and venturesome. Another continuity with the earlier pilgrimage narratives calls for more sustained attention: the temporal boundary of the early sixteenth century did not end English travellers' interest in seeking out the sites of the Holy Land. Although the greatest number of sixteenth-century documents in volume 2(i) were produced by Elizabethan England's commercial and diplomatic contacts with the Ottoman world – clustering geographically around Constantinople, Aleppo, Tripolis, Alexandria, and Algiers – a small number of Englishmen continued to record travels to Jerusalem and Bethlehem, taking the opportunity to do as their pre-Reformation forebears had done.

The itineraries of these travellers retraced the steps of a discredited devotional practice.[31] Hakluyt's three post-Reformation travellers – John Lok (1553), Laurence Aldersey (1581), and John Eldred (1583), all Protestants – approached the task of narrating travel to the Holy Land in distinctly different ways. After Eldred's three trading voyages between Babylon and Aleppo,

---

29 Actually, sources suggest direct trade may have been underway "as early as 1446," and it remained an important entrepot for Anglo–Levantine trade until the Ottoman conquest of 1566 (Dimmock, *New Turkes*, 22, 65, citing İnalcık and Quataert, *Economic and Social History of the Ottoman Empire*, 364–5).

30 The Matthew Gonson brought John Lok – another of Hakluyt's authors – at least part of the way to Jerusalem in 1553 (Lok, "Voyage of M. John Lok," 2[i]: 101). Susan Skilliter comments that after 1553, English ships do appear to have abandoned trade in the Mediterranean for several decades, as Antwerp became a more favourable source for Eastern goods (Skilliter, *William Harborne*, 6, 11).

31 Eamon Duffy's major study of pre-Reformation devotion has a valuable if brief section on attitudes to pilgrimage through the early 1500s, although he focuses principally on domestic shrines (*Stripping of the Altars*, 190–200). Essays by Morris and Keeble shed light on the changing idea of pilgrimage in post-Reformation England (Morris, "Pilgrimage to Jerusalem," 160–3; Keeble, "'To Be a Pilgrim'"). See also Matthew Dimmock on Protestant travel to Jerusalem and Susan Skilliter on William Harborne's intention to visit the Holy Land (Dimmock, *New Turkes*, 1–4; Skilliter, *William Harborne*, 131–3).

"desirous to see other parts of the countrey," he took ship from Tripolis, and visited "Rama, Lycia, Gaza, Jerusalem, Bethleem ... the river of Jordan, and the sea or lake of Zodome." The bare list is all Eldred provides: "of which places because many others have published large discourses, I surcease to write."[32] Eldred's bare listing strips Jerusalem and Bethlehem of any distinction *as* place, and his comment that these places had already been sufficiently written about implies that what had been or could be said about them tended towards geographical description rather than the personal experience of the traveller. (Eldred nonetheless, like some other English travellers, apparently did not hesitate to become a knight of the Holy Sepulchre.)[33]

Lok and Aldersey both made personal trips for which Jerusalem itself was the ultimate destination, embarking from Venice on ships apparently dedicated to transporting pilgrims.[34] Both men were captains from merchant families, who can be traced elsewhere in the compilation on voyages of commerce and diplomacy. Both shaped their narratives largely in the form of journals, whose daily entries made them akin to the shipboard records each may have kept as mariners, as well as to the daily itineraries of earlier pilgrim narratives. (Lok's journal in particular is sprinkled with nautical terms and observations: "the 23 we sayled all the day long by the bowline.")[35] To short notes of progress in space – "we came to Rama, which is tenne Italian miles from Joppa" – both add practical information about the commodities, population, fortifications, and allegiances of places through which they passed, along with longer passages of observation, description, and anecdote: the Venetian carnival, the gardens of Augsburg, vultures, brawls among pilgrims, the rescue of a ship's cat fallen overboard.

Both men were also attentive to the multiple faiths encountered around the Mediterranean. Aldersey's journal devotes three paragraphs to his observation of Jewish worship at a Venetian synagogue, the only such account in the

---

32 Eldred, "Voyage of M. John Eldred, 1583," 2(i): 271.

33 Foster, *Travels of John Sanderson*, 290.

34 In the late middle ages, Venice had developed a business model for conveying pilgrims to and around the Holy Land, including transport by sea. Although pilgrim galleys appear to have been less frequent after 1500, Morris describes the system as "remarkably stable" through the early decades of the sixteenth century (Sumption, *Pilgrimage*, 185–92; Morris, "Pilgrimage to Jerusalem," 142). Susan Skilliter offers evidence of preparations for a similar voyage to Jerusalem by William Harborne, the English emissary in Constantinople, but believes it did not take place (*William Harborne*, 131–3).

35 Lok, "Voyage of M. John Lok," 2(i): 102. See, for instance, *Pylgrymage of Sir Richarde Guylforde Knyght*.

compilation: "For my further knowledge of these people, I went into their Sinagogue upon a Saturday ... and I found them in their service of prayers, very devoute: they receive the five bookes of Moses, and honour them by carying them about their Church, as the Papists doe their crosse ... The Psalmes they sing as wee doe, having no image, nor using any maner of idolatrie: their error is, that they beleeve not in Christ, nor yet receive the New Testament."[36] Lok, in turn, paid detailed attention to a variety of Christian sites and practices, noting particularly when Greek Christianity differed from Catholicism. At Zante, he observed "their Altares, Images, and other ornaments," with the comment that "the Greekes have nothing to doe with [Western Christian friars], nor they with the Greekes, for they differ very much in religion"; at Limisso, he attended a Greek service, "of the which to declare the whole order with the number of their ceremonious crossings, it were to long. Wherefore least I should offend any man, I leave it unwritten: but onely that I noted well, that in all their Communion or service, not one did ever kneele, nor yet in any of their Churches could I ever see any graven images, but painted or portrayed."[37] Both men's interest in the religious use of images and ceremonies marks them as post-Reformation observers, sharing a kind of ethnographic interest in "superstition" that equally features in early English accounts of Indigenous North American and Inuit religious practices. Both reported with reserve on purportedly miraculous objects, as when Lok "not disposed would not go" with other pilgrims who detoured to see a cross reputed to have formerly hung unsupported in the air, and now to contain "3. drops of our lordes blood ... (as they say)," as well as "a little crosse made of the crosse of Christ ... closed in the silver" which covered the larger cross. Lok reported what "was tolde mee by my fellow pilgrimes" about the object's structure with scrupulous non-commitment: "you must (if you will) beleeve it is so, for see it you cannot."[38]

In many ways, these two narratives – albeit temporally divided by the death of Edward VI, the return to Catholicism under Mary I, and the restoration of Protestantism under Elizabeth – are quite similar. Where they differ most sharply is at the centre: in their treatment of the devotional practices associated with pilgrimage and their narration of encounter with the sights of the Holy Land itself. Aldersey set himself sharply apart from the Catholic pilgrims with whom he travelled, and was in consequence singled out by his shipmates as an Englishman and a heretic. On the outward-bound voyage by sea, when

36 Aldersey, "Voyage of M. Laurence Aldersey, 1581," 2(i): 151.
37 Lok, "Voyage of M. John Lok," 2(i): 103, 105.
38 Ibid., 2(i): 109. See also Aldersey's comment on Mount Olivet, discussed below.

the purser brought an image of the Virgin for the passengers to kiss, Aldersey stepped aside and "would not see it"; finally confronted, he directly refused to comply, "whereupon there was a great stirre: the patron and all the friers were told of it, and every one saide that I was a Lutheran, and so called me."[39] His marked abstention from the religious practices of the group, and the objections of other pilgrims and the friars accompanying them, provided him with the opportunity to make explicit doctrinal points, and the narrative highlights these moments of open standing apart from the rest of the group, its practices, and its beliefs. "There was also a Gentleman, an Italian ... and he tolde me what they said of me, because, I would not sing, Salve Regina, and Ave Maria, as they did: I told them, that they that praied to so many, or sought helpe of any other, then of God the father, or of Jesus Christ his onely sonne, goe a wrong way to worke, and robbed God of his honour, and wrought their owne destructions."[40]

By contrast, Lok's description of the pilgrims' communal hymn-singing carries none of Aldersey's disputational edge, and indeed makes fun of a friar who refused to participate:

the pilgrimes after supper, in salutation of the holy lande, sange to the prayse of God, Te Deum laudamus, with Magnificat, and Benedictus, but in the shippe was a Frier of Santo Francisco, who for anger because he was not called and warned, would not sing with us, so that he stood so much upon his dignitie, that he forgot his simplicitie, and neglected his devotion to the holy land for that time, saying that first they ought to have called him yer they did beginne, because he was a Fryer, and had been there, and knewe the orders.[41]

The evidence here is on the order of a dog that didn't bark: Lok's *neutral* description of the customary communal singing at first sight of the Holy Land becomes interesting mostly against the background of Aldersey's insistently critical account. In fact, nowhere in the text does Lok explicitly distance himself from the Catholic pilgrims and practices that surround him, a point that will bear revisiting below.

---

39 Aldersey, "Voyage of M. Laurence Aldersey, 1581," 2(i): 152.

40 Ibid., 2(i): 152. Aldersey's admonitory remarks can be compared with another English merchant's remarks on mediators and images at a dinner in Mexico, reported in Tomson, "Voyage of Robert Tomson, 1555," 3: 452–3.

41 Lok, "Voyage of M. John Lok."

Aldersey was prolix in describing the Holy Land itself, providing a detailed itinerary:

> Going out of the valley of Josaphat we came to mount Olivet, where Christ praied unto his father before his death: and there is to be seene (as they tolde me) the water & blood that fell from the eyes of Christ. A litle higher upon the same mount is the place where the Apostles slept, and watched not. At the foot of the mount is the place where Christ was imprisoned.
>
> Upon the mountaine also is the place where Christ stood when he wept over Jerusalem, and where he ascended into heaven.
>
> Now having seene all these monuments, I with my company set [forth] from Jerusalem, the 20 day of August.[42]

Aldersey visited the "monuments" that were for others canonical sites of pilgrimage; the 1511 narrative of Sir Richard Guildford's pilgrimage provides a broadly comparable description, albeit with notes that visiting some places granted "clene remyssyon" or "plenary remyssyon" of sins.[43] As with Lok, Aldersey's skeptical reserve about miraculous materials appears briefly in his parenthetical comment about the visibility of Christ's blood and tears. But the process of travel to these sites itself required no distancing comment. Aldersey attached place to scriptural event: these were loci of memory linked to a sacred text. By contrast, Lok's narrative breaks off on his arrival at Jerusalem, and resumes only once he had departed again on the homeward journey. In place of narrative, Lok supplied an official document certifying that he had visited the appropriate sites: "What I did, and what places of devotion I visited in Jerusalem, and other parts of the Holy land … may be briefly seene in my Testimoniall, under the hand & seale of the Vicar generall of Mount Sion, which for the contentment of the Reader I thought good here to interlace."[44] (The testimonial follows, in Latin; it is not translated.) The places of devotion visited by Lok and itemized in the document were largely the same listed in Aldersey's text, but his experience and observations in Jerusalem are displaced

---

42 Aldersey, "Voyage of M. Laurence Aldersey, 1581," 2(i): 153.
43 See, for instance, *Pylgrymage of Sir Richarde Guylforde Knyght*, fo. xv.r, xvi.r.
44 Lok, "Voyage of M. John Lok," 2(i): 107.

by the form attesting his presence at what we can presume is a canonical inventory of sites.[45]

For the vicar general who signed the testimonial, Lok had fulfilled all the requirements of pilgrimage.[46] His inclusion of this document raises a question of how this post-Reformation traveller, himself, thought about his journey, and what kind of story he thought himself to be telling. Throughout the narrative, from his departure from Venice on "my voyage to Jerusalem in the Pilgrims shippe" to his embarkation from Jaffa "the 15. of September being come from *our pilgrimage*," Lok's position in relation to the pilgrims with whom he travelled appears distinctly more ambivalent than is true for Aldersey's narrative. Symptomatic of this uncertain identification are the pronouns of Lok's concluding paragraphs: "The 30 in the morning *we* rowed to Sant Nicolo a litle Iland hard by uninhabited, but only it hath a Monastery ... after masse *wee* returned and went aboord. This day the patron hired a Barke to imbarke the pilgrims for Venice, but *they* departed not. In the afternoone *we* went to see the towne of Parenzo ... After supper *wee* imbarked ourselves againe, and that night *wee* sayled towards Venice" (emphasis mine).[47] Both the date and name attached to this prosaic and reticent narrative render even more intriguing this uncertainty about the traveller's ambiguous representation of the kind of travel he had undertaken. Little is known of Lok as an individual, and nothing of his religious convictions beyond what may be discernible from this narrative; most of his immediate family, however, were convinced adherents to reformed Christianity, as well as early and energetic participants in overseas

---

45 Another English pilgrim, late in the reign of Elizabeth, reported receiving a similar document: "having my Pattent sealed with the great seale of the Pater Guardian, and another Letter pattent, shewing that I washed in the water of Jordane: the 31. of. March I departed from Jerusalem" (Timberlake, *True and Strange Discourse*, 24). Matthew Dimmock notes that Timberlake was nonetheless insistent on entering Jerusalem as an Englishman and a Protestant, despite the difficulties this entailed (Dimmock, *New Turkes*, 1–5).

46 Compare the case of William Malim, headmaster and translator, who like John Eldred was made a knight of the Holy Sepulchre in Jerusalem during travels to the Near East in 1564. Although his biographer notes that he also supported "features of the old religion," such as confession, during his tenure as headmaster of Eton, Malim does not appear to have encountered any religious difficulties either before or after his journey; in 1569, he was given a prebendary in the diocese of Lincoln, "an appointment most unusual for one who had not been ordained" (Wright, "Malym, William"). His translation of Nestore Martinengo's account of the Ottoman siege of Famagusta, "Report of the Siege and Taking of Famagosta, 1571," is discussed in the next part of this chapter.

47 Lok, "Voyage of M. John Lok," 2(i): 102, 107, 112.

trade. John's father, Sir William Lok, had "strongly Lutheran convictions"; his sister Rose and sister-in-law Anne both became religious exiles after the accession of Mary Tudor, while both his brother Thomas and Rose's husband, Anthony Hickman, were jailed for helping Protestants to emigrate. Thomas "was commonly known to have entertained Knox, Foxe and Hooper at his home."[48] Only one of the siblings adopted a less radical response: Henry Lok accommodated himself to Catholicism, although his wife, Anne, left him to join Knox in Geneva. The youngest brother, Michael – about whom much more is known, through his connection with Hakluyt and with the voyages of Martin Frobisher particularly – spent most of the 1550s abroad conducting family business from the Canaries to Candia, and returned only after the accession of Elizabeth. We know from John Lok's later undertakings that he did not emigrate during the reign of Mary, or if so not for long.

Lok left for Jerusalem in late March of 1553, in the waning months of Edward VI's reign; many of his family members would become religious exiles under Mary, but her accession and the restoration of Catholicism lay in the future. It was an odd moment for an Englishman to go on pilgrimage. The date may align with one of the few known facts about his life, however. Soon after returning from his long and difficult journey, Lok would undertake one of the earliest English voyages to Guinea, funded by his brother Thomas and brother-in-law Anthony Hickman; the first English voyage to West Africa in 1553 had been both impressively profitable and fatal to a large proportion of officers and crew. These were dangerous voyages; perhaps we should understand his devotional travel as undertaken in the shadow of mortality.[49]

Lok's account, with what we know about his background, positions him undecidably between Protestantism and a legacy of older practices. Unlike Eden's print account of the 1554 voyage, Lok's pilgrimage narrative appeared for the first time in *PN* (1598–1600). If, as David and Alison Quinn supposes, it was "probably obtained from Michael Lok," the narrative was among family papers, and its attention to the details of fortifications, population, commodities, and allegiances would seem to comport with the interests of a merchant

---

48 Details about the Lok family rely on McDermott, "Michael Lok, Mercer and Merchant Adventurer," 1: 119–46; Lowe, "Throckmorton, Rose."

49 Hakluyt printed accounts of both voyages as prepared by Richard Eden, and printed in his 1555 *Decades*. See chapter 6 for further discussion. The wills made by seamen before embarking for Guinea in the period are discussed in Hair and Alsop, *English Seaman and Traders in Guinea*.

family already invested in the Levant trade.[50] We might set Lok's narrative alongside others in which Englishmen travelled outside their own confessional world and encountered the demand, coercive or merely social, to declare or manifest their beliefs and allegiances: for instance, the narratives of Englishmen held captive in or returning from the Catholic or Islamic worlds, many of which can be found in Hakluyt's second and third volumes.[51] Perhaps what Lok's narrative can tell us is simply that the hermeneutic pressure to declare and make manifest confessional allegiances did not operate continuously.

If Lok's reticence operates at the level of the document, Hakluyt's editorial reticence on the question of pilgrimage also deserves to be noted. While he declined to draw on the English pre-Reformation pilgrimage literature, he also declined (not uncharacteristically) to comment on pilgrimage as a problematic devotional practice. Samuel Purchas's later compilation provides a double counter-example: in 1600, the chaplain William Biddulph wrote from Jerusalem, "this famous place, where our sweet Saviour Christ vouchsafed once his blessed bodily presence," that his voyage was "*not* moved as Pilgrims with any superstitious devotion to see Relikes, or worship such places as they account holy; but as Travellers and Merchants" (emphasis mine).[52] As editor, Purchas was even more intent on castigating such improper ways of travelling and worshipping. When another traveller to the Holy Land lamented that "the enemies of Christ [are] the Lords of his Sepulcher," Purchas appended an extensive footnote, decrying attention to place and relic: "as for his Sepulcher, He is risen, he is not there ... Pilgrimages are good, when we are thereby made Pilgrimes from the world and our selves. Thy selfe is the holyest

---

50 Quinn and Quinn, "c&s," 2: 426; McDermott, "Lok, Sir William."

51 For such narratives in the compilation, see inter alia, Foxe, "Voyage of John Foxe"; Saunders, "Voyage of The Jesus, 1582"; Tomson, "Voyage of Robert Tomson, 1555"; Chilton, "Voyage of M. John Chilton, 1568"; Hortop, "Travels of Job Hortop"; Philips, "Voyage of Miles Philips." The first two narratives are discussed in the next section of this chapter; those by Hortop and Philips in chapter 6. Many additional sources on Englishmen in the New World have been found in the Spanish archives, and translated in Nuttall, *New Light on Drake*; Wright, *Spanish Documents Concerning English Voyages to the Caribbean, 1527–1568*; Wright, *English Voyages to the Spanish Main*. On narratives by English captives in the Ottoman Empire, see the texts and a valuable introduction by Nabil Matar in Vitkus, *Piracy, Slavery, and Redemption*.

52 Biddulph, "Letter [...] from Jerusalem," in Purchas, *Pilgrimes*, 2(viii): 1345. Biddulph's letters from the Levant had been previously printed volume as *The travels of certaine Englishmen* (London, 1609). The doctrine of merit as acquired by pilgrimage is discussed in an exchange described by Biddulph between a French Protestant, a Jesuit, and two friars (ibid., 1351).

place thou canst visit, if with faith and repentance made the Lords Temple ... The Fathers did, and wise men still doe visite these places, by folly perverted to superstition ... when Place hath more place than Grace."[53] While two of Purchas's weighty books invoked the *metaphor* of pilgrimage in their titles – *Purchas his Pilgrimage* (London, 1613) and *Hakluytus Posthumus, or Purchas his Pilgrimes* (London, 1626) – the editor clearly sought to evacuate the term of its reference to literal travel undertaken as a devotional practice.[54] While Hakluyt's prefaces and the margins of his book do occasionally register pointed editorial comments, this failure to make his own position explicit was not uncharacteristic. John Fox's captivity narrative, discussed below, provides a different but equally salient example of Hakluyt's silence at a moment when one might expect a polemic point about confession to be made by an editor who was also an Anglican minister and worked closely, at times, with Elizabeth's government.

Lok's and Aldersey's travel along these time-worn routes may have differed in their approach to meaning, but both engaged the political terrain of the present as well as the marks of a biblical past. Lok's narrative notes the Ottoman imprint almost everywhere; as his ship travelled along the shifting border between Venetian and Ottoman control, he saw castles which were "the Turkes, and ... did belong to Venetians," and places where a town under Ottoman control and its Venetian neighbour "continually skirmish together with much slaughter." When Venetian ships were sighted, the company hoped "to knowe the newes of the Turkes armie." On arrival in the Holy Land, he was told "by one of the shippe that had beene a slave in Turkie" that wearing green would offend against custom, as it was the Prophet's colour.[55] The merchant Eldred, as well, noticed the relics of violence just passed, overwritten by friendly mercantile travel but still legible in the form of deliberately unrepaired war damage and inscriptions. "This towne of Hammah is fallen and falleth more and more to decay ... but because it cost many mens lives to win it, the Turke will not have it repaired; and hath written in the Arabian tongue over the castle gate, which standeth in the midst of the towne, these words: Cursed be

---

53 Sandys, "Relation of a Journey, 1610," in Purchas, *Pilgrimes*, 2(viii): 1311.

54 A critique of "Hierosolymitan Pilgrimages" by Purchas appears in *Pilgrimes*, 2(viii): 1251–2. On English Protestants and the metaphor of pilgrimage, see Keeble, "'To Be a Pilgrim.'"

55 Lok, "Voyage of M. John Lok," 2(i): 104, 103, 103, 106. On the complex relations between Venice and the Ottoman Empire, see İnalcık, *Ottoman Empire*, 133–7.

the father and the sonne that shall lay their hands to the repairing hereof."[56] All three of the "travels" to Jerusalem described above, planned and made by individuals to destinations of personal interest, grafted their itineraries onto travel enabled by English diplomatic and commercial engagement with the Ottoman Empire and its North African provinces. Commerce left Eldred in the Near East and brought Lok as far as Cádiz, although as we've seen, Aldersey and Lok took advantage of the pilgrim ships still travelling from Venice for the last phase of their journeys. For these three documents, the interests of commerce sat comfortably alongside the main thrust of the narrative. The same is not true for the narratives of siege and captivity that follow, whose emphasis on violence, faithlessness, and existential conflict runs counter to the peaceful Anglo–Ottoman engagement Hakluyt would celebrate and document so extensively in this volume. These narratives contribute to a strand of identity-defining violence that can also be found in Hakluyt's narratives of maritime encounters with Spanish ships and raids on Spanish settlements and towns, as well as some encounters with Indigenous peoples of America.[57] We might say that the symbolic profit accrued by telling these stories apparently mattered to the editor, even as he advanced a program of material profit built on peaceful engagement and commerce.

CONFLICT

1 T. Docwra, tr., "A relation of the siege and taking of the citie of Rhodes, by Sultan Soliman [...] Anno 1522" (72–95)
2 N. Martinengo, tr. W. Malim, "A report of the siege and taking of Famagusta by Mustafa Bassa Generall of the great Turkes army, Anno 1571"[58] (117–30)

---

56 Eldred, "Voyage of M. John Eldred, 1583," 2(i): 268.
57 Not all violence was narrated in this way – see, for instance, raids on African towns, discussed in chap. 5.
58 Malim travelled to Turkey in 1564 and spent at least eight months there before touring other islands and cities in the eastern Mediterranean; he was one of three English merchants resident in Constantinople in the 1560s. A manuscript account describes "his great travayle by sea and land unto Hierusalem. Where he was made knight of the sepulchre as appeareth by his letters patent dated at Jerusaleme the 13th day of September ... 1564" (BL, Harleian MS 1116, fol. 69v, cited in Wright, "Malym, William"; Dimmock, *New Turkes*, 61).

3 "The voyage of John Foxe to the Streit of Gibraltar [...] Anno 1563. And his worthy enterprise and delivering 266 Christians from the captivity of the Turks [...] Anno 1577" (131–6)
4 "The voyage of the ship called The Jesus, to Tripolis in Barbary, Anno 1583" (184–91)

C.F. Beckingham supposes that if Hakluyt had a consistent purpose in the first part of volume 2, it must have been "to publicize the English connection [with the Near East], to show what opportunities there were for English merchants, and to record information that might have been useful to them."[59] Such an intention, and the peaceful commerce and diplomacy that it recognized, existed in tension with accounts of a past that was organized very differently. Hakluyt's dedication recalls an older history of the "incredible devotion, courage and alacritie" with which his countrymen participated in Christian military expeditions against Islamic powers.[60] The editor proposes these actions as models for emulation, even if that emulation was displaced from the East towards the West; Hakluyt urged England's "couragious increasing youth" to find "convenient employments" in the colonization of mid-Atlantic North America ("Virginia"), if not Ireland and Guiana, rather than in war to the East.[61] This displacement sought to manage celebration of the "alacritie" with which Englishmen had participated in war against Islam alongside "the happie renuing and much increasing of our interrupted trade in all the Levant" that had rendered such martial activities and attitudes inopportune.[62] In the complex landscape of late-sixteenth-century Europe, the Islamic empire of the Ottomans had become England's trading partner and potential ally.[63]

Just as with pilgrimage, the temporal break that Hakluyt describes between earlier religious conflict and later commerce was not total. The privileges granted Anthony Jenkinson by Suleiman I in 1553 predated the Ottoman

---

59 Beckingham, "Near East, North and North-East Africa," 1: 176.
60 Hakluyt, "Epistle Dedicatorie (1599)," sig. *2r.
61 Ibid., sig. *2v.
62 Ibid., sig. *3r–v.
63 For accessible overviews of developments in the multi-part political, military, and commercial relationships of England, Spain, France, and the Ottoman Empire, see Brotton, *Sultan and the Queen*; MacLean and Matar, *Britain and the Islamic World*, chap. 2. Other recent work on the subject will be found in the footnotes below.

conquest of Famagusta, for instance, which is narrated in the volume.[64] Both in practice and in the compilation, conflict continued into the sixteenth century, carried forward by narratives of Christian cities under siege and English seamen taken captive, physically and spiritually coerced. The examples discussed below were interspersed among largely *non*-narrative documents of Anglo–Ottoman diplomatic and mercantile engagement from 1553 on: letters, charters, and "commandments" that document amicable back-and-forth between the Turkey and Levant companies and their employees, Elizabeth's government and its representatives, the Ottoman government in Constantinople, and *its* representatives along the shores of North Africa. As Henry Turner has argued, such non-narrative records constitute a biography of the trading company as a "corporate person" – as such, they are charged with meaning in the context of Hakluyt's project.[65] Yet as a reading experience, these bureaucratic records pale in comparison with the dramatic narratives of conflict that we will now examine, all but one composed and presented to engage a popular audience. These extend into the late-sixteenth-century aspects of the religious conflict relegated by Hakluyt's preface to a time before.

Despite the thematic affinities of the four narratives I have listed, they are not associated in the compilation. The "Epistle Dedicatorie" identifies the siege of Rhodes as an example of English participation in the crusading order of the Knights Hospitaller, while later in the volume the siege of Famagusta helps to explain the interruption of England's "ancient" trade into the eastern Mediterranean as an effect of the city's fall and the altered political lines that resulted. Thomas Saunders's complex narrative on the fates of the *Jesus*'s crew,

---

64 "The Safe Conduct Granted by Sultan Soliman the Great Turke, to M. Anthony Jenkinson at Alepo in Syria, Anno 1553." Matthew Dimmock points out that these privileges went "unremarked in contemporary texts," but took on "greater national significance later, and would accordingly be reproduced later" (Dimmock, *New Turkes*, 49; Skilliter, *William Harborne*, 7–9).

65 "Richard Hakluyt's *Principal Navigations* records nothing less than the historical emergence of what has become, for us, the most familiar type of corporate person: the commercial corporation, in the form of trading companies organized according to the joint-stock method. A major purpose of Hakluyt's work is to provide a series of case histories of these enormous artificial persons, integrating their biographies into the larger historical narrative that he is seeking to tell about English nationhood and gathering together the different forms in which this corporate person begins to 'speak'" (Turner, "Toward an Analysis of the Corporate Ego," 111). For an overview of Anglo–Ottoman commerce before and during the period, see İnalcık and Quataert, *Economic and Social History of the Ottoman Empire*, 364–72.

taken captive in Tripolis, is set among documents describing the Anglo–Ottoman diplomacy that eventually freed most of them. John Fox's narrative of his captivity and escape is neither mentioned in the dedication, nor associated with other contents. Yet taken as a group, these texts provide a counter-story that weaves through this first part of volume 2 and its general celebration of peaceful Anglo–Islamic cooperation, a tension that extends into Hakluyt's dedication.[66] In different ways, all four challenge the pursuit of alliance and exchange, and the implicit claim that the "story" of Anglo–Ottoman relations can be framed chiefly in those terms.

Hakluyt's two sixteenth-century accounts of Christian cities besieged by Ottoman armies – the fall of Rhodes in 1522, and the fall of Famagusta, Cyprus, in 1571 – precede the resumption of regular trade that he assigns to the late 1570s.[67] Both accounts were translated soon after the fact by Englishmen with personal knowledge of the places, though not of the events described. Thomas Docwra held several offices in the Order of Saint John of Jerusalem on Rhodes and retained strong connections in Rhodes after becoming head of the order in England in 1501.[68] William Malim, the headmaster of St Paul's School (and earlier of Eton), had visited Cyprus, Constantinople, Antioch, and other places in the Near East in 1564; his previously printed translation of Nestore Martinengo's narrative of the siege of Famagusta was done to oblige the Queen's master of requests: "who remembring that I had bene at *Cyprus,* was willing that my penne should travell about the Christian & Turkishe affayres."[69] Unusually, Hakluyt included all of Malim's prefatory material from

---

66 Hakluyt, "Epistle Dedicatorie (1599)," sig. *3r. On evidence for Hakluyt's attitudes towards Islam, including in PN (1589), see Dimmock, "Hakluyt's Multiple Faiths," 223–4.

67 Matthew Dimmock provides a broader account of how Ottoman–European conflicts in the sixteenth century were represented in print for English audiences (*New Turkes*, chap. 1). As a comparison of available sources makes apparent, Hakluyt presented readers with only a selection of possible events and sources. Robert Brenner notes that Hakluyt also did not cover trade with the Ottomans undertaken by Venice Company merchants in the 1570s (*Merchants and Revolution*, 18).

68 Chibi, "Docwra, Sir Thomas." Dimmock notes a contemporary narrative of the siege of Rhodes that Hakluyt did not use: *The begynnynge and foundacyon of the holy hospytall* (London, 1524) (*New Turkes*, 23n23). The first chapter of *New Turkes* provides a good idea of comparable materials on pilgrimage, siege, and naval war with the Ottomans that Hakluyt did not include: the siege of Malta, for instance, or the battle of Lepanto.

69 Martinengo, "Siege and Taking of Famagusta, 1571," 2(i): 119. The translation had previously appeared as Nestore Martinengo, *A true report of all the successe of Famagosta* (1572).

the quarto publication of 1572: under a modestly contracted version of the original title are included a long dedication to the Earl of Leicester detailing Malim's experiences, a brief preface, a poem, and a description of Cyprus. Hakluyt drew on a different preface by Malim for a brief notice of another traveller, which hints at some familiarity, whether immediate or through common acquaintances.[70]

Docwra's French source is unknown. The introduction to his translation frames its narrative unambiguously as confessional war: "the great siege, cruel oppugnation, and piteous taking of the noble and renowmed [*sic.*] citie of Rhodes," held by a crusading order of knights in aid of "noble pilgrimes of the holy Sepulchre of Jesu Christ," by "this cruell bloodshedder, enemie of our holy Christian faith, Sultan Soliman."[71] The narrative juxtaposes ideally active Christian knights, noblemen, and merchants – characterized by their diligence, care, leadership, and selflessness – with skilled and powerful Ottoman antagonists who in the course of the narrative are sporadically referred to in denigrating terms as "cursed enemies," "dogges," and "houndes."[72] The narrative is not uniformly organized by such determined "othering," however. During the truce that began negotiations for surrender, men on the opposing sides seem to come together in a manner that relies on shared values of valour, and honour, and generosity.

Our ambassadors took their leave ... And there was given to each of them a rich garment of branched velvet, with cloth of gold of the Turkish fashion. Then Acmek basha took sir Passin, and led him to his pavillion, and intreating him right well, caused him to abide all that day and night: and in eating and drinking they had many discourses of things done at the siege, questioning each with other. And among all other things our ambassadour demanded of Acmek, and prayed him to tell for trueth how many men died of the campe while the siege was laied. The said Basha sware upon his faith and certified, that they were dead of the campe of violent death ... 64,000.men or more, beside them that died of sickness, which were about another 40.or 50.thousand.[73]

---

70 "Voyage of Sir Thomas Chaloner, 1541," 2(i): 99. Malim provided a dedication to Thomas Chaloner, *De republica Anglorum* (London, 1579); see Beckingham, "Near East, North and North-East Africa," 1: 179.

71 Docwra, "Siege and Taking of the Citie of Rhodes, 1522," 2(i): 72. Rhodes was strategically significant to a series of Ottoman rulers; as a base for the Knights of Rhodes, it controlled access to the eastern Mediterranean (İnalcık, *Ottoman Empire*, 29, 128).

72 Docwra, "Siege and Taking of the Citie of Rhodes, 1522," 2(i): 84, 88, 95.

73 Ibid., 2(i): 91.

When the knights finally sued for peace, Suleiman offered generous terms of surrender – "he promised by his faith for to let [the Grand Master] go with all his knights" – and generally fulfilled his promises, a point that will be important in discussion of Malim's narrative. Nonetheless, because the narrator finds this clemency unintelligible in light of Suleiman's character as a "cruell bloodshedder," he explains Suleiman's magnanimity by appeal to divine intervention: "God blinded him and would not that he should know his might."[74]

The rhetoric of this text announces that at Rhodes, not only armies but kinds of people were facing off. Yet on closer examination, it is apparent that this heavily defended border between "Turk" and Christian was permeable, in practice, to a variety of different figures. As well as armies, there were spies and traitors: a Jewish physician and a disaffected Portuguese knight spied for the sultan, while the grand master sent out spies in Ottoman dress; there were defectors, in both directions: "a Spanish renegado" (i.e., apostate) defected back *from* the Ottoman army, while "an Albanese fled to the enemies campe"; and there were impersonators: an expedition of Christians dressed as Turks successfully passed in the Ottoman camp, drawing off a number of "volunteers" then taken prisoner (one man's fluency in Turkish helped). As this linguistic fluency suggests, the narrative is full of evidence indicating earlier traffic across national, confessional, and linguistic lines: janissaries were overheard muttering in Greek, and the emissary who came from Suleiman to propose terms was a Genoese Christian.[75] Already within the city's walls were a number of "Turkish" slaves, whose role was complex. The women, who were domestic servants, treacherously plotted to fire their masters' houses during the first assault on the walls. The men, though falsely accused of rising up, loyally "did great service," their contribution to the defence of Rhodes so great that when "almost all the slaves and laborers were dead and hurt," one commander argued, it was no longer possible for the city to be defended at all.[76] Finally some number of Rhodians proved to be baptized converts from Islam; they emerged into visibility only at the narrative's end, when under the treaty they were returned to Turkey. Even before the walls came down, the hard

---

74 Ibid., 2(i): 91, 94.

75 Ibid., 2(i): 73, 78; 80, 85; 80; 85, 88. On the problems and misprisions associated with the early modern usage of "Turk" as a blanket term for Muslims and for Ottoman subjects, see MacLean, *Looking East*, 6–8.

76 Docwra, "Siege and Taking of the Citie of Rhodes, 1522," 2(i): 79, 89. On the critical importance of these slaves to the city's defence, see also Docwra, ibid., 2(i): 80, 87.

perimeter of the city that the knights defended proved to be permeable in multiple directions. This landscape of hybrid identities and allegiances stands out in contrast with a rhetorical frame that assumes implacable opposition and the defence of boundaries.[77]

The narrative Malim translated and introduced was written fifty years later, well into the realm of Elizabeth and only a few years before the first dispatch of English emissaries to the Sultan. Yet its language of heroic and unified Christian opposition to a barbaric infidel doubles down on the crusading rhetoric of the Rhodes narrative. Malim writes: "It mooveth me much to remember the losse of those ... notable Ilands [Rhodes, Chios, and Cyprus], to the great discomfort of all Christendome, to those hellish Turkes, horseleeches of Christian blood." He promises to tell about the Ottomans' "cruelty and beastly behaviour," their "unfaithfulnesse and breach of promise," and the "Venetians manly courage in defence of themselves, and their fortresse." Malim claims personal knowledge of the "cruelty and beastly behaviour" described in Martinengo's text, "having bene in Turky amongst them more than eight monaths together."[78]

As with the first siege narrative, much of the text is structured under headings related to the progress of the siege – "The first assault," "The second assault," and so on – and its procedural account provides detail on the diligence and courage of various named persons within the city. The most dramatic element comes after hostilities were concluded, and surrender had been negotiated on (again) generous terms. After signing terms of the city's surrender, the Ottoman commander Mustafa invited his Christian counterpart Bragandine to pay him a visit, a moment that echoes the courteous exchange between Passin and Acmek Basha at Rhodes. Mustafa "was very desirous both

---

[77] While I make this point at the level of the document, it echoes the broader picture drawn by historians. See, for instance, Fernand Braudel: "between the two enemy religions, it would be unrealistic to imagine a watertight barrier. Men passed to and fro, indifferent to frontiers, states and creeds. They were more aware of the necesseties of shipping and trade, the hazards of war and piracy, the opportunities for complicity or betrayal provided by circumstances" (Braudel, *Mediterranean World*, 2: 759). For religious conversion and the specific case of England, see also Matar, *Islam in Britain*. For a stimulating account of "exchange across [the] geographical and material boundaries" of European Christianity and Islam in terms of art objects, images, and techniques, see Brotton and Jardine, *Global Interests*. For overviews of work on Anglo–Ottoman relations (and literature concerning them) in the period, see (inter alia) the introduction to Dimmock, *New Turkes*.

[78] Martinengo, "Siege and Taking of Famagusta, 1571," 2(i): 119.

to see and know him, for his great worthinesse and prowesse, that hee had tried to be in him, and in the other of his Captaines and Souldiers, of whose manhood and courage he would honourably report, where soever he came, as occasion should serve thereunto."[79] Bragandine responded to the invitation, with its appeal to a shared set of values – "worthinesse and prowesse," "manhood and courage" – by bringing his men, unarmed, to a friendly meeting. On this account, Mustafa, "upon a sudden picked a quarrel unto them, especially burdening that noble ... with an untruth" (that he had violated the truce): in what follows, Bragandine's companions are killed; the surviving soldiers stripped and made slaves; and Bragandine himself, after public rituals of degradation and humiliation, is flayed alive, his skin stuffed and exhibited in all the towns along the coast of Syria. A marginal comment generalizes Mustafa's actions as "just Turkish dealing, to speake and not to meane."[80] The torture and killing of Bragandine thus allow for an exemplary contrast between his "constancie" and the shifts of "Turkish dealing": "He was most cruelly flaied quicke: with so great constancie and faith ... that [Bragandine] never lost or abated any jot of his stedfast courage, being so farre from any fainting, that hee at that present with most stout heart reproched them, and spake much shame of [Mustafa's] most traiterous dealing in breaking of his faithfull promise. At the last without any kind of alteration of his constancie, he recommending his soule unto almightie God, gave up the ghost."[81] The identities which emerge from this narrative are fully oppositional ones; Christians behave faultlessly, while "Turkish" behaviour is characterized not only in terms of barbarous cruelty but also as false and duplicitous. Hakluyt himself highlights the narrative's polemic point about "the oath of a Mahumetan" in the volume's Epistle Dedicatory, indeed suggesting that he has "revived" the narrative in order "that the posteritie may never forget" that such oaths are not to be trusted.[82] The evident incoherence of such suspicion with the celebration and promotion of activities that depended precisely on the viability of contracts and diplomatic agreements across confessional lines remains unresolved.

79 Ibid., 2(i): 127.
80 Ibid., 2(i): 127. The annotation is copied from Malim's 1572 quarto; Hakluyt reproduced such marginalia selectively, as Julia Schleck has shown for the Saunders narrative discussed below (Schleck, *Telling True Tales of Islamic Lands*, 131–7).
81 Martinengo, "Siege and Taking of Famagusta, 1571," 2(i): 128.
82 Ibid., 2(i): 119; Hakluyt, "Epistle Dedicatorie (1599)," 2(i): sig. *3r.

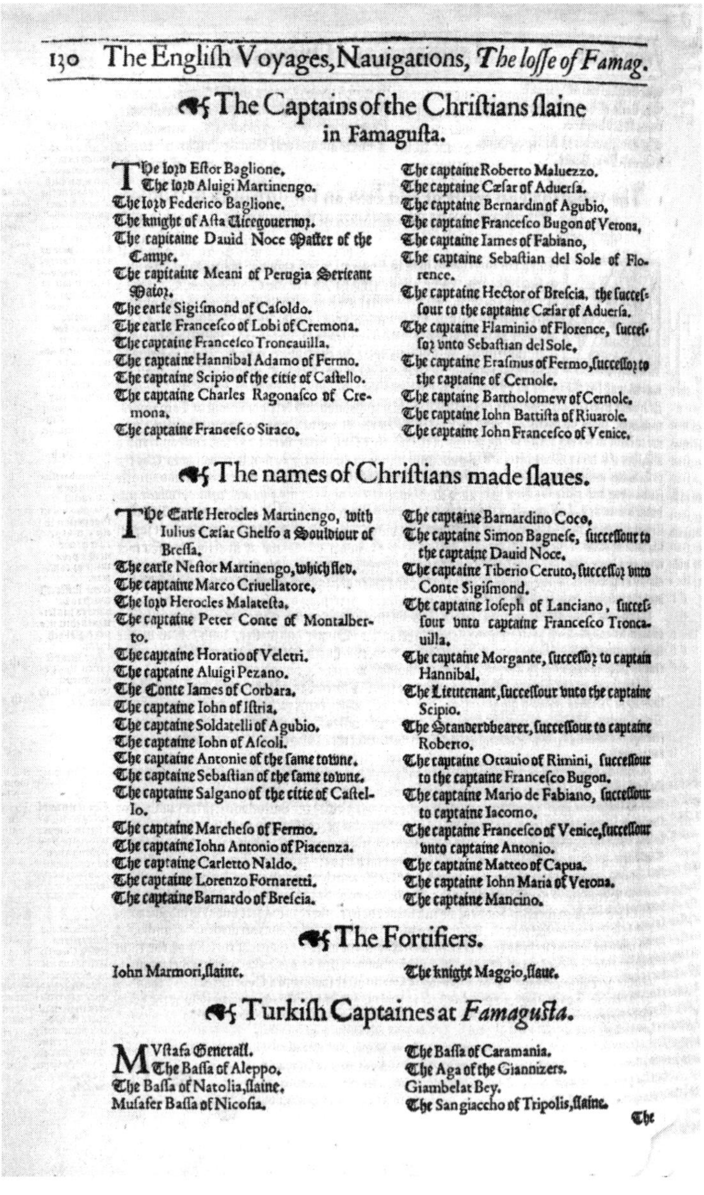

The Captains of the Christians slaine in Famagusta.

The lord Estor Baglione.
The lord Aluigi Martinengo.
The lord Federico Baglione.
The knight of Asta Vicegouernor.
The capitaine Dauid Noce Master of the Campe.
The capitaine Meani of Perugia Sericant Maior.
The earle Sigismond of Casoldo.
The earle Francesco of Lobi of Cremona.
The captaine Francesco Troncauilla.
The captaine Hannibal Adamo of Fermo.
The captaine Scipio of the citie of Castello.
The captaine Charles Ragonasco of Cremona.
The captaine Francesco Siraco.
The captaine Roberto Maluezzo.
The captaine Cæsar of Aduersa.
The captaine Bernardin of Agubio.
The captaine Francesco Bugon of Verona.
The captaine Iames of Fabiano.
The captaine Sebastian del Sole of Florence.
The captaine Hector of Brescia, the successour to the captaine Cæsar of Aduersa.
The captaine Flaminio of Florence, successor vnto Sebastian del Sole.
The captaine Erasmus of Fermo, successor to the captaine of Cernole.
The captaine Bartholomew of Cernole.
The captaine Iohn Battista of Riuarole.
The captaine Iohn Francesco of Venice.

The names of Christians made slaues.

The Earle Herocles Martinengo, with Iulius Cæsar Ghelso a Souldiour of Bressa.
The earle Nestor Martinengo, which fled.
The captaine Marco Criuellatore.
The lord Herocles Malatesta.
The captaine Peter Conte of Montalberto.
The captaine Horatio of Veletri.
The captaine Aluigi Pezano.
The Conte Iames of Corbara.
The captaine Iohn of Istria.
The captaine Soldatelli of Agubio.
The captaine Iohn of Ascoli.
The captaine Antonie of the same towne.
The captaine Sebastian of the same towne.
The captaine Salgano of the citie of Castello.
The captaine Marcheso of Fermo.
The captaine Iohn Antonio of Piacenza.
The captaine Carletto Naldo.
The captaine Lorenzo Fornaretti.
The captaine Barnardo of Brescia.
The captaine Barnardino Coco.
The captaine Simon Bagnese, successour to the captaine Dauid Noce.
The captaine Tiberio Ceruto, successor vnto Conte Sigismond.
The captaine Ioseph of Lanciano, successour vnto captaine Francesco Troncauilla.
The captaine Morgante, successor to captain Hannibal.
The Lieutenant, successour vnto the captaine Scipio.
The Standerdbearer, successour to captaine Roberto.
The captaine Octauio of Rimini, successour to the captaine Francesco Bugon.
The captaine Mario de Fabiano, successour to captaine Iacomo.
The captaine Francesco of Venice, successour vnto captaine Antonio.
The captaine Matteo of Capua.
The captaine Iohn Maria of Verona.
The captaine Mancino.

The Fortifiers.

Iohn Marmori, slaine.
The knight Maggio, slaue.

Turkish Captaines at *Famagusta*.

Mustafa Generall.
The Bassa of Aleppo.
The Bassa of Natolia, slaine.
Musafer Bassa of Nicosia.
The Bassa of Caramania.
The Aga of the Giannizers.
Giambelat Bey.
The Sangiaccho of Tripolis, slaine.

Figure 5.1 These lists of "the names of the captaines, and number of the people slaine, … likewise of them who were taken prisoners" after the Ottoman siege of Famagusta had been advertised on the title page of the pamphlet from which Hakluyt took his text.

Bragandine's resistance tells another, more implicit story: that the defeat of cities and bodies would never succeed in penetrating the core of the Christian self. Perhaps this story matters because while England had no strongholds to lose in the Mediterranean, resumption of direct trade by sea meant that, increasingly, English bodies were at risk of capture, with all that entailed. The experience of slavery was increasingly common for seamen in the sixteenth-century Mediterranean, with the galleys of both Muslim and Christian powers powered by enslaved rowers and a system of ransom that meant labour was not the only economic product of slavery.[83] A list of "the names of Christians made slaves" is provided at the conclusion of the account of Famagusta's fall, and Hakluyt also included two narratives of English mariners taken captive and enslaved by Ottoman counterparts. The captivity narratives of Fox and Saunders move the ground of violent opposition and resistance from the scale of the walled city to that of the ship's crew and, ultimately, the individual. These texts appear to be the earliest instances of a genre that would become increasingly popular; the two printed by Hakluyt are first and second on Nabil Matar's valuable list of English captivity narratives, 1577 to 1704, and a shorter narrative included in 2 (ii) is fifth on the list.[84] As Matar succinctly puts it, they are (like the narratives of siege warfare), "texts of confrontation between Christians and Muslims" animated by "religious/national purpose."[85] Like Malim's translation, both captivity narratives were published previously as quartos, although the Fox narrative survives only in a later version.[86] As we have seen, Hakluyt reproduced some of the editorializing marginalia from the original quarto edition of the fall of Famagusta, as well as the translator's prefatory material.

83 See, for example, Earle, *Corsairs of Malta and Barbary*, 12–13.
84 Matar, *Turks, Moors, and Englishmen*, 181–3. The shorter narrative is "Report of the Casting Away of the Tobie, 1593."
85 Matar, *Turks, Moors, and Englishmen*, 76.
86 Fox's narrative was entered in the Stationer's Register for 1579, though no extant copies of the 1579 quarto appear in the ESTC. An alternate version to Hakluyt's text later appeared as Anthony Munday, *The admirable deliverance of 266. Christians by John Reynard Englishman from the captivitie of the Turkes, who had been gally slaves many yeares in Alexandria* (London, 1608). Daniel Vitkus reproduces Hakluyt's text (with a helpful introduction) but adds a poem by Munday that is not present in Hakluyt's version or in the copy of the 1608 quarto reproduced in Early English Books Online (*Piracy, Slavery, and Redemption*, 70). Biographical evidence supports Munday's claim that "At Rome I was, when Fox did there arrive" to be presented to Pope Gregory XIII; he adds to his own testimony on Fox's veracity that "here's one was slave with him in thrall, / Lately returned unto our native land. / This witness can this matter perfect all" (Bergeron, "Munday, Anthony"; Vitkus, *Piracy, Slavery, and Redemption*, 70).

For the Saunders narrative, the only one of the two for which copies of the original survive, a much smaller proportion of the paratextual material accompanies the narrative into Hakluyt's compilation.[87] However, both narratives preserve unmistakably in their text a pointed moralizing of events characteristic of their original form. The narratives describe the fate of two ships' crews taken captive in Ottoman North Africa, and absorbed into regimes of forced maritime labour where they were subjected to violence, coercion, and indignity. (These regimes, in the circum-Mediterranean world, were organized along confessional lines; the Knights of Rhodes also engaged in slave taking from their base on Malta.) As the narratives suggest, the condition of enslaved captives in Ottoman North Africa varied widely.[88] Fox and others were able to move about with some freedom and practice trades; Martinengo had deliberately volunteered himself as a slave to improve his prospects.[89] The authors of both pamphlets nonetheless made escape from captivity into a providential narrative of deliverance.

"The woorthy enterprise of John Foxe an English man" begins with an attack by eight Ottoman gallies on an English ship trading into Spain in 1563. The crew resisted valiantly, knowing that their enemies' "mercy was nothing els but crueltie," and most intended to obey the boatswain's exhortation "to winne praise by death, rather then to live captives in misery and shame."[90] Nonetheless, they were overpowered and the survivors sent to the galleys. After thirteen or fourteen years, the gunner John Fox was one of only three Englishmen remaining among some two hundred and sixty odd Christian captives imprisoned in Alexandria for the winter while the galleys were in port.

Fox put his head together with another captive of some thirty years standing, Peter Unticaro, "a Spaniard borne, and a Christian" who had taken advantage of his captivity to run a "victualling house"; both men apparently had some freedom to come and go, Fox resourcefully earning a few extra meals here and there as a barber with the tacit permission of his jailor. The two agreed to take action against "the restraint of their libertie."[91] Recruiting

---

87 Saunders, *A True Discription and Breefe Discourse.* For discussion of the original quarto and analysis of changes made by Hakluyt, see Schleck, *Telling True Tales of Islamic Lands*, 128–45.

88 See, for instance, Matar, "Introduction"; *Turks, Moors, and Englishmen*, 78–81; Earle, *Corsairs of Malta and Barbary*, 80–6.

89 "I offred, and gave my selfe slave to one Sangiaccho del Bir" (Martinengo, "Siege and Taking of Famagusta, 1571," 2[i]: 128).

90 Foxe, "Voyage of John Foxe," 2(i): 131.

91 Ibid., 2(i): 132.

six other men, they gathered weapons, lured the permissive jail-keeper to them, and Fox killed him with a single blow of his rusty sword, addressing him in terms familiar from the siege narratives as "a bloodsucker of many a Christians blood." The conspirators released the other captives, fought their way through the guards, and seized a galley, which they took out to sea between the crossfire of two alerted forts. At sea, they survived famine to land at Gallipoli, Italy, where they sold the galley, divided the proceeds, and parted ways.

Daniel Vitkus comments that Fox's narrative as provided by Hakluyt "functions as an inspirational parable promoting the idea of divine favor for the 'Elect Nation' and its maritime enterprises."[92] Throughout, its author frames the experience of the captives in terms of scriptural parallels, and explains their vicissitudes as the result of divine intervention. When Fox and his companions achieve the impossible feat of sailing unscathed between the fire of two artillery batteries, like the Israelites at the Red Sea, Joshua at the walls of Jericho, or Daniel in the lion's den, they demonstrate that "such impossibilities can our God make possible." By contrast, the god of their opponents is "very much to blame, to suffer [the Turks] to receive such a gibe." [93] The hardships suffered by the men of the *Half-Moon* were not the dramatic martyrdom of Bragandine, but the common and protracted ones of forced labour and short commons; Fox's extraordinary endurance over a span of years is merely noted.[94] Yet though the Fox narrative lacks Martinengo's details of Ottoman cruelty and duplicity, its Old Testament rhetoric draws the line between Englishmen and Ottoman subjects with equivalent decisiveness, and it holds out a commensurate promise that even if cities and ships could not be fortified strongly enough to resist the Ottoman threat, the battle could be fought and won at the level of individual Christian men.

The second of the two captivity narratives tells a more complex story. Saunders's narrative describes the fate of the *Jesus* and its crew, taken captive at Tripoli (present-day Libya) in 1582.[95] The captivity narratives of Fox and Saunders originally appeared only a few years apart, in 1579 and 1587. Between those dates, however, fell the crucial, inflecting event of William Harborne's

---

92 Vitkus, *Piracy, Slavery, and Redemption*, 57.
93 Foxe, "Voyage of John Foxe," 2(1): 134.
94 Ibid., 2(i): 132.
95 The master of the *Jesus*, Andrew Diar, also served as master of the *Hopewell* on Martin Frobisher's 1578 voyage into the Arctic, an example of how wide and diverse the travels of English mariners could be in the period (McDermott, *Third Voyage of Martin Frobisher*, 34n5).

arrival in Constantinople as a credentialed factor and emissary. While Fox carved his way to freedom with only the help of a few motivated accomplices, the crew of the *Jesus* could call on the resources of the English and Ottoman states, as Hakluyt's selection of documents makes clear. The Saunders text is surrounded by the diplomatic correspondence that secured their freedom, as well as by documents describing Harborne's journey to Constantinople on his appointment as ambassador, Harborne's letters appointing English consuls at Alexandria and Tripolis, and so on. (Edward Barton, who served as Harborne's representative in freeing the prisoners, would succeed him as ambassador.) The correspondence implies that the *Jesus* was "stayed" and its master executed by a misunderstanding, and that the English had so organized their presence in the Ottoman world, and enjoyed such benevolent relations with its ruler, that the harassment experienced by its crew could occur only in marginal regions of the Ottoman dominions, and was easily redressed by an appeal to central power.[96]

The dissonance between the violence of captivity narratives and the implied neutrality of commerce was thus contained and, in a way, neutralized by the diplomacy that surrounded the story of the *Jesus*. Yet the narrative itself shows a number of complexities around matters of identity, resistance, and freedom that were fairly simple in the Fox narrative, recalling the blurred lines that were an unacknowledged part of Docwra's account of the siege of Rhodes.

Some basic outlines remain the same. Saunders calls out the "king" of Tripolis for repeatedly failing to honour promises: that he would trade with the English custom free, that he would reward a Spanish gunner who helped take the *Jesus*, that he would spare the master of the ship: "here all true Christians may see what trust a Christian man may put in an infidels promise."[97] Another lesson for Christian readers was to "see the wonderfull workes of God" shown in the judgments on those who harmed an English crew evidently under his protection: "there was none, neither Christian nor Turke that tooke the value of a peniworth of our goods from us, but perished both bodie and goods within seventeene moneths following.[98] The text itself complicates at least the first of these lessons, however: that untrustworthiness marked *non*-Christians. The *Jesus* was pursued in part because its French factor had smuggled aboard a European merchant avoiding his debt to an Ottoman merchant

---

96 This point was indeed advanced by Hakluyt's selection of documents on the Levant more broadly, and not only by materials relating to the voyage of the *Jesus*.
97 Saunders, "Voyage of The Jesus, 1582," 2(i): 185–7.
98 Ibid., 2(i): 186, 187.

who had consigned goods to him; the same factor had also cheated a Bristol merchant who loaned him money.[99] When the ship was taken and ransacked, "Christian caitifes likewise ... made spoyle of our goods, and used us as ill as the Turkes did." The sentence hardly makes clear which meaning of "caitiff" applies: are these *captives*, acting under compulsion, or *wretches, villains*, perhaps European men who had given their voluntary allegiance to the Ottoman state and were no longer Christians except by origin?[100] Or both? The one act of spoil Saunders details at some length does not clear up the question: an Ottoman gunner seizes a Geneva Bible belonging to one of the crew; is made to give it back; seizes it again; is reprimanded by his superior, who accuses him of wanting to "turne to Christianitie again: for he was a Renegado"; and then *again* seizes the book, threatening Saunders that if he complains again, "by Mahomet I will be revenged of thee."[101] The confessional identity of this figure can't really be stabilized, either within the text or for its readers – and the villainy of Christians who *are* clearly identified renders the attribution of faithlessness to Muslims *as* Muslims less intelligible.

One of the narrative's important subplots, which (as Jonathan Burton points out) "occupies nearly half of the account," concerns four Englishmen who had voluntarily converted or involuntarily *been* converted to Islam, and "turned Turkes."[102] The first was an unhappy boy from another English ship, the *Green Dragon*, who "did runne ashoare, and voluntarily turned Turke." The second and third were Richard Burgess and James Smith, young men from the *Jesus* who were first importuned to convert by the king's son, then introduced to James Nelson, the son of a yeoman of the Queen's guard already "inforced to turne Turke," and finally held down and forcibly circumcised, although both resisted violently. Burgess is quoted defiantly refusing to say the words of conversion: "A Christian I was borne, and so I will remaine."[103]

The narrative is riven with uncertainties about the national and confessional identities of these men, and how these identities could be affirmed or assigned. When Edward Barton arrived from Constantinople with an Ottoman justice, bearing letters commanding that the crew be set at liberty and the ship and goods restored, he entertained the men "lovingly" – but Burgess and Smith

---

99 Ibid., 2(i): 185.
100 OED, s.v. "caitiff."
101 Saunders, "Voyage of The Jesus, 1582," 2(i): 186.
102 Burton, *Traffic and Turning*, 97. The story of Burgess and Smith is discussed in Burton, 96–101.
103 Saunders, "Voyage of The Jesus, 1582," 2(i): 189.

were not available to him. Asking for them directly, he was told that "it was against their lawe to deliver them, for that they were turned Turkes."[104] Barton appears to have taken no further action. Like Fox, Burgess and Smith used violence against their captors. Along with James Nelson and the boy from the *Green Dragon* (now described as "the other *two* Englishmen, which the said king's sonne *had inforced* to become Turkes"; emphasis mine), Burgess and Smith conspired to lead an uprising of Christian slaves on a galley that was returning them, with their master, from Constantinople. Yet although these four Englishmen "with their swordes drawne, did fight against all the foresaid Turkes," the Christian captives (caitiffs in both senses) "falsely brake their promises" to join in the fight, and the three older men survived only to be put in chains.[105] The Englishmen were saved from hanging when the galley was taken by Venetian forces, who killed the Ottomans aboard and freed the Christian captives; yet the Venetians "would have killed the *two Englishmen* because they were circumcised, and become Turkes, had not the other Christian captives excused them, saying, that they were inforced to be Turkes, by the king's sonne, and shewed the Venetians also, how they did enterprise at sea to fight against all the Turks, and that *their two fellows* were slaine in that fight" (emphasis mine).[106] Not only did their uprising fail to succeed – in part because other Christians were faithless – but it did not affirm their identity as Christians. At the same time, the unhappy boy from the *Green Dragon* (also referred to "Master Blonkets boy"), who jumped ship and converted to Islam because he had heard that converts would be "well entertained," has been re-categorized as *forced* to convert. On page 190, James Nelson is said to have survived the fight, but on page 191 to have been killed by it. Nothing appears to be certain about these figures; nor can we tell how Burgess and Smith were able to make their way home without the aid afforded their shipmates, except that they travelled across Europe by land to arrive two months after the remaining company of the *Jesus* disembarked from a London ship that had been trading in the eastern Mediterranean.

Burgess and Smith's valiant and persistent defiance, their assertions that "a Christian I was born, and so I will remaine," seems to have impressed no one, failing to register them as Christians except on the word of the unreliable

104 Ibid., 2(i): 189–90.
105 "[T]he said Master Blonkets boy was killed, and the sayde James Smith, and our Purser Richard Burges, and the other Englishman, were taken" (Saunders, "Voyage of The Jesus," 2[i]: 190).
106 Ibid., 2(i): 191.

galley slaves. Simply as a result of what had been done to them and to their bodies, neither Ottoman law, the English emissary, nor even the Venetians appear to have viewed the two men as Christians. The readings of minds and bodies suggested by this narrative are (again) inconsistent with other documents. Most notably, Harborne's letter to Assan Aga, the son of a captured English merchant now "Eunuch & Treasurer to Hassan Bassa King of Alger," does not hesitate to affirm that "the fervent faith that ... I hear you have in our Lord Jesus Christ" and "faithful obedience like a true subject to her Majestie" could persist in an altered and recostumed body or an apparently converted mind. Harborne himself had put on Turkish clothes at the midpoint of his journey east, without apparent ill effect.[107]

Matar writes in an introductory survey of the *corpus captivitas*, the vast and diverse documentary archive on early modern English captivity, that "captivity narratives were written to assert English identity and authorize national commitment," to ease "reintegration into their national community."[108] Doubts about meanings and identities had to be cleared up. Yet both the narratives included by Hakluyt also introduce uncertainty. Saunders's narrative leaves uncertain not only the fate of James Nelson and the actual intention of the unnamed boy, but the status and identity of his two unfortunate shipmates. How could a Christian identity be convincingly maintained, in a world where neither confessional constancy nor heroic violence were probative?

The narrative of Fox introduces another kind of uncertainty, this time concerning the Spanish and Catholic world. Following their escape, Fox and his companions were "refreshed and eased" at a monastery in Gallipoli, Italy; Fox was presented by another Englishman to Pope Gregory XIII, who praised his heroic deeds and in turn commended him to the king of Spain. He served as a gunner in the Spanish army until returning to England "at such time as he conveniently could," some two or three years after the escape from captivity.[109] Far from downplaying Fox's trajectory through the heart of Catholic Europe, Hakluyt's version includes related testimonials and letters

---

107 Harborne, "Letter of William Hareborne to Assan Aga." The title notes that Assan Aga was "the son of Fran Rowley of Bristow merchant, taken in the Swallow"; the Swallow of London is second on the list of captured English ships that proceeds Harborne's letter in PN (1598–1600). On Assan Aga (also known as Samson Rowlie), see MacLean, *Looking East*, 103–5. On Harborne's dress, see Müller, "William Harborne's Embassies," 14–15.

108 Matar, "Introduction," 6, 36–7.

109 Foxe, "Voyage of John Foxe," 2(i): 135.

from the prior and brothers of Gallipoli, the "Bishop of Rome," and the king of Spain, documents less formulaic and more personal than the certificate Lok included to certify his pilgrimage. Writing in 1572, the translator Malim had found comfort in a "uniform preparation which is certainly concluded ... by very many Christian Princes ... against thse barbarous Mahometists"; Anthony Munday's 1608 quarto edition of Fox commented that the events narrated took place at a time when England and Spain were at peace (that is, in the early 1560s). The preconditions for Christian unity against Islam were less in evidence by the date of the quarto's original publication, in 1579, and certainly *not* present in 1589, the year after the defeat of the Armada, when Hakluyt first selected Fox's text for inclusion. Yet Hakluyt both included these ancillary materials detailing Fox's friendly reception by Catholic powers and refrained from comment – unless we attribute to him the subtitle that identifies the pope as merely "Bishop of Rome."

By 1599, Hakluyt would not have lacked for alternatives to Fox's narrative had he wished to exclude its friendly representation of Catholicism, or Fox's enlistment in the Spanish army. Two other English captivity narratives had appeared as quartos in the 1590s, one by a gunner named Edward Webbe, another by Richard Hasleton or Haslewood, who figures on a list of captives included in volume 2.[110] Both narratives had connections to the men who supplied Hakluyt with so many of the materials for his volume on the Levant. Hasleton's narrative was dedicated by its author to Richard Staper, a founding member of the Turkey Company and one of Hakluyt's sources, who was credited with intervening to free Hasleton; Webbe was freed, like the *Jesus* captives, by the mediation of Harborne and "ransome money gathered ... by the Marchants in the Citie of London."[111] In contrast to the Fox and Saunders narratives, these later texts detailed not only the experience of captivity in Ottoman North Africa, but the coercive and punitive pressure of Catholic states brought to bear on Protestants escaping from one captivity to fall into another. Hasleton's testimony in particular provides "a dramatic example of

---

110 Webbe, *Rare and Most Wonderfull Things*. Hasleton/Haslewood is associated with the Maria Martin both in the list published by Hakluyt, "In Tempore Romadan Beglergegi Argirae Spoliatae & Ereptae Naves, Merces, & Homines," and in the quarto publication, Barley, *Strange and Wonderfull Things*.

111 Barley, *Strange and Wonderfull Things*, sig. A3r–v; Webbe, *Rare and Most Wonderfull Things*, sig. C3v. On Staper, see below.

resistance to other faiths and other powers."[112] (Webbe's narrative also includes far more actual travel, though some may have appeared suspect to Hakluyt.)

Replacing one text with another comparable one was not unprecedented for Hakluyt, even as he sought to add both newer and older materials to *PN* (1598–1600). For instance, the editor improved on both John Mandeville's account of the East (doubtful authenticity, replaced with the narrative of Odoric) and Robert Baker's account of a voyage to Guinea in 1562 (bad poetry, replaced with a prose narrative).[113] But Fox's narrative and its appended testimonials remained. Absent clarifying evidence, we can't be certain whether and how Hakluyt's selections reflect religious, regional, or editorial priorities and commitments; the evidence here is, again, of a road *not* taken. Yet an editor who was as fully committed to Protestant English zealotry as we sometimes suppose Hakluyt to be might well have taken the opportunity of a new edition to improve on Fox's narrative of Catholic hospitality and employment by substituting Webbe or Hasleton's assertions of Protestant identity under persecution. Hakluyt's retention of Fox and of the two siege narratives is among the details of editing that move his project away from one kind of coherence and further towards being (as Nandini Das puts it) "a compendium that is forever fragmented, the product of multiple intellectual, political, and mercantile interests."[114]

COMMERCE IN THE EAST

1 "The voyage of master Caesar Frederick into the east India, and beyond the Indies, Anno 1563" (213–44)
2 "The long, dangerous, and memorable voyage of M. Ralph Fitch, merchant of London [...] to Ormuz, to Goa in the East India [...] to Siam, etc. begun in the year 1583, and ended in the year 1591" (250–68)
3 "The voyage of M. John Eldred to Tripolis in Syria by sea, and from thence by land and river to Babylon and Balsara. 1583" (268–71)

---

112 Vitkus, *Piracy, Slavery, and Redemption*, 72.
113 On Mandeville's treatment by Purchas and Hakluyt, see Fuller, "Real and the Unreal in Tudor Travel Writing." In *PN* (1598–1600), Hakluyt replaced "The first voyage of Robert Baker to Guinea. An. 1562" (*PN* [1589], 130–5) with "The Relation of One William Rutter." On Baker's poem, see Klein, "Robert Baker in Guinea."
114 Das, "Hakluyt's Two Indias," 119.

4 "A briefe remembrance of things to bee indevoured at Constantinople, and at other places in Turkie [...] written by M. Richard Hakluyt of the middle Temple, Anno. 1582" (160)
5 "Certaine other most profitable and wise instructions penned by the sayd M. Richard Hakluyt, for a principal English Factor at Constantinople" (161–5)

The previous section has highlighted some of the dangers of the East, as seen in the compilation: the violence of siege warfare, carceral violence against individuals, and threats both to religious identity and to the means of affirming it. In this last section, we will examine Hakluyt's representation of its profits and promise.

The great majority of the contents of volume 2(i) document trade and diplomacy between Elizabethan England and the Ottoman Empire in the last decades of the sixteenth century. Hakluyt published copious materials on the travels of Turkey Company and Levant Company merchants and the activities of English emissaries to the Porte, both narrative documents and the letters patent and other legal/diplomatic instruments that formalized the conditions of English presence.[115] His access may be explained by a personal connection with Richard Staper, one of the founding members of the Turkey Company and Levant Company (and subsequently the East India Company). While at Oxford, the young Hakluyt had been a pensioner of Staper's guild, the Clothworkers Company.[116] He thanked Staper in the preface to *Principall Navigations* (1589), for "furnish[ing] me with divers thinges touching the trade of Turkie, and other places in the East"; the dedication to *Principal Navigations* volume 2(ii) elaborates on the merchant's role in opening commercial and diplomatic relations with Constantinople. Hakluyt certainly had

---

115 On Hakluyt's combination of eyewitness account with official documents, see Müller, "William Harborne's Embassies," 12. The Turkey Company (1581) and the Venice Company (1583) would be subsumed into the Levant Company (1592); Brenner gives a detailed picture of the participants and their connection with other trades (Brenner, *Merchants and Revolution*, 16–21). Hakluyt printed letters patent for the Turkey and Levant Companies in PN 2(i).

116 "Chronology," 2: 269; Hakluyt, "Preface to the Reader (1589)," sig. *4v. David and Alison Quinn plausibly attribute many sources among the contemporary materials of volume 2(i) to the personal collections and archives of Staper, his fellow merchant Sir Edward Osborne, and William Harborne, Osborne's factor and subsequently English ambassador to Constantinople ("C&S"). Staper also provided Hakluyt with some materials on Brazil in PN 3, and was among the sponsors of the privateering expedition reported in PN 2(ii) (Flicke, "Voyage of Certaine Ships of London, 1591"). On this expedition, see chapter 6.

excellent access to materials on the Turkey trade and Elizabeth's correspondence with the Sultan; Matthew Dimmock indeed suggests that the occasional gaps in his coverage were tactical omissions aimed at advancing the company's interests.[117] Yet there are some distinctive features of these materials that make this part of the volume quite different from Hakluyt's sources on the Muscovy Company voyages documented in volume 1, an enterprise that (at least at the English end) was broadly comparable.

The year 1582, with Harborne's second voyage and first embassy to Constantinople, was arguably a watershed in English relations with the Ottoman world. The diplomatic and commercial engagements enabled by his presence and accreditation are evident in *PN* (1598–1600); the section on the Levant is rich in official letters, passports, commandments, and other documents relating to trade with English merchants and the conditions of their presence.[118] Yet despite this impeccable sourcing – or perhaps because of what Staper or Harborne chose to supply – Hakluyt's materials don't actually tell us much directly about the world of activities we glimpse through these official documents. The anonymous narrative of Harborne's voyage out, for instance, devotes a large part of its attention to a mutually suspicious and duplicitous encounter with the local government of Mallorca, and the rest to a thorough accounting of Ottoman court ceremony on the occasion of his arrival. (The latter offers parallels with the navigator Richard Chancellor's scrupulous narration of his movement through the physical and social geography of the Tsar's palace, discussed in chapter 4 above.)[119] Hakluyt's selection of documents from merchants trading in the Levant is in fact distinctly

117 For Hakluyt's reticence concerning the arms trade, see Dimmock, "Guns and Gawds: Elizabethan England's Infidel Trade," 215–18; for his careful editing of the diplomatic correspondence, see Dimmock, *New Turkes*, 89–90, 191–2; on his preferential treatment of Osborne and Staper over other merchants trading with Turkey, see Skilliter, *William Harborne*, 11–12, 186–7; Payne, "Hakluyt's London." Skilliter provides additional documents not present in *PN* (1598–1600) as well as surviving originals.

118 For the embassy, see the discussion and additional documents in Skilliter, *William Harborne*. For the Levant Company, see Andrews, *Trade, Plunder, and Settlement*, chap. 4; İnalcık and Quataert, *Economic and Social History of the Ottoman Empire*, 364–72. See also Hakluyt's use of available materials is covered in Beckingham, "Near East, North and North-East Africa."

119 "Voyage of the Susan, 1582," 2(i): 169–71; Chancellor, "Booke of the Emperor of Russia," 1: 238–9.

thinner than in the case of Muscovy.[120] Hakluyt did not include in the volume instructions to Levant Company merchants comparable to those for the Muscovy Company discussed in chapter 4; perhaps the company's expectations for documentation were different. Sea travel through the Mediterranean also did not generally call for the presence of expert navigators like Chancellor, Stephen Borough, or John Davis (for example), whose practice included production of regular records as well as the data necessary for making maps.[121] With two important exceptions, Hakluyt's selection of narrative material by English merchants and factors in this part of volume 2 appears to be tilted towards accounts of *personal* travel undertaken outside their employment by the company. The first exception would be several accounts of belligerent encounter between Spanish galleys and London ships bound for the eastern Mediterranean or belonging to Levant Company merchants; one of these is located in the volume's first half, the others with similar belligerent materials in the second half.[122] Hakluyt's most extensive narrative documentation of travel by Turkey Company or Levant Company merchants in the region on company business, however, concerns a single, multi-stage journey *beyond* Constantinople and indeed beyond the Ottoman Empire.[123] We turn now to that journey.

120 Beckingham, "Near East, North and North-East Africa," 1: 185. The diaries and letters of John Sanderson, a factor for the Turkey Company and its successors, provide a fascinating glimpse at the world of English merchants in the Levant (see Foster, *Travels of John Sanderson*).

121 On the particular differences between navigation in the Mediterranean and the North Atlantic, see Law, "Methods of Long-Distance Control," 241–3. One early voyage to Chios in 1550 was apparently planned by Sebastian Cabot as a "training mission" that provided valuable experience to a number of young English mariners, Chancellor among them (Bodenham, "Voyage of M. Roger Bodenham, 1550"). On this voyage, see Ash, *Power, Knowledge, and Expertise*, 107–8. Its captain, the Anglo-Spanish merchant Roger Bodenham, was also the source for a narrative of Mexico in volume 3; married to a Spanish wife, Bodenham sailed on at least one Spanish voyage to the Americas.

122 One was written by an associate of Hakluyt's and of the merchant John Newbery, another extracted from a pamphlet that does not survive, the third a report to Richard Staper and his associates (Jones, "Five Marchants Ships of London, 1586"; "Ten Marchants Ships of London"; Flicke, "Voyage of Certaine Ships of London, 1591"). See also "A Letter of M. John Newbery Sent from Alepo to M. Richard Hakluyt of Oxford, Ann. 1583."

123 This set of documents, and Hakluyt's alterations to the set in the second edition, are discussed in Das, "Hakluyt's Two Indias." Details below are drawn from Eldred, "Voyage of M. John Eldred, 1583"; Fitch, "Voyage of M. Ralph Fitch, 1591."

Ralph Fitch, John Newbery, John Eldred, and "six or seven other honest marchants" left London on the *Tiger* in 1583. From Tripolis (Syria), the company travelled by caravan to Aleppo – in both cities, there was an English consul – and from there to the Euphrates. Passing down the Euphrates to Fallujah by boat, they loaded their goods onto a hundred asses to go on foot across the desert to "the new city of Babylon" (near present-day Hillah, Iraq). From there, they descended the Tigris to Balsara (Basrah) on the Persian Gulf. Eldred and William Shales stayed six months there before returning to Babylon by barge, and then joining a caravan back across the desert to Aleppo. Eldred made two additional trips to Hillah, after which "as one desirous to see other parts of the country," he travelled to Jerusalem and other places in the region, producing the narrative mentioned earlier in this chapter. Eldred embarked for London on the *Hercules*, arriving in March of 1588.[124]

Meanwhile, Fitch and Newbery parted ways with Eldred at Basrah. They travelled on together to the island of Ormuz (near Bandar-e 'Abbās), where they were imprisoned by the Portugese and shipped to Goa to be examined by the Portuguese Viceroy there, and charged with spying. After being released by the intervention of some benevolent bystanders, they thought it best to disappear, and travelled widely in India before parting company at Agra in September 1585. Newbery was to head north to Lahore, returning home again via Ormuz, but disappeared somewhere en route. Fitch travelled east to the mouth of the Ganges, and onwards to Myanmar, Malaysia, and Sri Lanka before finally returning to England in April 1591.[125]

The activities of Eldred, Fitch, and Newbery had been richly documented by Hakluyt in the first edition of *Principall Navigations* (1589), which included letters to Hakluyt and others sent by the travellers from Aleppo, Babylon, Ormuz, and Goa, as well as a letter from Thomas Stevens, an English Jesuit known to Hakluyt who assisted the Englishmen in Goa. For the second edition, Fitch's return allowed the editor to add a complete narrative, for which the interest of English audiences would only have grown; by 1600, Eldred was a core member of the nascent East India Company, and both Fitch and Hakluyt attended meetings of the company to provide information on the region.[126]

---

124 Eldred, "Voyage of M. John Eldred, 1583," 2(i): 268–71.
125 On the significance of, in this voyage, the context of English engagement with India, see Habib, "'They Say.'" Less apparently momentous from a subcontinental perspective than an English one, the voyage does not appear in Indian sources; Habib examines Ralph Fitch's narrative for the traces it preserves of dialogue with Indian interlocutors.
126 Birdwood and Stevens, *Dawn of British Trade to the East Indies*, 10, 26, 123, 145.

Hakluyt also added an excerpt from the *Itinerario* of Jan Huyghen van Linschoten, who was in Goa at the time of Fitch and Newbery's imprisonment.[127]

Das comments on Hakluyt's additions that "[w]hile seemingly completing this story of [Fitch and Newbery's] adventures ... [t]he texts echo and contradict each other, illuminating pockets of uncertainty and gaps of knowledge.[128] The texts added to the second edition also include what Donald Lach refers to as Hakluyt's greatest editorial lapse, his inclusion of Cesare Federici's narrative of his travel in the East Indies alongside the narrative by Fitch; the juxtaposition makes visible Fitch's substantial plagiarism from Federici's work.[129] Federici travelled in the Indies from 1563 through 1581; his *Viaggio* (Venice, 1587) appeared in English translation as *Voyage and Travaile of M.C. Frederick into the East India* (London, 1588). Hakluyt's title specifies that the translation was done on board the *Hercules*, returning to London from Tripolis in 1588. This ship was the same one on which Eldred returned from the East in 1588. Federici's translator, Thomas Hickock, another merchant returning from Tripolis, surely discussed with Eldred the book he was translating – we might indeed suppose that the book entered Hakluyt's orbit through this coincidence of travel, since (as Lach points out) other works available on the continent supplied equivalent or better commercial details.[130]

Lach suggests that Fitch did not keep a diary of his travels, since the narrative he produced strikingly lacks "dates and exact references."[131] When Hakluyt requested an account of his travels, lacking anything on which to base a draft, perhaps he found in Federici's account ready phrasing for some memorable details: for instance, the practice of covering temples with gold leaf in Myanmar, or an extended description of the king's elephants that lacks only Federici's reference to a specific event.

---

127 With Hakluyt's encouragement, Linschoten's 1596 work was translated into English as *Discours of Voyages unto ye Easte and West Indies* (London, 1598). Another excerpt from *Discours*, on English raids on the Azores, appears in the second part of volume 2 ("Large Testimony").

128 Das, "Hakluyt's Two Indias," 121.

129 Lach, "Far East," 219. Hakluyt cited Federici as a source in his consultations with the East India Company; see Payne, "Hakluyt and the East India Company," 7–8; Taylor, *OW*, 2: 467.

130 Lach, "Far East," 1: 216–17.

131 Lach, *Asia in the Making of Europe*, 1: 479.

Federici: amongst all other Eliphants, he hath foure that be white, a thing so rare that a man shall hardly finde another king that hath any such, and if this king knowe any other that hath white Eliphantes, he sendeth for them as for a gift. *The time that I was there*, there were two brought out of a farre Countrey, and *that cost me something the sight of them*, for that they commaund the marchants to goe see them, and then they must give somewhat to the men that bring them; the brokers of the marchants give for every man halfe a duckat ... which amounteth to a great summe, for the number of merchants that are in that citie.

Fitch: among the rest he hath foure white elephants, which are very strange and rare: for there is none other king which hath them but he: if any other king hath one, hee will send unto him for it. When any of these white elephants is brought unto the king, all the merchants in the city are commanded to see them, and to give him a present of halfe a ducat, which doth come to a great summe: for that there are many merchants in the city. (emphasis mine)[132]

The similarities between the two texts, at some points, are so striking that they can be readily confused by less alert readers, an experience which alerted *this* reader to Fitch's plagiarism in the first place. Fitch's narrative records what were both new achievements (from the national perspective) and also, doubtless, personal experiences filled with excitement and challenge. Yet the text provides little sense of this newness, dominated by strings of place names distinguished by a sentence or two of information about government and custom. Longer sections offer more expansive cultural and commercial information about places of particular interest – yet (as above) these frequently repeat material already encountered in Federici's narrative.[133] Intrepid and creative as a merchant/traveller to places no Englishman had ever been, as a writer Fitch produced largely a sense of repetition.

A different kind of conspicuous repetition also characterizes the accounts of Fitch's fellow merchant Eldred, who travelled only as far as Baghdad and Basrah in modern Iraq. Eldred's description of the old city of Babylon and its ruins is marked throughout by his personal presence at a site, that "I John Eldred have often beheld at my good leasure." Yet despite Eldred's emphasis

---

132 Federici, "Voyage of Master Cesar Frederick, 1563," 2(i): 234; Fitch, "Voyage of M. Ralph Fitch, 1591," 2(i): 259. Hakluyt added in the margins to both passages, "Foure white elephants."

133 A close study of early modern European accounts of India can be found in Rubiés, *Travel and Ethnology*. On Federici particularly, see Rubiés, ibid., 303–6.

on eye-witness, his remarks on the supposed Tower of Babel echo details also found in Federici's observations: both men note that the tower was constructed using mats made of canes between the courses of bricks that remained in good condition given their antiquity, and that from a distance, the tower looked larger than its actual size ("almost as high as the stoneworke of Pauls steeple in London").[134] Here, as Joan-Pau Rubiés has remarked of regions further to the east, we are given details virtually every European observer was likely to notice and repeat in their own words as personal observations.[135] Such repetitiveness loomed especially large in places that Europeans *did* visit repeatedly or habitually, an issue Eldred recognized in the passage on the Holy Land cited earlier: "of which places because many others have published large discourses, I surcease to write."[136]

As he narrated his movements and activities in the East, however, Eldred also described a context of *practical* repetition, structured by routines and customary practices that preexisted his arrival. The English house at Tripolis, for instance, was organized "as it is the use of all other Christians of several nations."[137] Most strongly marked by the imprint of custom are his accounts of travel: down the Euphrates to Fallujah, from Fallujah over a "short desert" to Babylon, from Babylon down the Tigris to Balsara, upstream to Babylon again, and by caravan to Aleppo. Eldred travelled to Babylon twice more after the initial trip in 1584, each time returning "by the way aforesayd, over the deserts of Arabia." Three discrete itineraries are thus summed up in a single act of narration, which itself at times condenses many similar days: "in passing from Babylon to Aleppo, we spent forty days, traveling twenty, or four and twenty miles a day, resting ourselves commonly from two of the clock in the afternoon, until three in the morning."[138] Eldred's own travel was not the only form of repetition: in describing the conduct of the caravan between Babylon to Aleppo, or the river stages of the trip, he moves fluidly between his own experience ("we departed from thence with our camels the last of May with M. John Newbery") and something more general, both replicated in the practice of other merchants and replicating a customary practice:

---

134 Eldred, "Voyage of M. John Eldred, 1583," 2(i): 269. Cf. Federici, "Voyage of Master Cesar Frederick, 1563," 2(i): 215.
135 Rubiés, *Travel and Ethnology*, 116. See also Lach, *Asia in the Making of Europe*, 1: 533n298.
136 Eldred, "Voyage of M. John Eldred, 1583," 2(i): 271.
137 Ibid., 2(i): 268.
138 Ibid., 2(i): 270.

"*according to the maner of those that travell downe by water*, we prepared a small barke for the conveyance of our selves and our goods ... we *with all other sorts of marchants* bought us camels, hired us men ... furnished ourselves with rice ... and *every merchant* bought a proportion of live muttons, and hired certaine shepheards to drive them" (emphasis mine).[139] The repetitive, customary nature of the itineraries into which Eldred inserted his company is signalled by periodic shifts into present tense: "the marchants lie aboord the barke and the mariners upon the shores side as nere as they can unto the same ... the government and deciding of all quarels and dueties to be payed, the whole caravan committeth to one speciall rich marchant of the company." Many details of the travel Eldred describes echo Federici's fuller account of the same journey, but presumably Eldred and his companions were also *doing* what Federici had done and what merchants for generations had been doing, organizing the hazards of travel and commerce in well-understood ways to minimize their risk. (Federici's account, again, gives a much more vivid picture of what the personal and financial hazards of this trade could be.) If dramatic vicissitudes had a place in narratives of pilgrimage, the same was not true for a commerce it was hoped would become safe, profitable, and reasonably familiar.

Even as Elizabethan merchants ventured beyond the region of pilgrimage and crusade, this section of Hakluyt's compilation maps a space in which observation and action were matters of established practice, and even voluntary travel returned to sites visited by others whose experiences were similar. Despite the real novelties of Fitch's, Newbery's, and Eldred's travels, repetition seems less a single lapse than a structuring feature of these materials *and* the experiences they record. Eldred's account introduces one *distinctive* event only in its conclusion, describing the *Hercules* – the vessel on which the translator Hickock also sailed – as "the richest ship of English marchants goods that ever was knowen to come into this realm." This brief remark recalls the thematics of dramatic acquisition and loss in Hakluyt's older materials on travel in the near East and beyond. Whether in Babylon, Myanmar, or Jerusalem, however, the early modern travellers whose narratives he printed recorded none of the transformations suggested in the narratives of their predecessors. The stunning wealth of the goods they acquired is registered most visibly not in merchants' narratives, but in the associated documents Hakluyt largely printed in their stead.

139 Ibid., 2(i): 270.

Hakluyt's dedication suggests that a trade in rich goods was not the only kind of profit gained by trade with the Ottoman Empire; another was the cultural profit of a dialogue with distant powers. As the editor wrote in the epistle dedicatory to *PN* (1589), "Which of the kings of this land before her Majesty ... hath ever dealt with the Emperor of Persia ...? Who ever saw before this regiment, an English Ligier in the stately porte of the Grand Signor at Constantinople?" These rhetorical questions imply that a kind of prestige accrued from dealing with, being *recognized by*, powers beyond Europe. These were not, of course, dialogues in which sixteenth-century English envoys and merchants could impose terms. The occasional sense of deference, and of something to be gained in foreign encounters, emerges with particular clarity in a document by the editor's older cousin, Richard Hakluyt of the Middle Temple. Hakluyt the lawyer wrote a number of instructions for different kinds of travellers, many reproduced by his cousin the editor; we have seen his instructions to the Arctic navigators Pet and Jackman, imagining an encounter with the Chinese court, as well as instructions for a dyer bound for Persia in 1579.[140] In 1582, the elder Hakluyt prepared two more sets of instructions for the merchants who would accompany Harborne to Constantinople. Like his instructions to Morgan Hubblethorne, these are concerned with gathering intelligence that would benefit the cloth trade.[141] Unique to the instructions

---

140 "Instructions [1580]"; "Directions to M. Morgan Hubblethorne." The instructions to Arthur Pet and Charles Jackman are discussed in chapter 4. Both *DV* and *PN* (1589) include an additional set of instructions by the elder Hakluyt. David Quinn suggests that these notes "to bee given to one that prepared for a discoverie, and went not," were originally prepared for Sir Humphrey Gilbert's abortive voyage in 1578, then repurposed in *PN* (1589) as "The notes of Richard Hakluyt esquire, delivered for instruction to certaine gentlemen of master Frobisher's companie"; the text was not reprinted in the second edition of *PN* (Hakluyt, *DV*, sig. K1r; Quinn, *Richard Hakluyt, Editor*, 13; Hakluyt, *PN* [1589], 636). The lawyer also wrote "Inducements to the liking of the voyage intended to ... America": originals are John Brereton, *Discoverie of the North Part of Virginia*, and BL Sloane MS 1447 (neither included in *PN* [1598–1600]; both are reprinted in Taylor, *OW*, 2: 331, 343). Surviving correspondence and documents attest to the lawyer's broad geographical interests in American fisheries and the colony at Roanoke. *PN* (1598–1600) includes a variety of letters and other texts addressed to the elder Hakluyt from various travellers, including Anthony Parkhurst on Newfoundland, Henry Hawks on Mexico, and Ralph Lane on Roanoke. The particular interest in overseas enterprises among members of the senior Hakluyt's inn, the Middle Temple, is noted by Prest, *Rise of the Barristers*, 174.

141 On the cloth trade as an economic engine for the nation, see also the younger Hakluyt's "Particuler Discourse" (*PD*, 28–32).

for Constantinople, however, is a focus on the nation, both explicitly and in the interplay of what is "natural" and what is "foreign."

The first of these two documents presents a numbered list of objects to be sought ("Anile ... and also all other herbes used in dying ... to be brought into this realme") and actions to be done ("to endevour a vent of our Saffron"), both focused on benefiting the English trade in woollens for export. The second set of instructions, under the internal heading "Remembrances for master S.," proposes similar tasks: "in any wise, if Anile that coloureth blew be a naturall commodity of those parts, and if it be compounded of an herbe, to send the same into this realme ... Saffron the best of the universall world groweth in this realme ... See whether you can finde out ample vent for the same."[142] Yet the lawyer's instructions to Master S. spiral in towards these concrete assignments from a broadly general proposition about human nature: "all men confesse (that be not barbarously bred) that men are borne as well to seeke the common commoditie of their Countrey, as their owne private benefit." Of all the "infinite" number of things that might benefit England, the lawyer writes, "I finde that no one thing, after one other, is greater than Clothing, and the things incident to the same," because "There is no commoditie of this Realme that may set so many poore subjects on worke, as this doeth, that doeth bring in so much treasure, and so much enrich the merchant, and so much employ the Navie of this Realme, as this commoditie of our Wooll doeth."[143] The cloth trade was of such economic and strategic importance that the numerous tasks enjoined on Master S. – evidently not a clothier himself, since the lawyer advised him to familiarize himself with details of the trade before his journey – could be framed in grand terms as service to the nation.

Indeed, this second set of instructions speaks directly about England as a nation, territory, and idea. The instructions to Master S. begin by extolling England; not only does it have "the most excellent Wools of the world in all respects," it is blessed with a temperate climate, allowing its people to labour both winter and summer; its many falling rivers neither freeze nor dry up, but provide a continuous flow to power mills and "dresse clothes cheaply." Yet this

---

142 Hakluyt, Esq., "Things to Bee Indevoured at Constantinople, 1582," 2(i): 160; Hakluyt, Esq., "Instructions for a Factor at Constantinople," 2(i): 161, 162, 164. S. has not been identified, but Skilliter offers a conjectural identification with Richard Stanley, who carried a letter to the sultan from Queen Elizabeth in 1579; the letter is printed by Hakluyt (Skilliter, *William Harborne*, 48; Elizabeth I, "Answer of her Majestie to the Great Turke, 1579").
143 Hakluyt, Esq., "Instructions for a Factor at Constantinople," 161.

sense of advantage was only half the story; the lawyer also viewed English artisans as insular and liable to overvalue their own skills. S. was to send samples of Turkish cloth to the Dyers Hall, "partly to remoove out of their heads, the tootoo great opinion they have conceived of their own cunning, and partly to moove them for shame to endevour to learne more knowledge."[144] Foreign skills set a benchmark that English workers should strive to reach; foreign consumers would dictate the kinds of products they worked to make: "we are in our clothing trade to frame our selves according to the desires of forren nations ... thicke or thinne, broad or narowe, long or short, white or blacke."[145] An ideally temperate climate was not enough: in other dimensions, the English needed to think less grandly of themselves in relation to their foreign counterparts, and to understand their activities as subjunctively "framed" by the desires and capacities of "forren nations." The lawyer's suggestion of deference to foreign tastes and skills accompanies another, more surprising aspect of these instructions. In the instructions for Master S., the elder Hakluyt's general interest in materials for dyeing leads to a discussion of botany that opens more fundamental questions about what is actually "native" or "natural" in the first place.[146]

Plants are presumed to be the "naturall commodity" of particular regions (so that seeds and roots will be obtained there), but they *can* be transplanted and cultivated in other regions. Thus, both S. and the other unnamed merchant were to bring back samples: "all other herbes used in dying ... and all Trees, whose Leaves, Seedes, or Barkes, or Wood doe serve to that use, to be brought into this realme by Seed or Roote."[147] This practice of importing foreign plants, the lawyer continues, had been employed by the English since ancient times. Just as S. was now to bring back useful plants from the Ottoman Empire, earlier generations had brought to England some of the very plants now suitable for export; among these was saffron, originally brought in by a pilgrim. Foreign plants already present in the realm included not only recent exotica, like the tulips famously imported from Constantinople by the Dutch

---

144 Ibid., 2(i): 161, 163, 162.
145 Ibid., 2(i): 163–4.
146 In an intriguing essay on a cosmopolitan contemporary of Hakluyt's, John Gallagher cites the younger Hakluyt's associate John Florio using dyeing as a metaphor for language learning as (a third term) a mode of changing one's identity: "Let us see, if al the colours you have, are able, of naturall Englishmen, to dye us into artificial Italians" (*First Fruits* [London, 1578], fo. 106r, cited in Gallagher, "Italian London of John North," 104).
147 Hakluyt, Esq., "Things to Bee Indevoured at Constantinople, 1582," 2(i): 160.

naturalist Carolus Clusius; some (or so Hakluyt claims) were ones we might think of as native to England: apples for pies and cider, wheat for bread, barley for beer, even the "damask rose," brought by Thomas Linacre in the time of Henry VIII – all are described as foreign plants introduced to English soil in ancient times.[148]

At least at the level of the biome, then, England had never been simply English. Indeed, the lawyer's instructions seem to argue that the nation could hardly be itself *without* the admixture of foreign plants. Such imports were what had made the English civilized, things "without which our life were to be sayd barbarous: ... [which] the first inhabitants of this Iland found not here." Without the deliberate and persistent introduction of foreign species onto England's soil, the lawyer writes, "our life [had] bene savage now."[149] These are charged words: England itself would be barbarous without the interpolation and cultivation of exoteric plants – and in particular Turkish plants. And yet in the broader English literature on botany, plants aroused considerable anxiety precisely because "a flower ... is not simply imported into England, but, once imported, grows there, perhaps even becomes part of an English ecology."[150] These "denizens" – a metaphor used by herbalists – began to alter the matter of England itself.

148 Hakluyt, Esq., "Instructions for a Factor at Constantinople," 2(i): 165. On tulips, see also Goldgar, *Tulipmania*, chap. 1; Robinson, "Green Seraglios." This passing mention of Carolus Clusius hints at a broader network of connections, evident in the younger Hakluyt's collaboration with Clusius, Richard Garth, and James Garret (a Flemish apothecary resident in London) in producing the multilingual, illustrated volume of de Bry's *America* devoted to the Roanoke colony. On the two Hakluyts' connections with early modern botanists, see chapter 8.

149 Hakluyt, Esq., "Instructions for a Factor at Constantinople," 165.

150 Robinson, "Green Seraglios," 96–7. Deborah Harkness notes that John Gerard's *Herball* (1597), even though it silently incorporated the work of two Flemish botanists resident in London, Rembert Dodoens and Mathias L'Obel, registered clearly in its treatment of imported plant species a "marked ambivalence toward foreigners and foreignness," along with "anxieties about immigrants and foreign plant specimens" (*Jewel House*, 52, 54). Dodoens was the author of the "new herball" mentioned as a possible gift for the emperor of China in the lawyer's instructions to Pet and Jackman ("Instructions [1580]," 1: 441). The lawyer's instructions to Master S. do not engage directly with the actual immigration or presence of foreign persons. Nabil Matar has made clear the importance of actual Muslim presence in early modern England: "the Turks and Moors of the Muslim empires ... represented the most widely visible non-Christian people on English soil in this period ... Renaissance Britons were far more likely to meet or to have met a Muslim than a Jew or an Indian" (*Turks, Moors, and Englishmen*, 3).

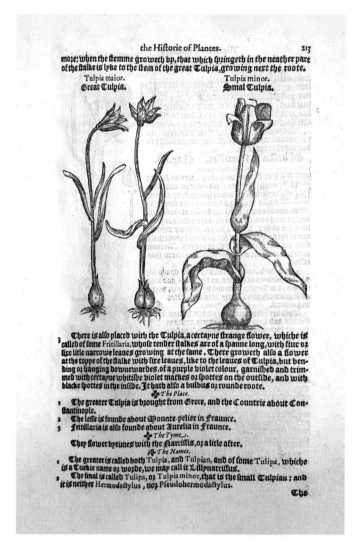

Figure 5.2 Tulips, an import from Constantinople, were introduced to England by Clusius (Dodoens, *Niewe Herball*).

These instructions return us to Hakluyt the editor's earliest narratives of travel to the East, which associated it with change and transformation, the acquisition of spiritual, material, and intellectual wealth. The transformations inaugurated by travel in those texts, if challenging for travellers, appeared to pose no challenge to Christian, English identity or the discourses around it. The sixteenth-century East provoked considerably more anxiety. If siege and captivity narratives held out the possibility that national and religious identity could survive sharp and protracted challenges, they also raised questions about such persistence, given cases where no defence of identity seemed to be adequate (the unwilling "converts" in Saunders's narrative) or where the boundaries of what is defended included national or confessional allegiances that would be otherwise unacceptable (Fox's accommodation with Roman Catholicism and service to Spain). These risks, of course, were the risks of distant travel, of being present in places where English subjects risked coercion and absorption. Hakluyt the lawyer's instructions look past the risks to English persons to how the realm as a whole might be altered by friendly accommodation with "Turkes and misbelievers."

The lawyer's instructions shared with a document we have examined earlier the idea that foreign trade was not simply an exchange of commodities, but precipitated dynamic processes of cultural change (see chapter 2). Yet the fifteenth-century "Libelle of Englyshe Polycye," praised for its sound policy by Hakluyt the editor, regarded foreign trade as having an almost wholly negative effect on the realm, corrupting and impoverishing even those who did not themselves venture beyond its borders to encounter the inferior and distasteful customs of other peoples. The elder Hakluyt's instructions suggest more than optimism about what might happen at the edges of English presence, or about the fortitude of English travellers: they present a fundamentally different idea of home. Instead of a realm walled and protected by the sea, the lawyer envisioned a managed transformation of nature, enabled by foreign imports, within the borders and the soil of the realm itself. The instructions project backwards into time immemorial a continued alteration of the biome as part of an ongoing history of self-cultivation and transformation, continually reaching beyond native resources and rejecting a nature untransformed by exchange.

We might wonder how to weight what is, after all, a single short document, and the lawyer's imprint on *Principal Navigations* (and its author) is not always easily discerned; he is a figure whose life and writings have been far less well-documented even than those of his reticent younger cousin, Hakluyt the editor.[151] Yet that imprint was real. We have already recalled the scene in which the lawyer instructed his young cousin, still a pupil at Westminster, by pointing

---

151 Christopher Tomlins provides a useful examination of the lawyer's views on colonization in *Freedom Bound*.

"with his wand to all the known Seas, Gulfs, Bays, Straights, Capes, Rivers, Empires, Kingdoms, Dukedoms, and Territories of each part, with declaration also of their special commodities, & particular wants, which by the benefit of traffic, & intercourse of merchants, are plentifully supplied."[152] Here, the lawyer taught young Hakluyt a classical and Christian understanding that the needs motivating commerce had been instantiated by providential design; commerce across seas and borders was no less than a matter of natural law.[153] The editor's most recent biographer writes of this moment in the lawyer's chambers, "This was Hakluyt's epiphany, his moment of conversion to his life's cause."[154] How to sort the benefits of contact from its risks – to persons and investments, but also to identities – was very much the question underlying the editor's materials on the trade routes and regions of volume 2(i).

[152] Hakluyt, "Epistle Dedicatorie (1589)," sig. *2r.
[153] For a history of this idea with extensive citations – some with particular pertinence to the younger Hakluyt – see Sacks, "Blessings of Exchange."
[154] Mancall, *Hakluyt's Promise*, 23. On this scene, see chapter 2.

6

West Africa and Beyond: Into the Tropics

THE SECOND PART OF VOLUME 2 is made up of voyages to "the southeast *without* the strait of Gibraltar" (emphasis mine).[1] Under this heading, Hakluyt gathered materials along a vast arc stretching from the Azores, around the Cape of Good Hope and across the Indian Ocean to Japan.[2] This chapter and the next will track these contents, focusing first on the Atlantic coast of Africa, and then on a substantial set of narratives relating episodes from the Anglo–Spanish sea war in the Atlantic. We begin with West Africa, however, which – as we have seen in chapter 3 – was one of the primordial targets of London's ambitious merchant and maritime community in the 1550s, as they sought to contact markets and resources beyond Europe and beyond the familiar waters of the Mediterranean and North Atlantic. Before we turn to the voyages and narratives themselves, Hakluyt's editing itself will repay attention (see appendix 1).

Despite its vast and varied geographical scope, Hakluyt gives the second part of the volume short shrift in the "Epistle Dedicatorie" prefacing the whole, a text weighted markedly towards the materials on the Levant and beyond found in the first half. Four pages of the six-page dedication discuss travels to

---

1 Volume 2(ii) begins with a new title and new pagination following page 312; the documents that follow are indexed in a separate catalogue of contents that follows that for the volume's first part.

2 As is Hakluyt's practice, narratives of voyages are accompanied by letters patent, lists of commodities, letters of information on neighbouring regions, and (for Morocco) diplomatic correspondence – this is generally correspondence between Elizabeth and Mulay Ahmad al-Mansur, although Hakluyt also included an account of the 1577 embassy to al-Mansur's predecessor, 'Abd al-Malik. For an account of Elizabeth's relations with Morocco that draws on Moroccan sources, see MacLean and Matar, *Britain and the Islamic World*, 48–61.

the Levant, the peaceful turn in Anglo–Ottoman relations, and new ventures in the Americas; a brief outline of the "chiefe contents of the second part" begins only on the penultimate page of the dedication. Once Hakluyt turns to materials "without the strait of Gibraltar" he passes rapidly over materials on Atlantic Africa to highlight materials on India, Sri Lanka, Japan, and China, omitting to mention narratives of the sea war at all:

I have here set downe the very originals and infancie of our trades to the Canarian Islands, to the kingdomes of Barbary, *to the mightie rivers of Senega and Gambra, to those of Madrabumbra, and Sierra Leona, and the Isles of Cape Verde, with twelve sundry voyages to the sultry kingdomes of Guinea and Benin, to the Isle of San Thomé, with a late and true report of the weake estate of the Portugales in Angola,* as also the whole course of the Portugal Caracks from Lisbon to the bar of Goa in India, with the disposition and quality of the climate near it under the Equinoctial line, the sundry infallible marks and tokens of approaching unto, and doubling of The Cape of good Hope, the great variation of the compass for three or four points towards the East between the Meridian of S. Michael one of the Islands of the Azores, and the aforesaid Cape ... whereunto I have added the memorable voyage of M. James Lancaster ... beyond Cape Comori, and the Isle of Ceylon ... I have likewise added a late intercepted letter of a Portugal revealing the secret and most gainful trade of Pegu ... and because our chief desire is to find out ample vent of our woolen cloth, the natural commodity of this our Realm, the fittest places ... I find for that purpose, are the manifold Islands of Japan, & the Northern parts of China, & the regions of the Tartars next adjoining ... And therefore I have here inserted two special Treatises of the said Countries. (emphasis mine)[3]

(Elided material deals at even more length with East and Southeast Asia.) The dedication thus elevates "memorable" or "gainful" voyages beyond the Cape of Good Hope while demoting the significance of voyages to North and West Africa.[4] Yet only two English narratives represent those more distant regions: a letter by the Jesuit Thomas Stevens about his sea journey to Goa, and an oral account (transcribed by Hakluyt) of James Lancaster's 1591 voyage into

---

3 Hakluyt, "Epistle Dedicatorie (1599)," sig. *3v–*4r.
4 For Hakluyt's engagement with the nascent East India Company, founded in the year after this volume's appearance, see Payne, "Hakluyt and the East India Company"; Mancall, *Hakluyt's Promise*, chap. 10. Documents can be found in Taylor, *OW*; Hackel and Mancall, "Richard Hakluyt the Younger's Notes for the East India Company in 1601."

the Indian Ocean, largely devoted to raiding Portuguese ships rather than engaging in exploration or trade.[5]

The distribution of materials across the geographical span of the second part of volume 2 presents a different kind of unevenness. After a brief section on Madeira and the Canaries, numerous accounts of voyages to Atlantic Africa follow: to Morocco from 1551, and to the sub-Saharan coast from 1553. Interspersed among these Atlantic voyages are a handful of translated sources on China, Japan, and the East Indies, the Stevens letter, and Lancaster's solitary English voyage into the Indian Ocean; a third substantial group of materials documents episodes in the sea war with Spain, including not only actions off the Azores but raids on the Iberian Peninsula itself. The preface's focus on the Indian Ocean, in short, does not correspond with a catalogue of materials weighted towards the Atlantic, and especially Atlantic Africa.

Certainly, China and the Moluccas, not Benin or Timbuktu, were the great goals of English thinking and planning. Yet if Hakluyt *wanted* to focus the second part of volume 2 on China and the East Indies, the materials he apparently *had* were narratives of long and dangerous voyages to the West African coast. These were written by participants in the voyages, precisely the kinds of primary sources that he has become famous for preserving and making public, and they record some of England's earliest and riskiest long-distance voyages. The second part of volume 2 thus registers tension between two agendas – one related to the editor's geographical priorities, evident in his framing, and one driven by the patterns of English voyages and their documentation, evident in his materials. This tension calls for attention to Africa's place in the explicit and implicit organizing systems of Hakluyt's work and that of his predecessor, Richard Eden – whose 1555 compilation provided detailed and important accounts of England's earliest West African voyages that Hakluyt reproduced.

---

5 "The Voyage of Thomas Stevens"; Hakluyt and Barker, "Memorable Voyage of M. James Lancaster, 1591." Stevens also figured in Ralph Fitch and John Newbery's experiences in Goa, discussed in chapter 4 (Fitch, "Voyage of M. Ralph Fitch, 1591"). Lancaster would become an important figure for the nascent East India Company, however. (His eventful voyages are collected in Foster, *Voyages of Sir James Lancaster to Brazil and the East Indies 1591–1603*.) The volume's remaining materials on East and Southeast Asia are a mixture of print and manuscript sources in translation, some intercepted as letters, some the spoil of captured ships, and many derived from the earlier collection of Richard Willes, a former Jesuit whose *History of travayle* (1577) expanded Richard Eden's 1555 collection, *Decades*.

AFRICA AND THE SYSTEMS OF HAKLUYT'S BOOK

Attending to Africa as a region demonstrates with particular clarity that the structures of *PN* (1598–1600) make some kinds of information harder to find than others. Although most of the compilation's African materials cluster in the second half of volume 2, African materials are dispersed into other parts of the compilation to an unusual degree.[6] As appendix 2 indicates, many voyages ultimately directed to the Americas or to the Pacific via the Straits of Magellan recorded significant time on the West African coast, and virtually all such voyages are found in volume 3; the exceptions are a voyage for Brazil shipwrecked "near Rio Grande in Guinie" (appendix 1, item 28) and an excerpt from the narrative of a slave-trading voyage by John Hawkins, duplicating the full account of that voyage in volume 3 (appendix 1, item 18). Hakluyt's organizing scheme typically privileged *destinations*, even ones that were not actually reached; thus, voyages nominally intended to transit the Straits of Magellan were understood as voyages *to* the Pacific rather than voyages to Africa, even if they lingered on the coast of Sierra Leone and failed to reach the Straits (see appendix 2).

Gathering together the African materials disaggregated by the editor would still not provide a complete picture of how knowledge about Africa circulated in the mercantile and maritime networks whose members are represented in *PN* (1598–1600), how these individuals engaged with Africa, and indeed how pervasive was this engagement. As early as 1481, rights of trade with "Guinea" were contested between English merchants and the king of Portugal, who sought to "stay" them from visiting the African coast; Hakluyt applauded comparable efforts to challenge Spanish claims of dominion in the Americas, but England's complex relations with Portugal and its empire did not receive equivalent attention.[7] Kim Hall notes "evidence that merchants had detailed knowledge of the mechanics of the trade" in enslaved Africans during Hakluyt's half century. Yet while Hakluyt gave extraordinary prominence to the merchant Robert Thorne's early proposals that the English explore northern routes to

---

6 For comparison, materials on East and Southeast Asia can be found in all three volumes. These are sorted according to the *route by which* they were reached (that is, by sailing east or west, travelling overland or sailing around the Cape of Good Hope). Africa, by contrast, was often intended as an intermediate destination on voyages ultimately aimed at the Americas or East Indies.

7 "Ambassage of John King of Portugale to Edward the 4, 1481."

the East Indies, as we have seen, Thorne's interests and investments in the South register only vestigially in *PN* (1598–1600), such that his engagement with Spanish exploration and Spanish practices of owning, employing, and trading in slaves remained largely buried in the archives until brought to light by the work of modern scholars.[8] In the compilation, English engagement with Africa is often a matter of passing references (not always readily visible in Hakluyt's index), names and biographies of investors, and the multiple itineraries of merchants, pilots, and authors whose complex travels must be reconstructed from a variety of print and manuscript sources.[9]

Disaggregated as it is, however, the evidence insists that both practical knowledge of Africa and the profits of contact with Africa had important circulation in England well in advance of the 1550s, not only in the presence of Africans themselves but in the activities of English merchants and mariners. Voyages to Africa appear early in the careers of voyagers like Martin Frobisher, Francis Drake, and Hawkins, lending weight to Hall's comment that "African voyages were truly the nursery to English seamen."[10] Following the thread a little further, the collaboration Drake received from free African communities in the New World was pivotal to the first of his celebrated raids on the Spanish West Indies, even as he continued to treat enslaved Africans as another form of booty.[11]

---

8 See chapter 3. Key sources include Ungerer, *Apprenticeship*; Dalton, "'Into Speyne'"; Dalton, *Merchants*.

9 Questions about the presence of African slavery, particularly, in Hakluyt's materials are not readily enabled either by Hakluyt or by his subsequent editors and indexers. Luke Ward's note that an African boy was given to Edward Fenton by Portuguese traders at Sierra Leone provides a test case (Ward, "Voyage of M. Edward Fenton, 1577," 3: 758–9). Entries under "slavery" in the index to the MacLehose/Hakluyt Society edition of 1903–5 direct the reader principally to materials on Muscovy, the Ottoman Empire, and the Americas; the sale of one African is the only trace of John Hawkins's three slave-trading voyages, and Fenton's slave is not mentioned. Hakluyt's own index to *PN* (1589) does not include a heading for slaves or slavery, and "Negroes," "Guiny," and "Sierra Leone" are no more informative; only his entry for "John Hawkins" includes the reference "he taketh 300 Negroes upon the coast of Guiny. 522 he saileth with them to Nova Hispania." Alison Quinn's index to *PN* (1589) directs readers from "Slaves" to a sub-heading under "Commodities," which indexes Hawkins's trading more completely; additional references are given as a sub-heading under "Negroes." The heading for Ward does record one of several transactions that took place; that for Fenton does not.

10 Hall, *Things of Darkness*, 19.

11 For sources on Drake, see chapter 10.

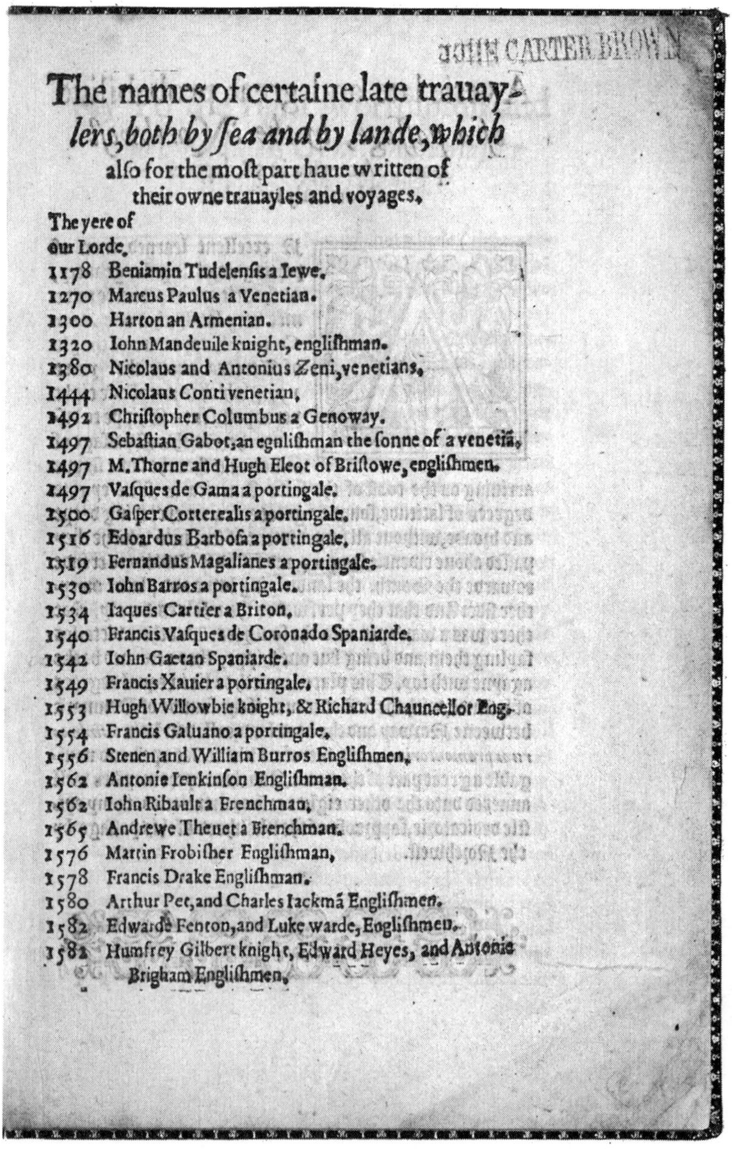

The names of certaine late trauaylers, both by sea and by lande, which also for the most part haue written of their owne trauayles and voyages.

The yere of
our Lorde.
1178 Beniamin Tudelensis a Iewe.
1270 Marcus Paulus a Venetian.
1300 Harton an Armenian.
1320 Iohn Mandeuile knight, englishman.
1380 Nicolaus and Antonius Zeni, venetians.
1444 Nicolaus Conti venetian.
1492 Christopher Columbus a Genoway.
1497 Sebastian Gabot, an englishman the sonne of a venetiā.
1497 M. Thorne and Hugh Eleot of Bristowe, englishmen.
1497 Vasques de Gama a portingale.
1500 Gasper Corterealis a portingale.
1516 Edoardus Barbosa a portingale.
1519 Fernandus Magalianes a portingale.
1530 Iohn Barros a portingale.
1534 Iaques Cartier a Briton.
1540 Francis Vasques de Coronado Spaniarde.
1542 Iohn Gaetan Spaniarde.
1549 Francis Xauier a portingale.
1553 Hugh Willowbie knight, & Richard Chauncellor Eng.
1554 Francis Galuano a portingale.
1556 Stenen and William Burros Englishmen.
1562 Antonie Ienkinson Englishman.
1562 Iohn Ribault a Frenchman.
1565 Andrewe Theuet a Frenchman.
1576 Martin Frobisher Englishman.
1578 Francis Drake Englishman.
1580 Arthur Pet, and Charles Iackmā Englishmen.
1582 Edwarde Fenton, and Luke warde, Englishmen.
1582 Humfrey Gilbert knight, Edward Heyes, and Antonie Brigham Englishmen.

Figure 6.1 Hakluyt listed notable travellers and writers on geography in the opening pages of his first compilation; among them are represented travels to Asia, the Near East, and the Americas, but none to Africa.

Why is so much about Africa so poorly visible to Hakluyt's readers? Distinguishing the effects of editing from the history discernible in the compilation and in the available archive, there are indications that Hakluyt habitually *de*centred Africa in ways that are not simply coincident with facts outside the text. In his early collection *Divers Voyages* (1582), no travels *to* Africa below the Sahara figure on the prominent lists of "writers of Geographie" and "travaylers, both by sea and by lande" that preface the volume. (For the list of writers, see figure 3.1.) In the manuscript treatise "Particuler Discourse" (1584), Hakluyt argued for the settlement of North America because "all other englishe trades are growen beggerly or daungerous," detailing the problems and obstacles to English trade with Morocco, Turkey, Western Europe, and Muscovy; but the chapter begins by dismissing "Bresill and Guynea where wee have little to doe."[12] While trade with Africa had faltered for some years after 1568, Hakluyt's remarks efface an ongoing history of engagement that is now poorly documented, in part because he did not document it.[13]

The historian of Africa P.E.H. Hair noted that although Hakluyt added important materials on the Canaries and on two early voyages to Barbary (Western Morocco) to the second edition of his compilation, he did not choose to print all of the African material that would have been available to him in manuscript, and indeed cut portions of several accounts already included in the 1589 edition.[14] The editor was instrumental in the translation and publication of two works on Africa by Filippo Pigafetta and Leo Africanus in 1597 and 1600, respectively, but neither work is represented in *PN* (1598–1600). (A note promises that the related seventh book of Leo's *Historie* would be "annexed to the end of this second volume," but no material from

---

12 Hakluyt, *PD*, 12. The third volume of *PN* includes a brief section of sources on Brazil; see Willan, *Studies in Elizabethan Foreign Trade*, 5–10. Kenneth Andrews notes that "Hakluyt failed to follow the story [of English trading voyages to Brazil] beyond 1581, though he must have known of subsequent trading ventures" (Andrews, *Trade, Plunder, and Settlement*, 241). The voyages are associated with correspondence to and from John Whithall, an English merchant settled in Brazil in the 1570s.

13 For instance, detailed advice about Benin to a merchant contemplating trade there, in a letter dated 1582, suggests that English trade there continued at some level during a period when no voyages are recorded by Hakluyt (Ryder, *Benin and the Europeans*, 79–82).

14 Hair, "Guinea," 192–203.

Leo is actually present there.)[15] Though materials collected after 1600 can to some extent be traced in Samuel Purchas's index to *Pilgrimes* (1625), C.R. Steele finds among them "only three items ... on Africa," a sharp contrast to the "vigor and enthusiasm" with which Hakluyt had continued to collect materials on the North (Russia, Greenland, Canada) and the East after the second edition had appeared.[16]

The text that failed to appear in volume 2, John Pory's translation of Leo's *Geographical historie of Africa* (1600), included a note of approbation by Hakluyt: he called Leo's geography "the verie best, the most particular, and methodicall, that ever was written, or at least that hath come to light, concerning the countries, peoples, and affaires of Africa."[17] Since Leo's work did not cover Africa comprehensively, Pory added a prefatory overview of the continent; yet Pory's account of the region actually reported on by English sources in Hakluyt's own collections – the coast from Sierra Leone to Benin – is both cursory and heavy on a range of supposed "naturall miseries" that are absent from first-person accounts. Pory's Guinea was so hot as to force the inhabitants to live nocturnally for most of the year, plagued by locusts, destitute of fruit trees; like Icelanders, the people of Guinea were said to sell their children, and even the kingdom of Benin was dismissed as a "rude and brutish nation."[18] The divergence from first-person accounts is indeed so great as to suggest that Pory did not consult Hakluyt's collections, an omission more remarkable because the two men were evidently in close contact in the 1590s; in the dedication to volume 3, Hakluyt wrote that he had "for these 3. Yeeres last past encouraged and furthered in these studies of Cosmographie and forren

---

15 The note on Leo Africanus follows Madoc, "Two Brief Relations Concerning Tombuto and Gago, 1594," 193. Hakluyt's involvement with publication of *A Reporte of the Kingdome of Congo* (tr. Abraham Hartwell) and *A Geographical Historie of Africa* (tr. John Pory) is noted in the paratext to each work (see Payne, *Guide*). The works by Hartwell and Pory are discussed in Hall, *Things of Darkness*, 25–44; Young, "Early Modern Geography and the Construction of a Knowable Africa."

16 Steele, "From Hakluyt to Purchas," 81. Purchas credits Hakluyt's collections for a copy (and perhaps a translation) of Pieter de Marees's account of Guinea, *Beschryvinge ende historische verhael, vant Gout Koninckrijckvan Guinea* (Amsterdam, 1602). On African sources collected by Hakluyt after the appearance of PN (1598–1600) see "Purchas as Editor," 1: 134–41; Hair, "Materials on Africa in Purchas."

17 Africanus, *A Geographical Historie of Africa*, 57.

18 Ibid., 42–3. (On Iceland, see chapter 3.) Compare the very different responses to the court of Benin, for instance, in Eden, "Voyage of M. Thomas Windam, 1553." On the inconsistencies of Pory's Leo (and claims that Africans sold their children), see also Morgan, *Reckoning with Slavery*, 126–31.

histories, my ... Learned friend M. John Pory."[19] When Hakluyt praised Pory's enlargement of Leo as diligent and faithful, he endorsed both the authority of Pory's error-ridden geography and a method that discounted the very first-hand sources on West Africa that he had recently published himself.

This survey of Hakluyt's activities solidifies an impression that West Africa was *generally* lower on the scale of his interests and values than other regions, and not only because he was particularly focused on the East Indies in 1599. That tilt might well reflect the priorities of his patrons and informants, whose collections and agendas are so markedly apparent in other parts of the collection; Hakluyt does not identify his sources directly.[20] But the overarching question of *why* sub-Saharan Africa might have been of less interest or importance to Hakluyt, why knowledge about it might have seemed less valuable to him (or his informants) than knowledge of other regions, can provide us with a useful heuristic.

Was this decentring of Africa simply explained by the circumstances of contact? Not necessarily, in my view. Consider a voyage funded by a group of city magnates, mustering several ships owned by the crown, captained by a high officer of the Navy who carried the Queen's commission, making first-hand observations in an extreme climate at the furthest extension of documented travel by English mariners, contacting a powerful ruler, and returning rich goods to its investors.[21] This was not the Northeast Passage search of 1553, treated by Hakluyt as an evident source of national pride and claims to ground-breaking achievement. Rather, it was a voyage to Guinea and Benin in the same year, funded by many of the same investors who

---

19 Hakluyt, "Epistle Dedicatorie (1600)," sig. A3v.

20 There is no direct evidence of Hakluyt's specific source or sources for African materials. The documents he prints had not been collected in a corporate archive (as was the case for the Muscovy Company), or provided by a named figure (as was the case for William Harborne and Richard Staper's materials on the Levant). Michael Lok is a likely candidate for some; William Towerson and Anthony Dassel, both members of the Muscovy Company, possible sources for others. Hair suggests that since Hakluyt obtained the materials on Muscovy in volume 1 from merchants who were also trading in Guinea, "it is almost certain that he tapped the same source for many of his Guinea accounts" (Hair, "Guinea," 200). Andrews considers each voyage to have been "separately financed as a terminable joint stock," with changing groups of participants; this surely had consequences for document retention (Andrews, *Trade, Plunder, and Settlement*, 104).

21 According to Alsop and Hair, Wyndham had been granted a royal commission to impress seamen and to punish them at sea, rights sought by later Guinea traders as well (*English Seaman and Traders in Guinea*, 147–9).

supported Willoughby and Chancellor's northern voyage.[22] Like the concurrent voyages intended to reach China by the North, voyages to West Africa were part of a novel and ambitious search for new markets and commodities (including gold) at a time of difficulties with continental markets and allied problems with the English coinage.[23] To an important extent, the southern and northern initiatives of the 1550s were undertaken by a common network of investors, thinkers, and mariners, and responded to the same incentives. When London merchants petitioned Queen Mary in 1555 to resist Portuguese requests to bar them from trading in Guinea, they treated the Muscovy and Guinea trades as equivalent assertions of their natural rights under "the common usage of the world": "We have of late resorted to sundry places, both towardes the south and north parties of the world, in both which we finde the governors and the people of the places well willing to receive us frindely and jentely."[24] Like voyages to the West Indies or Guiana, early voyages to West Africa were material expressions of an English right to navigate and trade in parts of the world claimed by other European powers, a right championed and celebrated by Hakluyt elsewhere.

In practice, these were different enterprises in many ways. Regions to the south of Europe were less of an unknown to the English than was true for the northeast. George Brooks notes that Portuguese information and Portuguese cargoes from Guinea had been reaching England since the late fifteenth century, when English merchants had to be actively prevented from accessing the trade, and even direct Portuguese trade with western Africa had been "preceded by centuries of indirect trade ... via Berber and Arab intermediaries."[25] William Hawkins made voyages to Guinea and Brazil in the 1530s, for which his son John was Hakluyt's (not very detailed) informant.[26] In the 1550s,

---

[22] "The early voyages to Guinea were promoted by groups of merchants who were almost all charter members of the Russia company" when it was founded in 1555 (Willan, *Muscovy Merchants of 1555*, 26).

[23] Ramsay, *City of London in International Politics*, 51; Gould, *Great Debasement*.

[24] Blake, *Europeans in West Africa*, 2: 355–6. (Original in State Papers Foreign, Mary, TNA, SP 69/7, no. 449.)

[25] Brooks, *Landlords and Strangers*, 121. On earlier English attempts at trading with Guinea, see "Ambassage of John King of Portugale to Edward the 4, 1481"; Hair and Law, "English in Western Africa," 245.

[26] "First Voyage of M. William Hawkins to Brasil, Anno 1530"; "First Voyage of John Hawkins to the West Indies, 1562"; Hair and Law, "English in Western Africa," 243. Archival material on the early Guinea and Brazil voyages is referenced in Williamson, *Sir John Hawkins*, chap. 1.

English trade with Guinea is thought to have developed as an extension of earlier trade with Western Morocco, itself initiated by merchants who were already trading in Spain and Portugal.[27] English voyages worked along a route pioneered by Portuguese navigators in the fifteenth century, and joined the French as interlopers in Luso–African trade. Even if navigation to West Africa was novel and dangerous for English seamen in 1553, it could hardly be claimed as an innovative discovery in the way that such claims would be made about the Muscovy voyages of the same era.[28] Of course, neither could voyages to the West Indies, but these were narrated as heroic defiance of Spanish claims in a way that never seems to have happened for Portuguese Africa.[29]

The financial and thus human organization of trade also differed between the South and North. The northeastern voyages were undertaken by a syndicate that would receive an early charter as the joint-stock Muscovy Company; soon, trade was accompanied with government-to-government agreements, exchanges of ambassadors, and resident factors. By contrast, the early decades of trade in Guinea were financed by changing groups of investors from year to year, albeit ones in which familiar names recur.[30] No company regulated the extent and nature of trade; no physical archive or corporate body existed to gather and retain documents; no resident factors or merchants maintained relationships and ensured continuity. At least on the evidence of Hakluyt's collection, few charters or letters patent were issued, and virtually no diplomacy undertaken. Although the crown actually participated financially in some African voyages (for instance, by supplying ships), the compilation's only letters patent for African trade date from the late 1580s and early 1590s

---

27 Willan notes "the presence of Spanish merchants [that is, English merchants trading primarily with Spain] among the promoters of the early Moroccan voyages," and a number would go on to trade with Guinea (*Studies in Elizabethan Foreign Trade*, 95, 100).

28 This point is made by Hair at the outset of his essay on Hakluyt's coverage of Guinea (Hair, "Guinea," 197).

29 Regarding Anglo–Portuguese conflict over trade with Guinea, see Andrews, *Trade, Plunder, and Settlement*, 110–12; Scammell, "English in the Atlantic Islands," 301. (Scammell misassigns William Towerson's 1557 voyage to 1577.) The sinking of William Winter's *Mary Fortune* by the Portuguese remains unmentioned in PN (1598–1600); compare the seizure of John Hawkins's *Primrose* in Spain (discussed in chapter 7).

30 Andrews, *Trade, Plunder, and Settlement*, chap. 5. The trade with Morocco may have begun on a similar basis, according to Willan, but soon "developed a more permanent and continuous organization based on factors residing in Morocco" (Willan, *Studies in Elizabethan Foreign Trade*, 101). Many of the merchants active in the Muscovy Company also invested in trade with Guinea (see the biographies in Willan, *Muscovy Merchants of 1555*). Names of other merchants and merchant families can be found in Alsop, "William Towerson."

(diplomatic relations with Morocco began in 1577, some twenty-five years after regular trade had been initiated). During the period covered by Hakluyt, neither merchants nor the crown initiated regular diplomatic or commercial relations with African rulers south of the Sahara.[31]

Thus, for West Africa, voyage *narratives* dominate the materials provided, with relatively few of the auxiliary materials Hakluyt typically categorizes as "Ambassages, Letters, Privileges, Discourses, and other necessary matters."[32] (Indeed, several items in that section are actually voyage narratives whose assignment to this category is unexplained.) Relatively few of these African texts had previously appeared in print. Unlike the captivity narratives found in 2(i) and the accounts of naval battles in 2(ii), accounts of long and (often) dangerous voyages to Africa were not transformed into ballads, broadsides, pamphlets, or free-standing quartos (the highest proportion of documents previously published as individual works is found in volume 3). The only previously printed sources among the African materials in volume 2(ii) are a description of the Canaries by the merchant and translator Thomas Nicholls (*A pleasant description*, 1583), and the two accounts of voyages to West Africa in 1553 to 1554 and 1554 to 1555 which had appeared in Eden's *Decades of the Newe Worlde* (1555) and, subsequently, in Richard Willes's expansion

---

[31] This lack of engagement contrasts with Portugese practice. For discussion of Luso–African diplomacy, see (for instance) Northrup, *Africa's Discovery of Europe, 1450–1850*, chaps. 1–2. Habib cites an "obscure" ten-year patent for trade with Africa granted in 1558 and mentioned in a 1788 report on African trade by the Privy Council, but Hakluyt does not reproduce the document (Habib, *Black Lives in the English Archives*, 67n8). On the Guinea charter of 1588, see the discussion by Gustav Ungerer, who views it as, in part, "a warrant for Dom Antonio's financial survival" (Ungerer, *Apprenticeship*, 81–6).

[32] The opposite is true for Morocco, however. Blake speculates that Hakluyt's contemporaries were "probably so familiar with the Barbary trade, which was flourishing at the time ... that he did not deem it worthwhile to record more details" after the trading voyages of 1551 to 1552 (*Europeans in West Africa*, 2: 273). Willan suggests an alternative explanation for the absence of narrative: "the trade had cased to be organized in those separate, self-contained, annual voyages which Hakluyt clearly preferred" over the "continuous 'traffic' between nations" (Willan, *Studies in Elizabethan Foreign Trade*, 101).

of *Decades, The History of Travayle* (1577).[33] Hakluyt used Willes's version of the text.[34]

Eden's two accounts of African voyages in the 1550s were in fact the *very first* narrative accounts of English travel beyond Europe to survive in their original printed form, and they mark a distinct shift in the production, survival, and (eventually) dissemination of the materials that editors like Hakluyt would begin to collect.[35] As we have seen, voyages before 1553 were rarely documented in even a rudimentary way, and Hakluyt had great difficulty in finding facts, let alone adequate sources, for this period. John Parker's bibliography of English overseas travel indicates that prior to 1550, no documents of *any* kind relating to English voyages had been printed for contemporary audiences, much less framed as part of the larger story of national achievement that Hakluyt wanted to tell in *Principal Navigations*.[36] Already important simply as sources on West Africa and on English trade and travel, Eden's accounts are also important for that part of the history of the book that attends to the transformation of travel into printed books.[37] That their inclusion was an afterthought, according to Eden, indicates the

33 PN (1589) included a verse narrative by Robert Baker (discussed below) on two Guinea voyages in 1562 and 1563 that appears to correspond to a non-extant news pamphlet, but was subsequently replaced by Hakluyt with a manuscript account by William Rutter. (Hakluyt's contents list for 2[ii] adds, "Described also in verse by Robert Baker.") Baker's original is given by David and Alison Quinn as *The brefe Dyscource of Roberte Baker in Gynney India Portyngyule and Fraunce & c.* (London, 1568) ("c&s," 2: 344). See also, Baker, *Travails in Guinea*; Klein, "Robert Baker in Guinea." On Nicholls (a factor for several important Guinea traders) and the Canaries, see Sebek, "Canary, Bristoles, Londres, Ingleses."

34 Hair, "Guinea," 1: 199.

35 Eden's account of the 1554 voyage also includes what is considered to be "the first English rutter for Atlantic ... voyaging" (Waters, *Art of Navigation*, 91, cited in Hair, "Guinea," 1: 200). On the sea journal as a basic form for Hakluyt's African narratives, see Hair, "Sixteenth Century English Voyages," 5.

36 Parker, *Books to Build an Empire*, chaps. 1–2. In the case of West Africa, as with other regions Hakluyt was able to offer only a brief account of a voyage to Guinea and Brazil by William Hawkins in 1530, found in volume 3, "First Voyage of M. William Hawkins to Brasil, Anno 1530."

37 On this transformation see, for instance, Warkentin, *Critical Issues in Editing Exploration Texts*. The process of putting travel into print unfolded differently in different national cultures, and in reference to different regions. Hair suggests that "the first generations of Portuguese experience in Guinea were too early to be communicated in print, and by the sixteenth century were too devoid of news value to compete with the excitement of contemporary discovery" (Hair, "Portuguese in Guinea 1444–1650," 11).

novelty of providing voyage narratives at all – particularly as Eden apparently had to compose them himself.

The narratives are best understood in the context of the varied activities, contacts, and conditions that characterized the different regions visited by Elizabethan mariners. Voyages of trade in the sixteenth century were concentrated on a small number of destinations along a strip of the coast stretching roughly from modern-day Liberia to western Nigeria; this coast was generally referred to as "Guinea," with occasional visits to the Benin Delta ("Benin") to the east. At "Sestos" (the River Cess in present-day Liberia), where English merchants bought malagueta pepper in the 1550s and 1560s, they entered an existing and well-developed trade, seeking to purchase a high-value commodity that required labour-intensive preparation. In exchange, the English brought textiles and metalware, both also produced in West Africa and available from other European traders; African traders could compare the quality and price of English goods with other sources, if they chose, or simply wait for a better offer. While Portugal claimed exclusive rights of trade, this part of the coast was relatively undefended by the Portuguese state (Hakluyt's texts register the competing presence of French ships in particular).[38] Even the 1555 ban on English trade with Guinea by Philip and Mary's government had a very limited effect in halting voyages like the ones led by William Towerson in the same year and those following.

When English ships continued south and east to access the trade in gold at Shamma and other towns east of El Mina (present-day Ghana), they entered a territory over which the Portuguese state sought to exercise effective control, from permanent forts established at El Mina, Axim, and Accra, and with naval squadrons patrolling the coast.[39] The result was a changing landscape of pro- and anti-Portuguese allegiances among African towns; a town that gladly traded gold for English metal and cloth in one year could be fortified with Portuguese cannon and soldiers the next. Even as they offered alternative trade outlets for local rulers who chafed at the Portuguese monopoly, the unpredictability

---

38 Once Portugal began to promote the sale of pepper from South Asia, a "true" pepper preferred by European consumers, interest in malagueta had declined, making the arrival of French and English purchasers in the 1530s, 1540s, and 1550s especially welcome to African producers. Portuguese efforts to deter interlopers were intermittent and ineffectual, perhaps even half-hearted given the diminished value of trade in an African commodity that competed with valuable imports from the Indian Ocean (Brooks, *Landlords and Strangers*, 282–6).

39 Blake, *Europeans in West Africa*, 1: 56.

of English presence, and their limited familiarity with coastal communities and languages, must have qualified their appeal as trading partners.

The English had a small number of trading contacts with Senegambia to the north, and the kingdom of Benin to the southeast; both were visited irregularly, and each has an interest that can't be given adequate weight in this chapter. A voyage to Senegambia in 1591 involved complicated negotiations between the English and Portuguese adherents of Dom Antonio, and gave a glimpse of the Saharan trade flowing towards the fort at Arguin Island; although one particular voyage is the focus of the narrative, the text notes multiple visits by "our ships" over the previous four years. Benin attracted merchants chiefly for its pepper, and was distinguished by an impressive city and court comparable (in English eyes) to London, as well as a monarch keen to find new trading partners once Portuguese interest had shifted towards the East Indies. Voyages to Benin took place in 1553, 1588, and 1589, but contacts were not sustained.[40]

The final part of the chapter examines materials from Hakluyt's concluding volume on the Americas and the Pacific that are nonetheless rich with information on a third section of coastal West Africa. Prevailing patterns of winds and currents meant that voyages intended for trans-Atlantic destinations would contact the coast well to the north of the River Cess, along a stretch from Cap-Vert in Senegal south to Sherbro Island in Sierra Leone (known to Hakluyt as Madrabumbra). These voyages fall into two groups. The first includes a series of voyages by John Hawkins and his associates in the 1560s seeking slaves to sell in the West Indies; the second includes a series of voyages aimed at entering the Pacific through the Straits of Magellan, 1577 to 1586. Sierra Leone had been riven by invasion and war in the decade and a half preceding Hawkins's arrival, a process generating war captives for the Portuguese slave traders who frequented rivers along the coast; slaves from Sierra Leone were prized by New World buyers.[41] The Sierra Leone estuary also offered an excellent harbour with readily available water, wood, and fresh food, making it a frequent and valuable port of call for mariners crossing the Atlantic.

On this part of the coast, the Portuguese presence was different again from the situations prevailing further south. The "Portingals" seen in these

---

40 "Voyage of Richard Rainolds and Thomas Dassell, 1591," 2(ii): 189. Ryder references a source on Benin that indicates at least one additional trading voyage, probably before 1578 (*Benin and the Europeans*, 84).

41 See for instance, Thornton, "Portuguese in Africa," 139–40. On the Mane invasions, see Rodney, *History of the Upper Guinea Coast*, chap. 4.

materials would often have been lançados or Luso-Africans, settled in mainland communities and serving as cultural brokers between African rulers, European visitors, and other communities within a broader region that included the Cape Verde islands. Richard Rainolds claimed that the Portuguese he encountered in Senegambia were "banished men or fugitives"; his perception of their alienated or disfavoured status may also reflect the presence of many New Christians (or, indeed, Jews who had been expelled from Portugal).[42] As Brooks comments, shipboard traders didn't always make distinctions among people they perceived as Portuguese on the grounds of language fluency, colour, and behaviour, but these differences existed and influenced the ways that Portuguese and Lusophone people in the sources interacted with the English.[43] The Portuguese who fought alongside their African neighbours when Hawkins raided their town on the Cacheu River certainly sought redress of their damages from the metropolis, but their affiliations and commitments to the Portuguese state may have been considerably looser than those of the garrisons at El Mina. (Equally, Portuguese informants who lured Hawkins into attacking a well-defended town may have been serving the interests of African communities in conflict with their neighbours rather than allying with a fellow European.)[44]

The trade that brought Hawkins to this coast necessitated both implied and overt violence, but even the long-distance voyages of the 1580s include more episodes of open conflict or aggression than seem entailed by the practical needs of the voyagers or nature of their contacts with African and Luso-African communities. The frequency of violence in both kinds of voyage distinguishes the voyages to Africa in volume 3 from the trading voyages gathered in volume 2(ii); this observation will provide a throughline for an examination of these voyages in the final section of the chapter. But we begin at the bibliographical beginning, with Eden's narratives from the 1550s, Eden's methods,

---

42 "Voyage of Richard Rainolds and Thomas Dassell, 1591," 2(ii): 192. His comment is cited in Blake's discussion of Portuguese lançados settled on the coast of Sierra Leone (Blake, *Europeans in West Africa*, 1: 27). Thornton describes Sierra Leone as "a large unofficial zone of private Portuguese" presence, where the state was unable directly to control or monitor settlement and trade ("Portuguese in Africa," 148–9; *Africa and Africans*, 60–3). See also Brooks, *Landlords and Strangers*, 159–61, 188–96.

43 Brooks, *Landlords and Strangers*, 203.

44 Sparke, "Second Voyage Made by John Hawkins, 1564," 3: 505; Kelsey, *Sir John Hawkins*, 62–5. Depositions related to the Cacheu raid are also discussed in Hair, "Protestants as Pirates, Slavers, and Protomissionaries."

and Eden's intellectual biography; these provide both a comparison and a foundation for Hakluyt's materials and editorial practice.

ENGLAND AND WEST AFRICA IN THE 1550S

1 Richard Eden, "The voyage of M. Thomas Windam to Guinea and the kingdom of Benin, Anno 1553" (9–14)
2 Richard Eden, "The voyage of M. John Lok to Guinea, Anno 1554" (14–23)
3 William Towerson, "The first voyage of Master William Towrson to Guinea ... 1555" (23–36)
4 William Towerson, "The second voyage of Master William Towrson to Guinea ... 1556" (36–43)
5 William Towerson, "The third voyage of the sayd M. William Towrson to Guinea ... 1557" (44–52)

Richard Eden's compilation, *Decades of the New World* (1555), included two narratives of voyages to West Africa in the years 1553 to 1554 and 1554 to 1555. The compilation centred on a partial translation of Peter Martyr's *De orbe novo* (Basel, 1533), along with selections from the *Historia general y natural* of Gonzalo Fernández de Oviedo y Valdés, the *Istoria de las Indias* of Francisco López de Gómara, and materials on Magellan's circumnavigation drawn from the works of Antonio Pigafetta and Maximilianus Transylvanus.[45] English interests also had a kind of place in the compilation, in the form of translated materials under the running head "Of Moscovie and Cathay." Eden did not include a narrative of Willoughby and Chancellor's 1553 voyage, however; his only sources related to the voyage are Edward VI's 1553 letters to any monarchs "inhabytinge the Northeast partes of the worlde" and the tsar's reply.[46] Instead, referring readers to an account of the voyage "largely and faythfully written in the Laten tonge by ... Clement Adams," Eden provided a grounding in geography and history that would enable his audience to understand such voyages as possible, necessary, and momentous.

Eden did not simply obtain and print narratives composed by merchants or mariners (as would become Hakluyt's usual practice) but composed them

---

45 As noted in chapter 2, Eden's working copy of *De orbe novo*, preserving his notes, is held in Johns Hopkins Special Collections.

46 Eden, *Decades*, fo. 305v–309r. *Decades* assigns page numbers to leaves (front and back, or recto verso) rather than sides. The unpaginated letter from the tsar follows fo. 309v.

himself, being "advertised of the same by thinformation of such credible persons as made diligent inquisition to knowe the truth hereof."[47] His hand lies heavily on these two texts, which were left largely intact by Hakluyt; one is writtren in the third person, while the second draws together a pilot's log, oral testimony, and learned geography. Eden should be considered to be their author, and that authorship draws his biography into our consideration of the narratives. Authorship matters because it is Eden's narratives – and specifically portions of the narratives that are his own original work – that yield some of the passages most frequently quoted in discussions of Hakluyt's African materials. We will begin by looking at the original context for Eden's texts in his biography and his writings – including *Decades*, in which the narratives first appeared.

A civil servant from a family of cloth merchants – Eden's father and uncle were among the initial investors in the Northeast Passage search of 1553 – he had geographical interests and learning comparable to Hakluyt's, graduating with a master's from Queens College Cambridge in 1544. Eden also had comparable connections in the world of long-distance trade and navigation, and published several books linked to the Muscovy Company's interests.[48] Yet his intellectual profile was distinctly different from that of Hakluyt. In addition to geography, Eden translated works on navigation (Martín Cortés), mining

---

47 Ibid., fo. 343v. Eden's role in the two Guinea narratives was much closer to what we might think of as "author" than to "transcriber" or "editor." While Hakluyt's most frequent practice was to use existing materials with some degree of editing, a number of narratives in *PN* (1598–1600) *were* "taken down" by him from oral information by travellers, or similarly composed after interviewing participants. No systematic study of these materials has been done, and they have as yet not been included among works "by" Hakluyt (see, for instance, Taylor, *OW*).

48 On Eden's relatives, see Gwyn, "Richard Eden Cosmographer and Alchemist," 22. Gwyn cites the *Calendar of Patent Rolls, Philip and Mary, 1554–55*, 2: 55–8; the Edens are not named in Willan, *Muscovy Merchants of 1555*. Andrew Hadfield suggests that *Treatyse of the Newe India* (1553) was prepared under the direction of the Earl of Northumberland, as part of his aim to promote English maritime expansion (Hadfield, "Eden, Richard"). Eden dedicated his 1561 translation of Martin Cortés, *Arte of navigation*, to the Muscovy Company. In the early 1570s, he is believed to have begun assembling accounts of the Muscovy Company voyages for the new iteration of his travel collections published after death by Richard Willes as *History of Travayle*, 1577 (Arber, *Three Earliest English Books on America*, xlviii; Gwyn, "Richard Eden Cosmographer and Alchemist," 34). Eden was employed in the treasury under Henry VIII and again under Philip and Mary; he served as secretary to Sir William Cecil in the early 1550s, and was a client of Sir James York, founding member of the Muscovy Company, promoter of voyages to Morocco and West Africa, and a key figure in the new discoveries and trades.

(Vannoccio Biringuccio), magnetism (Jean Taisnier), and anatomy (Andreas Vesalius). John Bale described him as a "cosmographer and alchemist," and his career evidences interests in both medical and metallurgical chymistry.[49]

All these disciplines, in their own ways, understood the terrestrial and celestial domains as systematically connected. Thus, as Eden's contemporary Robert Recorde wrote concerning medicine in a treatise on celestial navigation, "in physic the use of [astronomy] is so large ... that without it physic is to be accounted utterly imperfect."[50] The sun and other planets were thought to influence the constitution of the body and to generate the various metals out of a few primordial elements. Eden's interests connected him through multiple avenues to the science of place that we have examined in connection with Thorne's proposals for northern exploration in volume 1. While Thorne and others repeatedly celebrated the discovery that zonal theory was mistaken in predicting the tropics to be barren and uninhabitable, the framework of latitude nonetheless persisted as a way of understanding and modelling the human and physical geography of the globe. Arngrímur Jónsson's defence of Iceland, also in volume 1, testifies that its northern position licensed European cosmographers to claim that its nature and culture were aberrant or deficient compared to the temperate regions to the south. In the same way, regions in or near the belt of the tropics were still at times "thought to be incapable of sustaining civil societies, or even ... properly formed humans."[51] Eden's intellectual profile suggests that the conceptual systems linking the earth to the heavens through a theory of climate zones helped to structure and ground his expectations and presuppositions about regions "under the equator" and the nature of their populations. The evidence of his writing bears out this suggestion; Eden's expectations about the tropics bear the traces of a theoretical model that would have predicted their riches, and also framed their inhabitants and societies as defective.

---

49 J. Bale, *Scriptorum illustriu[m] maioris Brytannie* (1559), cited in Arber, *Three Earliest English Books on America*, xl. For context on the early modern materials sciences variously known as chemistry, chymistry, and alchemy, see Moran, *Distilling Knowledge*.

50 Recorde, *Castle of Knowledge*, sig. A6r. On this disciplinary association see, for instance, Cook, *Matters of Exchange*, 146; Siraisi, *Medieval & Early Renaissance Medicine*, 67; Clulee, *John Dee's Natural Philosophy*, 44–5. In addition to his edition of Vesalius's work on anatomy, Eden's own interest in medicine was also manifest in his attention to distillation and the preparation of chemical medicines, and in his references to the Italian physician Girolamo Cardano (for a transcript of Eden's autobiographical memorandum, see Arber, *Three Earliest English Books on America*, xlv–vi).

51 Davies, *Renaissance Ethnography and the Invention of the Human*, 27.

The "Two viages made owt of England into Guinea" come at the end of *Decades*, following an excerpt from Biringuccio's *Pyrotechnia* (1540). Eden's preface explains their presence. After delivering to the printer a manuscript that included materials up to and including the excerpt from *Pyrotechnia*, Eden writes, "I was desyred by certeyne my frendes to make summe mention of these viages ... that sum memory myght thereof remayne to owr posteritie if eyther iniquitie of tyme consumynge all thinges, or ignoraunce ... shulde hereafter bury in oblivion so woorthy attempts."[52] Originally, Eden "had not thought to have wrytten any thynge of these vyages [to Guinea] but that the liberalitie of master Toy [the printer] encoraged me to attempt the same."[53] The resulting narratives are rich in detail about events, observations, and results; Eden tells us far more about these voyages to Guinea than about the northern voyage of 1553. For the Muscovy Company voyages, Eden provided a great deal of geographical information, but no voyage narratives; for Africa, he provided voyage narratives that drew on participant testimony soon after the fact, framed with a "Breefe description of Afrike" that focuses primarily on North Africa with a brief (and inaccurate) notice of Guinea as a region with "no cities" and "very great desertes."[54] Eden's two narratives would be reproduced in *Principal Navigations* with only minor alterations. (Hakluyt's text is cited henceforth.)

The first voyage took place under Thomas Wyndham in 1553 to 1554. Wyndham had made two trading voyages to the western coast of Morocco in 1551 and 1552, as captain and part owner of the ship employed for them; in the following year, some of the same investors employed Wyndham and the *Lion* for the first of a series of trading voyages to Guinea. (At least two of the investors numbered among Eden's patrons.)[55] Wyndham was reasonably well informed for an English captain in the period; he was an associate of

---

52 Eden, *Decades*, fo. 343r.

53 Ibid., fo. 360r.

54 Ibid., fo. 344r–45r. An overwhelming focus on northern Africa also characterizes both William Prat's *Discription of the Contrey of Aphrique* (1554) and John Pory's later version of Leo Africanus, discussed above; both were (like Eden's *Decades*) translations and compilations. On these, see Young, "Early Modern Geography and the Construction of a Knowable Africa."

55 Williamson, *Sir John Hawkins*, 37, 41. Investors included Sir John York, Sir William Garrard, Sir Thomas Wroth, and Francis Lambert. James Alday gives additional names for the first voyage, listing only investors who died of "sweating sickness" before the voyage began; these included Henry Ostrich, believed to be Cabot's son-in-law ("First Voyage to Barbary, Anno 1551"). On Eden's relations with York and Garrard, see Gwyn, "Richard Eden Cosmographer and Alchemist," 18.

William Hawkins and may have heard directly of his earlier voyages to Guinea.[56] Yet to be well informed for an *English* captain was not to be sufficiently informed, and Wyndham was joined in his command by an expatriate Portuguese navigator, António Anes Pinteado. Pinteado had first-hand experience both of the relevant navigation and geography, and the logistics and practicalities of trading in Guinea; he also appears in fragmentary records as a consultant to Sebastian Cabot and others on the search for northern passage. Like Cabot, a navigator of Genoese or Venetian descent who had served as Spain's pilot major before returning to English service, Pinteado and his colleague Francisco Rodrigues brought expert knowledge to England's nascent attempts at distant navigations.[57] It was indeed in finding their way down the coast of West Africa that Portuguese navigators had developed the skills in celestial navigation that would catalyze Europeans' ability to access the rest of the globe by sea.[58] Yet as Eden tells the story, the Guinea voyage of 1553 turned on Wyndham's violent reaction against the authority of Pinteado's knowledge.

The expedition left London in August 1553. South of Madeira, Wyndham became "a terrible Hydra," removing Pinteado from command, stripping him of subordinates and "leaving him as a common mariner, which is the greatest despite and grief that can be to a Portugale or Spaniard, to be diminished of their honor, which they esteem above all riches."[59] On arrival at the River Cess ("Sestos"), the men were persuaded by Wyndham to disregard Pinteado's advice to make their voyage lading malagueta pepper there, and instead to press further south in search of gold. Near El Mina, they took a hundred and fifty pounds of gold in trade; again, Pinteado warned of the dangers of

56 "First Voyage of M. William Hawkins to Brasil, Anno 1530," 3: 700. Wyndham and Hawkins had collaborated in seizing the *Santa Maria de Guadeloupe* in 1544 (Alsop, "Wyndham, Thomas").

57 On Rodrigues, see Hair and Alsop, *English Seaman and Traders in Guinea*, 54n21. He is mentioned only briefly in the text as one of those who went upriver to Benin with Pinteado. On the need for such "clusters of knowledge," see Reinert, "Authority and Expertise at the Origins of Macro-Economics," 117.

58 On early Portuguese mapping of Africa, see Relaño, *Shaping of Africa*, chaps. 7–8. On Portuguese navigation, see (for instance) Rodger, "Atlantic Seafaring," 75–8; Domingues, "Portuguese Navigation"; Diffie and Winius, *Foundations of the Portuguese Empire, 1415–1580*.

59 Eden, "Voyage of M. Thomas Windam, 1553," 2(ii): 11. The expedition paused for a week at Madeira, and then mounted a raid on a smaller island to the south, an incident not recorded by Eden; the later importance of season and timing makes these delays consequential. The events of the voyage are narrated by Blake, *Europeans in West Africa*, 2: 284–8. Documents 123–32 also relate to the 1553–1554 voyage.

lingering on the coast at the wrong season, and again Wyndham overbore him.[60] The expedition continued east to Benin "under the equinoctial line" (Eden calls attention to this further southing), and merchants proceeded upriver to the court of Benin where Pinteado provided translation and helped to broker a trade in pepper.

At Benin, the English began to die. Eden attributes this morbidity to their intemperate behaviour; to ease the unaccustomed heat, the men ran into the water causing "sudden and vehement alterations" in temperature, and "having no rule of themselves" ate and drank palm wine and the fruits of the country "without measure."[61] Wyndham commanded Pinteado to return without waiting to conclude the trade then underway, then sickened and died himself. On Pinteado's return, the mariners abused and mistreated him, and insisted on leaving forthwith, abandoning in Benin the remaining merchants who had accompanied Pinteado to the king's court, as well as Wyndham's *Lion*. A few days later, Pinteado died "for very pensiveness & thought." Of some one hundred and forty men, barely forty came home, and many of these died after returning.[62]

After calling for Pinteado's return, Wyndham "all raging" broke into Pinteado's cabin and into the chests containing his personal possessions, and "spoiled" their contents: "such provision of cold stilled waters and suckets as he had provided for his health ... his instruments to saile by ... his apparel."[63] The contents of the chest were not only valuable to Pinteado, but represented what made him *of* value: his knowledge of the climate and ability to regulate or temper his body in it, by use of the quasi-medical provisions, and the

---

60 Eden, "Voyage of M. Thomas Windam, 1553," 2(ii): 12. On the importance of trading during the correct season, see for instance John Lok's comments in "Letter to the Marchants Adventurers of Guinea, 1561," 53.

61 Ibid., 2(ii): 12–13. This account of disease etiology conforms with the account by George Wateson, a physician whose work on disease in hot climates Hakluyt had originally intended to include in *Principal Navigations*: "the calenture ... Is the most usual Disease, happening to our Nation in intemperate Climates, by inflammation of the blood, and often proceeding of a moderate drinking of wine, and eating of pleasant fruits" (Wateson, *Cures of the Diseased*; Hakluyt, "Epistle Dedicatorie [1600]," sig. A3v). Mosquito-borne diseases were endemic along this coast (Brooks, *Landlords and Strangers*, 25).

62 Hair and Alsop, *English Seaman and Traders in Guinea*, 9. I have relied on Hair and Alsop for the hard details of the 1553–54 and 1554–55 voyages; theirs is the most detailed study of the texts and their history, drawing on archival sources in addition to the materials in Eden and Hakluyt. On Benin particularly, see also Ryder, *Benin and the Europeans*, 76–8.

63 Eden, "Voyage of M. Windam, 1553," 2(ii): 13.

specialized skills as a navigator represented by his instruments. In effect, Wyndham destroyed the capacities he lacked rather than seeking (if nothing else) to make use of them. The sentence in which Eden relates this episode concludes with Wyndham's illness and death, so that the emotional intemperance of destroying Pinteado's possessions appears homologous with, if not directly connected to, the intemperance that Eden believed contributed to the voyage's toll of deaths. The narrative concludes with a series of letters attesting to Pinteado's virtue and value; these are reproduced by Hakluyt.

Eden's narrative indicts Wyndham for his bad conduct, and particularly for his abuse of Pinteado and its consequences. Pinteado knew how to reach West Africa, where to trade, what for, and when; his knowledge made new regions and markets accessible to English mariners and merchants who did not possess the knowledge to reach them on their own. By contrast, the greed for gold, immoderate diet, unrestrained rage, and impatience of Eden's English mariners looks especially unattractive. This early celebration of English activities in effect condemns the failure to recognize and adequately value a foreigner's expertise.[64] The conflict between Wyndham and Pinteado may also have been a conflict *about* expertise, at a moment when the skills associated with navigation were themselves in a crisis occasioned by the advent of mathematical navigation and its challenge to the authority of a conservative body of practitioners. As Portuguese exploration of sub-Saharan Africa had both necessitated new techniques and fostered their development, the arrival of Pinteado and Sebastian Cabot in England brought a transformative technology that crucially enabled the challenging voyages undertaken in the 1550s.[65] Eden played a role in this transition: in 1561, the Muscovy Company pilot Stephen Borough returned from the Casa de Contratación in Seville with a new manual of navigation that, at his urging, the company would employ Eden to render into English. David Waters describes the resulting edition of

---

64 Michael Wyatt remarks on the broader picture of skilled "strangers": "there was a considerable amount of resentment that much of the skilled labour practiced in England in the sixteenth century was undertaken by foreigners" (*Italian Encounter with Tudor England*, 137).

65 John Law characterizes Portuguese celestial navigation as coordinating "documents, devices, and drilled people" (Law, "Methods of Long-Distance Control," 254). For specifics on the transfer of navigational expertise to England in the middle of the sixteenth century, see Ash and Sandman, "Trading Expertise." In a separate study, Eric Ash considers navigation as one instance of a growing culture of expertise in sixteenth century England, with interesting comparisons on the use of foreign experts in metallurgy (Ash, *Power, Knowledge, and Expertise*).

Martín Cortés's *Arte de Navegar* as "one of the most decisive books ever printed in the English language," providing "the key to the mastery of the sea."[66]

It was a moment for mathematics. The printer for Eden's *Decades, Arte of Navigation*, and *History of Travayle* (1577), a later expansion of *Decades* by Richard Willes, was a man named Richard Jugge, who commissioned or was given a gloriously intricate, personalized, mathematical instrument in the shape of a book with his nightingale *impresa* on the cover; from the workshop of Humfrey Cole, it unfolded to offer a compass, table of latitudes, and other tools related to the new navigational science (see plate 5).[67] Jugge's instrument is a material index of fascination with the new ways of spatial thinking that ultimately made possible long voyages to the South *and* the North, supported by the mathematics taught in Recorde's contemporary books. Yet Eden's translation of Cortés also provides evidence of the difficulties accompanying transition to a new mode of practice, and his complaints about the conservatism of practitioners were still being echoed by Edward Wright decades later.[68] The particular drama of the 1553 voyage thus conflates two larger concerns of its redactor/editor – the anxious relationship of Englishmen to foreign precedence in discovery and to the new mathematical expertise associated with navigation. In the northern voyages, that expertise was transferred at the outset to a generation of English navigators trained in the new technologies of instrument use, observation, calculation, and record keeping by figures like Cabot and Dee (himself educated on the continent); in these southern voyages, navigational expertise was initially embodied in the persons of Pinteado and Rodrigues, and its authority repudiated and ostracized by other mariners. By 1555, William Towerson was able to rely on an English navigator who had sailed with Wyndham and (the following year)

---

66 Waters, *Art of Navigation*, 104.

67 Cole was "the leading and most skilled maker" of instruments in late-sixteenth-century England; he also worked as an engraver (Bennett, *Divided Circle*, 74–5).

68 Eden's preface called for "preferment and maytenaunce of such experte men" who, without relying on "any rutter or Carde of Navigation," are able perform "longe and farre viages ... to discover unknowen lands and Ilands" (Cortés, *Arte of Navigation*, C4v–CC1r). A decade later, in a work that elaborated on Cortés's manual, William Bourne would also register the conservative reaction of pilots "wedded ... to their accustomed usage," who would mock those that observed the stars to determine latitude elaborated and even (Bourne, *Regiment for the Sea* [1574], cited in Wright, *Certaine Errors in Navigation*, sig. ¶¶4r). On the frictions around new methods, see Ash, *Power, Knowledge, and Expertise*, chap. 3.

John Lok. But the transfer and acquisition of expertise was never made explicit, much less celebrated, in connection with the African voyages.[69]

Despite these dramas and more than 50 per cent mortality, the 1553 voyage was profitable; investors were not deterred from setting out a second voyage the following year led by Lok, who we encountered in chapter 5 as a traveller to Jerusalem. Lok visited the River Cess, for pepper, and then a series of towns near São Jorge de Mina, exchanging cloth for gold; he omitted Benin, and turned for home (with much reduced loss of life) carrying pepper, ivory, and 400 pounds of gold. Eden's account of this second voyage raises a new set of issues: in this case, how to differentiate and adjudicate between the text's different sources. His text was built around the kernel of an unnamed pilot's log, apparently on the *Bartholomew* (thus, written by neither Robert Gainsh nor John Lok, who appear in the running heads for *PN* [1589] and [1598–1600], respectively).[70] He opened by emphasizing the pilot's authority, and assuring readers of his deference to it. This "expert Pilot" wrote from experience and expertise: "as he found and tried all things, not by conjecture, but by the art of sayling, and instruments perteining to the mariners facultie." Eden promised not to "change or otherwise dispose the order of this voyage so well observed by art and experience," but to provide it in "the sort and phrase of speech ... commonly used among them, and as I received it of the said Pilot."[71] Despite this disciplinary and linguistic deference, the pilot's log forms only part of his narrative. The transition, clearly marked, occurs roughly halfway through the text: "hitherto continueth the course of the voyage, as it was described by the said Pilot. Now therefore I will speak somewhat of the country and people, and of such things as are brought from thence. They brought from thence at the last voyage four hundred pound weight and odd of gold, of two and twenty carats and one grain in fineness: also the six and thirty butts of grains, & about two hundred and fifty Elephants teeth of all

---

69 This navigator was John Rafe or Ralph (Alsop, "William Towerson," 53). On the navigation of the Guinea voyages, see Waters, *Art of Navigation*, 89–94. Waters comments that records of these voyages indicate that "pilots still used roman numerals. In these calculation is possible only with the aid of an abacus" (ibid., 94). Paul Hair notes that the region's flat coast running mostly east to west was challenging for latitude-based navigation practices ("Sixteenth Century English Voyages," 7).

70 For evidence regarding the log's author, see Hair and Alsop, *English Seaman and Traders in Guinea*, 58–9n37.

71 Eden, "Voyage of John Lok, 1554," 14. The 1554 narrative is badly mispaginated in my copy text; page numbers given silently correct what is printed.

quantities. Of these I saw & measured some of nine spans in length."[72] It is clearly Eden, speaking in the first person, who tells us that that he had measured the tusks himself, and observed the head of an elephant in the house of the city merchant Sir Andrew Judde. Eden's direct contact with artifacts of the voyage grounds his own comments, like the pilot's, on autoptic evidence – but only momentarily. A discourse on "The description and properties of the Elephant" follows, reliant largely on classical sources that include Pliny's "continual war" between elephants and dragons, before Eden returns to autoptic evidence: "our men saw one drinking at a river in Guinea."[73] Eden thus supplements the log with both bookish additions and fragments of oral testimony. Appendix 3 provides an overview of the narrative's composition and editorial changes, complexities that have not always emerged clearly in the scholarship; Hakluyt's additions are also noted (see appendix 3).

Eden's remarks on "The people of Africa" share his methodologically hybrid approach to the elephant. Kim Hall also traces in this part of Eden's text an attention to the aesthetic values of whiteness (mediated through his description of elephant ivory) that, in turn, frames the description of Guinea's people that follows.[74] Drawing from Pliny, Josephus, Aristotle, the Psalms, and Gemma Frisius, his text populates Africa with marvels, monsters, and myths – cannibals, airy noises, men without heads, Prester John, the Queen of Sheba. As in the prefatory "Briefe description of Affrike," regions north of the Sahara are emphasized; both the Portuguese discoveries of the fifteenth and sixteenth centuries *and* the observations of English navigators are conspicuously absent, the only exception a reference to Cap-Vert as the place "to the which the Portugals first direct their course when they sailed to America, or the land of Brazil."[75] Eden's sole comment on the areas visited in 1554 to 1555 is the passage perhaps most frequently cited from these two texts, describing "the regions of the coast of Guinea" as inhabited by "a people of beastly living, without a God, lawe, religion, or common wealth, and so scorched and vexed with the heat of the sunne, that in many places they curse it when it riseth."[76] Yet this confused and derogatory account of the peoples of West Africa was evidently not conferred with the pilot's log, much less with Eden's

72 Ibid., 2(ii): 18.
73 Ibid., 2(ii): 18–19.
74 Hall, *Things of Darkness*, 50–3. (Note that in her discussion, the text is ascribed to the investor George Barne, for whom read "Eden.")
75 Eden, "Voyage of M. Thomas Windam, 1553," 2(ii): 10–11.
76 Eden, "Voyage of John Lok, 1554," 2(ii): 19.

own earlier account of Benin's ceremonious and well-regulated court.[77] Eden spoke, instead, from his library.

No more does Eden's description comport with the first-hand testimony that he introduces next: "Many things ... our men saw and considered in this voyage, woorthy to be noted."[78] The account of culture provided by men who had *been* in Guinea attends to many of the same ethnographic categories we also saw invoked in Jónsson's defence of Iceland: the construction of houses, diet, and agriculture, as well as dress, communication, and collaboration between towns. Africans appeared to European observers as underdressed, yet richly adorned with ivory, gold, and copper ornaments. Princes and nobles were identified, indicating a politically complex society characterized by order and deference to authority. Bread was observed to be baked out of "very faire wheate." In particular, mariners and merchants clearly noted the circumspection of Africans in trade: they used weights and measures in a systematic way and "will not lose any sparke of golde of any value."[79] By the account of Eden's informants, the inhabitants of Guinea largely lived in conformity with the natural laws that Europeans believed directed men to cultivate, fashion, and exchange the fruits of the earth. West Africa was not at all *terra nullius*, inhabited by people who lacked the capacity to develop law, religion, and commonwealth; quite the converse.[80]

Eden did not try to adjudicate meaningful differences between the different sources that flow into his narrative, nor to differentiate their respective claims

77 Eden, "Voyage of M. Thomas Windam, 1553," 2(ii): 12.
78 Eden, "Voyage of John Lok, 1554," 2(ii): 21.
79 Jennifer Morgan highlights the cultural significance of numeracy in later rationales for the Atlantic slave trade: "As travel writers and advocates of trade worked to construct an Africa ripe for the taking, they set about undoing decades of experience with politically and economically astute Africans" (*Reckoning with Slavery*, 59).
80 In one often cited passage, Towerson disparaged as "wild and idle" communities south of the River Cess whose inhabitants were less inclined to engage in trade, and not prepared to offer the quantity of goods that would interest a long-distance merchant; comments about the ugliness of women's breasts are also connected with this part of the coast ("First Voyage of William Towrson to Guinea, 1555," 25–7). As he remarks that "the Master did not know well the place," there was apparently some difficulty locating the places where the English had traded successfully before (Towerson, ibid., 2[ii]: 25, 28). In 1556, Towerson remarked again that on entering one river he found "no village," but only people who were "wild" and "not accustomed to trade" ("Second Voyage of Master William Towrson to Guinea," 37). "Wild" was not a usual or general descriptor for African communities, but used by Towerson on these two occasions specifically to describe communities not prepared to engage in the kind of trade he sought.

to authority: English mariners who had travelled to Africa coexist in his text with continental geographers who relied on a deeply mediated classical geography.[81] When he added Eden's narratives and much of their textual surround to volume 2(ii) of *Principal Navigations*, Hakluyt did not take the trouble to caution readers about Eden's account of "the wonders and monstrous things that are engendred in Africke," as he did for the valuable but perhaps not wholly reliable accounts of William de Rubriquis and John de Plano Carpini in the preface to volume 1.[82] The poor quality control evident in his endorsement of Pory is thus echoed in the African section of *PN* (1598–1600).

The methodological (or epistemological) confusion of Eden's second narrative did not persist, however. Three more voyages ensued in the 1550s, promoted by Miles Mording and several of his Muscovy Company associates and led by Mording's apprentice Towerson. Towerson employed a master (John Ralph) who had sailed with Wyndham in 1553 and with Lok in 1554, and followed a course similar to Lok's, trading at the River Cess and at similar locations on the Gold Coast near El Mina.[83] He wrote narrative accounts of

---

[81] The heterogeneity of this second narrative by Eden is noted by Emily Bartels ("Hakluyt and the Construction of Africa," 522–3). I differ from Bartels in seeing Eden's hybrid method and use of learned sources as distinctive, rather than typical of the African materials in Hakluyt; these were largely composed by merchants and mariners from observation, and on the model of regular record-keeping described in chapter 4 (in other words, for most voyages *only* the master's or factor's journal persists, without later additions). We diverge on several other matters of fact about the documents, but like Bartels, I am ultimately interested in understanding what lay behind them.

[82] See Hakluyt, "Preface to the Reader (1598)," sig. **1r. Readers will recall from chapter 4 that Hakluyt's standards for information on northern Asia were not uniformly stringent.

[83] Eden, "Voyage of John Lok, 1554," 2(ii): 17. Alsop places Ralph or Rafe on the Wyndham voyage (Alsop, "William Towerson," 53). Trade was briefly interrupted following the misfortunes of Towerson's third voyage, which included not only significant losses of ships and men, but also the loss of two key backers to imprisonment and death or to religious exile (John Lok's elder brother Thomas and Anthony Hickman, their brother-in-law); while both John Lok and the promoters of Towerson's voyages continued to be involved, Towerson concluded his apprenticeship and became a promoter and investor rather than a direct participant in overseas trade, active in the Muscovy, Eastland, and Spanish companies, promoting trade with Constantinople, backing projects by Christopher Carleill and Edward Fenton. Elsewhere in *PN* (1598–1600), Towerson appears as one of the Muscovy Company merchants who wrote a formal response to Christopher Carleill's proposals for a voyage to the Northwest in 1583 ("Articles on Behalfe of the Moscovian Marchants"). He was also among the backers of Edward Fenton's voyage in 1582, discussed later in this chapter. As Alsop comments, "his experience in

each voyage, presumably as reports to the voyage's promoters.[84] Towerson's narratives also exhibit a consistent form, essentially the kind of time-based reporting that also characterized reports to the Muscovy Company. With accumulating detail, his reports flesh out the comment Eden cites from "our men" that West Africans were "wary people in their bargaining," practiced in both the techniques and strategies of trade, and exploiting the opportunities offered by the competing presence of Portuguese, French, Dutch, and English merchants on the coast, all seeking to exchange European textiles and metalwork for gold, ivory, and pepper.

Towerson's detailed narratives also open a perspective on a passage near the end of Eden's narrative of the 1554 to 1555 voyage, which is worth quoting in its entirety; it falls among "other things that chanced ... in this voyage" and is written in Eden's own voice, mediating between oral testimony and learned framing:

There died of our men at this last voyage about twentie and foure, whereof many died at their returne into the clime of the colde regions, as betweene the Islands of Azores and England. [Margin: "Five blacke Moores brought into England."] They brought with them certaine blacke slaves, whereof some were tall and strong men, and could wel agree with our meates and drinkes. The cold and moyst air doth somewhat offend them. Yet doubtlesse men that are borne into hot Regions may better abide colde, then men that are borne in colde Regions may abide heate, forasmuch as vehement heate resolveth the radicall moysture of mens bodies, as colde constraineth and preserveth the same.[85]

Following the five men across subsequent narratives will provide a context for Eden's apparently inaccurate characterization of them as "blacke slaves," and enable us to unravel the threads of what were several connected ideas: disease, in the striking death toll of this and other voyages to West Africa in the period; latitude (and thus climate), as a factor in *dis*tempering bodies and thus triggering disease; and the idea of hot or cold regions as productive of differently constituted bodies, responding differently to changes in latitude and diet.

---

equatorial West Africa shaped the course and trajectory of his commercial success, professonal advancement, and marriage selections." For details of Towerson's later career, see Alsop, "William Towerson," 69–81.

84 For Towerson's connection with Mording, see Alsop, "William Towerson."

85 Eden, "Voyage of John Lok, 1554," 2(ii): 22–3. The marginal comment is Hakluyt's, another indication of his access to extra-textual information on this voyage.

In 1555, at the first town where Towerson's ships made an extended stay, an African man fluent in Portuguese asked them "why we had not brought againe their men, which the last yeere we tooke away"; the English answered that they were being taught the language and would "be brought againe to be a helpe to Englishmen in this Countrey."[86] Further east, they came to a town where in 1554, the *Trinitie* had previously been well received and an offer made to them of land to build a fort – but in 1555, "none ... would come neere us ... because that foure men were taken perforce the last yeere from this place."[87] Overtures of trade proved to be an attempt to lure the English into an ambush by the Portuguese; Towerson comments that this new alliance with the Portuguese, "whom before they hated," arose "because that the last yeere M. Gainsh did take away the Captaines sonne and three others ... with their golde, and all that they had about them."[88] Hakluyt highlights each of these moments with marginal comments: "The English in anno 1554 tooke away 5 negroes"; "Foure men taken away by the English"; "Master Robert Gainshes voyage to Guinea anno 1554."[89]

In 1556, several of the men kidnapped in 1554 accompanied Towerson back to the African coast, both as translators and brokers for trade; they were greeted joyfully by their family and acquaintances, and when asked about the whereabouts of the others ("Anthonie and Binnie"), reportedly answered that they "should bee brought home the next voyage." (At least one other man appears have returned on another, unidentified English ship elsewhere on the Mina coast in the same year.)[90] Towerson's first voyage indicates that at many points, he was able to communicate only by signs; the mediation of captives named as George, Anthonie, and Binnie would thus become another valuable form of foreign knowledge. Again, Hakluyt's marginalia to the 1556 voyage emphasize that the captives had been taken away by "Robert Gaynsh" and were "brought home by our men." At one point, the captive now referred to as George rejoined Towerson's group after following "at least 30 leagues

---

86   Towerson, "First Voyage of William Towrson to Guinea, 1555," 2(ii): 32.

87   Compare a voyage to Cap-Vert, where Africans took hostages as a response to captives taken by an English ship three weeks before (Wren, "Voyage of M. George Fenner, 1566," 59).

88   Towerson, "First Voyage of William Towrson to Guinea, 1555," 2(ii): 32, 34.

89   As noted above, Hakluyt added Gainsh's name, and his role as master of the *John Evangelist*, to the earlier narrative, apparently to elucidate these later references (Eden, "Voyage of John Lok, 1554," 2[ii]: 15).

90   Towerson, "Second Voyage of Master William Towrson to Guinea," 2(ii): 38, 39.

in a small boat," and assisted with some ongoing trade.[91] The former captives appear for the last time on Towerson's report of the 1557 to 1558 voyage, when "George and Binny came to us, and brought with them about two pound of golde."[92]

As Hakluyt's marginal comments repeatedly emphasize, the men who appear in Eden's narrative around the latitude of the Azores were certainly kidnapped; but their actions indicate that they were not slaves, but captives who returned to work as intermediaries in Anglo–African exchange, on a coast where such roles had become familiar.[93] These traces of the five captives across Towerson's reports and Hakluyt's marginalia re-embed them into a microhistory of actions, consequences, and answerability, as well as into the context of families and community. These textual traces differ strikingly from narratives of the actual slaving voyages undertaken by John Hawkins, or even the casual remarks on a later voyage of general trade by George Fenner that the English were offered "Negroes for ware" by Portuguese settlers in the Cape Verde islands, and later offered to sell "five Negroes" to a Portuguese ship.[94]

Within Hakluyt's compilations, the closest parallel to Eden's use of the term "slave" for Africans who were not, in the common sense of the word, enslaved occurs in Robert Baker's verse narrative of two trading voyages in the early 1560s, a text printed by Hakluyt in 1589 but replaced in the second edition. Baker's two poems refer repeatedly to African traders and leaders he encounters on the coast as "slaves." The poems are characterized by explicitly articulated and sharply negative ideas about African peoples and cultures; most of Baker's pejoratives appear remarkably disconnected from actual encounters or events, presented as fact (or as generalization) but *not* as

---

91 Ibid., 2(ii): 41.
92 Towerson, "Third Voyage of M. William Towrson to Guinea, 1557," 49.
93 See, for example, Northrup, "Gulf of Guinea and the Atlantic World," 177, 192. In 1555, English merchants claimed that three of their fellows had remained in Benin "to understand further of those countries and commodyties there, bring with them also certen others of that country into England and promising to retorne thether agen within shorte tyme" (Blake, *Europeans in West Africa*, 2: 357). However, this claim does not correspond with Eden's narrative of merchants abandoned on the 1553–54 voyage, the only documented visit to Benin at the time of writing.
94 Wren, "Voyage of M. George Fenner, 1566," 61, 64. Fenner is believed to have been a cousin to Thomas Fenner, who sailed with Drake on a number of voyages; Thomas had set out a voyage to Guinea in 1564 that turned back after taking damage from some French ships. (See Andrews, "Thomas Fenner and the Guinea Trade, 1564.") Thomas's close connection with Drake – who had sailed on all the Hawkins voyages – offers a possible explanation for a family interest in African trade.

observations.[95] When Baker claimed that he feared Africans as cannibals, for instance, he did not anchor this hoary trope in actions he had observed or even in evidence from which he had made inferences.[96] Like Eden (and unlike his compatriots writing in prose), Baker appears to have brought with him the preconception that the people of Guinea would be characterized by "beastly living" (or at least, he was willing to supply his print audience with these sensational preconceptions). In his text, the conflation of "African" and "slave" accompanies a constellation of negative associations also evident in Eden, but markedly less so in Hakluyt's other sources.[97]

In the context of *PN* (1598–1600), Eden's explicitly pejorative comments are unusual: in their content (which does not correspond to any reported observations from the voyage); in their *de facto* negative framing (Towerson disparaged principally people who were disinclined or unprepared to engage in trade); and in their mixed and bookish methodology, projecting old ideas

---

[95] See "First Voyage of Robert Baker," 133, 134, 135. Cast adrift on the coast after losing contact with their ship, Baker and his fellows considered whether to throw themselves on the mercy of Africans or the Portuguese; Baker refers to Africans as "brutish," and as "beastly savage people" who may be cannibals, while the Portuguese – more trustworthy, since Christians – might either hang the mariners or make them "Galey slaves" ("The Second Voyage of Robert Baker," 139; note mispagination in original). Baker – like Towerson, who was troubled by the uncovered breasts of African women – also took exception to African dress: a captain came to trade "as naked as my naile, Not having witte or honestie to cover once his taile" ("First Voyage of Robert Baker," 132). For Towerson, see "First Voyage of William Towrson to Guinea, 1555," 2(ii): 25, 26.

[96] For comparison, the Frobisher expedition into the Arctic found presumptive evidence for their judgement that the Inuit were cannibals in their consumption of raw meat and the discovery of discarded and damaged clothing that had belonged to five captured Englishmen (Best, "True Discourse," 68). Bernhard Klein remarks that Baker's ideas were at odds with his actual experiences (Klein, "Robert Baker in Guinea"). John Sparke wrote that the Mani-Sumba "live mostly by the spoile of their enemies, both in taking their victuals, and eating them also" but also notes that "we tooke ... of the Samboses none at all"; in other words, the claim of cannibalism was report rather than observation, although emphasized by Hakluyt's marginal comment "man-eaters" ("Second Voyage Made by John Hawkins, 1564," 3: 504). A manuscript account of John Hawkins's 1568 voyage to Sierra Leone does include an account of Mani-Sumba cannibalism following a battle "which oure owne men [did witnes]"; neither the manuscript nor the anecdote appears in the compilation (BL MS Cotton Otho VIII, fo. 28v, transcribed by Williamson, *Sir John Hawkins*, 509). On the Sumba as "man-eaters," see Rodney, *History of the Upper Guinea Coast*, 43–5, 56.

[97] This discussion focuses on vocabulary; on the theory and practice of slavery in sixteenth-century England, see part 3 below, and on Africans arriving in England before the Hawkins slaving voyages, see Habib, *Black Lives in the English Archives*, chaps. 1–2.

onto the scrim of witness reports that did not appear to support them. His voice has to be distinguished from the other voices braided together in the 1554 narrative, and his preconceptions from the observations made by others on the ground. But even as an apparent outlier, as a distinct voice, Eden's *ideas* about Guinea invite our scrutiny. He was after all *not* an outlier to the enterprise of English maritime and commercial expansion – on the contrary, he was closely involved with the planning, conceptualization, and print dissemination of distant voyages. And the suggestion that larger *systems* of thought animated Eden's negative conceptions about tropical Africa and Africans is borne out in his other writings (as well as in those of other authors).[98]

Eden's discussion of the five captives appears triggered by the onset of disease, which in turn he connected with the passage out of the tropics and into higher latitudes. Elsewhere, Eden considered latitude as an index of the sun's influence on terrestrial things. In his first compilation, he wrote that it was "a general rule, that nearest unto the south partes of the world betwene the two Tropikes under ye Equinoctial or burning lyne, where the sunne is of greatest forse, is the chiefest place where gold is engendered."[99] These links between rich metals and the heat of the tropics echo the proposals of the merchant Thorne; they were commonplace in discussions of the new geography.[100] Eden presented his "general rule" not only as the sum of empirical observations, drawing on "olde and new Histories, [and] dayly experience" for the knowledge that gold was to be found in Mexico and West Africa – but also as a theory grounded in and explained by "the principles of Natural Philosophy" expounded in "the Bookes of George Agric, and Albertus Magnus."[101] Agricola's and Albertus's work would have informed Eden's assertion that because the sun was "the chief instrument and mean that God uses"

---

98 For comparable examples of writing and thinking about Africa, see the discussions of André Thevet's and George Abbot's geographical writing in Vaughan and Vaughan, "Before Othello."

99 Eden, *A Treatyse of the Newe India*, sig. aa6r–v.

100 See chapter 3.

101 Eden, *A Treatyse of the Newe India*, sig. aa7v, aa6v. The works referenced are Georgius Agricola's *De re metallica* (Basel, 1556) and Albertus Magnus, *De natura locurum* (thirteenth century, various early modern editions); Eden cites the second title elsewhere in his preface. On Albertus's theory of place and its consequences for Spanish understandings of the Americas, see Wey Gómez, *Tropics of Empire*, 231–91. As noted above, Eden appended Vannocio Biringuccio's treatise on metals to his work on the Indies to inform readers of how the gold and silver found there was produced by "naturall generation" (Eden, *Decades*, fo. 325v; see Long, "Openness of Knowledge").

to generate, preserve, and alter sublunary creatures, attention to its movements could aid in understanding "the marvelous effects that [it] caused."[102] The philosophical understanding that Eden references in suggesting that gold was "engendered" where the sun was "of greatest force" held that gold was generated from a mixture of elemental substances subjected to heat (hence its prevalence in the tropics), just as silver – more "watery" – bore the influence of the moon and would be found in colder regions.[103]

This science of place did not ignore the influence of the sun on human bodies and temperaments. We can thus place into context Eden's comment that English merchants and mariners returning from Africa in 1555 began to sicken again as they reentered the "clime of the colde regions." The relative ease with which he believed the African captives to have adapted to the English diet and English climate may have indicated to him that the constitution of persons born nearer the equator was distinctive, more resilient, able to withstand environmental shocks without suffering the disease that Englishmen experienced in travelling to Africa.[104] Eden's references to climate and bodies in the passage in which Gainsh's captives first appear point towards this system of ideas, one that renders his thinking intelligible, if not coherent: elements of old cosmographies survived to jostle new sciences and data, and contradictions between books and eyewitness testimony remained unresolved.

The underpinnings of Eden's thinking offer us a heuristic rather than a sure guide to Hakluyt's other African materials; the compilation and the writings of those who supplied its contents are generally poor in the kinds of guiding evidence we can glean from Eden's writing and career, and neither Hakluyt himself, nor his traveller-authors, were equally forthcoming about the furniture of their minds.[105] Conceptual schemes only occasionally manifest

---

102 Eden, "Preface" to Cortés, *Arte of Navigation*, sig. CC2v.

103 Eden, *Decades*, fo. 333v–334r, 340v.

104 The already-cited text by Wateson argued that scurvy caused mariners to die "when they returned out of hot regions into cold climates" (Wateson, *Cures of the Diseased*, sig. C4r). See also Eden's preface to Cortés, *Arte of Navigation*, sig. CC3v. To place these ideas into a broader context, Sheldon Watts details a history in which Africans were seen both as immune to yellow fever/malaria, and as the agents by which Europeans became infected (*Epidemics and History*, chap. 6).

105 Geographical writing in sixteenth-century England was rich in empirical observations and conjectures about physical geography but relatively poor in explicit reflection, in contrast with the case of Spain, where a different colonial situation and institutional culture led to copious writings by prominent jurists and theologians but limited print circulation of first-hand reports by travellers. For a survey of reflective or theoretical

among what appear to be largely practical and atheoretical documents; for instance, George Best's discussion of Africa in the preface to his account of Frobisher's Arctic voyages drew together the "experience of our Englishmen" on the coast, knowledge about Africans resident in England, and cosmographical theory dividing the earth into zones of latitude. Africa could appear in a work on the Arctic because Best understood both to be extreme climates, outside the normatively temperate climate in which Europe and England were located; like Best, many English mariners might have personal experience of both.[106] At least for the educated among Hakluyt's mariners, merchants, and authors, it is plausible that Africa may have figured in a comparative system whose primordial categories were latitude or climate; situating the coast of Guinea latitudinally, as a region in the torrid zone, might have seemed to offer predictions or explanations about its peoples, resources, and environment. If thinking with climate was no longer a stable or coherent conceptual system, it nonetheless retained an influence in connecting latitude with degrees of civility – for instance, in the case of Iceland, whose far northern position led sixteenth-century Europeans to think of it as exotic, disordered, and uncivil.

Yet whatever the horizon of expectations provided by such ideas, the firsthand reports of English merchants and seamen did not draw on the language of marvels or monsters to describe the various peoples with whom they traded along the African coast, nor describe the region as an uninhabitable desert. In this way, the first-hand narratives found in *PN* 2(ii) differ sharply from the geography of editors like Eden and Pory. For those first-hand observers, the experience of disease and morbidity might have confirmed or activated understandings of tropical Africa as an extreme climate unfriendly to temperate life, yet even here English witnesses did not invariably characterize the African environment as deathly, dangerous, or even uncomfortable – on the contrary. An illustration may be instructive. Hakluyt printed parallel accounts of the voyage by a factor and a ship's master of a 1588 voyage that sought to revive

---

writing on the New World by Spanish authors, see Pagden, *Fall of Natural Man*. For a discussion of the cultures of geographical writing and map-making in sixteenth-century Spain, see Portuondo, *Secret Science*.

106 Best, "True Discourse," 3: 48–53. (This section of his text is separately titled in the volume 3 contents list as "Experiences and reasons of the Sphere to proove all parts of the worlde habitable.") Cassander Smith sets Best's often-cited discussion of colour – in the context of his thinking about climate – alongside Walter Ralegh's extended account of Guiana as another encounter with the tropics (*Black Africans in the British Imagination*, chap. 5). On English mariners, see Alsop, "From Muscovy to Guinea: English Seamen of the Mid-Sixteenth Century."

trade with Benin, and these describe sharply different perceptions and experiences in an almost identical environment.[107] This voyage experienced levels of disease and mortality comparable to those of 1553, phenomena that the factor Anthony Ingram, who travelled upriver to the court, linked directly to the West African climate and its interaction with English bodies: "(our natures at this first time not so well acquainted with that climate) we fell all of us into the disease of the fever."[108] Soon, Ingram wrote, "we had so many sicke and dead of our companie, that we looked all for the same happe, and so thought to loose both our ship, life, countrey and all."[109] During the same period, however, the ship's master, James Welsh, repeatedly recorded "faire weather" (10 February), days that were "faire and temperate" (7, 9 February, and 17 to 19 March), "a temperate day" (16 March), and only occasionally "a close soultry hot morning" (4 March).

Welsh's appreciation of Benin's weather extended to its "very gentle and loving" people, whose ingenuity impressed him: "They have good store of sope, and it smelleth like beaten violets. Also many pretie fine mats and baskets that they make, and spoones of Elephants teeth very curiously wrought." Welsh also found the African diet to be both pleasing and healthful for his English crew: "their bread is a kind of roots, they call it Inamia, and when it is well sodden I would leave our bread to eat of it, it is pleasant in eating, and light of digestion ... Our men upon fish-dayes had rather eate the rootes with oyle and vineger, then to eate good stockfish. There are great store of palme trees, out of the which they gather great store of wine, which wine is very white and very pleasant, & we should buy two gallons of it for 20 shels."[110] Where Eden explained English morbidity by the shock of extreme variations in climate and the men's immoderate insistence on "eating without measure of the fruits of the countrey, and drinking the wine of the Palme trees," Welsh found Benin to be temperate, with new foods that were pleasing and healthful, "light of digestion." This was not a place inimical to English bodies – on the contrary.

---

107 Ingram, "Voyage to Benin, 1588"; Welsh, "A Voyage to Benin [...] 1588." On the two voyages set forth under Welsh, and details of the trade, see Ryder, *Benin and the Europeans*, 81–4.

108 Ingram, "Voyage to Benin, 1588," 2(ii): 129.

109 Ibid., 2(ii): 130.

110 Welsh, "A Voyage to Benin [...] 1588," 2(ii): 129. The first of these two passages references ivory carvings that have now been much studied by art historians; see, for instance, the discussion and bibliography in Sobral, "Expansion and the Arts," 397–400; Gomes and Casimiro, "Afro-Portuguese Ivories."

Other Englishmen echoed Welsh: the chaplain John Walker wrote during his stay in the Sierra Leone estuary that "Where it is reported that the Coaste of Guynea is daungerous in contagyon of sycknesse we founde it very wholesome."[111] Walker's colleague Richard Madox noted that "above 50 men that wer before geven over to death" became "lusty and strong" after two weeks on shore there, with the benefit of fresh oysters, lemons, and bathing. "I told them the land was nothing so unholsom as yt was heald."[112] If Ingram and others experienced the African tropics as noxious and fatal, to others they were pleasant, appealing, and restorative. English experience of endemic disease and West Africa's unfamiliar tropical heat was real, but neither that experience nor the meanings attached to it were invariant. Eden's framing of tropical Africa as a place of aberrant nature, different bodies, and defective societies offers one potential context for the documents and interactions that ensued. Welsh's narrative provides some counterweight, and caution would in any case be warranted in generalizing from Eden to other witnesses about whom we know much less. Yet alert reading is warranted: we can't assume associations of ideas such as those manifest in Eden's writing *weren't* more widely held, at least in some attenuated form, not only by geographers and editors but by the investors who shaped voyages to Africa and the mariners and merchants who effected and recorded them.[113]

The last part of the chapter widens the survey of Hakluyt's African materials beyond the narratives of trade in volume 2(ii) to consider some narratives of

111 Donno, *An Elizabethan in 1582*, 310.

112 Ibid., 175. Paul Hair draws on testimony from English captives to conclude that the Hawkins crews experienced markedly higher mortality at Sierra Leone in 1568 (Hair, "Protestants as Pirates, Slavers, and Protomissionaries," 211–12). But William Hawkins told his companions in 1582 that "his uncle had comended this playce unto hym"; Madox comments that "I cold never hear grownd of reason why or how yt should be so unholsome, but only bare wordes whereunto I cold geve but bare credit" (Taylor, *Troublesome Voyage*, 81). Hair notes elsewhere that "the dangers of disease [on the West African coast] were less publicized in Portuguese accounts," which continued to see colonization as desirable – "a fond dream encouraged by the reality that a number of Portuguese did settle in Guinea" (Hair, "Portuguese in Guinea 1444–1650," 17).

113 The continuing influence of the classicizing, pejorative geography disseminated by Eden can be glimpsed again in John Speed's description of Africa on a 1626 map: "[Africa] in most parts hath scarce plenty sufficient to maintain her Inhabitants, and where there is, we shall meet with multitudes of ravening Beasts, or other horrible Monsters, enough to devour both it and us. In a word, there is no Region of the World so great an enemy to man's commerce ... so Pliny reports" (J.S., Map and Description of Africa, 1626, CO/700 African Photograph, TNA, cited in Morgan, *Reckoning with Slavery*, 121).

voyages to and then beyond Africa in volume 3. In contrast with the largely peaceful trade of volume 2, a striking degree and kind of violence threads through these documents, of a kind that appears both undermotivated and (in comparison with other parts of the compilation) undernarrated.[114] The narrative treatment of Anglo–African violence, resistance, and conflict can be usefully compared with parallel material on the West Indies (to which some of these voyages continued). The contrasting case of Anglo–Spanish conflict in the North Atlantic, copiously documented by Hakluyt in materials that adjoin narratives of African trade in the second half of volume 2, provides another point of comparison (see chapter 7). Both on their own, and against the background of comparable narratives elsewhere, these sources exhibit a violence that calls for scrutiny.

WEST AFRICA AND THE ENGLISH MARITIME WORLD

But nowe it is high time for us to weigh our ancre ... to get cleare of these boistrous, frosty, and misty seas, and with all speede to direct our course for the milde lightsome, temperate, and warme Atlantick Ocean, over which the Spaniards and Portugales have made so many pleasant prosperous and golden voyages ... Had they not continuall and yerely trade in some part or other of Africa, for *getting of slaves*, for sugar, for Elephants teeth, graines, silver, gold, and other precious wares, which served as allurements to draw them on by little and litle, and as proppes to stay them from giving over their attempts? (Hakluyt, "To the Reader," PN 1:*4v–*5r; emphasis mine)

1 "The first voyage of ... John Hawkins ... 1562" (3:500)
2 John Sparke, "The second voyage made by ... John Hawkins ... 1564" (3:501–21.
3 John Hawkins, "The third troublesome voyage of ... John Hawkins ... 1567, & 1568" (3:521–5)
4 Miles Philips, "The voyage of Miles Philips one of the company put on shore by sir John Hawkins, 1568" (3:469–87)
5 Job Hortop, "The travels of Job Hortop set on land by John Hawkins 1586 in the bay of Mexico" (3:487–95)
6 Luke Ward, "The voyage of M. Edward Fenton ... begunne in the yeere 1577" (3:757–68)

---

114 See Hair, "Sources on Early Sierra Leone: (21) English Voyages of the 1580s," 65.

7 John Sarracoll, "The voyage of M. Robert Withrington, and
  M. Christopher Lister ... Anno 1586" (3:769–78)
8 Francis Pretty, "The prosperous voyage of M. Thomas Candish ... 1588"
  (3:803–25)

Hakluyt's only apparent reference to slavery occurs, seemingly out of place, in the celebration of England's northern voyages that prefaces volume 1.[115] It arrives there whole: that is, enslaved persons were already commodities to be traded and West Africa identified as the source for that trade, along with the trades in "Elephants teeth, graines, silver, and gold" that the editor would document in volume 2(ii). Hakluyt's exhortation to "get cleare" of the North in order to access the resources of the South alluded to the known history of Luso-Iberian expansion; yet his comments also echo the long association of the torrid zone with the riches of precious metals and readily commodified people.[116] As this brief citation from volume 1 only begins to suggest, the apparently peripheral presence of the Atlantic slave trade during the period covered by *PN* (1598–1600) connects across the compilation in ways that are not always easy to recognize. In the remainder of this chapter, we look ahead to volume 3, and to materials on Atlantic Africa embedded in voyages to the Americas and beyond.

In the sixteenth century, English merchants who engaged with sub-Saharan Africa almost invariably treated the bilateral trade in goods and the triangular trade in slaves as the work of distinct voyages.[117] When Portuguese-speaking

---

115 This passage is among numerous references to slaves and slavery unmentioned in existing indexes; see note 9 above.

116 As Nicolás Wey Gómez has meticulously argued in *Tropics of Empire*, these associations and the medieval science behind them drew Columbus not only west but south, towards the American tropics.

117 On the evidence of the documents, English traders in goods occasionally acquired slaves in exchanges with the Portuguese. In 1566, George Fenner bought a small number of slaves from Portuguese traders in West Africa, and sold them to a Portuguese ship off the Lizard (Wren, "Voyage of M. George Fenner, 1566," 2[ii]: 64). Other early voyages intended for trade in goods avoided contact with the Portuguese, and did not report that slaves were offered to them for sale. Among later voyages that touched at Sierra Leone, only the accounts of Edward Fenton's voyage reported acquiring small numbers of slaves. Luke Ward and the chaplain John Walker both note the purchase of four slaves to replace crew who had died; Walker adds that they acquired "a boy ... exchanged for a boy wch [Ward] had before" (Ward, "Voyage of M. Edward Fenton, 1577," 3: 759; Taylor, *Troublesome Voyage*, 209). Both Ward and the chaplain Richard Madox record that the expedition traded one of their smaller ships, the *Elizabeth*,

Africans asked Towerson about Gainsh's captives, and complained to him about the Portuguese propensity to take captives for the slave trade, Towerson not only assured his interlocutors of the captives' return but proposed that the English might protect them against such mistreatment; Towerson's narratives and Hakluyt's frequent marginalia regarding these captives make clear that Gainsh's kidnapping was understood to pose a problem for later trade with the communities who were aware of it.[118] Yet the distinction suggested by Hakluyt's documents between activities undertaken by different crews and in different regions belies the shared context from which voyages and documents emerged. Although many more sixteenth-century voyages pursued a trade in goods than one in slaves, a number of the merchants who invested in bringing gold, spices, and ivory back from Africa also invested in the voyages intended to sell African slaves to buyers in the West Indies. Nor were such merchants a discrete, isolated group; *any* English merchant with the capacity to engage in trade with West Africa was also likely to be involved in the other emergent long-distance trades of the period, with Muscovy, Morocco, the Levant, and eventually the East Indies.[119] Thus while English involvement in the Atlantic slave trade during the sixteenth century appears to have been temporally limited to a series of voyages in the 1560s, this activity was broadly connected in its financial arrangements and personnel. Participation in the voyages, and profits from the sale of between fifteen hundred and two thousand persons, would have been diffused across the mercantile and maritime communities documented by Hakluyt. It also appears that captured or enslaved Africans in smaller numbers were taken up on voyages of other kinds.[120]

---

to Portuguese buyers in exchange for rice, ivory, and one slave, an eleven-year-old boy (Donno, *An Elizabethan in 1582*, 169, 172; Ward, "Voyage of M. Edward Fenton, 1577," 3: 758).

118 Towerson, "Second Voyage of Master William Towrson to Guinea," 2(ii): 39. John Sparke, the narrator of Hawkins's 1564 voyage, writes that the *Minion* – on a voyage of trade the same year – had indeed warned people at Cape Verde of "our comming, and our pretense [to have taken Negros there perforce]," suggesting that traders did not welcome slave-taking in the communities with whom they hoped to trade (Sparke, "Second Voyage Made by John Hawkins, 1564," 3: 503). The *Minion* would form part of Hawkins's small fleet in 1567, another indicator of the linked infrastructure of trade and slaving voyages.

119 See, for instance, the short biographies in Willan, *Muscovy Merchants*. Towerson's involvements provide an indicative case study (Alsop, "William Towerson").

120 The *Leicester Journal* of Drake's West Indies voyages of 1585–86, for instance, suggests that the men were taking the opportunity of collecting African slaves for themselves,

The practical conditions of the late sixteenth century did not favour English involvement in the Atlantic slave trade, whatever its profits for other nations. Thinkers like Hakluyt believed England's economy to suffer from a labour surplus rather than a labour shortage; new colonies and new export markets were imagined as a remedy for the problem of underemployment, rather than as large-scale agricultural and resource extraction enterprises requiring unfree labour.[121] John Hawkins and his associates saw demand from Luso-Iberian colonists in the New World as an economic opportunity, but Portuguese resistance on the West African coast, and legal and governmental barriers on the West Indian side, impeded English access to the Atlantic circuit of buying and selling slaves: mariners captured in Hawkins's attempt to force his way into the West Indian market were variously imprisoned, tortured, burned at the stake, condemned to the galleys, or put to service in Mexico. Of necessity, slave-trading voyages became acts of aggression against other European powers as well as acts of predation on Africans, with high returns but also significant added risk. These practical barriers and disincentives help to explain the relative paucity of programmatic slave trading among the voyages Hakluyt documented. We could indeed ask what explains its *presence*, given the investment of Hakluyt's generation in representing their countrymen and nation as morally superior to the Spanish, merciful rather than cruel, humane rather than barbarous, allies rather than tyrants.[122]

How was slavery conceptualized by the communities to which Hakluyt belonged? The compilation yields little direct evidence. In a consideration of legal foundations for settlement in the Americas, Sir George Peckham included the enslavement of war captives among principles that made up the "law of nations": "from the first beginning ... all men have agreed, that no violence

---

noting the determination "that none under the degree of ansient shulde keepe a Negro or other stranger" (Keeler, *Drake's West Indian Voyage*, 169).

121 See, for example, Hakluyt, *PD*, chap. 4. The late Elizabethan warrants concerning the removal of some Africans from England, apparently as a reward to a Baltic merchant who had redeemed a number of Englishmen captive on the Iberian Peninsula, cite the domestic surplus of labour and shortage of employment as a reason that their presence in the realm was undesirable (see Weissbourd, "'Those in Their Possession'").

122 While one passage in "Particuler Discourse" quotes Las Casas and Jean Metal on the "inborn savagery" of the Spanish as manifested in their practice of slavery in the Caribbean, their and Hakluyt's concern appears to be almost entirely with the enslavement of Indigenous people from the Americas. "Moores" appear only as escapees and rebels against the Spanish, in contrast with the "weak and feeble" Indigenous people, whose suffering provides the focus of the chapter (Hakluyt, *PD*, 55–60).

should be offered to Ambassadours: That the Sea with his Havens should be common: *That such as should fortune to be taken in warre, should be servants or slaves.* And that strangers should not bee driven away from the place or Countrey whereunto they doe come" (emphasis mine).[123] Peckham's comment reflected a juridical tradition rooted in classical antiquity. On this view, those captured in a war between states might be enslaved rather than killed, and slavery reflected the commutation of actual death into social death.[124] This rationale fit reasonably well with conditions in the Mediterranean, where, as we saw in chapter 5, the risk of captivity and enslavement was among the costs of doing business for English merchant shipping; Mediterranean slavery relied on conditions of endemic conflict between Christian and Muslim maritime powers.[125] Peckham drew on the law of nations principally as a legal basis for English rights of discovery in the Americas, however. (A Catholic investor in Humphrey Gilbert's northern settlement project, he had consulted with both Hakluyt and Dee.) His glancing reference to slavery may nonetheless suggest another climate of assumptions, this time drawing on contemporary legal thought rather than the science of place.

Peckham's writing suggests a debt to the Spanish jurist Francisco de Vitoria, whose expansive reflections on the legal framework for European engagement with the Americas would be deeply influential for the promoters of the Virginia Company.[126] Vitoria's work engaged with a range of questions posed by Spain's expanding global empire, including the trade in enslaved Africans. While he condemned "deceitful practices resulting in capture" of slaves, he did not consider the Atlantic slave trade itself to require a rationale beyond that afforded by the law of nations. Rights of making war, taking captives, and disposing of those captives were the prerogatives of sovereigns; the Portuguese, who channelled African slaves into the Atlantic world, could claim to have

---

123 Peckham, "True Reporte," 168. Peckham's text originally appeared as *A true reporte* (London, 1583).

124 See the classic study by Orlando Patterson, *Slavery and Social Death*, 5–8 and passim.

125 See Earle, *Corsairs of Malta and Barbary*, chap. 1.

126 On the English reception of work by Vitoria and fellow jurists of the Salamanca School, see Fitzmaurice, *Sovereignty*, chap. 3; Tomlins, *Freedom Bound*, 104–37 passim; MacMillan, *Sovereignty*, chap. 1. Vitoria discussed the permissible taking of slaves in war in *De Indis* 3.1 and *De Jure Belli* 3.3 (Vitoria, *Political Writings*, 283, 319). See, however, the discussion of theological arguments against Atlantic slavery as it was practised in Rodney, *History of the Upper Guinea Coast*, 119–21.

purchased them from African rulers who took captives in wars.[127] A second kind of argument for various forms of dispossession might invoke either religion or the lack of "civility" as potential grounds for denying natural rights to non-Europeans.[128] These ideas had deeper roots in Aristotelian thought, but according to Christopher Tomlins, were expressed explicitly with reference to slavery in Alberico Gentili's *De jure belli* (London, 1588), an important contemporary English work of political theory. Gentili, an associate of Hakluyt's and adviser to Queen Elizabeth, was Regius Professor of Civil Law at Oxford; he identified "a distinct population subject to slavery ... pirates and robbers; thieves and criminals; savages and brutes."[129]

As other scholars have shown, the actual legal status of slavery *in* England was far from clear, as was the status of Africans who had been enslaved before arriving in England. These silences and ambiguities have their own kind of legibility.[130] The contents of *Principal Navigations* remain reticent on the principles that animated the kinds of practice they document, and Hakluyt's

127 Herman Bennett has remarked on the "tacit recognition of [African] sovereignty" embedded in the view of slaves as war captives (*African Kings and Black Slaves*, 132). On Luso–African diplomacy, see, for instance, the overview and documents, respectively, in Northrup, "Africans, Early European Contacts, and the Emergent Diaspora," 39–43; Blake, *Europeans in West Africa*, vol. 1. After an initial phase of raiding, the Portuguese found it preferable to buy slaves in trade with African rulers (see for instance, Ryder, *Benin and the Europeans*, chap. 2). While English sources frequently identify African "captains" or "kings," no formal diplomacy appears to have been contemplated or undertaken by the English beyond the negotiations necessary for commerce. For a unique exception on the Fenton voyage (not reproduced by Hakluyt), see Taylor, *Troublesome Voyage*, 108–9.

128 Bennett helpfully links discussion of the late medieval legal traditions that would configure and respond to European contact with the Americas to the Luso-Iberian contacts with Africa which preceded that contact: for instance, the recurrent question of whether non-Christians properly exercised dominion over their own lands, decided in the affirmative by Innocent IV but reopened by later thinkers (*African Kings and Black Slaves*, chap. 3).

129 Tomlins, *Freedom Bound*, 422–3. On Gentili and Hakluyt, see Pirillo, "Balance of Power and Freedom of the Seas"; Hotman, Hotman, and van Meel, *Epistolae*. MacMillan considers that a generation of English civil lawyers "were taught the compilations of Justinian and Vitoria by Gentili or his colleagues in the professorships at Cambridge and Oxford" (*Sovereignty*, 46). Finally, Habib provides a survey of English court cases and decisions involving slavery in the sixteenth and early seventeenth century (*Black Lives in the English Archives*).

130 These archival silences have been remarked on and discussed by numerous scholars; see (inter alia) Habib, *Black Lives in the English Archives*; Weissbourd, "'Those in Their Possession'"; Smallwood, "Politics of the Archive."

unpublished texts of advice and theory – voluble on natural rights of discovery, navigation, and trade – pay no heed at all to the commerce with Guinea, a place "where wee have little to doe."[131] Yet even if we begin from the climate of assumptions that provided early modern thinkers with a rationale for slavery in broad terms, the practice of Hawkins and others will provide numerous examples of the gap between theories of who could be enslaved, and the business of slaving.

The voyages mounted by Hawkins in 1562, 1564, and 1567 were distinguished from the trading voyages of the 1550s and early 1560s by their aim: intended to buy, seize, or capture appreciable numbers of slaves on the African coast, Hawkins's ships did not seek to engage in trade with Africans other than as a pretext for taking captives (and that only once).[132] The practical origins of these voyages are well understood. According to Harry Kelsey, William Hawkins (the father) on his voyages to Africa and Brazil had met "Portuguese traders lading slaves for transport" across the Atlantic. His two sons, William the younger and John, joined other English merchants in entering the wine and sugar trade at the Canaries; the Thorne family too had employed a factor there, as indicated by a ledger entry included in *PN* (1598–1600).[133] An associate in Tenerife – Pedro de Ponte, a local magnate of Genoese descent – assisted Hawkins in conceiving, planning, and executing his three slave-trading voyages; Hawkins thus had access to commercial intelligence distinct from that developed through the trading enterprises of Towerson and others.[134]

---

131 Hakluyt, *PD*, 12.

132 At Cape Rojo in 1567, "with ... wares which the negros esteme they enticed the negros to come to them ... and ... our menne, thinking to sette uppon them to take them, they dowbted and fledde even as our menne pretended to doe their feat" (Williamson, *Sir John Hawkins*, 505; Kelsey, *Sir John Hawkins*, 64). The anonymous journal of the voyage, BL MS Cotton Otho E. VIII fo. 17–41, is transcribed by Williamson and cited in Kelsey's valuable biography.

133 "Briefe Note Concerning the Canarie Isles, 1526." (On the Thornes, see chapter 2.) Thomas Nicholls's description of the Canaries drew on his experience there as a factor for Thomas Lok, Anthony Hickman, and Edward Castelin, all active in trade with Guinea ("Description of the Canarie Islands," 2[ii]: 7). On Anglo–Canarian trade more generally, see Scammell, "English in the Atlantic Islands."

134 The report provided by Hakluyt touches lightly on the friendships at the Canaries that informed Hawkins of the market for slaves in Hispaniola and the ease with which they "might be had" in Guinea ("First Voyage of John Hawkins to the West Indies, 1562," 3: 500). Further details are provided by Kelsey, *Sir John Hawkins*, 10–13. Kelsey, in turn, cites Antonio Rumeu de Armas, *Los viajes de John Hawkins a America, 1562–1595* (Seville, 1947).

Financial backing, however, came from some familiar sources: names include Sir Lionel Ducket, Sir Thomas Lodge, Benjamin Gonson, Sir William Winter, and Thomas Bromfield.[135] The involvement of Gonson and Winter – both members of Elizabeth's Navy Board – heralded quasi-official support that would supply the seven hundred ton *Jesus of Lübeck*, one of the Queen's ships, for the later voyages of 1564 and 1567.

The terse, anonymous account of Hawkins's first voyage already manifests the practical information he had gained from his new Canarian partners, who also secured the services of a Spanish pilot. Rather than recreating the familiar itinerary of the Towerson voyages, which touched at the River Cess before continuing to Shamma and other towns on the Gold Coast, the Hawkins ships would scour the coast between Cap-Vert (Senegal) and the Sierra Leone estuary, destinations that were better positioned for a voyage across the Atlantic and offered opportunities to raid communities and take captives, as well as to take advantage of an existing trade in enslaved people.[136] Hakluyt's

---

135 Duckett was a member of the Muscovy Company, and invested in the Northwest Passage searches by Sir Martin Frobisher (1576–78) and John Davis (1585–87); he backed Hawkins in 1562, 1564, and 1567. Lodge was a member of the Muscovy Company, traded with Morocco, and invested in the trading voyages to Guinea of 1558, 1561, 1563, and 1564, as well as the 1562 voyage by Hawkins. Gonson was treasurer of the Navy and in 1567 became Hawkins's father-in-law; his father William owned the ship whose voyage to Chios is related in Hakluyt, "Voyage to the Iles of Candia and Chio, 1534 [and] 1535." Winter was surveyor of the Navy; he had invested in Wyndham's voyage in 1553 (Loades, "Winter, Sir William"). A Thomas Bromfield was one of the merchants associated with an attempted voyage to China in 1596, funded by Sir Robert Dudley ("Letters Sent in the Yere 1596, to the Emperour of China"). Among the list of gentlemen who sailed with Hawkins in 1564 were John Chester, son of Sir William Chester (member of the Muscovy Company, active in trading with Morocco, Persia, and Guinea), and Anthony Parkhurst (active in informing the Hakluyts on the Newfoundland fishery). A ship lost on the voyage of 1564–65 was co-owned by Chester and Sir William Garrard, a member of the Muscovy Company who invested in trade with Guinea as well as in the Hawkins voyages of 1564–65 and 1567–68 (Willan, *Muscovy Merchants of 1555*; Loades, "Winter, Sir William"; Parkhurst, "Letter Written to M. Richard Hakluyt of the Midle Temple, 1578"; Alsop, "Chester, Sir William").

136 For the 1560s voyages, I have relied chiefly on the account given in Kelsey's biography of Hawkins, which draws on English and Spanish archival sources (Kelsey, *Sir John Hawkins*, chaps. 1–4). In the region of Sierra Leone, "slavery ... was related to war," as "a series of invasions from the interior displaced many people, some of whom were enslaved" (Lovejoy, *Transformations in Slavery*, 43). For a more detailed history of Mane conquests, the resulting political and demographic landscape, and the consequences for a trade in slaves, see Rodney, *History of the Upper Guinea Coast*, chaps. 2, 4.

unattributed account of the 1562 voyage records that, travelling apparently directly to Tagrin Bay in Sierra Leone, Hawkins "got into his possession, partly by the sworde, and partly by other meanes, to the number of 300. Negros at the least," of whom almost half may have died during the Atlantic crossing.[137] The merchant John Sparke narrated the 1564 voyage in more detail. This expedition landed first at Cap-Vert, where Hawkins was thwarted by the *Minion*'s prior warnings of his intentions. Working south along the coast, he landed at one island where the people fled; lacking a pilot he was unable to go into the Rio Grande River, and so proceeded on to Sambula Island (perhaps Tamara Island, in the Îles de Los), inhabited by Sapi people "who before were ... conquered" by Mane invaders and enslaved by them. The expedition spent several days there "to take the inhabitants with burning, and spoiling their townes."[138] In another place, however, Hawkins was able to take advantage of an existing trade in people who had already been enslaved; in the "Callowsa River," Hawkins found two Portuguese ships at anchor, "dispatched his business, and so returned with two Caravels, loaden with Negros." On the way down river, Portuguese informants encouraged him to raid a town whose women, children, and gold were defended by only a few men – but the town was vigorously defended, and only ten captives taken, with seven Englishmen killed and a number more injured.[139] After the smaller ships had made several more sorties "about [their] trafficke," the English began to sicken and Hawkins set sail for the Indies, unable to delay long enough to gain more captives from a war impending between two local rulers. (He would learn that one king had been urged by "the Tangomangos" to take some English captives "to see what

---

[137] "First Voyage of John Hawkins to the West Indies, 1562"; Kelsey, *Sir John Hawkins*, 15.

[138] Sparke, "Second Voyage Made by John Hawkins, 1564," 3: 504; Brooks, *Landlords and Strangers*, 294–5. I have relied on Brooks for African and Portuguese history and placenames; his work occasionally transposes events from the two English voyages of 1564 and 1567. Rodney, however, suggests that the island raided by Hawkins was Sherbro Island, to the south (*History of the Upper Guinea Coast*, 61). John Sparke, as Kelsey notes, would later become mayor of Plymouth; he died in 1603 (*Sir John Hawkins*, 28; Hunneyball, "Sparke, John"). Although there appear to have been several relatives of the same name, a "John Sparke" travelled to Novgorod in 1566, and to Persia in 1568, on behalf of the Muscovy Company ("Voyage of Arthur Edwards, 1568," 389; "Voyage of Thomas Southam and John Sparke, 1566").

[139] Sparke, "Second Voyage Made by John Hawkins, 1564," 3: 505. The narrative suggests the Portuguese were simply mistaken, but local conditions suggests Hawkins was an unwitting tool in an intra-African conflict in which his interlocutors were also involved.

kind of people we were.")[140] That year, he sailed with some four hundred captives, arriving in Borbuta with some ill and near death. An additional slaving voyage in 1566 to 1567 was led by John Lovell, a relative and close associate of Hawkins, but not reported in either edition of Hakluyt's work.[141]

Hawkins's third voyage of 1568 was documented even more copiously than the second, as the result of a disastrous engagement at San Juan de Ulúa, the port for Veracruz, Mexico, where his ships put in to refit after a damaging storm. Caught in the harbour by a Spanish fleet, Hawkins would abandon five of his ships, leaving a disputed amount of goods, profits, and guns, as well as a number of his men; nearly a hundred more were put ashore near Tampico. Extant materials include narratives by Hawkins and by three returned captives (in volume 3), an anonymous journal, testimony in the Spanish archives by English captives and other informants, and complaints by Portuguese resident in Africa about losses to their shipping and town.[142] These sources allow us to expand on what was entailed in the 1562 account's "sworde, and … other meanes" or Sparke's remark that Hawkins "dispatched his business" of collecting slaves.

Hawkins arrived at Cap-Vert with six ships, making a night raid on a sleeping town but meeting vigorous, armed resistance and taking only "fewe" captives but "with great hurt and damage to our men."[143] The larger and smaller ships

---

140 *Tangomaos* was a term used for Portuguese, Cape Verdeans, and Luso-Africans who had assimilated to African dress and culture; another occurrence in the text distinguishes "tangomangos" from "Negroes" (Brooks, *Landlords and Strangers*, 191–2; Sparke, "Second Voyage Made by John Hawkins, 1564," 3: 514).

141 Sparke, "Second Voyage Made by John Hawkins, 1564," 3: 509; Kelsey, *Sir John Hawkins*, 40–6.

142 Kelsey comments that the extensive interviews with captives in Spanish archives make this the most completely documented English voyage of its day (*Sir John Hawkins*, 54). In addition to sources in PN (1598–1600), listed above, independently printed narratives include Hawkins, *True Declaration of the Troublesome Voyadge*; Hortop, *Rare Travailes of Job Hortop*. (No copy survives of the pamphlet by David Ingram, printed in 1582; the portion printed by Hakluyt in 1589 begins only after Ingram was put on shore in Mexico.) A transcription of the anonymous journal, BL MS Cotton Otho E. VIII fo. 17–41v, appears in Williamson, *Sir John Hawkins*. Sources from the Spanish and Portuguese archives, as well as the State Papers, are cited in Kelsey, *Sir John Hawkins*, chaps. 3–4.

143 Hawkins, "Third Troublesome Voyage of John Hawkins," 521; Williamson, *Sir John Hawkins*, 503. Hawkins had sailed with several dozen slaves who had remained unsold after John Lovell's voyage the previous year (Kelsey, *Sir John Hawkins*, 56, 302n56). Perhaps it was one of these men who taught him a remedy against wounds by poisoned arrows, as reported by Hortop ("Travels of Job Hortop," 3: 487).

and pinnaces travelled separately to a rendezvous at the Sierra Leone River, using the smaller draft vessels to enter coastal rivers and take slaves from Portuguese caravels; sources differ on whether this was trade, forced trade, or simply seizure.[144] One settlement on the Cacheu River was attacked and partially burned. These actions yielded something on the order of 150 captives when the flotilla regrouped in the Sierra Leone estuary. On the point of abandoning his slaving project in favour of trade, Hawkins was offered war captives by two African kings in return for his military aid in attacking a town on Konkaw Island. In all, the expedition collected 400 to 500 captives before turning west, including fifty persons taken as slaves by Lovell's voyage the preceding year, but not yet sold.[145]

Hawkins thus acquired slaves in three ways: some were captives in wars between African polities, persons whom Hawkins took or received from the victors. Some were seized or purchased from Portuguese ships; such persons had already been made slaves, through prior forms of violence.[146] Finally, Hawkins attempted to kidnap people from towns on shore. Met with fierce resistance, these raids were not markedly successful; in the face of African commercial sophistication and military and naval power, the Portuguese had long since turned from raiding to trade as a way of acquiring slaves.[147] What attracts notice are Hawkins's attempts to load the odds in his favour by raiding a town whose inhabitants were sleeping, or one said to be made up mostly of women and children.[148] While the principles cited by Peckham might provide a fig leaf for taking as a given the enslaved condition of war captives or already traded persons, a legal or ethical rationale for raids aimed at communities

---

144 Hortop, "Travels of Job Hortop," 3: 487–8. Kelsey cites Portuguese claims for damages following the voyages of 1564, 1566, and 1568, concluding that a combination of "purchase, intimidation, and outright theft" was used in acquiring enslaved people from Portuguese traders on the coast (Kelsey, *Sir John Hawkins*, 15, 24, 42, 62–4).

145 Kelsey, *Sir John Hawkins*, 56.

146 On the nature and rationale for conflicts in the region, see Rodney, *History of the Upper Guinea Coast*, 102–10. On enslavement in Africa more generally, Paul Lovejoy remarks that "Slavery was virtually always initiated through violence ... The most common type of violence has been warfare, in which prisoners were enslaved" (Lovejoy, *Transformations in Slavery*, chap. 1).

147 Thornton, *Africa and Africans*, 38–9. While Portuguese shipping was well-suited to other environments, shallow-water (versus deep draught) naval capability was important in the West African environment (Black, "Naval Capability," 21–2).

148 The failed night raid at Cap-Vert is described most fully in the anonymous journal (Hawkins, "Third Troublesome Voyage of John Hawkins," 3: 521; Williamson, *Sir John Hawkins*, 503).

that Hawkins believed to be incapable of defence, let alone aggression, is hard to imagine – and indeed left unstated in the narratives.

Hawkins appears to take as a given existing practices of capture, enslavement, and trade in enslaved persons, as if these did not require independent scrutiny or reflection. The silence on the rationale for slavery is not unusual in Hakluyt's sources in the sense that texts openly *reflecting* on the project of geographical expansion and the potential forms of encounter with peoples beyond Europe were much more the exception than the rule, something the fame of a few may obscure for readers not familiar with the whole span of Hakluyt's archive.[149] Yet this particular silence remains striking within a textual surround that was not silent on the affective dimension of being conquered, subject, or even enslaved. As we have seen, narratives of Mediterranean captivity presented the condition of slavery as intolerable to their protagonists, whatever individual freedoms they may have enjoyed. Narratives from the Anglo–Spanish sea war marked out compassion towards a defeated enemy, and the merciful treatment that it motivated, as traits of English national character sharply distinguished from the cruelty imputed to Spain; being captured by the Spanish was at least rhetorically a fate worse than death.[150] Affect could also be readily evoked in the Africa narratives when English death, injury, or captivity was in question. Sparke said of Hawkins that after an unsuccessful raid on an African town, "his heart inwardly was broken in pieces" for the deaths and injuries of his men."[151]

Accounts of the third Hawkins voyage juxtaposed the drama of English captivity, subjection, and deliverance in the New World with the mere business of a trade in captured and enslaved Africans. The ironies of this juxtaposition are manifold; the returned captive Job Hortop, for instance, defended Hawkins for abandoning his men when he retained enslaved Africans on board the remaining ships because "for them he might have had victuals, or anything needfull … which for gold nor silver he could not have had."[152] Indeed, as Herman Bennett comments, Hawkins "did not express concern about the loss of English lives or the plight of his surviving countrymen" when he brought

---

149 See especially Best, "True Discourse"; Harriot, "Briefe and True Report" (*PN*); Ralegh, "Voyage of Sir Walter Ralegh"; Peckham, "True Reporte."
150 These ideas are touched on in chapter 7; on ideas of mercy and inhumanity in English encounters in the Atlantic world, with Europeans and Indigenous peoples in the Americas alike, see also Fuller, *Remembering the Early Modern Voyage*, chap. 2.
151 Sparke, "Second Voyage Made by John Hawkins, 1564," 3: 506.
152 Hortop, "Travels of Job Hortop," 3: 491.

suit against Philip II in the High Court of Admiralty, seeking to recover only the value of slaves lost in the battle.[153] Yet the multiplication of narratives about the events at San Juan de Ulúa and their sequels surely testify to a general interest in the suffering of English captives as well as the perceived value of their information.[154]

Narratives by these captives themselves provide some of the few affective responses to the conditions of New World slavery in Hakluyt's volumes. In Mexico, the captive Hortop and his fellows were set to "card wooll among the Indian slaves, which drudgery we disdained, and concluded to beat our masters."[155] Miles Philips and others became in turn domestic servants – attending on Spanish masters alongside Indians and enslaved Africans – as well as overseers of Indian and African miners, and finally were consigned to the service of religious foundations. In the last of these roles, Philips supervised Indigenous workers set to build a new church. Thus he came to learn the "Mexican tongue," finding Indigenous labourers "courteous and loving"; he reported that – like Hortop and other English captives – "they and the Negroes also doe daily lie in waite to practise their deliverance out of that thraldome and bondage, that the Spaniardes doe keepe them in."[156] In *PN* (1598–1600), Philips's comment on "thraldome and bondage" registers an almost unique recognition of slavery as an affective experience for others.[157]

---

153 Bennett, *African Kings and Black Slaves*, 48–9.

154 The returned captive David Ingram, who claimed to have walked from Mexico to Nova Scotia, was interviewed with some seriousness by Sir Francis Walsingham and the colonial promoter Sir George Peckham (see "Certayne questions to be damaunded of Davy Ingram," in Quinn, *NAW*, 3: 212–13). Peckham cites Ingram as an authority (see, for instance, "True Reporte," 3: 169).

155 Hortop, "Travels of Job Hortop," 492, 494. See also the discussion of John Fox's captivity narrative, chap. 4.

156 Philips, "Voyage of Miles Philips," 479–81. Not all the English did seek to escape: sentenced only to a term of service, a number of captives remained in Mexico once it concluded, marrying Black, mestizo, or creole wives. On Philips, see further Fuchs, "An English Picaro in New Spain"; Helgerson, "I Miles Philips."

157 Both Francis Fletcher's manuscript journal of the Drake circumnavigation and the print account partly based on it, *World Encompassed* (1628), make reference to the "bloody cruelty" of Portuguese settlers on the Cape Verde islands towards both the original inhabitants and slaves imported from the mainland and North Africa, who revolted against this "intollerable Tyrranny" by fleeing to the mountains and conducting guerrilla war against the settlers (Drake, *World Encompassed*, 9; Penzer, *World Encompassed* [1926], 98). Hakluyt's "Famous Voyage" account soft-pedals what is an extended passage in Fletcher's journal,

Plate 1 Circumpolar charts, like this one by Mercator, allowed for better visualization of the polar regions.

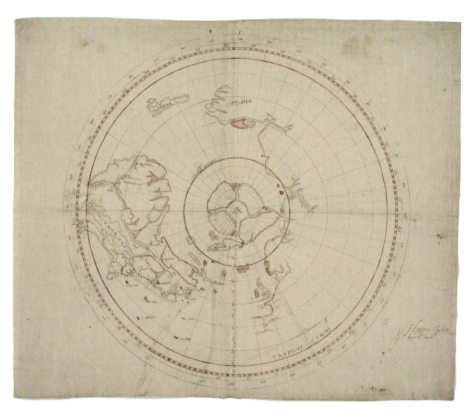

Plate 2 A polar chart by John Dee for Sir Humphrey Gilbert, who wrote an early treatise on the plausibility of a Northwest Passage.

Plate 3 The loxodromes drawn on this early seventeenth-century polar chart provide an example of what the "plat with spiral lines" provided to the Arctic navigators Pet and Jackman might have looked like. A foreshortened North America is at the bottom of the map, with the names of John Davis and Martin Frobisher placed to the north.

Plate 4 Ortelius's map of Iceland combined a geography of wonders with minutely detailed placenames, natural history, and cultural comment.

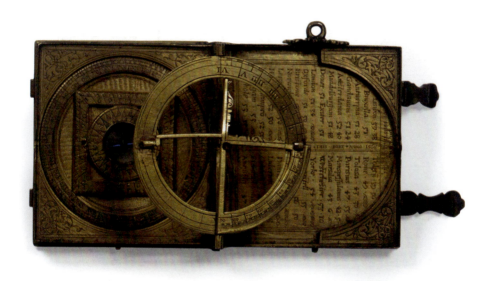

Plate 5 The instrument maker Humfrey Cole made this ingenious compendium for Eden's printer, Richard Jugge; each leaf of the "book" revealed new instruments, and the cover's impresa of a nightingale was a pun on Jugge's name.

Plate 6 Detailed charts, designed by Robert Adams and engraved by Augustine Ryther, were designed to assist readers in following Petruccio Ubaldini's narrative of the Armada battle.

Plate 7 This early seventeenth-century armillary sphere, a device used for modelling the movement of the heavens about the earth, resembles the object held by the child in de Bry's plate 8.

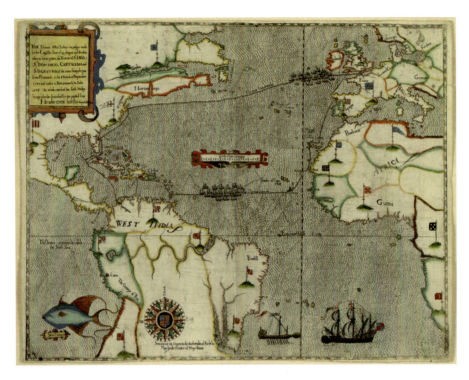

Plate 8 A map by Baptista Boazio, who sailed on the West Indies raiding voyage of 1585 to 1586, illustrates the course taken by Drake's fleet. The "Sea Connye" at bottom left relies on the drawings of John White, who was among the Roanoke colonists brought home by Drake.

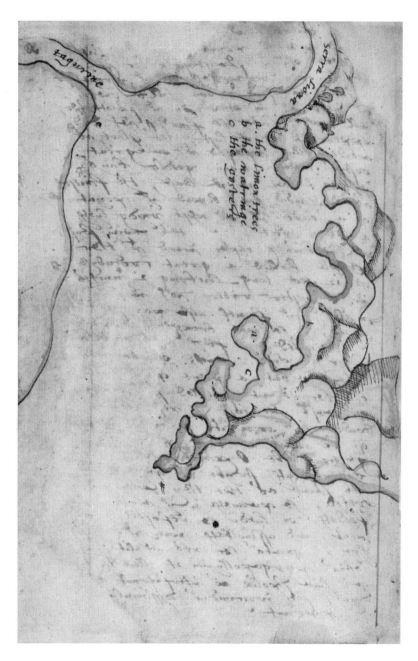

Figure 6.2 Edward Fenton's expedition lingered at Sierra Leone taking on water and provisions, long enough for Richard Madox to prepare this chart.

At least in volume 2, the third Hawkins voyage was followed by an interruption in recorded contacts with West Africa; these resumed only in the 1580s, when the sea war that began with the arrest of Hawkins's *Primrose* at Bilbão in 1585 abrogated concern that trading in Guinea might damage commercial relations with Spain and Portugal. Patents for trade with Benin and Senegambia were issued not long afterward.[158] Volume 3 yields another set of contacts, however. In the intervening years, a number of English voyages bound for the Straits of Magellan touched on the African coast, sometimes spending significant periods there: Drake in 1577 to 1580, Edward Fenton in 1582, Thomas Cavendish in 1586, and Robert Withrington and Christopher Lister for the Earl of Cumberland later in the same year. For these lengthy voyages, the Sierra Leone estuary provided an opportunity to wood, water, and take on fresh food, as well as (at times) to make repairs or confer on the course and conduct of the expedition. While Drake watered at the Cape Verde islands and paused only briefly at Sierra Leone on the last leg of his voyage, Cavendish spent somewhere between twelve and eighteen days in the harbour (accounts in the two editions of *Principal Navigations* differ).[159] The Cumberland expedition arrived a few weeks after Cavendish had departed, and remained almost a month (23 October to 17 November). In 1582, Fenton's expedition anchored at Sierra Leone for eight weeks, a longer stay than at any other point on the voyage, and long enough for the chaplain Richard Madox, the expedition's record-keeper, to draw a chart of the harbour. To this time on the ground we can add the accumulation of experience with Sierra Leone over multiple visits: the younger William Hawkins and the pilots Thomas Hood and Thomas Blacollar sailed with both Drake and Fenton, while Hood was present on the

merely mentioning that "the Moores, ... having bin slaves to the Portugals, to ease themselves, made escape to the desert places of the Island" ("Famous Voyage," 3: 731).

158 Andrews suggests during the 1560s, "plunder, reprisal and violence" from the Portuguese side made English trade with Guinea far less viable, while merchants did not want to sacrifice trade with the Iberian Peninsula for riskier and more distant markets; yet "[w]ith the outbreak of war in 1585 the possibility of trade to Guinea returned" (Andrews, *Trade, Plunder, and Settlement*, 110–12). (See chapter 7 on the events of 1585 and following.) William Hawkins, John's older brother, appears to have made a slave-trading voyage in 1582, not recorded in Hakluyt (Kelsey, *Sir John Hawkins*, 164). For unrecorded trade with Benin in the early 1580s, see note 13 above.

159 The instructions for Fenton's voyage specified a course via the Cape of Good Hope, "not passing by the streight of Magellan," but the shifting aims of the voyage resulted in an Atlantic crossing ("Instructions given to M. Edward Fenton," 3: 755; Taylor, *Troublesome Voyage*, xlii–liii).

Cumberland voyage as well. William Hawkins also transmitted some of the earlier experience of his uncle John Hawkins, alluding to earlier voyages also noted in the documents.[160]

Perhaps the most famous passage from the African sections of these voyages is the merchant John Sarracoll's description of how Withrington, Lister, and their men set fire to an African town. Sarracoll described coming upon a walled town that was finely built, with intricate streets, so cleanly kept "that it was an admiration to us all." Cumberland's men "entered with such fierceness, that the people fled all out of the town," and on departing, "our men ... set the towne on fire, and it was burnt (for the most parte of it) in a quarter of an hour."[161] Many readers may have first encountered Sarracoll and the burning town through a brilliant reading by Stephen Greenblatt. Greenblatt poses a series of questions:

Does the merchant feel that the firing of the town needs no explanation? If asked, would he have had one to give? Why does he take care to tell us why the town burns so quickly, but not why it was burned? Is there an aesthetic element in his admiration of the town, so finely built, so intricate, so cleanly kept? And does this admiration conflict with or somehow fuel the destructiveness? If he feels no uneasiness at all, why does he suddenly shift and write not *we* but *our men* set the town on fire? Was there an order or not?[162]

---

160 Taylor, *Troublesome Voyage*, 81. In the manuscript version of his account, Sarracoll referenced the "reporte of some men that were here [at Sierra Leone] with mr ffenton" (cited in Palmer, "All Suche Matters," 334). Sarracoll himself had sailed with Drake in 1577–80 (Andrews, *Last Voyage of Drake and Hawkins*, 41). William Towerson and George Barne, another investor in earlier Guinea trade, consigned cloth to Fenton's voyage for sale in the Moluccas, and Towerson's son Will sailed on Fenton's *Edward Bonaventure*.

161 Sarracoll, "Voyage of M. Robert Withrington, and M. Christopher Lister, 1586," 3: 770. Hakluyt's version of the text was much abridged from the apparent original, BL MS Lansdowne 100/3 fo. 23r–51r. A later account of the voyage was compiled for Cumberland's daughter, Lady Anne Clifford; a much-abbreviated version of that account appears in Samuel Purchas (*Purchas his Pilgrimes* 4: 1141). Sources on the expedition's sojourn at Sierra Leone are excerpted in Hair, "Sources on Early Sierra Leone." The log of the pilot Thomas Hood, Huntington Library HM 1648, provides an additional manuscript source. All three texts, along with the account prepared for Lady Anne Clifford, are compared (with particular reference to the passage cited) by Palmer, "All Suche Matters." In the constrained circumstances of early 2020, I briefly examined the Huntington manuscript but not the others, and have relied on Palmer's essay with particular gratitude.

162 Greenblatt, *Renaissance Self-Fashioning*, 194.

I will focus on two points from Greenblatt's analysis: Sarracoll's account is characterized by a kind of "moral blankness," and the violence being enacted and narrated is not only "casual [and] unexplained," but missing a sense of drama and catharsis, "the bloodbath that usually climaxes these incidents."[163] The clustering of voyages to Sierra Leone, and the deep documentary record provided, allows us to think about this burning town within the context of other voyages and other documents, including the manuscript record. It also matters, however, as one instance of a violence that seems peculiar to this group of sources.

Sarracoll wrote in the common form of a journal loosely based on daily reporting, a genre that characteristically deemphasizes causal connections or explanations; comparison with the original manuscript has shown that the narrative was vigorously pruned for publication. The quality of Sarracoll's text in PN (1598–1600) was thus not simply a reflection of his mind, and indeed (as Philip Palmer has pointed out), his expression of distress at seeing the town burn was among the passages excised from Hakluyt's text.[164] Yet a closer examination of the sources bears out Greenblatt's point that both affect and the narrative properties of explanation, cause, and meaning are strikingly underrepresented in records of this voyage. There are two manuscript witnesses to the voyage and the events described by Sarracoll: a copy of Sarracoll's original narrative, prepared under his direction for Lord Burghley, and a log by the pilot Thomas Hood.[165] Hood, too, gives an account of the burning of the town:

The 4 daye [of November 1586] our captayne went Ashor with 150 men to the negers towne and he toocke it And brout their rys abord and burnt ther toune And the negurs ran into the woods All saavyng sum that war slayn and thankes be to god we had never A man hurt but cam all safe abord agayne.[166]

The /5/ daye of november our men went a shor and fet rys abord and burnt the rest of the housys in the negurs towne and brout abord ropes and pullys

---

163 Ibid., 193.

164 "[Y]tt pytyed me muche to se yt for that yt was so fine athinge," transcribed and cited in Palmer, "All Suche Matters," 328.

165 Hakluyt's substantial cuts to Sarracoll's narrative are noted by Andrews, who suggests they were aimed at softening criticism of Withrington and at reducing the overall length (Andrews, "Latin America").

166 Transcription from HM 1648, fo. 21r, in Palmer, "All Suche Matters," 336–7.

that war som tangamangas and our bot went down to the outermost poynt of the ryver And burnt a towne and brout away all The rys that was in the towne. The /6/ daye we sarvyd god being Sunday. The /7/ daye of november we fet a bot full of rys.[167]

The log actually manifests the blankness of affect that is partially an effect of Hakluyt's cuts to Sarracoll's text: we burnt the towns, stole the rice, served God on the Sabbath. Again, form can tell us something more. While most the log's daily entries are devoted to navigational information, the expansiveness of Hood's narration on 5 and 5 November signals that he found these raids significant.

Hood's log adds several factual details: *this* town was attacked twice, and at least one other town was attacked in a similar way; at least on the first day, the Cumberland raiders killed several inhabitants before burning the town itself (Hood: "sum ... war slayn"; *Principal Navigations*: "the people fled all out of the towne"); and on each occasion the men seized stocks of rice from these towns, rather than simply finding it in various places in the countryside (Hood "our men brout away all the rys that was in the towne"; *Principal Navigations*: "we searched the countrey about [the town], where wee found in divers plaines good store of rice in stacks, which our men ... brought a bord"). Palmer suggests that rice was in fact the practical motivation for raiding these towns, since provisions for the long onward voyage were already low on some ships.[168]

That begs the question of violence, however. Four years earlier, Fenton had provisioned his ships at Sierra Leone by trading with the Portuguese in exchange for salt, inviting Portuguese and Africans to dine on board the flagship; he also exchanged gifts and a notably courtly letter with a local ruler who had sent him a monkey and the "great toothe of an Oliphant."[169] By

---

167 My transcription from HM 1648, fo. 21r, conferred with Palmer, 337. Palmer reads "set," but I believe "fet" (fetched) to be a preferable reading. On "tangamangas," see note 140 above.

168 Ward, "Voyage of M. Edward Fenton, 1577," 3: 659. Palmer confirms from the Saracoll ms. that food supplies were already dangerously low on some ships, partly as a result of dissension among the captains, and all three sources note that the men were also fishing (Palmer, "All Suche Matters," 338).

169 Fenton's journal, in Taylor, *Troublesome Voyage*, 108. A courtly letter, copied into the journal, accompanied Fenton's gifts; were it not that he was bound by particular orders, he wrote that "I would surely have seen the myselfe, Ledd thereunto aswell by the courtesey thow hast shewed me as the desier I have to see the greatnes and to have ussed some conferrance with the towchinge a further Amitie and traffique to be hade hereafter

contrast, Withrington appears to have been particularly dismissive of local norms. When Cumberland's ships arrived, a Portuguese-speaking informant told them that the local king would grant them permission to wood and water for a customary gift of wine and cloth. Withrington declined, thinking it "not good to give anything for that which they might take freely." English ships took wood and water "at pleasure" until their raid on the town, collected rice from the countryside over another two weeks, and departed. The 1586 visit thus began with refusal to acknowledge a local ruler's dominion, and concluded by treating cultivated and harvested rice as, like wood and water, a freely available natural resource.[170]

If Withrington's behaviour was high handed in comparison to Fenton, especially, Sarracoll's companions were nonetheless among a succession of English mariners who set fire to African towns – and here I return to the longer list of all Hakluyt's African materials. In 1557, Towerson and his men burned the town of Shamma, where they had traded before, "because the Captaine thereof was become subjected to the Portugals."[171] Although Towerson provides a *reason* for burning the town, as Cassander Smith points out, this was a place where the English had traded repeatedly and where, the previous year, "residents marveled at English weaponry and ... sought asylum" from the Portuguese. Smith comments that "the moment is most striking" in the actions, explanations, and details that are lacking: Towerson did not try to persuade people to trade, remind them of their alliance, or assume the role of protector suggested in his narrative of the preceding year.[172] In 1568, as we have seen, the Hawkins crews burned towns on the Îles de Los as they raided them for captives. Hawkins also used fire against houses "covered with dry palm leaves" when his forces participated in the siege of a town on Konkaw

---

betwixt the and the Queene my mistres subjects" (Taylor, ibid., 108–9). Fenton had been informed of the local political landscape by an earlier conversation with three Portuguese "having traffique in this River for Negroes, Rize and Oliphante teeth" (Taylor, ibid., 102). Ward's narrative in PN (1598–1600) does not include this letter, though Ward himself records sending gifts to an African queen.

170 On customary gifts, see Rodney, *History of the Upper Guinea Coast*, 85. Different narrative treatments of Withrington's refusal to make a customary gift are examined by Palmer; earlier expeditions had acquiesced to such requests, but the 1586 narratives suggest either a concern over being asked for too much or a simple refusal to acknowledge the rights on which such a request might be based (Palmer, "All Suche Matters," 334–5, 341).

171 Towerson, "Third Voyage of M. William Towrson to Guinea, 1557," 2(ii): 50.

172 Smith, *Black Africans in the British Imagination*, 47.

Island alongside three African kings.[173] On the same voyage, the master of his flagship, Robert Barrett, burned and looted a sizeable town on the Cacheu River, although he lost four men to the combined force of Africans and Portuguese defending it.[174] The narratives of Cavendish's 1586 voyage provided in the two versions of the compilation – by N.H. (1589) and Francis Pretty (1600) – both describe one or more similar events during the expedition's sojourn at Sierra Leone. N.H. writes that "having conference with the Negroes we fell at variance" and accordingly sacked the town; they subsequently also burned "some 150 houses because of their bad dealing with us and all Christians," including keeping a Portuguese man "in very miserable captivity." Pretty writes that Cavendish's men burned two or three houses in an "artificially builded" town of some hundred houses, "kept very cleane as well in their streetes as in their houses" and under a king to whom "good obedience" was used. A few sentences on the Portuguese castaway precede the burning, but lack the causal connection proposed by N.H. After he was "[e]spied … among the bushes onshore," the English "tooke and brought [him] away with us" as an informant, tying him up and interrogating him. While clearly taken captive by *Cavendish's* men, it is not apparent that he had been kept in captivity on shore rather than simply living in the community, as a number of Portuguese did along the coast.[175]

Strikingly, these attacks were narrated (at least) as directed primarily against fortified *towns* rather than human combatants. The English did not see these as mere clusters of hovels: Hakluyt's marginal comments to Sarracoll's text

---

173 Sparke, "Second Voyage Made by John Hawkins, 1564," 3: 504; Hawkins, "Third Troublesome Voyage of John Hawkins," 3: 522. The location is given by Brooks, *Landlords and Strangers*, 295.

174 This incident is not recorded by Hawkins; Portuguese demands for compensation and the anonymous journal are the chief sources (Kelsey, *Sir John Hawkins*, 64–5; Williamson, *Sir John Hawkins*, 506–7). Hortop describes a similar (or the same) attack taking place at the Rio Grande, *after* the siege at Konkaw Island (with some allowance for exaggerated numbers, the details match the Cacheu River): first seven caravels are taken, then a large, well-defended town attacked and burned with minor losses (Hortop, *Rare Travailes of Job Hortop*, sig. A4 r–v). The Hortop narrative in volume 3 adds a further detail matching the anonymous journal's account of the Cacheu River episode: after the caravels were brought out of the river, Francis Drake and Edward Dudley led a hundred soldiers back up river, fought with seven thousand men, and burned the town (Hortop, "Travels of Job Hortop," 3: 488).

175 N.H., "Famous Voyage of M. Thomas Candish, 1586," 809; Pretty, "Prosperous Voyage of M. Thomas Candish," 3: 804.

note include the comment, "Another great and fine towne of the Negroes."[176] The complexity and order of these built environments is already striking in Sarracoll's account of a town that was "so finely built, so intricate, so cleanly," but nowhere described more thoroughly than in Sparke's account of the towns Hawkins raided and burned at the Îles de Los in 1564:

> Their Townes are prettily divided with a maine streete ... and another overthwart street ... their houses are built in a range orderly in the face of the street ... [The houses are divided into rooms for different purposes.] In the middle of the towns there is a house larger and higher then the other ... This is the Consultation-house ... in which place, when they sitte in Counsell the King or Captaine sitteth in the midst, and in the Elders upon the floore by him: (for they give reverence to their Elders) ... There they sitte to examine matters of theft ... and take order what time they shall go to warres: and ... take order in gathering of the fruits in the season of the yeere, and also of Palmito wine ... and this surely I judge to be a very good order ... nothing is common, but that which is unset by mans hands.[177]

Sparke's text makes evident the association of the built environment with a political and social order: by implication, this is civility, the material embodiment of God's very plan for humanity. With the exception of N.H.'s text, no reasons are given to justify the violent destruction of these well-built and orderly towns.

Neither the presumed innocence nor the presumed savagery of the New World were projected onto West Africa's sophisticated trading coasts in these accounts – the English met people who appeared to them as virtually naked and yet were demonstrably conversant with ideas of property, craft, trade, wealth, and political power in ways they could not fail to recognize: "they required to know our measure, & our weight, that they might shewe their Captaine thereof"; "the Negroes enquired for fine cloth, and I opened two

---

176 Sarracoll, "Voyage of M. Robert Withrington, and M. Christopher Lister, 1586," 3: 770.
177 Sparke, "Second Voyage Made by John Hawkins, 1564," 3: 504–5. Coll Thrush comments on the hope that good planning in Jamestown could make for an orderly grid superior to the "higgledy-piggledy medieval welter of London streets" (*Indigenous London*, 39–40). See also William Pratt's claims that Africans were uncivil because they lacked fixed habitations, discussed in Young, "Early Modern Geography and the Construction of a Knowable Africa," 29–31.

pieces which were not fine enough, as they sayd."[178] In their inventories of African culture, English observers resorted only sparingly to the ethnographic tropes that so frequently appeared in other sources as signalling the incapacity of Indigenous societies in the Americas. The sources in *PN* (1598–1600) do not represent Africans as savages, cannibals, eaters of raw foods, or witches (imputations directed at Caribbean or Arctic peoples); rather, they were cultivators, builders of walls, dwellers in orderly towns, traders rather than innocent givers of gifts; politically organized and sophisticated, whatever their religious beliefs; and never purported to revere English technologies or persons as mysterious or divine. African dress *was* often treated as functionally equivalent to nakedness, yet the prevalent use of gold ornaments and sometimes scarification largely mitigated against associating "nakedness" with lack of sophistication, lack of resources, or lack of understanding about how to extract, transform, and craft what the earth yielded.[179] Although the sources relentlessly describe disease, it was the English – not Africans – who suffered from the invisible bullets of contagion, and weakened and died as a result.

Yet it remains evident in the actions of investors and planners, as well as in Hakluyt's disposition of materials, that West Africa – despite its commercial sophistication, and its resources of gold, ivory, and spices – was not regarded as a target of value for English trade, diplomacy, or geographical discovery. Voyages were neither celebrated nor durably recorded. This quiet demotion was accompanied by something more virulent. Even as men like Hawkins and Drake – who would react with lasting and self-righteous anger against Spanish cruelty and tyranny – packed captives into their holds in imitation of Spanish and Portuguese practice, the material evidence of African civility was itself attacked. The inglorious character of attacking towns full of women and children or whose inhabitants were sleeping, the infrequent success of such raids, and the direction of violence against the inanimate target

---

178 Towerson, "First Voyage of William Towrson to Guinea, 1555," 2(ii): 30; Towerson, "Second Voyage of Master William Towrson to Guinea," 2(ii): 42. Jennifer Morgan highlights the role of numeracy in arguments about civility and rationality; citing a similar passage from Eden's narrative of the 1554 voyage by Lok, she comments that "this recognition of the sophistication of African trade gave way to narratives that presented Africans as utterly ignorant of accounting" – "accusations of numerical ignorance" would eventually be joined with "those concerning the lack of civic norms" to found claims of enslavability (Morgan, *Reckoning with Slavery*, 61, 133).

179 Patricia Akhimie's work on the double-edged nature of "cultivation" in English conduct literature provided some inspiring tools for thinking about these different and distant texts (*Shakespeare and the Cultivation of Difference*).

of buildings make the violent moments of these materials not only hard to justify but hard to narrate successfully. The contrast could not be sharper with adjacent narratives of the Anglo–Spanish war, where conflicts described in sharp and specific detail were typically represented as against a superior force, accompanied by explicit displays of mercy to the defeated, and concluded with both moral and actual victory. We should be attentive to these adjacencies, and not take too much for granted the differences between theaters of action that Hakluyt's mariners inhabited almost simultaneously. In *PN* (1598–1600), something already troubled the interface between England and Black Africa. Both the vagaries of Hakluyt's editing, and the unthought violence of the later narratives, would come to find a language and a rationale that, in 1600, they did not yet wholly possess.

7

Belligerent Materials: Sea Fights in the Atlantic

Wherein also mention is made of certaine Sea-fights, and other memorable acts performed by the English Nation.

Principal Navigations, volume 2 (ii), title page

BELLIGERENT MATERIALS

THE 1615 TITLE PAGE OF WILLIAM CAMDEN'S *Annales rerum Anglicarum et Hibernicarum regnante Elizabetha* bore one illustration beneath its title: a scene of war at sea. By 1625, when the first English-language edition of the *Annals* appeared, this visual material had been expanded and elaborated: on the left-hand side, an engraved portrait of Elizabeth crowned with a halo of stars; on the right, the title encircled by five scenes from recent maritime history. Illustrated were Francis Drake's raid on the West Indies (1585–86), the first raid on Cádiz (1587), the defeat of the Armada (1588), the second raid on Cádiz (1596), and a map of South America showing Drake's engagement with the *Cacafuego* during the voyage of circumnavigation (1577–80). Whether in visual, textual, or cartographic media, these maritime actions were canonical moments of late-sixteenth-century English history, widely disseminated not only across a variety of media but also in multiple languages; all were documented in the second edition of *Principal Navigations*.

These materials were new to the second edition. In the preface to the first edition of 1589, Hakluyt had singled out several of these naval actions for notice, only to explain that they would not, in fact, be included in a collection devoted to voyages "of remote length and spaciousness" or "of search and discovery of strange coasts": "these (albeit singular and happy voyages of our renowmed countrymen) I omit, as things … without the compasse of my

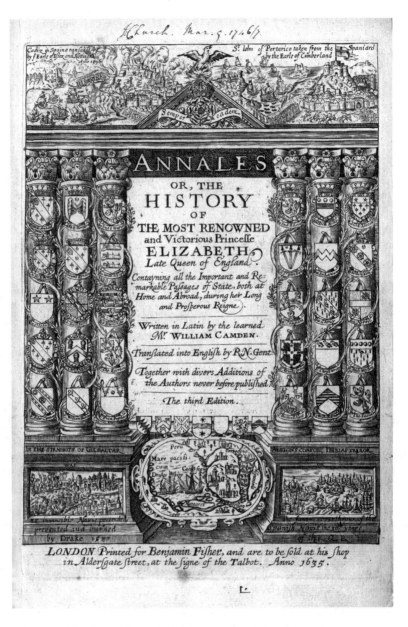

Figure 7.1 Naval victories and raids against Spanish and American towns line the frontispiece to the third edition of Camden's *Annales, or the History of the Most Renowned and Victorious Princesse Elizabeth* (1625).

prescribed limites."[1] The new parameters of the second edition allowed him to include voyages and actions in the Atlantic as well as materials on Britain itself, as we have already seen. Volume 1, devoted to the North and dedicated to the Lord Admiral Charles Howard, now closed with an account of the 1588 defensive action against the Spanish Armada – one of the great inflecting moments of England's maritime history – and an account of Howard and the Earl of Essex's 1596 raid on Cádiz.[2] Friends persuaded Hakluyt that these two narratives should come out without delay, suggesting that he had intended them for a later volume (the three volumes of the second edition appeared in successive years, 1598 to 1600).[3] The two actions taking place in the Caribbean and the Pacific appear in volume 3, with geographically related materials. The last of Camden's five actions, Drake's 1587 raid on Cádiz, also appeared in its geographically proper place, with other voyages in the Atlantic "outside the Straits of Gibraltar" in volume 2(ii). There, it joins a significant group of related sources, documenting belligerent encounters between English and Spanish ships in the Atlantic. This chapter will examine these Atlantic sources as a group.

It is hardly surprising to find narratives of maritime conflict with Spain in Hakluyt's collection. From the perspective of our own day as much as Hakluyt's own, the defeat of the Armada – like the circumnavigation of the globe by Drake and his companions in 1577 to 1580 – would seem obligatory to include among the "principal navigations ... of the English nation." In 1589, when both the victory of 1588 and the national celebrations commemorating it would have been fresh in memory, Hakluyt's restraint in excluding the defeat of the Armada demonstrates a remarkable commitment to the editorial principles of selection and ordering he had chosen to adopt. Ten years later, when volume 2 appeared with its revised scheme of coverage, he had accumulated many more materials of a similar kind: the raids on Cádiz and on Lisbon, encounters between merchant ships in the Levant trade and Spanish galleys, attempts at intercepting Spanish and Portuguese ships returning from the East and West Indies, and the actual capture of several carracks and their

---

1 Hakluyt, "Preface to the Reader (1589)," sig. *3v.
2 The volume's dedicatee, the Lord Admiral Charles Howard, had also been in command of both expedition; the Howards were linked to the Hakluyts by numerous ties of patronage (Taylor, *Tudor Geography: 1485–1583*, 124). Connections between the Hakluyt and Howard families are detailed in Payne, "Hakluyt, Aristotle, and Oxford," 8–20. Relevant documents can also be found in Taylor, OW.
3 Hakluyt, "Preface to the Reader (1598)," sig. **2v.

cargo. Some of these narratives from the sea war have played an outsized role in shaping perceptions of both *Principal Navigations* and the England whose naval history it records.

In an important chapter on *Principal Navigations*, Richard Helgerson wrote that Hakluyt's compilation contributed to a sense of national identity shaped by conflict with Spain: "Hakluyt's England define[d] itself in opposition to Spanish charity, Spanish cruelty, and Spanish ambition."[4] That opposition emerges with striking clarity in these accounts. If we might now argue for a more nuanced account of Anglo–Spanish relations in the period, Hakluyt's "belligerent materials" retain an undeniable importance for British naval history; that history, in turn, has traditionally been understood as the source of "the might and majesty of England," and a touchstone of national identity.[5] Nonetheless, Hakluyt's materials on the sea war have not themselves been examined *as* a group within the compilation; they are not (for instance) the subject of an essay in the *Hakluyt Handbook*, still a fundamental resource for study of Hakluyt's collections. Only a handful of individual documents in the proposed group – for instance, Walter Ralegh's "Last Fight of the *Revenge*" or Roger Marbecke's "Honorable voyage to Cadiz" – have been studied as written, circulated, and published texts.[6] The case to be made then is for examining as a discrete group within PN (1598–1600) the materials on the sea war distributed across the first two volumes of the compilation, but principally gathered in 2(ii) (see appendix 4).

Materials belonging to the proposed group are listed by volume in appendix 4, with a more detailed inventory of contents for volume 2(ii); a chronology of key events follows. As the chronology indicates, the contents of these materials lend them considerable coherence as a group: they relate events taking place in a relatively restricted set of locations, over a period of little more than a decade, and responding to a shared set of historical and political conditions. In contrast to the prominence given to the defeat of the Armada and the Essex-Howard raid on Cádiz on the title page of volume 1, and the attention to

---

4 Helgerson, *Forms of Nationhood*, 185. Two later studies by literary critics that complicate the idea of a national identity shaped by opposition are Fuchs, *Poetics of Piracy*; Greene, *Unrequited Conquests*.

5 Laughton, *Defeat of the Spanish Armada*, x.

6 Ralegh's "Last Fight," for instance, is discussed in some detail in Beer, *Sir Walter Ralegh and His Readers in the Seventeenth Century*, 3–7; Earle, *Last Fight of the Revenge*; Fuller, *Remembering the Early Modern Voyage*, chap. 1. Sources on Marbecke are cited below. Other materials have chiefly been edited and studied by naval and maritime historians; see, for instance, the publications of the Navy Records Society.

aggressive actions against the Spanish Americas in the epistle dedicatory to volume 3, Hakluyt draws little attention to the presence of narratives of naval war in the North Atlantic and Mediterranean in the second half of volume 2.[7] These belligerent materials are not mentioned in the prefatory material for the volume, and Hakluyt made only the most modest efforts to identify them to readers; the heading for the catalogue of contents for volume 2(ii) parenthetically adds "Sea-fights" to this section's "principall English voyages": "A briefe catalogue of the principall English Voyages made without the Straight of Gibraltar to the South and Southeast quarters of the world ... Wherein also mention is made of *certaine Sea-fights, and other memorable acts* performed by the English Nation" (emphasis mine). As appendix 4 shows, items in the second part of volume 2 are interspersed with materials on trade with West Africa and a few other smaller sets of materials (on the Canaries, Ethiopia and Morocco, voyages around the Cape, and accounts of China, Japan, and Pegu). Narratives of naval conflict in the waters between Gibraltar and Flores thus are juxtaposed with materials on trade and diplomacy with Morocco and sub-Saharan Africa. The logic of this arrangement was hodological, a function of itineraries vectored south and east "beyond the straits of Gibraltar." Could Hakluyt have seen these groups of materials as connected in more substantive ways?

Overall, the answer is a qualified no. Elizabethan England's engagement with Morocco was certainly animated by a mutual perception of the threat posed by Spain, but this element of Anglo–Moroccan exchanges was downplayed by Hakluyt, as Matthew Dimmock has noted; the Moroccan ambassador's brief appearance in Anthony Wingfield's narrative of the raid on Lisbon remains the sole trace of negotiations over potential collaboration against Spain.[8] Trade with sub-Saharan Africa had an element of intra-European aggression, to be sure: merchants were entering a region claimed by Portugal, which claimed a monopoly on trade and resisted intrusion (if with limited

---

7 See chapter 8 on Hakluyt's remarks in the dedication to volume 3.

8 Wingfield, "Voyage to Spaine and Portugale, 1589," 2(ii): 149; Dimmock, "Guns and Gawds: Elizabethan England's Infidel Trade," 217–19. An overview of Anglo–Moroccan relations in the period is provided in MacLean and Matar, *Britain and the Islamic World*, 49–61. See also Wernham, *Expedition of Norris and Drake*, xv, xxvii–viii, liii. Maclean and Matar draw on Moroccan sources; Wernham's compilation provides related English documents.

capacity).[9] Little was made of this angle in the narratives, however. Some of the aggressive encounters represented in the proposed grouping (items 3, 9, 10, and 14) involved English merchantmen returning from trade in the Levant, and merchantmen also participated in several of the naval actions documented in the book, joining the fleet gathered against the Armada in 1588 as well as raids on Cádiz (1587), Lisbon (1589), and the Azores (1591). As Robert Brenner explains, the hazards of the Levant trade had led merchants to build well-armed vessels that were also well suited for privateering. John Bird and John Newton, who funded a voyage to Benin in 1588, owned several such ships, and participated in actions like the capture of the *Madre de Deus*.[10] Yet we can see considerable overlap as well between names of merchants investing in trade with Africa and those trading in Muscovy. Unlike voyages to the Mediterranean, the trading voyages to the African coast did not require armed convoys, and the narratives associated with West Africa – where occasional violence is simply reported, as if in passing – differ sharply from a group of narratives centred on maritime conflict, where conflict between ships becomes a war of meanings and identities. The *dominant* impression produced by the alternation between materials on African trade and naval war is thus one of incoherence. It is hard to avoid speculating that Hakluyt located these narratives in 2(ii) simply because they needed to go somewhere, and other materials to fill out this part of the volume were either unavailable or of little interest to the editor. (Even so, the second half of volume 2 is more than one hundred folio pages shorter than the first.)

Despite their dispersion and their very modest advertisement by Hakluyt, both the common concerns of these belligerent materials and their common differences from the voyages of African trade that surround them suggest considering them *as* a group. Their chronological arrangement in 2(ii) also

---

9 English support for the Portuguese pretender, Dom Antonio, motivated both the 1589 attack on Lisbon and the 1588 letters patent for trade to Senegambia; however, Dom Antonio appears in the African materials only tangentially (see "Voyage of Richard Rainolds and Thomas Dassell, 1591," 190).

10 The London ships described in several narratives as engaging Spanish galleys were (all but one) returning from trade in the eastern Mediterranean; these narratives could easily have been associated with other Levant Company voyages in the first half of volume 2, rather than with the belligerent materials filling out the second half (on the belligerent capacities of Levant Company ships, see Brenner, *Merchants and Revolution*, 19). On Bird, Newton, and others, see Andrews, *English Privateering Voyages*. On the mutual imbrication of gentry and mercantile endeavours in the pages of Hakluyt's collection, see Helgerson, *Forms of Nationhood*, 163–81.

frames a history that unrolled between 1585 and 1596, distinct from the surrounding history of a trade with Africa beginning in the 1550s. Considered as a group, the multiple voices of these belligerent materials converge around a common rhetorical project: not only reporting on the sea war with Spain, but framing it as the confrontation of two distinct national characters and identities. Authors had repeated recourse to a recognizable set of rhetorical moves in telling their stories: for instance, the emphasis on English "mercy," deliberately shown to defeated enemies from a nation repeatedly characterized as inhuman and barbarously cruel. Yet the impression of an almost choral voice speaking from and about this homogeneously defined community belies a reality that was less harmonious. Among these accounts of men fighting together against a national enemy, both narration and the events it describes are *also* marked by internal differences, contestation, and even conflict between different interests. The use of common rhetorical strategies raises empirical questions about how something like a "common voice" came into being, and thus about authorship, the identity of the historical individuals who produced these texts. The second half of this chapter will track the particular "we's" and "I's" of Hakluyt's belligerent materials. First, however, we should map what they have in common, the contours of the "us" they represent and share.

"WE HAPPY FEW": WRITING AND FIGHTING IN THE FIRST-PERSON PLURAL

The Lorde is on our side, whereby we maybe assure o[u]rselves, o[u]r nombres are greater than theirs.

Sir Francis Drake to the Privy Council, 30 March 1588[11]

The *Primrose* narrative, which inaugurated both narratives and hostilities, will provide our first text for examination. In May of 1585, the ships of English and other northern European countries trading in Spanish ports were seized and held on orders from Philip II. Among them was the *Primrose*, whose escape was narrated in a contemporary pamphlet by the otherwise unknown Humphrey Mote, printed soon after the event; its author framed his report

---

11 Rodger, *Armada in the Public Records*, 42. The document transcribed is identified as State Papers Domestic 1588, S/P 12/209 No. 40, f. 77.

as both news and admonishment, "to the intent that it may be generally knowen to the rest of the English ships, that by the good example of this the rest may in time of extremitie adventure to do the like: to the honour of the Realme, and the perpetuall remembrance of themselves."[12] Mote was Hakluyt's source. As the story begins, with the *Primrose* lying at anchor off Bilbao after unlading its goods, several persons "seeming to be merchants of Biscay" came on board "bringing cherries with them" and stayed to be entertained to dinner by the master, despite his suspicions. Their boat returned with a consort and ninety-four men who boarded the vessel, took the master prisoner, and threatened him with violence to gain the vessel's surrender. Witnessing this, the men "seeing how with themselves there was no way but present death if they were once landed among the Spaniards ... resolved themselves eyther to defend the Maister, and generally to shunne that daunger, or else to die and be buried in the middest of the sea, rather then to suffer themselves to come into the tormentors hands."[13] In a "very bold and manly sort" the crew armed themselves and began to fire at the Spanish boarders, while others took up boar spears and lances. When asked to call them off, the master "answered that such was the courage of the English nation in defence of their own lives that they would slay them and him also: and therefore it lay not in him to do it." The boarders were eventually repelled with very one-sided casualties, and a few, including an official bearing a copy of Philip's commission for seizure of shipping, rescued from drowning and taken to England as prisoners. Mote concludes by calling his readers' attention to the various forms of exemplary upward loyalty displayed in the narrative: "the loving hearts of the servants to save their master ... yea, and the care which the master had to save so much of the owners goods as he might, although by the same the greatest is his owne losse in that he may never travell to those parts any more."[14] Perhaps to encourage such imitation, the crew's conduct is characterized not simply as sacrificial and spontaneous upward loyalty, but also as intelligent self-preservation, making explicit what the crew is said to have perceived as intuitively evident: namely, that violent resistance would be *safer* than surrender. That the master had not commanded and indeed could not halt their resistance underlines the force and immediacy of the men's perceptions and conclusions. That the perceptions and conclusions are *theirs*, perhaps not even collectively agreed

---

12 Mote, "Escape of the Primrose, 1555," 2(ii): 212. The original is Mote, *Primrose of London with her valiant adventure on the Spanish Coast* (London, 1585).
13 Ibid., 2(ii): 213.
14 Ibid., 2(ii): 114.

upon so much as the spontaneous result of identical understandings, is suggested by the train of reflexive pronouns with which their resolutions are described: "seeing how with *themselves* there was no way but present death ... they resolved *themselves* either to defend ... or else to die ... rather than to suffer *themselves*" to be taken. These particular forms of exemplary behaviour – the crew's spontaneous valour, the disinterestedness of the master – accord well with James Froude's classic account of the Elizabethan voyages and the conduct of Elizabethan mariners as uncalculated, unschooled, and unforced.[15]

The imperative to resist capture at any price – and thus (as a derivative) not to surrender even in the face of overwhelming odds – resonates through a number of these texts, along with the idea that surrender could lead to fates such as Catholicism or slavery that might be *worse* than death.[16] The corollary to this imperative was the view of one's enemy as "tormentors," who would unfailingly impose a fate worse than death on those who yielded. This depiction of the Spanish as cruel, tyrannical, and inhumane receives its fullest elaboration in Ralegh's account of the last fight of the *Revenge*, which buttressed its naval narrative with accounts of Spanish cruelties in the New World; as another example, Wingfield's narrative of the 1589 Cádiz expedition describes the "Spaniard" as an "implacable enemie to England, thirsting after our blood, and labouring to ruine our land, with hope to bring us under the yoke of perpetuall slaverie."[17] Representations of English conduct to vulnerable opponents as merciful and humane are as prominent among this group of narratives as the countervailing ones of Spanish *in*humanity and cruelty.[18]

15 Froude, "England's Forgotten Worthies," 382–3. On Froude's essay, see Fuller, *Voyages in Print*, 162–6.
16 Ralegh's story of Sir Richard Grenville's literally suicidal defiance may be the most celebrated or notorious example, but we have also seen this trope employed somewhat differently in the Levant materials discussed in chapter 5 (Ralegh, "Fight Betweene the Revenge and an Armada, 1591"). Hakluyt's collection also provides several examples of men who survived Spanish captivity and returned to tell a tale (see chapter 6). On Grenville's defiance and Ralegh's narrative, see Fuller, *Remembering the Early Modern Voyage*, chap. 2.
17 Ralegh, "Fight Betweene the Revenge and an Armada, 1591"; Wingfield, "Voyage to Spaine and Portugale, 1589," 2(ii): 153.
18 On pity, compare "Voyage of the Right Honorable George Erle of Cumberland to the Azores," Edward Wright's narrative of the Cumberland expedition, and "Taking of the *Madre de Dios*," 2(ii): 198. Hakluyt's marginal comments emphasize that "exceeding humanity [was] shewed to the enemy." On Wright's narrative and other examples of merciful behaviour towards Spanish captives, see Fuller, *Remembering the Early Modern Voyage*, chap. 2.

In Mote's report, for instance, the English crew of the *Primrose* regarded their assailants "with pity" and rescued several of them for medical care as, despite overwhelming superiority, a multitude of Spanish boarders drowned or left the ship soaked with their dying blood.

Numerical inequality between Spanish and English combatants, such as we see in Mote's account, forms another frequent motif among this group of narratives, not only as a fact but as something to be understood and interpreted. The defeat of the Armada and Richard Grenville's action in the *Revenge*, which opposed a single ship to the Spanish fleet, represent only the most prominent instances. Other examples can be found among Hakluyt's narratives of mercantile voyages, many of which were narrated (like the *Primrose* narrative) in contemporary pamphlets: for instance, a report in verse of the voyage that is independently represented in PN (1598–1600) by "The voyage of five marchants ships of London into Turkie, and their valiant fight in their returne with 11. Gallies, and two frigats of the King of Spaines."[19] The very title of the PN text, like those of items 9 and 10, foregrounds the inequality of forces engaged in conflicts from which, nonetheless, English ships and crews consistently emerged undefeated and almost unscathed.

The numbers (five against thirteen, ten against twelve, one against five) may well be fact. Yet naval history reminds us that, to understand the balance of forces in a particular engagement, care must to be taken in establishing the numbers that are to *be* compared: the number, kinds, and tonnage of vessels; the number and weight of guns; and the numbers of crew and soldiers are all factors to consider in characterizing combat as between equivalent or unequal forces.[20] The three items cited concern encounters between English merchant ships involved in the Levant trade and Spanish galleys, vessels whose architecture, proportions, and means of propulsion (whether sails or oars) gave them very different characteristics and capabilities.[21] The *rhetoric* of the

---

19 *Newes from Turkey, A true report in verse of a sea fight* [...] *by 5 Shipps of London against 11 Gallies & 2 Frigates* (London, 1586). An entry in the Stationer's Register attributes this non-extant pamphlet to "Thomas Ellis, mariner." David and Alison Quinn identify Ellis's pamphlet as the source for the *Principal Navigations* text, but the relationship between Ellis's verse narrative and the prose narrative attributed to Philip Jones by Hakluyt can only be conjectural ("C&S," 2: 345–6).

20 I am grateful to Andrew Lambert for alerting me to this set of issues. See, for example, discussion of Spanish and English naval forces in 1588 in Andrews, *Trade, Plunder, and Settlement*, 230–2.

21 For an appraisal of the relative strengths and weaknesses of Elizabethan sailing ships and oared galleys, see "Galley and the Galleon" (Rodger, *Safeguard of the Seas*, 204–20).

narratives, however, focuses principally on simple numbers of ships and crew.[22] The anonymous narrator of "The Valiant Fight by the *Centurion*" specified that the *Centurion* lost only four men from a crew of forty-eight, while estimating that the five galleys described in his narrative carried about two hundred soldiers apiece; Thomas White, in a merchant ship manned with "42 men and a boy," took two Spanish ships bound for the West Indies, in which were found "126 persons living, & 8 dead, besides those which they themselves had cast overboord."[23] Even encounters that would appear more evenly matched, like the one that opposed ten English galleons to twelve Spanish galleys, are treated *as* unequal, making much of the inequality in manning, and thus in the numbers available for boarding. "It pleased Almighty God greatly to encourage us all in such sort, as that the nearer they came the less we feared their great multitudes and huge number of men."[24] The effect of this rhetoric of quantities is to mystify outcomes, rendering them explicable only in terms of providential intervention or a special national virtue: as White writes, "it pleased God to give us the victory, being but 42 men and a boy ... for the which good successe we give God the only praise."[25]

Narratives about multi-ship actions often encouraged not only active resistance, but also lateral loyalties and associations. Several describe explicit agreements made to band together for mutual aid against Spanish aggression. Philip Jones describes one such association, between Levant Company ships preparing to run the gauntlet of Spanish galleys, in powerfully affective terms: "These ships in token of the joy on all parts conceived for their happy meeting, spared not the discharging of their Ordinance, the sounding of drums & trumpets, the spreading of Ensignes with other warlike and joyfull behaviours, expressing by these outward signes, the inward gladnesse of their mindes, being all as ready to joyne together in mutuall consent to resist the

---

22 In some cases, opposed forces seem unequal by any measure – as when two of Ralegh's pinnaces and their crew of sixty took on a Spanish fleet of twenty-four sails, with no loss of life, "a thing to be wondered at considering the inequality of number" (Evesham, "Voyage to the Azores, 1586," 121).
23 ?Hawes, "Valiant Fight by the Centurion, 1591," 2(ii): 169; White, "Taking of Two Spanish Ships, 1592," 2(ii): 194. (On the authorship of the pamphlet attributed to Hawes, see note 78.)
24 "Ten Marchants Ships of London," 2(ii): 167.
25 White, "Taking of Two Spanish Ships, 1592," 2(ii): 194. For the defeat of the Armada as a miracle, see van Meteren, "Vanquishing of the Spanish Armada, 1588," 1: 602. For a providential "secret stroke" that diminished Spanish resistance to the English fleet at Cádiz, see Marbecke, "Honourable Voyage to Cadiz, 1596," 1: 614–15.

cruel enemie, as now in sporting maner they made myrth and pastime among themselves."[26] By contrast, "The Valiant Fight by the *Centurion*" includes a monitory example of the dangers entailed by failing in such promises. In 1591, a number of smaller ships asked the master of the larger *Centurion* to travel in company with them from Marseilles, and "vowed in general not to fly one from another." In the heat of the subsequent fight, however, one of these smaller ships – the *Dolphin* – "lay aloof off and durst not come neere," while two others fled.[27] The anonymous author implies a didactic point: English (or Protestant) crews *ought* to assist their fellows even when not under attack and capable of escape themselves. Though the unhappy *Dolphin* went down with all hands when its powder was fired, the narrator comments that "sure, if it had come forward, and been an aid unto the *Centurion*, it is to be supposed that it had not perished." Such lateral associations, the narratives suggest, might be not only principled, elevating larger national or confessional loyalties above the interest of self-preservation, but (like the resistance of the *Primrose*'s crew) an aid to survival.[28] The *Dolphin* was not simply and clearly a negative example, however. The narrator raises two possibilities about the cause of the explosion: "whether it was with their good wills or no" that the ship blew up under close attack "was not known unto the *Centurion*."[29] Did the *Dolphin* blow up because a failure of cooperation left it isolated and vulnerable to attack? Or did its crew save their ship and themselves from capture by making the ultimate sacrifice? The observers' uncertainty allows the fate of this small ship to serve, ambidextrously, *both* as an example of the dangers attending upon a failure of mutual support, *and* as an example of heroic, suicidal resistance against capture by the Spaniards – just as, in the Azores action of 1591, Grenville ordered the master gunner of the *Revenge* to "split and sinke the shippe" when it was no longer possible to hold off the Spanish attack.[30]

This uncertainty bears noting. It allowed the coexistence in the narrative of two mutually exclusive explanations, both of which are rhetorically useful in different ways. But the careful attention to specifying what was and was not the subject of certain knowledge to observer informants *also* characterizes

---

26 Jones, "Five Marchants Ships of London, 1586," 2:(ii): 286.

27 ?Hawes, "Valiant Fight by the Centurion, 1591," 2(ii): 168, 169.

28 A similar point is made about two small Flemish ships in "Ten Marchants Ships of London," 2(ii): 167.

29 "Valiant Fight by the Centurion, 1591," 2(ii): 169.

30 Ralegh, "Fight Betweene the Revenge and an Armada, 1591," 2(ii): 172.

several of these narratives, and has its own rhetorical uses. For instance, the narrator of Drake's 1587 attack on Cádiz wrote that "the whole number of ships and barkes (*as we suppose*) then burnt, suncke, and brought away with us, amounted to ... (*in our judgement*) about 10000. tunnes of shipping" (emphasis mine).[31] The narrator's care to distinguish between what was (modestly) "not unknown to the world" and what is either "not known" or only "justly [to] be supposed" stands in opposition to *Spanish* reporters who are described as "greedy to purchase the opinion of their own affaires, and by false rumors to resist the blasts of their owne dishonours."[32] The careful search for evidence described by several narrators (for instance, "very diligent inquisition" into the numbers of English casualties in 1588) implies that a kind of objectivity underwrites their claims, as if to imply that English writers were practicing careful, unbiased journalism.[33]

This contrast between styles of expression takes another form in a passage on Spanish and English military music, again in "The Valiant Fight ... by the *Centurion*." Becalmed, the crew of the *Centurion* saw galleys coming up "in very valiant and couragious sort: the chiefe Leaders and souldiers in those Gallies bravely apparelled in silke coates, with their silver whistles about their neckes, and great plumes of feathers in their hattes." The Spanish began shooting and by 10 o'clock had boarded the *Centurion*: "who before their comming had prepared for them, and intended to give them so soure a welcome as they might. And thereupon having prepared ... they called upon God, on whom onely they trusted: and having made their prayers, and cheered up one another to fight so long as life endured, they beganne to discharge their great

---

31 "Voyage of Sir Francis Drake to Cadiz, 1587," 2(ii): 122. The authorship of this narrative is discussed below.

32 Ralegh, "Fight Betweene the Revenge and an Armada, 1591," 2(i): 170. Ralegh connects this allegation of habitually boastful and mendacious reporting with the disproportion between the "great and terrible ... ostentation" of the Armada and its failure in practice to "so much as sink or take one ship, bark, pinnace, or cockboat of ours" (ibid., 2[ii]: 170).

33 Van Meteren, "Vanquishing of the Spanish Armada, 1588," 1: 602. Other examples: "at Tirion in Barbary ... we heard report of the hurt that wee had done to the Gallies" ("Ten Marchants Ships of London," 2[ii]: 168); "what slaughter was done among the Spaniards themselves, the English were uncertaine, but by a probable conjecture ... they supposed their losse was ... great" (Jones, "Five Marchants Ships of London, 1586," 2[i]: 288). Roger Marbecke leaves the narration of "our returne home ... with the taking ... of Faraon" to "some other, whose chance was to be present at the action, as my selfe was not, and shalbe of more sufficient ability to performe it" (Marbecke, "Honourable Voyage to Cadiz, 1596," 1: 619).

Ordinance upon the Gallies."³⁴ The *Centurion*, unsupported by its smaller consorts, was grappled and boarded by five galleys. The Spanish battered the ship with gunfire until the mainmast was weakened, the sails holed, the mizzenmast and stern "made almost unserviceable." As the battle raged on,

the trumpet of the *Centurion* sounded forth the deadly points of war, and encourage them to fight manfully against their adversaries: on the contrary part, there was no warlike music in the Spanish galleys, but only their whistles of silver, which they sounded forth to their own contentment: in which fight many a Spaniard was turned into the sea, and they in multitudes came crawling and hung upon the side of the shippe, intending to have entred into the same, but such was the courage of the Englishmen, that so fast as the Spaniards did come to enter, they gave them such entertainment, that some of them were glad to tumble alive into the Sea, being remedilesse forever to get up alive.³⁵

The narrative suggests that silver whistles, along with silk coats and plumed hats, formed part of a *show* of valour and courage, making meaningless sounds that reflexively contented their producers but lacked the substantively martial, collective, and communicative *function* of the English trumpet "that sounded forth the deadly points of war."³⁶ Two other things merit notice here. The first is a personification of ships themselves as agents, represented not only as acting but also as feeling ("the little ships durst not come forward"); the second, use of a language of hospitality or recreation for talking about violence (the intention to give assailants "so sour a welcome as they might"). Both these tropes are exploited more fully in an account of Drake's raid on Cádiz in 1587.

This expedition followed on Drake's raiding expedition in the West Indies the preceding year, sacking Santo Domingo and Cartagena, destroying the fort at San Agustín, and relieving Ralegh's colony on Roanoke Island.³⁷ Drake

---

34 "Valiant Fight by the Centurion, 1591," 2(ii): 168.

35 Ibid., 2(ii): 168–9.

36 Compare Jones: "although they saw [the English ships] were farre out of their reach, yet in a vaine fury and foolish pride, they shot off their ordinance" (Jones, "Five Marchants Ships of London, 1586," 2[i]: 289). Trumpets were "a practical means of conveying orders" on early modern ships, used for signalling between ships as well as to accompany hailing, charging, or boarding another ship (Rodger, *Safeguard of the Seas*, 320–1).

37 The attempted seizure of the *Primrose* and the embargo authorizing it became a pretext for the West Indies expedition, which had already been in the planning stages (Rodger, *Safeguard of the Seas*, 248–9). See chapter 10 for discussion of that expedition and its narrative, "Famous Expedition of Francis Drake, 1586," 3: 534–48.

took a fleet of twenty-one ships to occupy the harbour at Cádiz, burn the shipping at anchor there, and then wait off Cape St Vincent, a position from which he "effectively threatened all inward-bound shipping from both the West and East Indies, and stopped the preparations of the Armada at Lisbon." Leaving the cape to cruise in search of prizes, he captured a Portuguese carrack before returning to Plymouth, having achieved "relatively little" towards the mission's ostensible aim of destroying elements of the Spanish invasion fleet, but producing a "devastating" effect on Spanish security and morale.[38]

This account exhibits many of the rhetorical devices we have already seen. Already cited is the ostentatiously careful estimation of "the whole number of ships and barks (as we suppose) then burnt, sunk, and brought away with us."[39] Along with this care not to overstate, conspicuous understatement is persistently employed, as in this description of the Spanish setting fire to their own ships: "We found little ease during our aboad there, by reason of their continuall shooting ... continually at places convenient they planted new ordinance to offend us with: besides the inconvenience which wee suffered from their ships, which, when they could defend no longer, they set on fire to come among us. Whereupon ... wee were not a little troubled to defend us from their terrible fire." While the burning ships caused "inconvenience," English crews "were thereby eased a great labour, which lay upon us day and night, in discharging the victuals, and other provisions of the enemie" from ships already captured.[40] This vocabulary of ease or offence, convenience and inconvenience – effectively, of sociability or even hospitality – is not unique to this particular passage. After their departure, ten galleys came out of harbour "as it were in disdaine of us, to make some pastime with their ordinance" – again, like Spanish words and music, Spanish artillery fire appears to be more show than function, so that this attack, like the convenient burning of laden ships, could be characterized (with irony) as a form of hospitality. Throughout the narrative, Spanish ships are personified in a drama of *social* competition: galleys were "glad to retire them ... under the Fort," acted "as it were in disdaine of us," and finally "for all their former bragging, at length suffred us to ride quietly."[41]

38 Rodger, *Safeguard of the Seas*, 251–3.
39 "Voyage of Sir Francis Drake to Cadiz, 1587," 2(ii): 122.
40 Ibid., 2(ii): 122.
41 Ibid., 2(ii): 122. Compare Marbecke, who writes that bad weather prevented Spanish ships and galleys from engaging the English invasion fleet, except for "Somme friendly and kind salutations sent one from the other in warlike manner, by discharging certain great pieces" ("Honourable Voyage to Cadiz, 1596," 1: 610–11).

Such personification of ships was of course a time-honoured convention. In these narratives, however, personification can produce particular effects. These are, after all, narratives about violence, and to represent that violence as a (largely pleasant) social interaction between non-human agents doubly distances us from its effects: ships themselves cannot feel. A displacement of agency appears to be another frequent feature of these narratives. When the Spanish at Cádiz destroyed their own ships and cargoes, relieving Drake's fleet of the "trouble" of taking them, the claim was that one's antagonists harmed *themselves*. After Cádiz, the narrator tells us, the Spanish admiral Álvaro de Bazán, Marquis de Santa Cruz, died not of physical wounds, but "of extreame griefe and sorrow" occasioned by "this strange and happy enterprize."[42] "The Valiant Fight ... by the *Centurion*" provides another striking image of violence as reflexive rather than transitive, not something done to opponents so much as something they do to themselves: "[m]any a Spaniard was turned into the Sea, and they in multitudes came crawling and hung upon the side of the shippe, intending to have entred into the same, but such was the courage of the Englishmen, that so fast as the Spaniards did come to enter, they gave them such entertainment, that some of them were glad to tumble alive into the Sea, being remedilesse forever to get up alive."[43] In this passage, even when *persons* emerge from the personified envelope of the ship, violence against them is narrated in a vocabulary of "entertainment," and the rejected guests are "glad" to drown themselves. Modesty and careful objectivity thus balance against a kind of gleeful euphemism.

Disavowing agency in a battle could imply more than that one's enemy defeated themselves; the "we" of these narratives could afford to be both outnumbered and inactive (at least rhetorically) because "God delivered them from the handes of their enemies and gave them the victory."[44] Emanuel van Meteren's account of "The miraculous victory achieved by the English fleet ... upon the Spanish huge Armada" is arguably the centrepiece of this group of documents, and from the title onwards van Meteren's text drives home in unmistakable terms the claim of divine intervention on behalf of a

---

42 "Voyage of Sir Francis Drake to Cadiz, 1587," 2(ii): 122.
43 "Valiant Fight by the Centurion, 1591," 2(ii): 169. See also Mote, "Escape of the Primrose, 1555," 2(ii): 113: "they came not so fast in on the one side, but now they tumbled so fast over boord on both sides."
44 "Valiant Fight by the Centurion, 1591," 2(ii): 169.

favoured nation.[45] To be sure, the providential strand of his narrative coexists with more practical explanations for the Armada's defeat, some that continue to be cited by naval historians: the rigidity of Philip's orders to Spanish commanders, and the advantages afforded the smaller English ships by their "dexteritie" and armament.[46] Nonetheless, van Meteren assiduously emphasizes the quantitative disparity of the opposing forces. A long list of Spain's assembled ships, materiel, and personnel takes up almost three folio pages early in the narrative. The "extraordinary" or "huge bigness" of Spanish ships, so large that some "contained within them chambers, chapels, turrets, pulpits, and other commodities of great houses," provided an object lesson on the need to rely, not on guns and manoeuvrability, but providential aid. "[A]lmighty God would have the Spaniards huge ships to be presented, not onely to the view of the English, but also of the Zelanders; that at the sight of them they might acknowledge of what small ability they had beene to resist such impregnable forces, had not God endued them with courage, providence, and fortitude, yea, and fought for them in many places with his owne arme."[47] The favourable outcome of confrontation between such numerically unequal forces could not be fully accounted for by practical reasons, van Meteren argued. Howard's letter to the Queen is cited to underline the point that human reason and judgement could not explain the English victory. Rather, in van Meteren's

---

45 In this, he echoes Hakluyt: "never was any nation blessed of Jehovah, with a more glorious and wonderfull victory ... But why should I presume to call it our vanquishing; when as the greatest part of them ... were onely by Gods out-stretched arme overwhelmed" ("Preface to the Reader [1598]," sig. **2r). Van Meteren was a merchant and historian, related to Abraham Ortelius, who served as consul and postmaster for the Dutch community in London (Harkness, *Jewel House*, 24–5). On his acquaintance with Hakluyt, see Quinn and Quinn, "Chronology." Van Meteren's Armada narrative forms part of his *Historia Belgica*, which appeared in various Latin and German editions from 1596 on; however, Anthony Payne and Michael Brennan have identified Hakluyt's immediate source as Bodleian Tanner MS 255, a compilation of excerpts prepared by Richard Robinson for Charles Howard (personal communication; on Robinson, see also Woudhuysen, *Sir Philip Sidney*, 199–201). The Tanner MS includes the poem by Theodore Bèze that appears at the conclusion of Hakluyt's version. Robinson appears also to have prepared an account of the 1596 Cádiz expedition, now Bodleian Rawlinson MS B 259, fos. 47r–61v. I am grateful to Anthony Payne for elucidating the manuscript background to these accounts.

46 Van Meteren, "Vanquishing of the Spanish Armada, 1588," 1: 593, 597. On Philip's orders and the advantages of English ship construction and ordnance, see, for instance, Mattingly, *Armada*, 253–4, 194–200. On warship design more generally, see Rodger, *Safeguard of the Seas*, 204–20.

47 Van Meteren, "Vanquishing of the Spanish Armada, 1588," 1: 592–4, 603.

words, "it is most apparent that God miraculously preserved the English nation."[48] This victory was not only terrestrial, and also not only of concern to England, as this account by a Dutch emigré suggests. In a year foretold by "ancient prophecies," the Armada aimed both at England and the Low Countries, and its defeat preserved them for the true faith of Protestant belief and practice. Van Meteren's addition of a poem on the Armada's defeat by the Calvinist theologian Theodore Bèze, "Ad serenissimam Elizabetham Angliae Reginam," underlines the international, Protestant dimension of the battle signalled by Hakluyt's selection of van Meteren's account as his source.

Van Meteren's text marshalled in one account of a critical national victory not only claims of divine intervention and a triumph over steep numerical disadvantage; many of the other rhetorical moves characterizing the shorter narratives of naval combat in volume 2 appear there as well. Among these are English clemency towards wounded enemies; "very diligent inquisition" to learn the full extent of English casualties, in contrast to the "false rumour" of an early Spanish victory; the ostentatious decoration of Spanish ships that would prove ineffective in battle; and the spontaneous participation of English volunteers alongside crews mustered under command.[49] The common ground of identity, defined by characteristic oppositions, remains clear. Yet Hakluyt's selected source also makes visible some surprising fault lines; these are suggested by comparison to another contemporary account of the battle that did *not* appear in PN (1598–1600), Petruccio Ubaldini's *Discourse concerninge the Spanishe fleete invadinge Englande in the yeare 1588* (London, 1590). Ubaldini's account of the battle, based on information from Howard, was accompanied by a companion volume of narrative maps illustrating the position on successive days, and the two together provided a lavishly detailed representation of the action for English readers (see plate 6).[50]

48 Ibid., 1: 602.
49 Ibid., 1: 592, 599, 600, 602.
50 Adams and Ryther, *Expeditionis Hispanorum*. (On the engraver Augustine Ryther, see Worms, "Maps and Atlases," 234; see also Hind, *Engraving in England*, 142–9.) Ubaldini's apparent original, in Italian with a dedication to Howard, is BL MS Roya 14 A x. (As noted above, Howard can also be linked with the van Meteren manuscript that was Hakluyt's source.) The BL catalogue entry adds that Ubaldini drew on "the [official?] account as contained in BL MS Cotton. Julius F x, ff. 95–101. Curiously enough the Italian was retranslated into English and appeared as printed for A. Ryther (*A Discourse Concerninge the Spanishe Fleete*, &c., 1590)." The catalogue entry also notes a second narrative by Ubaldini bound with the previous one, also in Italian, but written "at the request of Sir Francis Drake." Both are dated 15 April 1589.

Ubaldini presented the Armada battle as a strictly English story, emphasizing the advantage enjoyed by English forces because they were "all of one nation, of one toong, and touched with a greivous and equal hatred towards their enemies." By contrast, he offers several anecdotes pointing to the dangerous differences in "custom, language, and conceit" among the polyglot forces of Spain's multinational empire – for instance, when a Biscayan ship is said to have been blown up by its disaffected Flemish gunner.[51] Van Meteren told a more international story: he also stressed the interdependence of England and the Netherlands in resisting Spanish territorial aggression, recognized the key contributions of Dutch forces, and detailed the various commemorations and celebrations of the victory in the Netherlands.[52] Ubaldini's narrative, omitting mention of Dutch participation, instead celebrates the role played by London's citizens and merchants in the national mobilization. (He calls attention to a group of London ships, including the familiar *Centurion*, that "well entertained" some Spanish ships that attacked when they had become separated from the larger fleet.)[53] Both narratives close by describing a day of thanksgiving following the victory, when the Queen processed in triumph to St Paul's. Van Meteren focuses on the Queen and her "happy successe," in a manner that recalls his earlier encomium of her appearance to review the troops at Tillbury, "representing Tomyris that Scythian warlike princesse, or rather divine Pallas her selfe." Doubts are expressed about London, however; earlier in the text, he noted that London was considered a soft target by the Spanish, due to "the Citizens delicacie and discontinuance from the warres."[54] By contrast, Ubaldini frames the royal procession as a celebration of the City's contributions to the victory. The Queen was "desirous in triumphing manner to show her thankful mind unto the Londoners also, for the charges and pains they had undertaken all the year before, in the service of the crown of the Commonwealth, together with the increase of their own reputation, being accounted the foundation and chief stay with all the other parts of the reign."

---

51 Ubaldini, *A Discourse*, 7, 8–9.
52 See, for example, van Meteren, "Vanquishing of the Spanish Armada, 1588," 1: 591, 600, 603, 605.
53 Ubaldini, *A Discourse*, 6–7, 13. The *Mayflower* of London receives more qualified recognition on 14.
54 Van Meteren, "Vanquishing of the Spanish Armada, 1588," 1: 595, 601, 606. For another denigration of London, see ibid., 1: 597.

The text closes with a paean to the City as "more populous, more wealthie, more mightie, and more free, then ever it was heeretofore."[55]

Both the narratives by van Meteren and Ubaldini tell the story of a great victory – but they don't tell it in quite the same terms. Ubaldini's text is distinguished by a decidedly more domestic focus than the more internationalist account by van Meteren that appears in *PN* (1598–1600), and he singles out the City for particular praise. By contrast, van Meteren diminishes the contributions of London, bringing forward instead the participation of the Dutch both in the battle and its celebration. These choices distribute recognition in differing directions, and in recognizing who participated in the victory, they offer different configurations of the imagined communities whose victory it *was*, different values for "us." There may have been occasional or indeed external reasons for Hakluyt's selection of van Meteren's account over Ubaldini's – perhaps it reflected his friendship with van Meteren or (given the manuscript source) the urging of volume 1's dedicatee, Charles Howard, with whom the editor was connected by ties of patronage.[56] The effect, however, is to internationalize this most famous narrative of how England's boundaries were asserted and defended by naval valour, both in representing the contributions of "strangers" and indeed providing an account *by* a "stranger."

These divergent ideas of how the story should be told open a new set of questions. As we have seen, these narratives of naval war gesture to a community of feeling, identity, and belief, a "who we are" posited in opposition to "who they are." In widening the ambit of his collection to include actions of a kind he had deliberately if reluctantly excluded in 1589, Hakluyt found potent arguments for both national prowess and national unity. Even within the compilation itself, arranged by categories of time and space that seem to gesture towards no organizing argument, materials relating to the sea war provide a countervailing centripetal force. Confronting an enemy that these narratives defined as characterized by cruelty, ostentation, and divine disfavour, English mariners were unified, merciful, modest, loyal, reluctantly violent, and favoured by Providence. They formed a homogeneous community capable of defending the boundaries of selves, ships, and ultimately the realm itself against what was different from and opposed to them.

But that is only half the story. As a brief look at the two Armada narratives begins to suggest, the outlines of that larger community were not fixed, and it was neither homogeneous nor univocal. Were the citizens of London the

---

55 Ubaldini, *A Discourse*, 26–7.
56 On Hakluyt and the Howards, see note 2 above.

stalwart support of the kingdom, or its weakest links? What was the role of foreigners in enabling this national victory, and indeed in narrating it? Did the boundaries of community extend beyond England's shores? Although the texts in this group may seem to give voice to collective actions and understandings, they described events that by their nature generated multiple perspectives and experiences, and indeed were shaped by competing agendas, both personal and political. As in the case of the two Armada narratives, we can often recover alternative sources from the manuscript and print record, and these may inform on what Hakluyt's sources don't tell us, or tell us differently.

Examining those sources also raises some questions of attribution that speak to a broader feature of these materials as a group: despite their deep concern with claiming credibility and defining identity, in these narratives the simple question of who is speaking can be especially hard to answer. English mariners here as in other contexts are frequently represented in the first-person plural, as if an almost undifferentiated collective: "we" set sail; "we" descried the enemy; "we" showed mercy to the defeated. If in the belligerent context, the maritime convention of writing as "us" comes to suggest more than the occasional association of men moving together within the wooden envelope of a ship, the convention had a broader rationale both in the collective movement of men within a vessel, and in the kind of recording mariners were sometimes required to perform.[57] We might expect Hakluyt's commitment to naming his authors to be far more informative than it is for these materials, where attribution is frequently missing, misleading, or uncertain. The problem of authorial attribution is both a question in source study (one that bears on the mechanics of producing a common rhetoric), and a signal inviting us to pay close attention to the "we's" and "I's" that these narratives offer in opposition to Spanish "they's."

AUTHORSHIP AND THE "PAPER WAR": ATTRIBUTION AND IDENTITY[58]

Although all the voyages we are examining might appropriately be characterized as part of the Anglo–Spanish sea war of the 1580s and 1590s, they were of many different kinds. They ran the gamut from privateering cruises set in motion by private individuals, to large-scale naval and military expeditions of

---

57 Chapter 4's survey of instructions for voyagers examined writing practices that merged the hands of multiple authors, and multiple documents, into a single "book" recording the movement of groups of ships and men.

58 I borrow the term "paper war" from Hammer, "Myth-Making," 635.

national consequence, to voyages intended for ordinary commerce. They could involve mixed forces of royal, private, and merchant ships; single squadrons of ships personally owned by one or a handful of courtiers; or a group of ships belonging to members of a trading company. (In some cases, elements of all three kinds can be found in a single action.)[59] Some voyages were set out with a purpose of aggressive action against Spanish ships or Spanish towns; others found battle adventitiously. Different elements within a group of ships might have different capacities, orders, incentives, and aims. The sources *narrating* the voyages were themselves diverse in nature: substantial printed books, slim pamphlets, and manuscript sources of widely varied kinds. (The case of van Meteren suggests that Hakluyt might use manuscript sources even for a work in print.)

One account of a privateering expedition was originally embedded in a treatise on navigation as an example of the problems the treatise sought to address. Other print sources were pamphlets of the most ephemeral kind, some surviving only as entries in the Stationers Register. Known authors – and not all are known – included ministers, merchant captains, naval and army officers, courtiers, and mathematicians. Some are well known: Ralegh was a prominent figure at court, Roger Marbecke was chief of the royal physicians, van Meteren was consul for the Dutch community in London, Edward Wright was a mathematician and cartographer with a number of important publications. Others left little trace on history beyond the title pages of the pamphlets that appeared under their names: Humphrey Mote and John Hawes are otherwise unknown to print and to the *Oxford Dictionary of National Biography* (*ODNB*), though Hawes may have belonged to an important family of London merchants; Robert Flick and Nicholas Downton did not write for publication, though they can be traced on other voyages and in manuscript sources.[60]

---

59 Rodger notes that both merchants and courtiers invested in the privateering ventures of these years, and that "at every level the men, their expertise and money, their guns and equipment were freely interchanged with the Queen's ships" (*Safeguard of the Seas*, 294). To give a few examples, the capture of the *Madre de Deus* was undertaken by such a mixed force (see below). The purely military raid on Lisbon of 1589 (sometimes known as the counter Armada) was funded by a joint stock company with the Queen's participation, and questions of profit and payment are not absent from other military and naval narratives. A detailed account of the Lisbon expedition is given in Wernham, *After the Armada*.

60 On Hawes as a possible author, see note 78 below. The Hawes family more broadly was an important presence in the London merchant community, and Sir James Hawes, a clothworker, was Lord Mayor in 1574; on participation in overseas trade by

Finally, surrounding these accounts of a community joined together by values, confession, and determination against a common enemy, a manuscript record also testifies to strife between participants and hot contestation over what had happened, who was responsible (for better or worse), who profited, and who got to tell the story, publicly or at all. Looking for Hakluyt's sources calls our attention to the profile of these *other* sources on the events he records. What can we learn, given the precise conditions of knowledge, certainty, and uncertainty that characterize this group of materials, by paying attention to the perspectives of authors known and unknown, within and beyond PN (1598–1600)?

The difficulties in establishing authorship for these sources are, in a way, surprising. Hakluyt's editorial project was characterized by an intention to let original documents speak for themselves, assigning them to the "paynfull and personall travellers" who had created them and whose experiences they recorded. In his 1589 address to the reader, Hakluyt announced that "I have referred every voyage to his Author, which both in person hath performed and in writing hath left the same."[61] This editorial principle contributed to the compilation's characteristic "fragmentation," its attention to discrete, individual voices in contrast to the synthesis provided by comparable figures like André Thevet and Samuel Purchas. Yet Hakluyt's claim to have referred each voyage to a participant author was imperfectly realized, and not only in these belligerent materials. Recall the Guinea voyage of 1554.[62] The varying practices of modern scholars in citing this text are understandable: Richard Eden never supplied a name for the source he used in compiling the narrative for which he was himself ultimately responsible, and Hakluyt supplies several, but neither of the names provided in the texts' running heads was the author of the log Eden used. *That* author's name remains unknown.

Failures to value and record information dogged Hakluyt's efforts at commemorating many voyages before the reign of Elizabeth. Yet the problem of authorship for the more recent materials of PN 2(ii) was not a failure of memory – important though such failures are for the project as a whole.[63]

---

members, see Alsop, "William Towerson"; Croft, "English Mariners"; Willan, *Studies in Elizabethan Foreign Trade*, 16; Rabb, *Enterprise and Empire*, 310. Flicke and Downton are discussed further below.

61 Hakluyt, "Preface to the Reader (1589)," sig. *3v.
62 "Voyage of John Lok, 1554." See chapter 6.
63 The voyages of John and Sebastian Cabot may be the most obvious example of such failures to record; see chapter 3.

These voyages of the 1580s and 1590s in many cases left a significant documentary trail. For almost half of the actions represented by narratives in *PN* (1598–1600) (appendix 4, items 2, 6, 7, 11, 12, 13, and 15), archival sources outside the compilation register significant conflict between captains, between participants and the crown, between officers and crew, or some combination of the three. This manuscript record, in turn, allows us to appreciate where Hakluyt's narrators make choices (of speech or silence) that others made differently. At the very least, we can observe that whatever the unifying rhetoric of the accounts Hakluyt printed, participants apparently felt that there were many different stories to tell and that the differences mattered. Claire Jowitt notes that *both* editions of *Principal Navigations* "include accounts of bitter disputes between leading participants ... rarely are arguments resolved amicably."[64] In at least some cases, struggles over the narrative seem to have made dissimulated authorship attractive to some participants.

Among events reported in *Principal Navigations*, the clearest and best-known example of such contention is the 1596 attack on Cádiz by the Lord Admiral Charles Howard and Robert Devereux, the Earl of Essex. Hakluyt's narrator, Marbecke – a physician who accompanied Howard – presented the expedition as a heroic feat in the service of the queen, accomplished with exemplary piety as well as conspicuous success. Yet when Hakluyt provided this narrative in the first volume of his expanded compilation in 1598, its appearance proved sufficiently sensitive that it was hastily withdrawn.[65] References to the 1596 action nonetheless remain in volume 1's dedication, contents list, and preface to the reader, in which Hakluyt announced that he had relaxed his principles of geographical organization in order to include in a volume of northern voyages both the defeat of the Armada and "the honourable expedition under two of the most noble and valiant peeres of this Realme, I meane, the renoumed Erle of Essex, and the right honorable the lord Charles Howard, lord high

---

64 Jowitt, "Hero and the Sea," para. 5.

65 Surviving copies yield physical evidence that the "Cadiz leaves" were excised from printed copies, and a new title page printed, dated 1599 and omitting the 1598 title page's reference to "the famous victorie atchieved at the citie of Cadiz, 1596." The suppression may have been voluntary, and was at any rate not systematically enforced. Anthony Payne's detailed study of the 240 extant copies of *PN* (1598–1600) has shown that 115 copies *with* the "Cadiz leaves" survive in various states; of the entire range of extant copies, 130 copies (with and without the "Cadiz leaves") have a new title page (Payne, "Suppression of the Voyage to Cadiz," 2–3). An earlier version of Payne's article appeared as Payne, "Richard Hakluyt and the Earl of Essex."

Admirall of England, made 1596. unto the strong citie of Cadiz."[66] The suppression of the Cádiz narrative in volume 1 appears to have been the final episode in a larger struggle to control narratives about the action that began well before the fleet had returned to England. A brief summary may help to clarify how a "resounding tactical success" became the subject of controversy and even censorship.[67]

In June of 1596, a fleet of some hundred sail set out for Cádiz under the command of Howard; unlike most of the voyages discussed in this chapter, the expedition was solely funded by the crown. Howard's force arrived at Cádiz to destroy the Spanish naval fleet at anchor there, while a land army under the Earl of Essex took and occupied the city. Although it failed to prevent the burning of a *flota* with rich cargos, the expedition took "two new Spanish warships, 1,200 pieces of ordnance, and booty worth (on the Spanish estimate) twenty million ducats," also destroying thirteen warships, eleven Indies ships and a number of smaller vessels. The result was "a material and political catastrophe" for Spain.[68]

The messengers dispatched by Essex and Howard with a written report of the victory for Elizabeth and the Privy Council also carried numerous accounts by other hands and for other addressees. The result was a "welter of information … [that] opened the way for partisan debate in England" even as division and rivalry grew between elements of the forces remaining in Spain. Although members of the expedition "profited handsomely" by its spoils, the crown recovered only a fraction of what was taken; a financial investigation of the voyage was launched to identify mismanagement or malfeasance.[69] Senior officers sought to publicize their personal contributions, a competition aggravated by rivalry among the voyage's commanders – particularly Ralegh and the Earl of Essex. Both in his shaping of the expedition and the publicity campaign that followed it, Essex aimed at advancing an aggressive foreign policy agenda, one at odds with the policy of Elizabeth and her counsellors but attractive to more radical Protestants who "cast the war against Spain as

---

66 Payne, "Suppression of the Voyage to Cadiz," 7; Hakluyt, "Preface to the Reader (1598)," sig. **2v. The "late renoumed expedition and honorable voyage unto Cadiz" is mentioned in the dedication to Howard in volume I ("Epistle Dedicatorie [1598]," sig. *2v).
67 Payne, "Suppression of the Voyage to Cadiz," 4. My account relies on Rodger, *Safeguard of the Seas*, 284–7.
68 Rodger, *Safeguard of the Seas*, 286.
69 Hammer, "Myth-Making," 626.

an apocalyptic struggle."[70] Both Paul Hammer and Anthony Payne have detailed efforts by Essex to disseminate a partisan account of the voyage, composed by a secretary on his instructions, in the guise of a semi-anonymous letter from Cádiz. Its publication was suppressed by the queen, even as Thomas Nashe commented that printers were "gaping" for material on the victory – but manuscript copies of this and other Cádiz narratives appear to have circulated widely and enjoyed a "steady existence" in manuscript.[71] William Cecil, Lord Burghley, in turn, commissioned an authorized account of the action, completed and edited in draft but, ultimately, not disseminated. Given the potential for controversy, Payne concludes that "it was probably preferable from the queen's perspective not to allow anything at all about Cadiz into print."[72] Two years after the fact, Hakluyt's narrative in volume 1 was the first account of the action to appear, albeit still without the name of an author attached.

Manuscript and print accounts of the 1596 Cádiz expedition, including the one offered and then withdrawn by Hakluyt, have been examined as a case study in censorship, particularly as related to the changing politics of Elizabeth's court and the rise and fall of powerful figures such as Cecil, Ralegh, and Essex. A manuscript newsletter among Essex's papers, apparently referring to the Cádiz voyages, noted "there be proclamations sett owte agaynst the reporters of newes."[73] Stepping back from a detailed examination of court politics or

---

70 Payne, "Suppression of the Voyage to Cadiz," 8.

71 Nashe's letter is cited in Hammer, "Myth-Making," 632; Payne, "Suppression of the Voyage to Cadiz," 5. (Original: BL MS Cotton Julius 103, fo. 280r; McKerrow, *Works of Thomas Nashe*, 5: 194.) On manuscript circulation, see Hammer, "Myth-Making," 631–2. Hammer's examination of manuscripts yields further details of Essex's ongoing revisions and elaborations to the narrative produced by his secretary, Henry Cuffe, confirming our sense of the stakes in just how the story was presented and told. These authorial efforts on Essex's part were in addition to a broader, "multi-media propaganda campaign" that included sermons, public celebrations, visual imagery, a new hairstyle, a commissioned map, and gifts of stolen Spanish books to the Bodleian and King's College libraries (Hammer, "Myth-Making," 633–7).

72 Hammer, "Myth-Making," 628; Payne, "Suppression of the Voyage to Cadiz," 8.

73 Payne, "Suppression of the Voyage to Cadiz," 7. No official record of a proclamation or other censorship has been found, but other, less formal or public modes of suppression may have been in play. Payne suggests that the changes to Hakluyt's work were not necessarily the result of censorship or even direct pressure of a less formal kind; they might well have been a tactful gesture by someone close enough to the court to be sensitive to its currents ("Richard Hakluyt and the Earl of Essex," 19). On a related case of material withdrawn from *PN* (1589) during its print run, see Croskey, "Hakluyt's Accounts of Sir Jerome Bowes's Embassy to Ivan IV"; Stout, "'The Strange and Wonderfull Discoverie of Russia.'"

Elizabethan censorship, a more general point can be made: narrating or disseminating the story even of English victories could be a far from straightforward matter. A more particular point also bears considering. The correspondence of Essex's secretaries discussed attributing the narrative they had produced to "RG," "DT," or "RB," initials deliberately chosen to misdirect readers.[74] Such evidence introduces the possibility that some names attached to narratives of contested events may not in fact reveal the identity of "paynfull and personall travellers" (in Hakluyt's words) so much as a behind-the-scenes effort to shape public knowledge and understanding in particular ways. While Hakluyt's account of the 1596 Cádiz voyage was, indeed, a participant account that can be securely attributed (even if the editor chose not to do so), the broader picture of writing and suppression regarding the voyage cautions us that for these narratives of the Spanish war, the editor's claim to have attributed authorship and used participant accounts cannot be treated with complete confidence. Closer examination of his materials will make clear such caution is warranted.

Hakluyt's promises of attributing authorship as an editorial principle in 1589 probably owed something to local context, and in particular to his new disillusionment with the French cosmographer André Thevet, whose frequent failure to attribute documents and actions to their authors was thus implicitly criticized.[75] Nonetheless, the principle of attribution to authors who were also witnesses captures something distinctive about Hakluyt's methods, and provides us with a set of questions to ask about this group of documents. If no author is named, can authorship be established? Was the author – known or otherwise – a participant in the action? If an author's name is known, can that name tell us something about his relation to events, the circumstances of composition, or his relationship with other actors and stakeholders? If unknown, what can the document itself tell us about the circumstances underlying its composition? In a word, Hakluyt's editorial principles suggest a heuristic: who told these stories, why, and from where?

---

74 Hammer, "Myth-Making," 631.

75 Thevet's *New Founde Worlde, or Antarcticke* (London, 1568) was doubtless one of "those wearie volumes bearing the titles of universall Cosmographies which some men that I could name have published as their owne, being indeed most untruly and unprofitablie ramassed and hurled together" (Hakluyt, "Preface to the Reader [1589]," sig. *3v). Frank Lestringant has examined Hakluyt's relations with Thevet in meticulous detail (see, for instance, *Le Huguenot et le sauvage*, chap. 7).

Each of the major naval actions that figured in Hakluyt's collection left in its wake a very substantial archival trail of letters and dispatches, accounts, acts in council, legal materials, and diplomatic correspondence that documented shifting plans, multiple perspectives, and attempts at tallying the human and financial balance sheets of the voyage.[76] This broader record aids in contextualizing Hakluyt's sources as well as in appreciating the kinds of alternative sources, stories, and styles that did not appear in the compilation. Attentive readers have long noted that evidence internal to a text can sometimes locate otherwise unknown narrators on a particular ship or with a particular captain, implying distinct experiences, knowledge, and perspective, if not also loyalty; such evidence can sharpen awareness of an author's narrative and rhetorical choices. Texts also exhibit different habits in the extent to which they make visible individual voices or experiences; some remain entirely within the realm of the collective, narrating all actions as taken by "us," some move between "we" and "I," while others allow attentive readers to track distinct elements of the collective.[77] Such habits of style can always be described precisely, and attention to the empirical evidence of usage in the choice between "we" and "I" may speak to the larger question of how far "I's" or smaller values of "we" are distinct from a larger group, whether that be a ship, a fleet, or the nation itself. In thinking about whose a story it was, we will thus be considering evidence from the micro-scale of phrasing all the way up to the macro-scale of the larger archive (see appendix 5).

Appendix 5 separates the documents identified in appendix 4 into two groups: materials for which an author is known, and materials for which attribution is missing or problematic. The legend adds several further marked attributes: authors who were participants in the voyages they narrated; authors named by Hakluyt; and authors who were participants *and* identified

---

[76] Much of this record has been made available in editions and compilations by the Hakluyt Society, the Camden Society, and the Navy Records Society, along with valuable editorial introductions and commentary. The discussion that follows relies on this scholarship, and is enormously indebted to it. As such, however, it reflects a sampling of the archives rather than an exhaustive search.

[77] Two authors who were only incidentally at sea – Linschoten and Marbecke – provide a sort of control against which we can compare the practices of writers more habituated to the conventions of maritime writing; both move flexibly and naturally between the broader picture of movement and action in a group, and their own, more particular stories. Wingfield, a soldier, has particular habits that are again somewhat different from those of other authors in this section; his attention to named individuals recalls the siege narratives examined in chapter 5.

by Hakluyt. Also marked are authors who use the first-person singular at least once in contexts other than an address to the reader ("I assure you"); these represent the narrator as an individual actor whose actions and point of view are distinct from the larger group. As the appendix shows, roughly half of Hakluyt's documents in this group were participant accounts by explicitly named authors: items 5 (Evesham), 8 (Wright), 12 (Flicke), 13 (Linschoten), 14 (White), and 16 (Downton); for items 2 (Marbecke) and 7 (Wingfield), names of participant authors have been identified or confirmed from manuscript evidence.[78] Several additional narratives by named authors were probably or certainly written by non-participants, typically using the third person. If the minister and translator Philip Jones was indeed the author of the narrative under that name, there is no indication that he accompanied the ships travelling to Turkey whose action he narrates.[79] Ralegh was certainly not a participant in Thomas Howard's expedition to the Azores, which he narrated so memorably: though Ralegh "managed to inject into his prose the impression that he was an actual participant in the battle," his narrative was written in London.[80] Mote is unknown beyond his authorship of the pamphlet from which Hakluyt drew his rousing third-person account of the escape of the *Primrose*; the text offers no indication that he was a participant.

The tricky exception to these categories is the narrative of a 1589 expedition to Lisbon under Drake and Sir John Norris, "written (as it is thought)" by Anthony Wingfield. Framed with a first-person address *about* the account

---

78 The conjectural attribution of item 13 to Anthony Wingfield is discussed below. One might tentatively add item 10 to the list of participant narratives by named authors; both Hakluyt's text and its pamphlet source conclude with the line, "present at this fight master John Hawes merchant" (*Valiant and Most Laudable Fight by the Centurion of London, 1591*). Authorship remains conjectural – and Hawes, if he was the author, appears to be unknown beyond the fact that he was a merchant present on a Levant Company ship trading in the Mediterranean. (Another Hawes is noted by Purchas as captain of Cumberland's *Roe* in 1586; Purchas, *Pilgrimes*, 4[vi]: 1141.) Repeated attribution of actions to "the *Centurion*" and to "the Englishmen" hint at a perspective located outside the envelope of the ship and its company, features of style that might reflect redaction of oral testimony provided by Hawes or others by another hand. Exhibiting many of the rhetorical features noted earlier in the chapter, this document resists secure or meaningful attribution.

79 The practice of sending chaplains on trading expeditions appears to have been regularized by both the East India Company and the Levant Company in the seventeenth century, but is not attested in Hakluyt's materials (see Games, *Web of Empire*, chap. 7). The role of chaplains is discussed in chapter 10.

80 Lacey, *Sir Walter Ralegh*, 158.

that follows, that account itself does not differentiate Wingfield from other officers; his actions, like theirs, are narrated in the third person. Purportedly a letter from an unnamed military officer present on the expedition, the narrative begins by addressing a friend who had been misled by critical reports of the action; it closes with the request that its addressee treat the narrative as private, "not to be delivered to the publique view of the world."[81] Wingfield's name was suppressed altogether from the pamphlet version, *A True Copie of a Discourse* (London, 1589), and Hakluyt treats his authorship as conjectural; however, letters by Wingfield and Norris to Sir Thomas Wilkes discuss plans to publish the text (and Norris's concern that it would be "called in").[82] This was a controversial expedition, which left both Drake and Norris in disgrace with the queen; Wingfield's use of the third person comports with an intention to dissimulate authorship of a partisan account.

Participant accounts by named authors exhibit distinctive, if not uniform habits of style. Most visibly, they tend to narrate actions in the first-person plural, as done by "us" rather than "I" or "they."[83] Among these participant narratives, Edward Wright's account of a cruise off the Azores by the Earl of Cumberland's ships committed itself most thoroughly to the convention of collective narration, using "I" only in a short parenthetical remark about a plant observed on the voyage: "(Ceder I thinke)."[84] This narrative itself appeared concurrently in Wright's *Certaine errors in navigation* (1599), where it served to illustrate the hazards of old-fashioned navigational practices;

---

81 Wingfield, "Voyage to Spaine and Portugale, 1589," 2(ii): 143.

82 Wernham, *Expedition of Norris and Drake*, 294–5. Wingfield's account can usefully be compared with item 12, a report by Robert Flicke that seems actually to have been a report not written for publication; signed, dated, addressed to named recipients and opening with reference to an earlier dispatch, it concludes before many of the participating ships in the action had returned. Flicke's report supplements accounts by Ralegh and Linschoten (items 11, 13).

83 Linschoten and Marbecke, a merchant and physician who were seafarers only incidentally, were much freer in describing their individual actions, thoughts, and presence alongside the more collective experiences that participants had as a group. However, Payne comments that although Hakluyt retained Marbeck's use of "I," his edits "depersonalized" the account significantly, omitting Marbeck's name and occupation as well as "much personal detail concerning the lord admiral" (Payne, "Suppression of the Voyage to Cadiz," 16).

84 Wright, "Voyage of the Erle of Cumberland to the Azores," 2(ii): 158. Wright has also been recognized as an important collaborator on the globe published by Emery Molyneux in 1592 and following; Hakluyt announced the coming appearance of the globe in Hakluyt, "Preface to the Reader (1589)," sig. *4v.

prefatory material to the work makes clear that Wright's intent in publishing was to secure recognition as the author of a treatise that had been subject to plagiarism and misattribution since he had presented it to the Earl of Cumberland in manuscript some years earlier. Hakluyt himself identifies Wright in the headnote as an "excellent Mathematician and Enginier"; Wright's world map, which has an independent interest for its early use of the Mercator projection, appears in many copies of *PN* (1598–1600).[85] Within the Azores narrative itself, however, Wright maintains virtual anonymity. Evidence internal to the text locates Wright on Christopher Lister's *Victory* (and briefly as part of a boat party chased by "an huge fish").[86] On the list of captains and gentlemen that opens the narrative, he names himself with a flourish, as "Captain Edward Carelesse, alias Wright, who in Sir Francis Drakes West-Indian voyage ... was captaine of the Hope."[87] In the body of the narrative, its author stands out only by the negative evidence of his absence from visibility: unlike other captains, his own actions are never described or represented. The rich identifying and contextual information about text and author provided by Hakluyt's headnote, the world map, and the larger work from which the text has been extracted lie outside the frame of the narrative itself. Assertive as an author more generally, when he came to write about the Azores voyage Wright folded himself into the maritime "we."

Another captain of a trading voyage to Morocco, Thomas White, used the first-person singular only in the first sentence of his narrative about an encounter with two Spanish ships bearing religious goods to the West Indies: "in *my* returning out of Barbary in the ship called the *Amity* of London ... at four o'clock in the morning we had sight of two ships (emphasis mine)."[88] In the remainder, White is fully committed to the plural voice even for actions that seem as if they must have been his own as captain: "We then commanded their

---

85 Wright's map is present in 10 per cent of surviving copies; Arthur Hind speculates that it may have been sold separately from the book itself (Payne, *Guide*, 100–1).

86 Wright, "Voyage of the Erle of Cumberland to the Azores," 2(ii): 156. Purchas identifies him as captain of the *Margaret*, rear-admiral; the *Margaret* proved unseaworthy and returned to England with two prizes a few days out of Plymouth, presumably leaving Wright to transfer to Cumberland and Lister's *Victory* (Purchas, *Pilgrimes*, 4[vi]: 1,141).

87 Wright, "Voyage of the Erle of Cumberland to the Azores," 2(ii): 155. See also Cates, "Famous Expedition of Francis Drake, 1586," 3: 534.

88 White, "Taking of Two Spanish Ships, 1592," 2(ii): 193. The *Amity* appears to have been regularly employed in trade with Morocco (Willan, *Studies in Elizabethan Foreign Trade*, 245, 249). Payne notes that this voyage was an "example of City involvement in privateering" ("Hakluyt's London," 17).

captaines and masters to come aboord us ... we sent certaine of our own men aboord them."[89] The effect is to merge White into the collective of the English ship's company, whose prize had carried not only quicksilver for Spain's American silver mines, but a value-laden cargo of "bulles or indulgences, and guilded Missals or Service books." Intercepting these (as White implies) both hindered the practice of Catholic devotion in New Spain and (as he makes explicit) denied Philip the revenues to be raised by selling and taxing the indulgences.

"John Evesham, gentleman" narrated a raid on the Azores by two of Ralegh's pinnaces, again using "we," "us," and "our" to describe not only common movement but a sense of common purpose and shared achievement. (He candidly avows that "enrich[ing] ourselves ... was the cause of this our travail," and gestures towards a larger collective in the communal celebrations of the small fleet's return into Plymouth harbour, received "with triumphant joy, not only with great ordnance then shot off, but with the willing hearts of all the people of the town.")[90] It is impossible to place Evesham physically on either of the expedition's two ships. As an individual, he flickers briefly into view as one of a small boat party that cut out a ship and a caravel at Graciosa, when "the shot of *my* musket ... Happened to strike the gunner of the fort to death" (emphasis mine).[91] The passive and self-deprecating form of what might have been a brag suggests that the first-person *singular* entered Evesham's text only hesitantly.

Two participant narratives by London captains were less inhibited in representing their authors as "I." Nicholas Downton narrated a 1594 action between three of the Earl of Cumberland's ships and a carrack coming from the East Indies, which burned after a fierce struggle that killed one captain, disabled another, and seriously wounded Downton, captain of the *Sampson*; a second carrack put up stiff resistance, and was let go due to the loss of officers already suffered, and the "murmuring of some disordered and cowardly companions."[92] Hakluyt's header to the text describes Downton as "the discreet and valiant captaine," suggesting the possibility of a personal acquaintance, and a marginal comment suggests some personal knowledge: "Besides these 3 ships there was a pinnace called the Violet or the Why

---

89 White, "Taking of Two Spanish Ships, 1592," 2(ii): 194.
90 Evesham, "Voyage to the Azores, 1586," 2(ii): 121.
91 Ibid., 2(ii): 120–1.
92 Downton, "Firing and Sinking of The Cinquo Chaguas, 1594," 201.

not I."[93] The text appears based on a journal, each paragraph beginning with a date, but source and context are unknown; a reference in the text to "the 4 chapter in the first booke of the woorthy history of Huighen de Linschoten" suggests that it was composed or at least revised no earlier than 1598, when Linschoten's *Itinerario* appeared in English translation.[94] (Conceivably, Downton provided a report to Cumberland that he subsequently revised at Hakluyt's request.) In 1591, Robert Flicke, a member of the Drapers' Company, commanded a squadron of London ships sent to reinforce and relieve a fleet under Thomas Howard; Howard's aim had been to intercept the Spanish treasure fleet off the Azores. Flicke's squadron cruised off the Azores for several weeks without locating Howard's ships, but succeeded in taking several Spanish and Portuguese prizes (including "certain of the Indian fleete").[95] On their return, the ships still in company were driven into Plymouth harbour by a storm; Flicke's report "directed to Master Thomas Bromley, Master Richard Staper, and Master Cordall" was composed there, as he awaited instructions from them and from the Privy Council on the disposition of his prizes and their cargo.[96]

[93] Samuel Purchas printed extracts from Downton's journals on these East India Company voyages in *Purchas his Pilgrimes*; the first of these he marks as being among Hakluyt's papers.

[94] Downton, "Firing and Sinking of The Cinquo Chaguas, 1594," 2(ii): 200.

[95] Flicke, "Voyage of Certaine Ships of London, 1591," 2(ii): 177. Within the larger perspective afforded by reading all three narratives, the failed meeting of Flicke's and Howard's fleets proved to be critical; for want of the supplies Flicke's ships brought, Howard had landed his debilitated crews at Flores when they were surprised by the approach of Alfonso de Bazan's force, and the resulting delay in getting to sea left Grenville's *Revenge* hindmost and vulnerable to Bazan's galleons. Flicke's narrative lacks this perspective. Dated "Plymouth the 24 of October. 1591," his text opens with a reference to "my last of the twelfth of August," which "advertised you particularly of the accidents of our Fleete until then," indicating that it covered only a portion of the voyage; at the time of writing, he did not know the fate of consorts separated from him by weather, and as Howard had not yet returned, the outcome of the expedition remained uncertain.

[96] Staper, one of the prime movers in the Levant trade, appears to have provided Hakluyt with numerous documents in PN 2(i) ("C&S"). Thomas Cordell, a "magnate of the Levant trade," owned the *Centurion* and was "one of Cumberland's chief creditors" (Andrews, *Trade, Plunder, and Settlement*, 14; "Ten Marchants Ships of London," 2(ii): 167; Payne, "Hakluyt's London," 16–17). He and Flicke were both among the investors in Drake's 1587 voyage to Cádiz (Hopper, "Sir Francis Drake's Memorable Service, 1587," 27). Both Staper and Bromley were among the founding members of the Barbary Company, 1585 (Elizabeth I, "Letters Patent for a Trade to Barbary, 1585").

Both Downton and Flicke predominantly use the maritime "we" for collective actions and understanding ("we perceived her indeede to be a Carack"); like some other narrators, Flicke occasionally also renders decisions and orders in a passive voice that diffuses the agency of command ("it was thought good to send our boats furnished on shore"). Both use "I" for their own bodily experience ("I was shot in a little above the belly"; "it was ordered ... to have gone aboord myselfe") and for many actions specific to their professional roles as captain ("I commanded to give her the broad side"; "I caused a Flagge of Counsell to be put foorth"). Both also occasionally use "I" as a synecdoche for the ship and its company, a usage particular to captains ("I, in the *Sampson*, fetched her up in the evening"; "my selfe with the other two ships ... gave severall chases").

The largest clusters of first-person pronouns, for both authors, occur at moments that are also critical in their narratives. In Downton's narrative, a long paragraph describes the violent encounter with the *Cinque Llaguas* carrack, and the fire from which Downton's ship, grappled onto the carrack, only narrowly escaped. After all three of the English captains were wounded or killed early in the action, Downton's place had been taken by an able second in command; he remained capable of observing. (Hence Downton, captain of the fleet's smallest ship, became the narrator of the report.) The companies of the admiral and vice-admiral were left leaderless in the moment, and as Downton's men attempted to board the carrack they were "not manfully backed" by their fellows, emboldening resistance by the carrack's crew. This fracture in a collective effort caused Downton to distinguish between "the *Exchanges* men" and "my men." This long paragraph of actions turns to the first-person singular with particular frequency, both for present-tense expressions of opinion ("I must needs say") and for past-tense statements of perception ("I saw [the fire on the carrack] beyond all help"). As the coordination between ships and between officers and men faltered and fire from the *Cinque Llaguas* threatened the *Sampson*, the stylistic convention of the collective "we" was also interrupted. That "I" reappears later in the text as Downton considered how to board a second carrack, only to be deflected by the crew's "murmuring."[97] In Flicke's narrative, the singular first person

---

[97] Downton weaves between "I," "we," and "they" in this passage: "*I* consulted what course *we* should take in the boording. But by reason that *wee* which were the chiefe Captaines were partly slaine and partly wounded ... and because of the murmuring of *some* disordered and cowardly companions, *our* valiant and resolute determinations were crossed" (Downton, "Firing and Sinking of The Cinquo Chaguas, 1594," 2[ii]: 200–1).

coincides with a different kind of crisis, the "disorder" of his crews in pillaging several Portuguese and West Indian prizes.

> Whereas there were ... certaine summes of money taken from the company which they had thus purloyed and embeseled, and the same with some other parcels brought aboord my ship ... the company as pillage due unto them demanded to have the same shared, which *I* refused, & openly at the maine maste read the articles firmed by my Lord Treasurer and my lord Admirall, whereby we ought to be directed, and that it was not in *mee* any way to dispose thereof untill the same were finally determined at home. Hereupon they mutined and at last grew into such furie, as they would have it or els breake downe the cabbine ... whereby *I* was forced to yeeld, least the Spaniards which we had abord being many perceiving the same, might have had fit opportunitie to rise against us. (emphasis mine)[98]

Here the captain's assertion of his own authority over the crew, and his invocation of the formal articles issued by higher authorities to govern the voyage, were powerless in the face of desire and, perhaps, informal understandings about what was "due" to those who actually risked themselves in the action. Their fury threatened to dismantle not only the physical architecture of the ship, but its survival as an *English* ship within which a large number of Spaniards were prisoners.[99]

Both Flicke and Downton testify to the ability even of English merchant ships to tackle valuable and heavily defended Spanish shipping; it's easy to understand why these narratives are included among the set of "sea war" narratives in volume 2 despite their modest outcomes. But both texts are poor in the rhetorical features identified in the first half of the chapter. The encounters they describe are not narrated as victories against overwhelming odds, as a result of providential intervention, or as exhibitions of mercy, humanity, truthtelling, and careful empiricism. Violence is not described euphemistically, or characterized as self-reflexive. National character is not being limned against an oppositionally defined other, as in the texts by Mote, Jones, and Ralegh, or the various accounts of galley fights. Indeed, the "disorder" and "murmuring"

---

[98] Flicke, "Voyage of Certaine Ships of London, 1591," 2(ii): 177–8.

[99] While it concerns a narrative written from a very different experience of Anglo–Spanish conflict, Richard Helgerson's study of the emergence of the first-person singular in the narrative of the captive Miles Philips makes for a stimulating comparison (Helgerson, "I Miles Philips").

that both describe work against the sense of collective purpose and affect suggested in other texts. While we may not know exactly how the common tropes examined earlier came to enter the narratives that do exhibit them, it is instructive to notice when they are *missing*. Downton's and Flicke's reports appear to have been prepared for a relatively restricted audience, in contrast to voyages narrated in pamphlet form. Flicke addressed his text to stakeholders and owners; both accounts have an element of apology, attributing their mixed success at least in part to the "disorder" of their crews. Anthony Payne has tracked edits to the PN (1598–1600) version of Marbecke's Cádiz narrative that suggest an editorial interest in balance and impartiality, creating an impression of harmony and avoiding "attention to personal rivalries in telling his national story."[100] The Flicke and Downton narratives indicate that in volume 2(ii), Hakluyt was *not* engaged in this level of active editing, nor was he seeking to smooth out differences and produce greater uniformity among his texts (one hypothetical explanation for the common features explored in the first half of this chapter). The rhetorical and substantive differences of these two narratives are left in place, along with the message that not all on board *were* "on board" with the aims of the voyages as these were understood by their captains.

At least from the manuscript record known to this author, the reports by Downton and Flicke also do not appear to have been jousting against other narratives or other understandings, as was true for some of the narratives in this group, concerning larger, more contested events like the 1596 raid on Cádiz, the Lisbon expedition of 1589, or the 1591 cruise by Thomas Howard's fleet with which Flicke was officially connected. Such expeditions were larger in terms of the numbers of ships, the numbers of investors, the profit and loss sheets, and the sheer number of persons involved in combined land and sea operations. The direct involvement of the queen also made such actions inescapably political endeavours, domestically as much as internationally. Two narratives of contested events are among those for which identifying authorship has been especially problematic. These are items 6 and 15, narratives of Drake's raid on Cádiz (1587) with the taking of the *Saõ Phelipe*, and the capture of the *Madré de Deus* (1592). Neither account was attributed to an author by Hakluyt, and I believe that sources for both have been misidentified. Both involved some of the stakes that were missing from Downton's and Flicke's

---

100 Payne, "Suppression of the Voyage to Cadiz," 16–17.

narratives: political careers, aristocratic egos, and eye-watering spoils. Each presents different kinds of evidence and problems.

In 1592, the *Madre de Deus* became the second East Indian carrack taken by English privateers, after Drake's capture of the *Saõ Phelipe* in 1587. Carracks were challenging targets – the Portuguese East India trade went in ships of "fifteen hundred tons or more," which were "heavily manned and extremely difficult to board."[101] Both these ships were also consequential prizes, not only because of the vast riches they carried but because (as Hakluyt's source comments) their cargos "acquaint[ed] the English Nation more generally with the particularities of the exceeding riches and wealth of the East Indies."[102] Hakluyt himself received from the spoils of the *Madre de Deus* a book he characterizes as an "incomparable jewell," a treatise printed in Macao by the Portuguese Jesuit Duarte de Sande from which he extracted information on China.[103] Downton's men later used the *Madre de Deus* as a point of reference in guessing the size of the *Cinque Llaguas*: "some of them say, that she was bigger than the *Madre de Dios*, and some, that she was less."[104]

The queen had initially put Ralegh in command of the 1592 voyage, but recalled him shortly after departure; he returned to London before his fleet of some fifteen ships cleared Cape Finisterre, and would be in the Tower by the time they returned (printed narratives of the action are tactfully silent on his whereabouts). The larger part of the remaining ships, under Martin Frobisher, held station off the coast of Spain, while John Burgh commanded a smaller group of ships assigned to cruise off the Azores for prizes. The ten ships that eventually took the carrack after a day of hard fighting were a mixed group, however. Some of Burgh's ships had returned home; those remaining were joined by others belonging to the Earl of Cumberland, as well as two returning from a West Indian voyage under Christopher Newport. A manuscript account by Francis Seall, one of Cumberland's men, amplifies the narrative's brief reference, in volume 2, to a conference of captains

---

101 Rodger, *Safeguard of the Seas*, 281.

102 "Voyage of Sir Francis Drake to Cadiz, 1587," 2(ii): 123. The first English attempt at reaching the East Indies after the circumnavigations of Drake and Cavendish in the 1580s was the difficult voyage of James Lancaster in 1591–1593. The English edition of Linschoten's *Discourse* (London, 1598), encouraged by Hakluyt, would play an important role in disseminating practical information about the East Indies (Waters, *Art of Navigation*, 234). It is cited by Downton.

103 Hakluyt, "Epistle Dedicatorie (1599)," 2(ii): sig. *4r. The text appears in *PN* 2(ii) as de Sande, "Description of the Kingdome of China." See chapter 8.

104 Downton, "Firing and Sinking of The Cinquo Chaguas, 1594," 2(ii): 201.

(represented in Hakluyt's text – though not in other accounts – as summoned by Burgh).[105] According to Seall, the captains made an agreement specifying the terms of their cooperation and the division of any spoils they might take; such agreements appear to have been cited as enforceable in legal proceedings following other voyages.

[N]ow was left the Foresight of her Majesty, and five of my Lord's of Cumberland, the Roebuck and the Dainty, [which were] two ships belonging unto the fleet, which Sir Walter Ralegh should have proceeded to the sea with. These eight made a consortship together unto this effect: – that what soever within fourteen days, should be taken by them, or any of them eight, should, so far forth as the goods of any prize came unto, be proportionately levied out unto every venturer, according to the quality or burthen of his ship, both for tonnage and manage. Not long after this consortship, two ships came to the Islands, who before had been in the Indies; the one of them was named the Dragon, the other, the Prudence; which two ships stayed with us and made the number of our fleet ten.[106]

Competition and conflict over the spoils of the voyage arose among this motley fleet, despite their "consortship," virtually from the moment the carrack was first boarded, by men from Cumberland's *Tiger* and *Sampson*. Ships that were further away from the *Madre de Deus* struggled for their share of its cargo.[107] On arrival in England, the expedition's men and officers began hastily

---

105 "Taking of the Madre de Dios," 2(ii): 197; Kingsford, "Taking of the Madre de Dios," 90; Seall, "My Lord of Cumberland's Ships Voyage," 105–6. Kingsford provides a catalogue reference for Seall as BL MS Harley 540, which I was not able to confirm from the BL catalogue.

106 Seall, "My Lord of Cumberland's Ships Voyage," 2: 105–6. C. Newport and H. Merrick commanded the last two ships named; see Twitt, "Voyage of M. Christopher Newport [...] 1591." The Earl of Cumberland's ships included the *Tiger* (Capt. Norton), the *Sampson* or *Assurance* (Capt. Cocke), the *Phoenix*, the *Discovery*, and the *Gold Noble* (Capt. Downton), although the last two ships appear not to have been present when the carrack was taken (vide *Sea-Mans Triumph*). (See also Purchas's account of voyages to the Azores sponsored by Cumberland in *Pilgrimes*, 4: 1141–9.) For an example of legal proceedings involving the spoils of another mixed fleet and an agreement of consortship, see Andrews, *English Privateering Voyages*, chap. 5.

107 Seall, "My Lord of Cumberland's Ships Voyage," 108; Kingsford, "Taking of the Madre de Dios," 92–3. Kingsford cites the account in Purchas, *Pilgrimes*, and other archival sources. BL MS Lansdowne 70 includes numerous items from the Burghley papers relating to the carrack's prize goods.

disposing of what they had privately secured for themselves, and a spectacular dispersion of the carrack's rich goods ensued before officials could take account of the cargo on behalf of the crown and other stakeholders.[108] The rapid evaporation of the *Madre de Deus*'s cargo constituted sufficient emergency that Ralegh was released from the Tower and sent to Dartmouth under guard to halt the pillage. Once the remaining, unplundered cargo had been secured, the massive profits of the prize were distributed quite unevenly among the various adventurers and participants. When Hakluyt's narrative claimed that the spoils were "sufficient to yeeld contentment to all parties," the documents reviewed by Charles Lethbridge Kingsford suggest that that their actual distribution did not, in fact, content everyone.[109]

The narrative of this action included in *PN* (1598–1600) – "The Taking of the *Madre de Dios*" – offers no direct evidence of its source or the identity of its author. David and Alison Quinn's "Contents and sources" identifies Hakluyt's source as a pamphlet, *The Sea-Mans Triumph* (1591); though the pamphlet too is anonymous, the English Short Title Catalogue (ESTC) attributes it to Ralegh.[110] Close examination of *Sea-Mans Triumph* and "The Taking of the *Madre de Dios*" indicates conclusively that the first was not the source for the second: both are anonymous, third-person accounts of the action, but in content, emphasis, and style, these are entirely distinct narratives, making *Sea-Mans Triumph* an independent source on the action.[111] The differences between the pamphlet and the account in *PN* (1598–1600) merit attention

---

108 Burghley's papers testify to the complicated disputes that ensued over credit and over division of the spoils, both what was accounted for and distributed, and what had already been informally taken. See, for example, BL MS Lansdowne 70/28-70; and BL MS Lansdowne 115, f. 252 (in Andrews, *English Privateering Voyages*, 201–4). A number of related documents are printed in Kingsford, "Taking of the *Madre de Dios*." Burgh was killed in a duel with Ralegh's nephew, John Gilbert, two years later; this duel has sometimes been explained as a dispute over the spoils of the carrack (Andrews, *English Privateering Voyages*, 225n1).

109 "Taking of the *Madre de Dios*," 2(ii): 198. An overview of disputes over the spoils is given by Kingsford, some of whose sources are also printed in the volume ("Taking of the *Madre de Dios*," 92–8, 115–16, 118–19). See also Seall, "My Lord of Cumberland's Ships Voyage," 110–11.

110 Quinn and Quinn, "C&S," 2: 425.

111 The preface to *Sea-Mans Triumph* presents it as addressed to an unnamed patron by an author who had travelled down to the West Country following the fleet's return and spoken with "such as bare office and [were] principall officers in" the action. The text is dated, in conclusion, "Dartmouth Sept. 1592," reinforcing its presentation as a letter; the carrack arrived at Dartmouth 7 September.

here as an example of how much latitude authors could exercise in narrating the same events, and also – since the pamphlet was in print – as evidence that may inform on how Hakluyt chose between different available sources.

The account provided by Hakluyt, "The Taking of the *Madre de Dios*," opens by devoting a full folio page to Ralegh's commission, his preparations, his commitment to pursue the voyage, and his eventual return, leaving Frobisher and Burgh (under his orders) to execute the "worke of patience" of lying in wait for Spanish ships returning from the East or West Indies. Burgh succeeds Ralegh as focal character, and is treated – rather unusually – not only as an individual ("Sir J. Burgh demanded of him what was best to be done") but as a synecdoche for his ship, its company, and at times the fleet as a whole: "divers small caravels ... he intercepted"; "Sir John ... imbarqued himself, having only in company a small barke of threescore tunnes"; "Sir John Burgh receiving a canon perier under water, [was] ready to sinke." Indeed, the most frequent sentence construction used is "he" [verb] rather than "they" [verb] or "we" [verb] ("our men" occurs infrequently). That "he" most frequently signifies Burgh (standing for his ship, the *Roebuck* and his crew), but when other ships are in question, Hakluyt's narrator tends to follow a similar practice of referring to the names of their captains rather than (as more commonly) to ship names: "Sir J. Burgh concluded to intangle [the carrack]; and sir R. Crosse promised also to fasten himselfe to her at the instant." It is in other words the captains, in this narrative, to whom are attributed almost all significant actions, and their names subsume the names of the ships they commanded. Indeed, the narrator omitted naming the *Tiger* and *Sampson* at all, except as "my lord of Cumberlands two ships" (the captains' names are given as participating in Burgh's council); the omission aligns with an apparent desire to diminish the part played by Cumberland's ships in the assault on the carrack: "After [Sir Robert Crosse] had fought with [the *Madre de Deus*] alone three houres single, my lord of Cumberlands two ships came up, & with very little losse entred with sir R. Crosse, who had in that time broken their courages, and made the assault easie for the rest."[112] (Cumberland would later be accorded a far more generous share of the profits than Ralegh.)

The pamphlet *Sea-Mans Triumph*, by contrast, begins not with the queen's commission to Ralegh, but at a later moment of opportunistic improvisation: various English ships sent out to cruise for prizes that year had already "with the consent of their Admirals dispersed ... divers ways." Burgh's request to

---

112 All references in this paragraph are found in "Taking of the *Madre de Dios*," 2(ii): 196–7.

Thomson in the *Dainty* and Newport in the *Dragon* to "keepe him companie, offering manye large profferes" occurs almost immediately (the sequence by which the various groups of ships arrived and joined together differs in the two narratives). A list of additional ships participating follows, with owners and captains each named and given a few words of commendatory introduction. (For instance, Hugh Merrick of the *Prudence*, a minor player in the action, was "a man wel reputed for hys valour and skill in marine causes, and oftentimes as a man of choyce for his vertues, hath taken charge in her Majesties Navy.") Even the gunner of the *Dainty* receives this treatment as he asks permission to shoot at the carrack, beginning the assault: "The Gunner, whose name was Thomas Bedome, beinge a proper tall man, and had very good aime at any things, and good lucke withall, desired the Captaine, hee might give them a shoote, to lett them understande, that they were Englishmenne, and under her Highnesse, Commaunder of the Seas."[113] *Sea-Mans Triumph*'s careful accounting of ships and officers opens into a considerably more detailed narrative of the actual attack on the *Madre de Deus*: as *Sea-Mans Triumph* tells the story, after the *Dainty* began to fire on the carrack, "the nexte that came to her" was Burgh in the *Roebuck*, "the third was the golden Dragon ... the next was ... the Foresighte"; the *Phoenix* then called in the *Tiger* and *Sampson*, who bore up to support the *Foresight*, then actually boarded and took the carrack.[114] *Sea-Mans Triumph* distributes explicit credit and narrative visibility far more widely than Hakluyt's "The Taking of the *Madre de Dios*," with its tight focus first on Ralegh and then on Burgh (both as an individual, and as a synecdoche for his command).

We can assume that *Sea-Mans Triumph* was available to Hakluyt, and he certainly drew on pamphlets for other voyages. Both narratives share one recurrent trope: emphasis on the pity and compassion felt and expressed by English mariners towards the slain, wounded, and defeated crew of the *Madre de Deus*, "whose misery, our countrey menne (thoughe they were our hatefull enemies) greately bewayled." Hakluyt added a marginal note to his version of the text calling attention to the "Exceeding humanity shewed to the enemy."[115] Overall, however, *Sea-Mans Triumph* exhibits a greater number of the rhetorical moves identified in the first part of this chapter: the gunner who sought to initiate action in advance of the master's command, the hundred sailors who took a carrack with a crew of eight hundred, the framing of

---

113 *Sea-Mans Triumph*, sig. A4r, A4v, B1r, B3r.
114 Ibid., sig. B3v–B4v.
115 Ibid., sig. C1r; "Taking of the *Madre de Dios*," 2(ii): 198.

successful violence as "but the chance of warres, which was and is, as it pleaseth God," careful bracketing of facts as "supposed" and "reported."[116] *Sea-Mans Triumph* shares with other pamphlet narratives, especially, the sense that many hands could contribute to the national project of superiority over Spain; the preferential attention given by the PN narrative to the agency of gentlemen captains makes a noticeably different choice. In choosing the source he did print, Hakluyt was evidently not (or not solely) concerned with representing the sea war in a particular manner consistent across documents.

What other features of the narrative in PN (1598–1600) might have made it attractive to Hakluyt? That this account was written by someone eager to highlight Ralegh's devotion and dedication is unmistakable: it gave unusual prominence to Ralegh's contributions and efforts at a moment actually marked by his disgrace and imprisonment.[117] While Hakluyt's closest connections with Ralegh had been in the 1580s, perhaps that relationship continued to be a factor in the late 1590s; he is known to have consulted for Cecil on Ralegh's undertakings in Guiana.[118] "The Taking of the *Madre de Dios*" also adds a more strategic perspective to the account in *Sea-Mans Triumph*, which (like other pamphlet narratives) focuses on the successful battle and the fact of its outcome. After a short account of the actual battle and Burgh's disposition of prisoners, Hakluyt's narrator goes on to highlight the exceptional value of what was won in taking the *Madre de Dios*. Its cargo was rich, as shown in a list that has its own poetry:

The spices were pepper, cloves, maces, nutmegs, cinamon, greene ginger: the drugs were benjamin, frankincense, galingale, mirabolans, aloes zocotrina, camphire: the silks, damasks, taffatas, sarcenets, altobassos, that is, counterfeit cloth of gold, unwrought China silke, sleaved silke, white twisted silke, curled cypresse ... There were also ... carpets like those of Turky; wherunto are to be

---

116 *Sea-Mans Triumph*, sig. B3v, B4v, C1r, C2r.

117 "Sir Walter finding his honor so farre engaged in the undertaking of this voyage, as without proceeding he saw no remedy ... would in no case yeeld to leave his fleet now under saile" ("Taking of the *Madre de Dios*," 2[ii]: 195). An attribution of the PN (1598–1600) narrative *to* Ralegh seems far more plausible than his authorship of *Sea-Mans Triumph*, but positive attribution is not my focus here.

118 Lorimer, *Discoverie of Guiana (2006)*, lxxxvi–vii. In another essay, however, Lorimer suggests that by the 1590s, Hakluyt had become "impatient with Ralegh's mercurial temperament and short-lived enthusiasms," which had led him to abandon the Roanoke colony to whose success the editor had devoted such thought and effort ("Robert Cecil, Richard Hakluyt and the Writing of Guiana, 1595–1616," 110, 112).

added the pearle, muske, civet, and amber-griece. The rest of the wares were many in number, but lesse in value; as elephants teeth, porcellan vessels of China, coco-nuts, hides, eben-wood as blacke as jet, bedsteds of the same, cloth of the rindes of trees very strange for the matter, and artificiall in workemanship.

In the narrator's sole direct address to the reader, he calls attention to the capture's value as *information*. "I cannot but enter into the consideration and acknowledgment of Gods great favor towards our nation, who ... hath manifestly *discovered those secret trades & Indian riches*, which hitherto lay strangely hidden, and cunningly concealed from us ... Whereby it should seeme that will of God for our good is ... to have us communicate with [the Spanish] in those East Indian treasures, & by the erection of a lawfull traffike to better our means to advance true religion and his holy service" (emphasis mine).[119] (Even the dimensions of the carrack are said to have been carefully surveyed by the architect and cartographer Robert Adams.) Hakluyt's own interest in the *informational* value of the prize and its contents was indicated by his allusion to the captured treatise by Duarte de Sande in the volume's dedication. By 1599, the year in which volume 2 appeared, he was participating in meetings that would lead to the foundation of the East India Company the following year; an East India Company document that has been associated with Hakluyt, informing government of places where Spanish presence did and did not bar trade in the Indies, cited both Sande's treatise and an "intercepted Register ... of the whole government of the East India, in the Madre de Deos, 1592."[120] By 1600, the draw of East Indian trade may have had greater appeal than the kind of identity-defining project exemplified by the pamphlet narratives of the earlier sea war. Indeed, negotiations had already begun to explore the possibility of peace with Spain, formalized by treaty in 1604.

Hakluyt's account of Drake's 1587 attack on Cádiz, aimed at disrupting Spain's preparations for war, offers a final example of problems in attribution. This brief narrative of only two pages in folio again belies a voluminous

---

119 "Taking of the *Madre de Dios*," 2(ii): 198. The list comes from "the catalogue taken at Leaden hall the 15 of September, 1592."

120 Hakluyt, "Certaiyne Reesons why the English Merchants may trade into the East Indies" (now TNA CO 77/1, no. 17) in Taylor, *OW*, 2: 467. On the authorship and context for the document, and a list of works cited in it, see Payne, "Hakluyt and the East India Company." Payne dates "Certaiyne Reesons" to 1600. The account in *PN* (1598–1600) of Drake's capture of the *Saõ Phelipe* in "Voyage of Sir Francis Drake to Cadiz, 1587." On Hakluyt and the East India Company, see also Mancall, *Hakluyt's Promise*, 237–43.

manuscript record.[121] The narrative in *PN* (1598–1600), "The voyage of Sir Francis Drake to Cadiz ... 1587," appears to be based on a version of two brief letters, one by Thomas Fenner, captain of the *Dreadnought*, on 27 April, and the other by Drake himself, on 21 May; versions of both appeared in a pamphlet by Henry Haslop, *Newes Out of the Coast of Spaine* (London, 1587), and a version of Fenner's dispatch is transcribed in a miscellany on naval matters that belonged to John Dee, now in the British Library.[122] Perhaps more interesting in the present context, Hakluyt's text merges signed letters by two of the principal captains into a continuous narrative apparently written by one anonymous narrator; additional material before and after the two letters is not present in either of the other versions. Here is a case of participant narratives that lost their attribution when they entered *Principal Navigations*.

The introductory material to Haslop's pamphlet presents the two letters at its core *as* letters, if surrounded by several internal and implied layers of mediation: he has employed "such coppies as I have compassed ... conferd with divers that were eye witnesses." This allusion to "copies" makes the relationship of his source text to the original somewhat uncertain; he notes that Drake's "letters [were] at large" and "the coppies are common." (The title of the narrative claims it to be "written by *a* Gentleman of [Drake's] companie to one of his freends." But attribution, at least, is unambiguous: Haslop added Fenner's signature ("Your loving Cossin Thomas Fenner") to

---

121 Some of that record was generated by Drake's efforts to execute or court-martial his second-in-command, William Borough, efforts that Borough compared to the famous execution of Thomas Doughty, Drake's second-in-command during the circumnavigation of 1577 to 1580, in the Straits of Magellan. Borough survived to contest Drake's version of events, in proceedings that involved many of the expedition's other captains as witnesses. That complex episode will not concern us here beyond noting its presence (and its absence from the print record). Selections from the manuscript record are printed in Hopper, "Sir Francis Drake's Memorable Service, 1587"; Corbett, *Papers Relating to the Navy*. Doughty's execution is discussed in chapter 10.

122 BL Harleian MS 167, f. 104. Provenance is noted in the BL catalogue. The pages of Harleian 167 containing the dispatch, along with Drake's letter, are transcribed by Corbett in *Papers Relating to the Navy*, 111–16. According to Corbett, the first few lines of the Harleian document are illegible, but the text appears to be of a letter or dispatch that begins with the fleet's entrance into Cádiz harbour on 19 April (Corbett, ibid., 113n1). In a letter to Francis Walsingham on 17 May, Fenner referred to "my last letters of the accidents at Cadiz," presumably letters sent with Robert Crosse on 27 April; those had not been located by Corbett. The dispatch appears on the verso of another letter from Drake about the Cádiz victory, this one to John Foxe; on this letter, see chapter 10. Fenner's dispatch is cited in Stow, *Annales*, 1242.

the first section of the narrative; following the conclusion of Fenner's letter, a header introduces a second "Letter dated May 21," addressed to Master W. and signed "Your loving frend F. Drake." Both letters are written in the first-person plural.[123]

Hakluyt's text retains none of these markers of authorship. The text begins with a paragraph outlining the queen's formation of the fleet, listing the chief captains under Drake, and noting "certaine tall ships of London" as attached to the ships and pinnaces of her navy.[124] The substance of Fenner's letter follows, with largely only verbal differences from Haslop. The narrative in PN (1598–1600) reworks the first sentence of Haslop's Drake letter, putting it in the third person to give the appearance of continuous narration by someone other than Drake himself:

Haslop: you shal understand that since the departure of Captaine Crosse, we haue continued about Cape Saker.
PN: our Generall dispatched Captaine Crosse to England with his letters … After whose departure wee shaped our course toward Cape Sacre.[125]

While Haslop's version of Drake's brief letter concludes with the Marquis de Santa Cruz's refusal to engage him at Cascais, Hakluyt's text continues, shifting the "we" of Drake's and Fenner's letters to a third-person narrative in which Drake, "our General," "shaped his course" to the Azores, where "he took" a Portuguese carrack. "The whole company" then resolved to return home "to the great admiration of the whole kingdome." The final paragraph of Hakluyt's version echoes "The Taking of the *Madre de Dios*" in assessing the "extraordinary effects" of taking the *Saõ Phelipe.* "Caracks were no such bugs but they might be taken," and moreover they carried a rich trade from the East Indies of which the English nation was thus made aware.[126] That direct reference *to* the taking of the *Madre de Deus* dates the final stage of the text's reworking to 1592 at the earliest, five years after the original letters.

---

123 Haslop, *Newes out of the Coast of Spaine*, sig. A2v, A4r, A3r, A4r, B1r–B2v.
124 "Voyage of Sir Francis Drake to Cadiz, 1587," 2(ii): 121. According to Corbett, these were again Levant Company ships, whose admiral the *Merchant Royal* was commanded by Robert Flicke (Corbett, *Papers Relating to the Navy*, xviii).
125 Haslop, *Newes out of the Coast of Spaine*, sig. B1v; "Voyage of Sir Francis Drake to Cadiz, 1587," 2(ii): 122.
126 "Voyage of Sir Francis Drake to Cadiz, 1587," 2(ii): 123.

At least three hands contributed to what appears to the reader to be a single authored text, one in which we can trace only vestiges (in the shift of pronouns) of its multiply-authored origins. That unnamed author of the composite obscures the names of actual participant authors already disseminated in print. At least in this case, Hakluyt offers something very different from what we think of as his typical practice. This document has also been misattributed in the scholarship. David and Alison Quinn follow Julian Corbett in giving Hakluyt's source as "MS, Robert Long."[127] This narrative by the otherwise unknown Robert Leng, "The true Discripcion of the last voiage of ... Sir Frauncis Drake," survives in what appears to be a dedication copy presented to Lord Grey of Wilton, whose prefatory address "To the reader" suggests that it may have been intended for publication. Even without the positive identification of the Fenner and Drake letters as sources, Leng's text differs sharply enough from Hakluyt's that it is hard to imagine making one into the other, even with the kind of radical cuts required to reduce Leng's narrative to the much smaller compass of the account printed by Hakluyt.[128] Much longer than the Drake/Fenner dispatches, Leng's narrative is also distinguished by a florid celebration of Drake as a Christian hero.

With "Voyage of Sir Francis Drake to Cadiz," Hakluyt chose or fashioned a text that obscured the identities of the "paynfull and personall travellers" who were its authors, a text whose narrative perspective was a fictional composite of several distinct sources. He was apparently less committed than we might think to printing named authors able to answer for their work, or at least inattentive to many opportunities for doing so. The contrast between Leng's manuscript and the account in PN (1598–1600) also begins to suggest that Hakluyt was also not programmatically inclined to read events in this Anglo–Spanish struggle in markedly confessional terms – or at least that he was not prone to seek out narratives that would provide this perspective. (We will return to the topic of confessional rhetoric in chapter 10.)

---

127 Quinn and Quinn, "c&s," 2: 424; Corbett, *Papers Relating to the Navy*, xxiv–xxv. The BL catalogue describes Leng's narrative (BL MS Add'l 21620) as a small, vellum-covered quarto in its original binding, with a dedication to Lord Grey of Wilton and a preface to the reader accompanying the text; it is the only content in the volume. These features suggest that the volume was a presentation copy prepared for Grey. A transcription is printed in Hopper, "Sir Francis Drake's Memorable Service, 1587."

128 Hakluyt's narrative is two pages in folio compared with eleven pages in Hopper's transcript of Leng for the Camden Society. Leng's narrative may not have been available to Hakluyt; no other copies are identified by the BL catalogue.

A final point remains on the documents, and here we return to a very different image of the collective than the selfless, merciful, and loyal "we" associated with the mariners of the sea war. In his preface, Haslop represented his intent in publishing letters from Cádiz as not only celebrating Drake's service to his country, but also preempting or displacing the many, presumably critical rumours circulating about the Cádiz expedition. These rumours he attributed to "the multitude, as a many hedded beast, rumoring they knowe not what, and murmuring they know not whereat, some forward & wishing wel, others froward & discoraging the well minded."[129] Haslop's attribution of heterogeneous narratives to a murmuring, know-nothing populace is echoed in Wingfield's attribution of critical reports on the Lisbon expedition to inexperienced soldiers who "did long to be at home, where their discourses might be wondered at"; those insubordinate discourses informed "the blind opinion of this monster, a beast of many heades."[130] For Haslop and Wingfield, it was the "multitude" of the populace, or of raw recruits, who were to blame for critical speech about episodes of the sea war – who were, in effect, the fragmenters of the national community. Yet the manuscript record says something different (about the capture of the *Madre de Deus*, the 1587 and 1596 expeditions to Cádiz, the raid on Lisbon in 1588, or the 1591 cruise to the Azores): namely, that a good proportion of such critical speech came from knowledgeable, high-ranking officers (or sometimes, in fact, from Elizabeth's government). Then as now, the project of articulating collective actions and identities manifested a panoply of differing interests and narratives. The sea battles that contributed such memorable stories and images of unity and victory also generated a polyvocal record and a domestic struggle over what had happened and who, among the victors, really won.

These dissensions are not prominent in Hakluyt's representation of materials, although traces (as we have seen) can be discerned or suspected both in the details of a few narratives written for private audiences, and the general problems of connecting texts to authors who actually participated in a voyage. Nonetheless, with the exception of Marbecke's narrative of the voyage to Cádiz in 1596, Hakluyt does not appear to have treated them with a heavy editorial hand, neither adding features to texts that lacked them or smoothing out troublesome details. There is no evidence that the rhetorical commonalities of these belligerent materials were produced or even monitored by Hakluyt, while they lack the prominent emphasis and celebration accorded to the

---

129 Haslop, *Newes out of the Coast of Spaine*, sig. A2v.
130 Wingfield, "Voyage to Spaine and Portugale, 1589," 2(ii): 137, 154.

Armada and Cádiz narratives in the paratext of volume 1. (Indeed, Hakluyt might have viewed the draw on English shipping and personnel that attended the broader sea war as inimical to his interests in colonization and the exploration of new routes for trade.)[131] Much remains to be explained: how the common rhetoric came into being, and how and why these materials came into the compilation. What we can say is that this group of narratives is not at all straightforward in the ways that the imprimatur of Hakluyt might encourage us to think they are: they may be among the least straightforward documents in the compilation.

---

131 Anthony Payne, personal communication.

PART THREE

Americas and the Pacific

THE

THIRD AND LAST VOLVME OF THE VOYAGES, NAVIGATIONS, TRAFfiques, and Difcoueries of the *English Nation*, and in
some few places, where they haue not been, of ſtrangers, performed within and before the time of theſe hundred yeeres, to all parts of the *Newfound* world of *America*, or the *Weſt Indies*, from 73. degrees of Northerly to 57. of Southerly latitude:

As namely to *Engronland*, *Meta Incognita*, *Eſtotiland*, *Tierra de Labrador*, *Newfoundland*, vp *The grand bay*, the gulfe of *S. Laurence*, and the Riuer of *Canada* to *Hochelaga* and *Saguenay*, along the coaſt of *Arambec*, to the ſhores and maines of *Virginia* and *Florida*, and on the Weſt or backſide of them both, to the rich and pleaſant countries of *Nueua Biſcaya*, *Cibola*, *Tiguex*, *Cicuic*, *Quiuira*, to the 15. prouinces of the kingdome of *New Mexico*, to the bottome of the gulfe of *California*, and vp the Riuer of *Buena Guia*:

And likewiſe to all the yles both ſmall and great lying before the cape of *Florida*, *The bay of Mexico*, and *Tierra firma*, to the coaſts and Inlands of *Newe Spaine*, *Tierra firma*, and *Guiana*, vp the mighty Riuers of *Orenoque*, *Doſſekebe*, and *Maranon*, to euery part of the coaſt of *Braſil*, to the Riuer of *Plate*, through the Streights of *Magellan* forward and backward, and to the South of the ſaid Streights as farre as 57. degrees:

And from thence on the backſide of *America*, along the coaſtes, harbours, and capes of *Chili*, *Peru*, *Nicaragua*, *Nueua Eſpanna*, *Nueua Galicia*, *Culiacan*, *California*, *Noua Albion*, and more Northerly as farre as 43. degrees:

Together with the two renowmed, and proſperous voyages of Sir *Francis Drake* and M. *Thomas Candiſh* round about the circumference of the whole earth, and diuers other voyages intended and ſet forth for that courſe.

Collected by RICHARD HAKLVYT *Preacher, and ſometimes*
ſtudent of Chriſt-Church in Oxford.

¶ Imprinted at London by *George Biſhop*, *Ralfe Newberie*, and ROBERT BARKER.
ANNO DOM. 1600.

8

The Relations of Strangers: Covering the Americas

Of this *New world* and every speciall part thereof in this my third volume I have brought to light the best & most perfect relations of such as were chiefe actours in the particular discoveries and serches of the same, giving unto every man his right, and leaving every one to mainteine his owne credit. The order observed in this work is farre more exact, then heretofore I could attaine unto: for whereas in my two former volumes I was enforced for lacke of sufficient store, in divers places to use the methode of time only ... being now more plentifully furnished with matter, I always followed the double order of time and place ... I begin at the extreme Northerne limit, and put downe successi vely in one ranke or *classis*, according to the order aforesaide, all such voyages as have bene made to the said part ... Which methode I observe from the highest North to the lowest South.

Hakluyt, "Epistle Dedicatorie" (1600), sig. A2v

HAKLUYT'S DEDICATION TO VOLUME 3 rejoices that the amplitude of his materials on the Americas has allowed for what he views as an optimally clear mode of organization: this volume will exhibit a "farre more exact" distribution of materials into regional categories – fourteen in all – rather than employing the purely chronological organization forced on him in volumes 1 and 2 by the relatively scantier number of sources available. This wealth of materials, he continues, will allow him at times to provide multiple narratives on places or actions of particular interest. Yet the copious supply of materials on the Americas comes with a kind of asterisk: "[a]lbeit my worke do carry the title of *The English voyages*, as well in regard that the greatest part are theirs, and that my travaile was chiefly undertaken for preservation of their memorable actions, yet where our owne mens experience is defective, there I have bene careful to supply the same with the best and chiefest relations of strangers."[1]

---

1 Hakluyt, "Epistle Dedicatorie (1600)," sig. A2v.

While earlier volumes included impressive quantities of materials both in and translated from Latin, Hakluyt's third volume is distinguished by his reliance on sources from other European vernaculars, predominantly Spanish, French, and Italian.

Hakluyt's significant use and publication of materials by foreign authors, about foreign voyages, and in foreign languages has begun to be appreciated in the scholarship, as a counterpoint to his titular celebration of English voyages and travels.[2] (It is nonetheless still sometimes asserted that Hakluyt published *only* English voyages.) William Sherman notes that Hakluyt's career "began and ended with translations of foreign works," and Margaret Small comments that the second edition of Hakluyt's compilation included "many more foreign documents," overall, than the first edition of 1589.[3] Joan-Pau Rubiés has characterized Hakluyt's practice as (on the one hand) compiling accounts of English travel in his two large edited collections, while also publishing "a series of editions and translations of key texts" concerning the activities of other nations. Editions of Peter Martyr, Jacques Cartier, Duarte de Sande, Leo Africanus, and others, translated, funded, or set in motion by Hakluyt, appeared independently in a steady flow from 1580 onwards.[4] Yet – Rubiés continues – despite the "patriotic focus of *The Principal Navigations*," expressed in Hakluyt's clearly stated intention to publish and celebrate the activities of his countrymen, in the two collections the editor also "occasionally broke his own rules – that is, the separation of national and foreign narratives – in order to accommodate a number of particularly interesting texts within the collection, exploiting the best opportunity he saw to publicize them." The *English* focus of Hakluyt's documentation thus "coexisted in some tension with the practical needs of a wider proto-colonial project" for which a broader

---

2 The non-English sources of PN (1598–1600) are fully detailed in the *Hakluyt Handbook*; in addition to David and Alison Quinn's comprehensive "Contents and Sources," translated materials are given attention both in F.M. Rogers's chapter, "Hakluyt as Translator," and in the regionally focused essays in part 2, "Hakluyt's Use of the Materials Available to Him."

3 Sherman, "Bringing the World to England," 200; Small, "World Seen through Another's Eyes," 53. After the publication of PN (1598–1600), Hakluyt translated *Dialogues in the English and Malaiane languages* (London, 1614), from the Latin translation by Gothard Arthus of a Dutch original by Frederick de Houtman. Although the translation is attributed to Augustine Spalding, the minutes of the East India Company make evident that Spalding revised a translation previously done by Hakluyt (Payne, *Guide*, 112–13).

4 For a complete list of translations with Hakluyt's involvement, see Payne, *Guide*.

scope of information was useful and necessary.[5] As Rubiés suggests, the presence of foreign sources in *PN* (1598–1600) is more than merely exceptional. Indeed, we might say not so much that Hakluyt broke his own rules, but that his editorial rules were more nuanced than a simple distinction between English and foreign sources, reflecting a variety of imperatives that were sometimes in tension with each other.

Following the lead of Hakluyt's dedication, this chapter will explore his use of European vernacular sources in finer-grained detail, as a distinctive feature of the volume on the Americas. Earlier volumes, to be sure, were far from English-only, as we have noted in earlier chapters. Volume 1's translated materials come almost entirely from Latin, even in the case of contemporary authors (including Gerhard Mercator, Sebastian Münster, Sigismund Herberstein, Emanuel van Meteren, and Arngrímur Jónsson). Among a small number of vernacular sources in volume 2 are the narratives of Nestore Martinengo, the anonymous French writer translated by Thomas Docwra and Cesare Federici, as well as excerpts from the English edition of Jan Huygen van Linschoten, in whose translation and publication Hakluyt had a hand. Yet in volume 3, as Hakluyt turned his attention westwards towards parts of the world where English presence and knowledge were both still quite thin, the presence of vernacular works in translation grew to a flood, alongside accounts of English discoveries, colonial projects, attempts at circumnavigation, privateering, and raids. The last two forms of maritime encounter have provided a figurative language to describe the enterprise of textual translation. Barbara Fuchs suggests that piracy and privateering became a privileged metaphor for Elizabethan translation from Spanish in particular, whether of pragmatic military and geographic information or of purely literary texts: "During the Elizabethan era, translators from the Spanish turned repeatedly to an aggressive metaphorics that equates *imitatio*, or translation, with forcible taking."[6] Hakluyt himself made prominent use of this metaphorics, as we will see. Yet while the ideas of raiding and piracy may reflect some of the editor's imagined relations to Spanish sources, and indeed at times the actual provenance of these sources, this paradigm fails to characterize the much broader range of vernacular sources that Hakluyt included, or his relations to those sources.

    5 Rubiés, "Rise of an Early Modern Genre," 32.
    6 Fuchs, "Golden Ages and Golden Hinds," 324. On F.O. Mathiessen's use of such language to describe Elizabethan translations, see Sherman, "Bringing the World to England," 199.

This chapter will provide some indications both of the kinds of materials Hakluyt used, and the range of ways in which he negotiated their presence in the text and the facts that they recorded. Translation from the works, and languages, of Hakluyt's contemporaries always involved some kind of politics, and these politics differed from language to language; this survey of vernacular materials in volume 3 will accordingly be organized by language, grouping together languages whose situations were roughly comparable. The first part of the chapter will consider Hakluyt's use of original sources in Spanish and Portuguese; the second, sources in French and Italian. The final section of the chapter considers translations *out* of English and the relationships with scholars in the Low Countries that accompanied or were enabled by them. In particular, Hakluyt's involvement with Theodor de Bry's famous edition of Thomas Harriot's *Briefe and True Report of the New Found Land of Virginia* (Frankfurt, 1590) serves as a case study that locates the editor and his project of national celebration within a network of *trans*national correspondence and collaboration.

STOLEN SECRETS:
THE CASE OF SPANISH SOURCES

I have used the uttermost of my best endevour, to get, and having gotten,
to translate out of Spanish, and here in this present volume to publish such secrets of theirs, as may any way availe us or annoy them, if they drive and urge us by their sullen insolencies, to continue our courses of hostilitie against them.

Hakluyt, "Epistle Dedicatorie" (1600), sig. A2v

"Defects" in the English record led Hakluyt to introduce foreign sources for several regions of North America: present-day Eastern Canada and Florida, the central interior of North America ("Cibola ... and Quivira"), the Pacific coast of the Americas, and the American Southwest ("the backside of Florida and Virginia"), including particularly New Mexico. For all these regions, the editor either translated sources or reprinted translations already in print (as Rubiés indicates, several had been published either by Hakluyt himself or with his acknowledged encouragement).[7] Hakluyt's materials on the West

---

[7] Materials on the travels of Coronado, Fray Marcos de Niza, and Francisco de Ulloa were drawn from Ramusio. Hakluyt himself translated and published the travels of Fray Agustin Ruis and Antonio de Espejo, extracted from González de Mendoza, *Historia del gran Reyno dela China*. French materials are discussed in the next part of the chapter.

Indies and the Pacific received a different framing, however. The details he was able to gather on the rivers, ports, towns, cities, and provinces of the Spanish West Indies are characterized as resulting from successful acts of aggression ("by taking of their ships, and sacking of their townes and cities"), and their publication constituted another such act in a continuous programme that stretched from the harbours of Cartagena and Nombre de Dios to the London print shop. The epistle tells us something concretely about how Hakluyt wanted readers to understand his choice of Spanish sources as well as his own actions in printing them. Rather than conceding Spanish success in the exploration and colonization of the Americas, Hakluyt wished his publication of Spanish materials to be read as contesting their rights.

Some number of the items Hakluyt printed did, indeed, have a provenance linked to maritime war and privateering.[8] The most prominent such item, included in volume 2 as an account of East Asia, was Duarte de Sande's *De missione legatorum Iaponensium ad romanam curiam, rebusq[ue]* (Macau, 1590), which Nandini Das describes in her examination of how knowledge of Japan circulated in England before 1612 as principally "a series of humanist dialogues offering an account of the Tenshō embassy [to Rome in 1585]."[9] Sande's book was among the spoils taken from the captured *Madre de Deus* in 1592, by which "the secret trades and Indian riches, which hitherto lay strangely hidden, and cunningly concealed from us" by Spain were "manifestly discovered." As we have seen, the carrack was taken only after a fight so violent that "no man could almost step but upon a dead carcass or a bloody floor," and the cargo thus bloodily fought for was extraordinary.[10] Within the envelope of the carrack, Sande's treatise was "enclosed in a case of sweet Cedar wood, and lapped up almost an hundredfold in fine calicut-cloth, as though it had been some incomparable jewel."[11] Hakluyt here describes the book as a rich material object, whose structure communicated both its value and the will to secrecy surrounding it. Once it reached his hands, this precious object could become a text again, and circulate as information.

---

8 Paul Hammer notes that books were "a popular form of plunder" on raids into Spanish territory, and provides a list of some surviving volumes (Hammer, "Myth-Making," 637n92).
9 Das, "Encounter as Process," 1361.
10 "Taking of the Madre de Dios," 197, 198.
11 Hakluyt, "Epistle Dedicatorie (1599)," 2(i): sig. *4r. The text appears in volume 2(ii) as de Sande, "Description of the Kingdome of China."

Hakluyt was telling a story about his own publication as continuous with the work's original, violent seizure, but also one about a contrast between two information cultures. In a dedication to Walter Ralegh that prefaced his edition of René de Laudonnière's *L'histoire notable de la Floride* (Paris, 1586) before appearing in PN (1598–1600), he described that text as having been "conceled many yeeres" (presumably by its owner, the cosmographer André Thevet).[12] In the dedication to volume 2 of *Principal Navigations*, he referred again to this earlier publication, noting that he had had the voyages printed "at mine own charges ... Which by the malice of some too much affectioned to the Spanish faction, had been above twenty years suppressed."[13] The same vocabulary of revealing what had been concealed appeared in Hakluyt's editions and translations of the 1580s, in part aimed at promoting Ralegh's colonial projects.[14] In the dedication to his 1587 edition of Martyr's *De orbe novo*, he urged Ralegh to "reveal to us the courts of China and the unknown straits which still lie hid: throw back the portals which have been closed since the world's beginning at the dawn of time."[15] This representation of voyages

12 PN 3: 301. Hakluyt's collaborator on the prior French edition, Martin Basanier, wrote even more pointedly that "This history, being nonetheless [i.e., despite its value], suppressed and obscured for the period of twenty years or thereabout, I – aided by the diligence of Hakluyt – brought it out as if from a tomb, where it had so long lain useless, to put it where (it seemed to me by my frequent reading of it) the thing demanded)" (my translation). ([C]ette histoire ... estant neantmoins supprimee & esteinte ia par l'espace de vingt ans ou environ, ie l'ay tiree avec la diligence de Monsieur Hakluit ... comme du tombeau, où elle avoit ia si long temps inutile reposé, pour la mettre où il m'a semblé par la frequente lecture d'icelle qu'elle se demandoit; Taylor, OW, 2: 351–2.) Hakluyt and Basanier's unauthorized publication of a manuscript lent them by André Thevet is discussed by Frank Lestringant, *Le Huguenot et le sauvage*, 250–77.

13 Hakluyt, "Epistle Dedicatorie (1599)," sig. *3r.

14 Three works were dedicated to Ralegh by Hakluyt and his associates during the years Ralegh was actively supporting a colony in present-day North Carolina: *L'histoire notable de la Floride* (Paris, 1586); *De orbe novo Petri Martyris Angleri* (Paris, 1587); *A Notable Historie containing Foure Voyages [...] unto Florida* (London, 1587). In a letter to Ralegh dated 30 December 1586, Hakluyt made reference to pertinent information in a fourth publication that appeared without a dedication, *El viaje de hizo Antonio de Espejo* (Paris, 1586); a rare surviving copy of *El viaje* (BL C.32.a.32) was given to John Dee by Thomas Harriot, the mathematician and Roanoke colonist employed as an advisor by Ralegh (I am grateful to Anthony Payne for this detail). A transcript of the letter appears in Taylor, OW, 2: 353–6.

15 *De orbe novo* (Paris, 1587); translated in Taylor, OW, 2: 367 (original: Sinarum littora adhuc tibilatentia & freta recondita nobis aperito; portas ab orbis initio praescriptione temporum obseratas tuis reserato).

and their publication as discovery or revelation echoed John Foxe's claims about the revelatory nature of printing itself, and its role in a specifically anti-Catholic agenda. By printing, Foxe wrote, "tongues are knowne, knowledge groweth, judgement increaseth, books are dispersed, the Scripture is seene, the Doctours be read stories be opened, times compared, truth decerned, falshod detected, and with finger poynted, and all (as I sayd) thorough the benefite of printing. Wherfore I suppose that eyther the pope must abolish printing, or he must seek a new world to raygne over: for els, as this world standeth, printing doubtles will abolish hym."[16] Both Hakluyt's explicit statements and their implications echo Foxe's polemical framing.

So far, this evidence does not suggest that Hakluyt's work with non-English materials within, or beyond *Principal Navigations* poses any real challenge to a view of the work as a fundamentally nationalist, decidedly Anglo-Protestant project, within which the presence of work in translation enacts a successful appropriation of its content – a *translatio imperii*, as Eric Cheyfitz has suggested.[17] Yet I believe there is more to learn. Fuchs has argued that the master-metaphor of piracy in Elizabethan literary translation, drawn from the archive of actual piracy and privateering that Hakluyt did so much to preserve, served as an apologetic cover for a richer and more varied dialogue between English and Spanish traditions in particular.[18] In Hakluyt's work itself, just as piracy and privateering represent only part of the activities documented, the sources and kinds of his translated sources varied quite widely even in the case of Spanish and Portuguese materials. In the case of the French and Italian materials that are also generously represented in the compilation, the model of piracy is almost entirely inapplicable. (Indeed, the boundaries between "Spanish," "French," and "Italian" sources were not always firm; a number of Hakluyt's more substantive Spanish and French relations were drawn from Giovanni Battista Ramusio's widely disseminated print compilation, *Navigationi et viaggi* [Venice, 1550–59], and translated by Hakluyt from Ramusio's Italian.)

Hakluyt's narrative about his own practices of information management – that is, the narrative of secrets triumphantly seized and freely disseminated – equally captures only partially the range and variety of these practices.

---

16 Foxe, *Actes and Monuments* (1583), 1: 707.

17 Both Hakluyt's PD, and the materials on Ralegh's Roanoke colony by Thomas Harriot that appeared in PN (1598–1600) and in de Bry's 1590 edition, are discussed at various points in Cheyfitz's stimulating study of translation as practice and metaphor, *Poetics of Imperialism*.

18 Fuchs, *Poetics of Piracy*, 7–8.

Hakluyt's appointment as secretary and chaplain to the English ambassador to France in the mid-1580s offered opportunities for collecting information, but also managing its dissemination. His letters indicate that he was attentive to the desirability of metering information already in circulation about the voyages of Francis Drake, and, as Peter Mancall puts it, "worked the rumor mill."[19] More broadly, Samuel Purchas's notes of materials he had received from Hakluyt give some indication of how much Hakluyt *did not* publish, and we have other indications of his strategic reticences on sensitive subjects – like the selective presentation of information on trade in the Levant, as we saw in chapter 5.[20] The modes of secrecy to which his publishing projects responded were also more diverse than the deliberate suppressions instanced by the Sande volume, or Thevet's unpublished materials on the French colony in Florida. Foreign materials could be freely available in print, yet obscure to readers who lacked the languages to read them. Inattention could leave even domestic sources in obscurity unless actively recovered and circulated by scholars. Hakluyt's well-known articulation of his own "travail" in collecting materials makes this point in the dedication to volume 1: "I ... have brought to light many very rare and worthy monuments, which long have lien miserably scattered in mustie corners, & retchlesly hidden in mistie darkness, and were very like for the greatest part to have bene buried in perpetuall oblivion. The first volume of this work I have thus for the present brought to light."[21] This characterization of materials "hidden in mistie darknes" echoed the antiquary John Leland, a generation earlier. Leland wrote that the acts of Edward VI's forebears were "hitherso sore obscurid booth for lak of enprinting of *such workes as lay secretely yn corners*, and also bycause men of eloquence had not enterprisid to set them forthe yn a florisching style, yn sum tymes

---

19 On Drake, see Hakluyt's letter to Walsingham, 7 April 1585; in an earlier essay, I look more closely at Hakluyt's role in the embassy, and Mancall's biography provides an invaluable synthesis of outside events with Hakluyt's movements and writing (Taylor, *ow*, 1: 345; Fuller, "Richard Hakluyt's Foreign Relations," 45–50; Mancall, *Hakluyt's Promise*, 161–83). Mitchell Leimon and Geoffrey Parker have argued that Hakluyt's employer, Edward Stafford, was a double agent, an indication of the complications of this moment ("Treason and Plot in Elizabethan Diplomacy").

20 Samuel Purchas's notation of materials acquired from Hakluyt informs on materials in the editor's papers that did not appear in *PN* (1598–1600) (see the discussion and useful list in Steele, "From Hakluyt to Purchas"). Sources derived from Hakluyt's personal collection are also identified as such in Parker, "Contents and Sources of 'Pilgrimes.'" On unpublished Portuguese materials in Hakluyt's hands, see Strachan, "India."

21 Hakluyt, "Epistle Dedicatorie (1598)," 1: *2r.

pasted not communely usid in England" (emphasis mine).[22] These passages focus on the inaction of English writers, not the wilful, secret accumulation of the Vatican or the Spanish state, as the chief obstacle to a free circulation of knowledge in which "stories be opened." While the rhetoric of triumphant appropriation that hovers around Hakluyt's translations has rightly attracted the attention of scholars, its claims should be calibrated carefully against the actual contents of his volumes as well as against the evidence of his career.

Such caveats being registered, however, some of Hakluyt's Spanish sources *were* indeed, in some literal sense, "stolen secrets." A survey of Spanish materials in PN (1598–1600), as listed and identified by David and Alison Quinn, finds a number of documents that match this description (see appendix 6). Broadly speaking, these fall into three categories: eight items of depositions and testimony by Spanish and Portuguese captives, thirteen intercepted letters and reports, and seven rutters. Even given some amplification due to Hakluyt's habit of extracting parts of a single text as discretely titled items, these "Spanish secrets," whether taken from captives, taken with ships, or seized on land, make up a substantial group within the larger group of Spanish sources in volume 3. (A number of these sources came from captives taken by Drake, and several others narrated or responded to Drake's activities; I'll revisit some of these in chapter 10.) The closing pages of volume 3 are devoted to a "captive source": these materials on orders given to ships sailing to the West Indies by the Casa de la Contratación, and the examination administered to masters and pilots sailing to the West Indies, were the work of Pedro Diaz, captured by Richard Grenville in 1585. Captured documents and captive testimonies are not the only sources or kinds of sources from the Spanish-speaking world that appeared in the volume, however. A number of important *printed* works transmitting Spanish experience of the Americas were known to Hakluyt, and used to some extent in his work.

Hakluyt drew some of these materials from other compendia, and thus at a double linguistic remove. Sources on the travels of Fray Marcos de Niza, Francisco Vásques de Coronado, Hernando de Alarcón, Francisco de Ulloa, and Francisco Galí, as well as excerpts from Gonzálo Fernández de Oviedo's *Historia general y natural de las Indias*, came to Hakluyt through the works of Ramusio and Linschoten. A few works by Spanish and Portuguese authors, or written for and about Spanish interests, had been (or would be) edited and published by Hakluyt himself, in the original or in translation: *El viaje que hizo*

---

22 Leland, *Laboryouse journey [and] serche of Johan Leylande, for Englandes antiquitees* (1546), cited in Flower, "Laurence Nowell," 48.

Antonio de Espeio (Paris, 1586), the *De orbe novo* of Pietro Martire d'Anghiera (Alcalá, 1530; Paris, 1587), and Antonio de Galvão's *Tradado ... dos diversos & desuayrados caminhos* (Lisbon, 1563; trans. London, 1601). All three were used in PN (1598–1600), although only Antonio de Espejo's account of New Mexico, itself extracted from Juan González de Mendoza's *Historia ... de la China* (Madrid, 1586), appeared at length.[23] The Paris editions of *De orbe novo* and *El viaje* were both part of Hakluyt's efforts to publicize and support Ralegh's colonial projects in "Virginia," subsequent to his grant of letters patent for North America in 1584; as Kenneth Andrews points out, the editor laid claim to "extreeme travaile in the histories of the Spanyards."[24] Hakluyt also drew on his own translation of relevant materials from José de Acosta's *Historia natural y moral de las Indias* (Seville, 1590) to provide counsel to Robert Cecil regarding Ralegh's voyages to Guiana; an excerpt from the Guiana material is printed in the compilation.[25]

Some important Spanish sources were represented in PN (1598–1600) by brief excerpts from existing English translations: Francisco López de Gómara's *Las historia de las Indias y conquista de Mexico* (1552), translated by T. Nicholls as *The pleasant historie of the conquest of the Weast India* (London, 1596), and Martin Fernández de Enciso's *Suma de geographia* (1519), translated by J. Frampton as *Briefe description ... of the Weast India* (London, 1578). (A notable absence from these translated sources was the *Brevíssima relación* [1552] of Bartolomé de las Casas, which had appeared in English as *The Spanish Colonie* [London, 1583].)[26] The last two translations themselves could be understood

---

23 A French translation of Espejo by Hakluyt's collaborator Martin Basanier appeared as *Histoire des terres nouvellement descouvertes* (Paris, 1587). Robert Parke's translation of the larger work by Mendoza, *Historie of the Great and Mightie Kingdome of China* (London, 1588), acknowledges Hakluyt's "request and encouragement" (Payne, *Guide*).

24 Hakluyt, "Preface to the Reader (1589)," sig. *3v (cited in Andrews, "Latin America," 1: 235). On the motives for these publications, see Hakluyt's dedications to Ralegh in Taylor, *ow*. See also the essays in *Hakluyt Handbook*, vol. 1, by Andrews, Quinn, and Wallis.

25 Acosta, "Three Testimonies of Josepho de Acosta." Hakluyt's work with Acosta appears to date to 1596, after the return of a second expedition led by Lawrence Keymis; see Lorimer, *Discoverie of Guiana* (2006), lxxxvi–lxxxvii (original is TNA, SP12/235, no. 43). As Lorimer points out, Hakluyt alludes to these consultations in the dedication to volume 2, and they are also referenced in a letter to Cecil from Thomas Harriot (Lorimer, ibid., appendix 4, no. 5).

26 The English edition relied on an earlier French translation, *Tyrannies et cruautez des Espagnols* (Antwerp, 1579). The intense interest of this text for Protestants is exemplified in a lovingly precise manuscript translation and reproduction, with images, now in the

as acts of aggression or, indeed, revenge: the translators Frampton and Nicholls were both merchants who had been imprisoned by the Inquisition and their goods confiscated, and each, after his release and return to England, began to translate Spanish works of geography for publication in English.[27] Frampton argued that his translation of Enciso "revealed secrets that the Spanish nation was loth to have known to the world"; as in the case of Sande, print publication did not guarantee the free circulation of information.[28] Overall, however, Hakluyt drew on these major print sources quite minimally and chiefly in ways that bore directly on English projects: for instance, excerpts from López de Gómara's important history served as a witness to the Cabot voyages and a source on the fauna of regions explored by Coronado.[29] Overall, Spanish sources that were *not* stolen, but simply acquired in the open market of print, have a minimal footprint in Hakluyt's compilation. Considering PN (1598–1600) in relation to the larger universe of available print materials makes evident that the editor had little interest in disseminating information on Mexico, the Caribbean, or South America except as observed (or intercepted) by English merchants or mariners; examples of these observations would include the accounts of New Spain that Robert Tomson, John Chilton, Roger Bodenham, and Henry Hawks accumulated in their decades of business there.[30] The voluminous literature on the history of the Spanish invasion and

William Clements Library ("Tyrannies et Cruautez des Espagnols," 1582, Manuscripts M-07); a classic study of its role in the emergence of the "Black Legend" of Spanish colonialism is Maltby, *Black Legend in England.* Hakluyt cites Las Casas in PD.

27 R.C.D. Baldwin associates both men with "a translation programme of key Spanish texts" in navigation and medicine, overseen by Walsingham; their output included English editions of works by Francisco López de Gómara and Agustin de Zarate [Nicholls], Nicholas Monardes, Pedro de Medina, Bernardino de Escalante, and Martín de Enciso [Frampton]. (Nicholl's survey of the Canaries was briefly held back from publication because it was being "used to inform English naval operations ... in support of Dom Antonio's insurrection, which lasted from 1578 into 1582"; Baldwin, "Nicholls, Thomas.") See also Beecher, "Legacy of John Frampton."

28 Frampton, *Briefe description* [...] *of the Weast India* (London, 1578), cited in Fuchs, *Poetics of Piracy*, 25. Readers may recall that a translation of Enciso's work was provided to Henry VIII in the 1540s by Roger Barlow, Thorne's collaborator; however, Barlow's translation itself remained effectively secret in the archives and was evidently unknown to Frampton and his contemporaries (Taylor, *Brief Summe*).

29 See Hakluyt, PN (1598–1600), 3: 9, 380–2.

30 Tomson, "Voyage of Robert Tomson, 1555"; Bodenham, "Voyage of M. Roger Bodenham, 1564"; Chilton, "Voyage of M. John Chilton, 1568"; Hawks, "Voyage of Henrie Hawks, 1572." Their letters are reproduced in Taylor, OW.

settlement of the Americas, the nature of American societies and peoples, and the varieties of American flora and fauna makes only fleeting appearances in the compilation.

Significant exceptions occurred for what Hakluyt evidently considered to be, actually or prospectively, *English* spheres of activity. Thus, an eclectic array of sources provided accounts of expeditions shedding light on the lands and waters north and west of Mexico, whether into the interior (Fray Marcos de Niza, Francisco Coronado, Antonio de Espejo) or along the coast (Hernan de Alarcón, Francisco de Ulloa). These materials appear in two of volume 3's regional categories: "certaine voyages made from ... New Spaine to the 15 provinces of New Mexico, and to Cibola, and Quivira," and "Certeine voyages made for the discovery of the gulfe of California, and of the sea-coast on the Northwest or backside of America." While the second category included an extract from the "Famous Voyage" account of Drake's circumnavigation, first published in PN (1589) and appearing in its entirety later in volume 3, materials in these two categories were otherwise entirely of Spanish origin, though most were translated from the Italian of Ramusio's *Navigationi et viaggi* rather than directly from Spanish originals.[31]

Among these sources, however, one merits particular attention, coming directly from its Spanish original rather than through the mediation of the Italian editor: "The voyage of Antonio de Espeio ... to ... New Mexico." In 1582, Espejo had begun an overland journey to explore territories to the north of Mexico; on his return, a narrative of the voyage appeared in the second edition of González de Mendoza's *Historia ... Del gran reyno dela China ... Con un itinerario del Nuevo Mundo* (Madrid, 1586). Hakluyt must have immediately obtained a copy of the Madrid edition (there were multiple editions of González de Mendoza's text, not all containing the Espejo narrative), and as noted earlier, published a free-standing edition of Espejo in Spanish at Paris, also in 1586. A French edition by Hakluyt's collaborator Martin Basanier appeared in the same year.[32] The map actually accompanying Hakluyt's edition of Martyr's *De orbe novo* (1587) may have originally been prepared to accompany his 1586 edition of Espejo; Anthony Payne suggests that the map was not

---

[31] The passage duplicated as "Voyage and Course Which Sir Francis Drake Held" (3: 440–2) appears again as part of "Famous Voyage," 3: 736–8.

[32] *Histoire des terres nouvellement descouvertes* (Paris, 1586). Anthony Payne graciously shared unpublished work on Hakluyt and the Espejo text; for a treatment in print, see Payne, *Richard Hakluyt*, 87–9. The various editions of Mendoza and Espejo are detailed in *European Americana*.

ready in time (we will return to this map in the following section).[33] If this conjecture is correct, it only adds to the sense of an urgency in the handling of Espejo's text that invites us to understand its significance to Hakluyt.

Ricardo Padrón notes that the narrative's account of the human geography of New Mexico "arranges the indigenous societies encountered by Espejo in ascending order of civility along a route of travel from south to north," concluding with news of a people just a little further on whose cities exceeded Madrid in size; the presence of textiles and parasols resembling those found in China suggested that the peoples of New Mexico and beyond, in the temperate middle zones of North America, could be trading with their equally civilized Chinese counterparts.[34] In the Spanish context, as Padrón indicates, the Espejo expedition comported with hopes of connecting China to a larger, transpacific Spanish Indies, and contesting Portuguese claims to a sphere of influence that extended across all of Asia.[35] In the English (and French) context, it was of interest for how it could inform on the North American interior. In 1586, Hakluyt wrote to Ralegh in Paris suggesting that "in your enterprise of Virginia, your best planting will be about the Bay of the Chesepians" (asserting with some geographical vagueness that "our Cabot and the English did first discover" the region). Espejo's narrative about New Mexico suggested to him that Virginia colonists would find "rich silver mines up in the country in the latitude of 37 ½"; the editor evidently imagined the Maritimes, the Chesapeake, and the interior Southwest as loosely contiguous.[36] More publicly, in the dedication to volume 2 Hakluyt cited Espejo on the attractions of latitudes he understood as open to English discovery and occupation: "the Spaniards themselves in their own writings printed in Madrid 1586, and within a few months afterward reprinted by me in Paris ... as also in their intercepted letters come into my hand, bearing date 1595. They

---

33 Payne, *Richard Hakluyt: A Guide to His Books*, 91. Citation to Espejo are from the translated text in PN (1598–1600); his account was also independently published in English as *New Mexico* (London, 1587), apparently using Hakluyt's Paris edition as the base text. The English edition appears unconnected to Hakluyt, however. On Mendoza's *Historia*, see Padrón, *Indies of the Setting Sun*, 183–200.

34 Espejo: "many mantles of cotton straked with blew and white, like those that are brought from China"; "certaine shadowes or canopies like unto those which are brought from China" (Padrón, *Indies of the Setting Sun*, 196, 199; Espejo, "Voyage of Antonio de Espeio," 392, 393).

35 On this larger ambition, and the conceptual imbrication of Mexico and China, see Padrón, *Indies of the Setting Sun*.

36 Taylor, *OW*, 2: 355.

acknowledge the In-land to be a better and richer country than Mexico and Nueva Spania it selfe." The text as presented in PN (1598–1600) stressed that Espejo's journey towards ever more rich and well-governed regions kept "still the same NORTHERLY course" (emphasis in original).[37] Espejo's narrative, accessed by Hakluyt through González de Mendoza's book, became meaningful in the context of a theoretical and pragmatic view that "the north" was either available or destined to become an English sphere of activity; it pointed to continental North America as encompassing temperate latitudes that would favour abundance and civility. (Hakluyt's circulation of Espejo's text in France, discussed below, would evoke yet another dimension of its meanings for early modern readers.)

For East Asia and the Pacific, Hakluyt appears to have employed two very different kinds of foreign sources to supplement those associated with the circumnavigations of Drake (1577–80) and Thomas Cavendish (1585–88): Jesuit sources on China and Japan, and Spanish sources on the Pacific. The first, enabled by Portuguese trade and settlement, provided accounts of cultures more than narratives of voyages; they allowed the English to glimpse the courts and markets that mariners from Richard Chancellor to John Davis had tried to reach through the icebound waters of the North. The second reflected Spanish efforts to reach Asia through the Pacific, through a route departing from Mexico. These were voyages of exploration across a largely unknown ocean, which bore on English speculation about the topography of the northern Americas: how far north from California did the ocean extend, and how did the coastline run? What were the routes and distances from the west coast of North America to Japan and China? All were open questions of continuing interest, even if by 1600 the tide of practice was turning toward exploitation of the known route around the southern tip of Africa and through the Indian Ocean.

Despite Anglo–Spanish hostilities in the Atlantic and Caribbean, news about Spanish expeditions in the Pacific trickled into the compilation from social contacts between Hakluyt's informants and Spanish interlocutors, as well as from textual or cartographic sources. Examples include the Pacific voyages of Bernardo de la Torre, who accompanied Ruy López de Villalobos's expedition to the Moluccas in 1542 and the voyage of Andrés de Urdaneta, who

---

37 Espejo, "Voyage of Antonio de Espeio," 3: 394. By 1600, Hakluyt had also acquired an intercepted letter to a correspondent in Seville, dated 1590, with brief mention of an expedition sent from Mexico to pacify and subject "a great City called Cibola" to the Northwest ("Letter of Bartholomew Del Cano").

discovered a return route from the Philippines to Mexico in 1565, both alluded to in Humphrey Gilbert's treatise on the Northwest Passage, both sourced in Gilbert's conversations with an unnamed Spanish nobleman. Another set of conversations, this time in Mexico between the merchant Henry Hawkes and Diego Gutiérrez, a pilot, cartographer, and former cosmographer to Charles V, yielded news of Álvaro de Mendaña's discovery of the Solomon Islands in 1568 and some details on the Philippines. Embedded in English-authored texts, these conversations transferred Spanish information amicably across borders and languages.[38]

Purchas acquired from Hakluyt a manuscript account in Latin of Miguel López de Legazpi's voyage to the Philippines and establishment of a Spanish colony there. As Padrón notes, Legazpi's own narrative of the voyage remained unpublished, and indeed there was a general dearth of publication on the Philippines in Spain and Spanish America "until the early years of the seventeenth century, and these would not circulate widely."[39] Hakluyt's retention of such a document raises questions: surely publishing Legazpi's narrative would have been precisely the kind of triumph over Spanish secrecy that the editor heralded in his introduction. Absent more precise knowledge of *when* Hakluyt acquired the document, however – we know of his ownership only from a note by Purchas – arguments about its absence from PN (1598–1600) would be speculative.[40] Without ports on the Pacific coast of the Americas, and without access to the Pacific except by the very long route through the Straits of Magellan, England may simply have lacked the capacity to profit from these Pacific discoveries, as Spain's settlements in Mexico and Panama enabled it to do. Indeed, it was only after the capture in 1680 of a Spanish rutter that would become the Hack Atlas, that English predation on Spanish ships and settlement in the Pacific would become a serious and persistent threat.[41]

---

38 Wallis, "Pacific," 1: 224–5; Gilbert, "Discourse," 3: 15, 19–20; Hawks, "Voyage of Henrie Hawks, 1572," 3: 467–8. Gilbert believed he had heard that Urdaneta discovered the Northwest Passage, however, rather than how to navigate from the Philippines to Mexico.

39 Padrón ascribes this relative silence to Philip II's "tight control" of information relating to his overseas empire, and to the nature of these particular discoveries, more significant for enabling a lucrative trans-Pacific trade than for yielding rich resources or subject populations (*Indies of the Setting Sun*, 140).

40 Parker, "Contents and Sources of 'Pilgrimes,'" 2: 426–7.

41 Fabio López-Lázaro provides a fascinating perspective on the entry into the Pacific of William Dampier and other English pirates in his introduction to *Misfortunes of Alonso Ramírez*. I'm grateful to Joaquin Terrones for inviting me to become acquainted

Hakluyt did print another Spanish account of a voyage from Acapulco, to the Phillipines, onward to Macao, then Japan, and then back to Mexico. More a rutter than a narrative, Francisco Galí's account of a voyage in 1582 to 1584 was rich in useful and practical information, providing bearings, soundings, latitudes, landmarks, and distances for the route sailed; Hakluyt's headnote also calls attention to Galí's observations of evidence for a northern passage, as well as on the distance from North America to Japan, greater than the estimates provided in other texts. A note appended to the text comments that it was faithfully translated from the authoritative Spanish original into Dutch; originally addressed to the viceroy of the East Indies, it found its way into *PN* (1598–1600) through the *Itinerario* (Amsterdam, 1596) of Jan Huyghen van Linschoten, who had served as clerk to the bishop of Portuguese Goa. Soon after the work's publication in Dutch, Hakluyt had a copy of *Itinerario* in hand and urged it on an English translator; an English edition appeared shortly thereafter as *Discours of voyages unto ye Easte & West Indies* (London, 1598), but the text differs from that printed in *PN* (1598–1600), suggesting an independent translation into English of a text already "truely translated out of *Spanish* into lowe *Dutch verbatim* out of the Originall copie."[42] Multiply mediated as it was, and acquired through non-belligerent means, Linschoten's book and the sailing directions it provided would nonetheless devastate Portugal's control of trade with the East Indies. Cornelis de Houtman used them to sail to the East Indies in 1595 to 1597; Davis would sail with Houtman as pilot on a second voyage in 1598 to 1600, apparently at the behest of Essex, and immediately put his experience to use as pilot major for the first English trading voyage to the East Indies under James Lancaster in 1601.[43]

Other materials on East Asia were derived (immediately or otherwise) from Portuguese sources, or Jesuit sources reporting from Portuguese outposts. Textual and maritime relations between England and Portugal were distinct from those obtaining with Spain, even though, after 1580, Portugal was under the Spanish crown, and although Portuguese monarchs had staunchly resisted English intrusions into African markets. Dom António's rival claims to the

---

with Alonso Ramírez and the critical debates over his narrative, and to Bertie Mandelblatt of the John Carter Brown Library for a timely conversation about the Hack Atlas in March 2020.

42 Galí, "Voyage of Francis Gualle," 3: 447. On Hakluyt and the English publication of *Itinerario*, see Payne, *Guide*.

43 On Davis's participation in the 1601 voyage, see Markham, *Voyages and Works*, lxix–lxx. His narrative of the Houtman voyage appears in Purchas, *Pilgrimes*.

Portuguese throne enabled a hope that English support might peel away some part of Portuguese territory from Spain. Even if the popular uprising anticipated by Drake and Norris's raid on Lisbon (for instance) never quite materialized, English geographers had access to Dom António and his pilots, and Thomas Wyndham's colleague António Anes Pinteado was only one of a series of Portuguese navigators who provided important support to English voyages.[44] Hakluyt's materials on Africa and South Asia, regions claimed by Portugal, are only rarely accompanied with the language of "stolen secrets" so prominent for Spanish materials; beyond the spectacular example of Sande's treatise, captured with the *Madre de Deus*, only a single intercepted letter is said to reveal a "rich and secret trade" crossing the Sahara to the Portuguese fort at Arguin Island.[45] Hakluyt had access to some sources on "Portuguese" Asia through the mediation of Richard Willes, whose *History of travayle* (1577) revised and expanded Richard Eden's *Decades*. A member of the Jesuit order from 1565 to 1572, Willes was able to include "accounts of China and Japan ... never before printed in English."[46] These accounts translated works in print by the Portuguese soldier and captive Galeote Pereira and by the Jesuit historian of the Indies, Giovanni Pietro Maffei, whom Willes calls his "olde acquaynted friend," but his texts also included what David and Alison Quinn describe as Willes's "own composition from Jesuit sources."[47] The Portuguese pilots Nuño da Silva and Lope Vaz became sources of materials on the West Indies and the voyages of Drake after being captured by English ships in the Spanish Americas.

If the meanings and accessibility of Spanish and Portuguese sources were freighted by England's actual conflict and competition with Spain and Portugal,

---

44 On Hakluyt's contacts with Dom Antonio and his retinue in Paris, see Hakluyt, PD. The Portuguese pilot Simon Fernandez served both Humphrey Gilbert and Walter Ralegh as a navigator.

45 Petoney, "A Relation Concerning the Estate of the Island and Castle of Arguin."

46 Payne, "Willes, Richard"; the quotation is from Willes, *History of Travayle*, fo. 253v.

47 Willes's print sources are given by David and Alison Quinn as Galeote Pereira, *Novi avisi delle Indie di Portogallo* [...] *Quarta parte* (Venice, 1565); Giovanni Pietro Maffei, *Rerum a Societate Jesu in Oriente gestarum volumen* (Naples, 1573) (Quinn and Quinn, "C&S," 2: 427). See also Payne, "Willes, Richard." Willes's translation of Pereira's work on China from a Venetian edition originally included a compliment to the language skills of its addressee Elizabeth Morison, the daughter of the Countess of Bedford to whom the *History of Travayle* was dedicated; as he pointed out, she needed no translation of an Italian text. On female readers and patrons of geography in the 1570s, see Fuller, "Looking for the Women."

Hakluyt's own "language relations" also changed with changing political circumstances. Only five years after the final volume of *PN* (1598–1600) appeared, a 1605 letter to Hakluyt from Luis Tribaldos de Toledo, who had served as secretary to the Spanish ambassador in London, indicates very different conditions for the circulation of geographical information, inaugurated by a treaty signed by Philip III and James I to conclude the wars of their predecessors. Toledo's letter apparently fulfils a promise to continue through correspondence the professed friendship between its author and "my Hakluyt"; having conveyed Hakluyt's expressions of goodwill towards the Spanish royal cosmographer, Andrés García Cespédes, Toledo was also able to transmit from Cespédes "a certaine briefe yet very perspicuous Relation" of Juan de Oñate's expedition to New Mexico.[48] (Purchas, who printed the text found in Hakluyt's papers, provided marginal citations from the Spanish of Espejo to clarify the relationship of this information to Espejo's earlier expedition.) Toledo also, if more briefly and elliptically, provided Hakluyt with news on "the Coasts of the South Sea toward Cape Mendocino," and noted the absence of news on a voyage "to the Iland lately found out toward Nova Guinea," with a promise to "carefully advertise you thereof" when he knew more. Cespédes's "excellent Volume" drawing on material sent to the Council of the Indies was not yet licensed for publication – "they will not have all these things particularly to come to light" – but as María Portuondo has shown, the government of Philip III had already begun to shift its attitudes towards publishing materials on the geography of its expansive empire for reasons very similar to those on which Hakluyt's editorial projects were founded: "Rather than being kept secret for fear of usurpation or for defensive reasons, as had been the approach taken during most of the reign of Philip II, geographical knowledge had won a new currency. Its value now consisted in how well it served to buttress the Spanish monarchy's territorial claims. To achieve this, it had to be publicly deployed."[49] Secrecy had yielded to a programme that sounds much like Hakluyt's (or indeed, that of the Hakluyt Society during its Victorian decades).[50] Five years after Hakluyt's publication of stolen Spanish secrets

---

48 Purchas, *Pilgrimes*, 4: 1565–7.

49 Portuondo, *Secret Science*, 298. An account of Cespedes's career, and his interventions into the methods and institutions of Spanish cosmography, can be found in Portuondo, chap. 7.

50 See D. Quinn, "Hakluyt's Reputation," 1: 147; Fuller, *Voyages in Print*, 156–8. A broader retrospective of the Society's early years can be found in Hair, "Hakluyt Society: From Past to Future."

in PN (1598–1600), geographical information had become a matter of friendly correspondence across borders. We will return to suppler deployments of secrecy in the rest of the chapter.

CANADA IN TRANSLATION:
THE CASE OF FRENCH AND ITALIAN SOURCES

If the model of "stolen secrets" only partially (and temporarily) describes Hakluyt's use of Spanish materials in translation, it would be almost entirely misleading as a way of thinking about the compilation's French and Italian sources. Unlike Spain and Portugal, the various Italian states were not active rivals in trade and settlement beyond the Mediterranean; as Michael Wyatt writes, this was "an area Italians could not possibly have competed in, given the cumulative consequences of the political traumas the Italian peninsula had suffered throughout the 16th century."[51] Instead, as Elizabeth Horodowich points out, the Venetians she studies were "avidly collecting information about the Americas and mediating the dissemination of this knowledge to the rest of Europe."[52] European audiences frequently read about Spanish discoveries in Italian; Ramusio, in particular, made "painstaking efforts to side-step the Iberian embargoes of information," with results that (as we have seen) were prominent in the third volume of *Principal Navigations*.[53] Scholars have recognized that Ramusio's *Navigationi et viaggi* provided Hakluyt with a model as well as an appreciable amount of content.[54]

For Hakluyt, Italian was largely (and importantly) a language of mediation and collection rather than of first-person witness. The single exception in PN (1598–1600) – a voyage narrative in Italian and about Italians – was also especially prominent in the work of both Hakluyt and John Dee: the apocryphal narrative of Niccolò Zeno, relating a supposed Arctic voyage by two of his ancestors.[55] Horodowich has shown that Zeno's narrative was largely a

---

51 Wyatt, *Italian Encounter with Tudor England*, 141.
52 Horodowich, *Venetian Discovery of America*, 6.
53 Ibid., 6; van Groesen, *Representations of the Overseas World*, 41. On Ramusio, see Horodowich, ibid., chap. 3. For identification of Ramusio's materials in the two editions of *Principal Navigations*, see Quinn and Quinn, "c&s."
54 A helpful comparison of the two editors is provided by Small, "World Seen through Another's Eyes." See also "Italian and French influences," in Payne, *Guide*, 23–8.
55 Zeno, "Voyage of M. Nicolas Zeno." Ramusio reprinted the narrative from Niccolò Zeno, *De i commentarii* [...] *Et Dello scoprimento* [...] *de due fratelli Zenii* (Venice, 1558).

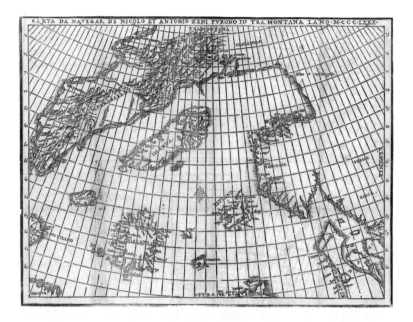

Figure 8.1 The Zeno brothers' apocryphal discoveries provided English geographical thinkers, mapmakers, and navigators with a number of place names, among them Estotiland, Frisland, and Drogeo.

pastiche of earlier sources, providing a convincing resolution to long debates over its veracity; the importance of Venice as a clearinghouse for geographic information, and as a centre for cartography, afforded its author ready access to the narrative's varied sources.[56] Yet the Zeno narrative of an Arctic full of populous, Latinate cities, reprinted by Ramusio, passed for geographical fact in learned circles. Marshalled along with other medieval materials in support of Dee's argument for an ancient English title to the North Atlantic, this work and its accompanying map also provided toponyms and hydrographic outlines used by Dee, as well as by Abraham Ortelius and Gerhard Mercator.[57] For his

---

56 Horodowich, *Venetian Discovery of America*, chap. 5. On mapmaking in Venice, see also Horodowich, chap. 4; Woodward, "Italian Map Trade 1480–1650," 779–91. Kirsten Seaver has also identified elements of the text apparently drawing on information from the northern cod fishery (Seaver, "Common and Usuall Trade," 1).

57 Sherman, *John Dee*, 183–5. A survey of Zeno's influence on both maps and geographic texts is provided by Lucas, *Voyages of the Brothers Zeni*.

part, Hakluyt reprinted the Zeno narrative in all three of his compilations; along with the proposals of Robert Thorne and some instructions by the elder Hakluyt, it was one of the few documents privileged in this way. *Divers Voyages* named "Nicolaus and Antonius Zeni" on a select list of "late travaylers, both by sea and by land," alongside Columbus, Cabot, Vasco da Gama, and Magellan.[58] In volume 3, the Zeno relation appeared among "Voyages ... for the finding of a Northwest passage" alongside the voyages of Martin Frobisher and John Davis; materials on both voyages would use Zenian toponyms, suggesting an effort to map this Venetian account back onto the actual Arctic that English mariners observed.[59] The Zeno relation served English interests, as circumstantial evidence of an Arctic civilization that Dee could argue was presumptively Arthurian, and predated any Spanish claim to the North Atlantic; while Zeno had sought to advance Venetian prestige with its publication, the Zeno relation appeared to its English readers to provide useful geographic and historical information without inciting any project that would challenge their own activities or assertions of precedence in the region. It sat comfortably alongside the Frobisher and Davis voyages that used it as a source.

Yet even if Italian editors and presses were prolific in producing and disseminating information about distant regions and seas, language could still make a work as important and well-known as Ramusio's *Navigationi et viaggi* effectively "secret" for English audiences. In the Latin preface to his edition of *De orbe novo*, Hakluyt noted that his intent in publishing it was so "that learned and industrious men, who have no knowledge, or only a little of the Spanish and Italian tongues, in which practically all works dealing with this subject ... are *obscured*, should not be deprived of so great and abundant a boon; and partly that ... our own island race, perceiving how the Spaniards began and how they progressed, might be inspired to a like emulation of courage" (emphasis mine).[60] The preface framed in surprisingly sharp terms a dual problem: the English, belated in their activities, needed to learn from

---

58 The list is found on the verso of the title page. Other contents that appear in all three collections are materials on the Cabots.

59 George Best compared his observations of "Friseland," on 20 June 1578, with "a description set out by two brethren Venetians, Nicholaus and Antonius Zeni ... they have in their Sea-cardes set out every part thereof" (Best, "True Discourse," 3: 62). Among the equipment for Frobisher's first voyage was "a great mappe universall of Mercator in printe," the (now lost) world map that "used much of the Zeno detail" (Waters, *Art of Navigation*, 530; Ruggles, "Cartographic Lure," 200–1). For Davis's use of the toponym "Estotiland," derived from the Zeno narrative, see Davis, "Letter to William Sanderson, 1586."

60 Taylor, *OW*, 2: 365.

and emulate the great deeds of other nations, and yet their ignorance of other vernaculars barred their access to useful and inspiring knowledge – even when that knowledge was widely available in print. (Hakluyt's concessive account of English belatedness here complicates the more celebratory account of "stirring abroad" in the prefaces to his Anglophone publications.)[61]

Spanish voyages were not the only ones Hakluyt believed would yield useful information to his compatriots, however. The preface to John Florio's 1580 translation of Jacques Cartier's two voyages – again, a work whose original passed into English through Ramusio's Italian – expressed the need for translation in similar terms. If Ramusio's volumes were "translated into English ... our Sea-men of England, and others, studious of Geographie, should know *many worthy secrets, which hitherto have been concealed*" (emphasis mine).[62] Although Hakluyt's name does not appear in the original, he animated and funded Florio's translation, and the preface is generally believed to have been his rather than Florio's, despite the latter's signature.[63] As the preface argues, the "concealment" of these Italian accounts of voyages undertaken by a French navigator was an artifact of inattention (or linguistic incompetence) on the part of their potential readers rather than – as in some other cases – the product of deliberate policy or positive actions to restrict their circulation. Language, not rarity, was indeed the bottleneck: William Sherman notes that for geography and travel writing, "books by (among others) Ramusio, Thevet, and de Bry ... clearly outnumber English publications in most of the major Elizabethan libraries we have catalogs for"; such books were widely available, needing only to be read by those best positioned to make use of their information.[64]

---

61 "Our nation ... in all former ages ... have bene men full of activity, stirrers abroad, and searchers of the remote parts of the world" (Hakluyt, "Epistle Dedicatorie [1589]," sig. *2v).

62 Cartier, *A Shorte and Briefe Narration*, sig. B2v. While the preface is signed by Florio, on the grounds of both style and content Frances Yates and E.G.R. Taylor view Hakluyt as the probable author (Taylor, *OW*, 1: 21–2; Yates, *John Florio*, 58–9).

63 Hakluyt noted in the preface to his *DV* that he had "caused ... Cartiers two voyages ... to bee translated" and "annexed to this present" volume (*DV*, sig. ¶3v). Anthony Payne's census of surviving copies finds only one exemplar that includes the Cartier translation, "with a contemporary binding instruction to include 'Florio ... iind'" (Payne, *Guide*, 83).

64 Sherman, "Bringing the World to England," 206. Many merchants and seamen, of course, were fluent in one or more additional languages; see, for instance, John Frampton's preface to his translation of Marco Polo: "manye Merchauntes, Pilots, and Marriners, and others of dyvers degrees, much bent to Discoveries, resorting to me upon seuerall

The Franco-Italian text of Cartier's voyages leads us to another group of vernacular European materials, one that Hakluyt was personally active in discovering, as well as translating and publishing. Sources either in French or concerning French voyages were the third most numerous group of materials in volume 3, after those pertaining to England and Spain; their variety, as well as their number, call for attention. Like the voyages of Cartier, some such sources were readily available to readers fluent in Italian through Ramusio's *Navigationi et viaggi*. Yet we can observe a diversity of cases. One narrative about the French settlement in northern Florida had originally appeared *in* English, when its author Jean Ribault sought refuge and help in London following the massacre of the colonists by Spanish forces.[65] Another French source in PN (1598–1600) was literally a stolen secret; a rutter seized from a French ship taken as a prize, it alerted English merchants and mariners to a profitable walrus fishery in the Gulf of St Lawrence.[66] Finally, an account of the Florida colony loaned to Hakluyt by the French cosmographer Thevet, and published by Hakluyt in Paris, led to charges and countercharges of deliberate, ideologically driven suppression (by Hakluyt), and theft and breach of trust (by Thevet); what had originally been a collegial exchange between scholars was reframed in terms that recall the reciprocal hostility of secrets stolen in the course of maritime aggression.[67] Hakluyt's French materials thus fall at multiple points on the spectrum from friendly exchanges to forcible taking. More readily accessible from friendly sources than Spanish or Portuguese materials, French materials were also caught up in national and commercial rivalries, as well as, at times, the internal politics of religious war.

French materials on North America had played a prominent role in Hakluyt's career from the outset, as his sponsorship of Florio's Cartier text suggests.

---

occasions, *toke so great delight with the reading of my Booke* [a Castilian edition of Marco Polo's travels], … that I coulde never bee in quiet, for one or for an other, for the committing the same to printe in the Englishe tongue" (emphasis mine; Frampton, *Travels of Marcus Paulus*, sig. *2r, cited in Beecher, "Legacy of John Frampton," 323).

65 Ribault, *Discoverye of Terra Florida.*
66 "The First Discovery of the Isle of Ramea," 3: 189–90.
67 Laudonnière, *L'Histoire Notable de La Floride* (Paris, 1586); printed by Hakluyt as multiple items under the in-text title, "A notable historie containing foure voyages made by certaine French Captaines into Florida" (*PN* 3: 301–62). Hakluyt contributed a poem to Martin Basanier's French edition; both Basanier (in the dedication) and Hakluyt himself (in the epistle dedicatory to volume 2) confirm that that this edition was printed "at mine own charges"; he translated the English edition himself (Payne, *Guide*, 87–92). Thevet's accusations are discussed in Lestringant, *Le Huguenot et le sauvage*, 255–8.

Divers Voyages also included Ramusio's account of the voyages of Giovanni da Verrazzano, made for François I, and the French cosmographer royal Thevet appeared on both the volume's prefatory lists of "certaine late writers of Geographie" and "certaine late travaylers ... which ... have written of their own travayles and voyages." (Thevet's *Singularitez de la France Antarctique* [1557] had been published in English several years earlier.) Hakluyt would initially pursue a personal acquaintance with Thevet during his employment at the English embassy in Paris during the years 1583 to 1588. The editor's sojourn in Paris provided him not only with a wealth of information on North America but the very idea that would become *Principall Navigations* (1589): "I both heard in speech, and read in books other nations miraculously extolled for their discoveries and notable enterprises by sea, but the English of all others for their sluggish security, and continuall neglect of the like attempts especially in so long and happy a time of peace, either ignominiously reported, or exceedingly condemned."[68] His response would be to assemble and publish of a record of English maritime achievements inviting "that just commendation which our nation do indeed deserve." Assembly of the first edition of *Principall Navigations* (1589) proceeded alongside the editor's efforts to collect and publish works on foreign travel, only occasionally in English. As we have seen, his years at the embassy also produced editions of Martyr's *De orbe novo*, Espejo's *Viaje*, and an edition of Laudonnière's *L'histoire notable de la Floride* (Paris, 1586); he also produced an English translation of Laudonnière's *A Notable Historie* (London, 1587).

Publication and printed matter were only one part of Hakluyt's interests during these years. The contemporaneous trade and colonization projects of Hakluyt's patrons made French knowledge of the northern Americas a target of interest as well as opportunity, and he played a strikingly active, personal role in seeking out both oral and written information on French activities there.[69] In letters to Francis Walsingham, the secretary of state, as well as in his treatise on colonization, "Particuler Discourse" (1584), the editor describes consulting both manuscript sources in French collections and a variety of French informants – cosmographers, naturalists, mariners, furriers – in quest

---

68 Hakluyt, "Epistle Dedicatorie (1589)," sig. *2r–v. Hakluyt's movements between Paris and London, and his contacts during these years, are detailed in Mancall, *Hakluyt's Promise*, chaps. 6–8. A more schematic outline can be found in "Chronology."

69 Hakluyt's letters from Paris and the dedications to works published in Paris can be found in Taylor, ow. Additional details can be found in the introduction and notes to PD.

of geographical information. Not all the fruits of Hakluyt's efforts made their way into the compilation. Étienne Bellenger's account of a voyage to the Maritimes and his information on the fur trade were cited liberally in "Particuler Discourse," and (according to David Quinn) informed the representation of Cape Breton on both the Molyneux globe and the world map by Edward Wright included in some copies of PN (1598–1600), but the account itself did not appear in either edition of the compilation.[70] The case of Bellenger reminds us that publishing information was not Hakluyt's only goal; more than a "midwife" who simply assisted other men's texts in coming to the world's view, Hakluyt might more accurately be viewed as a manager and broker of information who withheld as well as made public.[71]

The French sources that did appear in PN (1598–1600) cluster under three of volume 3's regionally focused headings: sections on the Maritimes and St Lawrence, and another on what Hakluyt called Florida, a broader region that extended to the north of the modern American state.[72] The short-lived Huguenot settlement in Hakluyt's Florida had struggled with food supply before falling victim to Spanish soldiers; it was of interest to Hakluyt as the site of a Protestant colony whose mistakes could inform the English colonial efforts of the 1580s. In the dedication to his translation of Laudonnière,

---

70 Bellenger's relation is BL MS Add. 14027, fo. 289–90v, printed in D. Quinn, *NAW*, 4: 306–8. Hakluyt apparently visited Rouen and obtained the relation, and (then or later) a map from Bellenger (Quinn, ibid., 4: 306). *PD* makes numerous references to information provided to him personally by "my frende Stephan Bellenger," whose voyage of 1583 apparently followed several previous voyages to maritime Canada. Hakluyt does not mention (or was not told) that a settlement had been intended. For details, see D. Quinn, "Voyage of Etienne Bellenger to the Maritimes in 1583"; Turgeon, *Une Histoire de La Nouvelle-France*, 109–12.

71 The language is from Parks, "Tudor Travel Literature," 1: 101. (The metaphor is discussed in Fuller, *Voyages in Print*, 142.)

72 In French usage, "Florida" extended as far north as the Gulf of Maine; for Hakluyt, however, "Florida" lay to the south of the English colony at Roanoke Island, in present-day North Carolina (on nomenclature, see Turgeon, *Une Histoire de La Nouvelle-France*, 104–5). Hakluyt did not include materials on the French settlement in Brazil either from André Thevet's *Singularitez de la France Antartique* (1558; English edition, 1568) or Jean de Léry's *Histoire d'un voyage faict en la terre du Bresil* (1578). As Joan-Pau Rubiés notes, Hakluyt owned a copy of Léry, perhaps acquired during his stay in Paris and through his closer acquaintance with André Thevet. Although Purchas would acquire Hakluyt's copy of the book and include Léry's material in *Pilgrimes*, Hakluyt's own writings yield "a striking lack of references" to Léry's work (Rubiés, "Texts, Images and the Perception of 'Savages,'" 121, 129n8). Hakluyt mentions the ministers who accompanied Villegagnon to Brazil in *PD*, but even there Léry is not cited by name (*PD*, 11).

Hakluyt pointed out that these accounts could forewarn English colonists "that by others mishaps they might learne to prevent and avoyde" the problems of provisioning, security, and unity that had been fatal to their French predecessors.[73] The colony's brief history also served him as a minatory example of confessional violence and Spanish "inhumanity," as suggested by the heading Hakluyt gave to one extract from a larger narrative: "The voyage of captaine Dominique Gourgues to Florida 1567, where he most valiantly, justly, and sharpely revenged the bloody and inhumane massacre committed by the Spaniards upon his countreymen, in the yeere 1565." Materials on French Florida thus presented Hakluyt with attractive rhetorical and informational opportunities. Yet the focus of activities under English patents of discovery in the 1580s lay considerably further north. The need for sources that could inform those projects and make them comprehensible and attractive, as well as practically successful, led Hakluyt to focus particular attention on materials relating to the region of the St Lawrence and the Maritimes, both areas considerably better known to the French than the English. The contents under these two headings are detailed in appendix 7.

Materials under the first heading, "Voyages to Newfoundland," are dominated by items relating to Humphrey Gilbert's patent of 1578; narrative accounts of the single voyage that resulted, adventitiously making landfall at the harbour already then known as St John's, are accompanied by an extensive halo of plans, promotion, and celebration.[74] Both Gilbert's formal claiming of Newfoundland for the crown and his death on the return voyage have lent this group of materials particular significance for later readers, and they have figured prominently in the reception history of Hakluyt's materials. "Voyages to Newfoundland" also includes a later, less well-known group of documents detailing English voyages in waters to the west of Newfoundland.[75] These voyages were inaugurated by the already-noted stolen source: a rutter for the Magdalen Islands found in the *Bonaventure*, a French ship taken as prize by a Bristol merchantman. In the compilation, the rutter is followed by a letter to the Lord Treasurer, William Cecil, from the *Bonaventure*'s captor, Thomas James, informing him that the *Bonaventure* had made "the discovery of an

---

73 Laudonnière, *A Notable History Containing Four Voyages* [...] *unto Florida*.
74 For background and other documents on Gilbert's project, see D. Quinn, *Voyages and Colonising Enterprises*; D. Quinn and Cheshire, *New Found Land of Stephen Parmenius*. Writing about the project is examined in Miller, *Invested with Meaning*; Fuller, *Voyages in Print*, chap. 1.
75 Useful context for these documents can be found in D. Quinn, *NAW*, 4: 56–80.

Island" with a rich walrus fishery yielding tusks, hide, meat, and oil. "If it will make sope, the king of Spain may burne some of this Olive trees," James added combatively; he had taken the prize on his way to join Thomas Howard, waiting off the Azores to intercept the Spanish treasure fleet.[76] The rutter's capture inaugurated an English effort to exploit what Hakluyt viewed as a "gainfull and profitable trade," exploiting marine resources in the Gulf of St Lawrence and the Strait of Belle Isle.[77]

Hakluyt's titular description of the *Bonaventure*'s 1591 voyage as a "discovery" was misleading, however; the English voyages that ensued entered not only challengingly unfamiliar waters, but a well-established sphere of existing French, Basque, and Indigenous presence and collaboration. (Charles Leigh's narrative gives a sense of the difficulties.)[78] Archival records (as well as the presence of European trade goods in the archaeological record) indicate that several decades before Hakluyt arrived in Paris, French ships making voyages to the Newfoundland fishery had begun to diversify their activities by hunting for whales and seals in the Strait of Belle Isle and trading for furs at Cape Breton, while the 1580s saw the development of a trade in furs that moved inland along the St Lawrence River ("Canada," in contemporary sources).[79] Bellenger's 1583 voyage to Acadia, related to Hakluyt, was thus neither an entirely new nor an isolated undertaking. Hakluyt's praise of Charles Leigh, George Drake, and Silvester Wyet as "the first ... of our owne Nation, that have conducted English ships so farre within this gulfe of S. Laurence" tacitly acknowledged that they were not *the* first. At the time of the appearance of *PN* (1598–1600), despite Hakluyt's exertions in gathering, even composing materials on these enterprises, the actual predominance of the French, Bretons, and Basques who "do yerely return from the sayd partes" remained largely unchallenged, and the promise of the rutter's stolen secrets unrealized. Hakluyt indeed complains that his compatriots remained "idle lookers on" despite the "manifold gaine" reaped by others.[80] In the wake of Gilbert's

---

76 James, "Letter to Cecil, 1591."

77 Hakluyt, "Voyage of M. George Drake," 3: 193. Although narrative records are poor, archival and archaeological investigations led Selma Barkham to conclude that "there may well have been as many as two thousand men using harbours every year along the Strait of Belle Isle during the second half of the sixteenth century" (Barkham, "Spanish Voyages to Terranova," 110). On this zone of interaction, see also Loewen, "Sea Change."

78 These materials are discussed at greater length in Fuller, "Canada in the English Geographical Imaginary."

79 Turgeon, *Une Histoire de La Nouvelle-France*, 107–12, 120–3.

80 Hakluyt, "Voyage of M. George Drake," 3: 193.

glorious assertion of English rights to a harbour already frequented by fishers of many nations, the remainder of this category quietly concedes – on a smaller scale – the kinds of failures and inaction that *PN* (1589) had set out to replace with a different story.

The next category in the volume's paratext, "the St. Lawrence and inland," overlapped geographically with its predecessor (Anticosti and the Magdalen Islands are *in* the Gulf of St Lawrence); it is here that we find the relations of Cartier, the Sieur de Roberval, and Jean Alfonse de Saintonge (also known as Fonteneau). These materials were newly added to *PN* (1598–1600), although all would have been in Hakluyt's hands when he returned from Paris in 1588. As appendix 7 indicates, the two categories of "Newfoundland" and "the St. Lawrence" have been sorted and organized so that each contains almost exclusively either English or French materials, disimbricating the actual complexity of European presence in the region. The "French" category of voyages into the St Lawrence includes principally materials before 1545, with the only contemporary materials being two letters relating to Hakluyt's research on Cartier and Canada in Paris. The effect is to signal the significance of the Cartier voyages, to be sure, but Hakluyt's volume categories also frame French activities in northern North America as having taken place primarily in the past. French voyages had generated a body of historical knowledge on which English planners could draw, but did not apparently belong on a continuum of activities extending into Hakluyt's own day.

Cartier's voyages held considerable interest for English geographers.[81] They were a focus for Hakluyt's research in France; he examined (but did not reproduce) a manuscript account of the second voyage and inquired about papers still in the possession of his family.[82] Although Cartier's voyage did not appear in the more narrowly focused first edition of 1589, *PN* (1598–1600) supplemented Florio's translations of the first and second voyages from Ramusio with the only known account of Cartier's third voyage into the St Lawrence and associated manuscript materials on the voyage of the Sieur de Roberval. The eventual disposition of the originals Hakluyt used is (typically) unknown; more unusually, so is their provenance – Hakluyt's is the only known version of the text. Thanks to his diligence, the acts and discoveries of an

---

81 John Dee alluded to "the massively wealthy dominion of Saguenay" in a 1578 memorandum to the queen, advising her on the legal grounds supporting the patent for discovery granted to Sir Humphrey Gilbert in the same year (document 1, in MacMillan, *Limits*, 38).

82 Hakluyt, *PD*, 83–5.

important French navigator were rescued from oblivion and made visible. In the following century, the French editor Melchisédech Thévenot would accordingly acknowledge a debt to Hakluyt for having preserved so many good things, including the works of "some of our French conquerors."[83]

Yet Hakluyt left the sequels of Cartier's voyages largely in the shadows. These sequels emerge as traces in the category's only contemporary materials, two letters from Cartier's great-nephew Jacques Noël to "John Growte," a student in Paris; they are contemporaneous with Hakluyt's time in Paris, and the second of the two might have accompanied the "aforesaid unperfite relation" of Cartier's third voyage that Hakluyt printed.[84] In his first letter, Noël wrote that Growte's brother-in-law "Giles Walter" had that morning shown him "a Mappe printed at Paris, dedicated to M. Hakluyt an English Gentleman"; this was a map of the Americas accompanying Hakluyt's 1587 edition of *De orbe novo*. Noël offered several corrections to its representation of the St Lawrence, indicated that he might have access to Cartier's materials, and requested that Growte provide him with a copy of this map "wherein all the West Indies, the kingdome of New Mexico, and the Countries of Canada, Hochelaga, and Saguenay are contained."

The map Noël alludes to was in some ways remarkable (see figure 8.2). "Based on a Spanish original," according to R.A. Skelton, the version that appeared in the Paris *De orbe novo* incorporated the most recent and sensitive English cartographic information: "data from Frobisher's Northwestern voyages, from Drake's circumnavigation and from Ralegh's colonial venture [that is, the colony at Roanoke Island, North Carolina] ... which must've been

---

83 Thévenot's remarks were included in a letter to John Locke from Nicolas Toinard, 14/25 August 1680, cited in Dew, "Reading Travels in the Culture of Curiosity," 39.

84 Hakluyt's language might be understood to indicate that Noel was responsible for providing to him the account of Cartier's 1540 voyage to the "countreys of Canada, Hochelaga, and Saguenay" that directly precedes the latter in PN (1598–1600): "Underneath the aforesaide unperfite relation that which followeth is written in another letter sent to M. John Growte student in Paris from Jaques Noel of S. Malo, the grand nephew of Jaques Cartier" (Hakluyt, PN 3: 236). (A "Steven Noel" is named as Cartier's nephew in Cartier, "Third Voyage of Jaques Cartier, 1540," 3: 324.) Scholars scrutinizing the materials closely have not reached consensus on the provenance of Hakluyt's text, however. Arthur Stabler proposes that Hakluyt obtained materials on the Cartier and Roberval voyages from André Thevet (cited in Lestringant, *Le Huguenot et le sauvage*, 329). Michel Bideaux considers the question of provenance to remain open (Cartier, *Relations*).

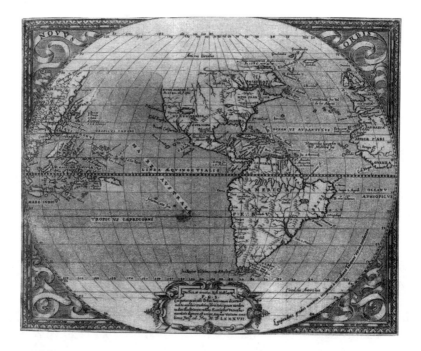

Figure 8.2 The map accompanying Hakluyt's edition of *De orbe novo* (Paris, 1587) visualizes the interior of North America and its waterways.

supplied by Hakluyt."[85] Its appearance attracted new information of equally high quality. Noël drew on his own knowledge and that of his great-uncle, both recorded in their papers, to correct the map's representation of the upper St Lawrence: "I hold that the River of Canada ... in that Mappe is not marked as it is in my booke, which is agreeable to the book of Jaqes Cartier: and that the sayd Charte doth not marke or set down the great Lake, which is above the Saults, according as the Savages have advertised us, which dwell at the sayd Saults."[86] Noël's verbal corrections were assiduously highlighted by Hakluyt in the margins: "The Saults are in 44. deg. and easie to passe"; "But 5. leagues journey to passe the 3. Saults"; "Ten dayes journey from the

85 Skelton, "Hakluyt's Maps," 65. Largely free of the Zenian cartography discussed above, the map locates Frobisher's discoveries correctly, placing "Meta Incognita" to the north of Labrador, separated from Greenland by a strait of water.

86 Noel, "Letter to John Groute by Jaques Noel," 3: 236. Noel's "booke ... agreeable to the book of Jaqes Cartier," presumably a private record, remains unknown.

Saults to this great Lake." All bear on a heading in the PN (1598–1600) text that appears to indicate a map present in the lost original of Cartier's third voyage: "Here after followeth the figure of the three Saults."[87] (Its absence in Hakluyt's version does not inform on its presence in his source text: as we have seen, his practice in the compilation was to extract map legends without reproducing cartographic images themselves.)

In a second letter, Noël responded to an inquiry – presumably relayed from Hakluyt – about surviving writings by Cartier. His letters testify not only that he had been able to consult Cartier's own map, but that he had personal knowledge of the Hochelaga region, and of how the St Lawrence ran above the rapids there: "I have seene the sayd River beyond the sayd Saultes." The letters also register that Noël's sons were *in* the region of the St Lawrence at the time of writing: "my booke ... is made after the maner of a sea Chart, which I have delivered to my two sonnes Michael and John, which at this present are in Canada."[88] (Alerted readers might find confirmation that French trade in the St Lawrence was renewed after 1581 in Christopher Carleill's proposal to pursue Gilbert's settlement project.)[89] Apart from this passing mention in an undated letter, none of the materials among voyages to "the St. Lawrence" make clear the nature or extent of renewed or continued French presence in the region.

What sparked Noël's interest in Hakluyt's publications, enough that he was ready to volunteer such valuable information – of a kind the editor could hardly have come by otherwise? His second letter is revealing about the kinds of speculation that Cartier's hydrography stimulated for both men. In a post-script, Noël requested that Growte send, in addition to the map accompanying Hakluyt's edition of *De orbe novo*, a "booke of the discovery of New Mexico." This book must have been Martin Basanier's translation of Espejo, *Histoire des terres nouvellement descouvertes* (Paris, 1586).[90] The second letter also transcribes two notes that had been "written in the hand of Jaques Cartier" on a chart

---

87 Cartier, "Third Voyage of Jaques Cartier, 1540," 3: 325.

88 Noel, "Letter to John Groute by Jaques Noel," 3: 236; Noel, "Another Letter by Jaques Noel," 3: 327.

89 Carleill, "Briefe and Summarie Discourse," 3: 187. The Noel family's activities are also detailed in Turgeon, *Une Histoire de La Nouvelle-France*, 126, 138. Turgeon describes evidence that French ships were outfitting at Bordeaux for voyages that included trading for furs on the shores of the St Lawrence as well as fishing for cod and whale. Remarks in PD indicate that Hakluyt had some awareness of this activity.

90 Noel, "Letter to John Groute by Jaques Noel," 3: 326. On the Espejo text, see section 1 of this chapter. Payne, *Guide*, 91.

drawn by the navigator, and these begin to show the valences where Cartier's exploration of the St Lawrence, and Espejo's relation of New Mexico, could be presumptively connected in a way that would make Cartier's nephew eager for a copy of the relation. The first note was affixed to the map beyond the place where the St Lawrence ("the River of Canada") divided: "By the people of Canada and Hochelaga it was said, That here is the land of Saguenay, which is rich and wealthy in precious stones. And about an hundred leagues under the same I found written these two lines following in the said Carde inclining toward the Southwest. *Here in this Countrey are Cinamon and Cloves, which they call in their language Canodeta.*"[91] In "Particuler Discourse," Hakluyt made reference to the same information about the St Lawrence above Hochelaga:

in the ende of that seconde relation this postscript is added as a special pointe: To witt that they of Canada say that it is the space of a moone (that is to say a moneth) to saile to a lande where Cynamon and cloves are gathered, and in the frenche originall which I sawe in the kinges Library at Paris in the Abbay of Saint Martines it is further put downe that Donnaconna the kinge of Canada in his barke had traveled to that Contrie where Cynamon and cloves are had, yea and the names whereby the Savages call those twoo spices in their owne langauge are there put downe in writinge.[92]

This testimony suggested to European readers not only that the hinterland of the St Lawrence might yield spices like those of the East Indies, but that the Indies themselves might be accessible by waters connected to the St Lawrence, and at no great distance. Certainly this was Hakluyt's reasoning; he noted in *Divers Voyages* that "[i]n the second relation of Jaques Cartier the 12. Chapter the people of Saguinay doe testifie that upon their coastes Westwarde there is a sea the end whereof is unknown to them."[93] Espejo's reports from the southwest of rivers and lakes trending towards the north appeared to dovetail with this testimony. Hakluyt carefully noted in his marginalia to Espejo not only "exceedingly rich Mines of silver" but reports

---

91 Noel, "Another Letter by Jaques Noel," 3: 236–7. Presumably, the river southwest of present-day Montreal, where the Ottawa joins the St Lawrence.

92 Ramusio, "Second Voyage of Jaques Cartier [...] 1535," 3: 232; Hakluyt, *PD*, 83. Hakluyt's consultation of Cartier's "french originall" and the detail of Donnaconna's travels were withheld from *PN* (1598–1600), present only in the manuscript treatise presented to Queen Elizabeth and a few of her counsellors (*PD*, xv).

93 Hakluyt, *DV*, sig. ¶2r.

of "a mighty lake" and of "a mighty River above 8 leagues broad" that "ran towards the North sea."[94] As he speculated in the margins, "Perhaps this River [in New Mexico] may fall into the Chespiouk bay, or into the great lake at Tadoac"; that is, either the Chesapeake, or the Great Lakes or Lac Saint-Jean, connected to the St Lawrence by the Saguenay River at Tadoussac.

Like Noël standing on a hill to look beyond the rapids, and trying to make sense of information that it was "ten dayes journey from the Saults" to a "great Lake, which is above the Saults, according as the Savages have advertised us," Hakluyt imagined watery connections that linked "the kingdome of Newe Mexico, and the Countreys of Canada, Hochelaga, and Saguenay."[95] If earlier he had used Espejo's text to advise Ralegh about attractive lands in the interior, placing Espejo in dialogue with Cartier highlighted the idea of a passage *through* North America to the south of the high latitudes where it had been sought by Frobisher, and was being sought by Davis at the time of writing. The correspondence with Noël indicates that others shared his conjecture that Espejo's New Mexico was potentially connected with, even close to regions of English and French activity to the northeast, and this thinking would persist for some little time; in 1595, Davis would cite Espejo's travels in support of a conjecture that "the distance is very small betweene the East parte of this discovered Sea and the [Northwest] passage wherein I have so painefully laboured."[96]

As Hakluyt selected and framed French materials in *PN* (1598–1600), they represented a layer of past discoveries and unfulfilled initiatives on which the English could build. Noël's letters remind us, of course, that French activities in North America were hardly a thing of the past. The details he volunteered in response to the valuable information proffered on Hakluyt's 1587 map also suggest that making knowledge public was not simply a one-way distribution, but an invitation to further transactions in kind, initiating occasions for thinking together about geographies still imperfectly known to Europeans. With that small exchange in mind, we turn now to Hakluyt's role in the transnational dissemination of English geographical knowledge.

---

94 Espejo, "Voyage of Antonio de Espeio," 3: 394–5. The editor was constantly attentive to evidence bearing on the unknown distance between Asia and North America; in the margins of the Mongol relations in volume 1, he noted that Mongol men wore clothes "like unto Frobisher's men," while women's dress resembled that of the women of Meta Incognita (Baffin Island/Qikiqtaaluk).
95 Noel, "Letter to John Groute by Jaques Noel."
96 Davis, *Worldes Hydrographical Discription*, sig. B7r.

TRANSLATIONS, TRANSMEDIATION, EXCHANGE: HAKLUYT'S FLEMISH CORRESPONDENTS

As we have seen, among the things Hakluyt learned in France was that news of English maritime activities did not travel; in the preface to *PN* (1589), he described his project of collecting and publishing information about English travel as animated by a desire to redress continental perceptions that the English were less active than other European nations in exploring unfamiliar regions and seas. If this was the motive behind *Principal Navigations*, publication on the continent – in Latin or one of the various European vernaculars – would have been a logical response. Yet Hakluyt chose to publish in English: which is to say, in a language that immediately narrowed the potential European audience for his collections, even as it extended the work's domestic audience to readers not at ease in Latin. George Hakewill spoke to the consequences of this choice some years after Hakluyt's death, when he wished "for the honour of the English name ... that his collections and relations had been written in Latin" – this was, of course, the choice Arngrímur Jónsson made for his own celebration of Iceland.[97] Even beyond the two editions of *Principal Navigations*, Hakluyt's extensive work in translation was almost entirely focused on bringing foreign materials into English rather than the reverse. During his time in Paris, he published numerous editions of works by foreign authors, but no translations of narratives by or about English travellers addressed to the continental audiences whose ignorance had inspired him. While we can't say what the appetite for such publications would have been, the field would hardly have been a crowded one. In a later dedication to his translation of António de Galvão's history of world exploration, Hakluyt comments that "for the space almost of fower thousand yeeres here set downe, our nation is scarce fower times mentioned."[98] The book he translated had been published in 1555, but by the date of *PN* (1589), the state of play was little better. Only two English voyage narratives had been published outside of England: a narrative of Drake's raids on the West Indies in 1585 to 1586, attributed to Walter Bigges, and Dionyse Settle's brief account of Frobisher's second voyage into the Arctic. The location of these imprints, in Leiden,

---

[97] Hakewill, *An apologie of the power and providence of God in the government of the world* (London, 1631), 253; cited in D. Quinn, "Hakluyt's Reputation," 137. For some reflections on the use of English in the period, see Helgerson, *Forms of Nationhood*, chap. 1. On Jónsson, see chapter 4 above.

[98] Galvão, *Discoveries of the World*, sig. A3v.

Cologne, Nuremberg, and Geneva, suggests a decidedly Protestant readership, but neither bears any trace of Hakluyt's involvement.[99]

Hakluyt made only one attempt to disseminate English travel narratives beyond England's shores, but that single initiative would prove enormously influential: this was Theodor de Bry's illustrated, multilingual folio edition of the mathematician and colonist Thomas Harriot's report on the English colony at Roanoke, *A Briefe and True Report* (Frankfurt, 1590).[100] A vital piece of evidence about Indigenous societies and English contacts with them, the book also provides rich evidence of Hakluyt's participation in the cosmopolitan scholarly networks already glimpsed in his correspondence with Mercator. Such networks had an important place in Hakluyt's intellectual life, and they continue to suggest adjustments to our understanding of the transnational dynamics of secrecy and making public described in the first section of this chapter.[101] As Hakluyt's exchanges with Noël remind us, while the editor's primary interest was in acquiring, extracting, and deploying foreign knowledge to English ends, in the course of his scholarly and consulting activities Hakluyt also transmitted information to foreign interlocutors. These exchanges took place largely through correspondence or (occasionally) in person, only rarely crossing over into the medium of print; Mercator's letters to Hakluyt and Dee in volume 1 of the compilation are among the occasional exceptions. The bilateral character of such scholarly exchanges differs sharply from the model of unilateral seizure under which Hakluyt introduced the copious translations of volume 3. Focused on communications between London and

---

99 *European Americana*, vol. 1, lists editions of Bigges, *A summary and true discourse of Sir Francis Drake's West Indian voyage* (London, 1589) in French and Latin (both Leiden, 1588) and German (Cologne, 1589); readers will notice that the two Leiden publications antedated the appearance of the work in English. Settle's *A true report of the last voyage into the West and Northwest regions* (London, 1577) appeared in French (Geneva?, 1578) and in German and Latin (Nuremberg, 1580).

100 Harriot, *A Briefe and True Report* (1590). De Bry would go on to publish materials on the voyages of Drake, Cavendish, and Ralegh, with later accounts of Jamestown and voyages from *Purchas His Pilgrimes* (1625); for a census of his publications, see van Groesen, *Representations of the Overseas World*, 493–507. Peter Mancall points out that the de Bry edition of Harriot and an English translation of Linschoten's *Itinerario* were the only two illustrated books with which Hakluyt was involved; on Hakluyt and visual images, see Mancall, "Visual World of Early Modern Travel Narratives," 87.

101 Matthew Day offers a stimulating discussion of publication and secrecy in an international context in "Richard Hakluyt's 'Principal Navigations' (1598–1600) and the Textuality of Tudor English Nationalism," chap. 5. On his relationship to the Dutch, see especially Day, 228–9, 244–5.

the Netherlands, such exchanges introduce another geopolitical context for the dissemination of geographical information that was Hakluyt's mandate.

During the period preceding publication of *PN* (1598–1600), Hakluyt's known non-English correspondents were all either from or resident in the Low Countries. Hakluyt corresponded with Mercator and referred to his son Rumold as "my friend." Ortelius, a Catholic geographer based in Antwerp, was an acquaintance of Hakluyt's elder cousin, and met William Camden, Dee and the younger Hakluyt on a visit to England in 1577; the editor alludes to letters from Ortelius.[102] Friendly correspondence did not imply an entirely open exchange of information, however; in "Particuler Discourse," Hakluyt complained – or bragged – that Ortelius had come to England in 1577 "to no other ende but to prye and looke into the secretes of Frobishers voyadge."[103] Ortelius's cousin Emanuel van Meteren, the Dutch consul in London, was also known to Hakluyt (and the source of the Armada narrative printed in volume 1). In 1594, van Meteren sought to recruit Hakluyt as a paid informant, relaying to him an inquiry from Jacob van Valcke, the treasurer of Zeeland; Valcke was seeking information about the Northeast Passage that would assist the voyage of Willem Barentsz, then in preparation. As we noted in earlier chapters, Hakluyt told van Meteren that "friends at Venice" could provide his employer with copies of Abū al-Fidā's text in Latin, and corrected some misunderstandings of John de Plano Carpini's account of his travels across Asia; both were viewed as potentially useful information on the regions that lay below the supposed passage.[104] But Hakluyt appears to have done more than assist in finding medieval manuscripts; he offered to provide Valcke with a digest of information on the Northeast and Northwest Passages, information he promised would be worth "many thousand pounds" and for which he requested a payment of twenty marks sterling.[105] An agreement was apparently entered into, and along with other old and new materials, Hakluyt may have supplied a narrative of Arthur Pet and Charles Jackman's Arctic voyage of

---

102 Hakluyt, *Divers Voyages*, sig. ¶2r; Taylor, *OW*, 1: 77–83; Hakluyt, *PD*, 76; Hakluyt, "Preface to the Reader (1598)," sig. **1r. Letters to and from the elder and younger Hakluyt can be found in Taylor, *OW*.

103 Hakluyt, *PD*, 76; Taylor, *OW*, 1: 12.

104 A letter from van Meteren to Valcke, and a letter from Hakluyt to van Meteren translated into Dutch by the latter, are both provided (in English) in Taylor, *OW*, 2: 417–20. Hakluyt also gratified van Meteren's request for materials on Cavendish's circumnavigation, which the latter subsequently published ("Chronology," 307, 311). See also D. Quinn, *Last Voyage of Thomas Cavendish*, 150–6.

105 Taylor, *OW*, 2: 419.

1580; a handwritten translation was found in the Barentsz encampment on Spitzbergen during later excavations.[106]

The circulation of geographical knowledge between London and the Netherlands profited both sides. Hakluyt was able to draw information *from* the Barentsz voyages for which he consulted, and he encouraged a translation of Gerrit de Veer's narrative account, *The True and Perfect Description of Three Voyages* (London, 1609), by William Philips, who had earlier translated Linschoten's work from Dutch.[107] We have already noted the usefulness of information on the East Indies provided by Linschoten's *Itinerario*; Linschoten's information would enable both Dutch and English ships to find safe, repeatable routes to the East Indies, opening the way for a regular and highly lucrative trade. Yet even among friends and allies, the circulation of information was not simply free, neither unrestricted nor free of costs. Hakluyt imposed a price for his "secrets" – *and* asked van Meteren to keep their arrangement itself "secret, for that imports me much."[108] Violent rivalry lay a few decades in the future, when the English and Dutch East India Companies would struggle over the Indies. Already, however, Hakluyt had to concede Dutch pre-eminence in Arctic discovery, albeit "with this proviso; that our English nation ... gave them good leave to light their candle at our torch."[109]

In one case, however, Hakluyt decided that sharing information publicly and freely beyond the channel would be advantageous. The de Bry edition of Harriot's report, to which we turn now, was (and remains) probably the single most influential sixteenth-century English text on the Americas, and in the period probably the most widely read outside of England itself. The core of the book was the slim quarto Harriot had published as a promotional pamphlet in 1588; his text was reprinted by Hakluyt in *Principall Navigations* (1589), as well as in the second edition of the compilation. Hakluyt had, of course, been involved in planning and promoting the Roanoke voyages from the beginning; his activities on Ralegh's behalf can be traced throughout the translations of the 1580s. It was apparently he that persuaded de Bry, an engraver whose Protestant convictions took him from the Low Countries to Frankfurt, to combine Harriot's text with engravings based on John White's related drawings as the first volume in what would prove to be a long series devoted to

---

106 "Chronology," 1: 307–8.
107 Payne, *Guide*, 108–9.
108 Taylor, *OW*, 1: 419.
109 Hakluyt, "Preface to the Reader (1598)," sig. *4v.

relations on the New World and the Indies.[110] Uniquely in de Bry's series, the Harriot volume was published simultaneously in English and French, as well as German and Latin, expanding its potential readership. In the concluding pages of this chapter, I want to look at some of the transactions and transformations involved in making Harriot's English text available to European audiences through de Bry's volume. The scholarship on de Bry's book is extensive, sophisticated, and as complex as its multi-media object, taking in not only the four distinct editions published in Frankfurt (and Harriot's source text) but also surviving watercolours and drawings by White and Jacques Le Moyne that correspond to de Bry's engravings; while the actual copies supplied to de Bry do not survive, these visual records have formed the basis of intensive investigation, including careful comparison with de Bry's images.[111] My own interest is very particular: to consider how the process of making this edition sheds light on Hakluyt's role in circulating information abroad, on his relations with his foreign collaborators, and on the final product as a text that is no longer simply English.

An accurate accounting of the inputs to de Bry's text requires us to think on a multi-year timeline. Harriot's own work had begun before he set sail for Roanoke, when he began to take language lessons from Manteo and Wanchese, the two men sent by the Roanoke leader Wingina to accompany Arthur Barlowe's 1584 scouting expedition back to London. It was during his work with them in 1585 that Harriot devised a "universall Alphabet ... first devised upon occasion to seeke for fit letters to express the Virginian speche"; a surviving page of this linguistic project bears what appears to be Manteo's signature.[112] Manteo continued to assist the English after returning to Roanoke on the 1585 voyage that also brought Harriot and White, a collaboration that afforded them unusual access to the domestic life of coastal Carolina communities. The detailed and even intimate information that both English witnesses were able to record on Indigenous lifeways and on the names and uses of plants testifies to the value of this collaboration. Coll Thrush makes

---

110 De Bry's preface credited Hakluyt as having "first Incouraged me to publish the Worke." De Bry was in London 1585–88, working on the illustrations to an English edition of Lucas Waghenaer, *Mariner's Mirror* (London, 1588), and on engravings of Sir Philip Sidney's funeral procession (van Groesen, *Representations of the Overseas World*, 63–4, 112–13).

111 See, inter alia, the essays in Sloan, *A New World*; Sloan, *European Visions*.

112 Harriot is cited in Kupperman, "Roanoke's Achievement," 10. On Harriot's alphabet, see Salmon, "English Origins of Algonkian Linguistics." On Manteo's signature, see Thrush, *Indigenous London*, 36.

the point more directly: "Although absent from the title-page of *A brief and true report*, [Manteo and Wanchese] and others were its coauthors."[113]

Following the colonists' return in 1586, Harriot prepared the text published as *Briefe and True Report* (1588), and reprinted by Hakluyt in *Principall Navigations* (1589). This publication, intended as a preliminary and undertaken without the aid of samples and notes he had lost on the return voyage, addressed potential investors and colonists, itemized Roanoke's natural resources, and described the culture of its people with only sporadic (but important) elements of event narrative. White, for his part, is believed to have produced an album or albums of watercolours, based on earlier sketches, for Ralegh and his circle; his drawings represented plants and fauna, as well as details of Indigenous life and plans of Indigenous towns on the island.[114] Once de Bry had agreed to take on the project, and after his return to Frankfurt, Harriot wrote captions in Latin to accompany the White drawings supplied to de Bry as the basis for engravings that would appear in his edition. (In other words, the sequence was first drawings, then captions, then – once these were in de Bry's hands – engravings with associated text.)[115] At this point, several additional collaborators became involved in work on the text: Harriot's English original (the 1588 text) had to be translated into Latin, French, and German, and Harriot's Latin captions into French, German, and English. French and Latin translations of the work are attributed to the famous naturalist Carolus Clusius (Charles de l'Écluse) and the German translation to "Christian," while Hakluyt himself translated Harriot's Latin captions for the English edition.[116]

Michiel van Groesen's recent study of de Bry has widened this group of collaborators to include two additional participants who remain unnamed in de Bry's texts: Richard Garth, an English civil servant, and James Garret, a

---

113 Kupperman, "Roanoke and Its Legacy," 6; Thrush, *Indigenous London*, 35. On the embedding of Indigenous knowledge and thought in Harriot's lists of Roanoke's natural products, see also White, "Invisible Tagkanysough."

114 Rubiés, "Texts, Images and the Perception of 'Savages,'" 126.

115 On this sequence, see Rubiés, ibid., 125; Stallybrass, "Admiranda Narratio," 21.

116 Clusius's initials appear on the title page of the Latin edition, and de Bry's address to the reader attributes both the French and Latin texts to the same person. Clusius was himself a notable translator, chiefly of works on botany; he produced translations from Flemish into French, Spanish into Latin, and French into Latin, as well as working with Harriot's text. As Peter Stallybrass notes, Hakluyt's translation into English was "set in type by German compositors who clearly had some difficulty with English," introducing some changes and errors (Stallybrass, "Admiranda Narratio," 12–13).

Flemish apothecary working in London.[117] Both were involved in producing, reviewing, and circulating multiple versions of the Latin text, and their correspondence regarding the translation links them not only with each other but with Clusius, Hakluyt, and de Bry.[118] These figures are worth pursuing; following the thread of their names begins to illuminate a set of connections that were not fully in view when (for instance) the *Hakluyt Handbook* was assembled. Hakluyt references Garth only once, but tellingly, praising Garth's collections in the address "To the Reader" in PN (1589). Here, the editor's delight in seeing with his own eyes the natural and cultural objects returned to London by distant voyages recalls Richard Eden's examination of elephant tusks and other African objects: "Whereas in the course of this history often mention is made of many beastes, birds, fishes, serpents, plants, fruits, hearbes, rootes, apparell, armor, boates, and such other rare and strange curiosities, which wise men take great pleasure to reade of, but much more contentment to see: herein I my selfe to my singuler delight have been as it were ravished and beholding all the premisses gathered together with no small cost, and preserved with no litle diligence, in the excellent Cabinets of my very worshipfull and learned friends M. Richard Garthe … and M. William Cope."[119] The modern introduction to PN (1589) could say of this rich passage only that "Garth is an obscure figure," for whom Hakluyt the lawyer witnessed a bond in 1575. Subsequently, however, he has been connected with a circle of friends and correspondents that included the younger Hakluyt along with Jean

---

117 Their correspondence is described in van Groesen, *Representations of the Overseas World*. Garret is among the group of "Lime Street naturalists" studied in Harkness, *Jewel House*. Clusius visited England in 1571, 1579, and 1581, and apparently became acquainted with both Garth and Garret there; see Raven, *English Naturalists*, 168–71; Egmond, *World of Carolus Clusius*.

118 Garth and Garret's correspondence with Clusius provides details of their role in producing and circulating Latin versions of Harriot's text. To summarize the account given by van Groesen, Hakluyt sent Garth's translation to de Bry, and another copy of Garth's translation was sent to Clusius by Garret. Clusius produced a Latin translation that Garret then reviewed and returned to him (van Groesen, *Representations of the Overseas World*, 112–16). The letters also discussed plans for dedicating the various print translations; the eventual dedicatees would range from Sir Walter Ralegh, Hakluyt and Harriot's patron (English edition), to the Archduke Maximilian III (Latin edition), whom Peter Stallybrass notes would become an active patron of the Counter-Reformation (Stallybrass, "Admiranda Narratio," 11).

119 Hakluyt, "Preface to the Reader (1589)," sig. *4v. For "William," read "Walter." Cope is also mentioned in the dedication to Hakluyt's edition of Galvão, *Discoveries of the World*. On his cabinet of curiousity, see Harkness, *Jewel House*, 33.

Hotman, William Camden, Laurence Humfrey, Thomas Savile, Alberico and Scipio Gentili, and the Hungarian scholar Stephen Parmenius, Hakluyt's "bed-fellow" at Oxford.[120]

Garth had interests that extended beyond those of the humanist circle captured by Hotman's letters, however. Hakluyt's preface places Garth among the early modern collectors who assembled "cabinets of curiosity" mingling artifacts and naturalia from around the world; he appears to have been a connoisseur of plants in particular. John Gerard's *Herball* (1597) mentions both Garret and Garth as "expert in the knowledge of plants," and Gerard consulted both men's gardens; he praised his "loving freind" Garret for his knowledge of tulips, and Garth was provided with plants received from Clusius.[121] Garret, as Deborah Harkness tells the story, warned Gerard's publishers that the forthcoming *Herball* was "cobbled together" – with many errors – from earlier publications by Matthias L'Obel and Rembart Dodoens.[122]

The cultures of collecting and botanical study in which we find Garth and Garret were pre-eminently ones of circulation and correspondence across oceans, languages, and national borders. Rumold Mercator's dedication to Garth of a 1587 world map strengthens our sense of the international connections and broader geographical interests implied by his cabinet. Garret's career was even more strongly marked by transnational exchanges. A practicing apothecary, he is described by Florike Egmond as also "an important intercontinental drugs merchant," professionally involved with the "long-distance trade in drugs and spices, which ... primarily concerned plants or plant-based in ingredients"; his brother Pietr was a wealthy merchant and apothecary in Amsterdam, equally involved with drugs and spices, with additional interests in sugar refining.[123] (Accessing the trade in East Indian spices directly, of course, was one of the ultimate aims of the projects Hakluyt celebrated.) Garret's geographical interests are even better documented than those of Garth; he invested in John Chidley's 1589 voyage, intended for the Pacific, hosting Chidley in his home and supplying a medicine chest for his ships. He

---

120 D. Quinn and Skelton, "Introduction," xlvii; D. Quinn and Cheshire, *New Found Land of Stephen Parmenius*, 12, 214–15. Correspondence among the members of this group can be found in Hotman, Hotman, and van Meel, *Epistolae*.

121 Gerard, *Herball*, 117, 145, 757. On Garth and Garrett's relations with other English naturalists, see Raven, *English Naturalists*, passim.

122 Harkness, *Jewel House*, 17.

123 Egmond, *World of Carolus Clusius*, 176–8. On the cultural context for Garret's activities, see (for example) Cook, *Matters of Exchange*, chap. 1.

Figure 8.3 Part of a 1587 world map dedicated to "Domino Richardo Gartho" by Rumold Mercator, in honour of Garth's support of geography and long friendship with his late father, Gerhard.

also interviewed the Japanese and Filipino boys brought to England by Thomas Cavendish in 1588, questioning them about star anise and cacao.[124] Charles Raven describes him as a "distributing agent for the curiousities and treasures which Drake and Ralegh were bringing back from their voyages."[125]

As with the study of Anglo-Saxon, the early modern culture of collecting and studying exotic plants may not have been at the centre of Hakluyt's own

---

124 Egmond, *World of Carolus Clusius*, 191–3. In PN (1598–1600), see also Pretty, "Prosperous Voyage of M. Thomas Candish"; Magoths, "Voyage of the Delight […] 1589."
125 Raven, *English Naturalists*, 192.

activities and interests, but he was evidently connected by acquaintance and friendship to the networks that these interests created.[126] In this milieu, ideas, images, texts, and objects derived from extra-European voyages circulated among European merchants, scholars, and aristocratic collectors. Objects, indeed, might travel more freely than texts: while the informational specifics of Drake's 1577 to 1580 circumnavigation may have been closely held by the English government, plants he had collected were described by Clusius as early as 1582, and other objects deriving from his voyages were present in the collections of at least one Leiden merchant with no apparent connections in England.[127]

Overall, the international publication of the Harriot/White materials that Hakluyt urged on de Bry amplified the project he had first undertaken in *Principall Navigations* (1589): making the record of English exploration and expansion known to the world at large, and presenting a model of interaction with Indigenous peoples in the Americas that served as a positive alternative to what he described privately in "Particuler Discourse" as "the proude and bluddy governement of the Spaniarde."[128] At the same time, making these materials available to the group of collaborators we have described saw them not only relocated in a new context, as part of a common book framed by de Bry's preface, images, and paratext, but also subject to additions and modifications beyond the scope of Hakluyt or Harriot's own interventions. The last two pieces of evidence related to the de Bry edition of Harriot's report both concern objects – or at least representations of objects introduced by de Bry to the visual images included in his edition. In different ways, both will tell us

---

126 These connections animate other passing references: as we have seen, the elder Hakluyt cited Dodoens's "new herball" in his instructions to a merchant travelling to Persia, and the younger Hakluyt's letters note that Matthias L'Obel's collaborator Pierre Pena assisted him with an introduction in Paris. Clusius, in turn, had become acquainted with Drake, Ralegh, and Philip Sidney on his visits to England. All three were patrons of the younger Hakluyt at different times, and Garet's reference to "le jeusne Hacblet" in a letter to Clusius regarding the translation project may suggest that both Hakluyts were known to Clusius (letter from Garet, Jacques Jr to Clusius, Carolus, 19 January 1589, in van Gelder, *Clusius Correspondence*).

127 Clusius, *Aliquot Notae in Garciae Aromatum Historium*; Egmond, *World of Carolus Clusius*, 162. (Garth is also referenced in *Aliquot Notae*.) Egmond notes that Clusius received naturalia from the voyages of Drake and other English seamen from both Garret and the English royal apothecary Hugh Morgan (Egmond, ibid., 179, 191–2). I am grateful to Bertie Mandelblatt for alerting me to the list of Drake materials in the collection of the John Carter Brown Library, including Clusius's book.

128 Hakluyt, *PD*, 43.

something about the benefits and costs of transnational collaboration and circulation in this sole instance of Hakluyt's publication *out* of English.[129]

Peter Stallybrass has tracked a cluster of significant additions to de Bry's representation of American plants in his engravings.[130] In the foreground of plate 16, "Their sitting at meat," de Bry's engraving added to the surviving drawing by White a display of objects that includes a pot, a tobacco pipe, and some staple Algonquian foods (walnuts, fish, corn, and clams); none of the added objects are mentioned in the caption by Harriot. Another set of additions appear in plate 20, "The town of Secota." Harriot's caption to the image notes that the people of Secota grow tobacco, sow corn, and grow pumpkins. While White's drawing represents only corn, and that with no great degree of accuracy, de Bry's engraving adds accurate depictions of ripe pumpkins, tobacco plants, and sunflowers, none of which are represented in other surviving drawings by White. Text on White's drawing indicates three fields where corn is "newly sprong," "greene," and "rype," and Hakluyt's translation of Harriot's caption nods to this distinction: "They sowe their corne with a certaine distance noted by H. other wise one stalke would choke the growthe of another and the corne would not come unto his rypeurs G. For the leaves thereof are large, like unto the leaves of great reeds." Although White distinguishes the three stages of growth by labels, his drawing represented these differences only gesturally; by contrast, the engraving provides precisely detailed images for all three stages of growth. Stallybrass examines surviving copies of the plates coloured by German painters, and finds that both plate 16 and plate 20 show detailed and accurate attention to the "divers colours" of American corn as described in the text of *Briefe and True Report*: kernels are carefully painted in white, red, yellow, and blue.[131] These additions suggest access to

---

129 This discussion of the collaborative making of de Bry's Harriot does not extend to the inputs of engravers and typesetters, for instance; my working assumption is that de Bry had editorial control of substantive additions to White's drawings of the kind that will be discussed below, and that for present purposes, he can reasonably be regarded as their agent.

130 Stallybrass, "Admiranda Narratio," 21. See also van Groesen on plate 21, an image of a Kewás that does not correspond with a surviving watercolour by White: "with distinctly Floridian features, the pagan god may have been observed and designed by Jacques Le Moyne, yet the decision to attach it to Harriot's *A Briefe and True Report* was made in Frankfurt" (van Groesen, *Representations of the Overseas World*, 222).

131 Stallybrass, "Admiranda Narratio," 28–9. Ralph Lane's letters to Walsingham and the elder Hakluyt confirm that American corn was of particular interest to the apothecaries and merchants among his colonists. His letter to Hakluyt singles it out for notice as a high yielding grain ("Guinie wheate") that yields both "corne" and "very good and perfect

Figure 8.4 De Bry's engraving of the gardens surrounding a Roanoke town was more botanically detailed than John White's original watercolour.

suger"; he reported to Walsingham that "our Physycyan here hath sente an assay to our Lord Sir Walter Rawlleye" (Lane, "Master Ralph Lanes Letter to M. Richard Hakluyt Esquire, 1585," 3: 254; D. Quinn, *NAW*, 3: 291). As this letter suggests, corn and other plants from Roanoke made their way to England. John Gerard apparently grew both tobacco and sunflowers; he accurately represents ears of corn in four colors in his *Herball*, though commenting that it "is of hard and evill digestion" (Gerard, *Herball*, 76–7, 614, 285).

information beyond what was provided in the White drawings that survive, and information of impressively high quality.

It is possible that the version of White's drawings supplied to de Bry differed from the surviving sets in precisely the ways noted by Stallybrass, though Harriot's captions do not reflect these differences. De Bry could also have drawn on additional materials provided by White, Harriot, and Hakluyt for which copies do not survive; van Groesen views it as likely that de Bry had copies of additional White images that he did not use in in the book, though the surviving record includes only one botanical drawing possibly relating to North Carolina. De Bry might have decided to improve on White's drawings of American people by incorporating information from such additional images, as he did in adding human figures to White's representation of clay pots and grills used for cooking in plates 13 and 14.[132] There is a third, complementary or perhaps even alternative possibility: de Bry might have drawn on the knowledge and collections of the naturalists who were at work on his translations to inform his representation of American plants. Plants themselves travelled, and a description of Clusius's famous garden at Leiden confirms that he would later experiment with growing corn, as well as other American plants. By the late 1580s he might well have studied corn, if not already cultivated it himself.[133] Ernst van den Boogaart speculates that Clusius may have suggested the addition of sunflowers and pumpkins to plate 20.[134] However it happened, it appears that de Bry was able to improve significantly on White's surviving drawings for the very specific case of American plants and foodstuffs. The implication is very strong that information continued to flow into the work after its materials left England; at the very least, the quality of that information

---

132 Van Groesen, *Representations of the Overseas World*, 146–7. The extant watercolours by White both have an English provenance, but the copies supplied to de Bry have not survived. Complicating the picture on what may once have existed, White lost many of his materials when boarding Drake's ships to leave the colony; originals and copies of his bird, fish, and reptile drawings survive, but with one exception the few surviving plant images are of plants from the West Indies, not North Carolina. (On White's drawing of milkweed and discussions with John Gerard, and on his drawings in general, see Hulton, *America, 1585*, 21, 182. On the alterations visible in plates 13 and 14, see Sloan, "John White's Watercolours," 180.)

133 A 1610 engraving by J.W. Swanenburg shows maize growing in the garden supervised by Clusius at the University of Leiden after 1593 (Stallybrass, "Admiranda Narratio," 30). Clusius was apparently in Frankfurt while the de Bry edition was in preparation.

134 Van den Boogaart, "Serialised Virginia," 114.

reflects the interests and expertise of the naturalists who contributed to the work's translations.

The final case of divergence between the Harriot/White originals and their transnational instantiation also involves an object, but this time an English one relocated from one of White's drawings to a new engraving devised by de Bry. Virtually no images either in White's drawings or de Bry's engravings register English people's presence in the sixteenth-century mid-Atlantic; we hear Harriot's first-person voice, and also see (as it were) through English eyes that look only outward.[135] The chief exception comes in the form of artifacts. De Bry's plate 8, "A cheiff Ladye of Pomeiooc," shows a woman holding a clay pot next to a girl who holds in one hand a doll in Elizabethan dress, and in the other an armillary sphere; the first was present in the surviving White drawing, the second added in the engraving. Harriot's caption notes the popularity of dolls as toys for children at Roanoke: "their yonge daughters ... are greatlye Diligted with puppetts, and babes which wear brought oute of England." The longer text of Harriot's "Reporte," however, draws attention to the attractions of technical objects like the armillary sphere rather than the small wares often designated as "trifles" (knives, mirrors, beads), much less "puppets and babes."

Most things they saw with us, as mathematical instruments, sea compasses, the virtue of the lodestone in drawing iron, a perspective glass ... burning glasses, wildfire works, guns, books, writing and reading, spring clocks that seem to go of themselves ... were so strange unto them, and so far exceeded their capacity to comprehend ... that they thought they were rather the works of gods and men, or at the least wise they had been given and taught us of the gods. Which made many of them to have such opinion of us, as that if they knew not the truth of God and religion already, it was rather to be had from us, whom God so especially loved.[136]

Objects like the armillary sphere thus figured as tokens of identity, allowing Harriot to contrast English skills in making and using technological instruments with the imputed incapacity of Indigenous peoples in the Americas to use or understand these objects except as magic or playthings (see plate 7).

---

135 This absence contrast sharply with the presence of Frenchmen in the plates accompanying de Bry's second volume, offering accounts of the French colony in Florida (see plates 33 and 35, in Le Moyne de Morgues, *Brevis narratio*).

136 Harriot, "Briefe and True Report" (*PN*), 3: 277.

Figure 8.5 The child in de Bry's engraving holds a doll in English dress and what appears to be a small armillary sphere (see plate 7).

Yet it is the doll, not the instrument, that reappears in de Bry's sole direct representation of English presence at Roanoke, in plate 2. Under the heading "The arrival of the Englishmen in Virginia," the engraving provides an accurately drawn large-scale map of Roanoke that enlarges detail from the map on plate 1. Several figures of Indigenous people have been placed on the plate 1 map to indicate presence, like the canoes shown inside the sound and the English ships shown along the islands of the Outer Banks; these figures are borrowed from other engravings in the book. The figures on plate 2, however, do not correspond to images elsewhere in the book; rather, they appear to have been designed *for* this plate and, in closeup, to tell a story.

The arriual of the Englishemen in Virginia. II.

THe sea coasts of Virginia arre full of Ilåds, wehr by the enrrance into the mayne låd is hard to finde. For although they bee separated with diuers and sundrie large Diuision, which seeme to yeeld conuenient entrance, yet to our great perill we proued that they wear shallowe, and full of dangerous flatts, and could neuer perce opp into the mayne låd, vntill wee made trialls in many places with or small pinness. At lengthe wee fownd an entrance vppon our mens diligent serche therof. After that wee had passed opp, and sayled ther in for af short space we discouered a migthye riuer fallnige downe in to the sownde ouer against those Ilands, which neuerthelesswee could not saile opp any thinge far by Reason of the shallewnes, the mouth ther of beinge annoyed with sands driuen in with the tyde therfore saylinge further, wee came vnto a Good bigg yland, the Inhabitante therof as soone as they saw vs began to make a great an horrible crye, as people which meuer befoer had seene men apparelled like vs, and camme a way makinge out crys likewild beasts or men out of theirwyts. But beengegentlye called backe, wee offred the of our wares, as glasses, kniues, babies, and other trifles, which wee thougt they deligted in. Soe they stood still, and perceuinge our Good will and courtesie came fawninge vppon vs, and bade us welcome. Then they brougt vs to their village in the iland called, Roanoac, and vnto theirWeroans or Prince, which entertained vs with Reasonable curtesie, althoug the wear amased at the first sight of vs. Suche was our arriuall into the parte of the world, which we call Virginia, the stature of bodee of wich people, theyr attire, and maneer of lyuinge, their feasts, and banketts, I will particullerlye déclare vnto yow.

Figure 8.6 This smaller-scale map showing the arrival of English ships at Roanoke is the only representation of the English among de Bry's engravings. Although captioned by Harriot, it does not correspond to a surviving watercolour by John White.

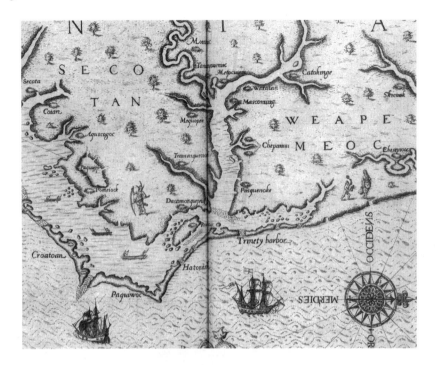

Figure 8.7 In this detail of de Bry's larger-scale map of the region, added figures of Indigenous men and women drawn from other engravings in the book include the woman and child shown in his plate 8 (figure 8.5), visible above the compass rose at bottom right.

Two gestures signal the moment of English arrival. On the island, the Indigenous man closest to the shore turns his face away from the bowmen who approach him to look back over his shoulder, towards the pinnace rowing across the sound. In the boat, we can see European hats and helmets, a flag, and a figure in the bowsprit holding an object in the hand that he stretches out towards the island. (Both the length of the arm and the tense angle at which it extends from the shoulder exaggerate this gesture.) Examining the image with the naked eye, we might think him to be holding a cross, and the blurred outline indeed appears vaguely cruciform. But a closer examination under high magnification reveals that he holds out a dressed doll, the replica in miniature of the doll seen in plate 8. Harriot's accompanying text, in Hakluyt's English translation, adds confidence to this identification by providing a narrative from which de Bry worked in crafting the image.

Figure 8.8 This enlargement of the arrival scene in de Bry's plate 2 (figure 8.6) does not reuse figures from other engravings, except for what appears (at high magnification) to be the doll represented in plate 8 (figure 8.5).

The sea coasts of Virginia are full of islands, whereby the entrance into the mainland is hard to find ... At length we found an entrance ... we came unto a good big island, the inhabitants thereof as soon as they saw us began to make a great and horrible crie, as people which never before had seen men appareled like us, and came away making outcries like wild beasts or men out of their wits. But being gently called back, *we offered them of our wares, as glasses, knives, babies [dolls], and other trifles*, which we thought they delighted in. So they stood still, and perceiving our goodwill and courtesy came fawning upon us, and bad us welcome. Then they brought us to their village in the island called, Roanoke, and unto their Weroans or Prince, which entertained us with reasonable courtesy, although they were amazed at the first sight of us. (emphasis mine)[137]

This moment may seem familiar in its resemblance to other European narratives of American encounter; Cartier, for example, recorded that in exchange for "hatchets, knives, beads, & other such like ware," the people he first encountered gave "whatsoever they had, til they had nothing but their naked bodies;

137 See figure 8.6.

for they gave us all whatsoever they had, and that was but of small value."[138] (These accounts of an all-for-little exchange can be usefully recalibrated by studies of how European trade goods were actually valued and used in Indigenous hands, and of a long-distance trade in exogenous goods and objects that adapted to European arrivals but certainly predated them.)[139] Yet in addition to these familiar misprisions of Euro-American trade, Harriot and de Bry's first contact narrative tells a story that does not exist in other accounts of arrival at Roanoke, and resists emplacement on a historical timeline.

Arthur Barlowe's report on the voyage of 1584 provides a detailed narrative of first contact at Roanoke that differs sharply from the Harriot/Hakluyt caption.

The third day we spotted one small boat rowing towards us, having them in three persons ... the third came along the shore side towards us, and ... walked up and down upon the point of the land next unto us: [we] rowed to the land, whose coming this fellow attended, never making the show of fear, or doubt. And after he had spoken of many things not understood by us, we brought him with his own good liking, aboard the ships. [He is given a shirt, a hat, wine, and food.] He departed, and went to his own boat again ... he fell a-fishing, and in less than half an hour, he had laden his boat as deep, as it could swim. [He divides the catch between the pinnace and the ship]. Which after he had (as much as he might,) requited the former benefits received, he departed out of our sight.

The next day there came unto us divers boats, and in one of them the king's brother, accompanied with 40 or 50 known, very handsome, and goodly people, and in their behavior as mannerly, and civil, as any of Europe...

The King is called Wingina, the country Wingandecoa, (and now by her Majesty, Virginia).[140]

In 1584, on this account, the English were themselves approached by a canoe with three men, who showed neither fear nor doubt, and courteous, reciprocal exchanges of gifts followed before, the next day, the colonists were met by

---

138 "First Voyage of Jaques Cartier, 1534," 3: 208.

139 See, for instance, Bradley, "Native Exchange and European Trade." On the use and value of copper cauldrons and glass beads, see Turgeon, *Patrimoines métissés*, chap. 2; Turgeon, *Une Histoire de La Nouvelle-France*, chaps. 3–4.

140 Barlowe, "Voyage of Amadas and Barlow, 1584," 3: 246.

people "as mannerly, and civil, as any of Europe."[141] If the scene on de Bry's plate 2 did not occur in 1584, it is equally inappropriate for the 1585 arrival that Harriot would have witnessed. That arrival was not a first encounter; as we have noted, Harriot had already begun to learn the language from Manteo and Wanchese, who had returned to England with Barlowe's crew the previous year. The surviving account of the settlers' arrival confirms the mutual familiarity of the colonists and their Indigenous neighbours: "The 3. [July 1585] we sent word of our arriving at Wococon, to Wingina at Roanoke."[142] Neither de Bry's engraving nor Harriot's caption correspond with these sources: even as they offer an iconic representation of the Roanoke colony's founding moment, the narratives of plate 2 can't be located in historical time.

I say "narratives" because, in effect, image and caption tell different stories. Harriot's caption, describing a moment that doesn't figure in his *Briefe and True Report*, suggests that a variety of small goods were offered as a response to the fear and retreat that greeted English arrival: "being gently called back, we offered them of our wares." De Bry's engraving condenses Harriot's narrative sequence; now, the English offer "wares" at or even before the moment of arrival. Those wares are conflated into the object held by the figure in the bows; de Bry has singled out the doll from among the trade goods described by Harriot's caption, and indeed from English artifacts depicted in other illustrations or named in *Briefe and True Report*. Jeffrey Knapp has emphasized the reliance of early English traders on "trifles," the small goods of knives, mirrors, and beads; but here is a *literal* toy.[143] In Harriot's original text of 1588, English artifacts underwrite a story about English technology as sufficiently impressive to Indigenous peoples in the Americas that it could serve as the opening wedge for English religion. His caption to plate 2 tells a different story of English gentleness and generosity, offering gifts or trade; it implies a silent critique of Spanish violence in the Americas, and imagines an American society to which European arrivals as such were novel and fearful. (The diplomatic overture described by Barlowe comports more plausibly with a history in which by 1584, Indigenous peoples had engaged with a variety of European mariners over the course of several decades.)[144] De Bry's image – an

---

141 The diplomatic nature of this encounter is stressed by Oberg, "Lost Colonists and Lost Tribes."
142 "The Second Voyage to Virginia by Sir Richard Grinvile for Sir Walter Ralegh, Anno 1585," 3: 253.
143 See, for example, Knapp, *Empire Nowhere*, 145.
144 See the documents in D. Quinn, *NAW*, 2: 550–66.

Easter egg, perhaps, for a few careful viewers – recasts *what the English had to offer* to the Roanoke bowmen he depicts: rather than the glass or the knife (or the armillary sphere), he chose the "baby." However we read this visual condensation – indeed, whether we choose to take such a tiny detail into account at all – de Bry's additions evidence the surrender of control that accompanied the spectacular publicity of this work's extra-insular dissemination, as the reciprocal of Hakluyt's triumphant assertion of dominance over the Spanish sources he translated into English and published.

This survey of translated sources on the Americas opened with Hakluyt's announcement of a plenitude that allowed for differences of method. De Bry's volume invites us to revisit another famous assertion of method, this one in the preface to *PN* (1589). Hakluyt promised to refer his sources to named authors who "both in person … performed and in writing … left the same"; we view this reliance on named, participant authors as distinctive to his methods.[145] (As we observed in chapter 7, the promise of first-person witness and reliable attribution was not always kept.) *Briefe and True Report* is a famous and important example of first-person witness by a careful observer, enhanced by an equally careful visual record. Yet behind the information signed for by the "I" (and eye) of de Bry's volume lay complex processes of mediation and translation, a traffic in ideas, texts, and material objects extended across multiple borders, languages, cultures, and disciplines. Indeed, as we have seen, Harriot's own text came to tell different stories as he prepared it for broader publication.[146] The authorial first-person voice was in some respects a choir, and Harriot's own hand assisted by multiple others, English and otherwise, whose names and interventions are not always visible.

The next chapter will turn to English voyages and English sources: the Northwest Passage searches of the 1570s and 1580s. These had their own relation to foreign sources. As Davis succeeded Frobisher in the quest for a northern route to China and the Moluccas, he drew on the Zeno relations for ideas of North Atlantic hydrography; Davis's reliance on the Zeno materials and his close association with Dee provide a clear intellectual genealogy for the idea he voices in *Worldes Hydrographical Discription*, that polar civilizations remained to be discovered to the north of the Inuit he actually encountered

---

145 Hakluyt, "Preface to the Reader (1589)," sig. *3v.

146 For an example of such reshaping, see the accounts of Guiana by Charles Leigh in Lorimer, *Discoverie of Guiana* (2006). On Hakluyt's editing of materials on India so as to "deliberately [highlight] the mingling of the scattered voices of 'strangers' and one's 'owne,'" see Das, "Hakluyt's Two Indias," 122.

(who did not look at all like the societies the Zeno described). These encounters, in Greenland and Arctic Canada, weave an ethnographic "us" and "them" through the Davis narratives. Yet, as we come to them following a chapter on Hakluyt's copious translations, the absence of other *European* presences in Davis's Arctic will be striking. In the absence of competitors or enemies, these materials also tell the story of English mariners negotiating their relations with each other. The challenging circumstances of Davis's voyages provide examples of how maritime communities were welded together, tested, broken, and reformed, both in writing and in practice – as well as of how one captain told this story.

9

Voyages in Search of a Northwest Passage: Identities at High Latitudes

IN THE CARIBBEAN AND THE PACIFIC as in the St Lawrence, whether they were mariners or writers, sixteenth-century Englishmen often had to craft a relationship with their European predecessors and competitors, as well as with Indigenous peoples and with the new landscapes and seascapes they encountered. Thus, as we have seen, many of the regional categories in volume 3 include substantial materials by and about the activities of other European nations. Yet at least for a few decades in the second half of the sixteenth century, Arctic America was a zone where the English claimed rights of discovery uncontested by other Europeans. English plans and projects did not have to reckon with the third term of a Spanish, French, Portuguese, or Dutch presence. Although the eastern Arctic was a zone of encounter with Inuit peoples in Greenland and in Baffin Island/Qikiqtaaluk, these encounters were not the central aim of the voyages. Less complex in their transnational engagements, the voyages produced an archive that is relatively straightforward in textual terms. A small number of authors, all named, all participants in the voyages, wrote a variety of texts that can be directly linked to aspects of their participation.

The materials under volume 3's heading of "Voyages undertaken for the finding of a Northwest passage, the north parts of America and ... the backside of Groenland" are (the Niccolò Zeno narrative excepted) almost exclusively English, extending towards the west the search for a northern passage whose beginnings were documented in volume 1. Hakluyt's materials begin with snippets of evidence relating to the northern voyages of John and Sebastian Cabot, Venetian and Anglo-Venetian navigators who sailed under a patent granted by Henry VII; these are followed by Humphrey Gilbert's theoretical treatise on the Northwest Passage, published in 1576 but originally composed in the 1560s. The bulk of materials under this heading, however, document two discrete sets of voyages intended to search for the passage: Martin Frobisher's voyages of 1576 to 1578, and John Davis's voyages of 1585 to 1587.[1] Like their counterparts in the northeast – the various voyages of Richard Chancellor, Stephen Borough, Arthur Pet, and Charles Jackman – these were remarkable for expertise and persistence rather than for the achievement of their optimistic goals, as ships laden with goods and instructions for trade and diplomacy with China skirted the boundaries of Arctic ice and traded opportunistically with the Inuit in furs, fish, and small metal goods. Despite evident failure to realize their original ambition, both enterprises were thoroughly documented by Hakluyt, emphasizing the prestige that the editor and his associates attributed to voyages that could be understood as part of a major national project.

The Frobisher voyages, in particular, have been the subject of a rich secondary literature that has explored an especially deep and varied archive. A lavishly funded enterprise that Deborah Harkness has characterized as "Elizabethan Big Science," they generated an extensive print and manuscript record, including multiple narratives as well as documents on their provisioning, planning, and finances. Their investors included the age's great and good, women as well as men. Returning three times to the same small island in Frobisher Bay (an inlet imagined to be the possible opening of a passage between America and Asia), the expeditions mined what was thought to be gold ore, built a house, buried provisions; these activities add to the Frobisher archive both significant material traces and an oral history.[2] The Davis voyages of the 1580s, by contrast, were less lavishly funded, and have remained less well known and less intensively studied. For these voyages, evidence is primarily textual, with Hakluyt's compilations as the principal source. Within the parameters of a study focused on *PN* (1598–1600) *as* a text, the specificity of this evidence provides an attractive opportunity as much as it does a limit.

The enterprise that resulted in Davis's three voyages began with John Dee's interest in the North (of which we have seen evidence in earlier chapters). This interest led him to purchase rights of discovery above 50 degrees north

---

[1] Hall, "First Voyage"; Settle, "Second Voyage of Frobisher, 1577"; Ellis, "Third Voyage unto Meta Incognita, 1578"; Wiars, "Report of Thomas Wiars, 1578"; Best, "True Discourse." For Davis's voyages, see below.

[2] Harkness, Jewel House, chap. 4. For a list of investors, see McDermott, *Third Voyage of Martin Frobisher*, 55–7. While the literature on Frobisher defies summary, an archaeological perspective is provided in Auger et al., "Decentring Icons of History." For a broader introduction to the scholarship, see the essays in Symons, *Meta Incognita*.

from Gilbert in 1580, and – after Gilbert's death at sea – to seek a patent in his own name with Davis and Gilbert's brother Adrian. Davis and Gilbert had known each other, in all likelihood, from their childhood in Devon; both were old associates of Dee's. Davis, like Chancellor several decades earlier, is thought to have been Dee's student in mathematics and navigation. After Dee's departure for the continent late in 1583, Davis and Adrian Gilbert pressed forward without him, and Gilbert was granted a patent for "search and discovery of the Northwest Passage to China.[3] Despite the list of associates claimed on Adrian Gilbert's patent, Davis's voyages were a far more modest affair than the voyages of the 1570s that precede in Hakluyt's volume.[4] The practical and financial failure of the Cathay Company, following on Frobisher's expansive claims to have located both a passage to Asia and an Arctic gold mine, had discredited the Northwest Passage search in the minds of many potential investors.

Davis made three voyages to Greenland, Baffin Island/Qikiqtaaluk, and Labrador. In general terms, the story goes as follows: in 1585, Davis led two ships up the west coast of Greenland, where they spent some time in the region of Nuuk in a bay to which they gave the name Gilbert Sound, then crossed the strait to make landfall near Cape Dyer, on the eastern coast of Baffin Island/Qikiqtaaluk. The expedition explored bays and inlets as they sailed south before turning east for home. In 1586, Davis took four ships, of

---

[3] "Letters Patents Graunted to M. Adrian Gilbert," 96. Comprehensive sources on Davis's life remain two nineteenth-century works by Clements and Albert Markham, respectively: Markham, *A Life*; Markham, *Voyages and Works*.

[4] The attached schedule as transcribed in Simon R. Neal's *Calendar of Patent Rolls* listed forty-five associates of Gilbert as members of the "Fellowship for the Discovery of the Northwest Passage": "Edward [de Vere], earl of Oxford, Francis [Russell], earl of Bedford, Robert [Dudley], earl of Leicester, Sir Francis Drake, Edward Osborne, lord mayor of London, Sir Lionel Duckett, William Fletewood, serjeant at law, Walter Rawley, Edward Dyer, John Hamond, D.C.L., Bernard Drake, Carew Raweley, Gawain Champernon, George Barnes, alderman of London, Richard Martyn, alderman of London, John Harte, alderman of London, Thomas Smyth, customer of London, Richard Younge, grocer, Thomas Owyn, John Chidleye, Richard Drake, Lawrence Radford, Tristram Gorge, Francis Penkvill, Philip Cole, Richard Fowell, John Hawkins, Martin Frobisher, Peter Turnor, doctor of physic, William Burroughe, Thomas Norton, Arthur Gilberte, John Davys, William Martyn, merchant, John Peryam, merchant, Lawrence Barham, draper, Walter Buggyns, merchant, Nicholas Gudrydge, merchant, William Easton, and Michael Locke, merchant." The patent along with its schedule can be found in TNA C 66/1243 mm. 32-4 (Neal, *Calendar of Patent Rolls 26 Elizabeth I (1583–1584) C 66/1237–1253*, no. 511).

which two were detached to explore to the east of Greenland. The others, under Davis, continued on to Gilbert Sound/Nuuk where they stayed for several weeks, then again coasted the western shores of Greenland northward. Landing briefly in the vicinity of modern Sisimiut to shift into the smaller of his remaining two ships, Davis again sailed west from Greenland, explored Cumberland Sound as a potential passage, and worked south along the coast of Baffin Island/Qikiqtaaluk and Labrador before turning home. Finally, in 1587, he led a pinnace and two ships to Gilbert Sound/Nuuk; the ships were detached for fishing, while Davis took the pinnace north to 72°40'N, was turned west by the ice, and again worked his way south before sailing for home. After this final voyage, the advent of the Spanish Armada in 1588 and the death of Francis Walsingham (a strong proponent of the Northwest Passage search) led to a long interruption in a project that would be resumed only in the early seventeenth century. Yet Davis remained a believer; he put the case that a search for northern passages should be renewed in a treatise that also summarized his earlier findings, *Worldes Hydrographical Discription* (London, 1595). (Hakluyt drew from the treatise a summary of the voyages.) At different times, Davis identified four places as possible passages warranting further exploration: a "free and open sea" to the north of the Davis Strait; Cumberland Sound, a large inlet on the eastern shore of Baffin Island/Qikiqtaaluk; the "furious overfall" of what would later be named the Hudson Strait, between Baffin Island/Qikiqtaaluk and Labrador; and a bay around 54° north, possibly Hamilton Inlet, Labrador.

Though Davis's voyages have generated a relatively slender bibliography of secondary literature, they were copiously documented by Hakluyt (see table 9.1).[5] Each of the three voyages is represented by at least two texts, each is documented by at least two people, and each produced at least one document in Davis's own hand. While there are many other instances of redundancy in the collection, Davis's presence among the authors of these documents makes this group of sources quite unusual. Narratives of the kind Hakluyt collected were only sporadically written by, rather than about, the captains who would later be celebrated as "explorers." As we have seen, actual logs were a product of many hands, while narrative accounts of voyages were often delegated to merchants, chaplains, or other non-mariners. Ralegh's *Discoverie of Guiana*, a first-person narrative detailing the voyage he planned

---

5 For a sampling of recent work, see Bennett, "Mecanicall Practises"; Craciun, "The Frozen Ocean"; Fuller, "Arctics of Empire"; Mahieu and Popelard, "'A People.'"

Table 9.1
Davis materials in *PN* (1598–1600), volume 3

Voyage	Narratives	Letters/reports	Ship's log	Overview
1585	Jane	[Davis MS., not included in *PN*]		Davis, from *Worldes Hydrographical Discription*
1586	Davis, Morgan	Davis		Davis, from *Worldes Hydrographical Discription*
1587	Jane	Davis	Davis	Davis, from *Worldes Hydrographical Discription*

and led in 1595, was more the exception than the rule.[6] The copiously documented "Frobisher voyages" adjoining these Davis materials in volume 3 are more typical, including no record by the hand of Frobisher himself. (Though figures like Frobisher and Francis Drake may have an occasional letter or commendatory poem over their names, these have often been suspected to have been partially or wholly composed, as well as actually written, by other hands.)[7] The second author, John Jane, was a merchant who sailed on all three of Davis's Arctic voyages and composed reports on the 1585 and 1587 voyages; he refers to Davis's main backer, the merchant William Sanderson, as "my uncle."[8] A third author, Henry Morgan, was responsible for only one document, narrating the course taken by two ships detailed for a more easterly course in 1586.

Unusual in including materials produced by their captain, materials relating to Davis's northwestern voyages in *PN* (1598–1600) are also temporally and formally diverse: they include a tabular ship's log with observations taken on board, brief letters written at the conclusion of a voyage, narratives written some time after the date of the letters, and (even more distant in time) Davis's synthetic account, extracted from *Worldes Hydrographical Discription* (1595). Thus, these materials offer exemplars from each of the different stages of processing that Ian MacLaren identifies as characteristic of travel writing, as rough logs and field notes are made into connected prose, into narrative, and

---

6 Hakluyt titled his version of this text as "Voyage of Sir Walter Ralegh."

7 On Frobisher as author, see Craciun, *Writing Arctic Disaster*, 209–14. On Drake, see Kelsey, *Sir Francis Drake*, 301–4.

8 Jane, "Third Voyage by John Davis, 1587," 3: 111.

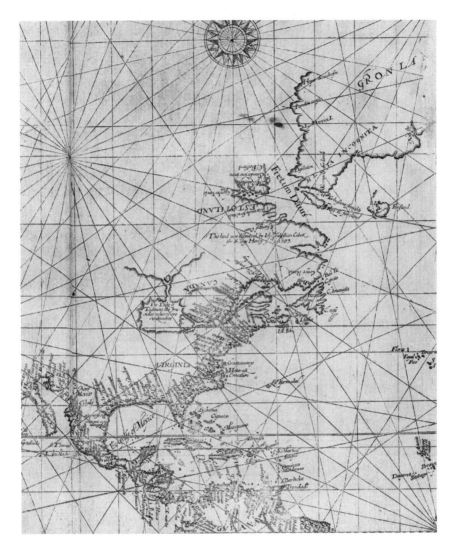

Figure 9.1 Edward Wright's 1598 world map assigns the navigator's name to "Fretum Davis."

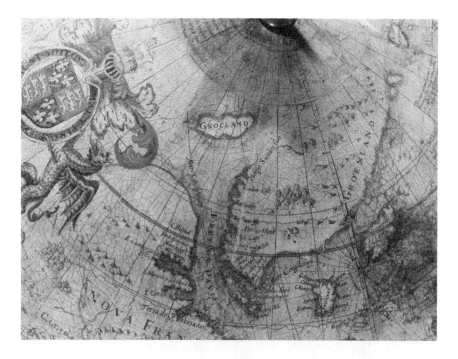

Figure 9.2 John Davis is credited with introducing Emery Molyneux, the maker of this globe, to the merchant William Sanderson, whose patronage supported both the globe and his own voyages of exploration.

then polished for various forms of publication.[9] Other surviving records are largely cartographic. Davis's voyages provided Edward Wright with coastlines and toponyms recorded on the world map accompanying some copies of *PN* (1598–1600) and (more copiously) on the various editions of the Wright-Molyneux globe.[10] Later, observations of magnetic variation attributed to Davis were marked on the revised world map Wright prepared for the second

---

9 See MacLaren, "The Evolution of Explorers"; MacLaren, "Generating Captain Cook and Paul Kane into Published Authors." More broadly, on editing the texts of explorers, see Warkentin, *Critical Issues in Editing Exploration Texts*; Craciun, *Writing Arctic Disaster*.

10 On the relationship of Wright's world map to *PN* (1598–1600), see Hind, *Engraving in England*, 1: 178–80.

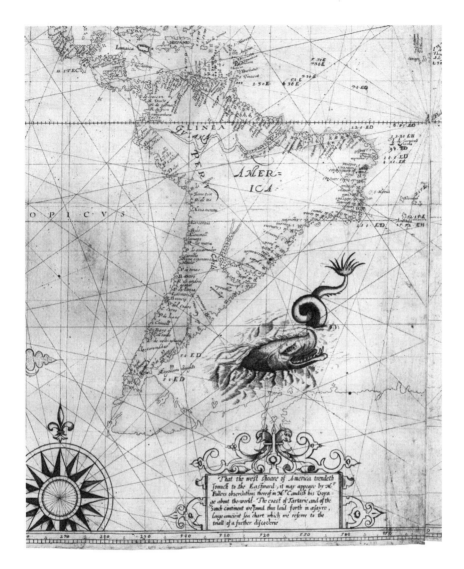

Figure 9.3 Initials on this 1610 version of Edward Wright's map represent observations of compass variation ("E" for East), and the observing navigators ("D" for John Davis). The two occurrences of "ED" off the coast of Patagonia suggest information derived from Davis's voyage into the Straits of Magellan in 1591.

edition of his *Certain Errors in Navigation* (London, 1610).[11] Hakluyt's "Davis documents" thus offer some unusual opportunities for thinking about voice and authorship in maritime travel writing. Earlier chapters have examined some practical determinants of maritime writing, as well as aspects of their style and rhetoric, within other categories of the paratext: voyages under the auspices of the Muscovy Company (in volume 1) and narratives relating to the Anglo-Spanish sea war of the 1580s (in volume 2[ii]). The documents authored by Davis and Jane will allow us to factor out some of the variables that complicate these earlier discussions: volume 1's multiple, discrete authors writing about enterprises over a wide geographical and cultural span; volume 2's uncertainties about authorship, non-participant authors, and documents that may have been redacted and shaped by multiple known or unknown hands. Here, two known authors, each represented by multiple texts, participated in a common set of voyages over a relatively short time span.

We will begin with scenes of encounter, a sample of the ethnographic materials through which Hakluyt's compilation "stressed the dissimilarities between the English and other peoples" even while describing exchanges between them.[12] The trajectories of these particular voyages, however – far from home and often far from populated land – will invite us also to examine the workings of communal identity in moments when Davis's companies were in effect encountering only themselves. From cooperation, through negotiation, through mutiny and back again, these narratives trace the evolutions of "we's" that were never static or entirely homogeneous.

"US" AND "THEM": EXCHANGES IN WESTERN GREENLAND

1 John Jane, "The First Voyage of M. John Davis ... 1585" (100–3)
2 John Davis, "The Second Voyage of M. John Davis ... 1586" (103–8)
3 John Davis, "Master Davis... His Letter to M. William Sanderson of London" (108)
4 Henry Morgan, "The Voyage and Course Which ... 2. Vessels of the Fleet of M. John Davis, Held" (109–11)

---

11 On Davis's involvement with the Molyneux-Wright globe, see Davis, *Worldes Hydrographical Discription*, sig. B6; Wallis, "First English Globe." On his patron William Sanderson, who funded Davis's voyages, the globe, and other enterprises of discovery, see McIntyre, "William Sanderson." Davis's report to Walsingham on the 1585 voyage is BL Lansdowne MS 46/21.

12 Cormack, "Good Fences," 652.

5 John Jane, "The Third Voyage Northwestward, Made by M. John Davis ... 1587" (111–14)
6 John Davis, "A Traverse-Book of M. John Davis Contayning All the Principall Notes and Observations Taken in His Third and Last Voyage to the Northwest" (115–18)
7 John Davis, "A Report of M. John Davis Concerning His Three Voyages" (119–20)

During each of his three voyages into the Arctic, Davis paused and spent several weeks in harbour somewhere in Nuup Kangerlua, a large fjord dotted with islands on the west coast of Greenland. After an initial visit to take on wood and water, he found it "convenient" as a final staging area before the push north and west, "stored with flote wood, & possessed by a people of tractable conversation."[13] In his 1586 letter to William Sanderson, Davis assigned a second name to this region, which he had initially named Gilbert Sound after his associate Adrian Gilbert: "the *Sunneshine*... hath been at *Island*, and from thence to *Groenland*, and so to *Estotiland*, from thence to *Desolation*, and to *our Marchants*, where she made trade with the people, staying in the countrey twentie days." Others used this toponym as well: Henry Morgan, purser of the *Sunneshine*, referred to a place in Gilbert Sound as "Merchants Isle," and John Jane's narrative of 1587 refers to a location either in or to the north of Gilbert Sound as "the shore of *our Marchants*, because there we met with people which traffiqued with us."[14] In the form of the place name "Merchants" – which persisted on maps at least through the seventeenth century – trade with the Thule Inuit encountered in the region of Nuuk left its mark on the textual and graphic record of the voyages alongside the names of Davis's friends and patrons.[15]

"Merchants" names Gilbert Sound as a place of commerce and exchange. These activities are relatively difficult to find in narrative accounts of the

13 Davis, "Second Voyage of John Davis, 1586," 3: 103.
14 Morgan, "Voyage and Course," 3: 110; Jane, "Third Voyage by John Davis, 1587," 112.
15 Davis's reference to the duration of the ships' stay makes the identification with Gilbert Sound in 64 degrees north unambiguous. However, maps of the period typically reproduce the coast line as depicted by Emery Molyneux's globe, with which Davis was associated, and Molyneux locates "Merchants Isle" distinctly to the north of Gilbert Sound (see figure 9.2). The textual record, which includes latitudes and distances, diverges in several places from the representation of Davis's discoveries on the globe. Strikingly, Molyneux represents *all* of Davis's "passages" except for the Davis Straits as landlocked bays or gulfs – including Hudson's Straits, the passage between Baffin Island/Qikiqtaaluk and Labrador. Subsequent maps appear to follow Molyneux rather than Davis.

voyages, but it is clear they occurred. In a letter following the voyage of 1586, Davis wrote to Sanderson that the *Sunneshine* and *Northe Starre* pinnace had acquired 500 full and 140 partial sealskins through trade in Greenland. Morgan's narrative of the course pursued by these two ships explicitly mentions acquiring only thirteen sealskins in trade on 30 August, the penultimate day of a roughly month-long residence in Gilbert Sound. The documents nonetheless make evident that other exchanges of goods, not narrated, had preceded this one on 30 August. As Morgan's account continues, one such episode of trade glimmers briefly in what then degenerates into an exchange of violence: "after we received the skins of them, the Master asked the carpenter to change one of *our boats which we had bought of them before*, and they would have taken the boat from him perforce, and when they saw they could not take it from us, they shot with their darts at us, and struck one of our men with one of their darts, and John Philp shot one of them into the breast with an arrow" (emphasis mine).[16] This dispute over an exchange of goods occasioned an escalating exchange of hostilities: buying turned into taking, and then into shooting. We have the impression of learning about the purchase of an Inuit boat only because the buyer's remorse it occasioned led to violence – in other words, trade registers in the narrative principally when it turns into something else. It is thus both hard to follow and easy to overlook.

Yet if these voyage narratives appeared disinclined to describe instances in which things like skins, kayaks, points, and ribbons changed hands without incident, they also make clear that English and Inuit people alike eyed each other's material surrounds and possessions attentively, and sometimes intrusively. Morgan provides a careful account of things "seen" or "found" by English observers at Gilbert Sound.

We ... saw their houses neare the Sea side, which were made with pieces of wood on both sides, and crossed over with poles and then covered over with earth ...

We found Foxes running upon the hilles ...

We did see dogs running upon the Islands ...

We ... found small pieces of wood upon the Islands, & some small pieces of sweete wood among the same ...

We found great Harts hornes ...

As for *the bones which we received of the Savages* I cannot tell of what beasts they be. (emphasis mine)

---

16 Morgan, "Voyage and Course," 3: 110. John Jane's account of the 1585 voyage also mentions purchase of Inuit "boats."

He also notes: "We found on shore three dead people, and two of them had their staves lying by them, and their old skinnes wrapped about them and the other had nothing lying by."[17] With the exception of the "bones which we received," which points to another non-narrated episode of trade or gift, these are not moments of bilateral exchange, in which things are offered for valuation, but unilateral moments of "finding" or discovery. Most of these observations appear to inventory Inuit cultural materials, animals, and other resources that, for Morgan, might inform on the prospects for trade and profit; Thomas Harriot's survey of "marchantable commodities" at Roanoke Island, which includes an account of the Indigenous inhabitants' material culture, might provide an analogy.[18] Animals, houses, pieces of wood, and the bodies of the dead with their grave goods appear in the narrative as available to observation, inventory, and description. Morgan was not the only Englishmen taking a good look at what the Inuit had, and had around them. In 1586, Davis and his men observed and described the contents of Inuit dwellings and kayaks but carefully "diminished nothing." In one instance, they left gifts, a gesture that on the face of it seems well meaning, if didactic: they looked, but gave instead of taking.[19] Yet the message communicated may not have been the one of disinterested English benevolence apparently intended. The first-order message communicated by a foreign object was of uninvited scrutiny and intrusion, which might happen at any time. Equally, the scrutiny of the dead and their belongings may not have appeared to Greenlanders as a neutral act.

We are on surer ground with English perceptions of how the Inuit responded to *their* material culture and how they practised giving and taking. Initially the Inuit were represented as generous, in terms that echo other European narratives of American encounter. In 1585, "they would by no meanes displease us, but would give us whatsoever we asked ... and would be satisfied with whatsoever we gave them ... They are very tractable people, void of craft or double-dealing."[20] The English were able to buy or acquire in trade kayaks; sealskin coats, gloves, and shoes; arrows; and paddles – all valuable goods, in

---

17 These are representative examples from one document, but could be duplicated from others. See, for instance, Davis's account of the second voyage: "we found the burial of these miscreants, with bags of their fish but took only one of them" (Davis, "Second Voyage of John Davis, 1586," 3: 105).
18 See Harriot, "Briefe and True Report" (*PN*), 3: 267.
19 Davis, "Second Voyage of John Davis, 1586," 3: 104, 107.
20 Jane, "First Voyage of John Davis, 1585," 3: 100. Compare, for instance, Ramusio, "First Voyage of Jaques Cartier, 1534," 3: 208.

an Arctic environment, and the product of skilled labour. Davis wrote to Walsingham following the voyage that "I have ... found an yle of very grate quantytie, not in any globe or map dyscrybed, yelding a sufficient trade of furre and lether."[21] He was almost certainly referring to the Nuuk region, "Gilbert Sound" – contacts to the west of the Davis Strait were considerably less friendly.[22]

When the *Mermayd* and *Mooneshine* returned in 1586, Inuit traders came in numbers bringing seal and deerskins, rabbits, fish, and birds. In numbers, they assisted in launching the pinnace being assembled there for the onward voyage. But soon, on 4 July, Davis found them to be "marvelous thievish, especially for iron." Although the Inuit continued to bring skins and fish, "seeing iron, they could in no wise forebear stealing." Initially, his language suggests, Davis laughed – his text characterizes these actions not as intentional, but as resulting from a failure of self-mastery, a form of helplessness in the face of desire and a failure to understand in a mature way how trade operated. Having initially formed a judgment that the Inuit were "tractable," he imagined himself as able to educate them, if he had time. But this initial response was soon displaced by hostility. When Davis returned from a brief exploration of the fjord, 7 to 9 July, although he perceived the Inuit as still "desirous in their fashion, of friendship and barter," he found his mariners deeply aggrieved because the ships' ropes and cables, as well as an anchor, had been destroyed or taken. Davis's own attitude finally "grew to hatred" when Inuit he had invited onto his own ship climbed up into the top and threw stones at the crew of the *Mooneshine*. (At this point, he describes their "nature" as "vile" or "devilish.")

In their nails, knives, and other metalwork, the English were in possession of a resource that had many uses in the Arctic. Although not produced there, iron was nonetheless familiar to Greenlanders, whether acquired in trade or by using meteoric iron or materials found at earlier Norse sites. (The site of the Norse "Western Settlement" lay further up Nuup Kangerlua, and might have been a rich source of metal goods.)[23] Davis's expedition brought

---

21 BL Landsdowne MS 46. Transcribed in Hakluyt, *PN* (1903–05), 7: xvi.

22 Jane wrote of the Greenlanders that "[t]hese people have great store of furres as we judge" ("First Voyage of John Davis, 1585," 3: 101). On Greenland as a rich source of such goods, see Seaver, *Frozen Echo*.

23 Kirsten Seaver estimates that this more northerly of the two main Norse settlements in Greenland was depopulated around the middle of the fourteenth century, earlier than the eastern settlement (*Frozen Echo*, 2). Archaeologists have documented

bracelets, knives, pins, needles, nails, and bells as gifts and trade goods.[24] Yet either the amount of goods offered or the terms on which they were offered became unacceptable, and his erstwhile trading partners began to take things that they were presumably unable to acquire in trade, with an edge of hostility expressed by cutting ropes and throwing stones. From the English perspective, things like an anchor, the cables to the ships' boats, the nails holding together a pinnace, couldn't be trade goods – they could not be replaced, and their absence could endanger not only the success of the voyage but even the survival of crews.[25] (Indeed, later on the 1586 voyage, the *Mooneshine* was reduced to a sheet anchor and a frayed cable, and in a storm off the coast of Labrador was nearly "driven on shoare among these Canibals"; two men had been slain, and two wounded in a previous encounter.)[26] The meanings and extra value of such English metalwork, and its critical importance in the context of the voyage, would not have been legible to the Inuit, but their actions came to be "read" not just as theft, but as hostility and threat.

Such dissonances in understanding underlie a longer narrative sequence in Davis's 1586 narrative that concludes with his taking an Inuit man captive.[27] Davis returned from exploring Gilbert Sound in a newly built pinnace to find that the anchor of the *Mermayd* had been stolen, and at the urging of the ship's master, he held hostage one man identified as the ringleader in order to obtain the return of the anchor. This proposed transaction seemed to be understood, and the anchor was returned. Yet once this was done, the English failed to complete the implied trade, as "the winde came faire, whereupon we weyed and set saile, and so brought the fellow with us."[28] Observing another man who followed briefly in his kayak and "made a kinde of lamentation," Davis

---

extensive use, manufacture, and circulation of iron artifacts across the western Arctic, both through contact with early Norse settlements but also through exploitation of meteoric iron in northwestern Greenland. See, inter alia, McGhee, "Contact between Native North Americans and the Medieval Norse."

24 Davis, "Second Voyage of John Davis, 1586," 3: 103; Jane, "Third Voyage by John Davis, 1587," 3: 112.

25 In 1587, again at Gilberts Sound, a partially assembled pinnace was stripped of several planks, Jane observes, for the iron in their nails. Intended for work on the discovery, the pinnace became unusable for the purpose ("Third Voyage by John Davis, 1587," 3: 112).

26 Davis, "Second Voyage of John Davis, 1586," 3: 108.

27 In 1587, John Jane simply writes that "the Master of the *Sunneshine* took of the people a very strong lusty young fellow" ("Third Voyage by John Davis, 1587," 3: 111). There is no mention of why he was taken or what became of him.

28 Davis, "Second Voyage of John Davis, 1586," 3: 104.

believed the captive to use gestures signifying that he was now dead, or would be dead. Eventually, he wrote, the captive became "reconciled," even integrated with his new community; yet Davis also appeared to recognize that for the captive and his fellows, this event was equivalent to a death. In the Atlantic world Davis inhabited, captivity was neither unusual nor solely inflicted by English crews on others; they too ran the gauntlet of captivity and its aftermaths, in the Mediterranean, in Baffin Island/Qikiqtaaluk, in West Africa, and elsewhere. But the same was not necessarily true for these Greenland captives and their communities.[29] To those left behind, Davis's failure to complete his side of the 1586 anchor-for-hostage exchange must have seemed gratuitous and faithless.

When Davis and his party returned for the third time in 1587, barter tipped quite quickly towards more violent and less consensual exchanges; the encounters of prior years must have left a residue for both parties. On arrival, Jane writes, the people "greeted us after the old manner," offering sealskins.[30] Immediately following this moment in the narrative, the Inuit stripped the ironwork from a pinnace being assembled from exploration, making it minimally usable, and soon after that shots and arrows were fired – notably, Jane speculates that the English crew were afraid to approach their counterparts. The narratives of these three voyages thus suggest that if offers of exchange or gifts were the opening gestures on both sides of this encounter, and each party possessed things that were of interest to the other, divergent understandings of how to give and how to take resulted in tension and even violence. This conflict and the forms of misunderstanding that gave rise to it are very well represented in the narratives. Yet also present, if less visible, are traces of the mutually acceptable exchanges surrounding them – the kind of thing that led to the toponym "Merchants." For instance, Davis's narrative of 1586 includes a vocabulary list that is noteworthy for both its length and its relative sophistication, including a mix of verbs, adverbs, and object nouns among the forty Greenlandic words represented. (By comparison, the word list obtained on Frobisher's 1576 voyage to Baffin Island/Qikiqtaaluk numbers only seventeen words, and all are concrete nouns, largely terms for body

---

[29] For comments on the Inuit experience of such captivities, see Seaver, "How Strange Is a Stranger?"

[30] Jane, "Third Voyage by John Davis, 1587," 3: 111.

M. *John Dauis*. 2.   Traffiques & Discoueries.   105

company should be the more vigilant to keepe their things, supposing it to be very hard in so short time to make them know their euils. They eate all their meat raw, they liue most vpon fish, they drinke salt water, and eate grasse and ice with delight: they are neuer out of the water, but liue in the nature of fishes, saue only when dead sleepe taketh them, and then vnder a warme rocke laying his boat vpon the land, hee lyeth downe to sleepe. Their weapons are all darts, but some of them haue bow and arrowes and slings. They make nets to take their fish of the sinne of a whale: they do all their things very artificially: and it should seeme that these simple therewith Islanders haue warre with those of the maine, for many of them are sore wounded, which wounds they receiued vpon the maine land, as by signes they gaue vs to vnderstand. We had among them copper oare, blacke copper, and red copper: they pronounce their language very hollow, and deepe in the throat: these words following we learned from them.

Their rude diet.
Their weapons.
Strange nets.
These Islanders warre with the people of the maine.
Copper oare.

Their language.

Kesinyoh, Eate some.	Conah, Leape.
Madlycoyte, Musicke.	Maatuke, Fish.
Aginyoh, Go fetch.	Sambah, Below.
Yliaoute, I meane no harme.	Maconmeg, Wil you haue this.
Ponameg, A boat.	Cocah, Go to him.
Paaoryck, An oare.	Aba, Fallen downe.
Asanock, A dart.	Icune, Come hither.
Sawygmeg, A knife.	Awennye, Yonder.
Vderah, A nose.	Nugo, No.
Aoh, Iron.	Tucktodo, A fogge.
Blete, An eye.	Lechiksah, A skinne.
Vnuicke, Giue it.	Maccoah, A dart.
Tuckloak, A Cagge or ellan.	Sugnacoon, A coat.
Panygmah, A needle.	Gounah, Come downe.
Aob, The Sea.	Sasobneg, A bracelet.
Mysacoah, Wash it.	Vgnake, A tongue.
Lethicksaneg, A seale skinne.	Ataneg, A seale.
Canyglow, Kisse me.	Macuah, A beart.
Vgnera, My sonne.	Pignagogah, A threed.
Acu, Shot.	Quoysah, Giue it to me.

The 7. of July being very desirous to search the habitation of this countrey, I went my selfe with our new pinnesse into the body of the land, thinking it to be a firme continent, and passing vp a very large riuer, a great flaw of winde tooke me, whereby wee were constrained to seeke succour for that night, which being had, I landed with the most part of my company, and went to the top of a high mountaine, hoping from thence to see into the countrey: but the mountaines were so many and so mighty as that my purpose preuailed not: whereupon I againe returned to my pinnesse, and willing diuers of my company to gather muscles for my supper, whereof in this place there was great store, my selfe hauing espied a very strange sight, especially to me that neuer before saw the like, which was a mighty whirlewinde taking vp the water in very great quantitie, furiously mounting it into the aire, which whirlewinde, was not for a puffe or blast, but continual, for the space of three houres, with very little intermission, which sith it was in the course that I should passe, we were constrained that night to take vp our lodging vnder the rocks.

The next morning the storme being broken vp, we went forward in our attempt, and sailed into a mighty great riuer directly into the body of the land, and in thiese, found it to be no firme land, but huge, waste, and desert Isles with mighty sounds, and inlets passing betweene Sea and Sea. Whereupon we returned towards our shippes, and landing to stoppe a floud, wee found the burial of these miscreants; we found of their fish in bagges, plaices, and caplin dried, of which wee tooke onely one bagge and departed. The ninth of this moneth we came to our ships, where wee found the people desirous in their fashion, of friendship and barter: our Mariners complained heauily against the people, and said that my lenitie and friendly vsing of them gaue them stomacke to mischiefe: for they haue stollen an anker from vs, they haue cut our cable very dangerously, they haue cut our boats from our sterne, and nowe since your departure, with slings they spare vs not with stones of halfe a pound weight: and wil you stil indure these iniuries? It is a shame to beare them, I desired them to be content, and said, I doubted not but al should be wel. The 10. of this moneth I went to the shore, the people following mee in their Canoas: I tolled them on shore, and vsed them with much courtesie, and then departed aboord, they following me, and my company. I gaue some of them bracelets, & caused seuen or eight of them to come aboord, which they did willingly,

Muscles.
A strange whirlewinde.

Great Islands.

Slings.

and

Figure 9.4 A word list gathered during John Davis's contacts with Greenlanders.

parts.)[31] There is no account of how Davis's vocabulary was obtained, during a stay of twelve days, from 29 June through 11 July; plausibly, it was at least added to by the captive Inuit man while he survived. But its existence testifies to multiple moments of voluntary give-and-take.

Many items on the Davis word list indeed name things given and taken in trade: boat, oar, dart, knife, iron, and so on. Yet as the inclusion of "Musicke" suggests, bartered objects were not the only means by which the Inuit and the English sought to find common ground. In 1585, Davis sailed with three musicians among his small crew, and the initial meetings between English mariners and their Greenlandic counterparts were punctuated with music and dancing. In 1586, the companies of the *Mooneshine* and *Mermayd*, and those of the *Sunneshine* and *Northe Starre* who arrived after them, played at leaping, wrestling, and football with the other men on shore; there is a suggestion that tackling became increasingly aggressive, but no record of injuries.[32] Davis expressed admiration both for the skill of Inuit wrestlers and for the craftsmanship he saw in Inuit goods.[33] The narratives of Frobisher's voyages to Baffin Island/Qikiqtaaluk in the previous decade provide a sharp contrast with such scenes of communal recreation. According to both accounts of the first voyage in 1576, almost immediately after Frobisher made landfall five Englishmen were taken captive by the Inuit and never recovered. Christopher Hall puts the first contact on 19 August, and the capture of the five men on 20 August.[34] George Best, who does not provide dates, adds the detail that, first, the Inuit "exchanged coats of seales, and beares skinnes and such like, with our men; and received belles, looking glasses, and other toyes, in recompense thereof againe."[35] Best connects these exchanges – involving "great curtesie, and many meetings" – with the men's capture, since they were led "contrary to their captaines direction ... more easily to trust" and thus made

---

31 Hall, "First Voyage," 3: 32. For more on the kinds of information to be gleaned from careful reading of such lists, see Wisecup, "Encounters, Objects, and Commodity Lists in Early English Travel Narratives." On Davis's list in particular, see Mahieu and Popelard, "'A People.'" Other wordlists in PN (1598–1600) can be found in Borough, "Voyage of the Aforesaide Stephen Burrough, 1557," 1: 293; Towerson, "First Voyage of William Towrson to Guinea, 1555," 2(ii): 27; Dudley, "Voyage of Sir Robert Duddeley," 3: 577–8.

32 Davis, "Second Voyage of John Davis, 1586," 3: 104; Morgan, "Voyage and Course," 3: 110.

33 Davis, ibid., 3: 104–5.

34 Hall, "First Voyage," 3: 31.

35 Best, "True Discourse," 3: 59.

themselves vulnerable in going ashore. This apparent courtesy followed by aggression led Best to characterize the Inuit as "subtile traitors" and "deceivers"; in response Frobisher took a captive of his own, and Best's account of the subsequent voyage in 1577 describes him as now "well acquainted with their subtill and cruell disposition." Although some exchanges ensued between the two groups in 1576, "neither part (as it seemed) admitted or trusted the others curtesie."[36] Wrestling appears in the narrative, but far from being a sport that men without a common language could play together, it served as a tactical alternative to shooting. One of Frobisher's men captured a fleeing hunter by using a "Cornish wrestling trick," and a record of the man's eventual autopsy revealed a serious chest injury that the examining physician attributed to the force with which he was tackled.[37]

Certainly, a wider range of gestures, objects, and meanings was exchanged at "Merchants" – tangibly and intangibly – than at Baffin Island/Qikiqtaaluk in the 1570s. Yet even though, in Greenland, both sides were disposed to trade – initially in ways that may have seemed or did seem not only satisfactory but generous – perhaps it isn't surprising that the Davis crews and the Greenland Inuit failed to find a persisting common ground. Against the landscape at least of other English encounters in Hakluyt's collection, the absence of techniques of mediation available elsewhere stands out sharply: for instance, the weights presented by African officials, or the lists of measures and prices in use in Russia or at different cities in the near East, or the bilingual intermediaries and translators that English travellers found (or more or less forcibly created) in other trading zones, such as Guinea. The difficulties of reaching a mutually satisfactory understanding seem to have grown rather than diminished over successive iterations of bargaining, to the point that more or less peaceful trade simply ceased – and with it, the kinds of provisional common ground fleetingly created or inhabited by men leaping, wrestling, and trading together at "our Merchants." Trade with Greenland was never more than ancillary to the aims of the voyages, after all.[38]

36 Ibid., 3: 63.
37 For this incident, see Best, ibid., 3: 64. The autopsy report on this man, who died a captive in London, can be found in D. Quinn, *NAW*, 4: 216–18. See also Cheshire et al., "Frobisher's Eskimos in England"; Fuller, *Remembering the Early Modern Voyage*, 52–5.
38 I am grateful to my colleague Whitney Newey for help in thinking about these exchanges from the perspective of an economist; he is of course not responsible for any misprision on my part.

Our awareness of the quiet give-and-take that was recorded only peripherally on the Davis voyages – at the macro-scale of the toponym, and the micro-scale of passing references – may highlight, reciprocally, the documents' *over*-representation of conflict. This preference contrasts with narratives in other areas of the compilation; in West Africa, for instance, comparable rhetorical opportunities were rarely exploited to the same degree by authors, even in the cases in which Anglo-African violence is clearly recorded. Yet in Greenland, as bare records were shaped into narratives, Jane, Davis and Morgan appear to have seen greater rhetorical profit in representing conflict than in commerce. Violent encounters consolidated and confirmed a sense of shared identity: recalling and reiterating that "we" were not "them." Yet to look at these documents through the lens of cross-cultural encounter presumes that in this situation of "us and them," the "us" can be treated as a unified corporate whole that is more or less homogeneous. That was not, of course, the case; in the next section, we will look more closely at the English side of things, and at the shipboard communities formed and represented in the course of Davis's voyages.

"WE" AND "I": FIRST PERSONS AT SEA

Style contributes to the presumption of unanimity. Even absent the conflictual framing of the belligerent narratives we examined in chapter 7, voyage narratives commonly employ the first-person plural: "we" set sail, arrived, were becalmed, etc. This narrative convention, as we have noted in earlier chapters, conjures the impression of a unified, corporate self. Such a convention seems natural – a ship's crew is compelled to move through space together in a way that a land army is not, and the concurrence of a crew and its officers, of ships in a common enterprise, was necessary for function, ultimately even for survival. Yet it *was* a convention of writing as well as, in practice, an aim that had to be approximated through many and ongoing efforts. In this section, the Davis materials allow us to examine in some detail the uses of this collective voice by two differently positioned authors, over the span of multiple documents. How and when did Jane and Davis make use of the collective first person rather than the individual "I," and what practical considerations were involved in organizing the collectivity of Davis's ships and crews into something that *could* be taken as a singular "we"? These are questions already asked from a somewhat different perspective. Narratives of the sea war were *predicated* on violent oppositions that almost required the cohesion of the group, practically as well as in terms of prose style. In examining them, we sought out the identities of individual writers in order to understand who was speaking, and on whose behalf. The Davis materials leave no ambiguities about authorship, and were written in very different circumstances, ones that in some respects lacked the centripetal pressures of the war. They will offer us a different kind of lens on the interplay of prose style and maritime community.

Jane's narrative of 1585 provides a simple example of what might be called the "maritime first person": an only occasionally individuated speaker who uses the first-person plural to write for, and as, the ship's company or fleet. Jane uses "we" 178 times: most frequently for collective movement ("we departed from *Dartmouth*"), but also for collective sensing and judgment: "we" discovered the land, it was the "most deformed ... that ever we saw." By contrast, he uses "I" only ten times: most frequently in connection with concrete actions and objects (I hallowed, I shook hands, I found many small trifles). Only once does Jane distinguish his own *perception* from that of his shipmates: "Our men sawe woods upon the rocks ... but I could not discerne them." Jane's presence as a distinct individual rarely interrupts the rhetorical unanimity of movement, perception, and feeling.

Jane's "we" does not have a uniform referent, however. Most frequently, it refers to the entire company of the ship or of the fleet collectively, identified with the vessel or vessels and moving as a unit: "we were run into a very deep Bay ... we cleared ourselves of the ice." At only two moments in the narrative does this collective "we" become disarticulated into different parts: the first time in hunting a polar bear, the second in managing an encounter with Greenlandic people.

> the *Captaine, the Master, and I* [we], being got up to the top of an high rocke, the people of the countrey ... made a lamentable noise, as *we* thought ... *we* hearing them, thought it had bene the howling of wolves. At last *I* hallowed againe, and they likewise cried. Then ... *we* made a great noise, partly to allure them to *us*, and partly to warne *our company* [larger "us"] of them. Whereupon *M. Bruton and the Master of his shippe*, with others of *their company*, made great haste towards us, and brought *our Musicians* with *them* from *our shippe*, purposing either by force to rescue *us* ... or with courtesie to allure the people. (emphasis mine)[39]

In this passage, members of the company – the larger "we" of the expedition – are distributed in different places, at elevations that make them more and less visible, and play different roles (from Jane's amateur "hallowing" to the

[39] Jane, "First Voyage of John Davis, 1585," 3: 100.

musicians' profession of courteous sound, and presumably the ability of others to exert "force"). Smaller groupings emerge within the whole – "the Captaine, the Master, and I," Jane as an individual, "our company," Bruton and the company of the *Mooneshine*, and finally the three musicians of the *Sunneshine*; these smaller groups cooperate to provide a layered and potentially flexible response to "them," the Greenlandic people whom the expedition was encountering for the first time. This corporate self acts cooperatively: if the whole breaks into parts, it is in order to pursue a common end.

Overall, Jane's depiction of cohesive and coordinated actions registers only the mildest of disturbances in the group's unanimity; Jane's pronoun usage shifts, however, as these small fissures open. On two occasions as the ships entered colder latitudes, Davis and the master increased the men's rations, first to raise their morale, then in response to their complaints.[40]

The *Captaine and the Master* [they] drewe out a proportion for the continuance of *our victuals* [us].

To encourage our men [them], *their allowance* was increased: the *Captain and the Master* [they] tooke order…

our men [they] fell in dislike of *their allowance* … *we* [us] made a new proportion … *we* restrained them from their butter and cheese. (emphasis mine)[41]

As Jane narrates the successive regulations of diet – *They* [officers] regulate *us* [company]. *They* [officers] regulate *them* ["our men"]. *We* [officers plus Jane] regulate *them* ["our men"] – we see his identification within the group shift. When scarcity highlights the disparities of power and need that distinguishes elements within the larger group, Jane's identification moves towards the smaller "we" of the ship's officers rather than the larger one of the ship's company.[42] (Indeed, several of the few instances of Jane's "I" occur in the phrase "the Captain, the Master, and I.") Jane's disposition to identify with Davis would become even more pronounced at moments of more serious crisis on a later voyage; in all, he accompanied Davis to sea on at

---

40 These complaints were not trivial; according to Cheryl Fury, dissatisfaction with provisions was a frequent cause for mutiny in the period (Fury, *Tides in the Affairs of Men*, 47).

41 Jane, "First Voyage of John Davis, 1585."

42 For thoughtful examinations of pronouns and role descriptors in Elizabethan travel writing, see Palmer, "All Suche Matters," 335–7; Helgerson, "I Miles Philips"; Jowitt, "Hero and the Sea." Jowitt focuses on the Cavendish-Davis voyage of 1591.

Table 9.2
Narration and identification in the Davis materials

	We	All occurrences of "I" (personal and global)	Global "I"
Jane, 1585	178	10	
Davis, 1586	92	50	32
Morgan, 1586	80	6	
Jane, 1587	126	4	
Davis, 1595	26	38	29

In this table, "global" indicates uses of the first-person singular when the first-person plural would be usual, as in the case of collective actions.

least three significant voyages of exploration, suggesting the development of a personal allegiance.

Davis's own narrative of the following year's voyage exhibits very different habits of expression than those of either Jane or Henry Morgan, a purser who composed the other 1586 narrative. Typically, Davis writes as "I"; while Jane used the collective "we" even for acts of perception and judgment, Davis used "I" not only for individuated actions, which are also described at a higher rate, but also *globally*, for actions that are clearly collective. (The usage in each narrative is mapped in table 9.2.) Davis's account of a brief scouting expedition provides a sample:

I went my selfe with our new pinnesse into the land ... a great flaw of wind tooke *me*, whereby *wee* were constrained to seeke succor ... *I* landed *with the most part of my company* and went to the top of a high mountaine ... *I* againe returned to my pinnesse ... willing *divers of my company* to gather muscles for my supper ... a mighty whirlwinde ... was in the course that *I* should passe, [so] *we* were constrained ... to take up our lodging under the rocks. (emphasis mine)[43]

In this passage, a personal "I," sometimes in association with "my company" (them), alternates both with "we" and with an "I" that clearly sweeps the collective under its wing. Looking at other documents by Davis's hand confirms these habits of expression: both the more frequent use of a personal "I," and the use of "I" as a synecdoche for "we." For instance, an entry in Davis's

---

43 Davis, "Second Voyage of John Davis, 1586," 3: 105.

transcribed log of the 1587 voyage reads, "since the 21 of this month *I* have continually coasted the shore of Gronland."[44] His use of the global or collective "I" was even more pronounced in the account Hakluyt extracted from *Worldes Hydrographical Discription*: "*I* was alone in a small barke of thirtie tonnes."[45] We can consider this preference as one that is potentially both stylistic and practical; that is, as both a rhetorical gesture of taking credit for the collective effort under his command, and an intent (or hope) that his crews and ships should work with a concerted harmony that made them effectively extensions of his own will. Yet on both the voyages of 1586 and 1587, the control suggested by Davis's synecdochic first person can be seen to waver, in both his capacities as captain and author.

In 1586, Davis sailed initially with four ships: "I departed from the port of Dartmouth for the discovery of the Northwest passage, with a ship of an hundred and twentie tunnes named the *Mermayd*, a barke of 60. tunnes named the *Sunneshine*, a barke of 35. tunnes named the *Mooneshine*, and a pinnesse of tenne tunnes named the *Northe Starre*."[46] The company sighted the southern tip of Greenland in mid-June, continued onto Gilbert Sound, where they stayed for several weeks, then again sailed north, landing near Sisimiut, Greenland in 66°30′N where the men, discouraged and cold, entreated Davis to consider their safety and his own and turn back. Davis, while empathetic, remained intent on continuing, "considering the excellencie of the businesse," and was resolved to avoid the disgrace and discredit of giving up the voyage. Considering the resources at his disposal, he elected to shift out of the 120-ton *Mermayd* into the smaller *Mooneshine* and "proceede in the action as God should direct me."[47]

When Davis wrote retrospectively about these voyages in 1595 (the text extracted by Hakluyt from *Worldes Hydrographical Discription*), he gave a different and more troubled account of how the courses of the *Mooneshine* and *Mermayd* came to diverge nine years earlier. "At this place the chiefe shipe wherupon I trusted, called the *Mermayd* of Dartmouth, found many occasions of discontentment, and being unwilling to proceede she there forsooke me. Then considering howe I had given my fayth and most constant promise to

---

44 Davis, "Traverse-Book," 117.
45 Davis, "Report of M. John Davis," 120. The third-person account of the taking of the *Madre de Deus*, discussed in chapter 6, similarly makes the captain into a synecdoche for his crew and ship ("Taking of the Madre de Dios").
46 Davis, "Second Voyage of John Davis, 1586," 3: 103.
47 Ibid., 3: 106.

my worshipfull good friend master William Sanderson, in one small barke of thirty tonnes ... *alone* without farther comfort or company I proceeded on my voyage" (emphasis mine).[48] The journal, written before 1589, had claimed a reasoned, prudential choice by Davis to proceed in his smaller ship, coloured by consideration for the men who feared to go further: "I determined," he writes, to shift into the smaller ship and send the less "convenient" one home. By 1595, the shift out of the *Mermayd* was no longer his choice, but reflected a betrayal of faith against which he was helpless and passive. This later narrative uses the language of failed romance: Davis, "alone without further ... company," is abandoned by the (singular, feminine) *Mermayd* (not by "them," the men).

As Davis continued (in this later version) to narrate the final voyage of 1587, he once again used the language of broken faith (and being "alone") to describe the failure of the two ships sent for fishing to make a promised rendezvous with the *Helen* pinnace, which he had taken north to explore.

I arived at the place of fishing and there according to my direction I left the two ships to follow that busines, taking their faithful promise not to depart untill my returne unto them ... and so in the barke I proceeded for the discoverie: but after my departure, in sixteene dayes the two shippes had finished their voyage, and so presently departed for England, *without regard of their promise:* my selfe not distrusting any such hard measure proceeded in the discoverie...

So coasting to the South I came to the place where I left the shippes to fishe, but found them not. Then being *forsaken & left* in this distresse referring my selfe to the mercifull providence of God, I shaped my course for England & unhoped for of any, God alone releeving me, I arived at Dartmouth. (emphasis mine)[49]

In 1595, there were good contextual reasons for Davis to tell the story in this strikingly affective way, and to describe himself as personally abandoned by others who had broken faith: in the intervening years, he had himself been accused of a similar and more consequential betrayal. In 1591, Davis and Jane sailed with Thomas Cavendish on what proved to be a failed attempt at circumnavigation; Davis wrote in a dedication to Charles Howard that he had been induced to accompany Cavendish by the promised opportunity "to search

---

48 Davis, "Report of M. John Davis," 3: 119.
49 Ibid., 3: 120. There is some ambiguity about place. Davis's log makes clear that the ships part company at Nuuk (Davis, "Traverse-Book," 3: 115–18). Yet the narrative account appears to suggest the parting took place off the coast of Labrador.

that North west discovery upon those backe partes of America."[50] Cavendish's small fleet became separated after an initial attempt at the Straits of Magellan, Davis and another captain taking their ships through the Straits into the Pacific and then east again while Cavendish and his two larger ships remained off the coast of Brazil. Before dying at sea, Cavendish accused Davis of breaking faith, deliberately abandoning him; he wrote to friends at home that Davis "hath been the death of me and the decay of the whole action ... [his] only treachery and running from me hath been an utter ruin of all."[51] When Davis returned from what was by any account a disastrous voyage, he was arrested, brought to London for questioning, and ultimately released. Davis alluded explicitly to these charges in a 1595 dedication to Charles Howard, complaining that "notwithstanding all this my labor to perfourme the voyage to his profite ... M. Candishe was content to account me to be the author of his overthrow, and to write with his dying hand that I ranne frome him, when that his own Shippe was returned many monethes before me."[52] In 1586, Davis wrote in the persona of an "I" whose companions were in many ways extensions of his own will, their agency and presence only intermittently acknowledged. When he retold the story in 1595, the altered circumstances of the moment licensed him to become powerless over the defections of those who *should* have been under his control, no longer the culprit but himself a victim of betrayal and abandonment both off the coast of Greenland in 1586 and in the Straits, in 1591.

Other facts about Davis's Arctic voyages were disconsonant with the picture he would later paint of an organizing self whose parts rebel and defect. Morgan's account of the 1586 voyage brings to the fore elements that are missing from Davis's parallel narrative, and these cast a different light on the story of abandonment and betrayal Davis would later tell about the voyage. Morgan writes that on 7 June, Davis directed the *Sunneshine* and *Northe Starre* to "seeke a passage Northward betweene Groenland and Island," while he sailed up Greenland's western coast.[53] After several weeks, the two ships turned back and proceeded to Gilbert Sound, where they had been directed to rendezvous with their consorts under Davis, but Davis had already taken the *Mermayd* and *Mooneshine* north. In Davis's own narrative, the *Sunneshine* and *Northe Starre* disappear from the narrative after being

---

50 Davis, *Seamans Secrets*, sig. ¶2v.
51 D. Quinn, *Last Voyage of Thomas Cavendish*, 52, 54.
52 Davis, *Seamans Secrets*, sig. ¶2v.
53 Morgan, "Voyage and Course," 3: 109.

enumerated in its opening paragraph; he mentions neither his charge to the second group of ships, nor the rendezvous they understood him to have set, one he declined to make. Only in the letter to Sanderson, written on his return, does he refer to their separate itinerary and activities, and lament the loss of the *Northe Starre* at sea with all hands. The broken rendezvous at Gilbert Sound remains unnarrated.

Given their various discrepancies and lacunae, one might say that the Davis documents as a corpus – despite their proximities of authorship, action, and time – do not quite hang together; they form a body whose parts their authors never intended to have assembled, yet which were joined together by Hakluyt.[54] Hakluyt's assembly invites us to read with a more critical eye a plain style that otherwise appears transparent and unmotivated. But workaday documents like these refer us not only to matters of rhetoric and style, but also to the practical challenges facing Elizabethan captains, who sought to make their motley fleets work together such that the collective "we" could become a reasonable approximation of reality. In these shifting identities and shifting accounts, we see authors navigating events and conditions that are external to them in even the most expansive sense of the first person: wind, seas, weather, unknown coastlines, unknown peoples. They did so as, or on behalf of, a collective whose actual heterogeneity in aims, capacities, and roles repeatedly emerged to shape the field of action. These practical experiences provide additional context for the work Davis performed, as captain and author, in shaping all that he commanded into a coordinated whole.

The list of ships that opens each of the three narratives by Jane and Davis reminds us that as captain, Davis sailed with ships of different burdens – from ten tons up through 120 – that were intended to play different roles in the collective enterprise of the voyage. Elizabethan ships were idiosyncratic in design to begin with, and the result would have been a fleet whose members had quite different sailing properties, yet needed to move together.[55] In his

---

[54] On a different but parallel case, see Nandini Das's comments on the second edition's added materials on Fitch and Newbery's journey to India in volume 2(ii): "While seemingly completing the story of the travellers' adventures, there are a number of problems with this amplification. The texts echo and contradict each other, eliminating pockets of uncertainty and gaps of knowledge" ("Hakluyt's Two Indias").

[55] On the variety of naval shipping (which might at times incorporate ships sold into the navy from the merchant marine), see Rodger, *Safeguard of the Seas*, 477–80. Only in the late 1570s did Matthew Baker, one of the queen's shipwrights, begin to build new hulls from designs on paper, enabling a design to be replicated across a class of ships (Rodger, ibid., 219).

narrative of the third voyage in 1587, Jane returned over and over to the poor qualities of the clinker-built *Helen* pinnace, a smaller ship eventually used (as had been the practice in other years) for the final westward stage of exploration. Compared to her companions the *Elizabeth* and *Sunneshine*, the *Helen* sailed "like a cart drawn with oxen," occasionally needing to be towed in light winds.[56] A mere three hours out, the *Helen* lost company because of a burst tiller, leading Davis to surmise that "the men had run away with her." Jane comments that "some of us were doubtful" this initial bad luck was the proverbial good omen since, unlike the other ships, "she was a Clincher" – in other words, built differently than the other ships. What reads as exasperation here about the failure of a smaller ship to keep up stirred real passions on some other voyages, when suspicions of intentional defection were more intense and prolonged.[57] (On Davis's voyage with Cavendish, the sequence of events that led to losing sight of Cavendish's *Galleon* began when the *Desire* "shot ahead" of the *Galleon* in a storm.) Doubts about human intentions surrounded the inevitable differences in how these motley ships performed.

A slightly different example of material disparities and their consequences would be the case of the *Mermayd* in 1586, the ship whose company Davis later accused of betraying his trust: "being unwilling to proceed, she ... forsook me." This was a case not only of dimensions but of ownership. In his earlier account, Davis writes that he chose to send the 120-ton *Mermayd* home from Greenland "by reason of her burden" (her larger size made her less "nimble" than the *Moonlight*) and "her great charge to the adventurers": while other ships appear to have been supplied by Sanderson or by Gilbert and Davis himself, the *Mermayd* was supplied by the Merchant Adventurers of Exeter. Guild records in the spring of 1587 indicate careful examination "of the accomptes of the last voiage in the Marmaide to China," including inquiry regarding a missing bale of cloth.[58] The Exeter merchants seem to have invested in expectation of more immediate and tangible returns, and according to Davis, did *not* adventure in the third and final voyage of 1587.[59] These details might invite us to speculate that the voyages' investors had different tolerances for risk to their capital, which – since some investors were also ship

---

56 Jane, "Third Voyage by John Davis, 1587," 3: 111.
57 On a voyage intended for "China and Cathay," Edward Fenton intentionally kept his smaller ships low on provisions, and considered turning his guns on consorts he suspected of plans to desert (Taylor, *Troublesome Voyage*, xliii, 209).
58 Cotton, *An Elizabethan Guild*, 84.
59 Davis, "Report of M. John Davis," 3: 120.

owners – perhaps played a role in Davis's calculations of which ship to use, or even in the disaffection of the *Mermayd*'s men. Different calculations about profit may also have played a role in the conduct of the *Sunneshine*'s company in 1587. On this voyage, a plan to detach two ships for fishing gave the enterprise some hopes of gain to offset the more distant and uncertain possibilities of finding a passage to Asia (and since Davis had set a rendezvous only a matter of weeks in the future, he seems not to have anticipated sailing *through* any passage found, much less staying to trade with the Chinese). Yet the company of the *Sunneshine* was so keen to go *directly* to the fishery, without an intermediate stop in western Greenland, that they threatened mutiny: "the Master told our Captain that he was afraid his men would shape some contrary course while he was asleep."[60] If Davis's own attention was fixed on the more distant horizon of an elusive trade route – and the preservation of his own reputation against "disgrace" – the men of the *Sunneshine* may have stood to profit more certainly from a catch in which they had shares than from supporting highly speculative discovery with which no one was likely to credit them.[61]

The need to yoke together different equipment, different objectives, and different (or changing) ideas of where to go and what to do, observed in the Davis voyages of the 1580s, was typical of many comparable enterprises in the period. (Edward Fenton's voyage of 1582, for instance, is described by one editor as "marked by ... irresolution, uncertainties, and delays" and "confusion stemming from divided intention.")[62] The examples I have pointed to highlight the ordinary difficulties of coordinating the movement of multiple ships with different sailing properties that were needed for different jobs, as well as the challenges of aligning and negotiating between the different "investment strategies" of those who contributed their goods and labour. As we have seen, managing these moving pieces so as to make a voyage cohere was not simple, and the practical challenges of doing so provided many small and large opportunities for centrifugal impulses to manifest themselves. At the level of narrative, Davis's shifting stories suggest that over time, even the same person's accounts of what happened, how ships moved and why, might come to diverge. When we take a closer look either at the "we" of writers like Jane and Morgan or the imperial "I" of an author-captain like Davis, the image of

60 Jane, "Third Voyage by John Davis, 1587," 3: 111.
61 Ibid., 3: 112. The financial arrangements for paying Davis's crews are unknown, but for the traditional practice of paying fishermen in shares, see Cell, *English Enterprise in Newfoundland 1577–1660*, 14–17.
62 Donno, *An Elizabethan in 1582*, 19.

the whole exhibits seams and tensions between its parts, even on voyages which, if their aim was speculative, were relatively harmonious in execution. Davis's language of betrayal and broken faith reminds us that there were sometimes sharper challenges. In the final section of the chapter, the Cavendish voyage of 1591 will allow us to examine a moment when the collective "we" threatened to fragment in irreparable ways.

CONSENT AND DISSENT AT HIGH LATITUDES

John Jane, "The Last Voyage of M. Thomas Candish ... Begun 1591" (842–52)

On the whole, these northern voyages appear to have been low in conflict (and in mortality). When the freezing, frightened companies of the *Mooneshine* and *Mermayd* expressed reluctance to continue on from Greenland, for instance, Davis characterized them sympathetically as having approached him "very orderly, with good discretion"; in turn, they appear to have yielded to his persuasion.[63] The men's reluctance to proceed did not constitute a challenge to his authority that had to be put down – their appeal was "orderly." Yet we might locate events like this petition in 1586, or the mutterings of the *Sunneshine*'s crew in 1587, towards one end of a spectrum of dissent: at the other end lies Henry Hudson's ship, limping back from another passage search in 1610 with empty, bloodstained cabins testifying to the crew's abandonment of the captain and his party, and to the violent death en route of the mutiny's alleged ringleaders.[64] When ships' companies fell out of agreement or when some fraction of them elected "to shape some contrary course" in defiance of the whole, the imagined communal identity of phrases like "We set sail from Dartmouth" could look very tenuous.

Voyages to high latitudes provide especially rich examples of such challenging moments, and Davis specialized in such projects, ones that lay at the edge of what Elizabethan expertise and technology could do. In the period covered by *Principal Navigations*, Davis sailed three times to the Arctic, and then to the Straits of Magellan with Cavendish. The experience of long, distant, and speculative voyages combined potentially enormous rewards with heightened

---

63 Davis, "Second Voyage of John Davis, 1586," 3: 104.
64 Hudson's voyages were documented in Purchas, *Pilgrimes*. Additional documents, including testimony to the High Court of Admiralty, can be found in D. Quinn, NAW, vols. 3–4.

risk of mortality; distance from the habits of home and the institutions that enforced them; and the fears and discomforts of sailing in bad weather, on short commons, and in dangerous and largely unknown waters. Like the large, costly, and politically loaded naval actions of the sea war, voyages in high latitudes exhibit the internal seams of the maritime "us," as well as its achievements. While the occasional conflicts that punctuated Davis's northwestern voyages were relatively low in intensity, his voyage to the Straits of Magellan with Cavendish in 1591 to 1593 was an altogether different story. The Cavendish voyage offers examples of conflict and negotiation ranging from verbal complaints, suggestions, and requests through more formal petitions and agreements to acts of open disobedience, conspiracy, and violence.

Unsuccessful voyages often left a wealth of information; legal proceedings generated records, and even informal accusations could motivate more than one participant to put forward his own version of events in writing. (Frobisher's voyages are as richly documented as they are, in part, because of the financial failure they occasioned.)[65] Cavendish's second attempt at a circumnavigation resulted in three full-length accounts, one printed by Hakluyt and two by Samuel Purchas, and important aspects of what happened remain either under debate or simply unknown: for instance, whether and how much Davis was to blame for "losing" Cavendish and his companions off the coast of present-day Argentina, or the circumstances that later led to Cavendish's unnarrated death at sea, even the circumstances in which a surviving manuscript account over Cavendish's name was produced.[66] This will not be the place to engage with those questions – or indeed, with comparisons between the three accounts – in any depth. But a brief outline of events will help us set in context a particular document in Hakluyt's collection that has considerable interest for issues of authorship, community, and identity. A testimonial signed for, and thus in the sense authored, by the companies of two ships on this voyage, it is an explicit,

---

[65] See, for instance, the financial records reproduced in McDermott, *Third Voyage of Martin Frobisher.* These include a long, unhappy screed by the enterprise's treasurer, Michael Lok.

[66] David Quinn remarks on a "discrepancy between the care, consistency, and neatness of the writing, and the physical condition into which, according to the manuscript, Cavendish himself had fallen. A man who is dying at sea would not normally produce a document so coherent in form or, indeed, in logical structure" (D. Quinn, *Last Voyage of Thomas Cavendish,* 3–6). For an account more critical of Davis, see Jowitt, "Hero and the Sea." On Purchas's use of the narratives by Cavendish and Anthony Knivet, see Fuller, "Writing the Long-Distance Voyage."

formal instance of the work involved in forming and maintaining communities at sea, as well as a case in which writing itself played an instrumental role.

Let us set the scene. When John Dee returned from the continent in 1589, he was visited at Mortlake by his old friend Richard Cavendish and Cavendish's nephew Thomas, who had distinguished himself by conducting a successful voyage of circumnavigation in 1586 to 1588 (also documented in Hakluyt's collection).[67] The younger Cavendish was evidently already planning a second attempt at sailing to the Indies by the same route, and it is likely that Dee recommended Davis to him as an expert navigator. Along with (again) Adrian Gilbert, Davis contributed a ship and some funds towards provisioning the voyage, expecting that once in the Pacific, he would be detached with one ship and a pinnace to search for the western opening of a Northwest Passage.[68] Cavendish's small fleet of five ships set sail in August 1591 on what would prove a disastrous voyage. The ships were over-manned, and disproportionately supplied with gentleman soldiers unable to sail them.[69] The victuals supplied were inadequate in quantity and quality. There was repeated disagreement over how to proceed, as accidents, weather, and time perturbed the original plan. Elements of the fleet lost contact and were unable to support each other. Sick men were abandoned on shore. Cavendish himself died somewhere off the coast of Brazil after accusing Davis of desertion, even as Davis's two ships were awaiting him in the Straits of Magellan in increasingly appalling conditions. The surviving accounts are by Jane; by Cavendish himself; and by Anthony Knivet, a young gentleman on Cavendish's ship who was among those left on shore, and survived to be captured by the Portuguese. Of these, Hakluyt printed only the first (though Purchas noted that the other two texts were present in Hakluyt's collection).[70]

---

[67] Fenton, *Diaries of John Dee*, 33–4; Pretty, "Prosperous Voyage of M. Thomas Candish."

[68] Davis, *Seamans Secrets*, sig. ¶2v. As noted in chapter 7, Davis survived the 1591 voyage to shift his field of operations to the Portuguese route first attempted by Lancaster, piloting first Dutch, and then English ships to the East Indies (see Markham, *Voyages and Works*). Although he appears to have gained the Earl of Essex as a patron, he never served again as captain; Cavendish's posthumous accusations may have dogged him.

[69] David Quinn provides an invaluable overview of the voyage in his introduction to *Last Voyage of Thomas Cavendish*. On the question of manning, see Hitchcock, "Cavendish's Last Voyage."

[70] For these and other sources found in Hakluyt's collection, see the table of contents to Purchas, *Pilgrimes*. Materials from Hakluyt's papers are also identified in Parker, "Contents and Sources of 'Pilgrimes.'"

The key sequence of events was roughly as follows. After an unsuccessful attempt on the Straits of Magellan, Cavendish's fleet sailed back towards Santos, Brazil, to rest, reprovision, and reconsider their course of action. In stormy weather, Davis's *Desire* lost sight of its companions off the coast of Patagonia, eventually finding only one other ship, the *Black Pinnace*. Davis polled the men – the *Desire* was Cavendish's ship, and its crew were largely Cavendish's followers – and on Jane's account, they agreed to look for him at Puerto Deseado. Both ships arrived damaged, low on provisions, and critically weak in stores. Davis proposed to divide his ships and men, sending the better-found *Black Pinnace* to search for Cavendish while the remainder of the company waited, with the *Desire*, where there were good supplies of water, mussels, and fish. But to the men, this plan to divide the company threatened simply to abandon most of them in a place where they would be murdered by "cannibals"; roused by two men identified by Jane as ringleaders, "the *whole company* joyned in secret … to murther *our Captaine and Master, with my selfe*, and all those which they thought were their friendes" (emphasis mine).[71] The boatswain revealed the mutiny before it could take effect, and Davis yielded to the wishes of his unhappy crews; efforts began instead to provision and refit *both* ships. Davis doubtless suspected (and if so, correctly) that Cavendish was in considerable distress, since his larger ships were not able to enter shallower harbours or approach the shore easily, but any attempt to rejoin was thus deferred; he therefore asked the men to sign a document that detailed how the ships had come to be separated, the efforts they had made to rejoin Cavendish, and the desperate situation in which they found themselves. The resulting "testimonial" was incorporated into Jane's narrative account, dated 2 June 1592, and is presented by Hakluyt as signed by Davis and the thirty-nine other men from the *Desire* and *Black Pinnace*, whose names (or in a few cases, identifying roles) are subscribed.[72] How can we think about this document, its authorship, and its agency, and what was enacted or put in place by the formal subscription of the men who signed?

While the "testimonial" has no exact counterpart in Hakluyt's collection, there are documents and practices that are in some way comparable. In one or two other instances crew are said to have presented their captains with written petitions. Only one such petition is included in the collection: following the narrative of John Chidley's failed attempt on the Straits in 1589 to 1590, Hakluyt adds "a petition made by certain of the company … unto the

[71] Jane, "Last Voyage of Thomas Candish," 3: 844.
[72] "The testimoniall of the companie of The Desire," in Jane, ibid., 3: 845–6.

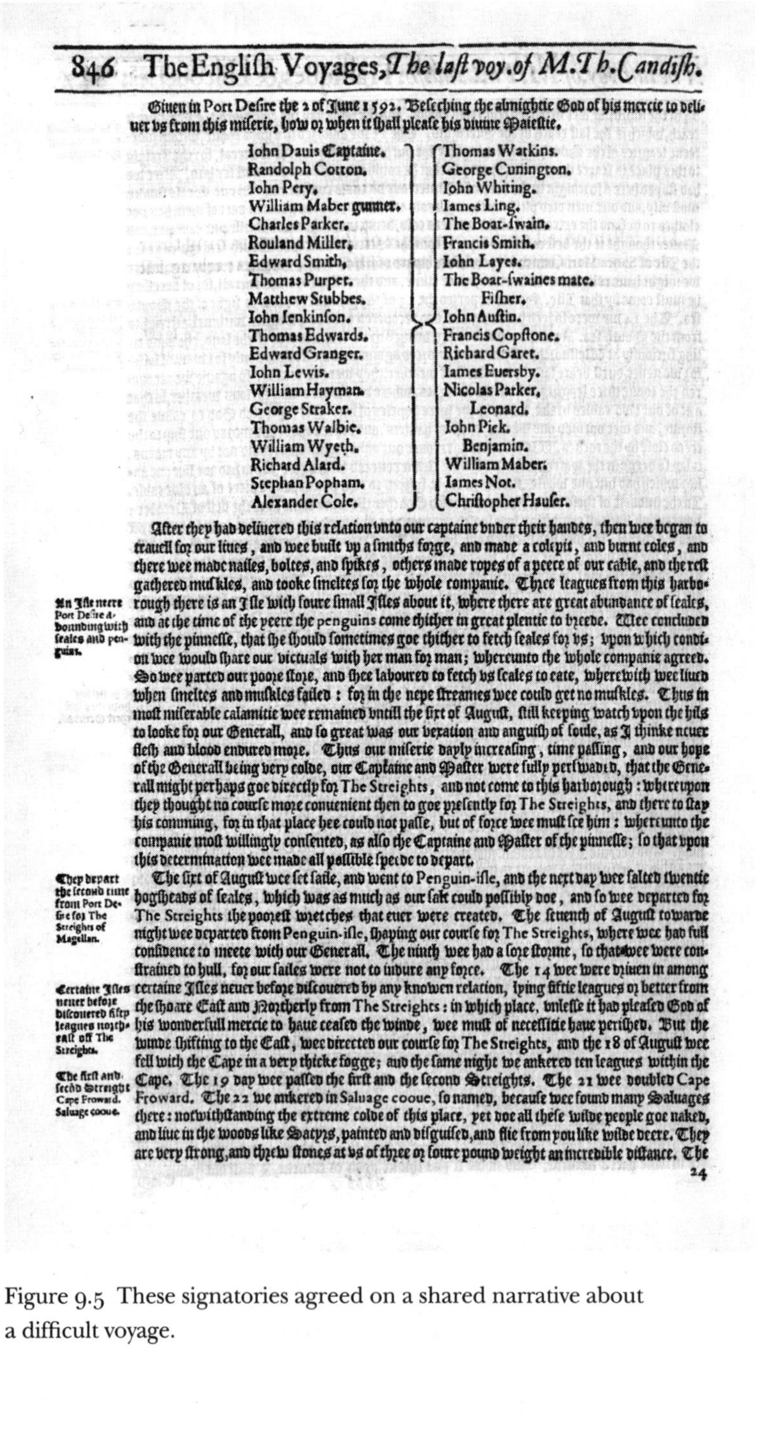

846　The English Voyages, *The last voy. of M. Th. Candish.*

Giuen in Port Defire the 2 of Iune 1592. Befeeching the almightie God of his mercie to deliuer vs from this miserie, how or when it shall please his diuine Maiestie.

John Dauis Captaine.	Thomas Watkins.
Randolph Cotton.	George Cunington.
John Pery.	John Whiting.
William Maber gunner.	Iames Ling.
Charles Parker.	The Boat-fwain.
Rouland Miller.	Francis Smith.
Edward Smith.	Iohn Layes.
Thomas Purper.	The Boar-fwaines mate.
Matthew Stubbes.	Fisher.
Iohn Ienkinfon.	Iohn Auftin.
Thomas Edwards.	Francis Copftone.
Edward Granger.	Richard Garet.
Iohn Lewis.	Iames Euersby.
William Hayman.	Nicolas Parker,
George Straker.	Leonard.
Thomas Walbie.	Iohn Pick.
William Wyeth.	Benjamin.
Richard Alard.	William Maber.
Stephan Popham.	Iames Not.
Alexander Cole.	Christopher Haufer.

After they had deliuered this relation vnto our captaine vnder their handes, then wee began to trauell for our liues, and wee built vp a smiths forge, and made a colepit, and burnt coles, and there wee made nailes, boltes, and spikes, others made ropes of a peece of our cable, and the rest gathered muskles, and tooke smeltes for the whole companie. Three leagues from this harborough there is an Isle with foure small Isles about it, where there are great abundance of seales, and at the time of the yeere the penguins come thither in great plentie to breede. Wee concluded with the pinnesse, that she should sometimes goe thither to fetch seales for vs; vpon which condition wee would share our victuals with her man for man; whereunto the whole companie agreed. So wee parted our poore store, and shee laboured to fetch vs seales to eate, wherewith wee liued when smeltes and muskles failed: for in the neye streames wee could get no muskles. Thus in most miserable calamitie wee remained vntill the first of August, still keeping watch vpon the hils to looke for our Generall, and so great was our vexation and anguish of soule, as I thinke neuer flesh and blood endured more. Thus our miserie dayly increasing, time passing, and our hope of the Generall being very colde, our Captaine and Master were fully perswaded, that the Generall might perhaps goe directly for The Streights, and not come to this harborough: whereupon they thought no course more conuenient then to goe presently for The Streights, and there to stay his comming, for in that place hee could not passe, but of force wee must see him: whereunto the companie most willingly consented, as also the Captaine and Master of the pinnesse; so that vpon this determination wee made all possible speede to depart.

An Isle neere Port Desire abounding with seales and penguins.

They depart the second time from Port Desire for The Streights of Magellan.

The first of August wee set saile, and went to Penguin-isle, and the next day wee salted twentie hogsheads of seales, which was as much as our salt could possibly doe, and so wee departed for The Streights the poorest wretches that euer were created. The seuenth of August towarde night wee departed from Penguin-isle, shaping our course for The Streights, where wee had full confidence to meete with our Generall. The ninth wee had a sore storme, so that wee were constrained to hull, for our sailes were not to indure any force. The 14 wee were driuen in among certaine Isles neuer before discouered by any knowen relation, lying fiftie leagues or better from the shoare East and Northerly from The Streights: in which place, vnlesse it had pleased God of his wonderfull mercie to haue ceased the winde, wee must of necessitie haue perished. But the winde shifting to the East, wee directed our course for The Streights, and the 18 of August wee fell with the Cape in a very thicke fogge; and the same night we ankered ten leagues within the Cape. The 19 day wee passed the first and the second Streights. The 21 wee doubled Cape Froward. The 22 we ankered in Saluage cooue, so named, because wee found many Saluages there: notwithstanding the extreme colde of this place, yet we all these wilde people goe naked, and liue in the woods like Satyrs, painted and disguised, and slie from you like wilde deere. They are very strong, and threw stones at vs of three or foure pound weight an incredible distance. The

Certaine Isles neuer before discouered fiftie leagues northeast off The Streights.

The first and second Streight Cape Froward. Saluage cooue.

24

Figure 9.5　These signatories agreed on a shared narrative about a difficult voyage.

master," complaining that the captain and the master's mate were behaving in a manner hostile to the company and its survival.[73] The presentation of the signed document as a consensus account formally adopted by the company also recalls the documentary requirements of the Muscovy Company; accounts and sometimes decisions were to be "set down in writing" and also "firmed" (signed), sometimes sealed or even notarized. Routines for keeping and reconciling inventories of goods and records of events were also prescribed in surviving instructions for Edward Fenton's East Indies voyage of 1582. The chaplain Richard Madox was appointed to keep a book recording details of deliberations by the captain's advisory council, with minutes to be dated and signed by all participants so that "every man shall knowe his doings must come to light and judgement at Retourne."[74] The Davis "testimonial" seems to aspire to the status of such an authorized record, bearing quasi-legal force, and capable of speaking authoritatively to those at home about decisions and actions on the voyage.

After conceding to the mutineers' demands, Jane writes, "the Captaine and Master ... made a motion to the companie, that they would lay downe under their handes the losing of the Generall, with the extremities wherein we then stoode; whereunto they consented, and wrote under their hands as followeth."[75] "They ... wrote": neither the testimonial nor Jane's surrounding narrative tells us in any detail how, and by whom, this particular record was composed or the process by which its contents were negotiated. With the notable exception of Jane himself, all hands appeared as signatories, even the two men named by Jane as the mutiny's ringleaders. But the production of a single narrative about what "we" did – a document that could be so signed – necessarily excluded the alternate memories and understandings these various individual people (and factions) may have held. The mutiny itself does not figure in the testimonial's narrative, even though it was directly implicated in Davis's choices of how to proceed. Including everybody meant not including everything, not

---

73 This petition, like the "testimonial" (and like Frobisher's letter addressed to his lost men in 1577), is set off from the surrounding context in PN (1598–1600) by a separate heading and a discrete entry in the table of contents. Examples of signed documents within narrative texts include Magoths, "Voyage of the Delight [...] 1589," 3: 840-2; Best, "True Discourse," 3: 70; Bigges and Cates, "Famous Expedition of Francis Drake, 1586," 543-4.

74 Document 10, "Preparatory notes by Arthur Atye," (BL MS Otho E VIII, 85v), in Taylor, *Troublesome Voyage*, 15. For the instructions, see "Instructions given to M. Edward Fenton."

75 Jane, "Last Voyage of Thomas Candish," 3: 844.

even the actual reason that Davis had not sailed from Puerto Deseado in search of Cavendish.

In agreeing together on a narrative that relieved them (and Davis) of blame in failing to rejoin Cavendish's ships, and that did *not* blame the mutineers either for conspiring the murder of their officers or delaying the search, the company once again found common ground. As they signed this memorandum of shared understanding, I would suggest that they also reinstituted a kind of social contract after the breach caused by the mutiny. At that moment, the implicit contract governing relations on shipboard had failed, while the institutions and forms of power that might have punished the men's dissent and imposed their compliance were simply too far away in space and time to operate. (Decisions both immediately before and after the testimonial are characterized as being "by a generall consent.") Yet the contents of the document secured only an understanding of the past, not (at least not explicitly) the principles on which the voyage would proceed. If we try to read the scenes that follow for an indication of how successfully the community had been in reconstituting itself, signs are ambiguous. On the one hand, Jane describes a burst of coordinated energy, with a range of disparate and necessary tasks being done by different parts of the group on behalf of the whole. "We began to travell for our lives, and wee built up a smiths forge, and made a colepit, and burnt coles, and there wee made nailes, boltes, and spikes, others made ropes of a peece of our cable, and the rest gathered muskles, and took smeltes for the whole companie." On the other hand, there is a sense of precariousness around anything recalling the fears of separation and abandonment that precipitated the mutiny: for instance, in negotiations between the companies of the *Desire* and the pinnace, "Wee concluded with the pinnace that she should sometimes goe [to an island] to fetch seals for us; upon which condition wee would share our victuals with her man for man; whereunto the whole companie agreed."[76] In the very need to negotiate these matters, the suspicion arises that ordinary commitments to mutual aid, coordination of movement, even the baseline goal of *collective* survival could no longer be taken as understood.

In the weeks that followed, the voyage proceeded through ever more desperate evolutions in and beyond the Straits, and Jane's account suggests that the technical expertise of Davis and the master provided them with new

---

76 Ibid., 3: 846. See also the later exchange between Davis and the principal mutineers (Jane, ibid., 3: 849–50).

and unarguable authority, as did their continuing good health relative to the increasingly moribund company. Here, for instance, is part of his account of the voyage east through the Straits:

our men were not able to moove ... and many of them ... were so eaten with lice, as that in their flesh did lie clusters of lice as big as peason, yea and some as big as beanes. Being in this miserie we were constrained to put into a cove for the refreshing our men. Our Master knowing the shore and every coove very perfectly, put in with the shore ... Here we continued until the twentieth of October; but not being able any longer to stay through extremitie of famine ... we put off ... but before night it blew most extreamely at Westnorthwest. The storm growing outrageous, our men could scarcely stand by their labor; and the Streights being full of turning reaches *we were constrained by discretion of the Captain and Master in their accounts to guide the ship* in the hell-darke night, when we could not see any shore, the chanell being in some places scarse three miles broad. But our captaine, as we first passed through the Straits drew *such an exquisite plat of the same, as I am assured it cannot in any sort be bettered*: which plat hee and the Master so often perused, and so carefully regarded, as that in memorie they had every turning and creeke, and in the deepe darke night without any doubting they conveyed the ship through that crooked chanell. (emphasis mine)[77]

Jane's "I" associates him firmly with Davis and the master, sharply distinct from the virtually supine crew ("our men") on whose behalf they guide the ship.[78] Not only still capable of action, they are the only ones capable of determining, using Davis's "exquisite plat" and their expert reckonings, where they were.[79]

What became of the mutineers? As conveniently happened on Hudson's last voyage as well, they did not survive. After successfully transiting the Straits into the Atlantic, the company of the *Desire* landed several times for water and provisions, and twice lost men on shore to attacks by Indigenous people

---

77 Ibid., 3: 849–50.

78 See also the particularly intimate scene on 10 October, at a moment when "we [had] yeelded ourselves to death, without further hope": "Our captain sitting in the gallery very pensive, I came and brought him some Rosa Solis to comfort him" (Jane, ibid., 3: 848). Jane then listened to Davis's prayer of confession, which he includes.

79 Compare Henry Hudson's attempt to monopolize knowledge of his ship's position by appointing the illiterate ship's carpenter, Philip Staffe, as master (Purchas, *Pilgrimes*, 3: 596–610).

and Portuguese colonists.[80] The company found itself in desperate case, low on water, with rotten barrels, missing cables and anchors, without having gained the provisions they had landed to seek; only a third of the number who had left England survived. Jane writes that at this moment, "recounting all our extremities, nothing grieved us more, then the losse of our men twise, first by the slaughter of the Canibals at Port Desire, and at this Ile of Placencia by the Indians and Portugals. And considering what they were that were lost, we found that *al those that conspired* the murthering of our captaine & master were now slain by salvages, the gunner only excepted" (emphasis mine).[81] In reporting "all" those involved with the mutiny as among those lost, Jane appears to forget that earlier in the text he had associated the mutiny with "the whole" of the crew. The community (what was left of it) had been made right by its ordeal: by tacit agreement, only the dead were to blame; and because they were dead, they could be mourned rather than condemned.

CODA

The documents examined in this chapter tell many stories, if often only in vestigial or fragmentary ways. First, there is the story of encounter. The Davis narratives de-emphasize common ground between English and Inuit actors in favour of conflict and difference, but in comparison with the textually and geographically adjacent Frobisher voyages, details allow us to glimpse a broader spectrum of cultural exchanges, peaceful as well as violent, consensual as well as forced. At the same time, and in a way that's characteristic of maritime writing, the various documents underplay distinctions between the various people engaged in the voyage – the bias of writing is toward large actions that are done together, whether these are articulated in the voice of a collective "we" or of the captain's representative, assimilating "I."

These writerly habits – emphasizing the opposition between "we" and "they," and smoothing "I's" and "he's" *into* a "we" – reflect to a degree the circumstances and requirements of both maritime writing and maritime practice. Their effect, however, is to contribute to a powerful sense of corporate identity that has left its mark on the reception of Hakluyt's book and the history it

---

80 Jane, "Last Voyage of Thomas Candish," 3: 850, 851.
81 Ibid., 3: 851.

records.[82] In his famous essay on *Principal Navigations*, James Froude wrote that "[t]he conduct and character of the English sailors ... was the free native growth of a noble virgin soil" rather than the result of training or discipline; claiming (inaccurately) that surviving orders governing conduct on shipboard were written collaboratively by officers and men, he characterizes both orders and the cultures they reflected and produced as the "spontaneous growth of common minds."[83] It does not diminish the extraordinary accomplishments of Davis, his officers, and his crews to say that Froude got it wrong. The maritime "we" was not homogeneous or stable. Common understanding and purpose could be elusive and transient, and when they existed, did not simply "grow." Concerted and ongoing efforts, both at the level of practice and of narration, were required to produce even the approximation of a corporate self.

Writing a testimonial may seem an undramatic response to threatened mutiny and murder. Jane's account of the actions Davis took to reconstitute community after the mutiny certainly lacked the ritual and sacramental elements that are so prominent in the "Famous Voyage" account of Francis Drake's voyage through the Straits of Magellan in 1578. Going ashore at the very place where Magellan had hanged his own mutineers, Drake summoned a jury to judge his second-in-command and then had him executed. Before the execution, Drake took communion with the condemned man; after it, he commanded the crew to make confession to his chaplain before all taking the sacrament together.[84] Jane's account of events in the far South years later lacks the theatricality and sanctioned violence of this performance (though this version of what had happened was further secured by the incidental death of two men identified as the mutiny's leaders). Nonetheless, the testimonial – a single narrative able to "manifest the trueth of our actions" in an agreed-upon fashion – must have required layers of negotiation, threat, and persuasion, as well as collation, redaction, and harmonizing of multiple perspectives, memories, and motives.[85] The case of the 1592 mutiny and its aftermath suggests

---

82 A more sustained look at corporate identity in PN (1598–1600) is provided in Henry Turner's stimulating essay on Hakluyt and joint-stock companies, "Toward an Analysis of the Corporate Ego."

83 Froude, "England's Forgotten Worthies," 382–3.

84 For an account of the trial drawing on manuscript sources, see Kelsey, *Sir Francis Drake*, 106–13. A surprisingly prolix account is provided in Hakluyt's brief account of the circumnavigational voyage, "Famous Voyage."

85 Jane, "Last Voyage of Thomas Candish," 3: 845.

the kind of work that went on under the surface of all of these voyages, and all of these voyage narratives, even if such work was willingly accepted or even normalized to the point of going unnoticed by those who performed it.

All of the documents discussed in this chapter negotiate between the ideal of unanimity, or at least seamless collaboration, and the practical need actively to shape or compel consent in common projects and narratives. Even relatively uneventful voyages involved decision points and branching choices that could be and were represented differently by different observers/narrators, or even by the same one at different times. Their narratives suggest the complex possibilities of representing identity as part of, or distinct from, a larger set. Because the rhetorical conventions, generic forms, and characteristic experiences visible in these documents are precisely *not* only individual but conventional and recurrent, especially in maritime contexts, I would suggest that the Davis materials can themselves be read, cautiously, as indicative of a larger class. Issues about this small set of documents thus also open into important questions about *Principal Navigations* as a whole: namely, how and how much the collection succeeded in representing and imagining unified corporate identities, from the scale of a ship's company to that of the nation; and conversely, what place and function it afforded diverse, disparate, and even foreign voices and perspectives. The role played by Hakluyt's collection in structuring and strengthening a coherent national identity has been a central claim about its importance for the last century and a half – that claim should be a provocation to investigation and analysis, not only a postulate. The case of the Davis voyages suggests that the notion of being together and being *one* was necessary for ships to move and stories to be told, and it was to a degree consensual. But it *was*, always, *made*: the process and conditions of making invite our attention and inspection.

From Davis, we will turn in the final chapter on volume 3 to Drake. Among English mariners, Drake pioneered both raids on the Caribbean and an ambitious reach into the Pacific and towards the Indies; he had many successors. In both their informational profile and the narratives of identity they encourage and transmit, the voyages of Drake provide the sharpest possible contrast with those of Davis – and a central element of what generations of readers have thought about when they thought about "Hakluyt." Drake was a central, perhaps *the* central figure in the privateering that, as we have seen, provided a language for Elizabethan literary translation. His voyages were acts of predation on Spanish settlements in the Caribbean and South America, as his circumnavigation began to break the Luso-Iberian monopoly on trade with the East Indies. Entering regions and markets the Spanish and Portuguese had sought to keep secret, Drake's voyages contributed to the compilation's supply of "stolen secrets," yielding documents translated by Hakluyt, as well as captured informants whose testimony he transcribed. His career, as it is represented in *PN* (1598–1600) and elsewhere, provides a central and celebrated example of the entanglements between literal and figurative plundering, maritime and textual aggression, that have linked Elizabethan translations to actual privateering and piracy. What is almost entirely missing from Hakluyt's representation of Drake's career, however, is Drake's own voice – or even the voice of anyone on board his own ships.

Not an author like Davis, Drake nonetheless took an active interest in shaping how he would be remembered, and these silences may in fact be an effect of that interest. The positive results of Drake's own authorial project would not emerge until after his death, but there is ample evidence in popular print and manuscript sources of what did emerge and circulate. Drake's career inspired some contemporaries to represent him as a fervently Protestant holy warrior; yet this facet of Drake's persona is – again – conspicuously missing from *PN* (1598–1600). Hakluyt's representation of Drake's career will thus invite a broader question about how, in fact, Protestant identity and conduct show up in this compilation authored by a clergyman, and return us to an overview of the compilation in conclusion.

10

Famous Voyages: The Caribbean and the Pacific

JOHN DAVIS, DESPITE THE BODY OF ARCTIC WATERS named after him, remains a relatively obscure figure. By contrast, Sir Francis Drake remains central, even unavoidable in any discussion of Elizabethan (or, indeed, English) maritime history, well beyond *Principal Navigations* – in which he also figures prominently. While PN (1589) famously provided the earliest printed account of the 1577 to 1580 circumnavigation, Drake's activities are found across all three volumes of PN (1598–1600). Ships under his command weave through the accounts of naval war distributed across volumes 1 and 2. He was in Africa with John Hawkins on the slaving voyages of the 1560s, and we also find him in the Mediterranean returning Turkish captives from the New World. Yet perhaps the most celebrated part of the record unrolls in the Caribbean and the Pacific, and thus in volume 3. Drake's incursions into the Spanish Americas began with the Hawkins voyages of the late 1560s, accompanied by threat but with the aim of trade. In the 1570s and 1580s, they continued into outright raids on circum-Caribbean towns and forts, on the Isthmus of Panama, and on Spanish and Portuguese shipping; in 1577 to 1580, Drake extended these raids past the Straits of Magellan to the coasts of present-day Chile, Ecuador, and Peru, and returned to England by completing an east-to-west voyage of circumnavigation. On his final voyage of 1595 he returned to the Caribbean with Hawkins.

The voyages of Drake in some ways stand for two larger sets of voyages and materials in volume 3, each populating a category of the paratext: privateering voyages to the West Indies ("English voyages to all the isles called Las Antillas, and to the foure greater islands ... as also along the coasts of Tierra Firma") and actual or attempted voyages through the Straits of Magellan ("voyages, some intended and some performed to the Streights of Magellan, the South sea ... the Malucos, and the Javas; and from thence ... [the whole globe of the earth being compassed] home againe into England"). In both cases, Drake was either an initiator or a very early participant in a particular type of enterprise; in both, numerous successors or imitators sought to repeat or improve on what he had done. That larger set of voyages provides some comparative context for the materials on Drake examined in this chapter, particularly in supplying a sense of what might have originally existed as part of the Drake corpus, but is no longer extant.

Drake's important career has, of course, generated a very copious literature, from the nostalgic productions of the seventeenth century to major studies by modern historians and biographers.[1] He has been viewed as a point of origin for what would become standard naval practices, from Julian Corbett's designation of Drake as the "the first great *sailing* admiral the world ever saw" to Claire Jowitt's more recent suggestion that Drake "established a precedent for the idea that one captain is sole master on a voyage" (emphasis mine).[2] The plethora of contemporary sources on Drake presents its own difficulties, exhibiting both important *lacunae* – such as the absence of primary sources on the circumnavigation – and particular documents and moments that have been circulated and recirculated with particular intensity: the West Indies voyage of 1585 to 1586, which was the subject of publication in multiple languages and media, Drake's 1587 letter to John Foxe, which circulated both in print and in numerous manuscript copies, or the iconic moments from the circumnavigation illustrated in Theodor de Bry's *America*, part 8.[3] Unusually, Drake also figured prominently in Spanish writing and archival documents.

Drake's career also presents numerous points of controversy, centred both around issues of leadership and around particular moments of empirical uncertainty such as the location of his "Nova Albion" landfall.[4] Within

---

1 Key sources for this chapter include: Kelsey, *Sir Francis Drake*; Kelsey, *Sir John Hawkins*; Keeler, *Drake's West Indian Voyage*; Andrews, *Last Voyage of Drake and Hawkins*; Wright, *Further English Voyages to Spanish America*; Wright, *English Voyages to the Spanish Main*; Nuttall, *New Light on Drake*; Vaux, *World Encompassed* (1854); Thrower, *Sir Francis Drake and the Famous Voyage*; Penzer, *World Encompassed* (1926).

2 Corbett, *Drake and the Tudor Navy*, 1: 59; Jowitt, "Hero and the Sea," para. 6. Jowitt sharpens a point also made by Parry, "Drake and the World Encompassed," 10.

3 Nuño da Silva's account of the circumnavigation and the text of *Summarie and True Discourse*, both accompanied with images, were included in de Bry's *America*, 8. On this volume, see van Groesen, *Representations of the Overseas World*, 496–7, 513.

4 Briefly, these would include his actions in support of Hawkins at San Juan de Ulua, his pursuit of a prize during the Armada battle, and his record of repeated charges against senior officers, resulting in one execution and the sole Elizabethan court-martial.

Hakluyt's compilation itself, the "Famous Voyage" account of Drake's 1577 to 1580 circumnavigation – the first to appear in print – presents unresolved questions about authorship, source, and even the date at which this unpaginated account was added to physical copies of *Principall Navigations* (1589). The modest aims of this chapter will not be to weigh in on these controversies, assess Drake's record of activity, or survey the literature. Rather, it will consider how this most celebrated of Elizabethan sea captains figures in *PN* (1598–1600) and what we can learn – about Drake and about Hakluyt's book – by following his career through the final volume of the compilation. Doing so will return us to the subject of information management, both in Hakluyt's persistent efforts to secure materials on Drake's voyages, and Drake's own interest in managing his reputation. The evidence on Drake's particular career in *PN* (1598–1600) stands out not only for the copious and distinctive character of what is present – in particular, the plurality of Spanish sources – but for the character of what is *absent*: missing are, first, any sources close to Drake himself, and second, the representations of Drake as a specifically Protestant hero that can be found in print and manuscript sources outside the compilation. Materials on Drake thus raise two kinds of editorial questions: first, what were the limits on Hakluyt's ability to record Drake's career, and second – more broadly – how do Hakluyt's materials, more generally, register religious identity? Although sources on Drake from the Spanish archives provide rich evidence about how Protestant convictions and practices manifested on at least some English ships, such evidence is surprisingly infrequent in *Principal Navigations*, not only in the case of Drake's voyages, but across the span of the compilation.

Drake began his career of distant voyages sometime in the 1560s. After several voyages to West Africa and the West Indies with John Hawkins and John Lovell, trading in enslaved West Africans with the colonists of New Spain, he initiated a different kind of project aimed simply at raids on Spanish settlements and shipping in the Caribbean; in a series of small voyages beginning around 1569, he and his crews probed the vulnerability of the Spanish West Indies and in particular the route transporting precious metals across the Isthmus of Panama. Four years after the last of these voyages, he set sail in 1577

(On the court-martial of the *White Lion*'s men, see Corbett, *Papers Relating to the Navy*; Fury, *Tides in the Affairs of Men*, chap. 2. Fury also covers the legal proceedings that led to Thomas Doughty's execution.) The nature and extent of Drake's discoveries at the southern tip of South America has also been a point of discussion; see Wallis, "Cartography of Drake's Voyage," 129–30.

on an expedition aimed at "armed commercial reconnaissance" of the American coast from Rio de la Plata through the Straits of Magellan and along the coast of modern Chile to roughly 30 degrees south, plundering Spanish settlements and shipping in the process.[5] While Drake was able to exploit the element of surprise as he worked north along the coast, rather than running the gauntlet of alerted Spanish squadrons on a return passage through the Straits, he elected to continue north, refit somewhere on the coast of North America, and then turn west; sailing across the Pacific to the East Indies, around Africa, and home in 1580, his one remaining ship completed the first European circumnavigation since the voyage of Magellan's company in 1519 to 1522, returning fabulous wealth to all who had invested in the voyage. As tensions between England and Spain grew in the middle of the 1580s, Drake was given command of a much larger expedition that raided a series of Spanish settlements around the Caribbean basin; the title of a published account numbers among those taken, "the townes of Saint Iago, Sancto Domingo, Cartagena & Saint Augustine."[6] Less materially profitable than the voyage of 1577, the voyage of 1585 to 1586 had a marked effect on morale and on perceptions of threat and capacity on both sides of the gathering conflict. After commanding ships and fleets in the naval battles and expeditions of 1587 to 1589, Drake was paired with Hawkins for what proved to be a final raid on the West Indies in 1595. The expedition did not succeed, finding the area both better defended and less wealthy than expected; first Hawkins, and then Drake succumbed to illness and died in the course of the voyage.

The second edition of *Principal Navigations* was assembled in the years immediately following this final voyage. That voyage, in turn, had succeeded years of diminished prominence following the Lisbon expedition of 1589, which had raised questions about Drake's command decisions.[7] Only a few years later, England and Spain would make peace, following the deaths of Philip II in 1598 and Elizabeth in 1603. Yet further in the future lay a posthumous rehabilitation of Drake's career in the 1620s, with the publication of important narratives on the West Indies voyages of the 1570s and on the

---

[5] On the planning and aims of the 1577 voyage, see Parry, "Drake and the World Encompassed," 3–5; Andrews, "Drake and South America."
[6] *A Summarie and True Discourse*. Andrews notes that Drake planned an expedition to Brazil with the Hawkins brothers in 1582; the expedition was diverted to the Caribbean, and is not documented in either edition of *Principal Navigations* ("Drake and South America," 57).
[7] See Wernham, *Expedition of Norris and Drake*.

voyage of circumnavigation, put forward by his nephew of the same name. In the year that the third volume of *Principal Navigations* appeared, Drake himself was gone and his reputation far from its apex. He remained, nonetheless, a central figure in Hakluyt's argument for the maritime achievements of his compatriots.

DRAKE IN *PRINCIPAL NAVIGATIONS* (1598–1600): PRESENCES AND ABSENCES

Let's begin with what Hakluyt's book had to tell us about Drake, and with an overview of his materials on Drake, both what is present (and where) and what is absent. Appendix 8 lists materials relating to Drake's voyages in the order which they occur. Appendix 9 lists the documents in chronological order, grouping them by the voyages to which they relate. While there are some surprises in Hakluyt's Drake materials, the first thing to strike a reader will be simply how many items there are, and how widely they are distributed across all three volumes of the compilation. The nineteen items I've identified as associated with Drake in appendix 8 are of many different kinds. Some narrate large or small voyages in which Drake was in joint or sole command (items 5, 6, 10, 16, 18, 20, and 22), some mention him briefly (items 2, 3, 7, and 11), some narrate actions in which he played a significant role without being in overall command (item 1), and some narrate voyages in which Drake participated without mentioning his presence (items 4, and 12–15). A noteworthy feature is the prominence of translated Spanish and Portuguese sources, largely stolen sources of the kind extolled by Hakluyt in the volume preface, and often evidence of the successes of English piracy or privateering. Such sources include information provided to either English or Spanish authorities by Drake's captives (items 8–9, 16, 23, and 25), as well as internal Spanish documents that bear on defensive preparations for Drake's arrival or return, in a zone of vulnerability that ranged from the coasts of the Iberian Peninsula to the Azores and Cape Verde islands, to the ports and coastal settlements of the Spanish Americas (items 17, and 19). Henry Savile's text (item 21) served as a rebuttal to a Spanish letter on the 1595 voyage that was found at the sack of Cádiz in 1596; the letter is also reproduced. On the other hand, while Spanish and Portuguese sources on Drake are numerous, relatively few of the listed sources present in *PN* (1598–1600) were closely based on shipboard logs or journals by English witnesses. In both the integration of Spanish sources and the paucity of first-hand *English* accounts, the Drake materials in volume 3 stand out as unusual within the compilation.

The earliest voyages in the compilation involving Drake, those led by Hawkins in 1566 to 1568, do not register his presence. There is an important story to tell that would follow the thread of these slave-trading voyages into Drake's early activities in the West Indies, considering his complex interactions there both with communities of free Africans and their descendants, and with the cargoes of "Negroes" on various ships Drake took as prizes. Within *Principal Navigations*, the means to follow this story do not exist, and its West Indian segment would be narrated in print only later, with the publication of *Sir Francis Drake Revived* (1626). While Drake figures in the belligerent materials clustered in the second half of volume 2, and the Armada narrative that concludes volume 1, those sources portrayed him as one among several commanders (for instance, the narrator of the Lisbon expedition followed the land army rather than sailing with Drake's fleet). The volume 3 voyages, by contrast, saw Drake largely in sole command of ships and squadrons, and the narratives accordingly foreground him. Sources in volume 3 focus on four voyages, all subsequent to those with Hawkins in the 1560s: the raid on Nombre de Dios in 1572, the circumnavigation of 1577 to 1580, the raid on the West Indies in 1585 to 1586, and the final West Indies voyage of 1595. Hakluyt took modest pains to represent this set of voyages as an arc, beginning with "The *first* voyage attempted and set foorth by the expert and valiant captain M. Francis Drake himself" (emphasis mine). Each voyage is represented by a narrative source; as appendix 9 shows, Hakluyt added a number of additional sources on the voyages of 1577 to 1580 and 1585 to 1586 by observers not present on Drake's ship, or present only for part of the voyage, whether these were English mariners on ships that returned by alternate routes (Cliffe), Spanish or Portuguese captives (Vas, da Silva, Morales, and Burgoignon), or Spanish administrators and civil servants (Bazan, Antonio, and Avellaneda).

Among the narrative sources, we can immediately remark one absence: no document by Drake himself is included (a point to which we will return). This feature sharply distinguishes the Drake materials from those associated with John Davis's voyages, for instance. Indeed, some key documents cannot be attributed to identified participants at all. Among the four main narratives indicated in bold in appendix 9, the first (item 15) is attributed to Lopes Vas, a Portuguese pilot captured by Robert Withrington and Christopher Lister at Rio de la Plata in 1586; this extract, which Hakluyt titled as Drake's "first voyage," was extracted from a longer manuscript relation by Lopes Vas detailing English activities in the Spanish Americas, from 1572 to 1587, and the full text appears later in the volume (item 24). Although Hakluyt provided partial narratives of the 1577 to 1580 voyage by the mariner Edward Cliffe and the Portuguese pilot Nuño da Silva, Drake's captive, narratives of the complete circumnavigation and of the West Indies voyage of 1595 (items 21 and 19) are both anonymous; the former is generally believed to have been compiled from journals by a non-participant, possibly Hakluyt, and the latter is judged by Kenneth Andrews to have been written by an unidentified "professional seaman" on board the *Phoenix*, under Bernard Drake.[8] (Henry Savile was also present on the voyage of 1595, though his text is a point-by-point rebuttal of Spanish claims rather than a narrative account.) The circumnavigation presented problems that we will return to later.

The ambiguous sourcing of voyage narratives on Drake in volume 3 is unusual among comparable materials. In the expanded selection of privateering voyages to the West Indies that Hakluyt added in PN (1598–1600), all but one of the voyages under captains *other* than Drake can be attributed to participant authors named in the text:

A relation of a memorable fight ... by 3. Ships of the honorable Sir George Carey.[9] (565–7)

A true report of a voyage undertaken for the West Indies by M. Christopher Newport ... *Written by M. John Twitt* of Harewich, Corporall in the Dragon. (567–9)

The voyage made to the bay of Mexico by M. William King Captaine.[10] (570–1)

A brief note of a voyage to the East Indies ... *Written by Henry May*, who in his returne homeward by the West Indies suffered shipwracke upon the isle of Bermuda. (571–4)

A voyage of the honourable Gentleman M. Robert Duddeley ... *Written [by Dudley] at the request of M. Richard Hakluyt.* (574–7)

---

8 Andrews, *Last Voyage of Drake and Hawkins*, 35, 80.

9 This text narrates the actions of the *Content*, one of the smaller of the flotilla's five named ships; its crew of twenty-three are named in a list that closes the narrative. Andrews suggests that its author is William King, master of the *Content* and apparent author of "The voyage made to the bay of Mexico," third on this list (Andrews, *English Privateering Voyages*, 107n2).

10 Probably by King; the narrative concludes, "I set saile."

The victorious voyage of Captain Amias Preston ... *Written by Robert Davie* one of the company. (578–83) (emphasis mine)[11]

By contrast, the only complete narrative of a Drake voyage that can be attributed to a named *English* participant is "Famous Expedition," an account of the West Indies voyage of 1585 to 1586; yet even there, authorship is problematic. Hakluyt made use of a previously printed book on the 1585 to 1586 voyage, *Summarie and True Discourse* (London, 1589). This work appears to have formed part of a significant publication project; as with Thomas Harriot's *Report* a few years later, illustrated editions quickly appeared on the continent. Indeed, two Leiden editions in French and Latin actually *preceded* the English edition of *Summarie and True Discourse,* delayed by preparations against the Armada, and two further editions in Latin (Nuremberg) and German (Cologne) would appear in 1589, while the text was reprinted again by de Bry in *Americae pars VIII* (Frankfurt, 1599).[12] These various editions of *Summarie and True Discourse* often included a series of town maps by Baptista Boazio, representing the various towns Drake's company had successfully attacked; a larger narrative map and chronology printed together as a broadside have also been attributed to Boazio (see plate 8).[13]

Both Boazio's images and the text Hakluyt reproduced clearly had their origins in eyewitness observation. But (unlike the 1588 text of Harriot's *Report*), here the original text itself had multiple authors. Hakluyt's headnote, "Published by M. Thomas Cates," referred to the 1589 text's dedication to the Earl of Essex, which was signed by Cates. Cates wrote that he had:

by chaunce recovered of late into my handes (after I had once lost the same) a copie of the Discourse of our late West Indian voyage, which was begun by Captaine Bigges, who ended his life in the said voyage after our departure from Cartagena, the same being afterwardes finished (as I thinke) by his Lieutenant Maister Croftes, or some other, I knowe not well who. Nowe finding therein a most true report ... I have presumed to recommend the publishing thereof ...

---

11 Titles given are those used in the text, rather than in the Catalogue of Voyages.

12 On the delay, see the prefatory material to *A Summarie and True Discourse.* For editions, see Alden and Landis, *European Americana,* vol. 1.

13 Boazio's maps include drawings of marine and land fauna by John White, who was among the Roanoke colonists Drake's ships brought back with them to England in 1586 (Keeler, *Drake's West Indian Voyage,* 316, 319).

my selfe having bene a member in the sayd actions, and was Lieutenant of Maister Carleils owne companie ... I can well assure the truth of this report. (emphasis mine)[14]

Walter Bigges, the one author of whose name Cates was certain, had indeed died before the text was completed. He numbered among the "land-Captaines" of a voyage that embarked a substantial number of soldiers, and his name appears in the text on a list of "men of name that died and were slain in this voyage, which I can presently call to remembrance"; he died after the fleet departed from Cartagena, probably among numerous victims of fever.[15] The other author or authors of his "Discourse" remain unidentified.

Summarie and True Discourse, Hakluyt's source, was thus from the outset a text by multiple hands. Its editor, Mary Frear Keeler, concludes from the surviving manuscript variant that the printed text (in all its English and continental versions) resulted from "considerable editing" of its original.[16] Numerous other accounts of Drake's West Indies voyage survive in manuscript (and appear in Keeler's volume for the Hakluyt Society): these include a journal kept by Christopher Carleill and then by his secretary, Edward Powell, aboard the *Tiger*, a London ship; a journal kept aboard the vice-admiral, Frobisher's *Primrose*; a journal kept aboard the rear-admiral, Francis Knollys's *Leicester*; and a "newsletter" associated with the *Tiger* journal in the manuscript record, apparently written in a hand resembling one of those found both in the journal and the manuscript of *Summarie and True Discourse*. Keeler suggests that Carleill, the chief military officer on the voyage, assembled documents relating to the voyage for Sir Francis Walsingham (his father-in-law). (Boazio, the mapmaker, appears to have been a follower of Carleill.) The conjecture that materials were assembled by Carleill for Walsingham (and presumably disseminated on the continent at Walsingham's direction) seems plausible and explanatory, although the reason for preferring the Bigges journal over Carleill's own as the basis for a narrative is uncertain. Behind the single document that Hakluyt reprinted were thus numerous hands, and numerous other *un*used documents that remained in manuscript.

---

14 *A Summarie and True Discourse*, n.p.
15 Bigges and Cates, "Famous Expedition of Francis Drake, 1586," 3: 534, 548; *Summarie and True Discourse*; Keeler, *Drake's West Indian Voyage*, 290.
16 Keeler, *Drake's West Indian Voyage*, 7. Details that follow rely on Keeler.

Notably absent from this picture are any materials from Drake's flagship, the *Elizabeth Bonaventure*, captained by Thomas Fenner.[17] Drake's secretary died during the voyage, leading to some difficulty in preparing its financial accounts, but Drake had additional clerical assistance from the chaplain, Philip Nichols, who would follow him to Cádiz in 1587.[18] Nichols was the "penner and deviser" of loyalty oaths administered to the members of the expedition at the Cape Verde islands, and apparent author of what would later appear as *Sir Francis Drake Revived* (London, 1626).[19] Indeed, the author of a newsletter addressed to Walsingham excused his brevity on the grounds that "our generall Sir Francis Drake promysed a whole and perfect booke of all such th[ings that] have happened throughout our whole voyadge," referring him to the "promysed booke" for fuller details.[20] Presumably this record was indeed created, but never circulated, and it has not survived – either among Hakluyt's materials or elsewhere. In its place, the narrative "by" Bigges received international dissemination.

Hakluyt's most recent biographer, Peter Mancall, views the West Indies voyage of 1585 to 1586 as "a decisive moment for Hakluyt," showing that "the Spanish could not in fact defend the extensive territories they claimed"; the possibility of safely undertaking English initiatives in North America thus gained appeal.[21] Still, Hakluyt did not print materials on the voyage in the first edition of 1589, when it would have been fresh in memory and clearly within the original parameters of the compilation. We might explain this absence by the separate publication of *Summarie and True Discourse* in London that year, though other voyage narratives – such as Harriot's *Briefe and True Report* or Wright's narrative of a voyage to the Azores – did appear in

---

17 Fenner was the author of dispatches from Cádiz, included along with Drake's in Hakluyt's "Voyage of Sir Francis Drake to Cadiz, 1587" (see chapter 7). He also served as Drake's vice-admiral on the Lisbon voyage of 1589. Kelsey suggests Fenner may have done some clerical work for Drake (Kelsey, *Sir Francis Drake*, 302). On Fenner's earlier trade in Africa, see Andrews, "Thomas Fenner and the Guinea Trade, 1564."

18 Keeler, *Drake's West Indian Voyage*, 61, 139–42, 145. The clerical role of chaplains on Fenton's voyage is discussed below; the Earl of Cumberland's chaplain John Layfield notes of a 1598 voyage to the Caribbean that "it suited his honor to use me in the dispatch of all things, which were to be done by warrant or direction under his hand" (Layfield, "A Large Relation of the Port Ricco Voiage [1596]," in Purchas, *Pilgrimes*, 4: 1,169).

19 Keeler, *Drake's West Indian Voyage*, 139–42.

20 Ibid., 106.

21 Mancall, *Hakluyt's Promise*, 169.

Hakluyt's collections very close to the time of their independent publication.[22] When Hakluyt did print a narrative of the West Indies voyage in PN (1598–1600), he used the 1596 second edition of *Summarie and True Discourse* for his text, and inserted a document – "A resolution of the Land-captaines, what course they think most expedient to be taken" – that is partially present in the *Leicester* journal but not in print editions of *Summarie*.[23] A picture emerges from this pattern of presences and absences: Hakluyt tried to document an important voyage in the second edition of *Principal Navigations* that had not been represented in the first, but remained unable to go beyond the source already in print, even though the presence of the "resolution" suggests that he devoted some effort to seeking out additional documents. Where Drake was concerned, as with the sea war narratives in volume 2(ii), Hakluyt did not – or perhaps was unable to – make good on his promise that he would "[bring] to light the best & most perfect relations of such as were chief actors in the particular discoveries and searches of the same, giving unto every man his right, and leaving everyone to maintain his own credit."[24] Relations by the "chief actor" were missing, while the actual authors of the 1585 voyage narrative used by Hakluyt were dead or unknown.

Examining Hakluyt's coverage of Drake's voyages in the first edition of 1589, completed during Drake's lifetime, may sharpen our understanding of how Hakluyt covered the voyages in 1600. A larger interest in celebrating Drake can certainly be discerned in PN (1589). Hakluyt's preface to the reader mentions among the materials regrettably excluded by its focus on distant voyages both the "good services" of Drake and John Norris on the Lisbon expedition of 1589 and, two years earlier, "the two most fortunate attempts of our famous Chieftaine Sir Frauncis Drake, the one in the Baie of Cales [Cádiz] upon a

---

22 Wright, "Voyage of the Erle of Cumberland to the Azores"; Wright, *Certaine Errors in Navigation*. (On Harriot's text, see chapter 8.) David Quinn, however, suggests that the publisher may not have allowed the reprint ("Early Accounts of the Famous Voyage," 35).

23 Bigges and Cates, "Famous Expedition of Francis Drake, 1586," 3: 543–4; Keeler, *Drake's West Indian Voyage*, 170–3, 304–5. This document was a signed record of the recommendation by Carlisle and other "land captains" that the expedition make for home after taking Cartagena; Keeler suggests that the original had been "distributed among the company" (Keeler, ibid., 171n1). The voyage of Edward Fenton may provide a useful case for comparison; key decisions by councils of the captains were carefully minuted, sometimes with signatures, in the official records of the voyage (see Taylor, *Troublesome Voyage*; Donno, *An Elizabethan in 1582*).

24 Hakluyt, "Epistle Dedicatorie (1600)," sig. A2v.

great part of the enimies chiefest shippes, the other near the Islands upon the great Carrack of the East India," omitted "as things distinct and without the compasse of my prescribed limit."[25] Hakluyt also lamented the absence of Drake's circumnavigation from the 1589 version of his work. In a passage that is well known for its bearing on a famous bibliographical crux, Hakluyt drew the reader's attention to the "memorable voyage of master Thomas Candish ... about the globe of the earth," of interest for itself but also remedying the lack of a similar account for Drake's voyage of 1577 to 1580. Hakluyt wrote that "I must confesse to have taken more than ordinarie paines, meaning to have inserted [an account of Drake's circumnavigation] in this worke: but being of late (contrary to my expectations) seriously delt withall, not to anticipate or prevent another mans paines and charge drawing all the services of that worthie Knight into one volume, I have yeelded unto those my freindes which pressed me in the matter, referring the further knowledge of his proceedinges, to those intended discourses."[26] Here, the editor makes visible his efforts to represent Drake's achievements in his collection, yet he claims to have been dissuaded from publishing an account of the circumnavigation that he had already assembled or procured, because a volume devoted exclusively to Drake's services at sea was then in preparation. Once that volume on Drake had failed to appear, and at some point *after PN* (1589) as a whole had been printed, Hakluyt added the unpaginated "Famous Voyage" account of the circumnavigation that now forms part of both editions of the compilation; both the date and source of this addition have occasioned considerable debate.[27] Hakluyt's preface confirms material evidence that "Famous Voyage" was a late addition to the 1589 volume; yet we also learn from this passage that Drake was to be the subject of what would have been a unique book project devoted to a single Elizabethan mariner – and that those preparing and supporting this project were protective of its impact, and of the intellectual property involved. Perhaps this dissuasion, which operated most visibly to prevent inclusion of a narrative dealing with the circumnavigation, also operated

25 Hakluyt, "Preface to the Reader (1589)," sig. *3v. A narrative of the voyage is discussed in chapter 7.
26 Hakluyt, "Preface to the Reader (1598)," sig. *4v.
27 David Quinn views this text as a skillful but hasty condensation ("Early Accounts of the Famous Voyage," 34–48). On dating the late addition of "Famous Voyage" to PN (1589), see Kelsey, *Sir Francis Drake*, 85–8, 177–9, 447–8; Payne, *Guide*, 9–10. Payne relies on detailed assessment of more than fifty surviving copies, concluding that "the bibliographical evidence is simply not exact enough to be of positive assistance to the historian in reconstructing events."

to discourage inclusion of the West Indies voyage; while the absence of Drake's circumnavigation would have been the most apparent to readers of *PN* (1589), if the proposed volume on Drake were to have covered "all the services of that worthie Knight," Hakluyt might have been discouraged or prevented from using *other* materials on Drake as well.[28]

Drake's voyage of circumnavigation was evidently subject to special forms of censorship and disinformation, both before his departure and after his return. There were certainly no substantive publications on the voyage of 1577 to 1580 despite the sensation it caused, and as W.T. Jewkes has shown, by the middle of the 1580s the lack of publicity on Drake's achievements was being lamented in ballads and pamphlets.[29] (Nonetheless, both during the circumnavigation and in the months following Drake's return, well-placed informants had enabled the Spanish ambassador in London, Don Bernardino de Mendoza, to send Philip frequent, timely, and detailed information about Drake's voyage, an index of its perceived importance.) On Harry Kelsey's account, Elizabeth sought accordingly to manage what even English officials knew about Drake's route or the plunder he had taken.[30] The French historian Lancelot-Voisin de la Popelinière heard that the Queen "kept to herself the memorials of his voyage, in order that they should not be published."[31] (These

---

28 Circumstances obtaining in 1588 to 1589 would have been materially different from the considerable secrecy obtaining during the months after Drake's return in 1580. David Quinn considers that even in 1589, Walsingham – who "had a dossier on Drake's activities" – was responsible for "the omission of the original narrative which Hakluyt possessed about the circumnavigation" (D. Quinn, "Early Accounts of the Famous Voyage," 35). Walsingham's stay on publication, he believes, would have resulted from the official displeasure directed towards Drake in the aftermath of the 1589 Lisbon expedition. My own sense is that, had Walsingham indeed dissuaded Hakluyt from publishing, Hakluyt would either have said nothing (as in the case of the Cádiz expedition, withdrawn from volume 1), or at least not created a story about a competing publication.

29 Jewkes, "Sir Francis Drake Revived," 113. Andrews comments that the voyage, officially intended for Alexandria, was accompanied by security arrangements whose "thoroughness and effiency ... were unsurpassed in the annals of Elizabethan maritime enterprise" ("Aims of Drake's Expedition," 726). On the impact of Drake's voyage, see (inter alia) Rodger, *Safeguard of the Seas*, 245. On the trickling out of information, see D. Quinn, "Early Accounts of the Famous Voyage."

30 Kelsey, *Sir Francis Drake*, chap. 8.

31 "Toutesfois qu'elle garde les memoires de sa navigation, afin qu'ils ne soient publiez. Je ne doute point que plusieurs ne luy persuadent de retenir telles instructions, afin qu'elles ne soient communiqués aux estrangers, ny mesmes à ses subjects" (La Popelinière, *Les Trois Mondes*, 3: 36).

appear to have included a journal and drawings produced by Drake's nephew John, later a prisoner of the Inquisition, as well a large map.)[32] Kelsey comments that although Kenneth Andrews is correct in calling Drake's circumnavigation "one of the most richly documented Elizabethan voyages," "it is equally true that there are almost no real first-hand accounts of the trip. The narratives that do exist have without exception been filtered through the hands and minds of clerks, copyists, editors, and interpreters."[33] This landscape of missing or problematic sources is generally understood to have resulted from early collection and retention of written accounts in the interests of the state. By contrast, Hakluyt was able to obtain and publish quite copious materials on Thomas Cavendish's circumnavigation of 1586 to 1588: *PN* (1589) included a narrative account, a 1588 letter on the voyage by Cavendish, and information drawn from a map of China obtained during the voyage, while *PN* (1598–1600) added a detailed rutter by Thomas Fuller, Cavendish's pilot, and replaced the narrative by N.H. in *PN* (1589) with one by Francis Pretty, who had also sailed with Cavendish.[34]

In both 1589 and 1600, conditions for publication about the Drake circumnavigation should have been quite different for someone with Hakluyt's connections and intentions. Even in 1587, Hakluyt had been given access to

---

32 Mendoza wrote to Philip II that Drake had presented the queen with "a diary of everything that had happened during the three years and a very large map" (cited and translated in Wallis, "Cartography of Drake's Voyage," 121). On John Drake's drawings as sources for another surviving map, see Kelsey, *Sir Francis Drake*, 179.

33 Kelsey, ibid., 85.

34 The *PN* (1589) source is N.H., "Famous Voyage of M. Thomas Candish, 1586." Sources in *PN* (1598–1600) are Pretty, "Prosperous Voyage of M. Thomas Candish"; Fuller, "Voyage of M. Thomas Candish." Hakluyt appears to have provided Pretty's journal to van Meteren several years before it appeared in volume 3 (D. Quinn, "Early Accounts of the Famous Voyage"). Robert Parke's translation of Mendoza's *Historia dela China*, "undertaken at the earnest request and encouragement of ... Master *Richard Hakluit*," details some of what was known and could be said about Cavendish's voyage in the year of this return: "your worshippe in your late voyage hath first of our nation ... discovered the ... *Luzones*, or *Philippinas*, lying neare vnto the coast of *China*, and ... brought home three boyes borne in *Manilla*, besides two other young fellowes ... borne in the mightie Iland of *Iapon* and ... sailed along the coast of *China*, not farre from the Continent" (Mendoza, *Historie of China*, sig. ¶2v). Sarah Maxwell notes that navigational information is *not* provided in the printed materials for either the Straits of Magellan or the Philippines, and suggests that "the English government enforced silence on this data" (Maxwell, "Philippines," 28). David Quinn suggests Hakluyt may have provided van Meteren with maps stemming from the voyage as well as manuscript accounts (D. Quinn, *Last Voyage of Thomas Cavendish*, 150–6).

Drake's improved cartography for the coast of Chile, represented on the map that accompanied his edition of *De orbe novo*.[35] In other words, the early suppression of information on the voyage does not seem sufficient on its own to explain the absence of a narrative from PN (1589) as it was assembled. Political considerations specific to the moment may have played a role, as some scholars have suggested, but these in turn do not seem to account for Hakluyt's inability to improve the brief "Famous Voyage" account for PN (1598–1600), a decade later. There, he supplemented his materials with narratives by Cliffe (who had served on one of the ships that did not accompany Drake through the Straits) and da Silva (who had sailed with Drake from his capture in the Cape Verde islands to the west coast of South America); the account by da Silva was taken from a print source, Jan Huygen van Linschoten's *Itinerario*.[36] These materials appear to be all Hakluyt had, could find, or could devise, even though a number of Drake's company remained active (and voluble) on other voyages; on the Edward Fenton voyage, for instance, Richard Madox heard them gossiping about their experiences on the voyage of 1577 to 1580.[37] We have seen that the editor at times exerted himself to take down oral accounts not only from aged survivors of voyages in the 1530s, but mariners of his own time. (One example was Edmund Barker, who sailed to the East Indies with James Lancaster in 1591.)[38] But no such interviews were done for Drake's voyages, and no unprinted materials on Drake are among those listed by Samuel Purchas as received with his collections. Similar conditions of secrecy and suppression – or at least, the missing primary sources that we believe to have resulted from them – do not seem to have pertained for other voyages "intended and ... performed to the Streights of Magellan." We have already noted the editor's ready access to materials relating to Cavendish's circumnavigation. As we have seen, Hakluyt printed John Jane's account of Cavendish's attempt at a second circumnavigation, and his library included two additional accounts of the 1591 voyage that were eventually

---

35 Wallis, "Cartography of Drake's Voyage," 130–1, 139.
36 Kelsey, *Sir Francis Drake*, 178.
37 See, for instance, Donno, *An Elizabethan in 1582*, 184, 208, 239.
38 Hakluyt, "Voyage of M. Hore"; Hakluyt, "Voyage to the Iles of Candia and Chio, 1534 [and] 1535"; Hakluyt and Barker, "Memorable Voyage of M. James Lancaster, 1591." Also by Hakluyt was the account of George Drake's voyage into the St Lawrence to hunt for walrus ("Voyage of M. George Drake").

published by Purchas.[39] Fenton's unsuccessful voyage of 1582 is also richly documented by Hakluyt.

One additional fragment of information contributes to this picture of a frustrated effort to publicize information on Drake's voyages, with bars to access that included a competing project under the aegis of Drake himself. Both in 1589 and 1600, Hakluyt drew on the narrative obtained from Lopes Vas for two extracts on early voyages to the West Indies by Drake in 1572 and by John Oxenham in 1575, presented as discrete narratives with individual titles.[40] The lengthy in-text title for the voyage of 1572 highlights both the source of the document, as testimony to the achievements of other English voyagers, and its status as the inception of Drake's career in command: "The *first voyage*, attempted and set foorth *by the expert, and valiant Captaine M. Francis Drake himselfe*, with the ship called the Dragon, and another ship, and a Pinnesse, to Nombre de Dios, and Dariene, about the yeere 1572. Written, and recorded by one Lopez Vaz, a Portugall borne in the citie of Elvas, in maner follow: which Portugale, with the discourse about him, was taken at the River of Plate by the Ships set foorth by the Right Honourable the Earl of Cumberland, in the yeere 1586" (emphasis mine).[41] This heading indicates some of what Hakluyt did not know about Drake's career. The raiding voyage of 1572 was not Drake's first voyage to the Indies "attempted and set forth by ... himself": in 1569, Drake had sailed to West Africa again with Hawkins before proceeding alone to the West Indies; in 1571, he sailed directly to the West Indies in the *Swan* pinnace.[42] When the account of the 1572 voyage compiled by Philip Nichols was eventually published in 1626, all three voyages were noted and framed in terms of a larger narrative. On Nichols's account, Drake's raids on Spanish towns and goods in the Indies sought to redress "wrongs received" at the hands of the Spanish on his slave-trading voyages with Lovell and Hawkins, respectively, in 1565 to 1566 and 1567 to 1568. The 1626 volume frames Drake's activities in terms of a "general vengeance" against wrongdoers, not only the Spanish viceroy who had surprised the Hawkins fleet

---

39 Knivet, "Admirable Adventures [...] of Master Anthonie Knivet"; Cavendish, "Master Thomas Candish His Discourse." These sources are discussed in more detail in Fuller, "Writing the Long-Distance Voyage."

40 For a similar argument – that journals on the 1572 voyage were "already preempted" for the writing project referenced in Drake's letter, and thus unavailable to Hakluyt – see Andrews, "Latin America," 237.

41 Vas, "First Voyage by Francis Drake, 1572," 3: 525.

42 Kelsey, *Sir Francis Drake*, 44–63.

in 1568, but also Philip himself; Nichols singled out for notice "the greatnesse of the person, by whom the first injury was offered ... the mightiest Monarch of all the world" and "the meannesse of him, who righteth himself ... an English captaine, a meane subject of her Majesties."[43] This was surely the kind of story about English valour and virtue that Hakluyt himself might have been happy to tell in 1589 or 1600, if he had the means to tell it.

The paucity of English sources on Drake in PN (1589) becomes especially striking given that Hakluyt appears to have been on familiar terms with Drake during the 1580s. In 1582, Hakluyt's dedication to *Divers Voyages* related Drake's support for the editor's proposal of a lectureship on navigation. He "liked so wel of the notion" that he offered to endow the lectureship with twenty pounds a year, with another twenty "to a learned man to furnish him with instruments and maps ... so readie he was, that he earnestly requested me to helpe him to the notice of a fitte man for the purpose, which I, for the zeale I beare to this good action, did presently and brought him one." Although the project ran aground on the candidate's request for a doubled fee, Hakluyt wrote that Drake "remaineth still constant, and will be, as he told me very lately, as good as his worde."[44] A 1589 dedication to Drake by Hakluyt's associate Philip Jones described the editor as "a man of incredible devotion toward yourself."[45] In preparing the second edition of *Principal Navigations*, Hakluyt exerted himself to locate and add materials on Drake, even though he did not apparently have access either to materials gathered by Walsingham (who died in 1590) or to papers held by Drake's family.[46] The results are a testimony to his efforts and persistence. The Spanish sources that he used, often performing his own translations and participating in the questioning of captives, did not only fill the gaps left by restricted access to English sources, but they also had affordances of their own: their presence resulted from successful acts of force, their testimonies to the impact of Drake's actions were the concession of an enemy, and though not exactly secrets, they also fulfilled his own programme of publishing things that would "annoy" Spain.[47]

---

43 Nichols, *Sir Francis Drake Revived*, 1–2.

44 Drake's support for the lectureship is alluded to again in a 1584 letter by Hakluyt to Walsingham (Hakluyt, *DV*, sig. ¶3v; Taylor, *OW*, 1: 208).

45 Meyer, *Certaine Briefe, and Speciall Instructions*, sig. A3v, cited in "Chronology," 1: 302.

46 D. Quinn, "Early Accounts of the Famous Voyage," 43.

47 Bazan, "Opinion of Don Alvaro Baçan"; Hakluyt, "Relation of Pedro Morales"; Hakluyt and Harriot, "Relation of Nicolas Burgoignon."

Hakluyt's efforts did not stop after the last volume of the compilation appeared: one of our few glimpses of the editor's day-to-day social life finds him dining at the Mitre Tavern in 1605 with a group that, surprisingly, included several of the Gunpowder Plot conspirators, and on the evidence of Sir Robert Cecil's informant, Hakluyt was there to meet an otherwise unknown merchant who had one of Drake's rutters in his possession.[48] The story of Drake in *Principal Navigations* is thus, in part, a story of what was not printed or narrated by Hakluyt because it was not available to him, and of the editor's resourcefulness in seeking out what he *could* print.

The narrative of the West Indian voyage crafted from Bigges's incomplete account is indicative of the particular shape taken by Hakluyt's materials on Drake. What volume 3 could offer about Drake was, like the sea war narratives, largely the result of distributed authorship. The English sources clearly focus *on* Drake, and yet always at a certain distance and from a perspective that is generally difficult to localize. Perhaps the easiest way to capture what is particular about them is to provide for comparison an utterly different source from the Caribbean section of volume 3, written by one of Drake's successors in efforts to tap the riches of the Spanish West Indies. Sir Robert Dudley began his narrative of a privateering voyage in the 1590s, written at Hakluyt's request, with several lines of autobiography: "having ever since I could conceive of anything bene delighted with discoveries of navigation, I fostered in my selfe that disposition till I was of more yeres and better ability to undertake such a matter." He continues that having hoped to undertake a voyage for the South Seas, he was constrained to fall back on the West Indies, "without hope there to doe anything woorth note: and so common is it indeed to many, as it is not woorth the registring. Neverthelesse, I have yeelded to your former importunity, and sent you this my journall to supply a vacant roome amongst your more important discourses."[49] Both Dudley's self-deprecation, and the first-person voice of this named author – indeed, the highly personal note of the prose – provide a clearest possible contrast with the mediations and lacunae of Hakluyt's Drake materials.

---

48 "Chronology," 1: 321. I am grateful to Matthew Day for sharing unpublished work that alerted me to this event lying both unnoticed and in plain sight; his insightful discussion of it falls within the larger ambit of a rewarding chapter on Hakluyt and national or religious "others" (Day, "Richard Hakluyt's 'Principal Navigations,'" 220).

49 Dudley, "Voyage of Sir Robert Duddeley," 3: 574.

To sum up: in Hakluyt's two compilations, I believe we see a pattern of absences around the figure of Drake. The absence of *one* missing source was attributed by Hakluyt to a competing publication project focusing exclusively on Drake; I am suggesting that the discouraging effects of this project on other publications may have extended to materials on Drake's American and Pacific activities more broadly.[50] Such a hypothesis would be one way of accounting for the pattern of materials found in volume 3: fewer English sources than we might expect, and few closely connected with Drake, with the difference mostly made up using captured sources or material already in print. Only for the voyage of 1595, following Drake's death, was Hakluyt able to print a source that Andrews views as "easily the best of the sea-journals relating to the voyage ... a detached record of the voyage by a professional seaman" that he considers more reliable and detailed than other surviving sources.[51] Even so, the text Hakluyt printed appears to pertain to the *Phoenix*, one of the expedition's smaller ships, rather than Drake's *Defiance*.

We have now reviewed Hakluyt's work in presenting materials about Drake, and begun to speculate from the shape of what appears to be absent from his presentation: first-hand accounts by English sources, and accounts by Drake himself or observers close to him. Some of these absences may be explained by pressures beyond the control of either man – in particular, efforts by Elizabeth's government to suppress information about the voyage of 1577 to 1580.[52] But Hakluyt's remarks about that voyage in the preface to *PN* (1589) suggest a complementary line of inquiry. If some gaps in the editor's documentation of Drake's voyages reflect *private* efforts to collect documents, what can we discern about that competing writing project, both the materials that may have been collected (by hands that were *not* those of Hakluyt) and the efforts made to organize those materials towards an eventual publication? Examining the textual representations of Drake's

---

50 The naval actions of volumes 1 and 2(ii) evidently fell into a different category, more national in character and with a different structure of command. However, Drake appears to have commissioned an account of the Armada victory by Petruccio Ubaldini as a gift to Christopher Hatton; bound with the account by Ubaldini referenced in chapter 6, it is now BL Royal MS 14 A XI. It is not evident from the catalogue whether this account differs substantively from that in Royal MS 14 A X, or only in the "more elaborate style" of its hand (BL catalogue).

51 Andrews, *Last Voyage of Drake and Hawkins*, 80.

52 See, for instance, David Quinn's argument that Walsingham restricted Hakluyt's publication in *PN* (1589) because Drake was politically problematic (D. Quinn, "Early Accounts of the Famous Voyage," 40–1).

career will require us to turn to materials that Hakluyt did not acquire, and to a publication project that was never entirely completed – a "lost book" manifest in traces and absences. The evidence will invite us to speculate about Drake himself as a kind of author, though one less like Davis than like Hakluyt himself.

DRAKE AND THE WRITTEN RECORD: OVERSEEING THE "COMMON BOOKE"

Unlike some comparable Elizabethan figures – Davis, Ralegh, and others – Drake evidently lacked an interest in producing writing for publication. He relied at times on amanuenses for documents over his signature, and he is not the named author of any document in PN (1598–1600) (though the partial, unstated dependence of one narrative in 2[ii] on one of his dispatches has been noted in chapter 7). Yet Drake appears to have had a pronounced interest in managing writing on and about his voyages. He was not the only captain who sought to manage potentially unfavourable accounts of his decision making, as we have seen, but the results suggest that he was unusually successful both in the scope of his efforts and in the ability to control what did appear in print. David Quinn writes that "there is no doubt whatever that Drake intended to publish under his own name a narrative of all his voyages." A letter to Queen Elizabeth over Drake's signature, dated 1592 but printed only decades later, announced that he was at work in "writing the Reporte" of his voyages, a discourse that would be presented to her when complete:

Madam, seeing *divers have diversly reported, and written, of these voyages and actions which I have attempted and made, every one endevoring to bring to light, whatsoever inklings or conjectures they have had; whereby many untruthes have bene published, and the certaine truth concealed:*[53] as I have thought it necessary my selfe, as in a Card to pricke the principal Points of the counsailes taken, attempts made, & successe had, during the whole course of my imployment in these services against the Spaniard, not as setting sayle, for maintainnig [*sic*] my reputation in mens judgment, but onely as sitting at Helme if occation shall be, for conducting the like actions hereafter: so I have accounted it my duty, to present this Discourse to

---

53 It is hard to know what print publications the sentence could refer to, as the only ones in print by 1592 would have been a handful of encomiastic pamphlets and ballads, *Summarie and True Discourse*, and *Principall Navigations* (1589). A more plausible construction of "published" might be as public discourses, speech, rumour.

your Ma'tie as of right ... humbly submitting my selfe to your Gracious censure, both in writing & in presenting: that posterity be not deprived of such help, as may happily be gayned hereby, and our present age (at least) may be satisfied, in the rightfulnes of *these actions, which hitherto have been silenced*, and your Servants labour not seeme altogether lost, not only in Travell by Sea and Land, but also in *writing the Reporte thereof, a worke to him no less troublesome, yet made pleasant and sweet, in that it hath beene, is, and shall be, for your Ma'ties content*; to whome I have devoted my selfe, live or dye.

Francis Drake
Jan. 1. 1592 (emphasis mine)[54]

(This assertion that Drake's actions had been "silenced" comes, curiously, three years after the appearance of *PN* [1589] and Hakluyt's "Famous Voyage" account of the circumnavigation.) If a text was actually delivered to Elizabeth, no trace of it has survived; possibly the letter was a draft left in Drake's papers.[55] Drake's death in 1595 presumably accounts for the long delay that ensued between the date given in the letter and the appearance of *Sir Francis Drake Revived* (1626) and *The World Encompassed* (1628) some thirty years later, both published by Drake's nephew of the same name.[56] The letter was prefaced to the first of these two works.

The title page of *Sir Francis Drake Revived*, where the letter appeared, describes the work as a synthesis of participant materials assembled by the chaplain who sailed with him on several later voyages: "Faithfully taken out of the Report of M. Christopher Ceely, Ellis Hixon, and others, who were in the same Voyage with him. By Philip Nichols, Preacher." We don't know precisely what is designated by "the Report," whether oral testimony or surviving journals. If the latter, either Drake or Nichols may have been collecting written materials considerably earlier than 1592 (the date of Drake's letter) or even 1589 (the date Hakluyt was told of the proposed publication); we can even imagine that Drake collected journals at the conclusion of his voyage. *World Encompassed* was based on a journal kept by Francis Fletcher, Drake's chaplain on the

---

54 Nichols, *Sir Francis Drake Revived*, sig. A3r–v.

55 David Quinn suggest the letter could have been written in either 1592 or 1593 (modern style); if the latter, it would have been impossible for Drake to complete a narrative before he was again employed, if the former, merely unlikely (D. Quinn, "Early Accounts of the Famous Voyage," 36–7).

56 For a comparative reading of Hakluyt's account of the circumnavigation and the one provided in *World Encompassed*, see Jowitt, *Culture of Piracy*, chap. 2.

circumnavigation; the journal was substantially redacted by another hand. It is also possible that Nichols transcribed information from surviving witnesses, as Hakluyt sometimes did; surviving analogues collected by the editor recount voyages as long ago as 1534 and 1536.[57] Whatever the nature of the sources and the date of their collection, Drake is credited with authorship even as Nichols appears on the title page; the nephew's preface to *Sir Francis Drake Revived* claims of his uncle that "this doer was partly the inditor." The title page specifies what this meant, describing the text as "reviewed also by Sir Francis Drake himself before his death, and much holpen and enlarged, by diverse notes, with his own hand here and there inserted." Drake's "indicting" amounted to reviewing, editing, annotating, and correcting the account produced from various sources by Nichols. A rare map by Nicola van Sype showing the coursetrack of the 1577 to 1580 circumnavigation also claims to have been viewed and corrected by Drake; Kelsey dates the map to the early 1580s, providing another defined date for Drake's editorial activity (see figure 10.1).[58]

As we think about this arc of narration, review, redaction, and publication, it may be useful to recall the practices of collecting shipboard writing on the rather different voyages set out by the Muscovy Company.[59] Collecting and collating materials by different hands was intended to produce a unified and corrected record, providing an accurate account of a route that could be followed by others, as well as of the kinds of trade that had been or could be undertaken. The instructions to create such a record served the company's interest in long-distance control of actions they could not observe or affect directly. Drake's voyages were of a different nature, but he also appears to have created records for authorities at home, even if the records themselves no longer exist. As we have seen, he promised a "whole and perfect booke of all such th[ings that] have happened" for the West Indies voyage of 1585

---

57 Hakluyt, "Voyage to the Iles of Candia and Chio, 1534 [and] 1535"; Hakluyt, "Voyage of M. Hore." However, Ralph Fitch's plagiarism of Cesare Federici suggests that it was difficult to produce a detailed narrative after the fact in the absence of a thorough journal on which to base it (see chapter 4).

58 Text on the van Sype map – poorly legible on the Library of Congress copy – is transcribed by Kelsey as "viuee et corige par le dict signeur drack" (Kelsey, *Sir Francis Drake*, 212). Helen Wallis suggests that van Sype copied the map from one sent to Henri IV, which is now BN MS Français 15454 fo. 133 (Wallis, "Cartography of Drake's Voyage," 143). The map Drake corrected would thus be the one requested from Walsingham by the French king. On dating the map, see Kelsey, *Sir Francis Drake*, 128, 179, 458n153.

59 See chapter 4.

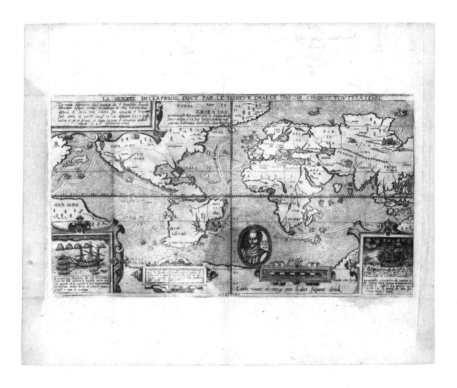

Figure 10.1 A legend on Nicola Sype's 1581 map of Francis Drake's circumnavigation affirms that it was viewed and corrected by Drake himself.

to 1586. Spanish witnesses testified that during the circumnavigation of 1577 to 1580, he "kept a book in which he entered his navigation" and drew images of naturalia, also carrying "painters who paint for him pictures of the coast in its exact colours"; on his return, Drake delivered a map and journal to the queen.[60] Even on the 1572 voyage, which may have been almost a family affair, we can imagine the need for at least minimal records to be kept for accounting and the purposes of navigation.[61] Yet the records collected by

---

60 On the West Indies voyage, see Keeler, *Drake's West Indian Voyage*, 106. On the records of the circumnavigation, see Nuño da Silva and Francisco de Zarate, in Nuttall, *New Light on Drake*, 207–8, 303.

61 Investment and ownership of vessels can inform indirectly on who would have expected to receive records and accounts for a voyage; see Kelsey, *Sir Francis Drake*, passim. Davis's "Traverse-Book," whose organization was an advance on common practice,

Nichols, at least, appear to have served primarily Drake's personal interests, as the raw material for representing "the whole course of my imployment in these services against the Spaniard" in a way that he found satisfactory. Thinking about the delivery or collection of records from a voyage invites us to a prior question about the kinds of records that would have been available to *be* collected. What kinds of record keeping might have been expected, even required, by Drake's various financial backers, or indeed (in the case of later, more ambitious voyages) by the Queen and Privy Council? What can we learn about the process of record keeping and Drake's involvement with it?

For the 1577 to 1580 voyage of circumnavigation, a set of instructions does survive for a reasonably close analogue: the voyage of Edward Fenton (1582); this voyage has already figured in chapter 6, since Fenton paused for some weeks at Sierra Leone. Fenton's voyage was a comparably long-range and strategic attempt to penetrate, in this case, the Portuguese sphere of influence in the East Indies; like Drake, Fenton contemplated leading his ships through the Straits of Magellan, though he had been specifically prohibited from doing so. Financial backers ranged from Drake himself through the queen. Fenton and his men were directed to generate copious written records, and did so; a wealth of documents record both the planning of the voyage and its execution.[62] In addition to the journals kept by Fenton and other captains, journals were kept by the voyage's two ministers, Richard Madox and John Walker, and as the expedition's official record keeper, Madox also kept minutes of meetings, discussions, and decisions by the council of captains.[63] The instructions for the voyage survive both in Madox's holograph journal and in *PN* (1598–1600). We can't assume Drake received the *same* instructions; their detail may have been, in part, a reaction to aspects of the earlier voyage that led Fenton's backers to seek greater oversight and answerability. The Fenton instructions can nonetheless give us a place to start in thinking about the kinds of records that might have been created (or expected) in 1577 to 1580, and

nonetheless provides some indication of the kinds of information regularly recorded by contemporary navigators, as does Thomas Hood's holograph logbook ("Traverse-Book"; Hood, "Red Dragon Logbook").

62 For backgrounds and documents, including a number not printed by Hakluyt, see Donno, *An Elizabethan in 1582*; Taylor, *Troublesome Voyage*.

63 Hakluyt printed the journal of one of Fenton's captains, as well as the instructions given to Fenton (Ward, "Voyage of M. Edward Fenton, 1577"; Privy Council, "Instructions given to M. Edward Fenton"). He made cuts to Ward's text in the 1600 edition.

thus the kinds of materials potentially available for Drake to "review, help, and enlarge" between 1580 and 1592.

Five items in Fenton's instructions concern record keeping. These require producing written records of consultation and decision making, disciplinary actions, and inventories of equipment and merchandise; Fenton was also directed to restrain the production of maps and charts.[64] Some requests echo instructions for earlier voyages. An inventory of equipment supplied and careful accounting for all trade was required by Sebastian Cabot in the 1550s

---

64 The relevant items are:

4. Item, ... of all ... your assemblies and consultations, ... a particular and true note [should] be kept, for which cause we appoint master Maddox minister ... to keepe a booke of all such matters as shall bee brought in consultation, and of all such reasons as shall be propounded by any person ... : what was resolved on, and by whose consent, who dissented there from, and for what causes ... and shall have to every acte, the handes of the General, and of all, or so many of the saide Assistants as will subscribe: which booke the said Master Maddox ... shall keep secret, and in good order to bee exhibited unto us, at your returne home.

5. Item, if there happen any person or persons ... should conspire, or attempt privatly or publikely, any treason, mutinie or other discord, ... upon just proofe made ... the same shall be punished ... And as well of the acts committed by any, as also of the proofe thereof, and of the opinions of you, and your Assistants, and the maner of the punishment, the Register shall make a particular and true note, in the booke of your consultation.

8. You shall make a just and true inventorie in every ship ... of all the tackle, munition, and furniture belonging to them ... and of all the provisions whatsoever, and one copie thereof under your hand ... to be delivered to the Earle of Leicester, and the other to the governour of the companie for them before your departure hence, and the like to bee done at your returne home of all things then remaining in the sayd ships ... with a true certificate how and by what meanes any parcell of the same shall have bene spent or lost.

17. Item you your selfe shall in the Gallion keepe one booke, and the Factors appointed for the same shippe another, wherein shall bee a just account kept, as well of the marchandise carried hence, as of those you shall bring home. And as well at your setting foorth, as from time to time, as exchange shalbe made, you shall set your hand to their booke, and they theirs to yours, and the like order shal you see that ... [the other captains and factors] shall use.

18. Item you shall give straight order to restraine, that none shall make any charts or descriptions of the sayd voyage, but such as shall bee deputed by you the Generall, which said charts and descriptions, wee thinke meete that you the Generall shall take into your hands at your return to this our coast of England, leaving with them no copie, and to present them unto us at your returne: the like to be done if they finde any charts or maps in those countries. (Privy Council, "Instructions given to M. Edward Fenton," 3: 755–6)

(items 8 and 17); the record to be kept of consultations and decisions (item 4) echoes William Borough's instructions to Arthur Pet and Charles Jackman's exploring voyage of 1580.[65] The two remaining instructions on record keeping appear distinctive to Fenton's voyage. One reflects the value of intelligence about the voyage's anticipated course through the Indian Ocean, as well as its political sensitivity: Fenton was directed to bar the unauthorized drawing of maps and charts, and to gather all existing cartographic materials for delivery to the Privy Council on his return (item 18). The second (item 5) required that the adjudication and punishment of mutinous conduct be recorded with a "particular and true note."

Thanks to item 4 in particular, the manuscript record gives ample evidence of the disagreements between the captains, between the captains and pilots, the seamen and merchants, the chaplains and everyone else. These took place over matters as basic as where and whether to water, revealing tensions between the pilots' practical experience, the voyage's written instructions, Fenton's commission, and the chaplains' concern with morality.[66] Madox's minutes of the various councils and of the often dissenting "opinions" of Fenton's assistants were signed by those concerned, creating a transparent and (like the testimonial of Davis's crews) agreed-upon version of events.[67] Given Drake's tendencies as a commander, at least on some better-documented voyages, it is hard to imagine that he presided over anything like the structure of consultation, debate, and signed opinions on major decisions that Madox was charged with recording. On the 1587 voyage to Cádiz, for instance, Borough complained to Drake that he seemed disinclined to consult or indeed inform his senior officers about key decisions. Borough's complaint was made in writing, and Drake required him to "burn or deliver" any copies of the letter, subsequently charging his senior captain with mutiny and desertion after Borough's *Golden Lion* was carried away by its crew. Cheryl Fury points out that this was the "sole recorded court-martial for mutiny in the later

---

65 Cabot, "Ordinances, 1553"; Borough, "Instructions and Notes, 1580," 1: 454.

66 For instance, as Madox wrote in in his diary for 26 June 1582: "the general [Fenton] wold not consent to water hear which thing the viceadmiral took yl, so dyd our master, but Furdinando [the pilot Simão Fernandes] had caried hym to this that the rather for want of water we myght robb" (Donno, *An Elizabethan in 1582*, 148).

67 On the desire of various council members to correct and edit his representations, see Madox's private diary (Donno, ibid., 263–4). For clarity, Madox provided both an ordered digest of discussions and, "for the better credyte of this book," an appendix of original memoranda by council members with their signatures (Donno, 289–90).

Elizabethan period."[68] Drake's style of command may have mitigated against both Madox's painstaking record of consultations and perhaps even the consultations themselves, while both his achievement and the extraordinary returns on the 1577 to 1580 voyage made their own, retrospective law. He would nonetheless have set out with the expectation of answering both to government and to the investors who funded the voyage, and – as we have seen – he certainly delivered written and cartographic records to the queen on returning.[69] Another requirement in Fenton's instructions may have been a reaction to events on Drake's earlier voyage for which thorough records had *not* been kept. The Privy Council's insistence that Madox keep careful records of judicial proceedings, including who voted on a case and how, unavoidably recalls Drake's execution of his second in command, Thomas Doughty, for "actions ... tending ... to contention or mutinie, or some other disorder."[70] Deliberations on Doughty's case seemingly left less satisfactory records.[71] Not only are judicial records absent, Doughty's execution was indeed surrounded by other issues about writing, including whether Drake had the authority to put someone to death at all.

This authority would have been provided by a written commission from the crown. Comparable documents survive for other voyages; Madox's official record of the Fenton expedition includes Fenton's commission from the queen as well as instructions from the Privy Council. According to Madox's text, Fenton's commission gave him authority "to order, rule, governe, correct and punyshe by imprisonment & violent meanes, & by death if the greatnes of the fawlt and necessytie shall so deserve, upon obstinate withstanding suche

---

68 Borough nonetheless retained a copy of the letter to send to Walsingham in his defence (Corbett, *Papers Relating to the Navy*, 123–31, 144, 149–85). On comparable debates over authority between Frobisher and Fenton, his lieutenant, on the 1578 voyage of Arctic exploration, see McDermott, *Third Voyage of Martin Frobisher*, 34. Further discussion is referenced in the same author's *Martin Frobisher: Elizabethan Privateer*. On the mutiny charge, see Fury, *Tides in the Affairs of Men*, chap. 2.

69 Letters from Bernardino de Mendoza, cited in Kelsey, *Sir Francis Drake*, 214–17. See also note 32 above.

70 "Famous Voyage," 3: 733.

71 For what appear to be allegations about Doughty's speech, transcribed from BL MS Harleian 6221, see appendix 1, Vaux, *World Encompassed* (1854). These papers relating to Drake's trial of Doughty belonged to Ralph Starkey, whom his biographer describes as devoted to "collection and transcription of state papers and other manuscripts" (Knafla, "Starkey, Ralph").

orders and articles as are delivered by us or by owr Councell."⁷² On at least one occasion – as Fenton threatened to hang the steward Esdras Draper – Madox wrote in his private diary that "the letters of authority are produced. They are scanned fully. Full power is given to one not inferior to the Queen." Fenton's declaration a few days later that "he had martial lau and wowld hang Draper at the mast" was followed by another that "he wold go throo the Sowth Sea to be lik Sir Fraunsis Drak."⁷³ Fenton's judicial actions, in other words, were authorized by documents available to his officers, and documented by the voyage's official scribe in conformity with the Privy Council's instructions; in interpreting their license, tellingly, he thought of Drake. It is certainly possible that Drake carried a similar royal commission, though some scholars are dubious.⁷⁴ What we do know from multiple sources is that he claimed the power to punish that it would have accorded him. His exercise of that power was not only under-authorized (relative to the expectations of the Fenton instructions) but suggestive of the intent to control access to documents and the means of producing them. The judicial proceedings that *would* have

---

72 Taylor, *Troublesome Voyage*, 60. The original is BL MS Cotton Otho E. VIII, folios 130–43, 173; it was not printed by Hakluyt. Similar powers were apparently given to Sir Thomas Wyndham on the Guinea voyage of 1553 (Fury, *Tides in the Affairs of Men*, chap. 2; Hair and Alsop, *English Seaman and Traders in Guinea*, 116, 148–9).

73 Donno, *An Elizabethan in 1582*, 191, 194. Taylor considers the Privy Council to have been anxious to limit Fenton's powers (*Troublesome Voyage*, xlvii).

74 Corbett, no fan of Doughty, considers it "almost certain that Drake had no express authority to inflict capital punishment" (*Drake and the Tudor Navy*, 1: 235). Kelsey notes that when Doughty's brother John brought suit against Drake for unlawful proceedings, rather than producing his commission Drake found means to avoid a trial. "We can only suppose that the commission did not exist" (*Sir Francis Drake*, 110). Nuño da Silva, alone among witnesses, reported to the Inquisition in Mexico City that when asked by what power he proposed to execute Doughty, Drake assembled all his men, "took out some papers, ... and read them in a loud voice. After reading them he showed them to the others and all saw and inspected them ... All present said that those papers were his and from her [the queen]" (translated in Nuttall, *New Light on Drake*, 378). This detail is present only in the Inquisition testimony, and not in the account printed by Hakluyt. (Don Francisco de Zarate claims to have been shown the commission by Drake, but as Andrews comments was "probably unable to read English"; "Aims of Drake's Expedition," 740.) The one corroborating English witness is a speech attributed to Doughty earlier in the voyage, asserting that "the General hath his authority from the highness the Queen's majesty and her Council such as hath not been committed almost to any subject afore this time: – to punish at his discretion with death or other ways offenders" (BL MS Harleian 6221, in Penzer, *World Encompassed* [1926], 169).

been more fully documented, under the requirements of Fenton's instructions, will repay further attention.

Doughty was originally the voyage's military commander, subsequently also captain of a Portuguese prize and Drake's *Pelican*, and by one account designated an "equal companion" in command with Drake and John Winter. He came into conflict first with Drake's brother, and then with Drake himself while the expedition was still crossing the Atlantic.[75] By the time Drake's ships made land at Puerto Deseado, Doughty had been removed from command and imprisoned, along with his brother. Drake is said to have accused him and his brother of being conjurers and witches, forbidding the men to speak with them, and commanding them on pain of death "not to set penne to papar ne yet to rede but what every man myght understand and se."[76] According to the chaplain Fletcher, Doughty had good command of Greek, along with "a Reasonable tast of Hebrew," and it may be that Doughty's languages both threatened an effectively encrypted means of private communication and (for some) evoked fears of witchcraft and conjuring.[77] Elizabeth Story Donno notes a parallel between Drake's concern about communications he couldn't read, and the extraordinary efforts required for Madox to keep a truly private record when both Fenton and Luke Ward, another captain, were "eager to pry into his papers" (Madox used the Greek alphabet as one mode of encryption).[78] Ward allegedly told him "that al notes showld be [taken] from al men," while Fenton was "sausy to read al my writings."[79] Madox concluded

---

75 The three are described as "eqwall companyons and frindly gentlemen" in John Cooke's narrative (BL MS Harleian 540, in Penzer, *World Encompassed* [1926], 142; Vaux, *World Encompassed* [1854], 187). A detailed account of events, drawing from manuscript sources, can be found in Kelsey, *Sir Francis Drake*, chap. 5.

76 Cooke's journal, in Penzer, *World Encompassed* (1926), 149, 153; Vaux, *World Encompassed* (1854), 195, 200.

77 Penzer, *World Encompassed* (1926), 125; Vaux, *World Encompassed* (1854), 63. On Madox's diary, with its use of classical languages, cipher, and pseudonyms, see Donno, *An Elizabethan in 1582*, 45–65. Greek and Hebrew characters were sometimes used for magical purposes.

78 Madox began his private diary with "a very clearly written explanation in English" that this brief journal would use Greek and Latin as an exercise in style; his candid and often scathing observations on events and personalities were protected by the use of classical languages, a system of pseudonyms, and actual cipher (Donno, *An Elizabethan in 1582*, 47–8).

79 Donno, ibid., 155–6, 240, 301. See also her discussion in the introduction, which includes additional references (ibid., 46–8). Fenton became particularly exercised by a reference to Drake's chaplain Fletcher in one of Madox's private letters, a result of

that he could not continue to maintain the daily register required by Fenton's instructions, given the captains' intrusive efforts to supervise and manage any writing at all; he believed that, given Fenton's intent to defy instructions that limited the geographical scope of the voyage, Fenton did not wish a written record of decisions to be kept.

Doughty was imprisoned and restrained from written communication, but a long voyage remained. When Drake's *Golden Hind* arrived at Port St Julian in the Straits of Magellan, the site where Magellan himself had executed members of his crew, Drake charged Doughty with "great matters," and impanelled a jury to inquire into them.[80] The ensuing trial and execution are narrated in "Famous Voyage," as well as, rather differently, in the late transcripts that survive of journals by Fletcher and John Cooke, a member of Winter's company on the *Elizabeth*.[81] The manuscript sources return us to questions about Drake's commission. Cooke reported an exchange between Drake and Doughty before the proceedings began: "why Generall, q[uo]d. he, I hope yow will let see yowre comyssyon be good. I warrant yow, aunswered he, my comissyon is good enowghe. I pray yow let vs then see it, qd. he, it is necessarye that it shuld be here shewed. Well, qd. he, yow shall not se it; but well, my masters, this fellowe is full of prating, bynd me his arms, for I will be saffe of my lyffe."[82] After the charges were read to the jury, Doughty asked Drake to allow him to undergo trial in England, offering to "set his hand to what so was there writen, or to any thinge els that he would sett downe."[83] Drake insisted that the jury deliberate first, and after his assurance that there was "no mattar of death," the jury found Doughty guilty of using words of "unkindness, and … some choler" against Drake. As he prepared to make an oration that would

misconstruing his Latin that again indicates how much Drake was on the minds of the voyagers of 1582.

80 Some historians consider the proceedings a "kangaroo court"; Fury takes a more positive view, affirming that Drake followed the process for court-martials, choosing "40 distinguished jurymen" led by a friend of the defendant to hear evidence (Parry, "Drake and the World Encompassed," 6; Fury, *Tides in the Affairs of Men*, 52).

81 Fletcher's journal is transcribed in BL MS Sloane 61, by John Conyers; John Cooke's, in BL MS Harley 540, by John Stow (Kelsey, *Sir Francis Drake*, 86). On the extant manuscript sources and their relation to Hakluyt's narrative see D. Quinn, "Early Accounts of the Famous Voyage"; Kelsey, *Sir Francis Drake*, 85–8. Wagner's edition of print and manuscript sources on the circumnavigation provides an overview (*Drake's Voyage around the World*).

82 Narrative of John Cooke, in Vaux, *World Encompassed* (1854), 202.

83 Cooke, in Vaux, ibid., 204.

conclude by asking the company as a whole to vote on death, Drake displayed a bundle of letters and papers, and said (in the words of the Cooke manuscript), "God's will I have left in my cabin that I should especially have had (as if he had there forgotten his commission ...) but truly I think it should have been showed to the uttermost if he had had it."[84] If Cook's account can be trusted, Drake's commission was missing at the moment when its authority was invoked to empower his controversial execution of Doughty, and never shown either then or later to anyone capable of reading it. Making the commission public would have clarified and stabilized the actual extent of Drake's authority; unread, its authority remained expansively indefinite. If we glimpse in later documents an intention to collect, reorganize, redact, and correct surviving records into a harmonized and authorized whole, in surviving accounts of the circumnavigation I believe we see Drake's hand intervening to prevent both writing and reading.

The largest and most suggestive piece of evidence on Drake's personal involvement with the records of 1577 to 1580 voyage is the encomiastic account of the circumnavigation in *World Encompassed* (1628). *World Encompassed* is considered to rely primarily on a redaction of the chaplain Fletcher's journal, with Cooke's journal as another redacted source: as an early editor noted, "the compiler and the chaplain were by no means of one mind."[85] Fletcher's journal was not an obvious choice for a narrative prepared by Drake and his associates. On the evidence of the surviving, partial transcript by John Conyers, the chaplain was at times markedly critical of Drake, and he was not among the favoured officers whom da Silva testified that Drake "had seated at his table, namely, the Captain, pilot and doctor."[86] Another narrative records that after Fletcher preached an injudicious sermon, Drake "excommunicated" his chaplain, requiring him to wear a paper that read: "Francis Fletcher, the falsest knave that liveth."[87] Yet even a critical record could be made to tell a more positive story, given sufficient oversight and editorial control. In the letter

---

84 Cooke, in Vaux, ibid., 205. In Cooke's account, Drake then read from the papers, which included correspondence about the voyage by Essex and Sir Christopher Hatton, and the queen's bill of adventure in the voyage. Kelsey notes that "several times during the expedition [Drake] claims to have a document from the Queen giving him such authority [to execute Doughty], but he never showed it to anyone, then or later" (Kelsey, *Sir Francis Drake*, 110, 452n59).

85 Vaux, *World Encompassed* (1854), xii.

86 Nuttall, *New Light on Drake*, 301.

87 The paper worn by Fletcher is described in Harleian MS. 280, fo. 81 (Vaux, *World Encompassed* [1854], 176; Kelsey, *Sir Francis Drake*, 202).

prefixed to *Sir Francis Drake Revived*, Drake promised that by "writing the Reporte" of his voyages, he would ensure that the "certaine truth" would replace "many untruthes [that] have bene published," opposing a singular, authorized narrative to the varied voices that had once sought to tell their own, varied stories. If Drake doesn't seem necessarily to have been "writing a report" in the sense of producing original text, he was clearly engaged in *managing* many kinds of writing acts, including collecting, supervising, and editing texts, *and* preventing the circulation (or even creation) of others. (Oral information was another matter, as we have already noted.)[88] Drake sought to determine how his story would be told and, while that story was in the making, to set limits to the ability of others either to access or produce information in writing independent of his control. At the periphery, those others may have included Hakluyt.

Such supervisory and editorial efforts at managing the production and circulation of writing form the greater part of what we might characterize as Drake's authorial work.[89] Yet Drake did sign his name to a small number of surviving texts, largely letters and dispatches; dispersed in different archival and print contexts, they have not as yet been gathered together. One such letter appears in the narrative of da Silva, having passed from English into Spanish, Dutch, and back into English again; others were printed in pamphlets, including the dispatch anonymously subsumed in Hakluyt's account of the Cádiz expedition of 1587.[90] Perhaps the most famous text over Drake's hand appeared in another such pamphlet publication, a letter also written in 1587 and addressed to the martyrologist John Foxe. The letter provides us with a glimpse at a text that appeared in print during Drake's lifetime, and surely with his cooperation. Extant in numerous manuscript copies, it is perhaps the most circulated piece of writing over Drake's signature.[91] Appended to Thomas

---

88 For gossip about the 1577–80 voyage, see (for instance) Donno, *An Elizabethan in 1582*, 184, 239. In the manuscript record, see the comments by John Saracoll, Fletcher, and others in BL MS Harleian 6221 (appendix I, Vaux, *World Encompassed* [1854]).

89 Drake also commissioned an Armada narrative by Ubaldini for presentation to Sir Christopher Hatton; I have not been able to examine the narrative, which is now BL Royal MS 14 A XI.

90 Da Silva, "Voyage of Nunno Da Silva," 3: 748; "Voyage of Sir Francis Drake to Cadiz, 1587." Drake also supplied a commendatory poem to Peckham, *True Reporte*, 1583. Other letters can be found in the State Papers; for a sample, see Corbett, *Papers Relating to the Navy*; Rodger, *Armada in the Public Records*.

91 Kelsey lists three manuscript versions: BL Harleian MS 167, fo. 104; Harleian MS 7002, fo. 8; and Folger V.a.321, fo. 39v–40 (Kelsey, *Sir Francis Drake*, 499n121).

Greepe's 1587 ballad on the West Indies voyage of 1585 to 1586, Drake's letter to Foxe provided breaking news of a raid on Cádiz aimed at disrupting Spanish plans of invasion; as significantly, it aligned Drake's activities at sea with the work of English Protestantism's great apologist, who had just died at the time of publication. Henry Haslop's 1587 news pamphlet on the Cádiz voyage referenced as already well known these "frendly lines full of love ... to that reverend father M. Fox," in which Drake "showes his devotion, and confirmes his religion."[92] Drake wrote:

where as it is most certayne, that the king doth not onely make speedy preparation in Spayne, but likewise expected a verye great Fleete from the Straytes, and dyvers other places, that shold joyne with his forces to invade England: We purpose to sette apart all feare of daunger, and by Gods furtheraunce to proceede by all the good meanes we can devise to prevent theyr comming, wherfore I shall desire you to continue faithfull in remembraunce of us in your prayers, that our purpose may take that good effect, as God may be glorifyed, his Church, our Queene and Country preserved, and these Enemies of the trueth utterly vanquished, that we may haue continuall peace in Israel. From aboord her Majesties good Ship the Elizabeth Bonaventure.

Your loving freende, and faythfull Sonne in Christ Jesus. Frauncis Drake.

Our enemies are many, but our protector commaundeth the whole world, let us all pray continually, and our Lorde Jesus wyll heare us in good time mercifully.

Frauncis Drake. Wrytten by the hands of M. Pynner.[93]

The letter to Foxe describes Drake's naval activities as not only defending queen and country, but also glorifying God and defeating the enemies of the truth. Foxe's prayers and Drake's war-making become two modes of a common enterprise.

This way of thinking about Drake's activities, of course, was quite widespread. As public understandings of his career emerged from the 1580s onward,

---

92 Haslop, *Newes out of the Coast of Spaine*, sig. A4r.
93 Greepe, *True and Perfecte Newes*, sig. C4r. For another example of secretarial writing, see Drake's dispatch to Walsingham, 27 April 1587: "pray pardon for not writing with my own hand. I am overcome with business" (Corbett, Papers *Relating to the Navy*, 109).

THE CARIBBEAN AND THE PACIFIC 445

among these was a tendency to represent him as a specifically Protestant hero (or villain, depending on your perspective) in a war of true against false belief. We can observe this framing of his voyages in Spanish sources: as Barbara Fuchs characterizes Lope de Vega's epic *La Dragontea* (1598), Drake "becomes the Dragon ... and the struggle against him becomes a cosmological battle of good against evil."[94] In other English sources, Drake would be likened to a variety of Biblical heroes. Both sides appeared to share the conviction that religion provided an appropriate frame for understanding Drake's voyages, and that he was himself the quintessential Protestant warrior, a "gran Luterano." Something like Drake's letter to Foxe surely would have appealed to an editor whose promotion of England's maritime activities was (as Christopher Hodgkins says of Hakluyt) informed by "the sense that England's imperial struggle was not merely against flesh and blood but above all against profound spiritual evil, incarnate in the papal Antichrist and his Spanish legions."[95] This text did not appear in *PN* (1598–1600), however. Drake's letter to Foxe brings to our attention this and other sources about the navigator that do *not* appear in Hakluyt's compilation, despite the circumstances of informational scarcity already described. In particular, we would learn relatively little about the confessional framing of Drake's career by reading *Principal Navigations*. One of the aims of this study focused *on* Hakluyt's book has been to revisit and scrutinize some of the broad claims about Hakluyt and his massive work sometimes made in more general studies. For scholars more specifically engaged with Hakluyt's work, the relation of his nationalism to his Protestantism, his historiography to his theology, have been a point of debate.[96] While Hakluyt's private views are recoverable, to the extent they are, through a

---

94 Fuchs, *Mimesis and Empire*, 143. For a more detailed examination of Drake's construction as a specifically Protestant hero, see Wathen, *Sir Francis Drake*, chap. 1.

95 Hodgkins, *Reforming Empire*, 57. See also Wright, *Religion and Empire*. (Factual claims in Wright's book should be treated with caution, however, and confirmed against subsequent scholarship.) A related view that Hakluyt's work anticipates "the English Black Legend in its final form" can be found in Maltby, *Black Legend in England*, 65. Broader studies referencing Drake sometimes conflate views expressed in *World Encompassed* with those of the chaplain Fletcher, whose journal it redacts; Maltby's book, for instance, suggests that Fletcher viewed Drake as little less than "an avenging angel of the Lord" (ibid., 74). The reality appears more complicated.

96 Key sources are Armitage, *Ideological Origins*, chap. 3; Sacks, "Richard Hakluyt's Navigations in Time"; Sacks, "Discourses of Western Planting." See also Boruchoff, "Richard Hakluyt and the Demands of Pietas Patriae"; Sacks, "'To Deduce a Colonie'"; Dimmock, "Hakluyt's Multiple Faiths."

handful of letters and manuscripts – none of his sermons survive – the question here will be whether and how his *publications* support a claim like the one made by Hodgkins and other scholars. Indeed, we might look beyond the role of a politicized Protestantism in shaping the record of voyages (by Drake and others) to ask how, in fact, Protestant belief manifests itself in *Principal Navigations*.

This empirical question is not an insignificant one, and ultimately not one that bears on Hakluyt alone. We have already noticed the role of several ministers (Madox, Fletcher, Walker, Nichols) in producing the records of events on which works such as Hakluyt's relied, and ministers are also recorded as being present on a number of key voyages (see appendix 10). Hakluyt, as we know, was himself a minister, who signed himself "Richard Hakluyt *Preacher*" on the title page to volume 3. His legacy materials, both published and unpublished, would be shaped into a definitively and explicitly Anglo-Protestant work by Purchas; the frontispiece to Purchas's *Hakluytus Posthumus* juxtaposes images of the children of Israel marching towards the New Jerusalem and the defeat of the Armada above the title itself.[97] Religious professionals thus played an integral role in creating the written record of Elizabethan voyaging, and we may well want to understand the nature of their impress on that record as well as the evidence of lay beliefs and practices that the record affords. Both the dimensions of *Principal Navigations* and the claims made about it make the case of Hakluyt worth studying. The final section of this chapter moves from Anglo-Protestant materials on Drake, to evidence about the religious practices of Drake and other English mariners, to evidence of Protestant practice in Hakluyt's compilation. Religious expression in the writing of Hakluyt's authors is quite common; but accounts of what English voyagers said and did as an expression of their religious identity prove to be far less so.

PROTESTANTS AND PRIVATEERS: CONFESSION AT SEA

A news ballad published shortly after Drake's return from the West Indies voyage of 1585 to 1586 made explicit a confessional, and not only naval and political, framing of the voyage. Thomas Greepe's *The True and Perfect News of the Worthy and Valiant Exploits, Performed and Done by That Valiant Knight Sir Francis Drake* (London, 1587) concludes with Drake's letter to Foxe; it opens with an

---

97 See Porter, "Purchas as Theological Geographer."

Figure 10.2 The frontispiece to Purchas's compilation mingles images of the Armada battle and the two circumnavigations with quotations from Scripture.

injunction that England rejoice, as God has blessed their queen with victory.[98] Drake is introduced as a hero of biblical stature:

First call to minde howe Gedeon,
But with thrée hundred fighting men
The Medians hoste he ouercame
A thousand to eche one of them.
He did suppresse Idolatry
The Lord gave him the victory.

So likewise by Gods mighty hande
Syr Frauncis Drake by dreadfull sworde
Did foyle hys foes in forraine lande,
Which did contemne Christes holy word.
And many Captives did sette frée
Which earst were long in misery.[99]

The voyage's double bearing as an English victory over Spanish defenders and a Protestant victory over Catholic practice is woven throughout the text. In Cape Verde, for instance, Drake and his men took and kept a town "With honour, fame, and victory: / Theyr Idoll gods eche where puld downe, / With all theyr fond Idolatry."[100] The ballad's brief reference to Drake's liberation of captives "which earst were long in misery" was elaborated in another contemporary text, Meredith Hanmer's *The Baptizing of a Turke* (London, 1586). Hanmer credited Drake's life as a "good Christian" for motivating one Turkish captive held in the West Indies to become a Protestant after Drake had freed him. Hanmer emphasized for his readers "what moved this *Turk* to becom a Christiā: not holie words, but workes, not the name of faith, but the viewe of fruites, not the learning of Clarks, but the lives of certain good Christiãs, whose love & kindnes did so ravish him (as he saide of himselfe) that he cõfessed the God of the christians to be the onely true God. And among others he named Sir *F. Drake* that worshipful knight, & *W. Haukins*

---

98 A valuable introduction is provided by David Waters in his edition of the text, Greepe, *True and Perfecte Newes* (1955). As noted above, publication of the Cates/Bigges account on the continent suggests the pertinence of Drake's West Indian raids for Protestant audiences beyond England.
99 Greepe, *True and Perfecte Newes*, sig. A4r.
100 Greepe, ibid., sig. B2r.

that worthy Captaine."[101] By contrast, when asked why he had resisted conversion during a quarter-century of captivity, the released captive reported that he "misliked in the Spaniard (which disswaded him from the [Catholic] faith) his cruelty in shedding of bloud, and his Idolatry in worshipping of Images."[102] It was at around the same time that Robert Leng's manuscript account of the 1587 Cádiz action represented Drake as England's "faithfull Moyses" and "our Ajax," a Protestant warrior in the larger conflict opposing God's "chosen" and a "sacred and swete pryncez" to the "enemye of Godes true Gospell."[103] As we saw in chapter 7, Leng's narrative was mistakenly identified by Corbett and Quinn as the source for Hakluyt's narrative of the action; there is no certainty that this text ever circulated beyond its addressee, Lord Grey of Wilton. Henry Haslop's pamphlet on the Cádiz action, *Newes Out of the Coast of Spaine* (1587), offers more evidence of confessional framing, this time in one of the dispatches Hakluyt did apparently use as a source on the voyage.[104] Haslop's text includes an additional paragraph in Thomas Fenner's dispatch that does not appear in the version printed in volume 2(ii) of Hakluyt's compilation. The missing paragraph elaborates precisely on the miraculous quality of English exploits at Cádiz, and their place in a larger history of divine intervention against Catholics and on behalf of the "blessed prince" Elizabeth.

It may seeme *straunge, or rather miraculous* that so great an exploit, should be performed with so small losse, considering the place so convenient, and their force so great ... But in this, as in all other our actions heretofore (although dangerously attempted, yet most fortunately performed) *our God wil, and hath alwaies made his infinite power to all papists apparant,* and his name by us his servants under our blessed prince (whose life the Lord prolong) to be continually glorified.

Your loving Cossin Thomas Fenner. (emphasis mine)[105]

---

101 Epistle Dedicatorie, Hanmer, *Baptizing of a Turke*, sig. 4r. Hanmer reiterates this appreciation of Drake and Hawkins in the text of his sermon.
102 Hanmer, ibid., sig. 4v.
103 Leng, "True Discripcion," 15.
104 See chapter 7 for discussion of the relationship between Haslop's pamphlet and Hakluyt's "Voyage of Sir Francis Drake to Cadiz, 1587."
105 Haslop, *Newes out of the Coast of Spaine*, sig. B1v. The language of the letter printed by Haslop is not dissimilar to another dispatch from Fenner to Walsingham printed in Corbett, *Papers Relating to the Navy*, 134–40.

While many elements of the documentary record are missing or problematic for Drake's voyages, some contemporary sources on his voyages circulated widely in print and manuscript: the letter to Foxe, Greepe's pamphlet, Fenner's dispatch. All three emphasize the confessional dimension of Drake's actions against Spain. In assembling *Principal Navigations*, Hakluyt elected not to use such sources, or (in the cases of Fenner's dispatch) provided a version that lacked its particular confessional framing.

The editor's own religious identity and commitment should not be ignored or underestimated. In the preface to volume 1, for instance, Hakluyt used language echoing Fenner's dispatch in describing the victory over the Armada as the work of Providence: "I think that never was any nation blessed of JEHOVAH, with a more glorious and wonderfull victory upon the Seas, then our vanquishing of the dreadfull Spanish Armada, 1588. But why should I presume to call it our vanquishing; when as the greatest part of them escaped us, and were onely by Gods out-stretched arm overwhelmed in the Seas, dashed in pieces against the Rockes, and made fearefull spectacles and examples of his judgements unto all Christendome?"[106] Yet across the span of *Principal Navigations* – and even in narratives that Hakluyt himself composed from notes or took down from oral information – he made sparing use of explicitly religious language. This claim modifies the picture provided by some twentieth-century scholarship. For instance, Louis B. Wright speculated that the "sanctimonious" narrative of Humphrey Gilbert's last voyage by Edward Hayes owed its vehement piety to revision by Hakluyt.[107] In fact, however, Hayes's explicit interpretation of England's colonial history in providential, even eschatological terms is unusual among documents in the compilation; in particular, it has no obvious analogues among documents in *Principal Navigations* known to have been transcribed or composed by Hakluyt.[108] This

---

106 Hakluyt, "Preface to the Reader (1598)," sig. **2r.

107 Wright, *Religion and Empire*, 24–5. Hayes, a participant in Gilbert's colonizing project, opened his text by arguing that England's colonizing projects would succeed (as Gilbert's did not) only to the extent that their motives were godly; history indicated to him that God had reserved the northern Americas for the English to settle and plant religion, furthering the movement of the Gospel from east to west and fulfilling the prophecy that "the worlds end approching," the Gospel would have been preached "thorowout the world."

108 As Philip Edwards points out, Hayes used similar eschatological language in a manuscript proposal ("Edward Hayes Explains Away Sir Humphrey Gilbert," 285–6). Edwards compares Hayes's passage on the circular movement of the Gospel with parallel arguments in a 1592 colonizing proposal that David Quinn has ascribed to Hayes and

THE CARIBBEAN AND THE PACIFIC 451

is not to say that Hakluyt did not share any of Hayes's views; he added marginalia calling out not only Hayes's congenial notion that northern America was "reserved for the English" but also that "the due time approcheth by all likelihood of calling these heathens unto Christianity. The word of God moveth circularly."[109] Yet whatever Hakluyt himself may have believed or expressed in his own preaching, he did not generally use either marginal comments, the opportunities of editing and transcription, or, indeed, his prefaces and dedications to bring forward eschatological views like those expressed by Hayes.[110]

Hakluyt largely abstained from adding pious terms and meanings as he edited his documents, sometimes (as in the case of Fenner's dispatch) even appearing to remove them. He also elected not to exclude from either edition of *Principal Navigations* more ecumenical materials like the captivity narrative of John Foxe, the pilgrimage of John Lok, or the colonial proposals of Sir George Peckham, a Catholic who was associated with the colonizing projects of Gilbert, Carleill, and (indeed) Hayes.[111] He printed the accounts of English captives who had suffered at the hands of the Mexican Inquisition after expressing (or failing convincingly to disavow) Protestant sentiments; but he printed them next to the narrative of Roger Bodenham, an Anglo-Catholic merchant who led the important Mediterranean voyage of 1550 before sailing with a group of Spanish ships to Mexico and settling comfortably

---

Christopher Carleill ("A discourse Concerning a voyage intended for the planting of Chrystyan religion and people in the North west regions of America," in D. Quinn, *NAW*, 3: 156, 158). Quinn also notes the presence of information derived from Hakluyt's French research in the Hayes/Carleill document.

109 Hayes, "Voyage by Sir Humfrey Gilbert," 3: 144–5.

110 Hakluyt's reticence may encourage us to turn to social contexts for indications of what he might have believed and assumed. David Sacks places Hakluyt in the social and theological context of Westminster Abbey, where he would be installed as a prebendary (or honorary canon) in 1602, and which provides at least strong circumstantial evidence for the outlines of his theology. The abbey records provide "a uniquely detailed record of Hakluyt's activities" from 1602 forward, suggesting his active participation in the life of this community ("Chronology," 316). In his valuable chapter, Sacks also argues that Hakluyt "believed – 'hoped,' perhaps, would be the better word – that the end of the present world order was near" (Sacks, "Discourses of Western Planting," 448).

111 Peckham included the narrative portion of Hayes's narrative within his own treatise (Peckham, "True Reporte," 1600). For the relationship between Hayes and Peckham, see Edwards, "Edward Hayes Explains Away Sir Humphrey Gilbert," 274. For more detail on Peckham's engagement with Gilbert's project and its aftermaths, see D. Quinn, *Voyages and Colonising Enterprises*. On Lok and Foxe, see chapter 5.

there.[112] The pictures of sources present in *PN* (1598–1600) thus troubles the claim sometimes made that Hakluyt was a Protestant zealot. Examining the editor's treatment of the Armada and Cádiz narratives that close volume 1, David Boruchoff concludes that Hakluyt sought to frame Anglo-Spanish conflict "within an ecumenical Christian economy," advancing "broadly Christian – rather than narrowly Protestant – ideals," and elevating those ideals over simple patriotism. While the inclusion of a congratulatory poem by the Calvinist Theodore Bèze makes Hakluyt's presentation of the Armada narrative less ecumenical than it might be, it is telling that *Principal Navigations* did not include perhaps the most central support of the Black Legend, Bartolomé de las Casas's *Brevísima Relación* (Seville, 1552) – a text Hakluyt knew, owned, and quoted liberally from in "Particuler Discourse."[113]

To appreciate the kinds of information that did not make its way into *Principal Navigations* – some of what a more energetic or polemically minded editor might have elicited from witnesses to depict Drake and his men as dismantlers of idolatry, even supposing a distaste for the doggerel of Greepe's pamphlet – we can turn to a surprising source. For the voyage of 1577 to 1580, *Spanish* witnesses testified expansively about the "Lutheran" conduct of Drake's crews:

And the said Lutherans robbed ... all the contents of a chest that was in the holy Church [at Huatulco], which consisted of sacred vestments and many gold and silver vessels used for daily service ... The witness ... went to the church, where he saw the picture of the mother of God, which was placed on the altar, broken into pieces and appearing to have been cut many times with a knife. The crosses that were there were also broken into pieces, and all the hosts from the box in which the unconsecrated wafers are kept were strewn on the floor and trampled upon. (Deposition of Bernardino López)

---

112 See the voyages of Robert Tomson, Job Hortop, Miles Philips, and Roger Bodenham in volume 3, and the Mediterranean voyage of Bodenham in volume 2(ii). On Tomson, see Conway, *An Englishman and the Mexican Inquisition, 1556–1560*. On Bodenham, see Croft, *Spanish Company*; Ash, *Power, Knowledge, and Expertise*, 106–7. On Hortop and Philips, see chapter 6 above. On another captive, interpreter, and spy mentioned briefly by Hakluyt, see Steggle, "Charles Chester and Richard Hakluyt."

113 Boruchoff, "Richard Hakluyt and the Demands of Pietas Patriae," 195. See also Sacks, "Rebuilding Solomon's Temple." On Hakluyt's use of Las Casas in "Particuler Discourse," see *PD*, xxvi.

[T]he boatswain of the Englishman's ship took a crucifix which belongs to witness, and seizing it by the feet struck its head against a table breaking it to pieces, saying "Here it is; here you go!" Seen by witness's face that he was grieved, the boatswain said "you ought indeed to be grieved, for you are not Christians but idolaters, who adore stocks and stones." (Deposition of Francisco Gómez Rengifo)[114]

Such acts of aggression against the devotional furniture of Spanish churches can be seen in relation to domestic policies and practices aimed at extirpating the use of religious images, vestments, plate, and so on in English churches following the Reformation, including by acts under Elizabeth.[115] Spanish deponents were not alone in testifying to iconoclastic behaviour on the voyage. The transcript of Fletcher's journal records that at Santiago in the Cape Verde islands, "we perceived the inhabitants were too superstitious according to the pope's anti-Christian tradition; for upon every cape, and small headland they set up a Cross ... One of the crosses myself and others did break down but with great dislike as well to some of our own company being so much addicted to that opinion as the Portugals themselves."[116] The "Anonymous Narrative" of the circumnavigation records that Drake himself rifled a church in Santiago de Chile, and gave the "spoyle" to his chaplain; the theft of "ornaments and belles" from the church was indeed among the complaints forwarded to Elizabeth's governor by the Spanish ambassador in 1580.[117] Yet what Greepe was happy to celebrate in broad strokes did not generally find its way into the print record. If Drake's crews seized the opportunity to profit both materially and ideologically from these encounters with their Catholic counterparts in the Atlantic islands and the Spanish Americas, English sources were reticent about the details of such literally iconoclastic actions and speeches; they are

---

114 Nuttall, *New Light on Drake*, 344, 353. On the boatswain's aggressive speech and actions towards devotional objects, see also Juan Pascual's testimony (ibid., 337).

115 Eamon Duffy follows both iconoclastic policies and resistance to them from the 1530s through the reign of Elizabeth in *Stripping of the Altars*.

116 Vaux, *World Encompassed* (1854), 21. For Fletcher's stinging comments on Catholicism as worship of "the base work and vile things of the earth," see Vaux, ibid., 16.

117 BL Harleian MS 280, in Vaux, 179–80. The Conyers transcript of Fletcher's journal does not cover this or subsequent parts of the voyage. For this incident in Nuño da Silva's testimony, see Nuttall, *New Light on Drake*, 261, 304. For Mendoza's complaints, see Nuttall, ibid., 412–5. The church at Huatulco, the subject of many questions by the inquisitors, does not seem to have figured in the complaint; Nuttall remarks on this absence (ibid., 416).

minimized in printed accounts, and no sources mention the spoliation of the church at Huatulco at all.

Protestantism was much more than an opposition to "idolatry," of course. We can also turn to Spanish witnesses for positive evidence of religious practices on board Drake's ships. A letter from the Mexican inquisitors to the archbishop of Guatemala requested that any persons taken prisoner by a "Lutheran corsair" should be asked whether they observed anyone not a member of the crew "joining the Englishmen in their sermons and prayers and litanies, communions and other ceremonies pertaining to their religion and sect." (Da Silva was suspected of participating in Protestant worship.)[118] The resulting scrutiny of Drake's prisoners and the heresy to which they might have been exposed yielded rich details of religious practice by Drake's officers and crew: the singing of psalms, silent prayer and individual reading, and the ubiquity of books among those worshipping, as well as the presence of a large copy of *Foxe's Book of Martyrs*, with hand-coloured illustrations. Drake deployed this copy of Foxe in discourse with his captives, lingering on "illuminated pictures of the Lutherans who had been burnt in Spain."[119] Witnesses generally identified Drake himself as the conductor of worship on shipboard; only one witness mentions preaching by Fletcher, the voyage's chaplain.[120] The relative invisibility of an actual Protestant minister in this testimony might be explained in part by the inquisitors' intent focus on Drake, but it appears that (with a few memorable exceptions) Drake took an increasingly prominent role in conducting religious services on his ship after the execution of Doughty.[121] Fletcher's single appearance in Hakluyt's "Famous Voyage" account of the circumnavigation was in giving communion to Drake and Doughty together;

---

118 Nuttall, *New Light on Drake*, 374–5.

119 Testimony of Simon Miranda, in Nuttall, ibid., 348. John King specifies that Drake's copy would have been the two-volume edition of 1576; although modestly less enormous and costly than the extravagant edition of 1570 that was placed in many English public settings, its presence in the confined quarters of the *Golden Hind* reflects a degree of commitment (*Foxe's Book of Martyrs*, 297–8). "Prayers and singing of Psalmes" are also attested in Drake, *World Encompassed*, 72, 81.

120 See the testimony of Juan Pascual; Simon de Miranda; Francisco Gomez de Rengifo (Nuttall, *New Light on Drake*, 325–7, 336, 348, 354–7). Fletcher's journal notes that he preached a sermon at the burial of two men killed by Patagonians (Penzer, *World Encompassed* [1926], 124; Vaux, *World Encompassed* [1854], 57).

121 Nuttall, *New Light on Drake*, 325, 336, 354–5; Kelsey, *Sir Francis Drake*, 170.

he fades from the record thereafter, and archival sources record that Drake "excommunicated" him in the East Indies for an injudicious sermon.[122]

Preaching and the use of the sacraments provide us with another optic to look for what is "Protestant" in the compilation, and the relative invisibility of Drake's chaplain in "Famous Voyage" will prove not to be unique. For the broader set of voyages Hakluyt records, traces of ministers and their actions are brief and rare, both in *PN* (1598–1600) and in related archival materials (see appendix 10). Their presence may be under-reported: Cabot's instructions for the Muscovy Company voyage of 1553 directed that morning and evening prayers should be conducted daily, by a minister on the admiral and by a merchant or learned person on the other ships, and Hakluyt's marginal comment to the list of personnel included in Willoughby's "True Note" notes next to the name of John Stafford, "A minister in the voyage." Stafford's ministry was evidently to be directed exclusively to his English companions; another item in Cabot's instructions directed the company "not to disclose to any nation the state of our religion, but to pass it over in silence."[123]

The actual presence of chaplains on several later voyages has already been noticed. Among voyages into regions claimed by Spain, we have encountered Madox and Walker for the Fenton voyage, Fletcher for Drake's circumnavigation, and Nichols for the 1587 raid on Cádiz – yet their presence is not discernible from Hakluyt's materials. The chaplain John Way, who sailed with Cavendish in 1586, is mentioned only once in the *PN* (1598–1600) account, as part of a landing party (Hakluyt's marginal comment calls him out as "John Way a preacher"); Thomas Hood's spare log of the Withrington and Lister voyage notes Sundays when "we sarvyd god," but the account by John Sarracoll (as edited by Hakluyt, at least) does not.[124] Roger Marbecke's account of the 1596 Cádiz expedition is characterized by the kinds of rhetoric visible in other belligerent narratives – for instance, attributing a naval victory to "the great mercy and goodnes of our living God" – but unusual in highlighting the presence of ministers and the practice of formal worship. Before setting sail, Marbecke notes, "the most holy name of our Omnipotent God" was invoked, and "his blessed and sacred Communion ... divers times most reverently celebrated." After the city was occupied, "the divine service was had, and a learned Sermon was made there by one master Hopkins, the ... Earle

---

122 "Famous Voyage," 3: 733; Vaux, *World Encompassed* (1854), 176.
123 Cabot, "Ordinances, 1553," 1: 227, 228; Willoughby, "True Copie," 1: 233.
124 Pretty, "Prosperous Voyage of M. Thomas Candish," 3: 811; Hood, "Red Dragon Logbook," fo. 21r.

of Essex his preacher."[125] As we have seen, however, Marbecke's narrative was withdrawn from PN (1598–1600) and is present only in some copies of the text.

Narratives where Protestants braved the Inquisition, faced imminent death in battle, or triumphed over Catholic antagonists, had one set of reasons for invoking religious identity and practice. Voyages that anticipated encountering or, indeed, living among Indigenous people had another. A minister named as Master Wolfall accompanied Frobisher's third voyage of 1578, which was intended to leave a colony to which he would have ministered; George Best adds that Wolfall hoped that he might "reforme those Infidels if it were possible to Christianitie." Wolfall's contacts with Inuit people, if any, are not reported, but he emerges twice in Best's text, both preaching sermons to the ships' companies and celebrating communion shortly before the expedition's return to England, "the first signe, seale, and confirmation of Christs name, death, and passion ever knowen in these quarters"; Hakluyt calls attention to this moment with a marginal note, "M. Wolfall a godly Preacher."[126] Frobisher's voyages were intended to locate a sea route through the Arctic, with an intended garrison emerging as a late plan. We might expect to find similar, or perhaps even more attentive recording of symbolic moments such as Wolfall's celebration of communion in Hakluyt's coverage of Roanoke, which Hakluyt's patron Walter Ralegh had from the outside intended as a colonizing venture. We have already examined Hakluyt's part in the wider dissemination of Thomas Harriot's account of the colony, *Briefe and True Report*, but this text was of course only part of the story; Ralegh's colonizing venture was attentively documented in PN (1598–1600), from the early scouting voyage of 1584, through multiple documents relating to the all-male settlement of 1585 to 1586; the small garrison of 1586; the colony of men, women, and families in 1587; and John White's failed search for the colonists in 1590. Harriot's efforts to declare "true doctrine ... and chiefe points of Religion" "in every towne where I came" were a rare attempt to evangelize; yet these varied documents bear few other indications of religious acts or identities.[127] A rare

---

125 Marbecke, "Honourable Voyage to Cadiz, 1596," 1: 607, 612, 615.
126 See Best, "True Discourse," 3: 84, 91. Cheryl Fury references a letter from the Privy Council to the bishop of Bath in 1578 concerning Wolfall's appointment, commenting that religious practice was necessary on shipboard (Fury, *Tides in the Affairs of Men*, 118, 134n130). Additional manuscript evidence of Wolfall's preaching to the company is provided in McDermott, *Third Voyage of Martin Frobisher*.
127 Harriot, "Briefe and True Report" (PN), 276–7.

exception occurs in White's account of the 1587 colony, which notes the christening of both Manteo and Virginia Dare, the infant daughter of Ananias and Eleanor Dare, but does so in the briefest of terms; neither christening is emphasized by the editor's marginalia, as Wolfall's service was.[128] Was there a minister in Roanoke? Such acts suggest that there was. In "Particuler Discourse," Hakluyt recommended that "one or two preachers for the voyage" be appointed, that Bibles and books of service should also be furnished, and that only artisans "which are protestantes" should be selected for the prospective colony.[129] (These comments, curiously, fall at the end of the text, under the heading of "Thinges forgotten," although the heading appears to indicate that they were to be integrated into a future draft which would then be "reduced into the best order.") Yet none of the documents printed by Hakluyt note the presence of a minister, and White's list of colonists does not identify a minister among the names of those who remained after his return to England.[130]

Hakluyt's failure to call attention to the two christenings at Roanoke is particularly surprising given the remarks on evangelization in "Particuler Discourse," which had been prepared in support of Ralegh's project. The text opens by proposing "thinlargement of the gospel of Christe" as the principal reason for English colonization: to "these poor people ... preachers should be sent." Even so, Hakluyt continues, despite "those of our nation that went with ffrobisher, Sr ffraunces Drake, and ffenton," he could not "name any one Infidell by them converted."[131] The emphasis of reformed Christianity on scripture over sacrament, which entailed requirements for language and literacy, renders it unsurprising that the fairly ephemeral encounters on these voyages did not result in more conversions; indeed, Hakluyt recommended that ministers sent to Roanoke not "ronne unto them rashly," but first learn the language and manners of their prospective converts, only then

---

128 Harriot's book does not mention these events, of which he surely knew.

129 Hakluyt, *PD*, 8, 127–8. In specifying the need to send Protestant rather than Catholic artisans, Hakluyt may have been thinking specifically of "Mynerall men," a category for which experts from Central Europe were often recruited; in fact, the man sent in 1585 was a Bohemian Jew, Joachim Gans (ibid., 193). On German miners and metallurgists in England, see Ash, *Power, Knowledge, and Expertise*, chap. 1; Baldwin, "Speculative Ambitions."

130 White, "Fourth Voyage to Virginia, 1587," 3: 284–5; White, "Names of All the Men, Women, and Children Safely Arrived in Virginia," 3: 285.

131 Hakluyt, *PD*, 11. On *PD*'s occasion see the introduction by David and Alison Quinn, xx–xxi.

transmitting "the swete and lively liquor of the gospel."[132] Manteo's conversion followed on such a process of acculturation – as we have seen in chapter 8, he had both spent time in England and engaged in serious and reciprocal language study with Harriot, one of only two Indigenous men to do so. A settled colony would evidently be required for there to be more. Given the nature of the conversion projects Hakluyt envisioned, such symbolic moments as the christening of Manteo and Virginia Dare would have to stand in, for some time, in the place of a broader evangelization that might eventually come. Given the aims that Hakluyt articulated in "Particuler Discourse," and his role in broadly publicizing the colony, we might expect such moments to be given particular emphasis.

The absence of such emphasis should surprise us. Roanoke was the sole English colonizing project that existed to be documented in PN (1598–1600); Hakluyt's engagement with the colony predated its inception, as we have seen, and he became both an investor in Roanoke and its greatest publicist.[133] Hakluyt's elder cousin received letters from Ralph Lane, the governor of the first group of colonists removed by Drake in 1586. David Quinn attributes to Hakluyt himself a brief account of that colony's departure and a resupply by Sir Richard Grenville later in the year, and White's account of his efforts to find the colonists in 1590 was addressed to the editor in warm terms: "as well for the satisfying of your earnest request, as the performance of my promise made unto you as my last being with you in England."[134] Hakluyt had particular (if not complete) access to both written records and eyewitnesses.[135] A different editor might have used this access to information and capacities for shaping it to highlight the religious character of English implantation and the sacramental acts that, at least symbolically, announced the arrival of the gospel on Virginia's shores, including a first, long-awaited conversion. The historical author of *Principal Navigations*, however, did not do so. The account in *World Encompassed* (1628) of Drake's acts of possession at Nova Albion, somewhere on the Pacific coast of North America, expressed the hope that through Elizabeth's rule, its people "might by the preaching of the Gospell, be brought to the right knowledge and obedience of the true and everliving

---

132 Hakluyt, PD, 8.

133 Hakluyt's name appears in a list of adventurers printed in PN (1589), 815–17.

134 Lane, "Master Ralph Lanes Letter to M. Richard Hakluyt Esquire, 1585"; Quinn and Quinn, "C&S," 2: 369; White, "Fifth Voyage to Virginia, 1590," 3: 287.

135 On sources Hakluyt was not able to obtain, however, see D. Quinn, "North America," 1: 246–7.

God." Hakluyt's "Famous Voyage" account attributes Drake's acceptance of dominion solely to a wish "that the riches & treasure thereof might so conveniently be transported to the enriching of her kindom at home."[136] The absence from *PN* (1598–1600) of what we might see as polemical texts that painted Drake's voyages as a kind of godly crusade was not simply an aberration that we might explain as particular to Drake, and thus perhaps explicable by the politics surrounding him. Rather, it appears symptomatic of a compilation in which at least at the surface of the text, the shaping role of Protestant belief was less often visible than Hakluyt's profession, and the historical reception of his work, might lead us to expect.

For an author like Hakluyt, authorship is largely a matter of choosing: choosing what to let in, and what to leave out. Ultimately, we sift these choices for significance, for moments when the editor seems to whisper that we should pause and direct our attention. Formally speaking, the beginnings and ends of books are a place to listen acutely for such editorial whispering. *Principal Navigations* opened with the conquests of King Arthur: how does it end? We might briefly recall the end of volume 1. There, Hakluyt moves from the Muscovy Company voyages to Muscovy and Persia, through the afterthought of Iceland, to what he calls the "double epiphonema" of the Armada battle and the 1596 raid on Cádiz. David Boruchoff supplies the contemporary definition of Hakluyt's term: "an amplifying of honestie, dignitie, profite, difficultie, or such other like, put at the end for the more mervelling."[137] We understand that these triumphs of England's maritime self-assertion against Spain, breaking though they do with the volume's geographical parameters, call back to and amplify both its dedicatory address to Charles Howard and the legendary victories of its opening pages. It was indeed with the "manifold Deliveries and Victories" of Elizabeth's "Warlike Fleets set forth to Sea against the Spaniards" that Purchas would conclude his own monumental collection.[138]

The heading to the last of volume 3's fourteen categories of materials gestures momentarily towards a different version of such an ending:

---

136 Drake, *World Encompassed*, 77; "Famous Voyage," 3: 738.
137 Richard Sherry, *A Treatise of the Figures of Grammer and Rhetorike* (London, 1555), 55r, cited in Boruchoff, "Richard Hakluyt and the Demands of Pietas Patriae," 195.
138 Purchas, *Pilgrimes*, 4: 1,891.

THE TWO FAMOUS VOYAGES HAPPILY Perfourmed round about the world, by Sir Francis Drake, and M. Thomas Candish Esquire together with the rest of our English voyages intended for the South Sea, the kingdomes of Chile, Peru, the backe side of Nueva Espanna, the Malucos, the Philippinas, the mightie Empire of China, though not so happy perfourmed as the two former; Whereunto are annexed certaine rare observations touching the present state of China, and the kingdome of Coray, lately invaded by Quabacondono the last monarch of the 66. princedomes of Japan.[139]

In the section that succeeds this heading, Hakluyt welds together fragments – the anonymous "Famous Voyage" and some partial English and Portuguese accounts of Drake's circumnavigation, fuller and more authoritative sources for Cavendish, a raft of deeply unsuccessful attempts on the Pacific by others, and a letter sent to the Emperor of China on a voyage that never returned, followed by Jesuit accounts of Japan and Korea. It is the collection's closest approach to the Chinese court where Hakluyt's cousin imagined Pet and Jackman arriving in 1580, or to Hakluyt's own grand invitation to Ralegh, in the Latin dedication to his edition of *De orbe novo*: "reveal to us the courts of China ... throw back the portals which have been closed since the world's beginning."[140] But *PN* (1598–1600) does not end there, looking across the Pacific towards the fading coursetracks of Cavendish and Drake; it ends with sources in translation, all three from Spanish, all concerned not with the secrets of Spanish discoveries, settlements, and wealth, but with process and procedure: the "sea-orders" of the Casa de la Contratación for ships sailing to the West Indies – lading, supply, manning, provisioning, and the organization of fleets; careening and caulking; and the examination process given to their pilots and masters along with other requirements and regulations. These sources illustrate Matthew Day's point that "paradoxically, foreignness is often invoked by Hakluyt not to condemn that otherness but to posit it as something to be replicated."[141]

The documents were written "upon the request and gratification of M. Richard Hakluyt" by Pedro Diaz, a Spanish pilot captured by Grenville in October 1585.[142] Following his capture, and although he was viewed as a flight risk, Diaz was nonetheless employed as a pilot on two voyages to Roanoke

---

139 Hakluyt, *PN* (1598–1600), 3: 730.
140 Taylor, *OW*, 2: 367.
141 Day, "Richard Hakluyt's 'Principal Navigations,'" 222–3.
142 Diaz, "Examination of the Masters and Pilots," 3: 868.

in 1586 and 1588; on the second, he succeeded in escaping, and once in Havana, provided Spanish authorities with a precise location for the colony to which he had twice piloted English ships.[143] He produced the documents printed by Hakluyt sometime in 1586 or 1587. Diaz's story provides a context within which to read the closing pages of *PN* (1598–1600), as a story about the persisting need for expert knowledge from beyond English shores, three decades after Thomas Wyndham had set sail to Africa with António Anes Pinteado (and, of course, about the costs of that knowledge). Nor were these documents an afterthought: taking up a theme touched on in the dedication to *Divers Voyages* and in letters to Walsingham, the concluding pages of volume 3 were anticipated in Hakluyt's initial dedication to Charles Howard in volume 1. While the first half of the dedication surveys Hakluyt's debts to Howard, and a history of the Howards' great deeds that continues through the defeat of a Spanish fleet and the occupation of a principal Spanish port, its remainder is a plea for institutions that would improve English seamanship "in imitation of Spaine." When Hakluyt read "the straight and severe examining of all such Masters as desire to take charge for the West Indies," he told Howard, "I greatly wished that I might be so happy as to see the like order established here with us."[144]

Principal Navigations opens with King Arthur, and an expansive imposition of British dominion over the North; its first volume is bookended with successful acts of violence. It closes on a different note, with translation, imitation, and an interest in technical expertise: soon, Hakluyt would broaden his circle of correspondents to include Spanish colleagues. At least as a public writer, Hakluyt was not committed to hardening the borders across which knowledge, or goods, or stories might travel. The case of Diaz invokes the benefits and risks of such commerce: even between warring states, movement took place. We close the book, thus, looking outwards from within a national community towards all of those with whom exchange is possible, on whatever terms – enemies, allies, partners intended and occasional – with the questions of what can be gained, what might be given in exchange, and what changes the absorption of foreign goods, knowledge, expertise, and persons may bring. That such exchanges will, indeed, take place is the founding supposition of Hakluyt's book.

---

143 Diaz's relation is printed in translation by D. Quinn, *NAW*, 3: 26–9. For Spanish efforts to find and suppress the colony, see ibid., 5: 56–7.

144 Hakluyt, "Epistle Dedicatorie (1598)," sig. *3r.

AFTERWORD

I hope that upon reaching this final shore, readers will understand a few things about Hakluyt's work clearly. Most centrally, I have tried to show that *Principal Navigations* does not support a view either of the work, or its author, in terms of strong, inflexible, ideological commitments, religious or nationalist. Hakluyt was a Protestant and a patriot, but a cosmopolitan and broad-minded one – at least as far as the public-facing evidence of print allows us to conclude. Those who think otherwise may examine the evidence and decide for themselves, after what will I hope at least be an orientation to this very complex book.

We began with Virginia Woolf's metaphor of the book as lumber room, which captures this idea of the book as a collection of objects, its covers a loose container for an accumulation of documents and events. Throughout this book, we have thought about these objects on their own terms, in relation to other objects, and in relation to the various logics that position them in the book. As we come to turn the last page, it may be useful to explore an alternate perspective that has come into view already – to think of *Principal Navigations* also as a collection of borders, of lines drawn across the field of its world. Such an idea has its material manifestation in cartographies that represent the course tracks of celebrated actors like Thomas Cavendish and Francis Drake, tracks that can be represented as lines, as a series of mathematically defined points, or as narrative. But the paths of travel, the stories and observations that adhere to them, and the places they connect are only the beginning of this collection of demarcations.

The boundaries of the collection itself are themselves another drawn line, and a crucial one. The presence of every item in the collection represents a positive choice on Hakluyt's part, and implies a quantum of labour, even of expense. As they crossed this border and entered the collection, the items Hakluyt admitted were shorn of many accompanying properties: material

Figure 11.1 The Molyneux globe displayed the coursetracks of the two circumnavigations by Drake and Cavendish, using dotted lines.

form, paratextual features like titles and dedications, images, original languages, the remainder of the larger texts of which they had once formed part. Some came accompanied with a small constellation of ancillary sources. All acquired new graphic and generic identities within the compilation as well as new meanings catalyzed by context and editorial framing. Behind the objects chosen for admission, in many cases, lay a trail of other items never considered, never known, or positively excluded.

Hakluyt's criteria of admission were irregular.[1] Some contents were offered, even pressed on him. Others had to be effortfully acquired. Some were searched out but denied to the editor, while other materials, seemingly easily identified, were never included and have been lost to time. Some of his choices, like the exclusion of John Mandeville's "Travels" and the relation of David Ingram from the second edition, have been read for meaning, as evidence of changing editorial principles and heightened standards of truth.[2] Yet if such principles governed these exclusions, they were not uniformly applied: the marvellous peoples of Central Asia described by Sigismund von Herberstein and Abū al-Fidā persisted without remark. Evidentiary standards for materials on West Africa, whether inside the collection or in associated sources, were surprisingly low even though the editor had ample sources for critical scrutiny of authors like Richard Eden or John Pory in the first-hand observations of English witnesses that he himself printed. Other choices of inclusion and exclusion challenge claims we might wish to make about the editor's standards, as these were expressed in his book. In 1600, Sir Humphrey Gilbert's treatise on the Northwest Passage still occupied eighteen pages in the opening section of volume 3; it was written, in the 1560s, by a military man with some learning but without experience at sea, and relied on an assembly of second- and third-hand evidence and hearsay for its speculative hydrography. In 1595, the Arctic navigator John Davis had published another treatise on the Northwest Passage, drawing not only on the classical authorities cited by Gilbert, but on his own three voyages in search of the passage, the experience of other English navigators, apparent reading of *Principall Navigations* (1589), a knowledge of mathematical navigation acquired through his tutelage by John Dee, and convictions grounded in a theology that no

---

[1] As Matthew Steggle writes, "We should beware of coming to Hakluyt with the expectation that we will find a monolithic consistency of purpose and technique, since his work is more interesting than that" ("Charles Chester and Richard Hakluyt," 78).

[2] See, inter alia, Parry, "Hakluyt's View of British History," 6–7; Ramsay, "Northern Europe," 155.

AFTERWORD

climate had been created impossible for human activity, passage, and trade. Hakluyt extracted the narrative, but left unused Davis's well-informed accounts of hydrography and temperature, the armature of theory that rendered plausible a route through the Arctic, and his fervent arguments that through the discovery of a northern passage to Asia, England was destined to spread the gospel to the infidels.[3] Gilbert's outdated, speculative, and secular proposals persisted in their stead. Each of Hakluyt's dividing lines makes a kind of sense, and can be understood as part of a larger logic; perhaps Gilbert's rank trumped Davis's experience, perhaps his text persisted by inertia. But the logics of the collection are multiple, and the criteria that govern the editor's choices responded to a variety of pressures.

To say "border" is also to invoke the dividing lines between nations and cultures. Such implicit dividing lines between England and the world's near and far peoples are among the most visible features of the book's contents. Lesley Cormack writes that "Hakluyt stressed the dissimilarities between the English and other peoples by describing strange customs and practices. By stressing odd and foreign attributes, he drew a distinction between the 'other' and the homely English reader."[4] Readers of this book, I hope, will by now be prepared to resist collapsing "Hakluyt" either with the book he edited or the materials it contained, but the point holds. To give one confirming example drawn unambiguously from Hakluyt's work as author, the entry for "women" in the index to *Principall Navigations* (1589) – a paratextual aid that he would not attempt to provide in 1600 – provides entries focused solely on foreign women and largely on the aberrant cultural or somatic properties that marked such women, not as individuals but types, as distinctly and deferentially "other."[5] No other representations of women are indexed.

And yet: these lines of cultural, national, or ethnic difference were by no means drawn in the same places or with the same exclusionary or contrastive

---

3 Davis writes (for instance): "what hindreth us of England (being by Gods mercy for the same purpose at this present most aptly prepared) not to attempt that which God himselfe hath appointed to be performed [i.e., the discovery of a Northwest Passage], ther is no doubt but that wee of England are this saved people by the eternal & infallible presence of ye lord predestinated to be sent unto these Gentiles in the sea" (*Worldes Hydrographicall Discription*, C6v).

4 Cormack, "Good Fences," 652.

5 "Women of Arabia, their apparell and ornaments. 232. Women paint their faces in Moscovie. 346. Breasts of women very long. 102. Women deadly and hurtfull in their lookis. 71. The undecent maner of riding used by the women of Moscovie. 409. Women bought and sold, and let out to hire in Persia. 425. The maners of the young

rigour. Ottomans, Muscovites, Spanish, Portuguese, and African customs, knowledge, and people were at times derided, excluded, and combatted, at others made the target of imitation, admiration, inclusion, or alliance, admitted as correspondents, envoys, or brokers. Confessional identities exhibit some of the same flexibility. And as Hakluyt looked back in time to craft an authorizing genealogy for the achievements of the present, the borders defining England itself, who was English, or what the English language itself was, grew less rather than more legible.

Hakluyt's book describes a world; along the trajectories of his travellers, information of new kinds accrued. Yet this accreted description is not neutral across the world that the book represents. Even taking into account the uneven distribution of English activity and presence, Hakluyt's prefaces and his allocation of space and place within the compilation express values and preferences, his own and those of the actors the book represents. Information may be gathered together in a way that gives priority to corporate actors over geographical location: this is true for the Muscovy Company voyages to Persia, located in "the North" (volume 1) even though Persia itself was located to the south of places located in the volume on "the South" (volume 2). Other information is dispersed, elevating ultimate or even intended destinations over regions contacted, sometimes at more length: this is often true for Newfoundland, Iceland, or West Africa. The dividing lines that disassemble these regions in the paratext seem to tell us that these are places that matter principally as a means to arrive somewhere else – just as Hakluyt curiously frames his volume-length celebration of England's northern voyages by announcing, "it is high time for us to weigh our ancre ... and with all speede to direct our course for the milde, lightsome, temperate, and warme Atlantick Ocean."[6] We, too, seek to organize what we can observe about the book and its contours. In reflecting on the values expressed in Hakluyt's organizing practices and the language of his documents, we sense at times the organizing pressure of other lines drawn on the globe.

The lines of latitude marking the limits of the sun's apparent motion were a function of the mathematical geography persistently advocated by Hakluyt, yet the lingering qualitative associations of latitude can be glimpsed at many moments in the compilation, in documents and editorial paratext; incoherent

---

women amongst the Savages of America. 530" (Hakluyt, *PN* [1589], sig. Ffff3r. For discussion of this index entry and the un-indexed occurrence of English and non-English women in the two editions of the compilation, see Fuller, "Looking for the Women").

6 Hakluyt, "Preface to the Reader (1598)," sig. *5r.

as the assumptions of earlier cosmography became after a century and more of empirical observation between the tropics and in the Arctic, mariners and scholars alike remained prone to assume that latitude informed on more than temperature and seasonal variation in the length of the day, and to find plausible that strange conditions might obtain in latitudes they considered to be extreme. More than seventy years after Robert Thorne cited Columbus's discoveries in the Caribbean to debunk cosmographical theories about the equatorial regions as an extreme climate, Davis made the same point, attempting to make plausible an Arctic open to navigation.[7] Even when thinking latitudinally, however, English writers made distinctions in practice between west and east across the band of the tropics: the tropical Caribbean, understood as a zone of abundance whose peoples had been tyrannically oppressed by Spain, and tropical Africa, *imagined* despite observed experience as a desert of hideous heat whose people remained beyond the pale of civility. These distinctions ran deep, even if they were never articulated as systematically as those along a north to south axis. Indigenous Americans were consistently indicated by the term "savages," but proposed as potential subjects, catechants, and even allies, implicitly or explicitly inviting the intervention of English voyagers and colonists who may have understood themselves to have been civilized by others.[8] West Africans, by contrast, were the target of no apparent thought at all, even as English mariners traded with them in exotic and mundane goods, burned their orderly towns, and converted them readily to property themselves – although slavery, as yet, did not exist in England as a legal category.[9] Nonetheless, despite the reverse travels into England of

7 Davis, *Worldes Hydrographical Discription*, sig. C4r–C5r.
8 See, for instance, the marginal comment on "Romane swords" as "teachers of civilitie" in Purchas, *Pilgrimes*, 4 (ix): 1,755.
9 The West Indian narratives of volume 3, as well as longer narratives of Drake's voyages published in the seventeenth century, are rich in references to captured ships whose cargo included enslaved Africans; only occasionally do we learn more. Traces of evidence suggests that some at least were not set on shore, but retained, whether to be sold again in the West Indies or brought to England (see, for instance, Nichols, *Sir Francis Drake Revived*, 38). Diego, an African or Afro-Caribbean man who first appears in Nichols's account of the 1572 voyage, apparently returned to England with Drake as a retainer of some kind (he was described as "Drake's man," and sailed on the voyage of circumnavigation). Nuño da Silva testified that Drake "carried [Diego] with him from his [Drake's] country"; other captives remarked his presence, because he spoke Spanish as well as English. He was among several crew members killed by Patagonians in the Straits (Nichols, *Sir Francis Drake Revived*, 15, 33; Nuttall, *New Light on Drake*, 302, 325; Vaux, *World Encompassed* [1854], 178–9).

Indigenous American visitors, captives, and envoys, it was African and Afro-Caribbean immigrants, voluntary or (especially) involuntary, who became not distant others but neighbours at home, even if this untheorized and unlegislated presence left only a handful of traces in Hakluyt's collection.[10]

The nation as imagined in *Principal Navigations* was not a stable term. Looking backwards in time, King Edgar's policing of England's maritime boundaries, King Arthur's expansive conquests, and the disdain for foreign goods articulated in "Libelle of Englyshe Polycye" were balanced against something more permeable, more in need of civilizing, and eventually more cosmopolitan. Whether in the form of objects, interviews, texts, correspondents abroad, or persons employed, captured, admitted as denizens, foreign knowledge and expertise was imported and domesticated as well, and the triumphal metaphor of piracy describes only a fraction of these exchanges. At the same time, within the envelope of national identity, the seafarers celebrated in the pages of *Principal Navigations* sometimes competed among themselves to control stories that could never be the property of single authors or doers except by a kind of fiction. The consensus account provided by unitary narratives was always the product of negotiation and mediation, some of the traces of which remain in the record of Hakluyt's text and even its varied physical copies. Those unitary narratives subsist alongside other versions, some that survive in other manuscript or print sources, some that can be inferred – through the evidence of wills, the evidence of context, the evidence of archaeology, or simply the understanding that other persons or peoples existed, in a past of historical experience that has its own descents and consequences. Not all the voices of these histories speak in the compilation; yet they may press against its borders, and make the contours of those borders more legible for us.

The lines Hakluyt drew, the limits of his attention and interest, give particular shape to the world his book mediates, and we have re-examined where and how those lines were drawn, as the work of an individual scholar rather than as a mimetic representation of either geographies or histories. To write *a* book about Hakluyt, to map the world of his book, also required drawing many lines. This book, too, has its limits, of attention, of expertise, and of length, and a great deal of *Principal Navigations* still remains outside them; reader, please take this map and better it with your own observations.

---

10 On Indigenous arrivals in London, see Thrush, *Indigenous London*; Vaughan, *Transatlantic Encounters*. On African and Afro-Caribbean presence, see Habib, *Black Lives in the English Archives*.

APPENDICES

APPENDIX 1

Contents of Volume 2(ii), in Order of Appearance

This appendix displays the contents of the second half of volume 2 in the order they would be encountered by readers. As the legend indicates, the list is marked up to differentiate materials added by Hakluyt to the second edition, materials categorized by Hakluyt as "Voyages," and materials relating to different regions. This listing indicates only *where* contents related to naval battles and raids appear in the volume; more detail on these materials appears in appendix 7.1.

Added in 1599: +
Categorized as "Voyages": †
Atlantic islands: #
Morocco and North Africa: &
West Africa: ℙ
East Asia and the Indian Ocean: %
[Naval battles and raids (not detailed)][1] (square brackets)

1. †# António Galvão, "The voyage of Macham the first discoverer of the Isle of Madera, in the yeere 1344" (Galvão, *Tratado* [...] *dos diversos & desvayrados caminhos* [...], 1563; probably translated by Hakluyt).
2. & "Note concerning the ayde and assistance given to king John the first of Portugale, by certaine English merchants, for the winning of Ceut in Barbary, Anno. 1415."
3. ℙ "The Ambassage of John the second king of Portugale to Edward the 4. King of England, to stay John Tintam, and William Fabian Englishmen, preparing for a voyage to Guinea, Anno 1481."
4. # "A briefe note conerning an ancient trade of English merchants to the Canarie Isles, Anno. 1526."
5. # "Thomas Nicholls, A description of the Canarie Islands, with their strange fruits and commodities" (Nicholls, *A pleasant description*, 1583).
6. +†& James Alday, "The first voyage to Barbary, Anno 1551."

---

[1] These materials are discussed in chapter 7.

APPENDIX 1

7. +†& James Thomas, "The second voyage to Barbary, 1551."
8. †℞ Richard Eden, "The voyage of M. Thomas Windam to Guinea and the kingdom of Benin, Anno 1553" (Eden, *Decades*, 1555).
9. †℞ Richard Eden, "The voyage of M. John Lok to Guinea, Anno 1554" (Eden, *Decades*, 1555).
10. †℞ "The first voyage of M. William Towrson marchant of London to Guinea, [...] 1555."
11. †℞ "The second voyage of M. William Towrson to Guinea and the castle of Mina. An. 1556."
12. †℞ "The third voyage of the sayd M. William Towrson to the coast of Guinea and the river of Sestos, Anno 1557."
13. ℞ "The commodities and wares that are most desired in Guinea."
14. +℞ "Certaine articles of remembrance delibered to M. John Lok, touching a voyage to Guinea, Anno 1561."
15. +℞ "John Lok, A letter [...] to the worshipfull company of marchants adventurers of Guinea, Anno 1561."
16. +†℞ "William Rutter, A voyage made to Guinea at the charges of Sir William Gerard, Sir William Chester, &c. Anno 1562."[2]
17. +℞ "A meeting at Sir William Gerards house for the setting forth of a voyage to Guinea, with the Minion of the Queenes, The John Baptist of London, and the Merline of M. Gonson, Anno 1564."
18. †℞ John Sparke, "A relation of the successe of the same voyage, taken out of a voyage of Sir John Hawkins to the West Indies."[3]
19. †℞ Walter Wren, "The voyage of M. George Fenner to Guinea and the Isles of Capo Verde, An. 1566."
20. †& "The voyage and ambassage of Master Edmund Hogan to the Emperour of Marocco, Anno 1577."
21. +†& "Joannes Thomas Freigim, The voyage of Thomas Stukely into Barbary, 1578."[4]

2 Features in both categories of the contents list.

3 Features in both categories of the contents list. The full text appears in *PN*, Volume 3 (see table 6.2, item 4).

4 Hakluyt added a paragraph on "divers other English gentlemen" who participated in the battle of Alcazar, including Christopher Lister, who subsequently served as captain on several voyages set forth by the Earl of Cumberland. Two narrated in *PN* include John Sarracoll, "Voyage of M. Robert Withrington, and M. Christopher Lister, 1586," and Nicholas Downton, "Firing and Sinking of The Cinquo Chaguas, 1594."

22. +% Galeote Pereira, "Certaine reports of the mighty Kingdome of China" (Richard Willes, *The history of travayle*, 1577, tr. *Novi avisi delle Indie di Portogallo* [...] *Quarta parte*, 1565).
23. +% Richard Willes, "A discourse of the Isle of Japan, and of other Isles in the East Ocean, &c." (*The history of travayle*, 1577; from various sources).
24. +% Duarte Sande, "An excellent description of the kingdome of China, and of the estate and government thereof" (*De missione legatorum Japonensium ad Romanum curiam*, 1590).[5]
25. †% Thomas Stevens, "The voyage of Thomas Stevens about the Cape of Buona Experanza unto Goa in the Est India, Anno 1579."
26. +% Peter of Lisbon, "A briefe relation of the great magnificence and rich traffike of the kingdome of Pegu beyond the East India."
27. +†% Richard Hakluyt/Edmund Barker, "The memorable voyage of M. James Lancaster about the Cape of Buona Esperanza [...] as far as the maine land of Malacca [...] begun in the yeere 1591."[6]
28. +⁜ "Certaine remembrances of a voyage intended to Brasil, and to the river of Plate, but miserably overthrowen neere Rio grande in Guinea [...] 1583."
29. ["The escape of the *Primrose* [...] 1585."]
30. & "The Letters patents granted [...] for a trade to Barbary, Anno. 1585."
31. †& "The voyage and ambassage of Master Henry Roberts to Mully Hamet Emperour of Marocco, Anno 1585."
32. & "Edicts and correspondence, Morocco."
33. [Cruises and raids.]
34. ⁜ "A patent graunted [...] for a trade to the rivers of Senega and Gambra in Guinea, Anno 1588."
35. +†⁜ James Welsh, "A voyage to Benin beyond the countrey of Guinea [...] set foorth in the yeere 1588."
36. ⁜ Anthony Ingram, "A relation concerning a voyage [...] to the kingdome and citie of Benin, An. 1588."
37. +†⁜ James Welsh, "The second voyage [...] to Benin in Africa, An. 1590."
38. +⁜ "An advertisement to king Philip the 2. Of Spaine, from Angola [...] An. 1591."
39. [Cruises, battles and raids.]

---

5   From a captured Portuguese carrack ("Taking of the Madre de Dios").

6   An additional narrative by a member of Lancaster's crew, taken up on the return voyage by a French ship in the West Indies, appears in *PN* 3 as May, "Voyage of Henry May, 1591, & 1592."

40. +℞ "A relation concerning the estate of the Island and Castle of Arguin, and touching the rich and secret trade from the inland of Africa thither [1591]."
41. +†℞ Richard Rainolds, "The voyage of Richard Rainolds and Thomas Dassell to the rivers of Senega and Gambra, neere the coast of Guinea, Anno 1591."
42. +℞ Laurence Madoc, "Two brief relations concerning the Cities and Provinces of Tombuto and Gago, and [...] the conquest thereof by the king of Marocco, and of the huge masse of gold, which he yerely receiveth thence for tribute [...] 1594."
43. +℞ "A briefe extract of a patent [...] for traffick betweene the river of Nonnia, and the rivers of Madrabumba and Sierra Leona, on the coast of Guinea, An. 1592."
44. [Actions at sea.]
45. +& "A report of the casting away of the Tobie [...] on the coast of Barbary [...] 1593."
46. +& "The letters of the Queens Majestie [...] unto the Emperour of Ethiopia, Anno 1597."

APPENDIX 2

West African Materials in Volume 3 (By Subheading)

This contents list accompanies the discussion of African materials in chapter 6; while the most readily visible materials on Africa are found in the second half of volume 2, a significant proportion of information about contacts with Africa is embedded in accounts of voyages to the Americas in volume 3.

ENGLISH VOYAGES UNDERTAKEN FOR THE FINDING OF A NORTHWEST PASSAGE

1. George Best, "Experiences and reasons of the Sphere to proove all parts of the worlde habitable" (pp. 41–56).

DIVERS VOYAGES MADE BY ENGLISH MEN TO [...] THE GREAT AND LARGE KINGDOME OF NEW SPAINE

2. Miles Philips, "The voyage of Miles Philips one of the company put on shore by sir John Hawkins, 1568" (pp. 469–87).
3. Job Hortop, "The travels of Job Hortop set on land by John Hawkins 1586 in the bay of Mexico" (pp. 487–94).

THE PRINCIPALL ENGLISH VOYAGES TO ALL THE ISLES CALLED LAS ANTILLAS

4. "The first voyage of the right worshipfull and valiant knight sir John Hawkins [...] made to the West Indies in the yere 1562" (p. 500).
5. John Sparke, "The second voyage made by the R. W. sir John Hawkins [...] to the coast of Guinie, & from thence to the isle of Dominica [...] Begun 1564" (pp. 501–21).
6. John Hawkins, "The third troublesome voyage of the right worshipfull sir John Hawkins [...] to the parts of Guinea, and the coasts of Tierra firma, and Nueva Espanna, Anno 1567, & 1568" (pp. 521–5).

7. Walter Bigges and Thomas Cates, "The famous expedition of Sir Francis Drake to the West Indies [...] in the yeers 1585, and 1586" (pp. 534–48).
8. "A declaration of the Capes and Islands as well of Madera, the Canaries, and The west Indies, as of the Açores, and the Isles of Cabo Verde" (pp. 624–7).

CERTAINE VOYAGES, NAVIGATIONS, AND TRAFFIQUES [...] TO DIVERS PLACES UPON THE COAST OF BRASILL

9. "The first voyage of M. William Hawkins of Plimmouth, father unto sir John Hawkins to Brasil Anno 1530" (pp. 700–1).

DIVERS ENGLISH VOYAGES, SOME INTENDED AND SOME PERFORMED TO THE STREIGHTS OF MAGELLAN, THE SOUTH SEA, ALONG THE COASTS OF CHILI [...]

10. "The famous voyage of Sir Francis Drake into the South Sea, and therehence about the globe of the whole earth, begunne Anno 1577" (pp. 730–42).
11. "The voyage of M. Edward Fenton and M. Luke Ward [...] intended for China, but performed only to the coast of Brasil, [...] begunne in the yeere 1577" (pp. 757–68).
12. "The voyage of M. Robert Withrington, and M. Christopher Lister intended for the South Sea [...] but performed onely to the Southerly latitude of 44. Degrees, begun Anno 1586" (pp. 769–78).
13. "The prosperous voyage of M. Thomas Candish esquire into the South Sea, and so round about the circumference of the whole earth, begun in the yere 1586. and finished 1588" (pp. 803–25).

APPENDIX 3

Eden's Narrative of John Lok's Voyage to Guinea (1554), in Decades *and in* Principal Navigations

This appendix accompanies the discussion of Eden's narrative in chapter 6.

L: Pilot's log
O: Personal observations by Eden; personal observations by mariners (reported)
W: Various written sources

Eden, *Decades*: The seconde voyage to Guinea.	Hakluyt, PN 2(ii): The second voyage to Guinea set out by Sir George Barne, Sir John Yorke, Thomas Lok, Anthonie Hickman and Edward Castelin, in the yere 1554. The Captaine whereof was M. John Lok.
Eden's introduction to the pilot's log (349v).	
"In the yeare of owre lorde M.D.LIII [...]" (349v–54r). L: Pilot's log from 11 October 1554 to 22 April 1555, then from 8°N to 42°N, followed by scattered notes.	Not present: log entries for 2 November to 17 November 1554. Marginal note added: "Robert Gainsh was master of the John Evangelist."[1]

---

1 Hakluyt's running heads in PN (1589) assign the voyage *to* Robert Gainsh; in PN (1598–1600), to John Lok. The anonymous pilot was evidently on the *Bartholomew*. (The third ship was the *Trinitie*.)

"Nowe therefore to speake somewhat of the contrey and people" (354r)
O: Eden's personal observations of gold, spices, elephant tusks, and an elephant's head returned to London.

Marginal note added: "Sir Andrew Judde" (in text: "This head divers have seene in the house of ... Sir Andrew Judde, where also I saw it.")

"The description and properties of the Elephante" (354r–55v)
W: Eden's survey of classical sources on elephants (and dragons).

"The people of Africa" (355v–58r)
W: Eden draws on classical geographers, scripture, and sixteenth-century cosmography.
O: The testimony of mariners used for some physical phenomena at sea: "sum of our men ... that were in this last vyage," "Rycharde Chaunceler toulde me that he harde Sebastian Cabot reporte ... (as farre as I remember)."

"Many thynges more owre men saw and consydered in this vyage" (358r–59r)
O: Personal observations by mariners of African dress and adornment, trade practices, houses, and diet.

Observations at sea and in London (359r–60r)
O: Partly by the mariners and partly by Eden: spices, shells on ships' keels, winds, English morbidity and latitude/climate, African captives and latitude/climate, variations in hair and skin colour.

Marginal note added: "Five blacke Moores brought in to England."

APPENDIX 4

The Anglo-Spanish Sea War in Volumes 1 and 2

Below are listed the contents of *Principal Navigations* related to naval engagements and belligerent encounters at sea taking place in European waters; these are discussed in chapter 7. As the list makes evident, most such materials are clustered in the second half of volume 2. The initials preceding each title indicate the nature of Hakluyt's source, whether it had been previously printed, and, if so, in what physical format. A chronology of events follows the list of materials.

MS: materials taken from manuscript sources
P: materials previously published as pamphlets
B: materials previously published as part of larger works in folio or quarto

VOLUME 1

1. [MS/B] "Vanquishing of the Spanish Armada [...] recorded in Latin by Emanuel van Meteren in the 15. book of his history of the low countries." Bodleian Tanner MS 255; also represented in *Historia Belgica* (1597).
2. [MS] "The honorable voyage unto Cadiz, 1596." BL Sloane MS 226.[1]

VOLUME 2 (I)

3. Philip Jones, "The voyage of five marchants ships of London into Turkie, and their valiant fight in their returne with 11. Gallies, and two frigats of the King of Spaines [...] Anno. 1586." Unidentified source.[2]

---

1 Additional mss. are listed in Payne, "Suppression of the Voyage to Cadiz," 16n49.
2 As noted in chapter 7, "C&S" mistakenly provides as source a non-extant news pamphlet by Thomas Ellis, *A true report in verse of a sea fight*, 1586.

VOLUME 2(1)

Other contents are in *italics*.[3]

Madeira and the Canaries, 1344–1526 (pp. 1–6)
Barbary, 1551–52 (pp. 7–9)
Guinea, 1553–66 (pp. 9–64)
Morocco and Barbary, 1577–78 (pp. 64–48)
Translated reports of China and Japan, varying dates (pp. 68–99)
T. Stevens to Goa, 1579 (pp. 99–102)
J. Lancaster to the Indies, 1591–94 (pp. 102–10)
Shipwreck on the Guinea coast, 1583 (pp. 110–11)

    4. [P] [Humphrey Mote],[4] "The escape of the Primrose, a ship of London, from before the towne of Bilbao in Biscay [...] Anno 1585" (pp. 112–14). *The Primrose of London with her valiant aduenture on the Spanish coast* [...], London, 1585.

A patent for trade to Barbary, 1585 (pp. 114–17)
Diplomatic exchanges with Morocco, 1585–87 (pp. 117–20)

    5. [MS] John Evesham, "The voyage made by two of Sir Walter Raleghs pinnaces [...] to the Azores [...] in the yere 1586" (pp. 120–1). BL Harley MS 167, fo. 113.[5]

    6. [MS] "The voyage of Sir Francis Drake to Cadiz [...] and his taking of the great East Indian Carak called the Sant Philip [...] Anno 1587" (pp. 121–23). Unidentified source.[6]

A patent for Guinea and three relations of voyages to Benin (pp. 126–33)
A letter to Philip II from Angola (pp. 133)

---

    3 Materials are listed in order of appearance in the volume, without respect to the categories of "voyages" and ancillary documents used in Hakluyt's "Catalogue" of contents.

    4 The author's name is provided in the original pamphlet publication, but not given by Hakluyt.

    5 Other documents under this name include the journal of a voyage to Egypt in PN 2(i), and a ms. account of the Norris-Drake expedition to Lisbon, 1589, for which the author served as a gunner on the *Gregory* of London. Evesham's narrative is printed in Wernham, *Expedition of Norris and Drake*, 226–36. The volume of naval sources in which the original is found was once owned by John Dee.

    6 As noted in chapter 7, "C&S" mistakenly attributes Hakluyt's text to Robert Leng or Long.

7. [P] Anthony Wingfield, "The voyage to Spaine and Portugale written (as it is thought) by Colonell Anthonie Wingfield, An. 1589" (pp. 134–55). *True coppie of a discourse*, London, 1589.
8. [B] Edward Wright, "The voyage of the Earl of Cumberland to the Azores, 1589" (pp. 155–66). *Certaine errors in navigation*, London, 1599.
9. [P] "A fight performed by ten marchants ships of London against 12 Spanish galleys, in the Streit of Gibraltar. An. 1590" (pp. 166–8). No extant copies of a pamphlet listed in the Stationers' Register ("C&S").
10. [P] "The valiant fight performed in the Streit of Gibraltar by the Centurion of London, against five Spanish gallies, An. 1591" (pp. 168–9). *The valiant and most laudable fight by the Centurion*, London, 1591.
11. [P] Walter Ralegh, "A true report of the fight about the Isles of the Azores, betweene the Revenge one of her Majesties ships, under the conduct of Sir Richard Grinvile, and an Armada of the King of Spaine, An. 1591" (pp. 169–75). Hakluyt's version is not identical with *A report of the truth of the fight about the iles of Açores*, London, 1591.[7]
12. [MS] Robert Flicke, "A voyage of certaine ships of London to the coast of Spaine, and the Azores, Anno 1591" (pp. 176–8). Unidentified source.
13. [B] "A large testimony of John Huighen van Linschoten concerning the worthy exploits atchieved by the right hon. the erle of Cumberland [etc.] about the Isles of the Açores [...] in the yeares 1589, 1590, 1591" (pp. 178–88). *Discours of voyages*, London, 1598.[8]

Materials on Senegambia, Timbuktu, and Sierra Leone (pp. 188–93).

14. [MS] Thomas White, "The taking of two Spanish ships laden with quicksilver and with the Popes Bulles, bound for the west Indies, by M. Thomas White in the Amitie of London, An. 1592" (pp. 193–4). BL Lansdowne MS 70/23.
15. [MS] "The taking of the mightie and rich Carak called the Madre de Dios, and of the Santa Clara a Biskaine of 600 tunnes, as likewise the firing of another great Carak called The Santa Cruz Anno 1592" (pp. 194–9). Unidentified source.

---

7 See Earle, *The Last Fight of the Revenge*. Among other materials by contemporary witnesses, Arthur Gorges's critical account was printed by Purchas, *Pilgrimes*, and Monson's can be found in *The Naval Tracts of Sir William Monson*.

8 I have not closely checked Hakluyt's text against the printed translation, with which he was involved.

16. [MS] Nicholas Downton, "The firing and sinking of the stout and warlike Carack called The Cinquo Chaguas, or The five wounds, by three ships of the R. H. the Earle of Cumberland, 1594" (pp. 199–201). Unidentified source.

The casting away of the Toby [...] *1593* (pp. 201–3).

The Queen's letter to the King of Ethiopia, 1597 (pp. 203–4).

CHRONOLOGY OF VOYAGES

1585: Philip's order for the arrest of English ships in Spanish ports. Attempted seizure of the *Primrose* at Bilbao (volume 2[ii], item 4).

1586: Ralegh's ships raid the Azores, capture Pedro de Sarmiento (volume 2[ii], item 5). Turkey Company ships attacked in the Mediterranean (volume 2[i], item 3).

1587: Drake attacks Cádiz, takes the *Saõ Phelipe* (volume 2[ii], item 6).

1588: Defeat of the Armada (volume 1, item 1).

1589: Drake and Norris raid Lisbon. Cumberland raids the Azores (volume 2[ii], items 7–8).

1590: Levant Company ships fight with Spanish galleys (volume 2[ii], item 9).

1591: The *Centurion* fights off galleys (volume 2[ii], item 10). T. Howard and Cumberland raid the Azores; loss of the *Revenge* (items 11–13).

1592: Two Spanish ships taken by a Barbary trader (volume 2[ii], item 14). *Madre de Deus* taken (item 15).

1594: Cumberland's ships burn the *Cinquas Llaguas* carrack (volume 2[ii], item 16).

1596: Howard and Essex sack Cádiz (volume 1, item 2).

APPENDIX 5

Authorship and Editing in Hakluyt's Materials on the Anglo-Spanish Sea War

This list breaks down materials on the sea war by details relating to their authorship. Hakluyt promised to assign each of his narratives to a named author who could attest to what he had personally seen; these materials indicate that only sometimes did the editor fulfill his promise to provide clearly attributed eyewitness accounts. Item numbers are the same used in appendix 4.

+: author named by Hakluyt
*: author was a participant[1]
^: author uses "I" in contexts other than address to the reader
Bold: author was a participant and named by Hakluyt
Bold italics: author was a participant, named by Hakluyt, and uses "I" in his text

KNOWN AUTHORS

1. + Emanuel van Meteren, "Vanquishing of the Spanish Armada."[2]
2. *^ [Roger Marbecke],[3] "The honorable voyage unto Cadiz, 1596."
3. + Philip Jones, "The voyage of five marchants ships of London into Turkie, and their valiant fight in their returne with 11. Gallies, and two frigats of the King of Spaines [...] Anno. 1586."[4]

---

1 I have construed "participant" fairly broadly, to include not only persons who took part in voyages, but someone like Linschoten (item 14) who was an eyewitness to some events at the Azores from a position on land.
 2 Van Meteren, the Dutch consul in London, was a correspondent and collaborator of the editor.
 3 Marbecke's authorship is clear in the manuscript record although omitted from PN.
 4 The minister and translator Philip Jones, who may be the author of this text, provided a dedicatory poem to PN (1589), and praised Hakluyt's forthcoming work in the dedication to his translation of Meyer, *Certaine Briefe, and Speciall Instructions*. Sherman

4. [Humphrey Mote],[5] "The escape of the Primrose, 1585." Mote appears to be unknown except as author of this text.
5. +*^ *John Evesham*, "The voyage made by two of Sir Walter Raleigh's pinnaces to the Azores, John Evesham, gentleman."
8. +* *Edward Wright*, "The voyage of the Earl of Cumberland to the Azores, 1589."
11. + Sir Walter Ralegh, "A true report of the fight [...] between the Revenge [...] and an Armada, 1591."
12. +*^ *Robert Flicke*, "A report of Mr. Robert Flicke [...] [re] the London supplies sent to my Lord Thomas Howard."[6]
13. +*^ *Jan Huyghen van Linschoten*, "A large testimony of Jan Huyghen van Linschoten Hollander" (Linschoten, *His discours of voyages* [London, 1598]).[7]
14. +*^ *Thomas White*, "The manner of the taking of two Spanish ships [...] bound for the West Indies, by M. Thomas White."[8]
16. +*^ *Nicholas Downton*, "The firing and sinking of the [...] carack called [...] The five wounds, by [...] Nicholas Downton."[9]

also attributes to Jones a 1586 manuscript proposal, "Concerning a Passage to be made from our North-Sea, into the Southe-Sea," now BL MS Harley 167, item 13 (Sherman, *John Dee*, 177, 245 n. 101).

5 Mote appears as author of the pamphlet source.

6 Flicke was a member of the Drapers' Company ("The Names qf the Suertyes to be bounde to her Ma'tie," Camden Society Miscellany V, 27). He served in the Cádiz expedion of 1587 and in the Lisbon expedition of 1589, adventuring 1,000 pounds; the commanders signed a letter attesting to his good service as captain of the *Merchant Royal* (Corbett, *Papers Relating to the Navy*, passim; Wernham, *Expedition of Norris and Drake*, 327-2). This report was addressed to Richard Staper and other members of the Levant Company.

7 Translated at Hakluyt's instance; he also drew on this work for Linschoten's account of his aid to Fitch and Newbery at Goa in PN 2(i), and for Nuño da Silva's relation of Drake's circumnavigation in PN 3 (Payne, *Guide*, 101-2). While the Quinns follow Zelia Nuttall and others in specifying a manuscript source, Kelsey asserts firmly that Hakluyt "used ... a translation from the Dutch version published earlier by Linschoten" (*Sir Francis Drake*, 88). Linschoten's name does not appear in the index to Nuttall's invaluable *New Light on Drake*, which compares Hakluyt's version of da Silva to the original in the Spanish archives. On the significance of Linschoten's work for English knowledge of the East Indies, see Waters, *Art of Navigation*, 234.

8 The two prizes were the "St. Francisco, and St. Peter" (BL catalogue entry, MS Lansdowne 70/100).

9 Downton is first recorded making a voyage in the *Robert* of London in 1590, from which he brought a prize into Portsmouth (Andrews, *English Privateering Voyages*, 89). In 1592, he was captain of the Earl of Cumberland's *Gold Noble*, but not present when other

UNKNOWN OR PROBLEMATIC AUTHORS

6. "The voyage of Sir Francis Drake to Cadiz, 1587." Source misidentified by Corbett and in "c&s" as Robert Leng.
7. +* "The voyage to Spaine and Portugale written (as it is thought) by Colonell **Anthonie Wingfield**, An. 1589." Wingfield's authorship is confirmed by correspondence about the plans for publication of this narrative.
9. "A fight performed [...] against 12 Spanish galleys, in the Strait of Gibraltar, 1590."
10. "The valiant fight [...] by the Centurion of London, 1591."
15. "The taking of the mightie and rich Carak called the Madre de Dios, and of the Santa Clara a Biskaine of 600 tunnes, as likewise the firing of another great Carak called The Santa Cruz Anno 1592." Source misidentified in "c&s" as *Sea-man's triumph*, an anonymous pamphlet attributed to Ralegh by ESTC.

---

ships in the squadron participated in taking the *Madre de Deus* carrack (Kingsford, "Taking of the Madre de Dios," 105). Downton invested with the Earl of Cumberland in a 1605 voyage to the Caribbean, and would later serve as the captain of several voyages for the East India Company. Purchas printed extracts from Downton's journals on these voyages in *Pilgrimes*; the first of the journals had been collected by Hakluyt (John Parker, "Contents and Sources of 'Pilgrimes'"). Downton's papers and other documents relating to the voyages have been edited for the Hakluyt Society (Foster, *The Voyage of Nicholas Downton*; Baigent, "Downton, Nicholas").

APPENDIX 6

Spanish Manuscripts in Principal Navigations, Volume 3 (Item Numbers from "C&S")

This appendix, accompanying the discussion of translated materials in chapter 7, briefly lists Spanish manuscript sources in volume 3, using the numbers assigned in David and Alison Quinn's "Contents and Sources of the Three Major Works." ("c&s" uses letters to indicate parts of *PN*, with "G" designating volume 3). Most of these sources were, in Hakluyt's phrase, "stolen secrets" obtained in the course of the sea war.

Depositions and testimony by captives: G.90,[1] 91, 119–20,[2] 175/184,[3] 196–8[4]

   1 This relation by one of Drake's Spanish captives was "taken from his mouth by Master Richard Hakluyt 1586." Morales' information included plausible numbers for the Spanish outpost at San Augustín as well as more suspect or exaggerated information about the Appalachians as "mountaines of golde and Chrystall Mines" (Hakluyt, "Relation of Pedro Morales"). Similar information is given in the following account by another captive.
   2 These two voyage narratives both formed part of testimony by Lopes Vaz, taken captive by the Earl of Cumberland's ships in 1586 (see Sarracoll, "Voyage of M. Robert Withrington, and M. Christopher Lister, 1586").
   3 As David and Alison Quinn note, some items are represented twice in Hakluyt's catalogue of materials, or divided into several discrete entries; thus, 175/184 indicates duplicate catalogue entries for the same source.
   4 According to David and Alison Quinn, obtained from Pedro Diaz, who had been captured by Sir Richard Grenville in 1585 ("c&s"); see chapter 10 and Diaz, "Examination of the Masters and Pilots."

Intercepted letters and reports:[5]   101, 106, 113,[6] 133,[7] 135, 136, 138,[8] 49–50,[9] 166, 167, 175, 187[10]

[5] Some materials in this category were in the possession of captives, as noted.

[6] Item 113 is "A relation of the haven of Tecuanapa" on the coast of Nicaragua, in the form of a detailed letter addressed apparently to the viceroy of Mexico; Hakluyt does not note that it was captured or intercepted.

[7] A rare survival in Hakluyt's hand. Bazan, "The Opinion of Don Alvaro Baçan." Hakluyt's holograph translation from the Spanish – both translation and original are included in PN (1598–1600) – corresponds to several missing pages from the original manuscript in the Biblioteca Nacional, Madrid; it is currently held at the Yale Center for British Art, Folio A 2018 4.

[8] This printed source was, as its original title stated, "found at the sacke of Cales" (Cádiz) in 1596.

[9] Items 149 and 150 are Spanish reports and letters about "El Dorado," included in the print version of Walter Ralegh's *Discoverie of Guiana* (1596) but separately titled in PN (1598–1600).

[10] Another document in the possession of Lopes Vaz, this was "an account of English activities in the Spanish empire 1572-87," a miscellany of information including "material for Drake's voyage obtained from Nuño da Silva" (Quinn and Quinn, "C&S," 2: 458; Wallis, "The Pacific," 1: 231).

APPENDIX 7

Materials on Eastern Canada in Volume 3

The materials on Eastern Canada listed below were organized by Hakluyt under three regional subheadings. These categories and their contents are described in chapter 8, which discusses Hakluyt's dissociation of French and English materials and the different treatments of two distinct kinds of English voyages, one set licensed by a patent for settlement, the other aimed at exploiting marine resources in the Gulf of St Lawrence. The first three documents under the heading of "Voyages made to Newfoundland" do not fall into either of these two categories.

※: English voyages relating to Humphrey Gilbert's patent and colonizing project
†: French voyages
℉: English voyages relating to the walrus fishery

VOYAGES MADE TO NEWFOUNDLAND, TO THE ISLES OF RAMEA AND THE ISLE OF ASSUMPTION, OTHERWISE CALLED NATISICOTEC, AS ALSO TO THE COASTS OF CAPE BRITON AND ARAMBEC

Richard Hakluyt, "The Voyage of the [...] Dominus Vobiscum [...] for the Discoverie of the North Partes" (p. 129).
Richard Hakluyt, "The Voyage of M. Hore, and Divers Other Gentlemen to Newfoundland, and Cape Briton, in the Yere 1536" (pp. 129–31).
Anthony Parkhurst, "A Letter Written to M. Richard Hakluyt of the Midle Temple, Contayning a Report of the True State and Commodities of Newfoundland [...] 1578" (pp. 132–4).
※ "The Letters Patents Graunted by Her Majestie to Sir Humfrey Gilbert Knight, for the Inhabiting and Planting of Our People in America" (pp. 135–7).
※ Stephanus Parmenius, "A Learned and Stately Poeme Written in Latine Hexamiters by Stephanus Parmenius Budeius, Concerning the Voyage of Sir Humfrey Gilbert to Newfound-Land, for the Planting of an English Colonie There" (pp. 138–43).

※ Edward Hayes, "A Report of the Voyage and Successe Thereof, Attempted in the Yeere of Our Lord 1583 by Sir Humfrey Gilbert Knight" (pp. 143–61).
※ Richard Clarke, "A Relation of Richard Clarke of Weymouth, Master of the Ship Called The Delight, Which Went as Admirall of Sir Humfrey Gilberts Fleete for the Discoverie of Norumbega 1583" (pp. 163–5).
※ Sir George Peckham, "True Reporte of the Late Discoveries [...] by [...] Sir Humfrey Gilbert Knight" (pp. 165–81).
※ Letters by and to Sir Francis Walsingham, 1582–83 (pp. 181–2).
※ Christopher Carleill, "A Briefe and Summarie Discourse upon a Voyage Intended to the Hithermost Parts of America [...] 1583" (pp. 182–7).
※ "Articles Set Downe by the Committies Appointed on Behalfe of the Company of the Moscovian Marchants, to Conferre with Master Carlile" (pp. 188–9).
† "The First Discovery of the Isle of Ramea [...] with the Ship Called The Bonaventure [...] Anno 1591" (pp. 189–90).
₽ Thomas James, "A Letter Sent to the Right Honourable Sir William Cecil [...] Concerning the Discoverie of the Isle of Ramea, 1591" (p. 191).
₽ Richard Fisher, "The Voyage of the Ship Called The Marigolde of M. Hill of Redriffe, unto Cape Briton and beyond, to the Latitude of 44 Degrees and a Halfe, Anno 1593" (pp. 191–3).
₽ Richard Hakluyt, "The Voyage of M. George Drake of Apsham, to the Isle of Ramea, in the Yere 1593" (p. 193).
₽ Silvester Wyet, "The Voyage of The Grace of Bristoll, up into the Gulfe of S. Laurence to the Northwest of Newfoundland, as Far as the Isle of Assumption or Natiscotec, Anno 1594" (pp. 194–5).
₽ Charles Leigh, "The Voyage of M. Charles Leigh, and Divers Others, to Cape Briton and the Isle of Ramea, 1597" (pp. 195–201).

VOYAGES MADE FOR THE DISCOVERY OF
THE GULFE OF SAINT LAURENCE TO THE WEST
OF NEWFOUNDLAND, AND FROM THENCE UP THE
RIVER OF CANADA, TO HOCHELAGA, SAGUENAY,
AND OTHER PLACES

† Giovanni Battista Ramusio, "The First Voyage of Jaques Cartier of Saint Malo, to Newfound-Land, the Gulfe of Saint Laurence, and the Grand Bay, Anno 1534" (pp. 201–12).

† Giovanni Battista Ramusio, "The Second Voyage of Jaques Cartier by the Grand Bay up the River of Canada to Hochelaga, Anno 1535" (pp. 212–32).

† Jacques Cartier, "The Third Voyage of Jaques Cartier unto the Countries of Canada, Hochelaga, and Saguenay, Anno 1540" (pp. 232–6).

† Jean Alfonse, "An Excellent Ruttier Shewing the Course from Belle Isle [...] up the River of Canada" (pp. 237–40).

† "The Voyage of John Francis de La Roche Knight, Lord of Roberval, with Three Tall Ships to the Countries of Canada, Hochelaga, and Saguenay, 1542" (pp. 240–2).

† Jacques Noel, "A Letter Written to M. John Groute Student in Paris by Jaques Noel of Saint Malo the Nephew of Jaques Cartier, Touching the Discoverie of His Uncle in the Partes of Canada 1587" (p. 236).

† Jacques Noel, "Part of Another Letter Written by Jaques Noel of Saint Malo" (pp. 236–7).

APPENDIX 8

Principal Navigations *Materials Related to Drake's Activities at Sea*

This list shows documents related to Drake broken down by volume, and in order of appearance. The same item numbers are used in appendix 7, which organizes the contents by the chronology of Drake's activities.

VOLUME 1

1. Emanuel van Meteren, "The Vanquishing of the Spanish Armada, Anno 1588" (1: 591–606).

VOLUME 2

2. John Newbery, "His third letter to Maister Leonard Poore, written from Goa [1584]" (2[i]: 248–50).
3. Laurence Aldersey, "The Voyage of M. Laurence Aldersey to the Cities of Alexandria and Cario in Aegypt, Anno 1586" (2[i]: 282–5).
4. "The Voyage of Sir Francis Drake to Cadiz [...] and His Taking of the Great East Indian Carak Called the Sant Philip [...] Anno 1587" (2[ii]: 121–3).
5. Anthony Wingfield, "The voyage to Spaine and Portugale written (as it is thought) by Colonell Anthonie Wingfield, An. 1589" (2[ii]: 134–55).

VOLUME 3

6. Ralph Lane, "An Account of the Particular Employments of the Englishmen Left in Virginia by Sir Richard Grinvile under M. Ralph Lane Their Generall, from the 17. of August 1585 Untill the 18. of June 1586. at Which Time They Departed the Countrey" (3: 255–64).

7. "The Relation of Pedro Morales a Spaniard, Whom Sir Francis Drake Brought from S Augustines in Florida, Touching the State of Those Parts" (3: 361).
8. Richard Hakluyt and Thomas Harriot, "The Relation of Nicolas Burgoignon, Alias Holy, Whom Sir Francis Drake Brought Also from S. Augustines" (3: 361-2).
9. "The voyage and course which sir Francis Drake held from the haven of Guatalco [...] To the Northwest of California [...] where [...] he graved his shippe, entrenched himselfe on land, called the countrey by the name of Nova Albion, and tooke possession thereof on the behalfe of her Majestie" (3: 440-2). Duplicates part of "Famous Voyage," below.
10. Miles Philips, "The voyage of Miles Philips one of the company put on shore by sir John Hawkins, 1568 [...]" (3: 469-87).
11. Job Hortop, "The travels of Job Hortop set on land by sir John Hawkins 1586 in the bay of Mexico" (3: 487-94).
12. "The First Voyage of the Right Worshipfull and Valiant Knight Sir John Hawkins [...] Made to the West Indies in the Yere 1562" (3: 500).
13. John Sparke, "The Second Voyage Made by the R. W. Sir John Hawkins [...] to the Coast of Guinie, & from Thence to the Isle of Dominica [...] Begun 1564" (3: 501-21.
14. John Hawkins, "The Third Troublesome Voyage of the Right Worshipfull Sir John Hawkins [...] to the Parts of Guinea, and the Coasts of Tierra Firma, and Nueva Espanna, Anno 1567, & 1568" (3: 521-5).
15. Lopes Vas, "The First Voyage Attempted and Set Foorth by the Valiant and Expert Captaine M. Francis Drake, with a Ship Called the Dragon, and Another Ship & a Pinnesse, to Nombre de Dios and Dariene, about the Yere 1572" (3: 525-6).
16. Alvaro Bazan, "The Opinion of Don Alvaro Baçan [...] Touching the Fleet of Sir Francis Drake Lying at the Isles of Bayona, [...] the 26 of October 1585" (3: 530-4).
17. Walter Bigges, "The Famous Expedition of Sir Francis Drake to the West Indies [...] in the Yeers 1585, and 1586" (3: 534-48).
18. Baptista Antonio, "A Relation of the Surveying, New Building Finishing, Making, and Mending of Certeine Ports, Harbours, Forts and Cities in the West Indies [...] by the King of Spaines Surveyous in Those Parts 1587" (3: 548-57).
19. "The Last Voyage of Sir Francis Drake & Sir John Hawkins, Intended for Some Special Services on the Ylands and Maine of the West Indies, Anno

1595. In Which Voyage Both the Foresaide Knights Died by Sicknes" (3: 583–90).
20. Henry Savile, "A Libell of Spanish Lies Written by Don Bernaldino Delgadillo de Avellaneda [...], Concerning Some Part of the Last Voyage of Sir Francis Drake: Together with a Confutation Thereof [...]" (3: 591–8).
21. "The Famous Voyage of Sir Francis Drake into the South Sea, and There Hence about the Globe of the Whole Earth, Begunne Anno 1577" (3: 730–42).
22. Nuño da Silva, "The Voyage of Nunno Da Silva a Portugal Pilot Taken by Sir Francis Drake at the Yles of Cabo Verde, and Caried along with Him as Farre as the Haven of Guatalco upon the Coast of New Spaine: With His Confession Made to the Viceroy of Mexico" (3: 742–8).
23. Edward Cliffe, "The Voyage of M. John Winter into the South Sea by the Streight of Magellan in Consort with Sir Francis Drake, Begun in the Yeere 1577. He Being the First Christian That Ever Repassed the Said Streight" (3: 748–53).
24. Lopes Vas, "A Discourse of the West Indies and the South Sea [...] Continued unto the Yere 1587" (3: 778–802).

APPENDIX 9

Principal Navigations *Materials* Related to Drake, by Voyage

Item numbers used below refer to order of appearance in *Principal Navigations*, as displayed in appendix 7. The main narrative sources for voyages on which Drake was in sole or joint command are identified in bold.

1562–67 Slaving voyages[1]	10 Miles Philips, "The voyage of Miles Philips one of the company put on shore by sir John Hawkins, 1568 [...]" (3: 469–87). 11 Job Hortop, "The travels of Job Hortop set on land by sir John Hawkins 1586 in the bay of Mexico" (3: 487–94). 12 "The First Voyage of John Hawkins" (3: 500). 13 "The Second Voyage Made by John Hawkins [...] 1564" (3: 501–21). 14 "The Third Troublesome Voyage of [...] Sir John Hawkins 1567, & 1568" (3: 521–5).
1572 Raid on Nombre de Dios	15 Lopes Vas, "**The First Voyage Attempted and Set Foorth by [...] M. Francis Drake [...] 1572**." Duplicates part of item 24.

---

1 Drake is named only in the relation of Miles Philips; additional details are provided by manuscript evidence.

PN MATERIALS RELATED TO DRAKE, BY VOYAGE   495

1577–80 Raids on Spanish Americas, circumnavigation	9 "The voyage and course which sir Francis Drake held from the haven of Guatalco [...] To the Northwest of California." Duplicates part of item 19. 21 **"The Famous Voyage of Sir Francis Drake [...] Begunne Anno 1577."** 22 Nuño da Silva, "The Voyage of Nunno Da Silva a Portugal Pilot Taken by Sir Francis Drake at the Yles of Cabo Verde." 23 Edward Cliffe, "The Voyage of M. John Winter [...] in Consort with Sir Francis Drake, Begun in the Yeere 1577." 2 John Newbery, "His third letter to Maister Leonard Poore, written from Goa [1584]."[2]
1585–86 Raids on the West Indies and Florida; removal of Roanoke colonists	3 Laurence Aldersey, "The Voyage of M. Laurence Aldersey to the Cities of Alexandria and Cairo in Aegypt, Anno 1586."[3] 6 Ralph Lane, "An Account of the Particular Employments of the Englishmen Left in Virginia by Sir Richard Grinvile under M. Ralph Lane" (3: 255–64).[4] 7 "The Relation of Pedro Morales a Spaniard, Whom Sir Francis Drake Brought from S Augustines [...]" (3: 361). 8 "The Relation of Nicolas Burgoignon, [...] Whom Sir Francis Drake Brought Also from S. Augustines" (3: 361–2). 16 Alvaro Bazan, "The Opinion of Don Alvaro Baçan [...] Touching the Fleet of Sir Francis Drake [...] 1585" (3: 530–4). 17 **"The Famous Expedition of Sir Francis Drake to the West Indies [...] in the Yeers 1585, and 1586"** (3: 534–48). 18 Baptista Antonio, "A Relation of the Surveying, New Building Finishing, Making, and Mending of Certeine Ports, Harbours, Forts and Cities in the West Indies [...] 1587" (3: 548–57).

2 In Ormuz, Newbery was questioned about Drake's activities in the Moluccas.

3 In Patras, Aldersey witnessed the return of twenty Turkish captives freed by Drake in the West Indies.

4 Lane's colonists were removed by Drake, who touched at Roanoke on his return from the West Indies.

1587–89 Naval war with Spain	1 Emanuel van Meteren, "The Vanquishing of the Spanish Armada, Anno 1588" (1: 591–606). 4 "The Voyage of Sir Francis Drake to Cadiz […] Anno 1587" (2[ii]: 121–3). 5 Anthony Wingfield, "The voyage to Spaine and Portugale […] An. 1589" (2[ii]: 134–55).
1595	19 **"The Last Voyage of Sir Francis Drake & Sir John Hawkins, Anno 1595."** 20 Henry Savile, "A Libell of Spanish Lies Written by Don Bernaldino Delgadillo de Avellaneda […], Concerning Some Part of the Last Voyage of Sir Francis Drake […]."

APPENDIX 10

Preachers and Voyages

This appendix, accompanying the discussion in chapter 10, identifies ministers who are known to have accompanied voyages represented in *PN* (1598–1600) and indicates the nature of the evidence for their presence. Voyages where this presence can be discerned from the text in *PN* (1598–1600) are in bold.

Date	Captain/destination	Preacher/documentation
1553	**Willoughby, Northeast Passage**	Master Stafford (see chapter 10, n. 123)
1572–73	Drake, West Indies	Philip Nichols (not a known participant) prepared a print narrative, *Sir Francis Drake Revived* (1626)
1578	Frobisher, Northwest Passage	Master Wolfall (see chapter 10, n. 126)
1577–80	**Drake, circumnavigation**	Francis Fletcher, journal, used as source for *The World Encompassed* (1628), transcribed in BL MS Sloane 61; Fletcher mentioned in "Famous Voyage" (*PN* 3) and in other manuscript and print sources
1582	**Fenton, attempted circumnavigation**	Richard Madox, official and private journals; John Walker, private journal and letters; both mentioned in Fenton's instructions and Luke Ward's narrative (*PN* 3), other manuscript sources
1585–86	Drake, Caribbean	Philip Nichols, mentioned in *Leicester* Journal[1]

---

1 Keeler, *Drake's West Indian Voyage*, 141–7.

1586–88	**Cavendish, circumnavigation**	John Way, mentioned once in narrative (see chapter 10, n. 124)
1587	Drake, Cádiz	Philip Nichols[2]
1588	Howard and others, defense against the Armada	"Preachers" mentioned in letters by John Hawkins regarding their sea wages[3]
1589	Drake and Norris, Lisbon	Leonell Sharp (chaplain to the Earl of Essex), Philip Nichols[4]
1595–96	Drake and Hawkins, Caribbean	The chaplain of the *Help*, mentioned in a Spanish document listing English casualties[5]
1596	**Howard and Essex, Cádiz**	Nine ministers present, six named in Roger Marbecke's narrative (*PN* 1): George Montaigne, William Alabaster, Leonell Sharpe, John Hopkins, Edward Doughtie, Theodore Price (see chapter 10, n. 125)
1598	Cumberland, Caribbean	John Layfield, author of a narrative account (from Hakluyt's papers; in Purchas, *Pilgrimes*)[6]

2 Corbett, *Papers Relating to the Navy*, 143, 161, 187.
3 Laughton, *Defeat of the Spanish Armada*, 2: 231, 317.
4 Hammer, "Sharpe, Leonell"; Wernham, *Expedition of Norris and Drake*, 29–31.
5 Andrews, *Last Voyage of Drake & Hawkins*, 234.
6 Purchas, *Pilgrimes*, 4(vi): 1155–76.

Tables, Figures, and Plates

TABLES

9.1 Davis materials in *PN* (1598–1600), volume 3   376

9.2 Narration and identification in the Davis materials   393

FIGURES

0.1, 0.2 Two parts of a 1598 world map by Edward Wright, found in some copies of *PN* (1598–1600). Courtesy of the John Carter Brown Library, Providence, RI.   xiv

1.1 "Catalogue of English voyages made by and within the Streight of Gibraltar," *PN* (1598–1600), volume 2. Courtesy of the Library of Congress, Rare Book and Special Collections Division, The Hans P. Kraus Collection of Sir Francis Drake. http://hdl.loc.gov/loc.rbc/rbdk.d0301.   9

1.2 "The first voyage of Master William Towrson to Guinea, 1555," *PN* (1598–1600), volume 2(ii): 23. Courtesy of the Library of Congress, Rare Book and Special Collections Division, The Hans P. Kraus Collection of Sir Francis Drake. http://hdl.loc.gov/loc.rbc/rbdk.d0301.   10

1.3 "A brief Catalogue of the principall English Voyages made without the Streight of Gibraltar," *PN* (1598–1600), volume 2. Courtesy of the Library of Congress, Rare Book and Special Collections Division, The Hans P. Kraus Collection of Sir Francis Drake. http://hdl.loc.gov/loc.rbc/rbdk.d0301.   15

PN (1598–1600), volume 1, t.p. Courtesy of the Library of Congress, Rare Book and Special Collections Division, The Hans P. Kraus Collection of Sir Francis Drake. http://hdl.loc.gov/loc.rbc/rbdk.do301.   24

2.1   "Ohthere's relation." © The British Library Board. Additional MS 47967 fo. 8r.   56

2.2   Gerhard Mercator and Rumold Mercator, "Asia," in *Atlas sive Cosmographicae meditationes de fabrica mvndi et fabricati figura* (Dusseldorf, 1595). Courtesy of Source gallica.bnf.fr/Bibliothèque nationale de France.   72

3.1   "Names of certaine late writers of Geographie," Hakluyt, *Divers Voyages* (1582). Courtesy of the John Carter Brown Library, Providence, RI.   80

3.2   Robert Thorne, *Orbis Vniuersalis Descriptio*, in Hakluyt, *Divers voyages* (1582). Courtesy of the John Carter Brown Library, Providence, RI.   81

3.3   Abraham Ortelius, "Asiae Nova Descriptio," *Theatrum Orbis Terrarum* 1570. Courtesy of the Norman B. Leventhal Map and Education Center at the Boston Public Library.   85

3.4   Documents by decade in *PN* (1598–1600), 1541–60   106

3.5   English voyages by decade in *PN* (1598–1600), 1541–60   106

4.1   Traverse board, ca. 1800. NAV 1698 © National Maritime Museum, Greenwich, London. Used by permission.   122

4.2   John Davis, "Traverse Book," *PN* 3: 117. Courtesy of the Library of Congress, Rare Book and Special Collections Division, The Hans P. Kraus Collection of Sir Francis Drake. http://hdl.loc.gov/loc.rbc/rbdk.do302.   123

4.3   Hugh Smyth or Smith, chart ca. 1580. © The British Library Board, Cotton MS Otho EVIII, f. 78. Used by permission.   127

PN (1598–1600), volume 2, t.p. Courtesy of the Library of Congress, Rare Book and Special Collections Division, The Hans P. Kraus Collection of Sir Francis Drake. http://hdl.loc.gov/loc.rbc/rbdk.do301.   154

5.1   A list of "the names of Christians made slaves," *PN* (1598–1600), volume 2(i): 130. Courtesy of the Library of Congress, Rare Book and Special Collections Division, The Hans P. Kraus Collection of Sir Francis Drake. http://hdl.loc.gov/loc.rbc/rbdk.do301.   182

5.2   Rembert Dodoens, *A niewe herball* (Antwerp, 1578). Courtesy of Houghton Library, Harvard University [f STC 6984].   204

6.1   "Names of certaine late travaylers," Hakluyt, *Divers Voyages* (1582). Courtesy of the John Carter Brown Library.   212

6.2   Richard Madox, chart of Sierra Leone harbour. © The British Library Board. BL Cotton MS Appendix XLVII fo. 39v. Used by permission.   257

7.1   William Camden, *Annales* (London, 1625), frontispiece. © The Trustees of the British Museum. Used by permission.   268

PN (1598–1600), volume 3, t.p. Courtesy of the Library of Congress, Rare Book and Special Collections Division, The Hans P. Kraus Collection of Sir Francis Drake. http://hdl.loc.gov/loc.rbc/rbdk.d0302.   316

8.1   "Carta de navegar," Niccolò Zen, *De i commentarii* (1558). Courtesy of the John Carter Brown Library, Providence, RI.   336

8.2   Detail, "Novus Orbis," in *De Orbe novo* (Paris, 1587). Courtesy of the John Carter Brown Library, Providence, RI.   346

8.3   Rumold Mercator, "Orbis terrae compendiosa descriptio" (Geneva, 1587). Courtesy of the John Carter Brown Library, Providence, RI.   358

8.4   Plate 20, "The Towne of Secota." Engraving by Theodor de Bry from a drawing by John White, in Thomas Harriot, *A Briefe and True Report* (Frankfurt, 1590). Courtesy of the John Carter Brown Library, Providence, RI.   361

8.5   Detail, plate 8, "A cheiff Ladye of Pomeiooc." Engraving by Theodor de Bry from a drawing by John White, in Thomas Harriot, *A Briefe and True Report* (Frankfurt, 1590). Courtesy of the John Carter Brown Library, Providence, RI.   364

8.6   Plate 2, "The arrival of the Englishemen in Virginia." Engraving by Theodor de Bry in Thomas Harriot, *A Briefe and True Report* (Frankfurt, 1590). Courtesy of the John Carter Brown Library, Providence, RI.   365

8.7   Detail, plate 1, "Americae pars, nunc Virginia dictu." Engraving by Theodor de Bry from a drawing by John White, in Thomas Harriot, *A Briefe and True Report* (Frankfurt, 1590). Courtesy of the John Carter Brown Library, Providence, RI.   366

502 TABLES, FIGURES, AND PLATES

8.8   Detail, plate 2, "The arrival of the Englishemen in Virginia." Engraving by Theodor de Bry, in Thomas Harriot, *A Briefe and True Report* (Frankfurt, 1590). Courtesy of the John Carter Brown Library, Providence, RI.   367

9.1   Detail of the Davis Strait from Edward Wright, "By the discouerie of Sr Francis Drake made in the yeare 1577," 1598. Courtesy of the John Carter Brown Library, Providence, RI.   377

9.2   Detail of Greenland and the Davis Strait on the Molyneux Globe (1603). Permission of the Masters of the Bench of the Honourable Society of the Middle Temple, London, to publish this image, is gratefully acknowledged.   378

9.3   Detail, map of the world, in Edward Wright, *Certain Errors in Navigation* (1610). Courtesy of the Beinecke Rare Book and Manuscript Library, Yale University. https://collections.library.yale.edu/catalog/2035678.   379

9.4   Greenlandic word list (Davis, "Second Voyage," PN [1598–1600], volume 3: 105). Courtesy of the Library of Congress, Rare Book and Special Collections Division, The Hans P. Kraus Collection of Sir Francis Drake. http://hdl.loc.gov/loc.rbc/rbdk.d0302.   387

9.5   Testimonial (Jane, "The last voyage of M. Thomas Candish [...] begun 1591," PN [1598–1600], volume 3: 845–6). Courtesy of the Library of Congress, Rare Book and Special Collections Division, The Hans P. Kraus Collection of Sir Francis Drake. http://hdl.loc.gov/loc.rbc/rbdk.d0302.   404

10.1 Nicola Sype, "La herdike enterprinse faict par le Signeur Draeck D'Avoir cirquit toute la Terre" (Antwerp, 1581). Courtesy of the Library of Congress, Rare Book and Special Collections Division, The Hans P. Kraus Collection of Sir Francis Drake.   434

10.2 Samuel Purchas, *Hakluytus Posthumus, or Purchas his Pilgrimes* (London, 1625), t.p. Courtesy of the John Carter Brown Library, Providence, RI.   447

11.1 Coursetracks, Molyneux globe (1603). Permission of the Masters of the Bench of the Honourable Society of the Middle Temple, London, to publish this image, is gratefully acknowledged.   463

PLATES

1 Gerhard Mercator, "Septentrionalium terrarum descriptio," [1595?]. Courtesy of the Norman B. Leventhal Map and Education Center at the Boston Public Library.

2 "Humfray Gylbert knight his charte. T.S. [i.e. John Dee] fecit." [ca. 1582–3] Elkins 42. Courtesy of the Free Library of Philadelphia, Rare Book Department.

3 Anon., early seventeenth century, circumpolar chart. Firenze, BNC, Portolano 20. By permission of the Biblioteca Nazionale Centrale di Firenze (BNCF).

4 Ortelius, *Map of Islandia*, plate 103, *Theatrum Orbis Terrarum* (London, ca. 1607). By permission of the Folger Shakespeare Library, Washington, DC.

5 Astronomical compendium, by Humfrey Cole, 1568. © History of Science Museum, University of Oxford, inv.36313. Used by permission.

6 Robert Adams, *Expeditionis Hispanorum in Angliam vera descriptio* (London, 1590). Courtesy of the Library of Congress, Jay I. Kislak Collection.

7 Armillary sphere, early seventeenth century. AST0634 © National Maritime Museum, Greenwich, London. Used by permission.

8 Baptista Boazio, "The famouse West Indian voyadge" (London?, 1589). Courtesy of the Library of Congress, Jay I. Kislak Collection.

BIBLIOGRAPHY

MANUSCRIPTS

Thomas Hood, "Red Dragon Ship Logbook, 1586–87," HM 1648, Huntington Library, San Marino, California.

MS Tanner 255, Bodleian Library, Oxford.

SOURCES IN *PN* (1598–1600)

Acosta, José de. "Three Testimonies of Josepho de Acosta Concerning the Mightie River of Amazones [...] and Likewise of the Empire of Dorado or Guiana." In *PN*, 3: 698–700.

Adams, Clement. "The Newe Navigation and Discoverie of the Kingdome of Moscovia, by the Northeast, in the Yeere 1553." In *PN*, 1: 243–55.

Alday, James. "The First Voyage to Barbary, Anno 1551." In *PN*, 2(ii): 7–8.

Aldersey, Laurence. "The Voyage of M. Laurence Aldersey to the Cities of Alexandria and Cairo in Aegypt, Anno 1586." In *PN*, 2(i): 282–5.

– "The Voyage of M. Laurence Aldersey to the Cities of Jerusalem, and Tripolis, in the Yeere 1581." In *PN*, 2(i): 150–4.

"The Ambassage of John the Second King of Portugale to Edward the 4. King of England, to Stay John Tintam, and William Fabian Englishmen, Preparing for a Voyage to Guinea, Anno 1481." In *PN*, 2(ii): 2.

"Articles Set Downe by the Committies Appointed on Behalfe of the Company of the Moscovian Marchants, to Conferre with Master Carlile." In *PN*, 3: 188–9.

Barlowe, Arthur. "The First Voyage Made to the Coast of Virginia by M. Philip Amadas, and M. Arthur Barlow, 1584." In *PN*, 3: 246.

Bazan, Alvaro. "The Opinion of Don Alvaro Baçan [...] Touching the Fleet of Sir Francis Drake Lying at the Isles of Bayona [...] the 26 of October 1585." In *PN*, 3: 530–34.

Beauvais, Vincent de. "The Long and Wonderful Voyage of Friar John de Plano Carpini [...] 1246." In *PN*, 1: 37–71.

Bede. "The Conquest of the Isles of Anglesey and Man." In *PN*, 1: 3.

Best, George. "A True Discourse of the Three Voyages of Discoverie." In *PN*, 3: 47–96.

Bigges, Walter, and Thomas Cates. "The Famous Expedition of Sir Francis Drake to the West Indies [...] in the Yeers 1585, and 1586." In *PN*, 3: 534–48.

Bodenham, Roger. "The Voyage of M. Roger Bodenham, with the Great Barke Aucher, to Candia and Chio, Anno. 1550." In *PN*, 2(i): 99–101.

– "The Voyage of M. Roger Bodenham to Sant Juan de Ullua in the Bay of Mexico, and from Thence to the City of Mexico, Anno 1564." In *PN*, 3: 455.

Borough, Christopher. "The Voyage of Christopher Burrough into Persia the Sixt Time, Anno 1579." In *PN*, 1: 419–31.

Borough, Stephen. "The Voyage of Stephen Burrough toward the River of Ob, Intending the Discovery of the Northeast Passage, Anno 1556." In *PN*, 1: 274–83.

– "The Voyage of the Aforesaide Stephen Burrough from Colmogro in Russia to Wardhouse [...] Anno 1557." In *PN*, 1: 290–5.

Borough, William. "Instructions and Notes Very Necessary and Needfull to Be Observed in the Purposed Voyage for Discovery of Cathay Eastwards [...] 1580." In *PN*, 1: 435–7.

– "Necessarie Notes to Be Observed, and Followed in Your Discoverie." In *PN*, 1: 383–4.

Cabot, Sebastian. "Ordinances, Instructions, and Advertisements of and for the Direction of the Intended Voyage for Cathay [...] 1553." In *PN*, 1: 226–30.

Camden, William. "A Chronicle of the Kings of Man, Taken out of M. Camdens Chorographie." In *PN*, 1: 10–16.

– "A Testimony, That the Britons Were in Italy and Greece, with the Cimbrians and Gauls, before the Incarnation of Christ." In *PN*, 2(i): 1.

Cano, Bartolomé del. "A Letter Intercepted of Bartholomew Del Cano, Written from Mexico the 30 of May 1590, to Francis Hernandez of Sivil." In *PN*, 3: 396–7.

Carleill, Christopher. "A Briefe and Summarie Discourse upon a Voyage Intended to the Hithermost Parts of America [...] 1583." In *PN*, 3: 182–7.

Cartier, Jacques. "The Third Voyage of Jaques Cartier unto the Countries of Canada, Hochelaga, and Saguenay, Anno 1540." In *PN*, 3: 232–6.

Chancellor, Richard. "The Booke of the Great and Mighty Emperor of Russia, and Duke of Moscovia, and of the Dominions Orders and Commodities Thereunto Belonging." In *PN*, 1: 237–42.

Chapman, Laurence. "The Voyage of Arthur Edwards Agent for the Moscovy Company, John Sparke, Laurence Chapman, Christopher Faucet, and Richard Pingle, Servants, into Persia, An. 1568." In *PN*, 1: 389–91.

Cheney, Richard. "The Voyage of Thomas Alcock, George Wrenne, and Richard Cheyney, Servants unto the Company of Moscovy Merchants in London, into Persia, Anno 1563." In *PN*, 1: 353–4.

Chilton, John. "The Memorable Voyage of M. John Chilton to All the Principall Parts of Neuva Espanna, and to Divers Places in Peru, Begun from Cadiz in Andaluzia, in March 1568." In *PN*, 3: 455–62.

Davis, John. "A Letter of Master Davis to M. William Sanderson of London, Concerning His Second Voyage." In *PN*, 3: 108.

– "A Report of M. John Davis Concerning His Three Voyages." In *PN*, 3: 119–20.

– "The Second Voyage of M. John Davis [...] 1586." In *PN*, 3: 103–8.

– "A Traverse-Book of M. John Davis Contayning All the Principall Notes and Observations Taken in His Third and Last Voyage to the Northwest." In *PN*, 3: 115–18.

Dee, John. "A Testimony of Master John Dee Touching the Voyage of Nicholas de Linna to the North Pole." In *PN*, 1: 122.

– "The Voyage of King Edgar with 4000 Shippes Round about His Large Monarchie, Anno 973." In *PN*, 1: 6–9.

Diaz, Pedro. "The Examination of the Masters and Pilots Which Sail in the Fleets of Spain to the West Indies." In *PN*, 3: 864–8.

Docwra, Sir Thomas. "A Relation of the Siege and Taking of the Citie of Rhodes, by Sultan Soliman the Great Turke: Wherein Honorable Mention Is Made of Divers Valiant English Knights, Anno. 1522." In *PN*, 2(i): 72–95.

Downton, Nicholas. "The Firing and Sinking of the Stout and Warlike Carack Called The Cinquo Chaguas [...] by Three Ships of the R. H. the Earle of Cumberland, 1594." In *PN*, 2(ii): 199–201.

Dudley, Sir Robert. "The Voyage of Sir Robert Duddeley to the Yle of Trinidad and the Coast of Paria [...] Anno 1594, & 1595." In *PN*, 3: 574–7.

Eden, Richard. "The Voyage of M. John Lok to Guinea, Anno 1554." In *PN*, 2(ii): 14–23.

– "The Voyage of M. Thomas Windam to Guinea and the Kingdom of Benin, Anno 1553." In *PN*, 2(ii): 9–14.

Edward VI. "The Letters of King Edward the Sixt, Written at That Time to All the Kings, Princes, and Other Potentates of the Northeast." In *PN*, 1: 230–2.

Edwards, Arthur. "Certaine Letters of Arthur Edwards Written out of Russia, Media, and Persia, to the Company of Moscovie Merchants in London." In *PN*, 1: 354–63.

Eldred, John. "The Voyage of M. John Eldred to Tripolis in Syria by Sea, and from Thence by Land and River to Babylon, and Balsara, Anno 1583." In *PN*, 2(i): 268–71.

Elizabeth I. "The Answere of Her Majestie to the Aforesaid Letters of the Great Turke, sent The 25 of October 1579, in the Prudence of London by Master Richard Stanley." In *PN*, 2(i): 138–40.

– "The Letters of the Queenes Most Excellent Majestie, Sent in the Yere 1596, to the Emperour of China, by M. Richard Allot and M. Thomas Bromefield, Merchants of London." In *PN*, 3: 852–4.

– "The Letters Patents Granted by Her Majestie to Certaine Noblemen and Merchants of London, for a Trade to Barbary, Anno 1585." In *PN*, 2(ii): 114–17.

– "The Letters Patents of Her Majesty Graunted to M. Adrian Gilbert and Others for the Search and Discovery of a Northwest Passage to China." In *PN*, 3: 96–8.

– "The Second Letters Patents Granted by the Queenes Majestie to the Right Wor. Company of the English Merchants for the Levant, in the Yere of Our Lord 1592." In *PN*, 2(i): 295–303.

Ellis, Thomas. "The Third and Last Voyage unto Meta Incognita, Made by M. Martin Frobisher, in the Yeere 1578." In *PN*, 3: 39–44.

Espejo, Antonio de. "The Voyage of Antonio de Espeio [...] to [...] New Mexico." In *PN*, 3: 383–96.

Evesham, John. "The Voyage Made by Two of Sir Walter Raleghs Pinnaces [...] to the Azores [...] in the Yere 1586." In *PN*, 2(ii): 120–1.

– "The Voyage of M. John Evesham by Sea into Aegypt, Anno 1586." In *PN*, 2(i): 281–2.

"An Excellent Ruttier for the Islands of the West Indies, and for Tierra Firma, and Nueva Espana." In *PN*, 3: 603–13.

"The Famous Voyage of Sir Francis Drake into the South Sea, and There Hence about the Globe of the Whole Earth, Begunne Anno 1577." In *PN*, 3: 730–42.

Federici, Cesare. "The Voyage of Master Cesar Frederick into the East India, and Beyonde the Indies, Anno 1563." In *PN*, 2(i): 213–44.

"A Fight Performed by Ten Marchants Ships of London against 12 Spanish Gallies, in the Streit of Gibraltar. An. 1590." In *PN*, 2(ii): 166–8.

"The First Discovery of the Isle of Ramea [...] with the Ship Called The Bonaventure [...] Anno 1591." In *PN*, 3: 189–90.

"The First Voyage of M. William Hawkins of Plimmouth, Father unto Sir John Hawkins to Brasil Anno 1530." In *PN*, 3: 700–701.

"The First Voyage of the Right Worshipfull and Valiant Knight Sir John Hawkins [...] Made to the West Indies in the Yere 1562." In *PN*, 3: 500.

Fitch, Ralph. "The Long, Dangerous, and Memorable Voyage of M. Ralph Fitch Marchant of London [...] Begunne in the Yeere 1583, and Ended in the Yeere 1591." In *PN*, 2(i): 250–68.

Flicke, Robert. "A Voyage of Certaine Ships of London to the Coast of Spaine, and the Azores, Anno 1591." In *PN*, 2(ii): 176–8.

Foxe, John. "The Voyage of John Foxe to the Strait of Gibraltar, in a Ship Called The Three Half-Moones, Anno. 1563 [...] and [...] Anno 1577." In *PN*, 2(i): 131–6.

Fuller, Thomas. "Certaine Rare and Speciall Notes Most Properly Belonging to the Voyage of M. Thomas Candish about the World." In *PN*, 3: 825–37.

Galí, Francisco. "The Memorable Voyage of Francis Gualle [...] from the Haven of Acapulco [...] to the Islands of the Lucones or Philippinas." In *PN*, 3: 442–7.

Geoffrey of Monmouth. "The Voyage of Arthur K. of Britaine to Island and the Most Northeastern Parts of Europe, Anno 517." In *PN*, 1: 1–2.

Gilbert, Sir Humphrey. "A Discourse [...] to Prove a Passage by the Northwest." In *PN*, 3: 11–24.

Hakluyt, Richard. "A Briefe Note Concerning a Voyage of One Thomas Tison." In *PN*, 3: 500.

– "A Briefe Note Concerning an Ancient Trade of English Marchants to the Canarie Isles, Anno 1526." In *PN*, 2(ii): 3.

– "A Preface to the Reader as Touching [...] This First Part." In *PN*, 1: sig. *4r–**2v.

– "Epistle Dedicatorie." In *PN*, 1: sig.*2r–*3v.

– "Epistle Dedicatorie." In *PN*, 2(i): sig. *2r–*4v.

– "Epistle Dedicatorie." In *PN*, 3: sig. A2r–3v.

– "An Epistle Dedicatorie to Sir Walter Ralegh, Prefixed by Master Richard Hakluyt before the History of Florida [...] 1587." In *PN*, 3: 301–3.

– "The Relation of Pedro Morales a Spaniard, Whom Sir Francis Drake Brought from S. Augustines in Florida, Touching the State of Those Parts." In *PN*, 3: 361.

– "The Voyage of the [...] Dominus Vobiscum [...] for the Discoverie of the North Partes." In *PN*, 3: 129.

– "A Voyage Made [...] to the Iles of Candia and Chio, about the Yeere 1534, Another Voyage [...] about the Yeere 1535." In *PN*, 2(i): 98.

– "The Voyage of M. George Drake of Apsham, to the Isle of Ramea, in the Yere 1593." In *PN*, 3: 193.

– "The Voyage of M. Hore, and Divers Other Gentlemen to Newfoundland, and Cape Briton, in the Yere 1536." In *PN*, 3: 129–31.

Hakluyt, Richard, and Edmund Barker. "The Memorable Voyage of M. James Lancaster about the Cape of Buona Esperanza [...] Begun in the Yeere 1591." In *PN*, 2(ii): 102–10.

Hakluyt, Richard, and Thomas Harriot. "The Relation of Nicolas Burgoignon, Alias Holy, Whom Sir Francis Drake Brought Also from S. Augustines." In *PN*, 3: 361–621.

Hakluyt Esq., Richard. "A Briefe Remembrance of Things to Bee Indevoured at Constantinople, and at Other Places in Turkie [...] Anno. 1582." In *PN*, 2(i): 160.

– "Certaine Other Most Profitable and Wise Instructions [...] for a Principal English Factor at Constantinople." In *PN*, 2(i): 161–5.

– "Directions given [...] to M. Morgan Hubblethorne, Dier, Sent into Persia." In *PN*, 1: 432.

– "Notes in Writing, besides More Privie by Mouth, That Were given [...] Anno 1580, to M. Arthur Pet, and to M. Charles Jackman." In *PN*, 1: 437–42.

Hall, Christopher. "The First Voyage of M. Martin Frobisher [...] Anno. 1576." In *PN*, 1: 29–32.

Harborne, William. "A Letter of William Hareborne [...] to Assan Aga, Eunuch and Treasurer [...] which [...] Was Sonne to Francis Rowley Merchant of Bristol, and Was Taken in an English Ship Called the Swallow." In *PN*, 2(i): 180.

Harriot, Thomas. "A Briefe and True Report of the Commodities [...] to Be Found and Raised in the Countrey of Virginia." In *PN*, 3: 266–80.

Hawkins, John. "The Third Troublesome Voyage of the Right Worshipfull Sir John Hawkins [...] to the Parts of Guinea, and the Coasts of Tierra Firma, and Nueva Espanna, Anno 1567, & 1568." In *PN*, 3: 521–5.

Hawks, Henry. "The Voyage of Henrie Hawks Merchant to Nueva Espanna [...] Written at the Request of M. Richard Hakluyt of Eyton in the Countie of Hereford Esquire, 1572." In *PN*, 3: 462–9.

Hayes, Edward. "A Report of the Voyage and Successe Thereof, Attempted in the Yeere of Our Lord 1583 by Sir Humfrey Gilbert Knight." In *PN*, 3: 143–61.

Herberstein, Sigismund. "A Voyage to the Northeast, Performed by Certeine Russes." In *PN*, 1: 492–5.

Hortop, Job. "The Travels of Job Hortop Set on Land by John Hawkins 1586 in the Bay of Mexico." In *PN*, 3: 487–94.

Incent, John, and Muscovy Company. "A Discourse of the Honourable Receiving into England of the First Ambassador from the Emperor of Russia [...] 1556 [...]." In *PN*, 1: 285–9.

Ingram, Anthonie. "A Relation Concerning a Voyage Set Foorth by M. John Newton, and M. John Bird, Merchants of London, to the Kingdome and Citie of Benin [...] An. 1588." In *PN*, 2(ii): 129–30.

"In Tempore Romadan Beglergegi Argirae Spoliatae & Ereptae Naves, Merces, & Homines." In *PN*, 2(i): 180.

James, Thomas. "A Letter Sent to the Right Honourable Sir William Cecil [...] Concerning the Discoverie of the Isle of Ramea 1591." In *PN*, 3: 191.

Jane, John. "The First Voyage of M. John Davis [...] 1585." In *PN*, 3: 100–3.

– "The Last Voyage of M. Thomas Candish [...] Begun 1591." In *PN*, 3: 842–52.

– "The Third Voyage Northwestward, Made by M. John Davis [...] 1587." In *PN*, 3: 111–14.

Jenkinson, Anthony. "The Voyage of Master Anthony Jenkinson from the Citie of Mosco in Russia to Boghar in Bactria, Anno 1558." In *PN*, 1: 324–5.

Johnson, Richard. "Certaine Notes Unperfectly Written by Richard Johnson [...] Which Was in the Discoverie of Vaigatz [...] 1556, and Afterwards among the Samoedes." In *PN*, 1: 283–5.

– "Notes and Observations [...] of the Severall Wayes from Russia to Cathay Over-Land." In *PN*, 1: 335–7.

Jones, Philip. "The Voyage of Five Marchants Ships of London into Turkie: And Their Valiant Fight in Their Returne with 11 Gallies and Two Frigats of the King of Spaine [...] 1586." In *PN*, 2(i): 285–9.

Jónsson, Arngrímur. "A briefe commentarie of Island: Wherin the errours of such as have written concerning this Island, are detected." In *PN*, 1: 515–90.

Lambarde, William. "A Testimonie of M. Lambard in His 'Archaionomia, Touching the Rights and Appendances of the Crowne of the King of Britaine." In *PN*, 1: 2–3.

Lane, Ralph. "An Extract of Master Ralph Lanes Letter to M. Richard Hakluyt Esquire, and Another Gentleman of the Middle Temple, from Virginia 1585." In *PN*, 3: 254–5.

"The Letters of the Emperour of Russia Sent to King Edward the Sixt, by Richard Chanceller." In *PN*, 1: 255.

"Libellus de Politia Conservativa Maris." In *PN*, 1: 187–208.

Linschoten, Jan Huygen van. "A Large Testimony of John Huighen van Linschoten Concerning the Worthy Exploits Atchieved by [...] English Captains about the Isles of the Açores [...] in the Yeares 1589, 1590, 1591." In *PN*, 2(ii): 178–87.

Lok, John. "A Letter [...] to the Worshipfull Company of Marchants Adventurers of Guinea, Anno 1561." In *PN*, 2(ii): 53–4.

– "The Voyage of M. John Lok to Jerusalem, Anno 1553." In *PN*, 2(i): 101–12, 1,599.

Madoc, Laurence. "Two Brief Relations Concerning the Cities and Provinces of Tombuto and Gago, and [...] the Conquest Thereof by the King of Marocco [...] 1594." In *PN*, 2(ii): 192–3.

Magoths, William. "The Voyage of the Delight a Ship of Bristol One of the Consorts of M. John Chidley Esquire [...] to the Streights of Magellan, Begun in the Yere 1589." In *PN*, 3: 839–42.

Marbecke, Roger. "The Honourable Voyage to Cadiz, Anno. 1596." In *PN*, 1: 607–19.

Martinengo, Nestore. "A Report of the Siege and Taking of Famagusta by Mustafa Bassa Generall of the Great Turkes Army, Anno 1571." Translated by William Malim. In *PN*, 2(i): 117–30.

May, Henry. "The Voyage of Henry May One of M. James Lancaster His Company, in His Navigation to the East Indies 1591, & 1592." In *PN*, 3: 573–4.

"The Memorable Voyage of Sighelmus Bishop of Shirburne, Sent by King Alphred unto S. Thomas of India, An. 883 [...]." In *PN*, 2(i): 5.

Mercator, Gerhard. "The letter of Gerard. Mercator to Richard Hakluyt of Oxford touching that discoverie [1580]." In *PN*, 1: 443–5.

– "The Voyage of Nicholaus de Linna, a Franciscan Friar, and an Excellent Mathematician of Oxford to All the Regions Situate under the North Pole, Anno 1360." In *PN*, 1: 121–2.

Meteren, Emanuel van. "The Vanquishing of the Spanish Armada, Anno 1588." In *PN*, 1: 591–606.

Morgan, Henry. "The Voyage and Course Which [...] 2. Vessels of the Fleete of M. John Davis, Held." In *PN*, 3: 109–11.

Mote, Humphrey. "The Escape of the Primrose, a Ship of London, from before the Towne of Bilbao in Biscay [...] Anno 1585." In *PN*, 2(ii): 112–14.

Muscovy Company. "Articles Conceived and Determined for the Commission of the Merchants of This Company Resident in Russia, and at the Wardhouse, for the Second Voyage, 1555." In *PN*, 1: 259–62.

– "Certaine Instructions, Delivered in the Third Voyage, Anno 1556. for Russia, to Every Purser and the Rest of the Servants." In *PN*, 1: 272–4.

– "Commission given [...] unto Arthur Pet, and Charles Jackman [...] for Discovery of Cathay, 1580." In *PN*, 1: 433–5.

– "Instructions given to the Masters and Mariners [...] 1557." In *PN*, 1: 295–7.

– "Instructions Made by the Company of English Merchants for Discovery of New Trades [...] 1582." In *PN*, 1: 453–5.

Newbery, John. "A Letter of M. John Newbery Sent from Alepo to M. Richard Hakluyt of Oxford, Ann. 1583." In *PN*, 2(i): 245–6.

Nicholls, Thomas. "A Description of the Canarie Islands, with Their Strange Fruits and Commodities." In *PN*, 2(ii): 3–7.

Noel, Jacques. "A Letter Written to M. John Groute Student in Paris by Jaques Noel of Saint Malo the Nephew of Jaques Cartier, Touching the Discoverie of His Uncle in the Partes of Canada 1587." In *PN*, 3: 236.

– "Part of Another Letter Written by Jaques Noel of Saint Malo." In *PN*, 3: 236–37.

Paris, Matthew. "The Voyage of a Certaine Englishman into Tartaria, and from Thence into Poland and Hungary, Anno 1243." In *PN*, 1: 20–1.

Parkhurst, Anthony. "A Letter Written to M. Richard Hakluyt of the Midle Temple, Contayning a Report of the True State and Commodities of Newfoundland [...] 1578." In *PN*, 3: 132–4.

Peckham, Sir George. "True Reporte of the Late Discoveries [...] by [...] Sir Humfrey Gilbert Knight." In *PN*, 3: 165–81.

Petoney, Melchior. "A Relation Concerning the Estate of the Island and Castle of Arguin, and Touching the Rich and Secret Trade from the Inland of Africa Thither, Written in the Yere 1[5]91." In *PN*, 2(ii): 188.

Philips, Miles. "The Voyage of Miles Philips One of the Company Put on Shore by Sir John Hawkins, 1568 [...]." In *PN*, 3: 469–87.

Pretty, Francis. "The Prosperous Voyage of M. Thomas Candish Esquire into the South Sea [...] Finished 1588." In *PN*, 3: 803–25.

"A Principall Ruttier [...] to Saile [...] to Saint Juan de Ullua in Nueva Espana." In *PN*, 3: 613–27.

Privy Council. "Instructions given by the R. H. the Lords of the Councell, to M. Edward Fenton Esquire." In *PN*, 3: 754–7.

Rainolds, Richard. "The Voyage of Richard Rainolds and Thomas Dassell to the Rivers of Senega and Gambra, Neere the Coast of Guinea, Anno 1591." In *PN*, 2(ii): 188–92.

Ralegh, Walter. "A True Report of the Fight about the Isles of the Azores, Betweene the Revenge One of Her Majesties Ships, under the Conduct of Sir Richard Grinvile, and an Armada of the King of Spaine, An. 1591." In *PN*, 2(ii): 169–75.

– "The Voyage [to Guiana] of Sir Walter Ralegh Himselfe." In *PN*, 3: 631–66.

Ramusio, Giovanni Battista. "The First Voyage of Jaques Cartier of Saint Malo, to Newfound-Land, the Gulfe of Saint Laurence, and the Grand Bay, Anno 1534." In *PN*, 3: 201–12.

– "The Second Voyage of Jaques Cartier by the Grand Bay up the River of Canada to Hochelaga, Anno 1535." In *PN*, 3: 212–32.

– "A Speciall Note [...] out of the Arabian Geographie of Abilfada Ismael." In *PN*, 1: 495.

"A Report of the Casting Away of the Tobie [...] on the Coast of Barbary [...] 1593." In *PN*, 2(ii): 201–3.

Rubriquis, William de. "The Journall of Frier William de Rubricis, Anno, 1253." In *PN*, 1: 93–117.

Rutter, William. "The Relation of One William Rutter Concerning a Voyage Set out to Guinea, Anno 1562. Described Also in Verse by Robert Baker." In *PN*, 2(ii): 54–5.

"A Ruttier Which Declareth the Situation of the Coast of Brasil [...]." In *PN*, 3: 728–30.

"The Safe Conduct Granted by Sultan Soliman the Great Turke, to M. Anthony Jenkinson at Alepo in Syria, Anno 1553." In *PN*, 2(i): 114.

Sande, Duarte de. "An Excellent Description of the Kingdome of China." In *PN*, 2(ii): 88–98.

Sarracoll, John. "The Voyage of M. Robert Withrington, and M. Christopher Lister Intended for the South Sea [...], but Performed Onely to the Southerly Latitude of 44. Degrees, Begun Anno 1586." In *PN*, 3: 769–78.

Saunders, Thomas. "The Voyage of a Ship Called The Jesus, to Tripolis in Barbary, Anno 1582." In *PN*, 2(i): 184–91.

"The Second Voyage of Ohthere into the Sound of Denmark." In *PN*, 1: 5–6.

"The Second Voyage to Virginia by Sir Richard Grinvile for Sir Walter Ralegh, Anno 1585." In *PN*, 3: 251–3.

Settle, Dionyse. "The Second Voyage of M. Martin Frobisher [...] Anno 1577." In *PN*, 3: 32–73.

Silva, Nuño da. "The Voyage of Nunno Da Silva a Portugal Pilot Taken by Sir Francis Drake [...] With His Confession Made to the Viceroy of Mexico." In *PN*, 3: 742–8.

Smith, Hugh. "The Discoverie Made by M. Arthur Pet, and M. Charles Jackman, of the Northeast Parts [...] 1580." In *PN*, 1: 445–53.

Southam, Thomas. "The Voyage of Thomas Southam and John Sparke by Land and River from Colmogro to Novograd in Russia, Anno 1566." In *PN*, 1: 365–9.

Sparke, John. "The Second Voyage Made by the R. W. Sir John Hawkins [...] to the Coast of Guinie, & from Thence to the Isle of Dominica [...] Begun 1564." In *PN*, 3: 501–21.

Stevens, Thomas. "The Voyage of Thomas Stevens about the Cape of Buona Esperanza unto Goa in the East India, Anno 1579." In *PN*, 2(ii): 99–110.

"The Taking of the Mightie and Rich Carak Called the Madre de Dios [...] Anno 1592." In *PN*, 2(ii): 194–9.

Thorláksson, Guðbrandur. "A letter written by the grave and learned Gudbrandus Thorlacius." In *PN*, 1: 590–1.

Thorne, Robert. "A Persuasion of Robert Thorne Merchant of Bristol, and Dwelling Long in Sivil in Spaine, to King Henry the Eight of Noble Memory, to Set Out and Further Discoveries to the North." In *PN*, 1: 212–14.

– "The Discourse of the Foresaid Robert Thorne, Written to Doctour Leigh." In *PN*, 1: 214–20.

Tomson, Robert. "The Voyage of Robert Tomson Merchant into New Spaine, in the Yeere 1555." In *PN*, 3: 447–54.

Towerson, William. "The First Voyage of Master William Towrson Marchant of London to Guinea, in the Yeere of Our Lord, 1555." In *PN*, 2(ii): 23–36.

- "The Second Voyage of M. William Towrson to Guinea and the Castle of Mina. An. 1556." In *PN*, 2(ii): 36–43.
- "The Third Voyage of the Sayd M. William Towrson to Guinea and the River of Sestos, Anno 1557." In *PN*, 2(ii): 44–52.

Turberville, George. "Certaine Letters in Verse, Written out of Moscovia [...] Touching the State of the Countrey, and Maners of the People." In *PN*, 1: 384–9.

Twitt, John. "The Voyage of M. Christopher Newport [...] 1591." In *PN*, 3: 567–9.

"The Valiant Fight Performed in the Streit of Gibraltar by the Centurion of London, against Five Spanish Gallies, An. 1591." In *PN*, 2(ii): 168–9.

Vas, Lopes. "The First Voyage Attempted and Set Foorth by the Valiant and Expert Captaine M. Francis Drake [...] to Nombre de Dios and Dariene, about the Yere 1572." In *PN*, 3: 525–6.

"The Voyage and Course Which Sir Francis Drake Held from the Haven of Guatalco [...] to the Northwest of California." In *PN*, 3: 440–2.

"The Voyage of Alexander Whiteman, Alias Leucander, under Canutus the Dane, to Palestine, Anno 1020." In *PN*, 2(i): 6.

"The Voyage of Ingulphus, Afterward Abbat of Croiland, unto Jerusalem, An. 1064." In *PN*, 2(i): 8–10.

"The Voyage of John Erigen, under King Alphred, to Athens, in the Yeere of Our Lorde 885." In *PN*, 2(i): 5–6.

"The Voyage of Octher to the North Parts beyond Norway." In *PN*, 1: 4–5.

"The Voyage of Sir Francis Drake to Cadiz [...] and His Taking of the Great East Indian Carak Called the Sant Philip [...] Anno 1587." In *PN*, 2(ii): 121–3.

"The Voyage of Sir Thomas Chaloner to Alger, with the Emperour Charles the Fift, Anno 1541." In *PN*, 2(i): 99.

"The Voyage of Swanus One of the Sons of Earl Godwin, unto Jerusalem, Anno 1052." In *PN*, 2(i): 6.

"The Voyage of The Susan of London to Constantinople, Wherein M. William Hareborne Was Sent First Ambassadour unto Zuldan Murad Can the Great Turke. Anno 1582." In *PN*, 2(i): 165–71.

"The Voyage of the Valiant Esquire M. Peter Read to Tunis in Barbarie 1538, Recorded in His Epitaph." In *PN*, 2(i): 99.

Ward, Luke. "The Voyage of M. Edward Fenton and M. Luke Ward [...] Intended for China, but Performed Only to the Coast of Brasil, [...] Begunne in the Yeere 1577." In *PN*, 3: 757–68.

Welsh, James. "A Voyage to Benin beyond the Countrey of Guinea Made by Master James Welsh, Who Set Foorth in the Yeere 1588." In *PN*, 2(ii): 126–9.

White, John. "The Fifth Voyage to Virginia Made by Master John White in the Yeere 1590." In *PN*, 3: 286–94.

- "The Fourth Voyage Made to Virginia with 3. Ships, Anno 1587. Wherein Was Transported the Second Colonie." In *PN*, 3: 280–4.
- "The Names of All the Men, Women, and Children Which Safely Arrived in Virginia, and Remained to Inhabit There Anno 1587." In *PN*, 3: 285.

White, Thomas. "The Taking of Two Spanish Ships Laden with Quicksilver and with the Popes Bulles, Bound for the West Indies [...] An. 1592." In *PN*, 2(ii): 193–4.

Wiars, Thomas. "The Report of Thomas Wiars Passenger in the Emanuel [...] 1578." In *PN*, 3: 44.

Willoughby, Hugh. "The True Copie of a Note Found in One of the Two Ships [...] Which Wintred in Lappia, Where Sir Hugh Willoughby and All His Companie Died, Being Frozen to Death, Anno 1553." In *PN*, 1: 232–7.

Wingfield, Anthony. "The Voyage to Spaine and Portugale Written (as It Is Thought) by Colonell Anthonie Wingfield, An. 1589." In *PN*, 2(ii): 134–55.

Wrag, Richard. "A Description of a Voyage to Constantinople and Syria Begun the 21 of March, 1593, and Ended the Ninth of August 1595: Wherein Is Shewed the Manner of Delivering the Second Present, by M. Edward Barton Her Majesties Ambassadour, Which Was Sent from Her Majestie to Sultan Murad Can, the Emperour of Turkie." In *PN*, 2(i): 303–7.

Wren, Walter. "The Voyage of M. George Fenner to Guinea and the Isles of Capo Verde, An. 1566." In *PN*, 2(ii): 57–64.

Wright, Edward. "The Voyage of the Right Honorable George Erle of Cumberland to the Azores." In *PN*, 2(ii): 155–66.

Zeno, Niccolò. "The Voyage of M. Nicolas Zeno and M. Anthony His Brother [...] Begun in the Year 1380." In *PN*, 3: 121–8.

GENERAL BIBLIOGRAPHY

Adams, Robert. *Expeditionis Hispanorum in Angliam vera descriptio. Anno Do. MDLXXXVIII*. London, 1590.

Africanus, J. Leo. *A Geographical Historie of Africa*. Translated by John Pory. London, 1600.

Akhimie, Patricia. *Shakespeare and the Cultivation of Difference: Race and Conduct in the Early Modern World*. Routledge Studies in Shakespeare 29. New York: Routledge, 2018.

Alden, John, and Dennis C. Landis. *European Americana: A Chronological Guide to Works Printed in Europe Relating to the Americas, 1493–1776*. 6 vols. New York: Readex Books, 1980.

Allen, W.E.D. "The Caspian." In Quinn, *Hakluyt Handbook*, 1: 168–75.

Alsop, James D. "Chester, Sir William (c. 1509–1595?), Mayor of London." In *ODNB*. https://doi.org/10.1093/ref:odnb/5240.
- "From Muscovy to Guinea: English Seamen of the Mid-Sixteenth Century." *Terrae Incognitae* 19, no. 1 (1987): 59–61.
- "The Career of William Towerson, Guinea Trader." *International Journal of Maritime History* 4, no. 2 (1992): 45–82.
- "Wyndham, Thomas (d. 1554), Naval Officer and Navigator." In *ODNB*. https://doi.org/10.1093/ref:odnb/30146.

Armitage, David. *Ideological Origins of the British Empire.* Cambridge, UK: Cambridge University Press, 2000.

Andrews, Kenneth R. "The Aims of Drake's Expedition of 1577–80." *American Historical Review* 73, no. 3 (1968): 724–41.
- "Drake and South America." In Thrower, *Sir Francis Drake and the Famous Voyage*, 49–59.
- ed. *English Privateering Voyages to the West Indies, 1588–1595: Documents Relating to English Voyages to the West Indies from the Defeat of the Armada to the Last Voyage of Sir Francis Drake.* Works Issued by the Hakluyt Society, 2nd series, 111. Cambridge, UK: Hakluyt Society, 1959.
- ed. *The Last Voyage of Drake and Hawkins.* Works Issued by the Hakluyt Society, 2nd series, 142. Cambridge, UK: Hakluyt Society, 1972.
- "Latin America." In Quinn, *Hakluyt Handbook*, 1: 234–43.
- "Thomas Fenner and the Guinea Trade, 1564." *The Mariner's Mirror* 38, no. 4 (1952): 312–14. https://doi.org/10.1080/00253359.1952.10658134.
- *Trade, Plunder, and Settlement: Maritime Enterprise and the Genesis of the British Empire, 1480–1630.* Cambridge, UK: Cambridge University Press, 1984.

Arber, Edward. *The Three Earliest English Books on America.* Birmingham: 1 Montague Road, 1885.

Armitage, David. *Ideological Origins of the British Empire.* Cambridge, UK: Cambridge University Press, 2000.

Ash, Eric. *Power, Knowledge, and Expertise in Elizabethan England.* Johns Hopkins University Studies in Historical and Political Science 2. Baltimore: Johns Hopkins University Press, 2004.

Ash, Eric, and Alison Sandman. "Trading Expertise: Sebastian Cabot between Spain and England." *Renaissance Quarterly* 57, no. 3 (2004): 813–46.

A Summarie and True Discourse of Sir Frances Drakes West Indian Voyage. London, 1589.

Auger, Réginald, William W. Fitzhugh, Lynda Gullason, Anne Henshaw, Donald Hogarth, and Dosia Laeyendecker. "Decentring Icons of History: Exploring the Archaeology of the Frobisher Voyages and Early European-Inuit Contact." In Warkentin and Podruchny, *Decentring the Renaissance*, 262–86.

Bahr, Arthur. *Fragments and Assemblages: Forming Compilations of Medieval London.* Chicago, IL: University of Chicago Press, 2013.

Baigent, Elizabeth. "Downton, Nicholas (bap. 1561, d. 1615), Sea Captain." In ODNB. https://doi.org/10.1093/ref:odnb/7986.

Baker, Robert. "The First Voyage of Robert Baker to Guinea. An. 1562." In PN (1589), 130–5.

– "The Second Voyage of Robert Baker to Guinea. An. 1563." In PN (1589), 135–42.

– *Travails in Guinea.* Edited by P.E.H. Hair. Liverpool: University of Liverpool Press, 1990.

Baldwin, Robert C.D. "John Dee's Interest in the Application of Nautical Science, Mathematics and Law to English Naval Affairs." In *John Dee: Interdisciplinary Studies in English Renaissance Thought,* edited by Stephen Clucas, 193: 97–130. Dordrecht: Kluwer Academic Publishers, 2006. https://doi.org/10.1007/1-4020-4246-9_6.

– "Nicholls, Thomas (1532–1601), Shipowner and Translator." In ODNB. https://doi.org/10.1093/ref:odnb/20124.

– "Speculative Ambitions and the Reputations of Frobisher's Metallurgists." In Symons, *Meta Incognita,* 2: 401–76.

– "Thorne, Robert, the Elder (c. 1460–1519), Merchant." In ODNB. https://doi.org/10.1093/ref:odnb/27347.

Bale, Anthony Paul, and Sebastian I. Sobecki. *Medieval English Travel: A Critical Anthology.* Oxford, UK: Oxford University Press, 2019.

Bale, John. *Scriptorum illustrium maioris Brytanniae [...] Catalogus.* Basel, 1559.

Barber, Peter. "Mapmaking in England, ca. 1470–1650." In Woodward, ed., *History of Cartography,* vol. 3, part 2: 1589–669.

Barkham, Selma. "The Mentality of the Men behind Sixteenth-Century Spanish Voyages to Terranova." In Warkentin and Podruchny, *Decentring the Renaissance,* 110–24.

Barley, William. *Strange and Wonderfull Things. Happened to Richard Hasleton, Borne at Braintree in Essex, in His Ten Yeares Traviles in Many Forraine Countries.* London, 1595.

Bartels, Emily. "Imperialist Beginnings: Hakluyt and the Construction of Africa." *Criticism* 34 (1992): 517–38.

Bately, Janet. "Introduction." In *The Old English Orosius.* Early English Text Society, supplementary series 6. London; New York: Early English Text Society by the Oxford University Press, 1980.

Bately, Janet, and Anton Englert, eds. *Ohthere's Voyages: A Late 9th-Century Account of Voyages along the Coasts of Norway and Denmark and Its Cultural Context.* Maritime Culture of the North 1. Roskilde: Viking Ship Museum, 2007.

Beazley, C. Raymond, ed. *The Texts and Versions of John De Plano Carpini and William De Rubriquis.* Works Issued by the Hakluyt Society, extra series 13. London: Hakluyt Society, 1903.

Beckingham, C.F. "The Near East: North and North-East Africa." In Quinn, *Hakluyt Handbook,* 1: 176–89.

Beecher, Donald. "The Legacy of John Frampton: Elizabethan Trader and Translator." *Renaissance Studies* 20, no. 3 (2006): 320–39.

Beer, Anna R. *Sir Walter Ralegh and His Readers in the Seventeenth Century: Speaking to the People.* Early Modern Literature in History. Basingstoke, UK: Macmillan Press, 1997.

Bennett, Herman L. *African Kings and Black Slaves: Sovereignty and Dispossession in the Early Modern Atlantic.* Philadelphia: University of Pennsylvania Press, 2019.

Bennett, J.A. "'Mecanicall Practises Drawne from the Artes Mathematick': The Mathematical Identity of the Elizabethan Navigator John Davis." In *Beyond the Learned Academy: The Practice of Mathematics 1600–1850,* edited by Christopher Hollings and Philip Beeley. Oxford, UK: Oxford University Press, forthcoming.

– *Navigation: A Very Short Introduction.* First edition. Very Short Introductions 514. Oxford, UK: Oxford University Press, 2017.

– *The Divided Circle: A History of Instruments for Astronomy, Navigation, and Surveying.* Oxford, UK: Phaidon, Christie's, 1987.

Benton, Lauren A. *A Search for Sovereignty: Law and Geography in European Empires, 1400–1900.* Cambridge, UK: Cambridge University Press, 2010.

Bergeron, David. "Munday, Anthony (bap. 1560, d. 1633), Playwright and Translator." In ODNB. https://doi.org/10.1093/ref:odnb/19531.

Bethancourt, Francisco, and Diogo Ramada Curto, eds. *Portuguese Oceanic Expansion, 1400–1800.* Cambridge, UK: Cambridge University Press, 2007.

Birdwood, George C.M., and Henry Stevens. *The Dawn of British Trade to the East Indies: As Recorded in the Court Minutes of the East India Company, 1599–1603.* London: H. Stevens and Son, 1886.

Black, Jeremy. "Naval Capability in the Early Modern Period: An Introduction." *Mariner's Mirror* 97, no. 2 (2011): 21–32.

Blake, John William, ed. *Europeans in West Africa: 1450–1560.* 2 vols. Works Issued by the Hakluyt Society, 2nd series, 86. London: Hakluyt Society, 1942.

Boemus, Joannes. *A Discoverie of the Countries of Tartaria, Scithia, & Cataya, by the North-East: With the Maners, Fashions, and Orders Which Are Used in Those Countries.* Translated by John Frampton. London, 1580.

Boogaart, Ernst van den. "Serialised Virginia: The Representational Format for Comparative Ethnology, c. 1600." In Sloan, *European Visions,* 113–19.

Boruchoff, David A. "Richard Hakluyt and the Demands of *Pietas Patriae.*" In Carey and Jowitt, *Richard Hakluyt and Travel Writing*, 187–96.
Bradley, James W. "Native Exchange and European Trade: Cross-Cultural Dynamics in the 16th Century." *Man in the Northeast* 33 (1987): 31–46.
Braudel, Fernand. *The Mediterranean and the Mediterranean World in the Age of Philip II.* New York: Harper and Row, 1976.
Brenner, Robert. *Merchants and Revolution: Commercial Change, Political Conflict, and London's Overseas Traders, 1550–1653.* Princeton, NJ: Princeton University Press, 1993.
Brereton, John. *A Briefe and True Relation of the Discoverie of the North Part of Virginia.* London, 1602.
Brewer, D. S. "Sixteenth, Seventeenth, and Eighteenth Century References to the Voyage of Ohthere." *Anglia* 71 (1953): 202–11.
Brooks, George E. *Landlords and Strangers: Ecology, Society, and Trade in Western Africa, 1000–1630.* Boulder, CO: Westview Press, 1993.
Brotton, Jerry. *The Sultan and the Queen: The Untold Story of Elizabeth and Islam.* New York: Viking, 2016.
Brotton, Jerry, and Lisa Jardine. *Global Interests: Renaissance Art between East and West.* Picturing History. London: Reaktion Books, 2000.
Bry, Johann Israel de, and Theodor de Bry, eds. *America.* 12 vols. Frankfurt, 1590–1634.
Burton, Jonathan. *Traffic and Turning: Islam and English Drama, 1579–1624.* Newark: University of Delaware Press, 2005.
Camden, William. *Britain, or A Chorographicall Description.* Translated by Philemon Holland. London, 1610.
Campbell, Mary Baine. *The Witness and the Other World: Exotic European Travel Writing, 400–1600.* Ithaca, NY; London: Cornell University Press, 1988.
Canny, Nicholas P., and Philip D. Morgan. *The Oxford Handbook of the Atlantic World.* 1st ed. Oxford, UK: Oxford University Press, 2011.
Carey, Daniel. "Hakluyt's Instructions: *The Principal Navigations* and Sixteenth-Century Travel Advice." *Studies in Travel Writing* 13 (2009): 167–85.
Carey, Daniel, and Claire Jowitt, eds. *Richard Hakluyt and Travel Writing in Early Modern Europe.* Works Issued by the Hakluyt Society, Extra Series 47. Farnham, Surrey, England; Burlington, VT: Ashgate, 2012.
Carley, James P. "Polydore Vergil and John Leland on King Arthur: The Battle of the Books." In *King Arthur: A Casebook*, edited by Edward Donald Kennedy. Arthurian Characters and Themes, vol. 1. New York: Garland Pub, 1996.
Cartier, Jacques. *A Shorte and Briefe Narration of the Two Navigations and Discoueries to the Northwest Partes Called Newe Fraunce.* Translated by John Florio. London, 1580.

- *Relations.* Edited by Michel Bideaux. Montreal, QC: Presses de l'Université de Montréal, 1986.
Cell, Gillian T. *English Enterprise in Newfoundland 1577–1660.* Toronto: University of Toronto Press, 1969.
Chancellor, Nicholas. "The 2. Journal of M. Arthur Pet and M. Charles Jackman [...] 1580." In *PN* (1589), 476–82.
Cheshire, Neil M., Tony Waldron, Alison M. Quinn, and David B. Quinn. "Frobisher's Eskimos in England." *Archivaria* 10 (1980): 23–35.
Cheyfitz, Eric. *The Poetics of Imperialism: Translation and Colonization from The Tempest to Tarzan.* Expanded ed. Philadelphia: University of Pennsylvania Press, 1997.
Chibi, Andrew A. "Docwra, Sir Thomas (d. 1527), Prior of the Hospital of St John of Jerusalem in England and Diplomat." In *ODNB.* https://doi.org/10.1093/ref:odnb/7726.
Clulee, Nicholas H. *John Dee's Natural Philosophy: Between Science and Religion.* London; New York: Routledge, 1988.
Clusius, Carolus. *Aliquot Notae in Garciae Aromatum Historium,* 1582.
Conway, G.R.G., ed. *An Englishman and the Mexican Inquisition, 1556–1560: Being an Account of the Voyage of Robert Tomson to New Spain, His Trial for Heresy in the City of Mexico and Other Contemporary Historical Documents.* Mexico City: Privately printed, 1927.
Cook, Harold John. *Matters of Exchange: Commerce, Medicine, and Science in the Dutch Golden Age.* New Haven, CT: Yale University Press, 2007.
Corbett, Julian Stafford. *Drake and the Tudor Navy, with a History of the Rise of England as a Maritime Power.* 2 vols. London, New York, and Bombay: Longmans, Green, and Co., 1899.
- *Papers Relating to the Navy during the Spanish War, 1585–1587.* London: Navy Records Society, 1898.
Cormack, Lesley B. "'Good Fences Make Good Neighbors': Geography as Self-Definition in Early Modern England." *Isis* 82, no. 4 (1991): 639–61.
Cortés, Martín. *The Arte of Navigation: Conteynyng a Compendious Description of the Sphere* [...]. Translated by Richard Eden. London, 1561.
Cosgrove, Dennis. "Images of Renaissance Cosmography, 1450–1650." In Woodward, *History of Cartography,* vol. 3, part 1: 55–98.
Craciun, Adriana. "The Frozen Ocean." *PMLA* 125, no. 3 (2010): 693–702. https://doi.org/10.1632/pmla.2010.125.3.693.
- *Writing Arctic Disaster: Authorship and Exploration.* Cambridge Studies in Nineteenth-Century Literature and Culture 104. Cambridge, UK: Cambridge University Press, 2016.

Crane, Nicholas. *Mercator: The Man Who Mapped the Planet.* 1st Amer. ed. New York: H. Holt, 2003.
Croft, Pauline. *The Spanish Company.* London, Leicester: London Record Society, 1973.
– "English Mariners Trading to Spain and Portugal, 1558–1625." *Mariner's Mirror* 69, no. 3 (1983): 251–66. https://doi.org/10.1080/00253359.1983.10655924.
Cronon, William. "Foreword." In Oslund, *Iceland Imagined,* vii-xii.
Cotton, William. *An Elizabethan Guild of the City of Exeter. An account of the proceedings of the Society of Merchant Adventurers, during the latter half of the 16th century.* Exeter: Printed for the Author by William Pollard, 1873.
Croskey, Robert M. "Hakluyt's Accounts of Sir Jerome Bowes' Embassy to Ivan IV." *Slavonic and Eastern European Review* 61 (1983): 546–64.
Dalché, Patrick Gautier. "The Reception of Ptolomy's Geography." In Woodward, *History of Cartography,* vol. 3, part 1: 285–364.
Dalton, Heather. "'Into Speyne to Selle for Slavys': English, Spanish, and Genoese Merchant Networks and Their Involvement with the 'Cost of Gwynea' Trade before 1550." In *Brokers of Change: Atlantic Commerce and Cultures in Precolonial Western Africa,* edited by Toby Green, 91–124. Oxford, UK: Oxford University Press, for the British Academy, 2012.
– *Merchants and Explorers: Roger Barlow, Sebastian Cabot, and Networks of Atlantic Exchange 1500–1560.* Oxford, UK: Oxford University Press, 2016.
– "Negotiating Fortune: English Merchants in Early Sixteenth-Century Seville." In *Bridging the Early Modern Atlantic World: People, Products, and Practices on the Move,* edited by Caroline A. Williams, 57–73. Farnham, UK: Ashgate, 2009.
Das, Nandini. "Encounter as Process: England and Japan in the Late Sixteenth Century." *Renaissance Quarterly* 69, no. 4 (2016): 1,343–68. https://doi.org/10.1086/690315.
– "Richard Hakluyt's Two Indias: Textual Sparagmos and Editorial Practice." In Carey and Jowitt, *Richard Hakluyt and Travel Writing,* 119–28.
Davies, Surekha. *Renaissance Ethnography and the Invention of the Human: New Worlds, Maps and Monsters.* Cambridge Social and Cultural Histories 24. Cambridge, UK: Cambridge University Press, 2016.
Davis, John. *The Seamans Secrets.* London, 1595.
– *The Worldes Hydrographical Discription.* London, 1595.
Day, Matthew. "Hakluyt, Harvey, Nashe: The Material Text and Early Modern Nationalism." *Studies in Philology* 104, no. 3 (2007): 281–305.
– "'Honour to Our Nation': Nationalism, *The Principal Navigations* and Travel Collections in the Long Eighteenth Century." In Carey and Jowitt, *Richard Hakluyt and Travel Writing,* 77–86.

- "Richard Hakluyt's 'Principal Navigations' (1598–1600) and the Textuality of Tudor English Nationalism." PhD thesis, University of York, 2004.
Dee, John. *General and Rare Memorials Pertayning to the Perfect Arte of Navigation.* London, 1577.
Dew, Nicholas. "Reading Travels in the Culture of Curiosity: Thévenot's Collection of Voyages." In *Bringing the World to Early Modern Europe: Travel Accounts and Their Audiences*, edited by Peter C. Mancall, 39–59. Leiden; Boston: Brill, 2007.
Diffie, Bailey W., and George D. Winius. *Foundations of the Portuguese Empire, 1415–1580.* NED-New edition, vol. 1. Minneapolis, MN: University of Minnesota Press, 1977.
Dimmock, Matthew. "Guns and Gawds: Elizabethan England's Infidel Trade." In Singh, *Companion to the Global Renaissance*, 1st ed., 207–22.
- "Hakluyt's Multiple Faiths." In Carey and Jowitt, *Richard Hakluyt and Travel Writing*, 219–28.
- *New Turkes: Dramatizing Islam and the Ottomans in Early Modern England.* Aldershot, UK; Burlington, VT: Ashgate, 2005.
Dodoens, Rembert. *A Niewe Herball, or Historie of Plantes.* Translated by Henry Lyte. Antwerp, 1578.
Domingues, Francisco Contente. "Science and Technology in Portuguese Navigation: The Idea of Experience in the Sixteenth Century." In Bethancourt and Curto, *Portuguese Oceanic Expansion*, 460–79.
Donno, Elizabeth Story, ed. *An Elizabethan in 1582: The Diary of Richard Madox Fellow of All Souls.* Works Issued by the Hakluyt Society, 2nd series, 147. London: Hakluyt Society, 1976.
Duffy, Eamon. *The Stripping of the Altars: Traditional Religion in England, c.1400–c.1580.* New Haven, CT: Yale University Press, 2005.
Earle, Peter. *Corsairs of Malta and Barbary.* London: Sidgwick and Jackson, 1970.
- *The Last Fight of the Revenge.* London: Collins and Brown, 1992.
Eden, Richard. *The Decades of the New World or West India.* London, 1555.
- *A Treatyse of the Newe India.* London, 1553.
Edwards, A.S.G. "A New Manuscript of The Libelle of English Policy." *Notes and Queries* 46, no. 4 (1999): 444.
Edwards, Philip. "Edward Hayes Explains Away Sir Humphrey Gilbert." *Renaissance Studies* 6, no. 3/4 (1992): 270–86.
Egmond, Florike. *The World of Carolus Clusius: Natural History in the Making, 1550–1610.* London; Brookfield, VT: Pickering and Chatto, 2010.
Elsner, Jaś, and Joan-Pau Rubiés. *Voyages and Visions.* Chicago, IL: University of Chicago Press, 1999.

Escobedo, Arthur. "The Tudor Search for Arthur and the Poetics of Historical Loss." *Exemplaria* 14, no. 1 (2002): 127–65. https://doi.org/10.1179/exm.2002.14.1.127.

Fenton, Edward, ed. *The Diaries of John Dee*. Charlbury, UK: Day Books, 1998.

Fitzmaurice, Andrew. *Sovereignty, Property and Empire, 1500-2000*. Ideas in Context 107. Cambridge, UK: Cambridge University Press, 2014.

Fleming, Juliet. "Afterword." *Huntington Library Quarterly* 73, no. 3 (2010): 543–52. https://doi.org/10.1525/hlq.2010.73.3.543.

– *Graffiti and the Writing Arts of Early Modern England*. Material Texts. Philadelphia, PA: University of Pennsylvania Press, 2001.

Flower, Robin. "Laurence Nowell and the Discovery of England in Tudor Times." *Proceedings of the British Academy* 21 (1935): 47–73.

Foot, Sarah. "Æthelstan [Athelstan] (893/4–939)." In ODNB. https://doi.org/10.1093/ref:odnb/8143.

Foster, William, ed. *The Travels of John Sanderson in the Levant 1584–1602*. Works Issued by the Hakluyt Society, 2nd series, 67. London: Hakluyt Society, 1931.

– ed. *The Voyage of Nicholas Downton to the East Indies, 1614–15: As Recorded in Contemporary Narratives and Letters*. Works Issued by the Hakluyt Society, 2nd series, 82. London: Hakluyt Society, 1939.

– ed. *The Voyages of Sir James Lancaster to Brazil and the East Indies 1591–1603*. Works Issued by the Hakluyt Society, 2nd series, 85. London: Hakluyt Society, 1940.

Foxe, John. *Actes and Monuments of Matters Most Speciall and Memorable*. 2nd ed. 2 vols. London, 1583.

Frampton, John, trans. *The Most Noble and Famous Travels of Marcus Paulus*. London, 1579.

Frantzen, Allen J. *Desire for Origins: New Language, Old English, and Teaching the Tradition*. New Brunswick, NJ: Rutgers University Press, 1990.

Froude, James Anthony. "England's Forgotten Worthies." In *Short Studies on Great Subjects*, 1: 358–405. New York: Scribner's, 1888.

Fuchs, Barbara. "An English Picaro in New Spain: Miles Philips and the Framing of National Identity." *CR: The New Centennial Review* 2, no. 1 (2002): 55–68. https://doi.org/10.1353/ncr.2002.0005.

– "Golden Ages and Golden Hinds; or, Periodizing Spain and England." *PMLA* 127, no. 2 (2012): 321–27.

– *Mimesis and Empire: The New World, Islam, and European Identities*. Cambridge Studies in Renaissance Literature and Culture 40. Cambridge, UK: Cambridge University Press, 2001.

- *Poetics of Piracy: Emulating Spain in English Literature*. Philadelphia: University of Pennsylvania Press, 2013.
Fuller, Mary C. "Afterword: Looking for the Women in Early Modern Travel Writing." In *Travel and Travail: Early Modern Women, English Drama, and the Wider World*, edited by Patricia Akhimie and Bernadette Andrea, 331–52. Lincoln: University of Nebraska Press, 2019.
- "Arctics of Empire: The North in *Principal Navigations* (1598–1600)." In Regard, *Quest for the Northwest Passage*, 15–29.
- "Arthur and Amazons: Editing the Fabulous in Hakluyt's *Principal Navigations*." *The Yearbook of English Studies* 41, no. 1 (2011): 173–89.
- "'His Dark Materials': The Problem of Dullness in Hakluyt's Collections." In Carey and Jowitt, *Richard Hakluyt and Travel Writing*, 231–42.
- "In the Round and on the Page: Canada in the English Geographical Imaginary, circa 1600." In Greer, *Before Canada*.
- "Missing Terms in English Geographical Thinking, 1550–1600." In *The State of Nature: Histories of an Idea*, edited by Mark Somos and Anne Peters, 28–60. History of European Political and Constitutional Thought 6. Brill, 2022.
- "Placing Iceland." In *Companion to the Global Renaissance*, 2nd ed., edited by Jyotsna Singh, 184–96. Blackwell Companions to Literature and Culture. Hoboken, NJ: John Wiley and Sons, 2021.
- *Remembering the Early Modern Voyage: English Narratives in the Age of European Expansion*. New York: Palgrave Macmillan, 2008.
- "Richard Hakluyt's Foreign Relations." In *Empire, Form, and Travel Writing*, edited by Julia Kuehn and Paul Smethurst, 2008.
- "The Real and the Unreal in Tudor Travel Writing." In *A Companion to Tudor Literature*, edited by Kent Cartwright, 475–88. Chichester, UK; Malden, MA: Wiley-Blackwell, 2010.
- *Voyages in Print: English Voyages to America 1576–1624*. Cambridge, UK: Cambridge University Press, 1995.
- "Writing the Long-Distance Voyage: Hakluyt's Circumnavigators." *Huntington Library Quarterly* 70, no. 1 (2007): 37–60.
Fury, Cheryl A. *Tides in the Affairs of Men: The Social History of Elizabethan Seamen, 1580–1603*. Westport: Greenwood Publishing Group, 2001.
Gallagher, John. "The Italian London of John North: Cultural Contact and Linguistic Encounter in Early Modern England." *Renaissance Quarterly* 70 (2017): 88–131.
Galvão, António. *The Discoveries of the World from Their First Originall unto the Yeere of Our Lord 1555*. Translated by Richard Hakluyt. London, 1601.

Games, Alison. *The Web of Empire: English Cosmopolitans in an Age of Expansion, 1560–1660*. Oxford, UK: Oxford University Press, 2008.
Gelder, Esther van, ed. *Clusius Correspondence. A Digital Edition-in-Progress*. 1st release. The Hague: Huygens ING, 2015. http://clusiuscorrespondence.huygens.knaw.nl.
Gerard, John. *The Herball or Generall Historie of Plantes*. London, 1597.
Gilles, Sealy. "Territorial Interpolations in the Old English Orosius." In *Text and Territory: Geographical Imagination in the European Middle Ages*, edited by Sylvia Tomasch and Sealy Gilles. Philadelphia: University of Pennsylvania Press, 1998.
Goldenberg, L.A. "Russian Cartography to ca. 1700." In Woodward, *History of Cartography*, vol. 3, part 1: 1,852–903.
Goldgar, Anne. *Tulipmania: Money, Honor, and Knowledge in the Dutch Golden Age*. Chicago, IL: University of Chicago Press, 2007.
Gomes, Mário Varela, and Tânia Manuel Casimiro. "Afro-Portuguese Ivories from Sierra Leone and Nigeria (Yoruba and Benin Kingdoms) in Archaeological Contexts from Southern Portugal." *African Arts* 53, no. 4 (2020): 24–37.
Gordon, Eleanora C. "The Fate of Sir Hugh Willoughby and His Companions: A New Conjecture." *Geographical Journal* 152, no. 2 (July 1986): 243. https://doi.org/10.2307/634766.
Gould, J.D. *The Great Debasement: Currency and the Economy in Mid-Tudor England*. Oxford, UK: Clarendon, 1970.
Gow, Andrew. "Gog and Magog on Mappaemundi and Early Printed World Maps: Orientalizing Ethnography in the Apocalyptic Tradition." *Journal of Early Modern History* 2, no. 1 (1998): 61–88.
Greenblatt, Stephen. *Learning to Curse: Essays in Early Modern Culture*. New York: Routledge, 2007.
– *Renaissance Self-Fashioning*. Chicago, IL: University of Chicago Press, 1980.
Greene, Roland. *Unrequited Conquests: Love and Empire in the Colonial Americas*. Chicago, IL: University of Chicago Press, 1999.
Greepe, Thomas. *The True and Perfecte Newes of the Woorthy and Valiaunt Exploytes, Performed and Doone by the Valiant Knight Syr Frauncis Drake, Not Onely at Sancto Domingo, and Carthagena, but Also Nowe at Cales and Uppon the Coast of Spayne, 1587*. London, 1587.
– *The True and Perfecte Newes of the Woorthy and Valiaunt Exploytes, Performed and Doone by the Valiant Knight Syr Frauncis Drake*. Edited by David W. Waters. Hartford: For HCT by CPR, 1955.
Greer, Allan, ed. *Before Canada: Northern North America in a Connected World*. Montreal and Kingston: McGill-Queen's University Press, forthcoming.

Groesen, Michiel van. *The Representations of the Overseas World in the De Bry Collection of Voyages (1590–1634)*. Leiden; Boston: Brill, 2008.

Grotius, Hugo. *The Free Sea*. Edited by David Armitage. Translated by Richard Hakluyt. Natural Law and Enlightenment Classics. Indianapolis, IN: Liberty Fund, 2004.

Guzman, Gregory G. "The Encyclopedist Vincent of Beauvais and His Mongol Extracts from John of Plano Carpini and Simon of Saint-Quentin." *Speculum* 49, no. 2 (1974): 287–307.

Gwyn, David. "Richard Eden Cosmographer and Alchemist." *Sixteenth Century Journal* 15, no. 1 (1984): 13.

Habib, Imtiaz. *Black Lives in the English Archives, 1500–1677: Imprints of the Invisible*. London: Routledge, 2008.

— "'They Say...': Indian Talk Back as Indiaspeak in Ralph Fitch's Account of India in 1583." *Sixteenth Century Journal* 47, no. 2 (2016): 305–25.

Hackel, Heidi Brayman, and Peter C. Mancall. "Richard Hakluyt the Younger's Notes for the East India Company in 1601: A Transcription of Huntington Library Manuscript EL 2360." *Huntington Library Quarterly* 67, no. 3 (September 2004): 423–36. https://doi.org/10.1525/hlq.2004.67.3.423.

Hadfield, Andrew. "Eden, Richard (c. 1520–1576), Translator." In *ODNB*. https://doi.org/10.1093/ref:odnb/8454.

Hair, P.E.H. "Discovery and Discoveries: The Portuguese in Guinea 1444–1650." In P.E.H. Hair, *Africa Encountered: European Contacts and Evidence, 1450–1700*, 11–28. Collected Studies. Brookfield, VT: Variorum, 1997.

— "Guinea." In Quinn, *Hakluyt Handbook*, 1: 197–207. London: Hakluyt Society, 1974.

— "Materials on Africa (Other than the Mediterranean and Red Sea Lands) and on the Atlantic Islands, in the Publications of Samuel Purchas, 1613–1626." *History in Africa* 13 (1986): 117–59.

— "Protestants as Pirates, Slavers, and Protomissionaries: Sierra Leone 1568 and 1582." *The Journal of Ecclesiastical History* 213 (1970): 203–24.

— "Sources on Early Sierra Leone: (14) English Accounts of 1582." *Africana Research Bulletin* 9, nos. 1–2 (1978): 67–99.

— "Sources on Early Sierra Leone: (21) English Voyages of the 1580s." *Africana Research Bulletin* 13, no. 3 (1984): 62–88.

— "The Experience of the Sixteenth-Century English Voyages to Guinea." *Mariner's Mirror* 83, no. 1 (1997): 3–13.

— "The Hakluyt Society: From Past to Future." In *Compassing the Vaste Globe of the Earth: Studies in the History of the Hakluyt Society, 1846–1996*, edited by P.E.H. Hair and R.C. Bridges, 7–48. Works Issued by the Hakluyt Society, 2nd series, 183. London: Hakluyt Society, 1996.

Hair, P.E.H., and J.D. Alsop. *English Seamen and Traders in Guinea 1553–1565: The New Evidence of Their Wills.* Lewiston, NY: E. Mellen Press, 1992.

Hair, P.E.H., and Robin Law. "The English in Western Africa to 1700." In *The Oxford History of the British Empire: Volume I: The Origins of Empire: British Overseas Enterprise to the Close of the Seventeenth Century, 1998.* Oxford, UK: Oxford University Press, 1998.

Hakluyt, Richard. *A Particuler Discourse.* Edited by David B. Quinn and Alison M. Quinn. Works Issued by the Hakluyt Society, extra series 45. London: Hakluyt Society, 1993.

– *Divers Voyages Touching the Discoverie of America* [...]. London, 1582.

– *The Principal Navigations, Voyages, Traffiques, and Discoveries of the English Nation.* 3 vols. London, 1598–1600.

– *The Principal Navigations, Voyages, Traffiques & Discoveries of the English Nation.* Glasgow: J. MacLehose and sons, 1903.

– *The Principall Navigations, Voyages and Discoveries of the English Nation.* London, 1589.

– *The Principall Navigations, Voiages, and Discoveries of the English Nation.* Edited by David B. Quinn and R.A. Skelton. 2 vols. Works Issued by the Hakluyt Society, extra series, 39. Cambridge, UK: Hakluyt Society and the Peabody Museum of Salem at the University Press, 1965.

Hall, Kim F. *Things of Darkness: Economies of Race and Gender in Early Modern England.* Ithaca, NY: Cornell University Press, 1998.

Hammer, Paul. "Myth-Making: Politics, Propaganda and the Capture of Cadiz in 1596." *The Historical Journal* 40, no. 3 (1997): 621–42.

Hanmer, Meredith. *The Baptizing of a Turke: A Sermon Preached* [...] *1586, at the Baptizing of One Chinano a Turke, Borne at Nigropontus.* London, 1586.

Harkness, Deborah E. *The Jewel House: Elizabethan London and the Scientific Revolution.* New Haven, CT: Yale University Press, 2007.

Harriot, Thomas. *A Briefe and True Report of the New Found Land of Virginia: Of the Commodities and of the Nature and Manners of the Naturall Inhabitants.* America 1, edited by Theodor de Bry. Frankfurt, 1590.

– *A Briefe and True Report of the New Found Land of Virginia.* Charlottesville, VA: Published for the Library at the Mariners' Museum by the University of Virginia Press, 2007.

Haslop, Henry. *Newes out of the Coast of Spaine: The True Report of the Honourable Service for England, Perfourmed by Sir Frauncis Drake in the Moneths of Aprill and May Last Past, 1587. Upon Cales.* London, 1587.

Havens, Earle. "Americana Vetustissima: Richard Eden's Annotated Copy of Peter Martyr's Decades of the New World." In *Other People's Books: Association Copies and the Stories They Tell*, edited by Susan F. Rossen, 23–8. Chicago, IL: Caxton Club, 2011.

Hawes, John. *The Valiant and Most Laudable Fight Performed in the Straights, by the Centurion of London against Five Spanish Gallies [...]*. London, 1591.

Hawkins, John. *A True Declaration of the Troublesome Voyadge of M. John Hawkins to the Parties of Guynea and the West Indies: In the Years of Our Lord 1567 and 1568*. London, 1569.

Helgerson, Richard. *Forms of Nationhood: The Elizabethan Writing of England*. Chicago, IL: University of Chicago Press, 1992.

— "'I Miles Philips': An Elizabethan Seaman Conscripted by History." *PMLA* 118, no. 3 (2003): 573–80.

Herendeen, Wyman H. *William Camden: A Life in Context*. Woodbridge, UK; Rochester, NY: Boydell Press, 2007.

Hind, Arthur M. *Engraving in England in the Sixteenth & Seventeenth Centuries; a Descriptive Catalogue with Introductions*, vol. 1, 3 vols. Cambridge, UK: Cambridge University Press, 1952.

Hitchcock, R.F. "Cavendish's Last Voyage: Purposes Revealed and Concealed." *Mariner's Mirror* 87, no. 1 (February 2001): 5–14.

Holtz, Grégoire. "Hakluyt in France: Pierre Bergeron and Travel Writing Collections." In Carey and Jowitt, *Richard Hakluyt and Travel Writing*, 67–76.

Hodgkins, Christopher. *Reforming Empire: Protestant Colonialism and Conscience in British Literature*. Columbia: University of Missouri Press, 2002.

Hopper, Clarence, ed. *Sir Francis Drake's Memorable Service Done against the Spaniards in 1587*. Camden Miscellany 5. Westminster: Printed for the Camden Society, 1863.

Horodowich, Elizabeth. *Venetian Discovery of America: Geographic Imagination in the Age of Encounters*. Cambridge, UK: Cambridge University Press, 2018.

Hortop, Job. *The Rare Travailes of Job Hortop*. London, 1591.

Hotman, François, Jean Hotman, and Jan W. van Meel. *Francisci et Joannis Hotomanorum Patris et Filii, et Clarorum Virorum Ad Eos Epistolae*. Amsterdam, 1700.

Hulton, Paul. *America, 1585: The Complete Drawings of John White*. Chapel Hill: University of North Carolina Press; British Museum Publications, 1984.

Hunneyball, Paul. "Sparke, John (c.1574–1640), of The Friary, Plymouth, Devon." History of Parliament Online. Accessed 11 July 2021. http://www.histparl.ac.uk/volume/1604-1629/member/sparke-john-1574-1640.

İnalcık, Halil. *The Ottoman Empire; the Classical Age, 1300–1600*. Translated by Norman Itzkowitz and Colin Imber. Reprint. Late Byzantine and Ottoman Studies 1. New Rochelle, NY: Aristide D. Caratzas, 1989.

İnalcık, Halil, and Donald Quataert. *An Economic and Social History of the Ottoman Empire, 1300–1914*. Cambridge; New York: Cambridge University Press, 1994.

Jackson, Peter, and David Morgan, eds. *The Mission of Friar William of Rubruck: His Journey to the Court of the Great Khan Mongke, 1253–1255*. Works Issued by the Hakluyt Society, 2nd series, 173. London: Hakluyt Society, 1990.

Jardine, Lisa, and William Sherman. "Pragmatic Readers: Knowledge Transactions and Scholarly Services in Late Elizabethan England." In *Religion, Culture, and Society in Early Modern Britain: Essays in Honour of Patrick Collinson*, edited by Anthony Fletcher and Peter Roberts, 102–24. Cambridge, UK: Cambridge University Press, 1994.

Jewkes, W.T. "Sir Francis Drake Revived: From Letters to Legend." In Thrower, *Sir Francis Drake and the Famous Voyage*, 112–20.

Jones, Evan. "England's Icelandic Fishery in the Early Modern Period." In *England's Sea Fisheries: The Commercial Sea Fisheries of England and Wales since 1300*, edited by David Starkey, Chris Reid, and Neil Ashcroft, 105–10. London: Chatham, 2000.

Jones, Evan T., and Margaret M. Condon. *Cabot and Bristol's Age of Discovery*. Bristol, UK: University of Bristol, 2016.

Jowitt, Claire. *The Culture of Piracy, 1580–1630: English Literature and Seaborne Crime*. Burlington, VT: Ashgate, 2010.

– "The Hero and the Sea: Sea Captains and Their Discontents." *XVII–XVIII. Revue de La Société d'études Anglo-Américaines Des XVIIe et XVIIIe Siècles* 74 (2017). https://doi.org/10.4000/1718.888.

Keeble, N.H. "'To Be a Pilgrim': Constructing the Protestant Life in Early Modern England." In Morris and Roberts, *Pilgrimage*, 238–56.

Keeler, Mary Frear, ed. *Sir Francis Drake's West Indian Voyage 1585–86*. Works Issued by the Hakluyt Society, 2nd series, 148. London: Hakluyt Society, 1981.

Kelsey, Harry. *Sir John Hawkins: Queen Elizabeth's Slave Trader*. New Haven, CT: Yale University Press, 2003.

– *Sir Francis Drake: The Queen's Pirate*. New Haven, CT: Yale University Press, 1998.

Kendrick, T.D. *British Antiquity*. London: Methuen Press, 1950.

King, Edmund. "Ingulf (c. 1045–1109), Abbot of Crowland." In *ODNB*. https://doi.org/10.1093/ref:odnb/14422.

King, John N. *Foxe's Book of Martyrs and Early Modern Print Culture*. Cambridge; New York: Cambridge University Press, 2006.

Kingsford, Charles Lethbridge, ed. "The Taking of the Madre de Dios, Anno 1592." In Laughton, *Naval Miscellany*, vol. 2, 85–121.

Klein, Bernhard. "'To Pot Straight We Goe': Robert Baker in Guinea, 1562–64." In Carey and Jowitt, *Richard Hakluyt and Travel Writing*, 243–56.

Knafla, Louis A. "Starkey, Ralph (d. 1628), Archivist and Merchant." In *ODNB*. https://doi.org/10.1093/ref:odnb/26317.

Knutson, Roslyn L. "A Caliban in St. Mildred Poultry." In *Shakespeare and Cultural Traditions: The Selected Proceedings of the International Shakespeare Association World Congress, Tokyo, 1991*, edited by Tetsuo Kishi, Roger Pringle, and Stanley Wells. Newark: University of Delaware Press; Associated University Presses, 1994.

Knapp, Jeffrey. *An Empire Nowhere: England, America, and Literature from Utopia to The Tempest*. Berkeley: University of California Press, 1992.

Koester, David. "The Power of Insult: Ethnographic Publication and Emergent Nationalism in the Sixteenth Century." In *Central Sites, Peripheral Visions: Cultural and Institutional Crossings in the History of Anthropology*, edited by Richard Handler, 8–40. Madison: University of Wisconsin Press, 2006.

Krogt, Peter van der. *The Globes of Hondius: A Most Important Pair of Globes Showing the Results of the Earliest Dutch Exploration Voyages to the East Indies*. Utrecht: Antiquariaat Forum, 1991.

Kupperman, Karen Ordahl. "Roanoke and Its Legacy." In Harriot, *A Briefe and True Report of the New Found Land of Virginia* (2007), 1–7.

– "Roanoke's Achievement." In Sloan, *European Visions*, 3–12.

Lacey, Walter. *Sir Walter Ralegh*. New York: Atheneum, 1974.

Lach, Donald F. "The Far East." In Quinn, *Hakluyt Handbook*, 1: 214–22.

– *Asia in the Making of Europe*. 3 vols. Chicago, 1965.

Laudonnière, René de. *A Notable History Containing Four Voyages [...] unto Florida*. London, 1587.

Laughton, John Knox, ed., *Naval Miscellany*, vol. 2. Publications of the Navy Records Society 40. London: Printed for the Navy Records Society, 1912.

– ed. *State Papers Relating to the Defeat of the Spanish Armada, Anno 1588*. 2 vols. Publications of the Navy Records Society 1–2. London: Printed for the Navy Records Society, 1894.

Law, John. "On the Methods of Long-Distance Control: Vessels, Navigation and the Portuguese Route to India." In *Power, Action, and Belief: A New Sociology of Knowledge?*, edited by John Law. London; Boston: Routledge and Kegan Paul, 1986.

Leimon, Mitchell, and Geoffrey Parker. "Treason and Plot in Elizabethan Diplomacy: The 'Fame of Sir Edward Stafford' Reconsidered." *English Historical Review* 111, no. 444 (1996): 1,134–58.

Le Moyne de Morgues, Jacques. *Brevis narratio eorum quae in Florida Americae provi[n]cia Gallis acciderunt*. In *America* 2, edited by Theodor de Bry. Frankfurt, 1591.

Leng, Robert. "The True Discripcion of the Last Voiage of [...] Sir Frauncis Drake." In Hopper, *Camden Miscellany*, 10–23.

Lestringant, Frank. *Le Huguenot et le sauvage: l'Amérique et la controverse coloniale, en France, au temps des guerres de religion (1555–1589)*. Genève: Droz, 2004.

Levy, F.J. *Tudor Historical Thought.* Huntington Library Publications. San Marino, CA: Huntington Library, 1967.
Lewis, C.S. *English Literature in the Sixteenth Century.* Oxford, UK: Clarendon Press, 1954.
Loades, David. *England's Maritime Empire: Seapower, Commerce and Policy, 1490–1690.* London: Longman, 2000.
– *John Dudley, Duke of Northumberland 1504–1553.* Oxford, UK: Oxford University Press, 1996.
– "Winter, Sir William (c. 1525–1589), Naval Administrator." In *ODNB.* https://doi.org/10.1093/ref:odnb/29769.
Loewen, Brad. "Sea Change: Indigenous Navigation and Relations with Basques around the Gulf of Saint Lawrence, c. 1500–1700." In Greer, *Before Canada.*
Long, Pamela O. "The Openness of Knowledge: An Ideal and Its Context in 16th-Century Writings on Mining and Metallurgy." *Technology and Culture* 32, no. 2 (1991): 318–55.
– "Trading Zones in Early Modern Europe." *Isis* 106, no. 4 (2015): 840–47.
López de Gómara, Francisco. *The Pleasant Historie of the Conquest of the Weast India, Now Called New Spayne.* Translated by Thomas Nicholls. London, 1578.
López-Lázaro, Fabio T. *The Misfortunes of Alonso Ramírez: The True Adventures of a Spanish American with 17th-Century Pirates.* Austin: University of Texas Press, 2011.
Lorimer, Joyce. "Robert Cecil, Richard Hakluyt and the Writing of Guiana, 1595–1616." In Carey and Jowitt, *Richard Hakluyt and Travel Writing,* 105–17.
– ed. *Sir Walter Ralegh's Discoverie of Guiana.* Works Issued by the Hakluyt Society, 3rd series, 15. London: Hakluyt Society, 2006.
Lovejoy, Paul E. *Transformations in Slavery: A History of Slavery in Africa.* 3rd ed. African Studies 117. Cambridge, UK: Cambridge University Press, 2011.
Lowe, Ben. "Throckmorton [née Lok; other married name Hickman], Rose (1526–1613)." In *ODNB.* https://doi.org/10.1093/ref:odnb/67979.
Lucas, Frederick W. *The Voyages of the Brothers Zeni.* London: Henry Stevens Son and Stiles, 1898.
Lydon, Ghislaine. "Saharan Oceans and Bridges, Barriers and Divides an Africa's Historiographical Landscape." *Journal of African History* 56, no. 1 (2015): 3–22. https://doi.org/10.1017/S002185371400070X.
MacCrossan, Colm. "Framing 'the English Nation': Reading between Text and Paratext in The Principal Navigations (1598–1600)." In Carey and Jowitt, *Richard Hakluyt and Travel Writing,* 139–52.
MacLaren, Ian S. "Generating Captain Cook and Paul Kane into Published Authors: Case Studies of a Book History Model for Exploration and Travel Writing." *Papers*

of the Bibliographical Society of Canada/ Cahiers de La Société Bibliographique Du Canada 54, nos. 1–2 (2016): 7–56.

– "In Consideration of the Evolution of Explorers and Travellers into Authors: A Model." *Studies in Travel Writing* 15, no. 3 (1 September 2011): 221–41. https://doi.org/10.1080/13645145.2011.595926.

MacLean, Gerald M. "East by North-East: The English among the Russians, 1553–1603." In Singh, *Companion to the Global Renaissance*, 1st ed., 163–77.

– *Looking East: English Writing and the Ottoman Empire before 1800.* Basingstoke, UK; New York: Palgrave Macmillan, 2007.

MacLean, Gerald M., and Nabil I. Matar. *Britain and the Islamic World, 1558–1713.* Oxford, UK: Oxford University Press, 2011.

MacMillan, Ken. *Sovereignty and Possession in the English New World: The Legal Foundations of Empire, 1576–1640.* Cambridge, UK: Cambridge University Press, 2006

– ed. *John Dee: The Limits of the British Empire.* Westport, CT: Praeger, 2004.

Mahieu, Marc-Antoine, and Mickaël Popelard. "'A People of Tractable Conversation': A Reappraisal of Davis's Contribution to Arctic Scholarship (1585–7)." In Regard, *Quest for the Northwest Passage*, 71–88.

Maltby, William S. *The Black Legend in England: The Development of Anti-Spanish Sentiment, 1558–1660.* Durham, NC: Duke University Press, 1971.

Mancall, Peter C., ed. *The Atlantic World and Virginia, 1550–1624.* Chapel Hill, NC: Published for the Omohundro Institute of Early American History and Culture, Williamsburg, VA, by the University of North Carolina Press, 2007.

– *Hakluyt's Promise: An Elizabethan's Obsession for an English America.* New Haven, CT: Yale University Press, 2007.

– "Richard Hakluyt and the Visual World of Early Modern Travel Narratives." In Carey and Jowitt, *Richard Hakluyt and Travel Writing*, 87–101.

Marenbon, John. "John Scottus [called John Eriugena, John Scottus Eriugena] (fl. c. 845–c. 870), Theologian." In *ODNB*. https://doi.org/10.1093/ref:odnb/24940.

Markham, Albert Hastings, ed. *The Voyages and Works of John Davis, the Navigator.* Works Issued by the Hakluyt Society, 1st series, 59. London: Hakluyt Society, 1880.

Markham, Clements R. *A Life of John Davis, the Navigator, 1550–1605, Discoverer of Davis Straits.* New York: Dodd, Mead and Company, 1889.

Matar, Nabil I. "Introduction: England and Mediterranean Captivity, 1577–1704." In Vitkus, *Piracy, Slavery, and Redemption*, 1–52.

– *Islam in Britain, 1558–1685.* Cambridge, UK: Cambridge University Press, 1998.

– *Turks, Moors, and Englishmen in the Age of Discovery.* New York: Columbia University Press, 1999.

Mattingly, Garrett. *The Armada*. Boston: Houghton Mifflin, 1962.
Maxwell, Sarah. "The Philippines: A Link between Thomas Cavendish (1560–1592) and Sir Robert Dudley (1574–1649)." *IMCoS Journal* 155 (2018).
Mayhew, Robert J. "William Camden and Brittania." In *Britannia*, by William Camden, xiii–xxiii. London: Thoemmes, 2003.
McDermott, James. "Chancellor, Richard." In ODNB. https://doi.org/10.1093/ref:odnb/5099.
— "Lok, Sir William (1480–1550), Mercer and Merchant Adventurer." In ODNB. https://doi.org/10.1093/ref:odnb/16951.
— *Martin Frobisher: Elizabethan Privateer*. New Haven, CT: Yale University Press, 2001.
— "Michael Lok, Mercer and Merchant Adventurer." In Symons, *Meta Incognita*, 119–46.
— ed. *Third Voyage of Martin Frobisher to Baffin Island 1578*. Works Issued by the Hakluyt Society, 3rd series, 6. London: Hakluyt Society, 2001.
McGhee, Robert. "Contact between Native North Americans and the Medieval Norse: A Review of the Evidence." *American Antiquity* 49, no. 1 (1984): 4–26. https://doi.org/10.2307/280509.
McIntyre, Ruth. "William Sanderson: Elizabethan Financier of Discovery." *William and Mary Quarterly*, 3rd series, 13, no. 2 (1956): 184–201.
McKerrow, R.B., ed. *Works of Thomas Nashe*. 5 vols. London: Sidgwick and Jackson, 1910.
McKisack, May. *Medieval History in the Tudor Age*. Oxford, UK: Clarendon Press, 1971.
Meale, Carol. "'The Libelle of Englyshe Polycye' and Mercantile Literary Culture in Late-Medieval London." In *London and Europe in the Later Middle Ages*, edited by Julia Boffey and Pamela King, 181–228. London: University of London, 1995.
Mendoza, Juan Gonçalez de. *Historia de las cosas mas notables. Ritos y costubros del gran Reyno dela China*. Madrid, 1586.
Meyer, Albrecht. *Certaine Briefe, and Speciall Instructions for Gentlemen, Merchants, Students, Souldiers, Marriners*. Translated by Philip Jones. London, 1589.
Miller, Shannon. *Invested with Meaning: The Raleigh Circle in the New World*. Philadelphia, PA: University of Pennsylvania Press, 1998.
Monson, William. *The Naval Tracts of Sir William Monson*. Edited by M. Oppenheim. London: Printed for the Navy Records Society, 1902.
Montalbano, Kathryn. "Misunderstanding the Mongols: Intercultural Communication in Three Thirteenth-Century Franciscan Travel Accounts." *Information and Culture* 50, no. 4 (2015): 588–610.
Moran, Bruce T. *Distilling Knowledge: Alchemy, Chemistry, and the Scientific Revolution*. New Histories of Science, Technology, and Medicine. Cambridge, MA: Harvard University Press, 2005.

Morgan, Jennifer L. *Reckoning with Slavery: Gender, Kinship and Capitalism in the Early Black Atlantic*. Durham, NC: Duke University Press, 2021.

Morris, Colin. "Pilgrimage to Jerusalem in the Late Middle Ages." In Morris and Roberts, *Pilgrimage*, 141–63.

Morris, Colin, and Peter Roberts, eds. *Pilgrimage: The English Experience from Becket to Bunyan*. Cambridge, UK: Cambridge University Press, 2002.

Mote, Humphrey. *The Primrose of London with Her Valiant Adventure on the Spanish Coast*. London, 1585.

Müller, Sabine Lucia. "William Harborne's Embassies: Scripting, Performing and Editing Anglo-Ottoman Diplomacy." In *Early Modern Encounters with the Islamic East: Performing Cultures*, edited by Sabine Schülting, Ralf Hertel, and Sabine Lucia Müller, 11–26. Transculturalisms, 1400–1700. Farnham, UK; Burlington, VT: Ashgate, 2012.

Neal, Simon R., ed. *Calendar of Patent Rolls 26 Elizabeth I (1583–1584) C 66/1237–1253*. List and Index Society, v. 287. Kew, UK: List and Index Society, 2001.

N.H. "The Famous Voyage of M. Thomas Candish Esquire Round about the Globe of the Earth [...] Begunne in the Yeere 1586." In *PN* (1589), 809–13.

Nichols, Philip. *Sir Francis Drake Revived*. London, 1626.

Lund, Niels. "Ohthere [Óttarr] (fl. 871–899), Explorer." In *ODNB*. https://doi.org/10.1093/ref:odnb/20650.

Northrup, David A. "Africans, Early European Contacts, and the Emergent Diaspora." In Canny and Morgan, *Oxford Handbook of the Atlantic World*, 38–54.

– *Africa's Discovery of Europe, 1450–1850*. Oxford, UK: Oxford University Press, 2002.

– "The Gulf of Guinea and the Atlantic World." In Mancall, *Atlantic World and Virginia*, 170–93.

Nuttall, Zelia, ed. *New Light on Drake: A Collection of Documents Relating to His Voyage of Circumnavigation, 1577–1580*. Works Issued by the Hakluyt Society, 2nd series, 34. London: Hakluyt Society, 1914.

Oberg, Michael Leroy. "Lost Colonists and Lost Tribes." In Sloan, *European Visions*, 101–5.

Orgel, Stephen. *The Reader in the Book: A Study of Spaces and Traces*. Oxford, UK: Oxford University Press, 2015.

Oslund, Karen. *Iceland Imagined: Nature, Culture, and Storytelling in the North Atlantic*. Seattle: University of Washington Press, 2011.

Ortelius, Abraham. *Theatrum Orbis Terrarum*. Antwerp, 1570.

Ovenden, Richard, and Stuart Handley. "Howard, Lord William (1563–1640), Antiquary and Landowner." In *ODNB*. https://doi.org/10.1093/ref:odnb/13947.

Padrón, Ricardo. *The Indies of the Setting Sun: How Early Modern Spain Mapped the Far East as the Transpacific West*. Chicago, IL: University of Chicago Press, 2020.

Pagden, Anthony. *The Fall of Natural Man: The American Indian and the Origins of Comparative Ethnology*. Cambridge, UK: Cambridge University Press, 1986.

Palmer, Philip S. "All Suche Matters as Passed on This Vyage: Early English Travel Anthologies and the Case of John Sarracoll's Maritime Journal (1586–87)." *Huntington Library Quarterly* 76, no. 3 (2013): 325–44. https://doi.org/10.1525/hlq.2013.76.3.325.

Parker, Joanne. "Ruling the Waves: Saxons, Vikings, and the Sea in the Formation of an Anglo-British Identity in the Nineteenth Century." In Sobecki, *The Sea and Englishness*, 195–206.

Parker, John. *Books to Build an Empire: A Bibliographical History of English Overseas Interests to 1620*. Nico Israel, 1965.

– "Contents and Sources of 'Pilgrimes.'" In Pennington, *Purchas Handbook*, 2: 383–464.

Parks, George B. *The Contents and Sources of Ramusio's "Navigationi."* New York: New York Public Library, 1955.

– *Richard Hakluyt and the English Voyages*. New York: American Geographical Society, 1928.

– "Tudor Travel Literature." In Quinn, *Hakluyt Handbook*, 1: 97–132.

Parry, Glyn. *The Arch-Conjuror of England: John Dee*. New Haven, CT: Yale University Press, 2011.

Parry, John H. "Drake and the World Encompassed." In Thrower, *Sir Francis Drake and the Famous Voyage*, 1–11.

– "Hakluyt's View of British History." In Quinn, *Hakluyt Handbook*, 1: 3–7.

Patterson, Orlando. *Slavery and Social Death : A Comparative Study*. Cambridge, MA: Harvard University Press, 1982.

Payne, Anthony. "Hakluyt and the East India Company: A Documentary and Bibliographical Review." *Journal of the Hakluyt Society*, February 2021.

– "Hakluyt, Aristotle, and Oxford." In *Hakluyt and Oxford: Essays and Exhibitions Marking the Quartercentenary of the Death of Richard Hakluyt in 1616*, edited by Anthony Payne, 1–34. London: Hakluyt Society, 2017.

– "Hakluyt's London: Discovery and Overseas Trade." In Carey and Jowitt, *Richard Hakluyt and Travel Writing*, 13–24.

– *Richard Hakluyt: A Guide to His Books*. London: Quaritch, 2008.

– "Richard Hakluyt and the Earl of Essex: The Censorship of the Voyage to Cadiz in the Principal Navigations." *Publishing History* 72 (2012): 7–52.

– "The Suppression of the Voyage to Cadiz in Hakluyt's 'Principal Navigations.'" *Journal of the Hakluyt Society*, December 2021.

– "Willes, Richard (1546–1579?), Poet and Geographer." In *ODNB*. https://doi.org/10.1093/ref:odnb/29444.

Peckham, Sir George. *A True Reporte, of the Late Discoveries, and Possession, Taken in the Right of the Crowne of Englande, of the New-Found Landes*. London, 1583.

Pennington, L.E., ed. *The Purchas Handbook*. 2 vols. Works Issued by the Hakluyt Society, 2nd series, 185–6. London: Hakluyt Society, 1997.

Penzer, N.M., ed. *The World Encompassed and Analogous Contemporary Documents Concerning Sir Francis Drake's Circumnavigation of the World*. London: Argonaut Press, 1926.

Pirillo, Diego. "Balance of Power and Freedom of the Seas: Richard Hakluyt and Alberico Gentili." In Carey and Jowitt, *Richard Hakluyt and Travel Writing*, 177–86.

Pliny. *The Historie of the World, Commonly Called the Naturall Historie of C. Plinius Secundus*. Translated by Philemon Holland. London, 1601.

Poe, Marshall T. *A People Born to Slavery: Russia in Early Modern European Ethnography, 1476–1748*. Ithaca, NY: Cornell University Press, 2000.

Pope, Peter. *Fish into Wine: The Newfoundland Plantation in the 17th Century*. Chapel Hill: University of North Carolina Press, for the Omohundro Institute, 2004.

– *The Many Landfalls of John Cabot*. Toronto: University of Toronto Press, 1997.

Porter, H.C. "Purchas as Theological Geographer." In Pennington, *Purchas Handbook*, 1: 181–9.

Portuondo, María M. *Secret Science: Spanish Cosmography and the New World*. Chicago, IL: University of Chicago Press, 2009.

Prest, Wilfrid R. *The Rise of the Barristers: A Social History of the English Bar, 1590–1640*. Oxford; New York: Clarendon Press; Oxford University Press, 1986.

Purchas, Samuel. "The Churches Peregrination by This Holy Land Way, and Warre into Mysticall Babylon." In Purchas, *Pilgrimes*, 2: 1245–71.

– *Hakluytus Posthumus, or Purchas His Pilgrimes*. 4 vols., 1625.

Puttenham, George. *The Arte of English Poesie Contrived into Three Bookes [...]*. London, 1589.

Quinn, Alison M. "The Modern Index to the 'Principall Navigations.'" In Hakluyt, *Principall Navigations*, 1965.

Quinn, David B. "Early Accounts of the Famous Voyage." In Thrower, *Sir Francis Drake and the Famous Voyage*, 33–48.

– ed. *Hakluyt Handbook*. 2 vols. Works Issued by the Hakluyt Society, 2nd series, 144–5. London: Hakluyt Society, 1974.

– "Hakluyt's Reputation." In Quinn, *Hakluyt Handbook*, 1: 133–52.

– ed. *Last Voyage of Thomas Cavendish, 1591–92*. Chicago, IL: Newberry Library, by the University of Chicago Press, 1975.

– ed. *New American World: A Documentary History of North America to 1612*. 5 vols. New York: Arno Press and Hector Bye, 1979.

– "North America." In Quinn, *Hakluyt Handbook*, 1: 244–53.

- *Richard Hakluyt, Editor: A Study Introductory to the Facsimile Edition of Richard Hakluyt's "Divers Voyages" (1582)*. Amsterdam: Theatrum Orbis Terrarum, 1968.
- *Sir Francis Drake as Seen by His Contemporaries*. Providence, RI: John Carter Brown Library, 1996.
- "The Voyage of Etienne Bellenger to the Maritimes in 1583: A New Document." *Canadian Historical Review* 43, no. 4 (1962): 328–43.
- ed. *Voyages and Colonising Enterprises of Sir Humphrey Gilbert*. 2 vols. Works Issued by the Hakluyt Society, 2nd series, 83–4. London: Hakluyt Society, 1940.

Quinn, David B., and Neil M. Cheshire. *The New Found Land of Stephen Parmenius*. Toronto: University of Toronto Press, 1972.

Quinn, David B., and Alison M. Quinn. "A Hakluyt Chronology." In Quinn, *Hakluyt Handbook*, 1: 263–331.
- "Contents and Sources of the Three Major Works." In D.B. Quinn, *Hakluyt Handbook*, 2: 338–460.

Quinn, David B., and R.A. Skelton. "Introduction." In Hakluyt, *The Principall Navigations*, 1965.

Rabb, Theodore K. *Enterprise and Empire: Merchant and Gentry Investment in the Expansion of England, 1575–1630*. The Emergence of International Business, 1200–1800, 3. London; New York: Routledge/Thoemmes Press, 1999.

Raleigh, Walter A. "English Seamen of the Sixteenth Century." In *The Principal Navigations, Voyages, Traffiques & Discoveries of the English Nation*, by Richard Hakluyt, 12–120. Glasgow: J. MacLehose and Sons, 1903.

Ramsay, G.D. "Northern Europe." In Quinn, *Hakluyt Handbook*, 1: 155–60.
- *The City of London in International Politics at the Accession of Elizabeth Tudor*. Manchester, UK: Manchester University Press, 1975.

Raven, Charles E. *English Naturalists from Neckam to Ray: A Study of the Making of the Modern World*. Cambridge, UK: Cambridge University Press, 1947.

Recorde, Robert. *The Castle of Knowledge*. London, 1556.
- *The Whetstone of Witte*. London, 1557.

Regard, Frédéric, ed. *The Quest for the Northwest Passage: Knowledge, Nation and Empire, 1576–1806*. London: Pickering and Chatto, 2012.

Reinert, Sophus A. "Authority and Expertise at the Origins of Macro-Economics." In *Antonio Serra and the Economics of Good Government*, edited by Sophus Reinert and Rosario Patalano, 112–42. London: Palgrave Macmillan, 2016.

Relaño, Francesc. *The Shaping of Africa: Cosmographic Discourse and Cartographic Science in Late Medieval and Early Modern Europe*. Aldershot, UK; Burlington, VT: Ashgate, 2002.

Ribault, Jean. *The Whole and True Discoverye of Terra Florida*. London, 1563.

Richardson, William. "Watson, Anthony." In *ODNB*. https://doi.org/10.1093/ref:odnb/28828.

Roberts, Gareth Ffowc, and Fenny Smith, eds. *Robert Recorde: The Life and Times of a Tudor Mathematician*. Cardiff, UK: University of Wales Press, 2012.

Robinson, Benedict S. "Green Seraglios: Tulips, Turbans, and the Global Market." *Journal for Early Modern Cultural Studies* 9, no. 1 (2009): 93–122.

Rodger, N.A.M. *The Armada in the Public Records*. London: HMSO, 1988.

– "Atlantic Seafaring." In Canny and Morgan, *Oxford Handbook of the Atlantic World*, 71–86.

– *Safeguard of the Seas: A Naval History of Britain 660–1649*. New York; London: Norton, 1998.

Rodney, Walter. *A History of the Upper Guinea Coast, 1545–1800*. Oxford Studies in African Affairs. Oxford, UK: Clarendon Press, 1970.

Ronay, Gabriel. *The Tartar Khan's Englishman*. London: Phoenix, 2001.

Rubiés, Joan-Pau. "From the 'History of Travayle' to the History of Travel Collections: The Rise of an Early Modern Genre." In Carey and Jowitt, *Richard Hakluyt and Travel Writing*, 25–41.

– "Instructions for Travellers: Teaching the Eye to See." In Rubiés, *Travellers and Cosmographers*, 139–90.

– "New Worlds and Renaissance Ethnology." In Rubiés, *Travellers and Cosmographers*, 157–97.

– "Texts, Images and the Perception of 'Savages' in Early Modern Europe: What We Can Learn from White and Harriot." In Sloan, *European Visions*, 120–30.

– *Travel and Ethnology in the Renaissance: South India Through European Eyes, 1250–1625*. Cambridge, UK: Cambridge University Press, 2000.

– *Travellers and Cosmographers: Studies in the History of Early Modern Travel and Ethnology*. Variorum Collected Studies Series CS888. Aldershot, UK; Burlington, VT: Ashgate, 2007.

Ruggles, Richard I. "The Cartographic Lure of the Northwest Passage: Its Real and Imaginary Geography." In Symons, *Meta Incognita*, 1: 179–256.

Ryder, A.F.C. *Benin and the Europeans, 1485–1897*. Ibadan History Series. London: Longmans, 1969.

Sacks, David Harris. "Discourses of Western Planting: Richard Hakluyt and the Making of the Atlantic World'." In Mancall, *Atlantic World and Virginia*, 410–53.

– "Rebuilding Solomon's Temple: Richard Hakluyt's Great Instauration." In *New Worlds Reflected: Travel and Utopia in the Early Modern Period*, edited by Chloe Houston, 17–55. London: Routledge, 2016.

- "Richard Hakluyt's Navigations in Time: History, Epic, and Empire." *Modern Language Quarterly* 67, no. 1 (2006): 31–62. https://doi.org/10.1215/00267929-67-1-31.
- "'To Deduce a Colonie': Richard Hakluyt's Godly Mission in Its Contexts." In Carey and Jowitt, *Richard Hakluyt and Travel Writing in Early Modern Europe*, 197–218.
- "The Blessings of Exchange in the Making of the Early English Atlantic." In *Religion and Trade: Cross-Cultural Exchanges in World History, 1000–1900*, edited by Francesca Trivellato, Leor Halevi, and Catia Antunes. Oxford, UK: Oxford University Press, 2014.

Salmon, Vivian. "Thomas Harriot (1560–1621) and the English Origins of Algonkian Linguistics." In *The Study of Language in 17th-Century England*, 143–72. Amsterdam Studies in the Theory and History of Linguistic Science. Amsterdam: Benjamins, 1979.

Saunders, Thomas. *A True Discription and Breefe Discourse, of a Most Lamentable Voiage, Made Latelie to Tripolie in Barbarie, in a Ship Named the Jesus.* London, 1587.

Savile, Henry. *Rerum Anglicarum scriptores post Bedam praecipui, ex vetustissimis codicibus manuscriptis nunc primum in lucem editi.* London, 1596.

Scammell, G.V. "The English in the Atlantic Islands c. 1450–1650." *Mariner's Mirror* 72, no. 3 (1986): 295–317.

Schleck, Julia. "Forming the Captivity of Thomas Saunders: Hakluyt's Editorial Practices and Their Ideological Effects." In Carey and Jowitt, *Richard Hakluyt and Travel Writing*, 129–38.
- *Telling True Tales of Islamic Lands: Forms of Mediation in English Travel Writing, 1575–1630.* Selinsgrove, PA: Susquehanna University Press, 2011.

Schotte, Margaret. "Expert Records: Nautical Logbooks from Columbus to Cook." *Information and Culture: A Journal of History* 48, no. 3 (2013): 281–322. https://doi.org/10.1353/lac.2013.0015.

Seall, Francis. "A Treatise of My Lord of Cumberland's Ships Voyage, and of Their Taking [...] of the Great Carrack Lately Brought into Dartmouth." In Laughton, *Naval Miscellany*, vol. 2, 99–113.

The Sea-Mans Triumph: Declaring the Honorable Actions of Such Gentlemen Captaines and Sailers, as Were at the Takinge of the Great Carrick, Lately Brought to Dartmouth. London, 1592.

Sears, Jayne, and Francis R. Johnson. *The Lumley Library: The Catalogue of 1609.* London: Trustees of the British Museum, 1956.

Seaver, Kirsten A. "'A Very Common and Usuall Trade': The Relationship between Cartographic Perceptions and 'Fishing' in the Davis Strait circa 1500–1550." *British Library Journal* 22, no. 1 (1996): 1–26.

- "How Strange Is a Stranger? A Survey of Opportunities for Inuit-European Contact in the Davis Strait before 1576." In Symons, *Meta Incognita*, 2: 523–52.
- *The Frozen Echo: Greenland and the Exploration of North America, ca. A.D. 1000–1500.* Stanford, CA: Stanford University Press, 1996.
- *Maps, Myths, and Men: The Story of the Vinland Map.* Stanford, CA: Stanford University Press, 2004.

Sebek, Barbara. "Canary, Bristoles, Londres, Ingleses: English Traders in the Canaries in the 16th and 17th Centuries." In Singh, *Companion to the Global Renaissance*, 1st ed., 279–93.

Sherman, William H. "Bringing the World to England: The Politics of Translation in the Age of Hakluyt." *Transactions of the Royal Historical Society* 14 (2004): 199–207.
- *John Dee: The Politics of Reading and Writing in the English Renaissance.* Amherst, MA: University of Massachusetts Press, 1995.
- "John Dee's Role in Martin Frobisher's Northwest Enterprise." In Symons, *Meta Incognita*, 1: 283–98.
- "The Place of Reading in the English Renaissance: John Dee Revisited." In *The Practice and Representation of Reading in England*, edited by James Raven, Helen Small, and Naomi Tadmor, 62–76. Cambridge, UK: Cambridge University Press, 2006.
- *Used Books: Marking Readers in Renaissance England.* Material Texts. Philadelphia: University of Pennsylvania Press, 2008.

Shirley, Rodney W. *The Mapping of the World: Early Printed World Maps, 1472–1700.* Holland Press Cartographica, v. 9. London: Holland Press, 1983.

Simmons, J.S.G. "Russia." In Quinn, *Hakluyt Handbook*, 1: 161–7.

Singh, Jyotsna G., ed. *A Companion to the Global Renaissance.* 1st ed. Blackwell Companions to Literature and Culture. Chichester, UK ; Malden, MA: Wiley-Blackwell, 2009.

Siraisi, Nancy G. *Medieval and Early Renaissance Medicine: An Introduction to Knowledge and Practice.* Chicago, IL: University of Chicago Press, 1990.

Skelton, R.A. "Hakluyt's Maps." In Quinn, *Hakluyt Handbook*, 1: 48–73.

Skilliter, Susan A. *William Harborne and the Trade with Turkey, 1578–1582: A Documentary Study of the First Anglo-Ottoman Relations.* Oriental Documents 1. Oxford, UK: Oxford University Press, for the British Academy, 1977.

Sloan, Kim, ed. *European Visions: American Voices.* London: British Museum, 2009.
- "John White's Watercolours." In Sloan, *A New World*, 93–223.
- ed. *A New World: England's First View of America.* Chapel Hill: University of North Carolina Press, 2007.

Small, Margaret. "A World Seen through Another's Eyes: Hakluyt, Ramusio, and the Narratives of the *Navigationi et Viaggi*." In Carey and Jowitt, *Richard Hakluyt and Travel Writing*, 45–56, 2012.

– "From Jellied Seas to Open Waterways: Redefining the Northern Limit of the Knowable World." *Renaissance Studies* 21, no. 3 (2007): 315–39.

– "From Thought to Action: Gilbert, Davis, And Dee's Theories behind the Search for the Northwest Passage." *Sixteenth Century Journal* 44, no. 4 (2013): 1041–58.

Smallwood, Stephanie E. "The Politics of the Archive and History's Accountability to the Enslaved." *History of the Present* 6, no. 2 (2016): 117–32.

Smith, Cassander L. *Black Africans in the British Imagination: English Narratives of the Early Atlantic World.* Baton Rouge: Louisiana State University Press, 2016.

Smith, John. *The Complete Works of Captain John Smith (1580–1631).* Edited by Philip L. Barbour. 3 vols. Chapel Hill: University of North Carolina Press, 1986.

Sobecki, Sebastian I. "Introduction: Edgar's Archipelago." In Sobecki, *The Sea and Englishness*, 1–30.

– *Last Words: The Public Self and the Social Author in Late Medieval England.* Oxford, UK: Oxford University Press, 2019.

– ed. *The Sea and Englishness in the Middle Ages: Maritime Narratives, Identity and Culture.* Cambridge, UK: D.S. Brewer, 2011.

Sobral, Luis de Moura. "The Expansion and the Arts: Transfers, Contaminations, Innovations." In Bethancourt and Curto, *Portuguese Oceanic Expansion*, 390–459.

Spenser, Edmund. *Edmund Spenser's Poetry: Authoritative Texts, Criticism.* Edited by Hugh Maclean and Anne Lake Prescott. 3rd ed. A Norton Critical Edition. New York: Norton, 1993.

– *The Shepheardes Calender: Conteyning Twelue Æglogues Proportionable to the Twelve Monethes.* London, 1579.

Stafford, Pauline. *Unification and Conquest: A Political and Social History of England in the Tenth and Eleventh Centuries.* London: E. Arnold, 1989.

Stagl, Justin. *A History of Curiosity: The Theory of Travel, 1550–1800*, vol. 13. Studies in Anthropology and History. Chur, Switzerland; Langhorne, PA: Harwood Academic Publishers, 1995.

Stallybrass, Peter. "Admiranda Narratio: A European Best Seller." In Harriot, *A Briefe and True Report* (2007), 9–30.

Steele, C.R. "From Hakluyt to Purchas." In Quinn, *Hakluyt Handbook*, 1: 74–96.

Steggle, Matthew. "Charles Chester and Richard Hakluyt." *Studies in English Literature 1500–1900* 43, no. 1 (2003): 65–81.

Stout, Felicity. "'The Strange and Wonderfull Discoverie of Russia': Hakluyt and Censorship." In Carey and Jowitt, *Richard Hakluyt and Travel Writing*, 153–63.

Stow, John. *The Annales of England: Faithfully Collected out of the Most Autenticall Authors, Records, and Other Monuments of Antiquitie.* London, 1600.

Summit, Jennifer. *Memory's Library: Medieval Books in Early Modern England.* Chicago, IL: University of Chicago, 2008.

Sumption, Jonathan. *Pilgrimage: An Image of Mediaeval Religion.* Totowa, NJ: Rowman and Littlefield, 1975.

Swanton, Michael James, ed. *The Anglo-Saxon Chronicle.* New York: Routledge, 1998.

Symons, Thomas H.B., ed. *Meta Incognita: A Discourse of Discovery: Martin Frobisher's Arctic Expedition, 1576–1578.* 2 vols. Hull, QC: Canadian Museum of Civilization, 1999.

Taylor, E.G.R., ed. *A Brief Summe of Geographie.* Works Issued by the Hakluyt Society, 2nd series, 69. London: Hakluyt Society, 1932.

– "A Letter Dated 1577 from Mercator to John Dee." *Imago Mundi* 13 (1956): 56–68.

– ed. *Original Writings and Correspondence of the Two Richard Hakluyts.* 2 vols. Works Issued by the Hakluyt Society, 2nd series, 76–7. London: Hakluyt Society, 1935.

– ed. *The Troublesome Voyage of Captain Edward Fenton 1582–1583.* Works Issued by the Hakluyt Society, 2nd Series, 113. Cambridge, UK: Hakluyt Society, 1959.

– *Tudor Geography: 1485–1583.* New York: Octagon Books, 1968.

Taylor, F. "Some Manuscripts of the 'Libelle of Englyshe Polycye.'" *Bulletin of the John Rylands Library* 24 (1940): 376–418.

This Is the Begynnynge, and Contynuaunce of the Pylgrymage of Sir Richarde Guylforde Knyght. London, 1511.

Thornton, John. *Africa and Africans in the Making of the Atlantic World, 1400–1680.* Cambridge, UK: Cambridge University Press, 1992.

– "The Portuguese in Africa." In Bethancourt and Curto, *Portuguese Oceanic Expansion*, 138–60.

Thrush, Coll. *Indigenous London: Native Travelers at the Heart of Empire.* New Haven, CT: Yale University Press, 2016.

Timberlake, Henry. *A True and Strange Discourse of the Travailes of Two English Pilgrimes.* London, 1603.

Tomlins, Christopher L. *Freedom Bound: Law, Labor, and Civic Identity in Colonizing English America, 1580–1865.* Cambridge, UK: Cambridge University Press, 2010.

Tuck, Richard. *The Rights of War and Peace: Political Thought and the International Order from Grotius to Kant.* Oxford, UK: Oxford University Press, 2001.

Turgeon, Laurier. *Patrimoines métissés: contextes coloniaux et postcoloniaux.* Paris; Laval: Maison des sciences de l'homme; Presses de l'université Laval, 2003.

- *Une histoire de la Nouvelle-France: Français et Amérindiens au XVIe siècle.* Paris: Belin, 2019.
Turner, Henry S. "Toward an Analysis of the Corporate Ego: The Case of Richard Hakluyt." *Differences* 20, no. 2–3 (January 2009): 103–47. https://doi.org/10.1215/10407391-2009-006.
Tyacke, Sarah. "All at Sea: Some Cartographical Problems in the North." *IMCOS Journal* 111 (2007): 38–42.
- *Before Empire: The English World Pictures in the Sixteenth and Early Seventeenth Centuries.* Hakluyt Society Annual Lectures. London: Hakluyt Society, 2001.
- "Chartmaking in England and Its Context, 1500–1660." In Woodward, *History of Cartography*, vol. 3, part 1: 1722–53.
Ubaldini, Petruccio. *A Discourse concerninge the Spanishe fleete invadinge Englande in the yeare 1588.* London, 1590.
Ungerer, Gustav. *The Mediterranean Apprenticeship of British Slavery.* Madrid: Editorial Verbum, 2008.
Urness, Carol. "Purchas as Editor." In Pennington, *Purchas Handbook*, 1: 121–44.
Van Duzer, Chet. "A Northern Refuge of the Monstrous Races: Asia on Waldseemüller's 1516 Carta Marina." *Imago Mundi* 62, no. 2 (June 2010): 221–31. https://doi.org/10.1080/03085691003747159.
Vaughan, Alden T. "Sir Walter Ralegh's Indian Interpreters, 1584–1618." *William and Mary Quarterly* 59, no. 2 (2002): 341–76. https://doi.org/10.2307/3491741.
- *Transatlantic Encounters: American Indians in Britain, 1500–1776.* Cambridge, UK: Cambridge University Press, 2006.
Vaughan, Alden T., and Virginia Mason Vaughan. "Before Othello: Elizabethan Representations of Sub-Saharan Africans." *William and Mary Quarterly* 54, no. 1 (January 1997): 19. https://doi.org/10.2307/2953311.
Vaux, W.S.W., ed. *The World Encompassed by Sir Francis Drake.* London, 1854.
Vitkus, Daniel J., ed. *Piracy, Slavery, and Redemption: Barbary Captivity Narratives from Early Modern England.* New York: Columbia University Press, 2001.
Vitoria, Francisco de. *Political Writings.* Edited by Anthony Pagden and Jeremy Lawrance. Cambridge Texts in the History of Political Thought. Cambridge, UK: Cambridge University Press, 1991.
Wagner, Henry R. *Sir Francis Drake's Voyage around the World; Its Aims and Achievements.* San Francisco, CA: J. Howell, 1926.
Wallis, Helen. "Edward Wright and the 1599 World Map." In Quinn, *Hakluyt Handbook*, 1: 69–73.
- "The Cartography of Drake's Voyage." In Thrower, *Sir Francis Drake and the Famous Voyage*, 121–63.

- "The First English Globe: A Recent Discovery." *Geographical Journal* 117 (1951): 275–90.
- "The Pacific." In Quinn, *Hakluyt Handbook*, 1: 223–33.

Warkentin, Germaine, ed. *Critical Issues in Editing Exploration Texts: Papers Given at the Twenty-Eighth Annual Conference on Editorial Problems.* Toronto, ON; Buffalo, NY: University of Toronto Press, 1995.

Warkentin, Germaine, and Carolyn Podruchny, eds. *Decentring the Renaissance: Canada and Europe in Multidisciplinary Perspective, 1500–1700.* Toronto, ON; Buffalo, NY: University of Toronto Press, 2001.

Warner, J. Christopher. "Elizabeth I, Savior of Books: John Bale's Preface to the Scriptorum Illustrium Maioris Brytanniae […] Catalogus (1559)." In *John Foxe and His World*, edited by Christopher Highley and John N. King, 91–129. St. Andrews Studies in Reformation History. Aldershot, UK; Burlington, VT: Ashgate, 2002.

Warner, Sir George, ed. *The Libelle of English Polycye: A Poem on the Use of Sea-Power 1436.* Oxford, UK: Clarendon Press, 1926.

Waters, David W. *The Art of Navigation in England in Elizabethan and Early Stuart Times.* New Haven, CT: Yale University Press, 1958.

Wateson, George. *Cures of the Diseased, in Remote Regions: Preventing Mortalitie, Incident in Forraine Attempts, of the English Nation.* London, 1598.

Wathen, Bruce. *Sir Francis Drake : The Construction of a Hero.* Cambridge, UK; Rochester, NY: D.S. Brewer, 2009.

Watts, Sheldon. *Epidemics and History: Disease, Power and Imperialism.* New Haven, CT: Yale University Press, 1999.

Webbe, Edward. *The Rare and Most Wonderfull Things Which Edw. Webbe an Englishman Borne, Hath Seene and Passed in His Troublesome Travailes.* London, 1590.

Weissbourd, Emily. "'Those in Their Possession': Race, Slavery, and Queen Elizabeth's 'Edicts of Expulsion.'" *Huntington Library Quarterly* 78, no. 1 (2015): 1–19.

Wernham, R.B. *After the Armada: Elizabethan England and the Struggle for Western Europe, 1588–1595.* Oxford, UK; New York: Clarendon Press; Oxford University Press, 1984.

- ed. *The Expedition of Sir John Norris and Sir Francis Drake to Spain and Portugal, 1589.* Aldershot, UK; Brookfield, VT: Temple Smith, for the Navy Records Society, 1988.

Wey Gómez, Nicolás. *Tropics of Empire: Why Columbus Sailed South to the Indies.* Transformations: Studies in the History of Science and Technology. Cambridge, MA: MIT Press, 2008.

Whitelock, Dorothy. *The Anglo-Saxon Chronicle.* New Brunswick, NJ: Rutgers University Press, 1961.

White, Ed. "Invisible Tagkanysough." *PMLA* 120, no. 3 (2005): 751–67. https://doi.org/10.1632/003081205X63840.

William of Malmesbury. *William of Malmesbury's Chronicle of the Kings of England: From the Earliest Period to the Reign of King Stephen.* Edited by J.A. Giles. London: George Bell and Sons, 1904.

Williams, Ann. "Edgar [called Edgar Pacificus] (943/4–975), King of England." In *ODNB*. https://doi.org/10.1093/ref:odnb/8463.

Williams, Jack. "The Lives and Works of Robert Recorde." In *Robert Recorde: The Life and Times of a Tudor Mathematician*, edited by Gareth Roberts and Fenny Smith, 7–24. Cardiff, UK: University of Wales Press, 2012.

Williamson, James Alexander. *Sir John Hawkins: The Time and the Man.* Oxford, UK: Clarendon Press, 1927.

Willan, Thomas Stuart. *Studies in Elizabethan Foreign Trade.* Manchester, UK: Manchester University Press, 1959.

– *The Muscovy Merchants of 1555.* Manchester, UK: University of Manchester Press, 1953.

Willes, Richard, ed. *The History of Travayle in the West and East Indies: And Other Countreys Lying Eyther Way, Towardes the Fruitfull and Ryche Moluccaes: As Moscovia, Persia, Arabia, Syria, Aegypte, Ethiopia, Guinea, China in Cathayo, and Giapan: With a Discourse of the Northwest Passage.* London, 1577.

Wisecup, Kelly. "Encounters, Objects, and Commodity Lists in Early English Travel Narratives." *Studies in Travel Writing* 17, no. 3 (2013): 264–80.

Woodward, David, ed. *The History of Cartography: Cartography in the European Renaissance*, vol. 3 (6 vols). Chicago, IL: University of Chicago Press, 1987.

– "The Italian Map Trade 1480–1650." In Woodward, *History of Cartography*, vol. 3. part 1: 773–803.

Woolf, Virginia. "The Elizabethan Lumber Room." In *The Common Reader*, 1st series, 61–72. New York: Harcourt Brace, 1925.

Worms, Laurence. "Maps and Atlases." In *The Cambridge History of the Book in Britain. 1557–1695*, edited by John Barnard and D.F. McKenzie, 4: 228–45. Cambridge, UK: University Press, 2002.

Woudhuysen, H.R. *Sir Philip Sidney and the Circulation of Manuscripts, 1558–1640.* Oxford, UK: Oxford University Press, 1996.

Wright, Edward. *Certaine Errors in Navigation.* London, 1599.

Wright, Irene A., ed. *Documents Concerning English Voyages to the Spanish Main, 1569–1580.* Works Issued by the Hakluyt Society, 2nd series, 71. London: Hakluyt Society, 1932.

– ed. *Further English Voyages to Spanish America, 1583–1594: Documents from the Archives of the Indies at Seville Illustrating English Voyages to the Caribbean, the Spanish*

Main, Florida, and Virginia. Works Issued by the Hakluyt Society, 2nd series, 99. London: Hakluyt Society, 1951.

— ed. *Spanish Documents Concerning English Voyages to the Caribbean, 1527–1568*. Works Issued by the Hakluyt Society, 2nd series, 62. London: Hakluyt Society, 1929.

Wright, Louis B. *Religion and Empire: The Alliance between Piety and Commerce in English Expansion, 1558–1625*. Chapel Hill: University of North Carolina Press, 1943.

Wright, Stephen. "Malym [Malim], William (1533–1594)." In *ODNB*. https://doi.org/10.1093/ref:odnb/17883.

Wyatt, Michael. *The Italian Encounter with Tudor England: A Cultural Politics of Translation*. Cambridge, UK: Cambridge University Press, 2005.

Yates, Frances A. *John Florio: The Life of an Italian in Shakespeare's England*. Cambridge, UK: Cambridge University Press, 1934.

Young, Sandra. "Early Modern Geography and the Construction of a Knowable Africa." *Atlantic Studies* 12, no. 4 (2015): 412–34.

Zeno, Niccolò. *De i Commentarii Del Viaggio in Persia [...] Et Dello Scoprimento Dell'isole Frislanda, Eslanda, Engrouelanda, Estotilanda, & Icaria, Fatto Sotto Il Polo Artico, Da Due Fratelli Zeni, m. Nicolò Il k. e m. Antonio*. Venice, 1558.

INDEX

Page numbers in italics indicate references to illustrations.

'Abd al-Malik, 207n2
Abū al-Fidā, 136–7, 141, 352, 464
Acapulco (Mexico), 332
Accra (Ghana), 220
Acmek Basha, 178, 180
Acosta, José de, 326
Adams, Clement, 83–4, 86–8, 110–12, 111nn6–7, 114–18
Adams, Robert, 309; charts by, plate 6
affect, in texts, 116, 125, 131, 255–6, 260–1, 277, 395
Africa: in *PN* (1598–1600), 208–23, 245; Portugal and, 216–17, 218n31, 220–2, 236. *See also* West Africa; *specific places*
Africans: in England, 235, 236, 254, 467n9, 468; Mani-Sumba, 238n96; Sapi, 252; as traders, 233, 265. *See also* captives and captivity; *specific places*
Agra (India), 195
Alarcón, Hernando de, 325
alchemy, 225. *See also* metal, Inuit use of; metallurgy and mining
Aldersey, Laurence, 165–9, 173–4
Aleppo (Syria), 195, 198

Alexander the Great, 71
Alexandria (Egypt), 156; Christian captives in, 184; English consul at, 186
Alfred (King), 46nn61–2, 54–5, 57–8, 60, 163
al-Mansur, Mulay Ahmad, 207n2
ambassadors: to England, 128n50, 334, 424, 453; to France, 324; to the Ottoman Empire, 186, 192n116; to Spain, 79, 89–90
Americas, claims to, 26n5, 32, 105, 248, 321, 372
Amsterdam (Netherlands), 41, 357
Andrews, Kenneth, 326, 418, 425, 430
Anglorum navigatio ad Muscovitas (Adams), 87, 112
Anglo-Saxon: Dee and, 45; Hakluyt (editor) and, 54, 58; manuscripts in, 55, 55n94, 58; printing of, 59; Recorde, and, 57; study of, 31, 32n17; translation into, 54–5
Anglo-Saxon Chronicle, 44, 46
Anglo–Spanish sea war, 207, 244, 255, 267, 380, 452; narratives of, 273–87
Annales rerum Anglicarum et Hibernicarum regnante Elizabetha (Camden), 267, 268
"Anonymous Narrative," 453

Anticosti (Quebec, Canada), 344
Antonio (Dom), 221, 332
Antwerp (Belgium), 165n30;
  markets at, 84
Arctic, theories about, 92,
  94–7. *See also* Northeast
  Passage; Northwest Passage;
  specific places
Argentina, 401
Arguin Island (Mauritania), 333
armillary spheres, 363, plate 7
arms, trade in, 193n117
Arte de Navegar (Cortés), 229–30
Arthur (King), 25n2, 31, 33, 77, 143;
  conquests of, 25–6, 33n22, 37;
  Lambarde on, 59; polar regions
  and, 35, 37, 39–40
Ash, Eric, 125, 229n65
Assan Aga (Samson Rowlie), 189
astrolabes, 36
Atlantic slave trade, 104, 233n79;
  J. Hawkins and, 245–55; Hakluyt
  (editor) and, 101n62
*Atlas of the Counties of England and
  Wales* (Saxton), 41
authorship, 29, 459; and attribution,
  287–314; and F. Drake, 414, 419,
  430–5, 442–4; Eden and, 224; in
  first person, 380, 429–30; identity
  and, 390–6, 401–5, *404*; by
  merchants, 119–20 128, 131; by
  ministers, 432–3, 435, 437–9,
  440, 446
Axim (Ghana), 220
Azores (North Atlantic), 207–9, 416;
  raids on, 272, 295, 297–8

Babylon (Iraq), 195, 198–9
Bacon, Roger, 63
Baffin Island (Nunavut, Canada),
  372, 374–5, 386, 388–9
Baghdad (Iraq), 197

Baker, Robert, 191, 219n33, 237–8,
  238n95
Bale, John, 30, 34n24, 158, 160,
  160n13, 225
Balsara. *See* Basrah
Baptizing of a Turke, The (Hanmer), 448
barbarity, in England, 203; of Mongols,
  72–5; of Ottomans, 180–1, 190,
  203; of Spanish, 105, 247, 273,
  275, 342
Barbary Company, 299n96
Barbary kingdoms (North Africa),
  208, 213
Bárdarson, Ivar, 38
Barentsz, Willem, 352–3
Barker, Edmund, 426
Barlow, Roger, 101–5, 327n28
Barlowe, Arthur, 354, 368–9
Barrett, Robert, 263
Bartels, Emily, 234n81
barter, 384, 386, 388–9
Barton, Edward, 186–7
Basanier, Martin, 322n12, 328,
  349n67, 347
Basrah (Iraq), 195, 197–8
Battle of Hastings, 30
Batu (general), 73
Bazán, Álvaro de (Marquis of Santa
  Cruz), 282, 311
Beazley, Raymond, 74
Beckingham, C.F., 161, 175
Bede, 30–1, 52
Bedome, Thomas, 307
Behaim, Martin, 63
Bellenger, Étienne, 341, 343
Benin (kingdom in Nigeria), 209, 215,
  258, 272; court of, 213n13, 221,
  228; Eden and, 228, 233; trading
  voyages to, 213n13, 220, 221;
  weather in, 242; Welsh and, 242;
  Wyndham voyage and, 228
Bennett, Herman, 249n127, 255

INDEX

Best, George, 19, 93, 94n43, 125, 337n59, 456; on Africa, 241; on Inuit, 388–9; "Treatise of the sphere," 94n43
Bethlehem (Israel), 166
Bèze, Theodore, 283n45, 284, 452
Biddulph, William, 172
Bigges, Walter, 350, 420–1
Bird, John, 272
Biringuccio, Vannoccio, 225–6
Boazio, Baptista, 419–20, plate 8
Bodenham, Roger, 82, 194n121, 327, 451
Bodleian Library, 29n10
Boemus, Joannes, 133
Book of Martyrs (Foxe), 454
Book of Revelation, 70
Borbuta (West Indies), 253
Borough, Christopher, 109, 138
Borough, Stephen, 76, 86, 121, 134, 229; on Indigenous Siberians, 138–9, 148; navigational expertise, 138n81, 194
Borough, William, 87, 110, 138n81; F. Drake, court-martial efforts against, 310n121; instructions by, 120–1, 124–6, 128, 437
Boruchoff, David, 452, 459
botany, 202–3, 357, 362. *See also* plants
Bowyer, Robert, 55
Bowyer, William, 55
Bragandine (military commander), 180–1, 183, 185
Branham, Hugh (minister), 143
Brazil, 101, 192n116, 219n36, 232, 250, 403
Brenner, Michael, 283n45
Brenner, Robert, 272
Brevis commentarius de Islandia (Jónsson), 142–50, 225, 233
Brevísima Relación (de las Casas), 326, 452

Briefe and True Report (Harriot), 19, 125, 255n149, 354, 355, 383, 421–2; de Bry edition, 320, 351, 353–6, 359–70, 356
"Briefe commentarie." See *Brevis commentarius de Islandia*
Briefe description … of the Weast India (Enciso), 326
Britain: boundaries of, 42–61; Edgar's circumnavigations of, 43; Norse in, 53
British Library catalogue, 284n50, 312n127, 430n50
Brittania (Camden), 31, 41, 52, 64, 158
Bromfield, Thomas, 251, 251n135
Bromley, Thomas, 299
Brooks, George, 216, 222
Bukhara (Uzbekistan), 140–1
Burgess, Richard, 187–8
Burgh, John, 303–4, 306, 308

cabinets of curiosity, 357
Cabot, John, 77–8, 88, 372
Cabot, Sebastian, 78, 82, 86–9, 101–2, 372, 455; instructions by, 119–21, 131–3, 436; papers of, 78; Pinteado and, 227, 229; voyage for the Moluccas, 101–2
Cacheu River (Guinea-Bissau), 222, 254, 263, 263n174
Cádiz (Spain), 13, 25, 313; F. Drake, raid on (1587), 267, 269, 272, 279–82, 302, 309–13, 310n122, 443–4, 449; Essex-Howard raid on (1596), 14, 151, 267, 269–70, 290–3, 302, 416; narrative by Marbecke on, 151, 302
Camden, William, 53, 158, 267, 268, 269, 357; dedicatory poem in *PN*, 32; *Chronicle of Man* and, 52; medieval materials and, 31, 47n66, 64–5; nationalism and, 41–2; Ortelius and,

39n37, 41, 136, 352. See also
Brittania; Annales rerum Anglicarum et Hibernicarum regnante Elizabetha
Campbell, Mary, 67
Canada, 371; French and Italian sources and, 335–49
Canary Islands (North Atlantic), 208–9, 213, 218, 250
cannibalism, 70, 71, 74, 132, 139, 141, 232, 238nn95–6, 265, 403
Canute (King), 59, 161
Cape Breton (Nova Scotia, Canada), 341, 343
Cape Finisterre (Spain), 303
Cape of Good Hope (South Africa), 91, 95, 97, 207–8
Cape St Vincent (Portugal), 281
Cape Verde islands (West Africa), 222, 237, 256n157, 258, 416, 453
capital punishment, 439, 439n74, 442
captives and captivity, 243n112, 247–9, 275, 412, 448, 468, 495n3; in Africa, 221, 236–7, 240, 246, 250–5; in the Americas, 256, 388–9, 451; in Greenland, 386; in the Mediterranean, 105, 183–4, 190, 252; narratives of, 158, 174, 183–9, 183n86, 186, 205, 451; Spanish and Portuguese, 275n18, 325, 416–17, 428, 454, 486
Cap-Vert (Senegal), 221, 232, 251–3
Carelesse (Wright), Edward, 297
Carey, George, 418
Caribbean. *See* West Indies
Carleill, Christopher, 234n83, 347, 420, 451
carracks, 269, 281, 298, 300, 305, 423; significance of taking, 303, 309. *See also* ships
Cartagena (Colombia), 280, 321
Cartier, Jacques, 318, 338–9, 344–9, 367

cartography and cartographers, 41, 55, 288, 309, 347; control of, 437; Davis and, 378–80, *377, 378, 379*; F. Drake and, 425–6, 433, *434*, 438, *463*, plate 6, plate 8; Frobisher's voyages and, 345, 346n85, *377, 378, 463*; Iceland and, 143, 144, plate 4; information in, 345; Hakluyt (editor) and, 36–7, 63; instructions regarding, 126, 436; mathematical, 95, 108, 297; naval battles and, 267; North America and, 345–8; Northern Asia and, 63, 70–1, *85*, 85–6; planar, 95; Spain and, 331; Venice and, 336, *336*. *See also* globes; maps; rutters; *specific makers*
Casa de la Contratación, 86, 229, 325, 460
Castle of Knowledge, The (Recorde), 57
Cataño, Leonardo, 104
Cates, Thomas, 419
Cathay Company, 374
Catholics and Catholicism, 32, 167–8, 171, 189–91, 248, 298, 352, 449, 451
Cavendish, Richard, 402, 460, 462
Cavendish, Thomas, 358, 398; circumnavigation (1586–1588), 263, 330, 358, 425, 460, 462, *463*; circumnavigation attempted (1591–1593), 330, 395, 400–3; Davis and, 395–6, 400–3, 406; death, 396; in Sierra Leone, 258, 263
Cecil, Robert, 326, 429
Cecil, William, Lord Burghley, 31, 55, 224n48, 260, 292, 308, 342
Ceely, Christopher, 432
Central Asia, 62; information on, 85–6. *See also* Mongols
Certaine errors in navigation (Wright), 296, 380
Cespédes, Andrés García, 334

Cess, River (Liberia), 220–1, 227, 231, 233n80, 251
Chancellor, Nicholas, 129, 138
Chancellor, Richard, 76–7, 99, 111, 111n6, 114–18, 194; Chios voyage, 194n121; materials from, 107–8; on Muscovy, 112–13; Muscovy Company and, 109–10; navigation and, 82, 117, 121; Northeast Passage search, 82–4, 87
chaplains. *See* ministers
Charles V (King), 89, 331
charts. *See* maps
Chesapeake (Virginia, United States), 329, 349
Chester, John, 251n135
Chester, William, 251n135
Cheyfitz, Eric, 323
Chidley, John, 357, 403
Chile, 426
Chilton, John, 327
China, 208–9, 328–30, 370, 460
Chios (Greece), 164–5, 194n121
christening, 448, 457
Christian IV (King), 149
Chronicle of Man, 52–3, 59–60, 162n22
Chronicles (Holinshed), 160
Chronicon ex chronicis (John of Worcester), 45
Chronicon Hierosolymitanum, 160
Cibola (New Mexico, United States), 327
civility: Africa and, 265; built environment and, 147, 263–4; far North and, 54, 139, 141, 144; Iceland and, 147, 149; latitude and, 241, 330
Cliffe, Edward, 417, 426
Clifford, Anne, 259n161
climate. *See* cosmography
cloth, 5; Eden and trade in, 224; Hakluyt (editor) and trade in, 209; making of, 202; trade in, 48, 66, 84, 100, 103, 133, 200–2, 220, 231, 259n160, 264
clothing and dress, 66, 179, 189, 233, 238n95, 265, 349n94
Clothworkers Company, 192
Clusius, Carolus, 203, *204*, 355–6, 356n118, 357, 359; garden of, 362
Cnoyen, Jacobus, 37–8
Cnut. *See* Canute
Cole, Humfrey, 230, plate 5
Columbus, Christopher, 60, 76–7, 88–9, 92, 467
Commelin, Jerome, 31
confessional or religious identity, 20, 172, 178–9, 187, 189, 205, 278, 342, 466; Drake and, 446–50, 452–5, 458–9; Hakluyt (editor) and, 172, 312, 445, 450–2, 458–9. *See also* Catholics and Catholicism; christening; converts and conversion; ministers; Protestants and Protestantism; religions
Constantinople (Turkey), 192, 194; Hakluyt (Esq.), Harborne as emissary at, 186, 193; instructions and, 200–2; tulips and, 202, *204*
converts and conversion, 59, 457–8; between Islam and Christianity, 179, 180n77, 187–8, 448–9
Cooke, John, 441–2
Cope, William, 356
Corbett, Julian, 312, 413, 439n74, 449
Cormack, Lesley, 465
Coronado, Francisco Vásques de, 325, 327
corporate identity, 176, 124, 390, 392, 408–10, 466
Cortés, Hernán, 88
Cortés, Martín, 224, 230
Cosa, Juan de la, 71

cosmographers, 38, 63, 102–3, 136, 214, 293, 331, 334
cosmography, 109, 114, 147, 466–7; Eden and, 225, 239–40; as mathematical discipline, 92–6; and theory of climate zones, 92–4, 144–6, 225, 241. *See also* Arctic, theories about; navigation; tropics
Cotton, Robert, 31
Counter-Reformation, 356n118
Crosse, Robert, 306
Crovan, Godred, 53
crusades, 8, 29, 156–7; metaphor of, 459
Cuffe, Henry, 292n71
Cumberland, Earl of (George Clifford), 258–9, 262, 296–8, 303–4, 306, 427
Cumberland Sound (Nunavut, Canada), 375
Cyprus, 156, 177

Dalton, Heather, 100, 101n62, 102, 104–5
Dare, Ananias, 457
Dare, Eleanor, 457
Dare, Virginia, 457–8
Das, Nandini, 191, 321, 397n54
da Silva, Nuño, 333, 418, 426, 439n74, 442–3
Dassel, Anthony, 215n20
Davie, Robert, 419
Davis, John, 19, 91, 140, 371; authorship and style, 375–7, 390–1, *393*, 393–6; T. Cavendish, and, 395–6, 400–3, 406; on climates, 93, 94n43; compass variation and, *379*; Dee and, 373–4, 402; A. Gilbert and, 374, 381, 398, 402; Greenland and, 374–5; Indonesia and, 332; Jane and, 392, 409; Molyneux and, *378*; mutiny and, 399, 405, 412; Northwest Passage searches by, 191, 349, 370, 373–6, 378, 381–90, 394, 399–400, 464–5, 467; Sanderson and, 376, *378*, 381–2, 395, 397, 398; secondary literature on, 373, 375; technical expertise, 402, 406–7; Zeno materials and, 337
Davis Strait (North America/Greenland) 375, *377*, *378*, 384
Day, Matthew, 351n101, 429n48, 460
de Bry, Theodore, 351, 353–6, 413, 419; *Americae VIII*, 413, 419; engravings by, 360–70, *361*, *364*, *365*, *366*, *367*; Hakluyt (editor) and, 320, 353
Decades of the Newe World (Eden), 28, 102, 218, 223–4, 226, 230, 333
Dee, John, 82, 118, 138n81, 310, 322n14, 464; Arthurian conquest of Arctic and, 35; R. Barlow texts and, 103; Cavendish and, 402; circumpolar map by, 95, plate 2; Davis and, 370, 373–4; diaries of, 33, 33n22; Edgar and, 43–4, 47, 51, 60; English rights to North Atlantic and, 336–7; H. Gilbert and, 344n81, 373–4; Hakluyts and, 33–4, 34n24; medieval materials and, 32–4, 34n24; G. Mercator and, 37, 351; on Nicholas de Linna voyage, 35–6, 40; northern regions and, 373–4; Orosius manuscripts and, 55, *56*, 58; Ortelius and, 39; Smith chart, *127*, 128; R. Thorne proposals and, 98; Zeno narrative and, 39, 335–7
De jure belli (A. Gentili), 249
de la Torre, Bernardo, 330
Denmark, 54, 142, 145
De orbe novo decades (Peter Martyr), 28, 322, 326, 328; translated by Basanier, 339n67
De orbe novo decades (1587), edited by Hakluyt, 223, 337, 340; dedication

to Ralegh, 150, 322, 340, 460;
map in, 345, *346*, 347, 426
Derbent (Russia), 71
Diaz, Pedro, 325, 460–1
diet: civility and, 146–8, 238n96, 265; health and, 228, 240, 242, 243
Dimmock, Matthew, 177n67, 193, 271
diplomacy, 8; Anglo–American, 369; Anglo–Moroccan, 217–18, 271; Anglo–Ottoman, 155, 157–8, 175–7, 186, 192–3; Anglo–Persian, 83; Anglo–Russian, 109; Luso–African, 218n31, 249n127. *See also* ambassadors
Discourse concerninge the Spanishe fleete invadinge Englande in the yeare 1588 (Ubaldini), 284
Discourse of a discoverie (H. Gilbert), 55
Discours of voyages unto ye Easte and West Indies (van Linschoten), 332
Discoverie of Guiana (Ralegh), 375
disease, 228, 265, 407, 420; ideas about climate and, 228n61, 235, 239–40, 240n104, 241–3; scurvy, 240n104
Divers Voyages (Hakluyt), 99, 213, 348, 428, 461; Cartier's relations and, 338n63; R. Thorne and, 79, *81*, 90, 95; Verrazzano and, 340; Zenos and, 337
Docwra, Thomas, 177–8, 319
Dodoens, Rembert, 133, 203n150, 357, 359n126
Donno, Elizabeth Story, 440
Don River (Russia), 71
Doughty, John, 439n74
Doughty, Thomas, 310n121, 438, 439n74, 440–2, 454
Downton, Nicholas, 288, 298, 300–2
Dragontea, La (de Vega), 445
Drake, Bernard, 418
Drake, Francis, 5, 11, 20, 258, 462; Cádiz raid, 267, 269, 279–82, 309–13, 310n122, 443–4, 449; career of, 414–15; circumnavigation, 256n157, 269, 327, 330, 345, 415, 418, 424–5, *434*, 435, 460; Clusius and, 359n126; command style, 437–8; death, 415; "Famous Voyage" account of, 19, 125, 409, 414, 423–6, 432, 441, 454, 459–60; T. Fenner and, 237n94; J. Foxe and, 310n122, 413, 443–6, 454; Greepe and, 446, 448; Hakluyt (editor) and, 324, 416–31; Haslop and, 310–12; J. Hawkins and, 412, 417, 427; legal proceedings and, 310n21, 438, 441–2; Lisbon raid, 333, 422; maps and, 434, *434*; privateering and, 410–11; religious identity and, 446–61; slaving voyages, 412, 414; Spanish sources and, 325; West Indies and, 267, 280, 350, 415, 418, 427, 443–4, plate 8; writing by, 431–3, 442–3; written record and, 431–46
Drake, George, 343
Drake, John, 425
Draper, Esdras, 439
Drapers' Company, 299, 484n6
Drogeo (apocryphal place), *336*
Ducket, Lionel, 251, 251n135
Dudley, Robert, 251n135, 418, 429
Duffy, Eamon, 165n31
Dutch East India Company, 353
Dyer, Edward, 34n24

East Asia, 321, 330
East India Company, 4, 295n79, 353, 485; Eldred and, 195; Fitch and, 195; formation of, 309; Hakluyt (editor) and, 195, 196n129, 208n4, 299n93, 309, 318n3; Lancaster and, 209n5; Staper and, 192

East Indies (Indonesia), 196, 209, 311, 410, 415; attacks on ships returning from, 269, 281; claims to, 89–90; cosmography and, 93–4; Fenton voyage to, 405; Linschoten and, 332, 353; northern route searches and, 211. *See also* Moluccas

Eden, Richard, 28, 218–20, 222–43, 224n48, 289; on C. Adams, 87n24; on S. Borough, 138n81; S. Cabot and, 102; narrative, 111n7; publishing history and, 219–20, 219n35; on West Africa voyages, 225–40

Edgar (King), 30, 51–2, 468; administrative reforms by, 44; as naval hero, 44–6; sources on, 44–8; voyages by, 43; xenophilia of, 46, 46n61

Edward III (King), 38

Edward VI (King), 87, 171; death of, 167; Northeast Passage searches and, 82, 102, 117, 223

Edwards, Arthur, 87

Edwin of Northumberland (King), 30, 52

Egmond, Florike, 357

Eldred, John, 165–6, 170n46, 173–4, 195–9

elephants, 197, 231–2, 245

Eliot, Hugh, 90

Elizabeth (Queen), 41, 46, 91; death of, 415; F. Drake and, 424, 430–1; Essex-Howard expedition and, 291; A. Gentili and, 249; Moroccan correspondence, 207n2; Ottoman correspondence, 193; Protestantism and, 167

Ellis, Thomas, 19

El Mina (Ghana), 220, 222, 227, 231, 234

Enciso, Martin Fernández de, 326–7

England, 76–7; economic issues, 48–9, 83–4; historiography of, 31–2; history, pre-modern, 26–7, 59–60; languages of, 50–1, 54–5, 58–9; long-distance trade and, 82–4, 87–8; the North as reserved for, 91, 95, 97, 138; Protestant Europe and, 284–6; religious conflict in, 170–1; Reformation, and, 46, 157–8, 165; Spain and, 84, 267, 269–70, 415, 461–2; territorial identity, 46, 52–3, 60. *See also* Anglo–Spanish sea war; Britain; national identity; Protestants and Protestantism; Spanish Armada

English Short Title Catalogue (ESTC), 305

Eriugena, John, 163

Espejo, Antonio de, 327, 329–30, 334, 340, 347–9. See also *El Viaje que hizo Antonio de Espeio*; González de Mendoza, Juan

Essex, Earl of (Robert Devereux), 269–70, 290–3, 332

ESTC. *See* English Short Title Catalogue

Estotiland (apocryphal place), 39, *336*, 337n59, 381

Euphrates River, 195, 198

Europe, conflicts with Ottoman Empire, 177–83; conflicts with Mongols, 70, 73

Evander, 50–1

Evesham, John, 156, 298

expertise, 77, 83, 124, 288n59, 373, 461; in botany, 357, 363; conflicts about, 229–30; from foreigners, 41, 86–7, 202, 227, 229, 461; of navigators, 87, 101, 103, 121, 138n81, 194, 227, 230–1, 400, 402, 406–7, 468

Ezekiel, 70

Fallujah (Iraq), 195, 198

INDEX

Famagusta (Cyprus), siege of, 176–7, 180–1, *182*
Federici, Cesare, 196–9
Fenner, George, 237, 245, 450
Fenner, Thomas, 237n94, 310, 310n122, 311–12, 421, 449
Fenton, Edward, 234n83, 257, 262, 399, 426–7; East Indies voyage, 405; instructions, 435–41, 436n64; in Sierra Leone, 258, 261; slavery and, 211n9, 245n117; Straits of Magellan and, 435
Ferdinand (King), 60
Fernandez, Juan, 104
first-person voice, authority of, 26n5, 363, 370, 375. *See also* pronouns in travel writing
fisheries and fishing, 336n56, 395, 399; Hakluyt (Esq.) and, 33, 200n140; at Iceland, 38n35, 145–6; at Newfoundland, 251n135, 343–4; in the St Lawrence, 339, 343, 347n89
Fitch, Ralph, 159, 195–7
Fletcher, Francis (minister), 256n157, 432, 440–2, 453–5
Flick, Robert, 288
Flicke, Robert, 299–302
Florida (United States), 324, 339, 341, 341n72, 342
Florio, John, 338–9, 344
Fox, John, 173, 177, 183, 183n86, 184–6, 188–91
Foxe, John, 58–9, 323, 443, 445, 450–1, 454; F. Drake, letter to, 413
Frampton, John, 326–7
François I (King), 340
French, sources in, 335–49
Friseland (apocryphal place), 33, 33n22, 39, *336*, 337n59
Frisius, Gemma, 144, 232
Frobisher, Martin, 19, 171, 303, 349–50, 376, 420; Africa voyages, 211; Baffin Island/Qikiqtaaluk voyages, 39, 373, *377*, *378*, 386, 388–9; Best and, 94n43, 241; cannibalism claims and, 238n96; Cathay Company and, 374; Dee and, 39; gold and, 94n44; investors and, 251n135; *Madre de Deus* and, 303, 306; Orkney and, 53n85; Ortelius and, 39, 352; Zeno and, 337
Frothingham, Christopher, 111n7
Froude, James, 20, 51, 275, 409
Fuchs, Barbara, 319, 445
Fuller, Thomas, 425
fur, 141, 343, 347n89, 373
Fury, Cheryl, 437

Gainsh, Robert, 231, 236, 240, 246
Galí, Francisco, 325, 332
Galvão, Antonio de, 326, 350
Gama, Vasco da, 76–7
Ganges River (India), 195
Garrard, Chester, 251n135
Garrard, William, 251n135
Garret, James, 355, 356n118, 357, 359n126
Garret, Pietr, 357
Garth, Richard, 355–6, 356n118, 357, *358*
Gelandium (apocryphal place), 33
General and Rare Memorials (Dee), 33, 43, 47
Gentili, Alberico, 249, 357
Gentili, Scipio, 357
Geoffrey of Monmouth, 25n2, 30–1, 35, 38–9
Geographical historie of Africa (Leo), 213–14
Gerald of Wales, 36, 64
Gerard, John, 203n150, 357
Gestae Arthuri, 38
Gilbert, Adrian, 374, 381, 402

Gilbert, Humphrey, 200n140, 398, 465, plate 2; colonizing project, 450n107, 451; Dee and, 374; Newfoundland and, 342–3; Northwest Passage treatise, 331, 372, 464; Ohthere and, 55, 57
Gilbert Sound (Greenland), 374–5, 381, 381n15, 382, 384–5, 394, 396–7
Gilles, Sealy, 54
globes, 63; by Molyneux, 41, 296n84, *378*, 381n15, *463*
Goa (India), 195–6, 208, 209n5
Godwinson, Harold, 30, 52
Gog, 70–1
Gold Coast (West Africa), 234, 251
gold and silver, 196, 229; in Arctic, 94n44, 373–4; English need for, 49, 84, 216; in Muscovy, 50; in North America, 329, 348, 486n1; in Panama, 414; in tropics, 90, 105, 239–40, 245; in West Africa, 220, 227, 231, 233, 235, 244, 246, 252, 265
Golden Palace, 50
Gonson, Benjamin, 251, 251n135
Gonson, Matthew, 165n30
Gonson, William, 251n135
González de Mendoza, Juan, 326, 328, 330
Gourgues, Dominique, 342
Gow, Andrew, 71
Graciosa (Azores), 298
Great Lakes (North America), 349
Greenblatt, Stephen, 259–60
Greenland, 19, 38–9, 140, 143, 371–2, 374–5; exchanges in, 380–90, 394, 396
Greepe, Thomas, 443–4, 446, 450, 452–3
Gregory XIII (Pope), 183n86, 189
Grenville, Richard, 275n16, 276, 278, 325, 458, 460

Groesen, Michiel van, 355
Growte, John, 345
Guatemala, 454
Guiana, 19, 175, 216, 241n106, 308
Guildford, Richard, 169
Guinea (region in West Africa), 220; Baker on voyages to, 191, 219n33, 237–8; Eden on voyages to, 223–40; Lok voyage to, 171, 231–4, 235; Pory on, 214; Towerson voyages to, 234–7; trade rights with, 210, 216–17, 220; Wyndham voyage to, 226–31. *See also* West Africa; *specific places*
Gulf of St Lawrence (Canada), 339, 343–4
Gutiérrez, Diego, 331
Güyük Khan, 67–8

Hack Atlas, 331
Hair, P.E.H., 213, 243n112
Hakewill, George, 350
Hakluyt, Richard (editor): as author, 6, 459; correspondents and, 38, 40–1, 63, 75, 136, 334–5, 340–1, 356–7, 461; as cosmopolitan, 41–2, 59, 462; Dee and, 32–40; F. Drake and, 427–9; editorial methods and principles of, 136–7, 161, 269, 287, 289, 293, 308, 312–13, 370; editorial shaping by, 98, *106*, 107–8, 161, 174, 186, 208–9, 451–2, 462, 464–8; life information, 5, 49–50, 192, 324, 340; maps and, 36–7, 297, 345–6; Muscovy Company and, 110; oral accounts transcribed by, 164, 428, 450; Ralegh and, 308, 322, 326, 329, 349, 356n118, 456, 460; research by, 28–9, 64, 136, 160–1, 213–14, 324, 340–1, 344–9, 422, 429; Spain and, 334–5, 428, 451–2, 461–2; Staper and, 192,

193n117; translations and, 317–19, 322, 325–6, 337–9, 340, 350–70, 428
Hakluyt, Richard, Esq. (lawyer), 21, 141; Dee and, 33, 33n22; on England, 201–2; on foreign encounters, 200; instructions from, 124, 132–4, 200–2, 200n140, 205; G. Mercator and, 352
Hakluyt Handbook (Quinn), 270, 356
Hakluyt Society, 103, 334
Hakluytus Posthumus or Purchas his Pilgrimes (Purchas), 27, 173, 214, 446, *447*
Hall, Christopher, 388
Hall, Kim, 210, 232
Hamilton Inlet (Labrador, Canada), 375
Hammer, Paul, 287n58, 292–3
Hanmer, Meredith, 448
Harborne, William, 185–6, 189, 193, 215n20
Hardråde, Harald, 52
Harkness, Deborah, 203n150, 357, 373
Harriot, Thomas, 125; Dee and, 322n14; Hakluyt (editor) and, 456; Latin version of text by, 356, 356n118; Roanoke report, 320, 351–70, 383, 457n128, 486
Harvey, Gabriel, 29n11
Hasleton, Richard, 190–1
Haslop, Henry, 310, 313, 444, 449
Hasse, John, 87
Hawes, James, 288n60
Hawes, John, 288, 288n60, 295n78
Hawkes, Henry, 327, 331
Hawkins, John, 210–11, 238n96, 264, 414; crew of, in Sierra Leone, 243n112; F. Drake and, 412, 417, 427; slave trade voyages, 105, 221–2, 237, 247, 250–5, 258, 264; West Indies raid, 415

Hawkins, William (brother of J.H.), 250, 258n158
Hawkins, William (father of J.H.), 78, 216, 227, 250
Hawkins, William (nephew of J.H.), 243n112, 258, 259
Hayes, Edward, 450–1
Helena (Empress), 156–8
Helgerson, Richard, 88, 270
Henry VI (King), 48
Henry VII (King), 78, 86, 88, 372
Henry VIII (King), 31, 79, 84, 86, 203, 224n48; R. Barlow, proposal to, 102; dissolution of monasteries by, 31; R. Thorne, proposal to, 91–2, 98, 102
Herball (Gerard), 203n150, 357
Herberstein, Sigismund von, 60, 135–7, 139, 319, 464
Hickman, Anthony, 171, 234n83, 250n133, 477
Hickock, Thomas, 196
Hillah (Iraq), 195
Hispaniola (West Indies), 100; English factor at, 103
Histoire des terres nouvellement descouvertes (Basanier), 347
Histoire notable de la Floride, L' (Laudonnière), 322, 340
Historia de las Indias y conquista de Mexico, Las (López de Gómara), 326
Historia ... Del gran reyno dela China ... Con un itinerario del Nuevo Mundo (González de Mendoza), 326, 328
Historia general y natural (Oviedo y Valdés), 223, 325
Historia natural y moral de las Indias (Acosta), 326
Historiarum adversos paganos (Orosius), Old English, 52, 55
History of travayle (Willes), 219, 230, 333

Hixon, Ellis, 432
Hochelaga (Quebec, Canada), 347–8. *See also* Canada; St Lawrence River
Hodgkins, Christopher, 445–6
Holinshed, Raphael, 160
Hondius, Jodocus, 41
Hood, Thomas, 258, 259n161, 260–1, 455
Horodowich, Elizabeth, 335
Hortop, Job, 255–6
Hotman, Jean, 356–7
Houtman, Cornelis de, 332
Howard, Charles, 13, 395–6; Armada battle and, 151, 269, 283–4; Azores expedition, 295; Cádiz raid and, 151, 269–70, 290–3; Hakluyt (editor) and, 151, 269, 286, 459, 461
Howard, Thomas, 299, 302, 343
Howard, William, 31, 64
Hubblethorne, Morgan, 200, 200n140
Hudson, Henry, 400, 407
Hudson Strait (Canada), 375
Humfrey, Laurence, 357
Hungary, 73

Iberian Peninsula, 209, 416; trade with, 84, 258n158
Iceland, 241, 466; Arthur and, 25–6; Christianity in, 148; diet, 147; Jónsson defence of, 142–50, 225, 233, 350; Ortelius map of, plate 4; trade with, 38n35, 48, 142n94
Îles de Los (Guinea), 252, 262, 264
India, 156, 195, 208
Indian Ocean, 207, 209
information: censorship and suppression, 290–3, 321, 424–6, 425n34, 436; as commercial intelligence, 124; management of, 29, 323–5, 331, 334, 351–3, 414; oversight by captains, 432–3, 437, 440–1, 442–3; publication of sensitive, 322, 325, 333, 339, 345, 410, 426
Ingram, Anthony, 242
Ingram, David, 464
Ingulf, 162–3
Innocent IV (Pope), 62, 249n128
inquisition, 327, 425, 439n74, 451, 454, 456
instructions for travellers, 108, 110, 113n10, 118, 121–2, 159; by W. Borough, 120, 125–8, 437; by Cabot, 119–21, 130–3, 435–6; by Dee, 119; by Hakluyt (Esq.), 133–4, 200–3; by Muscovy Company, 124–34; by Privy Council, 436–9; to clothworkers, 124
interpreters, 30, 43, 67–8, 73–4, 86, 236, 389, 452n112
Inuit, 19, 370, 373, 383–6, 388–9
Inventio Fortunata, 37–8
Ireland, 25–6, 175
iron, 94, 384–5, 388. *See also* metal, Inuit use of
Isabella (Queen), 60
Isle of Man (United Kingdom), 52–3
Istoria de las Indias (López de Gómara), 223
Italian sources, 335–49
Itinerario (Linschoten), 196, 299, 332, 353, 426
Ivan IV (Tsar), 82
ivory, 133, 231–2, 233, 242n110

Jackman, Charles, 40, 76, 83, 129–35, 142, 352; instructions to, 126, 128, 200
James, Thomas, 342–3
James I (King), 334
Jane, John, 376, 380–1, 386, 390, 426; T. Cavendish and, 395, 402–3; Davis and, 409; on mutiny, 405; pronoun usage by, 391–3, 407
Japan, 208–9, 330, 332, 460

Jenkinson, Anthony, 83, 110, 140, 175
Jerusalem, 157, 159, 162–3, 164n27, 165–6, 169, 169–74, 195, 199
Jewkes, W.T., 424
John, Lord Lumley, 64, 111n6, 160
John of Worcester, 30–1, 45
Johnson, Richard, 87; language skills, of, 140–1; on northern peoples, 138–40
joint-stock companies, 217. *See also specific company names*
Jones, Philip (minister), 277, 295, 301, 428
Jónsson, Arngrímur, 142–50, 225, 233, 319, 350
Jowitt, Claire, 290, 413
Judde, Andrew, 232

Kara Sea (North Asia), 142
Keeler, Mary Frear, 420
Kelley, Edward, 34n24
Kelsey, Harry, 250, 424, 433
King, William, 418, 418n9
Kingsford, Charles Lethbridge, 305
Klein, Bernhard, 238n96
Knapp, Jeffrey, 369
Knights Hospitaller, 176
Knights of Rhodes, 178n71, 184
Knivet, Anthony, 402
Knollys, Francis, 420
Kola Peninsula (Russia), 82
Konkaw Island (Sierra Leone), 254, 262–3, 263n174
Korea, 85, 460
Krantz, Albert, 144

Labrador (Canada), 375
Lach, Donald, 196
Lac Saint-Jean (Quebec, Canada), 349
Lahore (India), 195
Lambarde, William, 31, 58–9
lançados, 222

Lancaster, James, 95, 208–9, 209n5, 332, 426
Lane, Ralph, 458
languages, knowledge of, 140–1, 338–9n64, 354, 440; word lists, 386, *387*, 388, 388n31. *See also* Anglo-Saxon; Latin; Portuguese; Spanish
Lapland (Finland), 25
la Popelinière, Lancelot-Voisin de, 424
las Casas, Bartolomé de, 326, 452
Latimer, Henry, 102–3
Latin, 350; Hakluyt's use of, 27, 30, 36, 58; translation into, 356, 356n118
latitude, observations of, 120, *123*, 230, 231n69, 332, 381n15, plate 5. *See also* cosmography
Laudonnière, René de, 322, 340–1
Law, John, 229n65
law: and culture, 115; slavery in, 247–9, 467; and trade, 247. *See also* laws; legal documents; legal proceedings; letters patent; rights of discovery
laws: of nations, 247–8; of nature, 50, 147, 205, 232–3
Lee, Edward, 79, 89–90, 101
legal documents, 192, 215n21, 304n106, 405, 438–9, 439n74, 441–2. *See also* letters patent
legal proceedings, 222, 310n21, 413–14, 439–42; consortships and, 304; records of, 401
Legazpi, Miguel López de, 331
Leigh, Charles, 343
Leland, John, 324
Le Moyne, Jacques, 354
Leng, Robert, 312, 449
Leo Africanus, 213–15, 318
letters patent, 33, 88, 156n2, 192, 207n2, 217, 272n9, 326, 374
Leucander, 161
Levant, 155–206, 324. *See also* Barbary kingdoms; Levant Company;

Ottoman Empire; *specific places*; *specific trading companies*
Levant Company, 156n2, 158–9, 192–4, 193n118, 272n10, 277, 311n124
"Libelle of Englyshe Polycye," 47–50, 60, 205, 468
Liberia, 220
libraries, 39, 63, 136, 292n71, 338, 426; Hakluyt (editor) and, 29, 426; monastic, 31, 32n17; private, 29, 31 (*see also under individual names*); royal, 102, 348; shipboard, 39
Linacre, Thomas, 203
Linschoten, Jan Huyghen van, 196, 299, 319, 325, 332, 353, 426
Lisbon (Portugal), 295; raids on, 272, 288n59, 302, 313, 333, 415, 422
Lister, Christopher, 258–9, 297, 417
Llwyd, Humphrey, 41
Loades, David, 83
L'Obel, Mathias, 203n150, 357, 359n126
Lodge, Thomas, 251, 251n135
logs and logbooks, *122*; by S. Borough, 121, 139; Davis and, 131n36, 376, 394–5; Eden and, 224, 231–3, 289; format of, 121–2, *123*, 124; by Hood, 260–1, 455; by Smith, 130; by Willoughby, 112, 117–19, 121
Lok, John, 156, 165, 165n30, 166–74, 231, 451; family of, 171, 234n83
Lok, Michael, 171, 215n20
London, 198, 221, 334, 339; the Spanish Armada and, 285–7; de Bry in, 354n110; Dutch and, 203n148, 203n150, 283n45, 288, 351–3, 355–6; Indigenous Americans in, 354, 389n37, 468n10; maps of, 133; merchants and ships, 84, 154, 190, 194, 216, 272n10, 276–80, 285, 288n60, 297–302, 311, 374n4, 420; prominence as market town, 59; Spanish embassy in, 334, 424, 425n32
Lope de Vega, Félix, 445
López de Gómara, Francisco, 223, 326–7
López de Villalobos, Ruy, 330
Loshak (fisherman), 138–9
Louis IX (King), 62
Lovell, John, 253, 414, 427
loxodromes, plate 3
Lucar, Cyprian, 98–9, 103
Lucar, Emanuel, 98
Luso-Africans, 222, 253n140

Macao, 332
MacCrossan, Colm, 161
MacLaren, Ian, 376
McDermott, James, 114
MacMillan, Ken, 34n24
Madeira (North Atlantic), 209, 227
Madox, Richard (minister), 243, 243n112, 245n117, 426, 436n64, 455; records kept by, 405, 435, 437–40; Sierra Leone estuary chart, 257, 258
Maffei, Giovanni Pietro, 333
Magdalen Islands (Quebec, Canada), 342, 344
Magellan, Ferdinand, 89, 101, 409, 415
magnetic variation, 120–1, 138, 208, 378, *379*
Magnus, Olaus, 144
Magog, 70–1
Maillard, Thomas, 104
Malaysia, 195
Malgo (King), 33
Malim, William, 170n46, 174n58, 177–80, 183
Mallorca (Spain), 193
Malta, 177n6, 184
Mancall, Peter, 324, 421

Mandeville, John, 191, 464
Mani-Sumba, 238n96
Manteo, 354, 369, 457–8
maps, *336*, *434*, plate 5, plate 6, plate 8; circumpolar, 95, 128, plate 1, plate 2, plate 3; charts and, 126, *127*, 128, 257, 258, 347–8; loxodromes on, 126–8, plate 3; planar maps, 95; of Roanoke, 364–6, *364*, *366*; of the world, *xiv–xv*, 36, 36n28, 71, *81*, 88n25, 297, 337n59, 341, *346*, 378, 379–80. *See also* cartography and cartographers
Marbecke, Roger, 288; Cádiz narrative by, 151, 270, 279n33, 281n41, 290–1, 294n77, 296n83, 302; ministers and, 455–6
Marco Polo, 70–1, 75, 85, 136
marginalia, 8, *10*, 29n11; Gainsh in, 246; on Mongol materials, 65–6
maritime writing, 19, 121–4, 294, 380, 408; authorship and attribution in, 287–314; conventions and style in, 296–7. *See also* instructions for travellers; logs and logbooks; pronouns in travel writing
Martinengo, Nestore, 177, 180, 184–5, 319
Martyr, Peter (Martire d'Anghiera, Pietro), 79, *80*, 318. See also *Decades of the Newe World*; *De orbe novo decades* (Peter Martyr); *De orbe novo decades* (1587)
Mary I (Queen), 82, 167, 171, 216, 220
Matar, Nabil, 183, 189, 203n150
mathematics, 35–6, 229–30, 363, *364*, 374, 462, plate 5, plate 7; cosmography and, 92–3, 96, 108; Davis and, 374; Dee and, 32, 95, 138n81, 374; Harriot and, 322n14; Lucar and, 98; navigation and, 121, 229–30; numeracy, 233n79; Recorde and, 57, 93, 230; Wright and, 288, 297
Maurice of Nassau, 41
Maximilian III (Archduke), 356n118
May, Henry, 418
Mayhew, Robert, 41
Mediterranean, 155–6, 158, 161; armed convoys and, 272; English presence in, 156; English trade and, 164–5, 165n30; faiths in, 166–7; navigation in, 194n121; slavery in, 183, 248. *See also specific places*
Memorials. See *General and Rare Memorials*
Mendaña, Álvaro de, 331
Mendoza, Bernardino de, 424, 425n32
Mercator, Gerard, 65, 79, 319, 336; circumpolar map by, 36, 95, plate 1; Dee and, 37–9, 351; in *Divers Voyages*, 79; and Hakluyt (editor), 34, 35–8, 40, 63, 136n73, 351–2; on de Plano Carpini, 63, 65, 70n145; on Northern Asia, 71, 72, 75, 85; polar regions and, 36–41; Zeno materials and, 336, 337n59
Mercator, Rumold, 357, *358*
Mercator projection, 297
Merchant Adventurers of Exeter, 398
merchants, English: Americas and, 101, 104, 355, 360n131; the Armada and, 285; Atlantic islands and, 103, 250; Baltic and, 30; Brazil and, 213n12; Bristol and, 99; Constantinople and, 158, 174n58, 192; customs of, 198–9; Indonesia and, 309; instructions to, 118, 124, 128, 131, 200–2; the Levant and, 193, 197; Morocco and, 104, 217, 226; Muscovy and, 83, 114, 217n30; the Northeast Passage and, 82, 86, 87, 224; the Northwest Passage and, 373n2, 396; Persia and, 83, 141;

privateering and, 272, 288n59; in Spain, 99–108, 217, 274, 327; South Asia and, 195–7; West Africa and, 155, 210, 215–17, 216n22, 220–1, 228, 235, 237n93, 245–6, 251n135; in West Indies, 103. *See also names of companies*
merchants, Italian, 48, 103, 104, 250
Merchants Isle (Greenland), 381, 381n15
Merrick, Hugh, 307
metal, Inuit use of, 384, 385; latitude and, 146, 224, 239, 245; theories about, 94, 225, 239–40; as trade good, 220, 235, 373, 384–5. *See also* alchemy; gold and silver; iron; metallurgy and mining
metallurgy and mining, 224, 298, 329, 348, 457n129
Mexico, 247, 256, 327, 331–2, 414; Inquisition in, 451, 454
ministers, 288, 456–9; on ships, 295n79, 435, 446. *See also under* authorship; *specific names*
Moluccas (Indonesia), 90, 101, 209, 330, 370
Molyneux, Emery, 41, 341, 378, *378*, 381n15, *463*
monasteries, 170, 189; Henry VIII's dissolution of, 31
monetary policy, 84
Mongols, 30, 134; accounts of, 61–75; Europe invaded by, 73; Gog and Magog and, 70–1, 72
monstrous races, 69–70, 137
Mording, Miles, 234
Morgan, Henry, 376, 381–2, 390, 393
Morocco, 104, 108, 207n2, 209, 217, 218n32; trade with, 217n30, 271
Mote, Humphrey, 273, 276, 288, 295, 301
Mount Hekla (Iceland), 145–6

Munday, Anthony, 183n86, 190
Münster, Sebastian, 144–5, 319
Muscovy, 16n21, 55, 110n4; R. Chancellor on, 113, 115; empire of, 70, 108, 135, 216; Herberstein on, 60, 135; sea route to, 60, voyages to, 77, 81–3
Muscovy Company, 82–7, 102, 109–41; Dee and, 33, 43n38; Eden and, 224, 226, 229–30; Hakluyt (editor) and, 88, 108–10, 466; Hakluyt (Esq.) and, 33; instructions and records of, 405, 433, 455; Northeast Passage and, 87, 109–19, 126–34, 138–40; Northwest Passage and, 234n83; Persia and, 83, 140–1, 252n138, 466; Recorde and, 57; Towerson and, 234n8, West Africa and, 216n22, 217n30, 234–5, 251n135, 252n148. *See also* instructions for travellers
music and musicians, 65, 132, 279–80, 388, 391–2; hymn-singing, 168; psalm-singing, 167, 454
Mustafa (Ottoman commander), 180–1
mutinies, 403, 405, 407, 409
Myanmar, 195–6, 199
myth, 26, 31

Nashe, Thomas, 292, 292n71
national identity, 51; *Brittania* and, 20; captivity and, 105, 189, 205; F. Drake and, 20; *Principal Navigations* as document of, 4, 270, 410; trade and, 159, 201–5
naval conflict, narratives of, 269–72; archival trails of, 294; authorship and attribution in, 287–314; first-person plural writings, 273–87; numerical comparisons in, 276–7
navigation: celestial, 120, 225, 229n65; cosmography and, 96; instruction

and training in, 86, 194n121, 230, 428, 460; instruments for, 120, 121, *122*, 228, 230, 231, 363; lack of skills in, 82, 121, 296; Mediterranean and North Atlantic differences, 194n121; transfer of expertise in, 86, 102, 229n65, 229–31; voyage instructions and, 120–2, 124, 126; writing practices and, 8, 120–4, *123*, 125–9, 139, 194, 261. *See also names of individuals*
Navigationi et viaggi (Ramusio), 27, 60, 109, 335, 337, 339
Navy Board, 251
Nelson, James, 187–9
Netherlands, 285; geographical knowledge circulation and, 351–3
Newbery, John, 136, 195–6, 198
New Christians, 222
Newes Out of the Coast of Spaine (Haslop), 449
Newfoundland (Canada), 95, 344, 466
New Mexico (United States), 327–9, 334, 348–9
Newport, Christopher, 303, 307, 418
Newton, John, 272
New World. *See* Americas, claims to; North America; West Indies
N.H. (writer), 263–4, 425
Nicholas of Lynn, 35–6, 38, 40–1, 143
Nicholls, Thomas, 218, 326–7
Nichols, Philip (minister), 421, 427–8, 432–3, 435, 455
Nigeria, 220
Niza, Fray Marcos de, 325
Noël, Jacques, 345–7, 349, 351
Nombre de Dios (Panama), 321, 417, 427
Norris, John, 295–6, 422; Lisbon raid, 333
North Africa, 184. *See also* Barbary kingdoms; Morocco

North America: early voyages to, 77–8, 88–9, 90–1, 98; French in, 339–49; Hakluyt (editor) and, 175, 213. *See also specific places*
North Atlantic, 370; Arthurian conquests in, 25–6; English rights to, 36n27, 39–40, 336–7; navigation in, 194n121
North Carolina (United States). *See* Roanoke
Northeast Passage, 76–7, 108, 141; S. Borough, search for, 138–9; Chancellor and Willoughby search for, 82–3, 87–9, 111–18; Pet and Jackman search for, 40, 129–35, 142
Northumberland (United Kingdom), 30
Northwest Passage, 94n43, 251n135, 374, 402; Davis searches for, 91, 370, 464–5, 467; Frobisher searches for, 19, 39; H. Gilbert on, 331, 372, 464
Norway, 52–3, 59, 114, 143
Notable Historie, A (Laudonnière), 340
"Nova Albion" (placename), 413, 458
Novaya Zemlya (Russia), 82, 137–8
Nowell, Lawrence, 55, 58
Nuuk (Greenland), 374–5, 384
Nuup Kangerlua (Greenland), 381, 384

ODNB. See *Oxford Dictionary of National Biography*
Odoric (Friar), 160
Ögödei Khan, 73
Ohthere, 54–61, 77, 99
Oñate, Juan de, 334
oral testimony, 38, 54, 295n78, 340, 373, 426, 432; Eden and, 224, 232, 235; transcribed by Hakluyt (editor), 78, 208, 224n47, 411, 426, 450, 486

Order of Saint John of Jerusalem, 177
Orkney Islands (United Kingdom), 26, 52; Norse and, 53n85
Ormuz (Iran), 195
Orosius, Paulus, 52, 54, 56, 58, 60
Ortelius, Abraham, 63, 75, 133, 143–4, 336; Asia map, 85; Camden and, 41, 136, 352; Dee and, 39, 352; Iceland map, plate 4; van Meteren and, 283n45, 352; Siberia information, 85
Osborne, Edward, 192n116, 193n117
Oslund, Karen, 148
Ottoman Empire, 70, 155–6, 158, 173–6, 194; Elizabeth correspondence with, 193; English engagements with, 174, 192–3; European conflicts with, 177–84, 177n67; Hakluyt (editor) and, 155, 175–7; trade in, 200–2
Oviedo y Valdés, Gonzalo Fernández de, 223, 325
Oxenham, John, 427
Oxford Dictionary of National Biography (ODNB), 288

Pacific, 19, 76, 90, 95, 210, 221, 269, 330, 460; the Philippines, 331–2. *See also* Cavendish, Thomas; Drake, Francis; Magellan, Ferdinand
Padrón, Ricardo, 329, 331
pagination, 11, 16, 21
Palmer, Philip, 260
Pan, 50
Panama, 97, 331, 414
Paris, Matthew, 62, 64, 72–3
Parker, John, 219
Parker, Matthew, 31
Parkhurst, Anthony, 251n135
Parks, George B., 13, 17, 112, 118
Parmenius, Stephen, 357
Parry, Glyn, 40

"Particuler Discourse" (Hakluyt), 29n11, 213, 247n122, 340–1, 348, 352, 359; *Brevísima Relación* and, 452; evangelization in, 457–8
Patagonia (Chile), 403
Patent Rolls, 31
Patmer, Henry, 102
Payne, Anthony, 283n45, 292, 292n73, 302, 328
Peckham, George, 247–8, 254, 451
Peerse, Gories, 144, 146–7
Pena, Pierre, 359n126
pepper, 94, 220n28, 308; trade in, 220–1, 227–8, 231, 235
Pereira, Galeote, 333
Persia, 83, 108, 156, 200, 466
Persian Gulf, 195
Pet, Arthur, 40, 76, 83, 129–35, 142, 352; Borough, W., and, 87, 126, 128; instructions to, 126, 128, 200
Philip II (King), 82, 220, 256, 273, 283, 334, 415, 424, 425n32, 428; English ships and, 274
Philip III (King), 334
Philippines (Pacific), 331–2
Philips, Miles, 256
Philips, William, 353
Philp, John, 382
Pigafetta, Antonio, 223
Pigafetta, Filippo, 213
pilgrimages, 164n27, 165n31, 174n58, 177n68, 199; Hakluyt (editor) and, 156–8, 161–2, 172–3, 451; narratives of, 165–74; Purchas and, 172–3
Pinteado, António Anes, 227–30, 333, 461
piracy, 249, 416; metaphor of, 323
plagiarism, 196–7
Plano Carpini, John de, 92, 137, 234; Mongols and, 62–3, 66–70, 67n134, 70n145, 73–4, 134–5; Siberia

information from, 85; van Meteren and, 352
plants, 354; collecting, 357–9; drawings of, 360, 362; import and export of, 201–3. *See also* botany; spices; specific plants
Pleasant historie of the conquest of the Weast India, The (López de Gómara), 326
Pliny, 69, 70n145, 75, 85, 232
Plymouth (United Kingdom), 281, 298
PN (1589). See *Principall Navigations*
PN (1598–1600). See *Principal Navigations*
polar route, 98–9n56; R. Barlow and, 102; Davis and, 91n38; R. Thorne and, 89–99
Ponte, Pedro de, 250
Port St Julian (Argentina), 441
Portugal, 90, 195, 208–10, 232; Africa and, 216–17, 218n31, 220–2, 236; claims to throne, 332–3; J. Hawkins, slave voyages and, 252, 254; Pacific and, 330; pepper trade, 220n28; slave trade and, 245, 247; trade rights claims, 220, 271
Portuguese (language), 222, 236, 245–6, 262; Hakluyt (editor) and, 323, 324n20, 325–6, 332–3
Portuondo, María, 334
Pory, John, 214–15, 234, 241, 464
Powell, Edward, 420
Preston, Amias, 419
Prester John, 232
Pretty, Francis, 263, 425
Principall Navigations (Hakluyt), 4n3, 29–30, 79, 464; Adams narrative in, 87n24; alterations to, 292n73, 414, 423; assembly of, 340; assertions of method in, 7, 13, 116, 136–7, 267–9, 289, 293, 370; R. Baker, poems in, 191n113, 219n33, 237–8; T. Cavendish in, 263, 425; N.

Chancellor, journal in, 129–30; dedication to, 149, 156, 200, 205–6, 340; Dee and, 33–4; differences from *PN* (1598–1600), 5, 11–13, 14, 29–30, 101, 111n7, 129–30, 156, 160n13, 161, 191n113, 196, 213, 231, 263, 286, 344, 425; F. Drake and, 421, 422–4, 426, 428, 430n52; "Famous Voyage" in, 328, 412, 414, 423; R. Garth in, 356; index for, 211, 465; motive for, 149, 340, 350; N.H. narrative in, 263; preface to, 49–50, 110, 116, 192, 326, 338, 356; A. Quinn, index to, 211n9; D. Quinn on medieval sources for, 160n13; R. Thorne in, 79; Wright-Molyneux globe and, 296n84
Principal Navigations (Hakluyt), *106*, 107; coherence of, 44, 74, 191, 397, 397n54; connections across, 11–12, 66, 70, 175; fragments and excerpts in, 25, 27, 160–1; genres of writing in, 7–8, 110, 111–19; indexes and, 4, 211n9, 465; marginalia and paratext in, 7–8, *9*, *10*, 29n11, 181; material withdrawn from, 290–3; medieval materials in, 13–14, 42–74, 159–64; motivation for, 150, 340, 350; omissions and silences in, 100–3, 105, 136, 157, 172–3, 190, 193, 211, 213–14, 445, 452, 455, 457–9; organization of, 5, 7–9, 11–12, 124–5, 150–1, 210, 459, 461; reception, history of, 4, 20, 51, 410; religion in, 446–61; translated materials in, 319 (see also *Principal Navigations*, volume 3)
Principal Navigations, volume 1 (Hakluyt): beginning and end of, 25–6, 150–1, 459, 461; characteristics of, 13–14, 26, 319; epistle dedicatory, 13, 83, 290–1,

291n66, 324, 461; marginalia and paratext, *24*, 37n29, 38n35, 65–6, 143; preface, 53, 78, 144, 234, 269, 283n45, 352, 353, 433, 450, 466

Principal Navigations, volume 2 (Hakluyt): characteristics of, 14, 16–17, 155–9, 175–6, 193–4; epistle dedicatory, 14, 16, 157, 160, 175–6, 181, 207–8, 329–30, 322; marginalia and paratext of, *9*, *10*, *15*, 16, *154*, 235–7, 246

Principal Navigations, volume 3 (Hakluyt): characteristics of, 17–20, 317–19; conclusion of, 460–1; epistle dedicatory, 17, 215, 228n61, 271, 317, 320–1, 422; investors in, 288n59; marginalia and paratext of, *316*, 348–9, 446, 451, 457, 459–60; privateering expeditions, 288, 303, 323, 416

Privy Council, 83, 273, 299, 435; S. Cabot and, 86, 102; Essex and C. Howard, report to, 291; Fenton and, 437–8; Madox and, 438

Procopius, 160

pronouns in travel writing: alteration of, 311–12; first-person singular, 62, 87, 89, 116, 162, 232, 297–8, 300–1, 301n99, 390; first-person plural, 118, 287, 295, 296, 297–8, 390, 397; mixed use of, 170, 300, 391, 392n42, 392–4; reflexive, 275; third person, 116, 224, 295, 296, 306, 311

Protestants and Protestantism, 31–2, 284; evangelization and, 456–8; iconoclasm and, 167, 448–9, 452–3; printing and, 322–3; religious services, 454–6. *See also* confessional or religious identity; ministers

Prynne, Edward, 102

Ptolemy, 93

Puerto Deseado (South America), 403, 406, 440

Purchas, Samuel (minister and editor), 27, 34n24, 214, 446, 459; T. Cavendish, materials and, 426; F. Drake, materials and, 426; Hakluyt's library and, 28, 29n10, 324, 331; Legazpi narrative and, 331; pilgrimage and, 172–3

Purchas his Pilgrimage (Purchas), 173

Pyrotechnia (Biringuccio), 226

Qikiqtaaluk. *See* Baffin Island

Quinn, Alison, 87, 111n6, 219n33, 276n19, 305, 312, 457n131; index by, 4n6, 60, 211n9; on M. Lok as source, 171; on Spanish materials, 325; on Staper as source, 192n116; on Willes, 333

Quinn, David, 87, 111n6, 219n33, 276n19, 305, 312, 449, 450–1n108, 457n131, 458; on F. Drake, 431, 432n55, 441n81; on Hakluyt (Esq.) instructions, 200n140; on M. Lok as source, 171; on G. Peckham, 451n111; on *PN* (1589) sources, 160n13; on Spanish materials, 325; on Staper as source, 192n116; on Walsingham, 424n28; on Willes, 333

"Quivira" (placename, North America), 327

Rafe, John, 231n69

Rainolds, Richard, 222

Ralegh, Walter, 67, 288, 301, 329, 460; Azores expedition and, 295, 298; Cádiz and, 291–2; Clusius and, 359n126; Guiana and, 241n106, 375; Hakluyt (editor) and, 150, 322, 322n14, 326; Harriot and, 356n118; letters patent, 326; *Madre de Deus* and, 303–8; on *Revenge*, 270, 275,

275n16; Roanoke and, 280, 345, 349, 353, 355, 456–7
Ralph, John, 234, 234n83
Ramusio, Giovanni Battista, 5, 27, 60, 109, 335–40; Abū al-Fidā and, 136. See also *Navigationi et viaggi*
Raven, Charles, 358
Recorde, Robert, 57, 93, 225, 230. *See also specific works*
Red Sea, 185
Reformation, 158, 165, 453
Reinert, Sophus, 83
religions: Buddhism, 68; eastern Christianity, 68–9, 167; Islam, 68, 157. *See also* Catholics and Catholicism; converts and conversion; ministers; Protestants and Protestantism
Rerum Anglicarum Scriptores (Savile), 160
Rerum Muscovitarum commentarii (Herberstein), 60, 135
Rhodes, siege of, 176, 178–80
Ribault, Jean, 339
rights of discovery, 26, 32, 35, 40, 105, 247–8, 344n81; voyage narratives and, 26n5
Rio Grande (river, West Africa), 210, 252, 263n174
Roanoke (North Carolina, United States), 19, 89, 280, 322n14, 341n72, *361*, 456–8; English arrival at, accounts of, *364*, *365*, 366–70, *367*; commodities at, 383; Harriot report on, 320, 351, 353–5, 359–60, 362–3, 366, 368–70, 383. *See also* "Virginia"
Roberval, Sieur de (Jean-François de La Roque), 344
Robinson, Richard, 283n45
Rodrigues, Francisco, 227, 230
Roman Empire, 161
Ronay, Gabriel, 74

Rubiés, Joan-Pau, 12, 198, 318–19, 341n72
Rubriquis, William de, 62–3, 65–7, 70–1, 73–4, 234; Buddhism and, 68; Islam and, 68
Russia. *See* Muscovy; Siberia
Rut, John, 98
Rutter, William, 219n33
rutters, 219n35, 331, 332, 339
Ryther, Augustine, plate 6

S. (Master), 201–2, 203n150
Sacks, David, 451n110
saffron, 201–2
Saguenay River (Quebec, Canada), 349
St John's (Newfoundland and Labrador, Canada), 342
St Lawrence River (Quebec, Canada), 341–9
Saintonge, Jean Alfonse de, 344
Sambula Island. *See* Îles de Los
San Agustín (Florida, United States), 280
Sande, Duarte de, 303, 309, 318, 321, 324, 333
Sanderson, William, 41, 376, *378*, 381–2, 395, 398
San Juan de Ulúa (Mexico), 253, 256, 413n
Santiago de Chile, 453
Santo Domingo (Dominican Republic), 280
Santos (Brazil), 403
São Thomé, 104
Sapi people, 252
Sarracoll, John, 259–64
Sartach Khan, 67
Saunders, Thomas, 176, 183–5, 187, 189
Savile, Henry, 31, 160, 416
Savile, Thomas, 357
Saxton, Christopher, 41

Scotland, 46, 48; Norse and, 53n85
Scriptorum illustrium maioris Brytanniae ... catalogus (Bale), 30
Scriptorum majoris Brytannie (Bale), 160
Seall, Francis, 303–4
Seamans Secrets (Davis), 94n43, 124n37, 395–6
Sea-Mans Triumph, The, 305–8
Seaver, Kirsten, 38, 63
secrecy, 321–5, 327, 331, 333–5, 351–3, 353, 424–6. *See also* information
Selden, John, 29n10
Senegambia, 221–2, 258
Settle, Dionyse, 19, 350
Seville (Spain), 101n62; English merchants and cosmographers in, 99–108
Shales, William, 195
Shamma (Ghana), 220, 251, 262
Shepheardes Calendar (Spenser), 51
Sherbro Island (Sierra Leone), 221
Sherman, William, 29n11, 35, 43, 47, 318, 338
ships: *Amity*, 297; *Bartholomew*, 231; *Black Pinnace*, 403; *Bonaventure*, 342–3; *Cacafuego*, 267; *Centurion*, 277–80, 282, 295n78; *Cinque Llaguas*, 300, 303; *Content*, 418n9; coordinating movement of, 95n99, 396, 398n57, 460; *Dainty*, 304, 307; *Defiance*, 430; *Desire*, 398, 403, 407; *Dolphin*, 278; *Dominus Vobiscum*, 98; *Dragon*, 307, 427; *Edward Bonaventure*, 82, 87, 114, 117; *Elizabeth*, 398, 441; *Elizabeth Bonaventure*, 421; *Exchange*, 300; *Foresight*, 307; *Galleon*, 398; *George*, 129–30; *Golden Hind*, 441, 454n119; *Golden Lion*, 437; *Green Dragon*, 187–8; *Half-Moon*, 185; *Helen*, 395, 398; *Holy Crosse*, 164; *Hercules*, 195–6, 199; *Jesus*, 176, 185–8; *Jesus of Lübeck*, 251; *Leicester*, 420, 422; *Lion*, 226, 228; *Madre de Deus* (ship), 13, 288n59, 302–9, 311, 321; materials captured with, 333; *Matthew Gonson*, 163; *Mermayd*, 384–5, 394–6, 398–400; *Minion*, 252; *Mooneshine*, 384–5, 392, 394, 396, 400; *Moonlight*, 398; *Northe Starre*, 382, 388, 394, 396–7; *Pelican*, 440; personification of, 282, 395; *Phoenix*, 307, 418, 430; *Primrose*, 258, 273–4, 276, 295, 420; properties of, 139, 276, 309, 397, 398, 399, 403; *Revenge*, 275–6, 278; *Roe*, 295n78; *Roebuck*, 304, 306–7; *Sampson*, 300, 304, 306; *Saō Phelipe*, 302–3, 311, 423; *Sunneshine*, 381–2, 388, 392, 394, 396, 398–9; *Tiger*, 195, 304, 306, 420; *Trinitie*, 236; *Victoria*, 89; *Victory*, 297; *White Lion*, 414n4; *William*, 129–30
Shorte and briefe narration (Cartier); Hakluyt (editor) and, 338–9
Siberia, 85, 95, 137, 142; S. Borough and, 138–9, 148; Johnson and, 139–40
Sidney, Henry, 82, 115
Sidney, Philip, 359n126
Sierra Leone, 238n96, 243, 251, 257, 258, 260–1; J. Hawkins, crew in, 243n112; slave trade and, 211n9, 221, 245
Sierra Leone River, 252, 254
Sighelmus, 163
Sigtrygsson, Godred, 53
Sir Francis Drake Revived (Nichols), 417, 421, 432–3, 443
Skelton, R.A., 345
Skilliter, Susan, 165n30
slaves and slavery, 105, 244, 275; in Americas, 247n122, 256; Atlantic

INDEX

trade in, 105, 245–7; Drake and, 237n94, 412, 417, 427; Fenton and, 211n9, 245n117; J. Hawkins and, 105, 210, 221–2, 237, 247, 250–5, 258, 264; in indexes, 211n9; legal status of, 249–50; in Mediterranean, 183–4, 248; rationales for, 233n79, 248, 255; in Spain, 104; sovereignty and, 249n127; R. Thorne and, 104–5, 107n82; war and, 247–9, 252, 254

Small, Margaret, 144, 318

Smith, Cassander, 262

Smith, Hugh, 127, 128, 130, 142

Smith, James, 187–8

Solomon Islands (Pacific), 331

Southeast Asia, 155–6

Spain: communication with, English, 330–1, 334–5; conflict with, English, 269–88, 415, 445, 448–50, 453–4, 459; English merchants in, 89, 100–4, 451–2; intelligence gathering, 424, 425n32; as model, 70, 84, 105, 244–5, 265, 460–1; rhetoric about, English, 273, 275, 277–86, 319, 321–3, 342, 448–9, 455

Spanish Armada, 25–6, 267, 276, 375, 450, 452; C. Howard and, 151, 269, 283–4; van Meteren on, 282–3, 283n45, 284–6; Ubaldini on, 284–6

Spanish Colonie, The (Las Casas), 326. See also *Brevísima Relación*

Spanish (language), 338n64, 467n9; Hakluyt (editor) and sources in, 319, 320–30, 334

Sparke, John, 238n96, 252–3, 255, 264, 455

Speculum Historiale (Vincent of Beauvais), 62n112

Speed, John, 243n113

Spenser, Edmund, 51

spices, 91, 94, 246, 265; Canada and, 348; *Madre de Deus* and, 308; trade in, 48, 89–90, 164, 246, 357–8. See also pepper; saffron

Sri Lanka, 195, 208

Stafford, John, 455

Stallybrass, Peter, 360, 362

Staper, Richard, 190, 192, 192n116, 193, 193n117, 299

Stationer's Register, 183n86, 288

Steele, C.R., 214

Stevens, Thomas, 195, 208–9

Strait of Belle Isle (Newfoundland, Canada), 343

Strait of Gibraltar, 16, 155, 207–8, 269, 271

Straits of Magellan (South America), 91, 258; Cavendish and, 396, 400–1, 403; Chidley and, 403; Davis and, 19, 379, 396, 400–2, 406–7; T. Doughty, execution in, 310n121; F. Drake and, 20, 409, 412, 441; Fenton and, 435; Pacific voyages and, 210, 221, 331; R. Thorne and, 95, 97

style, 294, 295n78, 296, 305, 350, 390–1, 397; Hakluyt (editor) on, 50–1

sugar, 48n70, 104, 105, 244, 250, 357

Suleiman I (Sultan), 175, 178–9

Suma de geographia (Enciso), 326

Summarie and True Discourse (Bigges/Cates), 419–22

Swanus, 162–3

Tacitus, 59

Tagrin Bay (Sierra Leone), 252

Taisnier, Jean, 225

Tamara Island. See Îles de Los

Tampico (Mexico), 253

Taqwīm al-buldān (Abū al-Fidā), 137

Tartars, 73–4

Taylor, E.G.R., 102–3
temperate climates, 92, 92n39, 201–2, 244. *See also* cosmography
Theatrum Orbis Terrarum (Ortelius), 143
Thévenot, Melchisédech, 345
Thevet, André, 289, 293, 324, 338–40, 341n72
Thomas (Saint), 163
Thorne, Nicholas, 79, 101n62, 103; ledger book, 100
Thorne, Robert: R. Barlow and, 101–3; S. Cabot, voyage and, 101–2; cosmography and, 92–6, 225, 467; Dee and, 98; documents in *PN*, 79, 89–99; editorial treatment by Hakluyt, 14, 79–81, *80*, 98–9, 108, 210–11, 337; map by, *81*; mercantile career of, 100–5, 250; slavery and, 104–5, 107n82
Thrush, Coll, 354
Tigris River, 195, 198
Timbuktu (Mali), 209
time: in organization of narratives, 8, *9–10*, 11; in organization of *PN*, 156
Tison, Thomas, 100, 103
Thorláksson, Guðbrandur, 143
Toledo, Luis Tribaldos de, 334
Tomlins, Christopher, 249
Tomson, Robert, 327
Torne, Juan, 104
torrid zone. *See* tropics
Towerson, William: African voyages by, 220, 230, 233n80, 234–7, 246; later career of, 234n83, 259n160; Shamma burned by, 262
Tradado ... dos diversos & desuayrados caminhos (Galvão), 326
trade, 100; in drugs and spices, 357; Eden and, 224; exports from England, 48, 84, 201, 208; identity and, 159; and imports to England, 48–9, 202–3; imports to England, problems with, 83–4; imports to England, theory and policy of, 50, 206, 216, 309; Levant and, 157–8, 164–5, 172, 175–7, 183, 186, 192–4, 200; Morocco and, 209, 217–18, 226; Muscovy and, 81, 83; Persia and, 81, 109, 124, 140; record-keeping and, 433; West Africa and, 217, 246. *See also* barter; fisheries and fishing; merchants, English; merchants, Italian; *specific companies*; *specific commodities*
trading zone, 57, 57n97
translations: English need for, 324, 327, 338, 338n63; in *PN*, 318–49; of English materials, 350–1; of Harriot's text, 353–60
translators, 183–4, 196, 199, 218, 295, 319, 327, 332, 355, 483; Hakluyt (editor) as, 318, 339, 340, 355. *See also* interpreters; *specific works*
Transylvanus, Maximilianus, 223
traverse boards, 122, *122*
Treaty of London, 334
Treaty of Tordesillas, 90
Treaty of Zaragoza, 89
Treatyse of the Newe India (Eden), 102
Tripolis (Lebanon), 136, 186, 195–6, 198
Tripolis (Libya), 177, 186
Tromsø (Norway), 114
tropics, 225, 239; diseases in, 243; as torrid zone, 92, 92n39, 144. *See also* cosmography
True and Perfect Description of Three Voyages, The (de Veer), 353
True and Perfect News of the Worthy and Valiant Exploits, Performed and Done by That Valiant Knight Sir Francis Drake, The (Greepe), 446, 448
True Copie of a Discourse, A (Wingfield), 296

"True Discripcion of the last voiage of ... Sir Frauncis Drake" (Leng), 312
Tudor, Mary, 171
tulips, 202, *204*, 357
Turberville, George, 159
Turkey Company, 159, 190, 192, 194
Turner, Henry, 176
Twitt, John, 418
Tyacke, Sarah, 36–7, 126n45, 128n47

Ubaldini, Petruccio, 284–6, plate 6
Ulloa, Francisco de, 325
Ungerer, Gustav, 101n62, 104–5, 107n82
Unticaro, Peter, 184
Urdaneta, Andrés de, 330

Valcke, Jacob, 136, 352
van den Boogaart, Ernst, 362
van Meteren, Emanuel, 136, 151, 288, 319; Hakluyt (editor) and, 352; Ortelius and, 283n45, 352; Plano Carpini and, 352; on Spanish Armada, 282–6, 283n45
van Sype, Nicola, 433; map by, *434*
"Van Yslandt" (Peerse), 144
Vardø (Norway), 82, 114, 116, 134
Vas, Lopes, 417, 427
Vaygach Island (Russia), 126, 129, 138–9
Vaz, Lope, 333
Veer, Gerrit de, 353
Venice (Italy), 173; geographic information and, 336; synagogue in, 166–7; voyages to Jerusalem and, 166, 166n34
Venice Company, 177n67, 192n15
Veracruz (North America), 253
Verrazano, Giovanni, 77, 340
Vesalius, Andreas, 225
Viaggio nell'India orientale, et altra l'India (Federici), 196

Viaje que hizo Antonio de Espeio, El (ed. Hakluyt), 325–6, 340, 347–9. See also *Histoire des terres nouvellement descouvertes* (Basanier); *Historia ... Del gran reyno dela China ... Con un itinerario del Nuevo Mundo* (González de Mendoza)
Vincent of Beauvais, 62, 62n112, 63, 65
violence in PN narratives, 461; in the Anglo–Spanish sea war, 280, 282, 301, 308; in the Arctic, 382, 386, 390, 408; Drake and, 409; in the Levant, 174, 183, 186, 188–9, 192; Spanish, in the Americas, 342, 369; in West Africa, 222, 244, 254, 260–6, 272, 274, 390
"Virginia" (placename), 175, 326, 329, 368. See also Roanoke
Virginia Company, 248
Vitkus, Daniel, 183n86, 185
Vitoria, Francisco de, 248
volcanoes, 145
Voyage and Travaile of M.C. Frederick into the East India (Fitch), 196

Waldseemüller, Martin, 63
Wales (United Kingdom), 46
Walker, John (minister), 243, 245n117, 435
Wallis, Helen, 41, 425n32, 433n58
Walsingham, Francis, 99, 340, 424n28, 461; Carleill and, 420; Davis and, 384; death of, 375; T. Fenner and, 310n122
Walsingham, Thomas, 31
Walter, Giles, 345
Wanchese, 354, 369
Ward, Luke, 211n9, 245, 440
Waters, David, 229
Way, John, 455
weather: in Benin, 242; on Northeast Passage voyage, 130; recording, 120

Webbe, Edward, 190–1
Welsh, James, 242–3
West Africa, 93, 155; English editors and, *106*, 107–8, 210–23, 223–35, 238–41, 466; as temperate, 242–3; trade with, 215–18, 226–9, 234–7, 241–2, 246, 271; violence and, 390. *See also* Benin; Guinea; Sierra Leone; *specific places; specific voyagers*
West Indies, 19, 269, 281, 325, 329, 412, 417; F. Drake, raid on, 267, 280, 350, 412, 415, 418, 443–4, plate 8; F. Drake, voyages to, 427; J. Hawkins, slave trade and, 247; slave-trading voyages to, 221, 414
Wey Gómez, Nicolás, 239n101, 245n116
Whetstone of Witte, The (Recorde), 57
White, John, 353–5, 359–60, *361*, 362–3, 456–8
White, Thomas, 277, 297–8
Whiteman, Andrew, 161–3
White Sea route to Muscovy, 60–1, 114–15
Wilkes, Thomas, 296
Willes, Richard, 218–19, 230, 333
William I (King), 163
William of Malmesbury, 31, 45–6, 46n61, 59
William of Normandy, 53
Willoughby, Hugh, 76–7, 82–4, 87, 107, 110–12, 115–16; company of, 455; voyage log, 117–19, 121

Wingandecoa (North America), 368
Wingfield, Anthony, 151, 271, 275, 295–6, 295n78, 313
Wingina, 354, 368–9
Winter, John, 440–1
Winter, William, 251
Withrington, Robert, 258–9, 262, 417
Wococon (North Carolina, United States), 369
Wolfall, Mr (minister), 456–7
Wolsey, Thomas, 89
women, 59, 66, 73, 179, 238n95, 252, 254, 333n47, 349n94, 373, 456, 465
Woolf, Virginia, 3–8, 462
World Encompassed, The (Drake), 432, 442, 458
Worldes Hydrographical Discription (Davis), 370, 375–6, 394
Wright, Edward, 230, 288, 421; Azores narrative, 296–7; world map, 341, *377, 378, 379*
Wright, Louis B., 450
Wright-Molyneux globe, 378
Wyatt, Michael, 335
Wyet, Silvester, 343
Wyndham, Thomas, 226–30, 234, 234n83, 333, 461

York, James, 224n48

Zeno, Niccolò, 335–7, *336*, 372
Zeno brothers, 39, 143, 335–6, 337, 370